PLAYBILLS TO PHOTOPLAYS

To Grammy + Papa,

Love,

Elizabeth Engel

Playbills to Photoplays

Stage Performers
Who Pioneered the Talkies

Edited with Foreword by Brenda Loew
Introduction by Don Wilmeth

New England Vintage Film Society, Inc.
Newton, Massachusetts

To order additional copies of this book, contact:
Xlibris Corporation
1-888-795-4274
www.Xlibris.com
Orders@Xlibris.com
70647

CONTENTS

Dedicated to Marcus Loew

"One of the first film industry pioneers
to recognize the power of movie stars
and promote them heavily."

20th Century American Leaders Database
Harvard Business School
www.hbs.edu/leadership/database/leaders/marcus_loew.html
(accessed 7.8.10)

Epigraph
Excerpt from
Sunset Boulevard (1950) movie script
by Charles Brackett, Billy Wilder, D. M. Marshman, Jr.
March 21,1949

GILLIS
I know your face. You're Norma
Desmond. You used to be in
pictures. You used to be big.

NORMA
I am big. It's the pictures
that got small.

GILLIS
I knew there was something
wrong with them.

NORMA
They're dead. They're finished.
There was a time when this business had the eyes of the whole
wide world. But that wasn't good
enough. Oh, no! They wanted the
ears of the world, too. So they
opened their big mouths, and out
came talk, talk, talk...

GILLIS
That's where the popcorn business
comes in. You buy yourself a bag
and plug up your ears.

NORMA
Look at them in the front offices --
the master minds! They took the
idols and smashed them. The
Fairbankses and the Chaplins and
the Gilberts and the Valentinos.
And who have they got now? Some
nobodies -- a lot of pale little
frogs croaking pish-posh!

Illustrations

Anything But Silent: The Film Legacies of Charlie Chaplin and Buster Keaton

Talkers Fast and Smooth: Lee Tracy and Warren William

Eddie Quillan: A Study in Versatility

Twelve year old Spencer Tracy in his first long pants. © United Press International. Private collection...445

Spencer Tracy's portrait for Ripon College's Eastern Debating Team, 1922. © Ripon College...446

Spencer Tracy in his dressing room when he appeared in *Uncle Tom's Cabin* (1924). Photo courtesy Wisconsin Center for Film and Theater Research. 456

March 3, 1986, *Playbill* for a one-night-only tribute to Spencer Tracy, Majestic Theatre, NYC. Participants included Katharine Hepburn, Stanley Kramer, Sidney Poitier, Jason Robards, Frank Sinatra, Susie Tracy, and host Robert Wagner. A benefit for the American Academy of Dramatic Arts, it included the showing of a documentary *The Spencer Tracy Legacy: A Tribute by Katharine Hepburn*, a beautiful written tribute by Hepburn and a list of the sponsors. PLAYBILL® is a registered trademark of PLAYBILL Incorporated, NYC. All rights reserved. Used by permission. Private collection. 460

Spencer Tracy (*far left*) in the George M. Cohan Broadway play *Yellow* (1926). Also shown: Chester Morris (*far right*). Private collection...463

Cast of *The Cat and the Canary*. Spencer Tracy, *top, left*. Grand Rapids Herald. 6.9.25. Used with permission, Grand Rapids History and Special Collections Center, Grand Rapids Public Library. Emily Deming Collection (no. 149-1-10.S). 466

The Morgan Brothers—Ralph, Frank . . . and *Carlyle*

Young Ralph Morgan as a stage actor with a small inset of 1933 film actor portrait of Ralph by Frank Powolny (same year Ralph became first president of Screen Actors Guild). Courtesy Screen Actors Guild. 486

Young Frank Morgan in Chicago as a stage actor with a small inset of smiling Frank in 1936 RKO film *The Dancing Pirate* (when he was also a Screen Actors Guild board member). Courtesy Screen Actors Guild...492

Index

About
New England Vintage Film
Society Inc.

New England Vintage Film Society Incorporated is a non-profit 501c3 tax-exempt charitable educational organization established to advance the relevancy of classic and vintage American films from Hollywood's Golden Age to today's world. New England Vintage Film Society Incorporated programs include publishing; lecturing; film screenings; and exhibiting Hollywood memorabilia to educate, enlighten, enrich, and entertain.

New England Vintage Film Society Incorporated published *Playbills To Photoplays: Stage Performers Who Pioneered the Talkies*, a compilation of twenty-eight essays and over one hundred photographs, to chronicle the lives and career paths of early twentieth-century performers who transitioned from entertaining on stage before live audiences to acting in the new technological medium of sound films, commonly known as talkies.

Playbills To Photoplays: Stage Performers Who Pioneered the Talkies explains the social, political, economic, historical, and cultural issues that shaped each performer's body of work, acting technique, persona, and public following over time.

To order *Playbills To Photoplays: Stage Performers Who Pioneered the Talkies* or to learn more, visit www.starsofstageandscreen.com.

In 2009, New England Vintage Film Society Incorporated published *Spencer Tracy, Fox Film Actor: The Pre-Code Legacy of a Hollywood Legend*, endorsed by Robert Osborne, host of Turner Classic Movies (TCM). The book is a unique collection of essays and rare images celebrating legendary two-time Academy Award—winning actor Spencer Tracy's outstanding legacy of early screen performances in Fox's lively Depression era pre-Code films.

To learn more about *Spencer Tracy, Fox Film Actor: The Pre-Code Legacy of a Hollywood Legend* or to order the book, visit www. spencertracyfoxfilmactor.com.

Ms. Brenda Loew, president, New England Vintage Film Society Incorporated, served as editor for both titles, guiding all phases of the publication process.

For more information about New England Vintage Film Society, Inc. visit www.nevintagefilm.org.

Foreword

This book is very personal to me—it has its roots in my family's history.

The inspiration for *Playbills To Photoplays: Stage Performers Who Pioneered the Talkies* originated with a Freeport, Maine man who contacted me as the ninth owner of a 1928 Marr & Colton theatre pipe organ that once belonged to my great-uncle, E. M. Loew, the theatre chain magnate. Hearing the restored theatre pipe organ play transported me back to the era of early twentieth-century American entertainment and brought tears to my eyes. The pipe organ was originally installed in E. M. Loew's Thompson Square Theatre, 179 Main Street, Charlestown, Massachusetts. The theatre, built circa 1915 as a "neighborhood" theatre, had 650 seats on the main floor and 250 in the balcony. Following the introduction of sound movies, the organ was removed from the theatre and relocated to one of the Loew houses in Milton, Massachusetts.

Hollywood royalty, heads of state, and other celebrities were often invited guests at the Loew Estate in Milton. My great-uncle was very good friends with his neighbor Joseph P. Kennedy Sr., President John F. Kennedy's father. I was fortunate to know my great-uncle; and I learned much about Hollywood, politics, and the entertainment business from him. Just as Marcus Loew's father had done two generations earlier, my great-uncle E. M. Loew emigrated from Vienna, Austria. Penniless, he arrived in the United States in 1911 at age thirteen, lived with relatives in New York City, and worked at various odd jobs before opening his first theatre at the age of eighteen. His life was reported on by the press like a Horatio Alger rags-to-riches story. E. M. Loew's chain of indoor and "open air" drive-in movie theatres was—at one time—the largest east of the Mississippi. My great-uncle also owned Bay State Raceway in Foxboro, Massachusetts (the current site of Gillette Stadium, home of the New England Patriots) and the famous Latin Quarter nightclubs in New York City, Boston, and Palm Island (Miami), Florida, managed by Barbara Walters's father, Lou.

Written with passion and depth, the biographical essays in this compilation describe the lives, struggles, and careers of many legendary early twentieth-century American entertainment icons—Hollywood royalty my great-uncle would tell stories about. Before he died in 1984, E. M. Loew gave me permission to write the story of his life. Perhaps someday I will. In the meantime, *Playbills To Photoplays: Stage Performers Who Pioneered the Talkies* remains faithful to the show business legacy I have been left.

I am proud that my branch of the Loew family tree played a role in the evolution of America's entertainment industry as vaudeville, silent films, and the legitimate stage yielded to the arrival of the "talkies" revolution and Hollywood's Golden Age.

Brenda Loew
August 2010
Newton, MA
Playbills To Photoplays:
Stage Performers Who Pioneered the Talkies

Acknowledgments

Playbills To Photoplays: Stage Performers Who Pioneered the Talkies could not have been published without the cooperation of many people and institutions. On behalf of New England Vintage Film Society Incorporated, I wish to thank the following individuals for investing their time, energy, and passion towards making *Playbills To Photoplays: Stage Performers Who Pioneered the Talkies* a reality:

Audrey Marie Johnson, for her steadfast enthusiasm and solid professional skills; Cyndi Tracy, for her early flat-out support; and writers Abigail Adams, Ben Bergin, Cinzi Lavin, Professor Don Wilmeth, Elizabeth Engel, Erik Hanson, Helaine Feldman, Howard Oboler, Dr. James Fisher, Jan Merlin, Jon Steinhagen, Judy Samelson, Kal Wagenheim, Lauren Milberger, Matthew Bowerman, Professor Maurizio Giammarco, Michael Jackson, Susanne Robertson, Travis Stewart, Val Sherman, Valerie Yaros, Dr. William Russo, and Zanne Hall, for their contributions of entertaining, well-researched essays.

I must also thank the following staff and organizations for their assistance with this book:

Dr. William D. Mett and www.redskelton.com; Ruth Van Stee, Grand Rapids (MI) Public Library; Dorinda Hartmann, Assistant Archivist, Film and Photo Archive, Wisconsin Center for Film and Theatre Research; Andrew Prellwitz, Ripon College Library; Cheryl Gratz, Xlibris; Laura Leff, President, International Jack Benny Fan Club; Screen Actors Guild;

Playbill.com; University of Texas Press, Journals Division; and www.goldenageofhollywood.ning.com.

Presenting the life histories of each and every stage performer who pioneered the talkies would simply have been an impossible undertaking. We attempted to include as many personalities in this compilation as we realistically could. Thanks to all of you for playing a key role in preserving the stories of the show business performers included in this book—entertainers whose lives and careers chronicle an essential period of American entertainment history . . . such stuff that dreams were made on.[1]

Brenda Loew, President and Editor
New England Vintage Film Society Inc.
Playbills To Photoplays: Stage Performers Who Pioneered the Talkies
Spencer Tracy, Fox Film Actor: The Pre-Code Legacy of a Hollywood Legend
Newton, MA

---

[1]   Shakespeare, *The Tempest*, 1610.

Introduction

A NEW PROFESSION: *THE MOVIE STAR!*

Don B. Wilmeth

FILM VERSUS THE STAGE

Students of film and those of theatre history are becoming ever more aware of how little they know of each other's fields. As a theatre historian, I admit that my understanding of the nuances, methods, and developments of filmmaking and its history is basic at best. There has been a long-standing bias that has tended to create a chasm between appreciation and interest in the two media. That early film owed much to the nineteenth-century stage—its techniques and production methods, its literature, its talent pool (after all, there was no other), and even its acting styles—has long been accepted. Yet much of what is still acknowledged by many as "fact" has been effectively challenged over the past forty years or so, especially as the result of more sophisticated and critically astute studies of nineteenth-century theatre (and vaudeville) and the serious efforts by film historians to pay careful attention to the early years of American film (as an understanding of how few examples still exists became evident) and, as importantly, to share knowledge with theatre scholars.

Some of the misunderstanding and confusion has been due to attitudinal stances; other problems of knowledge and perception have been caused by early scholarship often riddled with error and incorrect conclusions that for decades have been accepted and passed down without much question. The best example of both is likely A. Nicholas Vardac's *Stage to Screen: Theatrical Method from Garrick to Griffith*. When published in 1949 Vardac was judged to be a pioneering effort that explained—in rather blatant and absolute terms—the relationship between the late Victorian stage and early motion pictures. Vardac certainly based his arguments and conclusions on the right kind of sources—photos, press clippings and reviews, promptbooks, set designs, and other similar primary sources—yet his findings are colored by an attitude common to fifty years ago. As David Mayer has recently explained this, "Vardac offers a narrative of separation: of one medium, the stage, failing and being supplanted by a newer, more technically adept medium, cinema, which could achieve the effects and illusions and maintain an environmental 'realism,' which allegedly was believed to elude the paint-and-canvas scenery, which the theatre offered." Vardac, unfortunately, writing on a topic of fairly recent serious interest in the late 1940s, depended on too many inaccurate and rather naïve accounts of the stage, as well as a dated and skewered notion of the period under examination, which, as Mayer notes, led him to treat "this period of time as a vast solidified and undifferentiated lump." The result is an extremely influential study that leads Vardac and his adherents (such as Ben Brewster and Lea Jacobs—see sources consulted) to minimize subtleties, nuances, developments, and changes in the Victorian stage over a long period, resulting in a picture of the stage of the time, says Mayer, that was "all coarse, crude, pandering to low common-denominators, noisy, performed by unsubtle actors roaring their tirades and gesturing extravagantly." To Mayer this criticism is similar to the sort "modern" film critics level against much silent film.

Mayer and other film and theatre historians who focus on the intersections of the two media, especially during the early years of filmmaking, find that Vardac and his "school" largely ignore historical context (especially for the stage), except to be derogatory. Such an attitude about the stage and the screen from the last quarter of the nineteenth century to the introduction of sound movies has been largely altered, thanks to the sophisticated and critically astute studies of the stage of the last half of the nineteenth century by such scholars as Martin Meisel, Michael Booth, Peter Brooks, Stephen Johnson, and David Mayer, among others. And film historians of the formative years such as Charles Musser have been doing similar good in deepening our understanding and appreciation of early film, as Musser did in his *Before the Nickelodeon* and other studies. Brewster and Jacobs, similarly serious film scholars, in their recent *Theatre to Cinema* offer much of value in their analysis, including a useful and generally sensible critique of Vardac, yet even Brewster and Jacobs (which I nevertheless recommend) state that "popular melodrama rapidly disappeared from the live stage once moving pictures took over its subject-matter and adapted its techniques." This conclusion is categorically nonsense, for melodrama to this day (not necessarily the same as seen in the nineteenth century, although revivals of those plays are often very successful and with a truthful acting style seem quite contemporary) is the American theatre's major form of serious drama; it certainly did not disappear. It might have been well if Brewster and Jacobs had depended less on Vardac and on a dated and distorted notion of late Victorian acting as "overlarge and unrealistic" or specifically of melodrama acting, as Mayer explains, "as a series of poses and frozen gestures." Mayer points out that even a respected film critic like Roberta Pearson labels gestural action in silent screen acting as "histrionic," that is "stagey." Melodrama, it might be noted, is still interpreted by far too many serious scholars in a pejorative manner, whereas it is as legitimate a genre of drama as farce or even as tragedy.

My objective here is not to offer a potted summary of Mayer's important study of the theatrical influences on the landmark films of D. W. Griffith (although I admittedly recommend the book strongly to anyone interested in the intersection of film and the stage from the 1890s to the 1930s); yet I would quote and underscore, as I attempt to provide context and historical perspective for this collection of essays, one of Mayer's conclusions and refutations of Vardac's overstated beliefs that "as the stage ran out of steam, it surrendered to film."

Rather, concludes Mayer, "what he does not recognize is the extent to which there was a long period of exchange of technology and effects between the stage and film, stage plays incorporating film sequences, film intercutting with live moments. There were no fixed boundaries but, rather, a continual series of fluid interchanges." And finally, Mayer offers in his book clear evidence "of a bewildering range of histrionic diversity, which, rather than taming screen acting, allowed and encouraged oversized performance in films well past the moment when it was claimed to have disappeared." Surely this collection helps to illustrate this point and to carry a sense of acting diversity well into the twentieth century.

THE ARRIVAL OF THE SCREEN ACTOR

In an important guide to a film series organized and presented by the American Federation of Arts in 1986 (see *Before Hollywood* in sources consulted), film historian Charles Musser provides a succinct chronology of the actor's status in early film and provides a useful summary for us, leading up to the 1920s and the beginning timeframe for most of the essays in this volume. Unapologetically, I will draw heavily from Musser's essay in order to provide some perspective.

Up to 1915 the young film industry had undergone some astounding transformation; these changes had a major impact on the status of the actor. The earliest films were little more than novelties. The interest was in action, not acting. The people on screen were little more than part of the scenery. Musser notes that until at least 1904 "production personnel, non-professionals, and stage actors took turns performing for the camera." All on-screen talents were equal—and largely anonymous. With the rise of story films in 1903-04 actors became more essential elements in production, though scenery often retained its dominance. Slowly actors were called upon to create a rudimentary character, and though the screen actor did not yet exist, motion picture acting began to emerge as a more unified practice. Acting in films was part-time work, and filmmakers rarely cared much about the level of talent in use; casting calls were rare. Names of casts were rarely revealed. As nickelodeons demanded more one-reel story films, permanent stock companies of actors were created, with salaries that provided steady income and prevented film actors from drifting back to vaudeville or the legit stage. Musser states that by 1908 there was a growing group of people who had become professional moving picture actors.

But cinema had a low status in its early history, and an anti-cinematic bias prevailed for decades. Entering the film industry on a permanent basis was a complicated decision. Furthermore, "film acting was considered less artistically demanding than stage performance." Even vaudeville (low in the estimation of most legitimate, serious actors) required a focus, staying power, and discipline not necessary for most film performers. Cinema had little demand for well-developed character psychology or even a vivid personality, as did the stage. But film began to expand stories (drawing on other narrative forms, including the vaudeville sketch [see "Who's Charley?" below]) and developed a hierarchy of characters, the basis for the subsequent Hollywood "star system." Audiences began to recognize talent that appeared often in short films and gave them nicknames, not knowing their real names.

And as more close-ups were used, actors' personalities came across as well. By necessity and as a result of public pressure, actors' names began to be used; and leading players were treated as stars, as least on a basic level. By mid-1912, notes Musser, several film companies were using head titles to credit leading actors; and by the teens the star system began to emerge, which, in turn, forced filmmakers to focus more attention on specific performers (and to pay them more), giving star film actors a status similar to that of the stage actor. Yet cinema was not yet accepted as an art form by "the better classes of the community" (including many legitimate stage actors).

As Musser suggests, the feature film helped to elevate film's status (some starring major stage actors like the divine Sarah Bernhardt), as did the adaptation of successful full-length stage vehicles. Slowly actors were beginning to realize that a screen career—if material was carefully chosen—could increase their following, earn them more money, and even provide them artistic challenges. But such attitude changes came slowly for many.

A BAKER'S DOZEN

A surprisingly large number of well-established legitimate New York stage actors eschewed offers to appear on the screen—at least on a permanent or even semi-permanent basis. Hard statistical evidence is scarce, but anecdotal reports certainly seem to support this notion, even by the early 1930s. During the heyday of the golden age of American movies, and certainly at the height of the studio system, from the 1930s to the 1950s, there seemed to have been little concern about an actor's previous training or experience on stage. The emerging studios chose to mold their own talents. Jeanine Basinger persuasively illustrates how the studios developed a "star-making machine," based on a practical business plan that literally "manufactured illusions."

A December 1930 *Theatre Guild Magazine* poll of eight New York critics listed the thirteen outstanding stage actors in America, according to their judgment. These were (1) Alfred Lunt, (2) Lynn Fontanne, (3) Eva Le Gallienne, (4) Helen Hayes, (5) Dudley Digges, (6) Katharine Cornell, (7) Ruth Gordon, (8) Paul Muni, (9) Tom Powers, (10) Richard Bennett, (11) Walter Huston, (12) Alla Nazimova, and (13) Edward G. Robinson.

Of these examples, the top three had few film credits. As previously noted, a sizable number of successful stage actors were surprisingly snobbish about screen acting, and this may well have been the case with a number on this list. Lunt (1892-1977) and Fontanne (1887-1983), in their heyday, were the best-known acting couple in the United States; yet between 1923 and 1943, they appeared together in only eight films, most in the 1920s and none particularly notable. Perhaps their stage styles, often considered over-deliberate and genteel, simply did not work on screen (their only modest success—and an unhappy experience for them—was *The Guardsman* in 1931). Certainly their attitude toward film was typical of many stage actors who considered live performance in legitimate theatre an art form, whereas acting to a camera was a craft and one that allowed the actor little control. Even today the argument is often made that film actors often require little "real" talent, since the director, the camera operators, editors, and numerous others create the on-screen performance as much or more than the actor. James Cameron's recent *Avatar* tells his story largely without blood and flesh actors! With endless repetition and retakes, almost anything is possible—today as in the past—whereas the stage actor, through lengthy rehearsal, has one chance at each performance to get it right. The Lunts, for example, held in disdain gifted stage actors who deserted the stage for the lure of Hollywood, with its large salaries, long-term contracts, California weather, frequent change in assignment (as contrasted with the New York stage's relatively lengthy engagements in one role), and the well-advertised social life and celebrity of the film actor. The Lunts also believed, as did other actors—and many today—that the stage was a more satisfactory and fulfilling medium not only for the actor but also for the audience than was the movies (and especially television).

The great actor, director, and translator (Ibsen, Chekhov, etc.) Eva Le Gallienne (1899-1991), number three on the *Theatre Guild* list, and despite enormous contributions to the American theatre, is almost forgotten in the public consciousness because of the paucity of her film roles. Her love was the stage, and film had little interest to her (her one late credit of note was in 1980's *Resurrection*).

Helen Hayes (1900-93), often called The First Lady of the American Theater—as were Fontanne and number 6, Katharine Cornell—did not eschew film roles, continuing to appear in films (and television) long after her stage retirement in 1971. She did, however, cast her lot largely with the theatre during a lengthy career. Yet while she was able to appear on stage in 1971 (she was featured as Mary Tyrone in *Long Day's Journey into Night*), she specialized more and more in cameo character roles in film (e.g., *Airport* in 1970). Her screen appearances thus assure her place as a film icon while she remained a mainstay of twentieth-century theatre history.

Dudley Digges (1879-1947), an Irish-born and trained character actor, is the great exception among the top five, with over fifty film credits (forty between 1929 and 1946) and a reputation not only as a fixture of the Broadway stage but also as an actor often in demand in supporting film roles (yet his is not a household name, and his image would likely not be identified by most film buffs in a lineup). Number six, Katharine Cornell (1893-1974), one of three reigning actresses on the Broadway stage along with Fontanne and Hayes during the second quarter of the twentieth century (best remembered for her Elizabeth Barrett in *The Barretts of Wimpole Street* in 1931), had theatre credits that are lengthy and numerous, ranging from Shakespeare to Chekhov, Shaw, Christopher Fry, and Somerset Maugham. Of all the "outstanding stage actors" on the *Theatre Guild* list, Cornell was probably the most devoted to the theatre, even more so than Lunt-Fontanne and Le Gallienne. In the early thirties she turned down a number of film roles that won other actresses Oscars (O-lan in *The Good Earth* and Pilar in *For Whom the Bell Tolls*, for example). Between 1920 and 1930 legit theatres outside New York decreased in number, many converting to film palaces; the Depression reduced live theatre even more: during the 1927-8 Broadway season, the number of stage productions reached a record of 280; by 1939-40 this had been reduced to 80. The temptation to accept film roles must have been great, but Cornell simply became even more determined to stay in the theatre in order to help keep it vibrant and important. Ultimately, she appeared in only one film role, as Juliet reciting a short few lines from *Romeo and Juliet* in *Stage Door Canteen* (1943), a wartime propaganda film that starred many of Hollywood's best actors, under the auspices of The American Theatre Wing. But her appearance was an indication of her support of the troops, not a desire to be in the movies.

Of the remaining names on the list, all had film credits, to varying degrees. Tom Powers (1890-1955) might be the most unique, in that before a lengthy stage career in Broadway musicals and dramas, he had appeared in more than seventy silent films (1911-17). In 1944 he returned to Hollywood (first as the murder victim in 1944's *Double Indemnity*). Subsequently, into the 1950s, he appeared in over eighty film and television roles (most often as a middle-aged businessman or a military/police officer. Ruth Gordon's (1896-1985) career in both film and theatre is well-known. Despite a film acting career that began with an appearance as an extra in a silent film in 1915 and ending with iconographic roles in such cult films as *Rosemary's Baby* and *Harold and Maude*, her stage career was equally noteworthy, if less permanently memorable, as was her career as playwright and, with her second husband, Garson Kanin, screenwriter.

Paul Muni, Richard Bennett, Walter Huston, and Edward G. Robinson are best remembered today for their film work; yet each had a notable stage career. Muni (1895-1967) appeared in only twenty-five films during a long career, including the pre-Code classics in the 1920s, *Scarface*, and *I Am a Fugitive from a Chain Gang*; yet he learned his trade in New York's Yiddish theatre in the teens and early twenties and returned often to the stage during his career, appearing in his last major stage role in 1955—Henry Drummond in *Inherit the Wind*. Bennett (1870-1944)—father of actresses Constance, Barbara, and Joan—had a long and distinguished stage career beginning in 1891 (*Damaged Goods*, *He Who Gets Slapped*, *Winterset*, *They Knew What They Wanted*, and as Robert Mayo in *Beyond the Horizon*). He reprised his *Damaged Goods* appearance in its silent movie version in 1914, his film debut. Other than the role of Major Amberson in 1942's *The Magnificent Ambersons*, his twenty-seven film roles did not match the excellence of his stage parts. Huston (1884-1950) is still admired for his 1948 appearance in *The Treasure of the Sierra Madre* (for which he won an Academy Award for Best Supporting Actor), but his reputation is also enhanced by such stage appearances as *Knickerbocker Holiday* in 1938 with his rendition of "September Song." Robinson (1893-1973), Bucharest born, had a modest New York stage career (beginning in 1913), appearing first in film in 1916 and graduating to stardom in the 1930s (he deserted his stage career in 1930, and largely threw his lot with film thereafter). One of many actors who saw his career flourish in the new sound film era, he made only three films prior to 1930 but appeared in fourteen films in 1930-1932. Often cast as the "tough guy" (especially in the 1930s and 1940s), Robinson over a fifty-year career appeared in 101 films. And finally, the Russian-born Alla Nazimova (1879-1945) came to the United States in 1905 as an experienced and well-trained stage actor, acclaimed for her appearances in the plays of Ibsen (in English). Her stage fame faded by 1918 (though apparently, based on her rank in the *Theatre Guild* list, her transformative stage personae lingered); and for a decade she appeared in such films as *Camille* and *Salome*, returning by the early 1930s (perhaps aiding her reputation and rank) to the stage (in 1931 she appeared as Christine in O'Neill's *Mourning Becomes Electra*).

The above baker's dozen represent fairly typical patterns of legitimate actors' migrations from stage to film (and often back) during the American film's golden age. Certainly the stage was the major training ground for almost all actors during the 1920s-1940s. Yet like a few of the outstanding actors in the *Theatre Guild* list, other superb actors avoided film almost completely, choosing to commit themselves to the stage and staunchly believing that theirs was an art form while acting to a camera was no more than a craft—or even a fluke. A great example, whose historically significant performances never received permanency (that is, in recorded form), was the actor Walter Hampden (1879-1955), known as Dean of the American Theatre and contemporary with the group profiled above, yet little known as a film actor. Hampden's life, recently chronicled by Geddeth Smith, illustrates how he dedicated most of his career to Shakespearean roles on stage (Hamlet, Henry V, Shylock, Othello) and his one greatest non-Shakespearean role of Cyrano de Bergerac. Yet none can be seen on film (or television); we must get our clues as to his great stage performances by looking at his few film depictions, notably in *Sabrina*, *The Vagabond King*, and *All About Eve* (in which he played "the Old Actor"). Unfortunately, since Hampden made so few films, and most, made late in his career, were small or cameo roles, we have no real record of Hampden in his full and considerable powers. It is regrettable that Hampden and others like him left so few records of their acting prowess.

Conversely, a large number of performers trained in less prestigious and poorer-paying popular entertainment forms—vaudeville, circus, burlesque, even minstrelsy—were far more eager and pleased to make this transition from stage to screen, especially after the introduction of sound, as argued in James Fisher's essay on Al Jolson and Ruby Keeler. The intersecting of vaudeville and film is another poorly explored topic, although a sizable number of good vaudeville studies (many unpublished theses) have been undertaken in recent years, beginning with Robert C. Allen's unpublished dissertation in 1977. A surprisingly large number of the performers profiled in this collection fall into the category of vaudeville trained or at least vaudeville experienced: Mae West, the Marx Brothers, Charlie Chaplin, Buster Keaton, Al Jolson, Cary Grant, James Cagney, Clifton Webb, Burt Lancaster, Eddie Cantor, W. C. Fields, Red Skelton, Fred Astaire, Marie Dressler, Ed Wynn, Eddie Quillan—and Charley Grapewin—but interestingly not Harold Lloyd.

WHO'S CHARLEY?

Many of the film performers discussed in this collection followed a fairly predictable series of steps from unknown stage performer to headliner to largely unknown or uncredited film extra (often in silent films) and then to roles in "talkies" and, if all went well, stardom and celebrity status. I believe more typical are the lives of those in this volume that never truly reached stardom and struggled for survival (such as Frankie Thomas, Eddie Quillan, and Charles Wagenheim), or, like the example to follow, reached success in films late in life after a circuitous route with plenty of bumps and detours. The road traveled by such performers is difficult to track since lesser-known actors—vaudevillians and itinerant stage actors in small stock companies or "on the road"—leave fractured records and rarely find their ways into stage or film histories. Such is the case with the following case study, although fortunately his comic talent reached headliner status (and years of experience) before carving a late career in the talkies.

Charles Ellsworth Grapewin (known professionally as Charley Grapewin) was born in Xenia, Ohio, on December 20, 1869—some incorrectly say 1875—well before appearing in film was an option! Some orientation might be helpful. The year prior to Charley's birthday, the "leg show" was essentially introduced to the American scene by Lydia Thompson and her British Blondes, combining burlesque with pulchritude in tights, P. T. Barnum's famous New American Museum burned down, Dan Castello's Circus became the first to make a transcontinental tour, and celluloid was developed by inventor John Hyatt. The year of Charley's birth was noted theatrically, among other events, for the opening of New York's Booth's Theatre (called the temple of art by its builder, actor-manager Edwin Booth) about a year before Charley's birth. Booth, who died in 1893, was still very much at the top of his profession. Other notable theatre and entertainment events in 1869 include the management of Augustin Daly, head of one of New York's last great stock companies; the publication of Ned Buntline's *Buffalo Bill, the King of Border Men*, the first of some 550 dime novels about Cody, the icon who starred in the Wild West exhibition (and made early films about his life); the opening of one of California's first important theatres, the California Theatre, built on Bush Street in San Francisco; the first appearance of stage magician Alexander Herrmann (d. 1896) in New York; and Madame Rentz's Female Minstrels was credited as the first American burlesque show. The minstrel show by 1869 was America's most successful form of entertainment, variety and musical comedy were on the rise, vaudeville was not yet America's favorite form for all kinds of amusement, and the American circus entered its "Golden Age" during the decade following the Civil War (Barnum did not enter the circus business until 1871). Grapewin then had some options if he was to enter the "show business," but movies were not one of them.

Some years ago I acquired a small archive of scrapbooks that had belonged to Grapewin, about whom I knew essentially nothing (other than his role as Uncle Henry in *The Wizard of Oz*). Though these scrapbooks are dominated by largely unidentified photographs and undated clippings, they nonetheless document some key events in his journey to Hollywood and his film career, which, though fairly brief (other than a period in 1900 when he made two short silent films; see below), lasted from 1931 to about 1944. And even more tantalizing non-film aspects of his career are hinted at but fail to provide solid facts. So what did Charley do from, say 1879 until 1931, when he began his serious film career (at age sixty)? That's more than half a century!

Not surprisingly, Charley apparently ran away from home at age ten to join the circus—working first (in his teens) as a roller-skating acrobat, according to one account (and there are few documented ones), and a couple of press interviews—and soon graduated to the high-wire and trapeze. Apparently he also juggled, for a photo in one of his scrapbooks shows him with Indian clubs in hand. Other photos and clippings suggest that Grapewin was certainly physically fit, enjoyed sports, and later in life was a dedicated fisherman. A series of newspaper articles—most undated but apparently from the summer of 1912 (when Charley was in his forties)—reveal that while living in New Jersey and touring in vaudeville, he was the captain of a semi-professional baseball team known as Grapewin's National Stars (sometimes called the Invincibles) that soundly beat most of its opponents. He was the owner of this team for a number of years.

Grapewin apparently left the circus in Portland, Oregon, subsequently joining a series of regional stock companies, and began to write short plays that featured him (or could) in the star parts (in the late 1920s and early 1930s some ten records of titles by Grapewin can be found in copyright records, most likely short plays used in vaudeville). It is possible that he returned to the circus in the 1880s and spent the better part of that decade moving between stage work and the circus trapeze. Possibly circa 1890 he landed a part in a New York production (*Little Puck*), though I've yet to verify this. We do know that in 1895 or 96 Charley married actress Anna Chance (b. 1875), daughter of baseball great Frank Chance (d. 1924) who also managed the Chicago Cubs to four National League championships (1906-10). Charlie and Anna remained a devoted couple until her death in 1943. For the remainder of Grapewin's stage career, Anna was his leading lady in his various comic sketches.

In 1900 (September and October), essentially when he entered vaudeville, Grapewin first ventured into films—albeit only long enough to make two silent comic "shorts" filmed by Frederick S. Armitage, then an American Mutoscope and Biograph cameraman and ultimately cinematographer on 423 early films (the last in 1917). Grapewin's films were *Chimmie Hicks at the Races* (Charley as Hicks who pantomimes watching a horse race, making several bets, ultimately losing all his money, and at the end on his knees praying for forgiveness), only twenty-two feet in length, and *Chimmie Hicks and the Rum Omelet* (directed by Cecil M. Hepworth). According to Kemp Niver, Grapewin appeared in a third short film three years later, *Jimmie Hicks in Automobile*, this time filmed by G. W. Bitzer, an even more prolific cinematographer than Armitage (almost one thousand credits; ultimately collaborator with D. W. Griffith, including the controversial *Birth of a Nation* in 1915). Grapewin's third comic short (twenty-nine feet in length) shows Charley in an automobile demonstrating various driving maneuvers.

Apparently this was the end of Grapewin's early film career—modest and undistinguished. Although Grapewin was adept at pantomime and had a pliable and comically effective face, for some reason he failed to find a long-term place in silent films. But chapter two for him in movies lay ahead.

Given his writing proclivity and his career doing verbal humor in comic sketches, perhaps he was unsatisfied doing brief pantomimic bits. Several unverified Internet sources credit Grapewin as the author of the first vaudeville sketch ("The Mismatched Pair") without dancing or singing. Perhaps. One of the more interesting scrapbooks in my Grapewin archive is a press book that covers 1913-17 (the earliest book of clippings is for 1901-2). Charley and Anna at this point lived in West End, a neighborhood in Long Branch, New Jersey (also during his baseball days). Vaudeville tours in this period, with his own small company, at various times included such sketches as *Poughkeepsie, The Awakening of Pipp* (which toured for several years and was billed as "The Rip Van Winkle of Vaudeville"), *Stuck, The Immortal Pipp, A Common Occurence, Above the Limit, Up-to-You John Henry* (by George V. Hobart), and, at the end of his vaudeville career, *Jed's Vacation.*

A sense of Grapewin's professional life is suggested by the towns he played for short periods of time (from one-night stands to a week or so). The press book dates from November 1913 and indicates that he toured eight months a year, while spending the balance of his year in Long Branch where he designed and built an elaborate home filled with theatrical memorabilia, a billiard's room, and probably a shop (Charley was a talented woodworker building tables with inlaid tops). Grapewin had clearly earned a position of some importance, for he and Anna toured the Keith circuit, one of the strongest and most respected of the numerous vaudeville circuits available (see "Trav S. D.'"s discussion and others that touch on vaudeville). He and his company in November appeared as headliners at The Garrick in Wilmington, Delaware; Atlanta's Forsyth Theatre; and Union Hill, New Jersey's Hudson Theatre. In December appearances included an engagement at New York's Palace (apparently an annual event for the Grapewins), the pinnacle of first-class vaudeville (headlined here by the great comic Bert Williams on loan from Florenz Ziegfeld.) In January Grapewin moved west, with engagements over the next several months in Louisville, Grand Rapids (the local press notes that in *The Awakening of Mr. Pipp* "whatever [Charley] says hits the bull's eye, and he holds his audience in the hollow of his hand"); Toledo, Hamilton (Canada); Buffalo (with stage and silent screen star Valeska Suratt on the bill); Detroit (Sophie Tucker as headliner); and then back to the East Coast (Brooklyn, Philadelphia [with comic Nat M. Wills and Ed Wynn in *The King's Jester*], Norfolk [with the Astaires], Atlantic City [as a featured act], Baltimore, Brooklyn again, and Coney Island).

This short period is typical of Grapewin's subsequent and previous years (through 1917). It is worthy of note that late in this tour Grapewin is reviewed most favorably (date not given) in *The New York Dramatic Mirror*. At this point Charley has chosen to give up Mr. Pipp (the bibulous role; Charley was known as one of the best "tipplers" in the profession) because audiences had begun to be so convinced by his "stewed" condition to believe that he could only do a "tank" part. To counter this impression, he wrote *Poughkeepsie: A Domestic Comedy* with a role quite the opposite from Pipp and, as the author of this review (Walter J. Kingsley) notes, this part (as a traveling salesman) was more like Grapewin who "is inclined to be abstemious." Regardless, it was the laughing hit of the New York area season, and Grapewin "is one of the cleverest farceurs this country has ever produced." Another article noted that Grapewin's new sixteen-minute sketch at the Orpheum "stopped the show." For the balance of 1914 Grapewin and company traveled widely, received superb notices, and clearly were an audience favorite. While in Poughkeepsie the press noted that this was his third visit there in twenty years, a good hint as to his longevity in vaudeville.

After a lengthy tour of California during spring 1915, Grapewin apparently had momentarily grown tired of his *Poughkeepsie* character and in Peoria returned to Pipp, to great acclaim, but announced that he "would bury" Pipp at the end of this engagement after sixteen years (having been born in Wilmington, Delaware).

By February 1916 Grapewin and Anna were back at the Palace playing *Poughkeepsie* with Ruth St. Denis, Fannie Brice, and Hilda Spong on the bill; and then by spring they were touring the Midwest. By the summer he was back in New Jersey at his ocean front cottage, promoting his amateur baseball team the Grapewin National Stars. With the fall of 1916 came another season on the Keith circuit, still performing *Poughkeepsie*. The remaining tour was essentially a duplicate of previous seasons. In his press book Grapewin includes a handwritten list of engagements from July 30, 1916, through mid-February 1918. The tour began at Coney Island, and the list ends with Louisville, Kentucky, with seventeen stops in between. In December he and Anna reappeared at the Palace with Lady Lucile Duff-Gordon, dress and costume designer, and her fashion revue (*Fleurette's Dream at Peronne*) with a dozen mannequins and a million dollars in clothing, as the headliner. But Grapewin was the real hit of the show and received six curtain calls. During the spring of 1918 Charley and Anna introduced a new sketch, *Jed's Vacation*, a sequel to *Poughkeepsie*, with the Grapewins in their now-familiar characters from that sketch (traveling salesman and wife). Grapewin's press book ends with an ad for B. F. Keith's in Atlantic City (with Sophie Tucker as headliner) in early July 1918.

The next decade of Charley's life is unclear. Apparently he left the vaudeville stage in 1919 after some three decades of stage experience, rising to the head of his profession. From the numerous reviews in his press book, it is clear that he was a favorite wherever he appeared, retracing his steps to major stops on the Keith circuit every season and then returning to his New Jersey retreat for the summer months and an annual indulgence in his favorite sport, baseball. Sketchy evidence indicates that he went to work for General Motors for a time, invested his money wisely (he must have done well financially as a vaudeville headliner), had a net worth of some $2 million, and at some point in this decade retired and moved to California. In late 1929, however, he discovered that his net worth had dwindled to $200. Turning to one of his previous talents, writing, Grapewin apparently earned some income with four books, including *The Town Pump: An American Comedy*, written in collaboration with Anthony Hillyer (Los Angeles, 1933). At the same time, the film industry discovered by the late 1920s that the talking picture was not the fad that Thomas Edison had predicted, and as James Fisher explores in his essay on Jolson and Keeler. And Charley Grapewin had found his second act in the movies. Here he was, living in California, adept at reading comic lines with a well-honed expertise after decades on stage, a flexible seasoned performer, and of an age that made him a valuable, in-demand asset to films as an old codger character actor.

From 1929 to 1951 Grapewin had an extraordinary film career, appearing in over one hundred films, most significantly from the mid-1930s to the mid-1940s, dating, it is worth noting, from his mid-sixties to his late seventies. His five earliest films from 1929 were all comic shorts, all but one also starring Anna Chance. It is worth noting that his earliest film in this group was *Jed's Vacation*, which, it might be recalled, was his last vaudeville sketch in 1918. Indeed, it seems likely that several, if not all, of these short comic films were based on vaudeville sketches (his second, *House Cleaning*, sounds very much like his popular sketch *Poughkeepsie*). The debt owed to vaudeville by early film transcended the acquisition of stage talent trained in variety, like Charley and many others discussed in the pages that follow, but dozens of early film shorts—both comic and dramatic—were either adapted or based on sketches seen in vaudeville. Even longer narrative films owed much to theatre technique and source material, as David Mayer, discussed at the beginning of this introduction, has persuasively illustrated in his recent book on D. W. Griffith.

These early Grapewin films—and many later ones—are mostly forgotten or forgettable, with Charley often seen in small roles—Pop or Gramp this; Dr. That, Judge What's-his-name; an unnamed drunk; Professor Jones; or, more significantly, as he was seen in two of his more important films in 1937, the Old Father in *The Good Earth* (with Paul Muni), based on Pearl S. Buck's Nobel Prize—winning novel, and Uncle Salters in *Captain Courageous* (based on Rudyard Kipling's story). Today his considerable reputation (though few today know his name) as a film icon rests on a handful of memorable character roles (including the above two): Dr. Tatum in *Anne of Green Gables* (1934), Mr. Dave McComber in *Ah, Wilderness!* (1935, based on Eugene O'Neill's only comedy), Gramp Maple in *The Petrified Forest* (1936), Uncle Henry (when he was almost seventy) in *The Wizard of Oz* (1939; one of his smallest but best remembered parts), Grandpa in *The Grapes of Wrath* (based on Steinbeck's novel and directed by John Ford in 1937), and Jeeter Lester in *Tobacco Road* (1941, the role in the John Ford film, with screenplay based on Erskine Caldwell's novel and Jack Kirkland's play that made Charley a true star). In the early 1940s he had the recurring role of Inspector Queen in the Ellery Queen film series starring Ralph Bellamy. And finally, in 1941 he played the small role of California Joe in the Western epic *They Died with Their Boots On*, starring Errol Flynn as George Armstrong Custer. His final role, in 1951, was as Grandpa Reed in the modest but affecting film *When I Grow Up*, starring the young actor Bobby Driscoll.

Charley and Anna had retired to California in the late 1920s. With successful film roles under his belt during the late 1930s—and more to come—the Grapewins built a new home in the largely undeveloped town of Corona, a suburb of Los Angeles. Like their cottage in New Jersey, Charley no doubt designed this new commodious house. The ground breaking was in March 1939, and the large home—christened "Grape-Inn"—was completed by the fall. It was apparently located on a small lake or pond, for the Grapewins had their own private pier, and fishing was a popular pastime at their address (which was No. 1 Grapewin Avenue).

The Grapewins apparently had a few happy years before Anna's death in 1943. Charley had a handful of films ahead of him prior to his death from natural causes on February 2, 1956. The Grapewins had no children; his estate was left to his long-time housekeeper. The street where Charley lived and died is today Grapewin Street.

AND NOW, A STELLAR CAST OF MOVIE STARS

SOURCES CONSULTED

Allen, Robert C. "Vaudeville and Film, 1895-1915: A Study in Media Interaction." PhD dissertation. University of Iowa, 1977.

Ashby, LeRoy. *With Amusement for All: A History of American Popular Culture since 1830*. Lexington: University Press of Kentucky, 2006.

Barrow, Kenneth. *Helen Hayes: First Lady of the American Theatre*. New York: Doubleday, 1985.

Basinger, Jeanine. *The Star Machine*. New York: Knopf, 2007.

Before Hollywood: Turn-of-the-Century Film from American Archives. New York: American Federation of Arts, 1986.

Booth, Michael. *English Melodrama*. London: Herbert Jenkins, 1965.

Brewster, Ben, and Lea Jacobs. *Theatre to Cinema*. Oxford: Oxford University Press, 1997.

Brooks, Peter. *The Melodramatic Imagination*. New Haven: Yale University Press, 1976.

Brown, Jared. *The Fabulous Lunts*. New York: Atheneum, 1986.

Fuller, Kathryn H. *At the Picture Show: Small-Town Audiences and the Creation of Movie Fan Culture*. Washington: Smithsonian Institution Press.

Grapewin, Charley. Archive of scrapbooks owned by the author.

Johnson, Stephen. "Evaluating Early Film as a Document of Theatre History: The 1896 Footage of Joseph Jefferson's *Rip Van Winkle*." *Nineteenth Century Theatre*. Vol. 2, no. 2 (1992): 101-22.

Lambert, Gavin. *Nazimova: A Biography*. New York: Knopf, 1997.

Mayer, David. *Stagestruck Filmmaker: D. W. Griffith and the American Theatre*. Iowa City: University of Iowa Press, 2009.

Meisel, Martin. *Realizations: Narrative, Pictorial, and Theatrical Arts in Nineteenth-Century England*. Princeton, NJ: Princeton University Press, 1983.

Mostel, Tad, with Gertrude Macy. *Leading Lady: The World and Theatre of Katharine Cornell*. Boston: Atlantic-Little, Brown, 1978.

Musser, Charles. *Before the Nickelodeon: Edwin S. Porter and the Edison Manufacturing Company*. Berkeley: University of California Press, 1991.

Nasaw, David. *Going Out: The Rise and Fall of Public Amusements*. Cambridge: Harvard University Press, 1993.

Niver, Kemp R. Ed. Bebe Bergsten. *Early Motion Pictures: The Paper Print Collection in the Library of Congress*. Washington: Library of Congress, 1985.

Pearson, Roberta. *Eloquent Gestures: The Transformation of Performance Style in the Griffith Biograph Films*. Berkeley: University of California Press, 1992.

Peters, Margot. *Design for Living: Alfred Lunt and Lynn Fontanne: A Biography*. New York: Knopf, 2003.

Robinson, David. *From Peep Show to Palace: The Birth of American Film*. New York: Columbia University Press, 1996.

Runkel, Phillip M. *Alfred Lunt and Lynn Fontanne: A Bibliography*. Waukesha, WI: Carroll College Press, 1978.

Schweitzer, Marlis. *When Broadway Was the Runway*. Philadelphia: University of Pennsylvania Press, 2009.

Sheehy, Helen. *Eva Le Gallienne: A Biography*. New York: Knopf, 1996.

Smith, Geddeth. *Walter Hampden: Dean of the American Theatre*. Madison and Teaneck: Fairleigh Dickinson University Press, 2008.

Toll, Robert C. *The Entertainment Machine*. Oxford and New York: Oxford UP, 1982.

Wilmeth, Don B., ed. *The Cambridge Guide to American Theatre*. 2nd revised, updated edition. Cambridge and NY: Cambridge University Press, 2007.

CLARK GABLE - Metro Goldwyn - Mayer   CG-12

Journeyman Gable

Erik Christian Hanson

Most people don't know that Clark Gable had a theatrical career. His journey to stardom began at age seventeen when the "King" of Hollywood saw a play at the Akron Music Hall. It changed his life. His reaction to Richard Walton Tully's *The Bird of Paradise*: "I'd never seen anything as wonderful in my life" (Harris, 11). His excitement would be confirmed because he became a regular at the Music Hall. He wasn't paid to work as a *callboy* (someone who tells the actors when it is time to go on); however, he didn't seem to mind. He treated Akron Music Hall like a learning place, a place where he could imbibe everything about the stage actor's lifestyle. One would assume movies would have been the influence that inspired Clark's acting pursuits, but it was the stage that appealed to him most:

> When he'd attended movies (silent and monochrome in those days), he'd never felt any interest in becoming an actor. Perhaps he'd needed the stimulation of a live performance, of hearing words spoken, to realize what magic an actor could perform (Harris, 12).

At the age of twenty-one, Gable would attempt to garner that magic by teaming up with a migrant tent show in Akron that did plays and musicals in small towns (Harris, 16). He wasn't hired for his acting skills, though; he was hired to do the grunt work since his physique warranted it. "I got the job only because they needed someone with muscles to do the heavy work" (Gable quoted in Harris, 16). Quite content to be involved, in any capacity, with a group that traveled the country doing what he loved, he would soon have to contend with Mother Nature who had other plans for his burgeoning acting career: a storm in Montana ended the tent show's tour (Harris, 17).

It was back to reality for Clark. After bouncing from a lumber mill to a department store in Portland, Oregon, he would befriend an employee that belonged to a theater group called the Red Lantern Players. When word came through the store that the Astoria Players, a stock company, were coming to town in search of talent for their summer tour, Clark decided to take a crack at auditioning. But the Brooks Brothers suit he bought would prove fruitless given the result of his audition. The managing director of the company, Rex Jewell, stated, "He seemed to me to lack the slightest gift for the stage with nothing, absolutely nothing to offer then or in the future" (quoted in Harris, 19). Apparently tent show experience wasn't going to cut it. "Nothing to offer," though, would be reconsidered since Clark had something to offer the tour: his muscles.

The tour for the Astoria Players, much like the traveling tent show, was short-lived. Clark was forced to find work at a lumber company, then, after quitting there, at a newspaper called the *Oregonian*. While working in the classified department at the paper, he received news that Josephine Dillon, an acting coach with Broadway experience, wanted to start her own theater group. To get her group kick-started, Dillon invited directors, actors, and playwrights to a play reading at her home. Clark made an appearance but remained silent throughout; he was a wallflower, trying to soak in everything he heard.

His eagerness to learn would quickly rub off on Dillon who saw something in him that others didn't. She not only served as his "live-in companion" (25) shortly thereafter, but she became his mentor and wife as well. Like a sequence out of George Bernard Shaw's *Pygmalion*, she gave him a full-fledged makeover. "She paid to have his teeth repaired, his hair restyled, and his eyebrows plucked" (Harris, 24). Once the physical attributes of Clark were tailored to her liking, Dillon tackled his acting skills, or lack thereof. To combat his clumsiness on stage, she taught him how to control his body. His voice came next. Its high pitch needed to be corrected if he wanted to be considered for strong, masculine roles.

Coming to the conclusion that roles would be aplenty in Hollywood (on stage and in motion pictures), Dillon convinced Gable to leave Portland. But Hollywood's abundant opportunities seemed to be a myth since Clark's first taste of Hollywood had him working as a mechanic before finally landing, with Dillon's assistance, extra work in films. The free time, if and when he had some, was devoted to play auditions.

On stage, he'd soon become a spear-carrying guard in *Romeo and Juliet* and an army member in *What Price Glory?*, a play he was initially rejected for. Director Lillian Albertson couldn't shake the sound of his voice, a voice he and Dillon had been trying to correct. "It wasn't quite heavy enough to match his general makeup. He looked the hardy, virile type, but he sounded like a pansy when he read the tough and salty dialogue" (Albertson quoted in Harris, 33). Dillon stepped in to save the day and convinced Albertson to hire him for the role with the promise that she could fix his voice in time for the play's production.

Next, Gable would play a prosecutor in *Madame X* and a reporter in *Chicago*. But instead of enjoying the minimal success he was having on the stage, Dillon, his toughest critic, would be there to critique his every move. What else would you expect from the person who created him? "When permitted to attend rehearsals, she took copious notes and later drilled him on his deficiencies. On opening nights she always occupied a front-row seat. At intermissions she would rush to his dressing room with advice and suggestions" (Harris, 35).

Apparently the advice from Dillon, whether it unnerved Clark or not, would pave the way for the press to start complimenting his performances and for stock company scouts to start pursuing him. After catching one of his *Chicago* performances, a scout from a company in Houston, Texas, "offered him a full season's contract, running from the autumn of 1927 through the spring of 1928. The salary was a guaranteed $150 weekly, with the roles changing as often as the plays—once a week" (Harris, 40). Clark was ambivalent about the idea of joining a stock company (a group that performs different plays weekly) since he had the opportunity to join a vaudeville circuit, which, if it succeeded, could land him on Broadway. Dillon intervened yet again and "forced him to go to Texas" (Harris, 41).

Texas was the right choice. Working for a stock company allowed Clark to acquire a sense of discipline that Dillon had tried for years to provide. "Besides acting ten performances per week, he attended daily rehearsals of the next play on his agenda. He had to store two roles in his memory at the same time and make sure that he didn't mix them up when he went onstage" (Harris, 43).

After bit parts in the stock company's plays, Clark became a star in Houston after his performances in *Craig's Wife* by George Kelly and *Anna Christie* by Eugene O'Neill. He had "acquired so many fans that the theater ran out of photos and had to dole out rain checks" (Harris, 44). Mondays became "Clark Gable Nights."

As his popularity soared, so did Dillon's confidence in him. She felt he was ready for Broadway. Even though their relationship was souring at this point, Clark would, slowly but surely, get his feel for the New York scene, arguably the most difficult scene to succeed in theatrically. When asked to give his impression of said scene, Clark replied, "I'd heard how the New York critics could make or break an actor. I wanted to see exactly what they would do to me" (Harris, 49).

His first taste of Broadway came when he starred in and received positive notices for his performance in *Machinal*. But getting the boot from two plays shortly thereafter—*House Unguarded* (which landed on Broadway without him) and then, *Gambling*—would humble Clark considerably and force his mind to consider the possibility that exits from both shows might "raise doubts about his talent among casting agents and producers" (50). The doubts would only increase when two other plays he starred in (*Hawk Island* and *Blind Window*) would fizzle after takeoff, never making it to Broadway.

The age of thirty was approaching, and Clark wasn't where he wanted to be. He was aging in an industry where age matters, and he wasn't the talk of the town like he was in Houston. To make matters worse, talkies arrived. Plays would feel the impact of their arrival considerably.

> Talkies had taken away the last competitive edge that plays and vaudeville had over movies. Because of the expense involved in putting on a live production, admission prices needed to be much higher than for movies. But an exhibitor rented cans of film and needed to employ only a projectionist and house staff. Even in the best of times a ticket to a live event was a luxury item for many people and purchased sparingly (55).

One play that wasn't seen sparingly that season was *The Last Mile* by John Wexley, starring Spencer Tracy. The play (especially Tracy's performance) was taking Broadway by storm; a West Coast production would soon follow. Fortunate that Lillian Albertson was directing the production in Los Angeles and San Francisco, Clark would land the role of "Killer" Mears. With so much talk surrounding the performance of Tracy, Clark would, after being advised by Albertson, have to find his own approach to the role.

Clark's approach, albeit different than Tracy's, would assure his entrance into the world of film after praise from a theater critic like this came:

> I must have seen every one of Gable's previous plays in Los Angeles, yet I had trouble remembering them. His work had not been outstanding. But in the role of the convict sentenced to walking that "last mile" to the electric chair, Gable literally knocked everyone in the audience between the eyes with the fierce, bloodthirsty, vindictive and blasphemous way he tore that part open (Schallert quoted in Harris, 60).

Some actors "tear a part open" and never get discovered. Some take acting class after acting class and only get extra work. Others never find an agent. Some actors, like Clark, endure grueling journeys.

Clark Gable's journey led to starring roles *It Happened One Night* (1934), *Mutiny on the Bounty* (1935) and, eventually, *Gone With the Wind*. "The dashing, mustachioed image of Rhett Butler in *Gone with the Wind* [1939] remains indelibly associated with the name Clark Gable," but his trials and tribulations as a theatrical actor merit our attention and respect.

Bibliography

Harris, Warren G. *Clark Gable: A Biography*. New York: Random House, 2002.
TCM.COM. 2009. Classic Film Union. 7 Sept. 2009 <http://fan.tcm.com/service/displayKickPlace.kickAction?u=4555518& as=66470&b=>.

Red Skelton: A Personal Remembrance

Zanne Hall

One of those rare performers of the old days who not only made the transition from stage to radio to film and television but also starred in these venues was Red Skelton who I came to know when he was on tour through my hometown of Pittsburgh, Pennsylvania, in 1971. It was one of those serendipitous relationships where you meet someone and feel an immediate kinship that affects your entire life. Red was a Shriner and played at their Syria Mosque performing arts center, a beautiful Middle Eastern—like edifice that has since been razed to make way for, of all things, a parking lot.

In 1923, when Red was ten years old, he had the luck to meet Ed Wynn while he was selling newspapers outside of the Pantheon Theatre in Vincennes, Indiana. Wynn was playing in a vaudeville show and brought Red backstage to watch the acts. The lad was bitten hard by the show business bug. Why not? His father, who died shortly after he was born, was a former clown with the Hagenbeck-Wallace Circus, so performing was already in his blood. Considering himself a clown first and foremost became important throughout his life. As an accomplished painter, he drew mostly clown compositions.

At fifteen he knew he wanted to make a living in the entertainment world and worked wherever he could, including medicine shows, showboats, burlesque, vaudeville and circuses. It was on this hectic proving ground where he developed an eclectic education, honing the many characters that became later well-known to his audiences. His act consisted of pantomime, pratfalls, funny voices, and sight gags; and it continued this way throughout his career. He took serious stock of his self-worth and was covetous of the characters he created. I saw this trait when I spent time with him backstage.

I worked as an usherette (read "aspiring actress") at the Mosque where Red was appearing for a few days. We became fast friends, and he asked me to come in early so that we could spend time together before he went onstage. I couldn't wait to get there each night. One time, I showed up extra early and walked into his empty dressing room that had been prepared for his arrival. The bright round lights that surrounded the makeup mirror were on, his costumes were laid out, and a pitcher of water (no sports bottles then) and cups were on a side table. The famous brown crumpled fedora that he utilized for various characters like Clem Kadiddlehopper and Junior, the Mean Widdle Kid, sat on his makeup table. I couldn't resist putting it on my head. I began play-acting his various characters in the mirror. When he came into the room, I proudly showed him my imitations. He wasn't pleased. My heart sank, and I thought that my acting might've been less than perfect. He looked at me and said quietly but sternly, the words still burning in my head: "Imitation is not the sincerest form of flattery. Imitation is *stealing*." He had changed gears and was now my mentor as Ed Wynn had been for him. I sensed this remark came from his early years on the stage when a performer's act was his or her livelihood. If another performer did a bit better, then the bit or the act became theirs and not the originator's; so the creator was forced to find a new act, hopefully one that was unstealable.

Red began working on the stage in the early thirties during vaudeville's death rattle. Radio and talking film were overtaking the era like wildfire. Many performers looked for work elsewhere if they wanted to continue working in front of audiences. Red emceed the walkathon circuit where he met his first wife, Edna Stilwell, in Kansas City when he was seventeen. She too was an usherette. A walkathon was a sad exhausting fad where couples "danced" for hours, sometimes days, until they dropped—literally. The last couple to continue moving around the floor, even clinging to one another zombie-like, was awarded a prize. In the Depression, anything was appreciated. Trying to be glib with wild antics to make people stay awake sharpened his improvisational skills.

A minor vaudevillian star, "Uncle" Jim Harkins saw Red's act and encouraged the young comedian and Edna to venture to New York to hook up with an agent, Tom Kennedy, who had seen Red's walkathons in New Jersey and liked his banter with the audience. They negotiated a contract, and Kennedy had Red doing clubs along with the slowly dwindling vaudeville circuit. He also negotiated movie deals with minor roles for the upcoming comedian.

The end of the 1930s were lucky years for him. He got his break in radio and film at that time. His first radio appearances were on *The Rudy Vallee Show*, and a few years later he garnered his own comedy radio series *The Raleigh Cigarette Program* consisting of the various characters and bits that audiences were already becoming familiar with. His 1938 film debut was in *Having Wonderful Time*, which was based on a 1937 play by Arthur Kober. Much of Red's impromptu antics ended up on the editing floor owing to time constraints, but that didn't deter him from starring in numerous movies in the 1940s and beyond while still maintaining his radio series.

He was happiest when professionally busy, and busy he was, but in 1944 he was drafted by the U.S. Army and went in as a private. He liked to joke, "I was the only celebrity who went in and came out a private." During this time he divorced Edna and married Georgia Davis, who he had introduced me to. I remember she was a tall pretty red-haired lady with sad eyes. I didn't know at the time that they had a tumultuous relationship, and he would divorce her later that year. A few years after that, she would commit suicide by gunshot.

He had a very hectic military life, not unlike his professional life; and in addition to his military duties, he never turned down requests to entertain officers. Often, his shows were late at night, and the combination of trying to fulfill his military obligations during the day led to a nervous breakdown. He was discharged in 1945 and resumed his radio and movie career. Harboring a profound sense of patriotism, he sold war bonds in 1945, touring with the Ozzie and Harriet band.

I didn't know what Red's political party of choice was, but he was deeply patriotic and conservative. This is where we crossed swords, but I never really told him how much for fear of ending our fledgling friendship. At the height of the Vietnam War, my generation saw patriotism as a stranglehold. Red performed for Vice President Spiro Agnew, President Nixon's mouthpiece, who called my generation "Yippies, Hippies, Yahoos, Black Panthers, lions and tigers alike. I would swap the whole damn zoo for the kind of young Americans I saw in Vietnam." (The quote is very famous and can be found on many websites, including QuotationsBook.com, ThinkExist.com, UBR.com, and the60sofficialsite.com). Red deemed it a privilege to be drafted, but this was not World War II. At that time, there was a very clear definition of tyrants who desired to break apart the world and rule over the spoils. To my peers, the Vietnam War seemed pointless and hazy. Red was very firm with me when he emphasized that Communism's spread had to be stopped in Vietnam. I remember talking to him about politics one time while sporting an armband on my jacket with "May Day" written across it. May Day was a pivotal month set aside for demonstrations to end the war. Knowing he was from a generation a world apart, I put my hand over the armband, covering it. Whenever I came in early to meet with him, I turned my jacket inside-out. His generation cheered the war effort, but it was my generation who was fighting and dying in it.

I think his conservatism, along with the fact that times were changing, led to his show being cancelled in 1971. CBS was not happy that he wasn't attracting younger audiences and cancelled him after sixteen years. He felt betrayed. I also remember that he cautioned me against "blue" humor and said that it was cheap to go for a dirty laugh. This world was also changing. This was now the world of the post-Lenny Bruce comedians such as George Carlin and Richard Pryor who spoke to the anti-war "Yippies, Hippies," etc.

Red and I shared a passion for clowns, and I told him that I was creating a clown character for children's parties I called Skeffington. "Skeffy the Clown . . . I like that," he smiled. I also told him that I had applied to Ringling Bros. Clown College, but he talked me *out of* pursuing a clown career until graduating from college. That was probably the first and last time Red Skelton ever told anyone *not* to become a clown. He most likely recalled his uneducated youth where he skipped high school graduation to go on the road to support his family. I also confessed to him that I got incredibly nervous whenever I went onstage, and he laughed that he used to lose his lunch before performances. He told me that he still got nervous before going out in front of an audience but that the energy helped keep him focused. I remember one time I was backstage with him before he went on. He liked my being there as a support. The stage was lit up like the sun while just a few feet away the wings were in moonlight. He put his arm around my waist, and I did likewise. I felt something hard around his middle and realized he was wearing a back brace of some kind. This was surprising as he had the agility of an acrobat when he was onstage with no hint of a back problem. His energy was much younger than his chronologic years. He looked at me and smiled, unloosed his arm from around my middle, then stepped a few feet toward the stage, mentally preparing himself to go on. Standing straight as a poker, his brown fedora in his hands, his eyes closed, and his head bowed, he entered a meditative state. I later drew a watercolor of that poetic image.

Children's Hospital, just a few blocks away from the Syria Mosque in Oakland, is a famous U.S. hospital. One of the things it originated in 1971 was the "Mr. Yuk" symbol, a round green face that looks as though it's swallowed something bad. The idea started with the hospital's pediatrician, Dr. Richard Moriarty; and the illustration was created by a grade school student, Wendy Brown. This sticker was utilized by mothers who affixed it to poisonous household items that were dangerous for their children to ingest. Red visited the hospital, as he did many children's hospitals, not only because he was a kind man but because of the tragedy he suffered from the loss of his young son to leukemia. Our friendship bond became even stronger when I told him my mother was a nurse there who worked on the worst floor: neurology. Most of the children in this ward never recovered.

Red was a very loving person, and his aura attracted people wherever he went. He could stand alone in one spot for only a brief moment because people wanted to be with him, to talk to him, not because of his fame but because they wanted to be near the person *within* that fame. He was approachable. He genuinely loved people and loved making them laugh. He is quoted many times, as well as in Arthur Marx's biography, as saying, "I believe we were all put on this earth for a purpose . . . . I was put here to make people laugh." I consider myself extremely lucky that he touched my life in such an unforgettable, life-long memory. His warmth reached out to his audiences when he bade them at the end of every show "Good night and may God bless."

Reinventing the Public Self: Four Vaudevillians Who Got a Hollywood Makeover

"Trav S. D."

The institution of American vaudeville (circa 1880-1930) was second to none in providing talent for the medium that replaced it. The best-known vaudeville veterans among the Hollywood stars of the thirties were its comedians, performers like the Marx Brothers, Mae West, W. C. Fields, Stan Laurel, and countless more. That this should be so is not surprising. When these larger-than-life clowns brought their acts to the silver screen, they brought a bit of vaudeville with them. It was in their jokes, their mannerisms, their costumes, and in their little extra skills (such as juggling or ability on a musical instrument) that added a little magical extra to their performances. But the fact is, vaudeville's shadow was much longer than that. Its legacy was everywhere, and not always in so obvious a manner. Some of its prominent progeny were hiding in plain sight.

That the broader public doesn't associate names like Cary Grant, James Cagney, Clifton Webb, or, little bit later, Burt Lancaster clearly and irrevocably with the variety stage that spawned them is a mysterious historical quirk, having more to do, I think, with the changing tastes of a maturing audience than any premeditated campaign to lock the hats and canes in the attic. That quality historian Henry Jenkins calls the "vaudeville aesthetic," encompassing bizarre, surreal comedy as well as containing a steady stream of constant jarring surprises (frequently literal vaudeville turns) enjoyed its greatest heyday in the very early thirties. Increasingly, however, audiences (and therefore studios) sought stories: recognizable, believable heroes in plausible narratives following the old Aristotelian plot structure. Naturally, the shift was relative. Hollywood still cranked out fantasy. Those supposedly real heroes happened to be uncommonly handsome and witty, and the stories, while not *Duck Soup*, were not exactly *The Bicycle Thief* either. And because of this, the astute observer can still spot the small subtle touches of vaudeville brought to the screen with them.

One of the greatest transformations came in the career of Cary Grant. Starting out as a teenaged tumbler in the British Music Hall with Bob Pender's Knockabout Comedians, young Archie Leach (his real name) toured the provinces for a couple of years, before the outfit crossed the Atlantic in 1920 to try American vaudeville. The troupe opened at the legendary Hippodrome (Broadway's biggest theatre) in a revue called "Good News," which ran for nine months. In 1921 they toured the Keith circuit, with a final gig at the Palace in 1922.

Pender returned to the United Kingdom, but Leach chose to stay in the United States. He got some work doing stilt walking in

Coney Island. Then he went on in "Better Times," the sequel to "Good News," at the Hippodrome, with some fellow Pender veterans. Booked as "The Walking Strangers" the group did a vaudeville act, working the Panatages wheel in 1924. Archie moved into the National Vaudeville Artist's Club, making himself generally available as a substitute. He was a valuable man to have around. His skills included juggling, acrobatics, unicycle, comic sketches; and (not to be sneered at) he was an excellent straight man. He worked in the latter capacity, for example, for Milton Berle at Proctor's Newark. During these years of struggle, he became good friends with Burns and Allen. He studied Burns and Zeppo Marx as examples of some of the top straight men in the business.

In the late 1920s, he began to move into musical comedy. He was cast in the 1927 Hammerstein musical *Golden Dawn*. In 1929, he did *Boom Boom* for the Shuberts with Jeanette McDonald. He worked in various Shubert shows for three years. Then his friend and colleague Fay Wray went to Hollywood to star in *King Kong*. Wray persuaded Leach to make the move himself in late 1931, where he signed at Paramount as Cary Grant.

That carefully wrought name and persona was invented—fashioned with all the care and diligence of the old vaudevillian he'd always been. Grant became prized in motion pictures for his suave, sophisticated style, a manner of talking, moving, and dressing that bespoke, above all, class. But it was an illusion. Raised in a lower middle-class home—the offspring of a struggling, alcoholic father, and a controlling, dotty mother (she was later institutionalized)—he might just as easily found himself clerking in a bank. Hence, that mysterious quality of humility that always added another layer to roles that in lesser hands might have seemed lightweight and superficial. And, of course, the third level is the legacy of his training as an acrobat, his wonderful facility for physical comedy, whether face-pulling, pratfalls, or double takes. Surely that training had something to with his ability to run through a cornfield like a track star in *North by Northwest* at the age of sixty.

An interesting contrast with the life and career of Grant is that of his contemporary James Cagney. On the face of it, the two were on parallel tracks: born within five years of each other (Cagney in 1899, Grant in 1904), born to impecunious families with alcoholic fathers, an apprenticeship in vaudeville and the Broadway stage, and Hollywood film careers that spanned roughly the same time period from the early 1930s through the 1960s. Grant and Cagney had even been members of the same vaudeville act, although at different times.

But here the similarities end. Where Grant's well-known persona was a carefully wrought masterpiece of artifice, Cagney built his reputation and career on being one of the most truthful dramatic actors to come out of the studio system. So indelible is the impression that he made in a series of gritty Warner Bros.' gangster pictures that the public largely forgot (if it ever knew) that this Hollywood tough guy started out in show business as a vaudeville hoofer. But Cagney never forgot.

"Vaudeville is where I learned my business," he once said, "and truth to tell, it's where I had the most fun."

His idol as a young man had been George M. Cohan, the ultimate song-and-dance man. When Cagney got to portray him in the 1942 film *Yankee Doodle Dandy*, it wasn't just another bio-pic for him; he was realizing the ambition of a lifetime. For a glance at Cagney the hoofer, this is the film to watch.

He started taking acting classes at the Lennox Hill Settlement House. Early parts included a drag role in *Every Sailor* at the Eighty-sixth Street Theatre and a chorus part in *Pitter Patter* on Broadway. In 1921, he was cast in a vaudeville three act—Parker, Rand, and Cagney—filling the spot that had just been vacated by Archie Leach. The trio toured for six months before breaking up. He was in two Lew Fields musicals

Ritz Girls of 19 and 22 and *Snapshots of 1923*. He teamed up for a while with a man named Victor Kilian, doing dancing and comedy. In 1922 he married Frances "Willie" Willard, who became his vaudeville dance partner. They spent the years 1923-24 working vaudeville three-a-days, and even some five-a-days.

It was Kilian who brought about the sea change in Cagney's career. Kilian had important contacts in the legit theatre and persuaded Cagney to try out for the role of a drifter in Maxwell Anderson's *Outside In* (1925). Cagney got outstanding reviews in the part from such important writers as Robert Benchley—including effusive praise for a ten-minute stretch where Cagney didn't talk at all! There followed a stretch of other Broadway roles, culminating in George Kelly's *Maggie the Magnificent* (1929) and Marie Baumer's *Penny Arcade* (1930). The latter play was adapted into the film *Sinner's Holiday* by Warner Bros., launching Cagney's film career and his long association with criminal parts. Today, he is usually associated with movie likes *Public Enemy* (1931), *Angels with Dirty Faces* (1938), and *White Heat* (1949). His formative years growing up rough and tumble in the slums gave his performances in such yarns an authenticity that few could match. As a consequence it is usually Cagney the mobster we think of first, not the star of musicals like *Footlight Parade* (1933), *Something to Sing About* (1937), and *Yankee Doodle Dandy* (1942).

Another vaudeville dancer whose Hollywood screen output made little, if any, use of his broad variety training was Clifton Webb. Webb's trajectory couldn't have been more different from Grant's and Cagney's. Far from going into show business to escape a colorless origin, Webb (born Webb Parmalee Hollenbeck) was a child prodigy who was driven into show business by a domineering stage mother. A frustrated actress, Mrs. Hollenbeck pushed young Webb into dancing school at the age of seven. When the father objected, she pushed him too—right out of the family.

The boy she raised was a perfect man of the theatre. He was to become one of the top dancers in the business, a professional opera singer, and an Academy Award-nominated actor (twice). At age seven he made his professional debut at Carnegie Hall in a children's play called *The Brownies*. He followed this with the lead in *Oliver Twist* and a play called *The Master of Carlton Hall*. A remarkable person by any measure, he graduated from high school at age thirteen, then studied painting and opera. In 1911, he sang with the Aborn Opera Company in Boston. Parts in *La Boheme*, *Madame Butterfly*, and *Hansel and Gretel* followed.

By the midteens, Castle Mania was sweeping the land. As a trained dancer, Webb was in a position to take advantage of the craze. He teamed up with Bonnie Glass, and then Mae Murray, performing on the Keith circuit and in nightclubs, and teaching private classes at the Webb Dance Studio. After this, he would add eccentric dances to his more traditional ballroom repertoire, and he partnered with Mary Hay and Gloria Goodwin. By the late twenties, he was headlining at the Palace.

Throughout the twenties and thirties he starred in musical and straight plays in both New York and London, and had numerous roles in silent films. But it wasn't until he was fifty-one years old when he was cast in the film *Laura* (1944) that he became the movie star that he is primarily known as today. He went on to star in the original version of *The Razor's Edge* (1946), the popular "Mr. Belvedere" series (1948-51), *Stars and Stripes Forever* (1952, in which he portrayed John Philip Sousa), the original *Titanic* (1953), and many others into the 1960s. His impeccable grace in these performances must almost certainly be owing to his long experience as a dancer, though we seldom get to see him do it.

By the late 1930s, when Burt Lancaster went into show business, there wasn't very much left of vaudeville. A tough but highly intelligent kid from the streets of New York, Lancaster's interest in gymnastics had kept him out of trouble. When still a teenager, he became a professional trapeze artist, working circuses and the few vaudevilles that remained with his partner Nick Cravat.

During his hitch in World War II, he picked up acting in the USO. Immediately upon his discharge, he tried out and landed a part in a Broadway show that flopped. His Hollywood break was a film called *The Killer* (1946), and from there his career took off. He was one of the most versatile men in Hollywood, essaying serious dramas, westerns, crime-thrillers, and comedies. He always remained proud of his acrobatic skills, however, and sought to show them off to good advantage whenever he could. Because of this, he may also be said to be the last of the swashbucklers. Certain of his vehicles were tailored around his ability to swing on a bar high above the ground wearing leotards. These included *The Flame and the Arrow* (1950) and *The Crimson Pirate* (1952)—both of which featured Nick Cravat as a mute sidekick—and *Trapeze* (1956).

A long list of traditional thespians who went on to Hollywood stardom had done time in vaudeville as well: people like the Barrymores, Walter

Huston, Frederick March, and scores of others. But unlike the performers in this brief survey, their one and only specialty had always been acting itself. The vaudeville training in other specialties like acrobatics, slapstick, crosstalk comedy, and song and dance gave this handful of movie actors a unique bag of tricks most of their contemporaries (and most current movie actors) sorely lacked. In subtle ways, vaudeville enriched their performances, even if their origins in the variety theatre were downplayed.

Bibliography

Godfrey, Lionel. *Cary Grant: The Light Touch*. St. Martin's Press, 1981.

McCabe, John. *Cagney*. Alfred A. Knopf, 1997.

McCann, Graham. *Cary Grant: A Class Apart*. Columbia University Press, 1998.

Nelson, Nancy. *Evenings with Cary Grant*. William Morrow and Company, 1991.

Wansell, Geoffrey. *Haunted Idol: The Story of the Real Cary Grant*. William Morrow and Company, 1984.

The Silence Is Over: Stars Tackle the Talkies

Elizabeth Engel

More than any other technological advance in the history of filmmaking, the advent of sound forever changed the movie business. All of Hollywood—from the directors to the theater owners—was forced to either adapt or become obsolete. Although every aspect of the business was affected, it was the actors who endured the most scrutiny. For the first time in the history of film, people were going to be able to hear their favorite stars speak. The heroic soldier, the femme fatale, and the villain, once only seen, could now be heard as well. For some actors, this was an opportunity to ascend to stardom; for others, it proved to be their undoing.

The trouble with sound was that the voices of some actors did not measure up to their larger-than-life, on-screen personas. As seen in the movie *Singin' in the Rain*, the glamorous heroine might have a screechy, high-pitched voice that was unsuitable for her smoldering image. Filmmakers attempted to solve this problem with a technique known as voice-doubling. If a leading man's voice didn't measure up to his physique, the studio would simply find another voice that did and synchronize the two. This practice, which was not widely publicized, resulted in scandals for the actors involved and ultimately went out of fashion. Good looks alone were not enough for movies anymore. The actors had to be able to talk.

When Al Jolson appeared in *The Jazz Singer* in 1927, he was already one of America's most popular singers and performers. According to an early review in *The New York Times*, "few men could have approached the task of singing and acting so well as [Jolson] does in this photoplay [Hall, 24]." Jolson, with his vaudevillian background, was a true entertainer. And Warner Bros., one of the smallest studios at the time, was betting on Jolson's esteemed reputation as an entertainer when they enlisted him in the project. In the film, Jolson plays Jack Robin, the son of a cantor, who leaves home to perform in vaudeville and later achieves fame and success as a singer. The film was written especially for Jolson and chronicles his own life as a cantor's son and rise to fame.

The Jazz Singer is in essence a silent film with a series of talking scenes and song interludes. Still, it was the first film to integrate sound. After Jolson finishes the opening song "Dirty Hands, Dirty Face," he delivers the first words ever spoken in a motion picture: "Wait a minute, wait a minute. You ain't heard nothing yet. Wait a minute I tell ya, you ain't heard nothing." These few words foreshadowed the future of what was to come in Hollywood. *The New York Times* reported, "His 'voice with a tear' compelled silence, and possibly all that disappointed the people in the packed theater was the fact that they could not call upon him or his image at least for an encore [Hall, 24]." Although studios were reluctant to fully embrace sound and continued to make silent films for the next few years, *The Jazz Singer* marked the end of the silent film era.

After *The Jazz Singer*, silent film stars under contact at the major studios were immediately tested for sound. The careers of some top-paid stars were ruined because their voices were not acceptable or their accents were too thick. In contrast, other stars fared extremely well during the transition, and the addition of sound only propelled their success at the box office. Greta Garbo, John Barrymore, and Norma Shearer were among the silent film actors who made a harmonious transition into the "talkies." Other actors, such as John Gilbert, were not as fortunate.

As the son of stage actress Ida Adair, Gilbert was immersed in the world of acting since birth. While touring with his mother's theater troupe, Gilbert appeared on stage whenever a script called for a child's part, even playing the occasional girl's part. After his mother died when he was only fourteen, Gilbert spent some time in doing odd jobs before he decided that acting in movies was the only career for him. He began humbly, doing extra work and nearly starving for several years, before ascending to stardom. The tall and handsome Gilbert was tagged "The Great Lover of the Silver Screen" for his romantic roles and perfervid magnetism on screen. He was the quintessential matinee idol, adored by female moviegoers everywhere. His popularity during the silent film era was comparable to that of Rudolph Valentino.

Tragically, Gilbert's career came to a crashing halt in 1929 with his first talking picture, *His Glorious Night*. According to actress Colleen Moore, he was "one of Hollywood's greatest stars of the silent screen and the most tragic victim of the advent of sound [Moore, 205]." Some say Gilbert's voice was not deep enough, not natural, and too "stage-bound." Others thought that his voice had nothing to do with his fall from stardom. "I never have believed, then or now, that it was Jack Gilbert's voice that ruined him . . . . What ruined Jack Gilbert were three little words," said Moore (Moore, 206). In *His Glorious Night*, Gilbert repeats, "I love you, I love you, I love you." When Gilbert professed these words, audiences began to giggle. It appeared that the audience was laughing at the tenor of Gilbert's voice. However, the reason why they were laughing may have had more to do with the fact that the mainly female audience was embarrassed to hear a man tell a woman that he loved her (Moore, 206). In 1929, a public declaration of love was laughable, not romantic.

John Gilbert's career never recovered. His decline was accelerated by his alcoholism and feuding with MGM's Louis B. Mayer. Mayer and Gilbert hated each other and clashed periodically. The 1926 wedding of actress Eleanor Boardman and director King Vidor was rumored to be a double wedding with John Gilbert and Greta Garbo. However, Garbo never showed up. After stalling the wedding, Eleanor told Jack, who was standing in the hallway, that they couldn't wait any longer. Mayer, emerging from the guest bathroom, snidely remarked to Gilbert, "What's the matter with you, Gilbert? What do you have to marry her for? Why don't you just fuck her and forget about it?" (Fountain, 131). Gilbert, who had been drinking, surged toward Mayer, grabbed him by the throat with both hands, pushed him backward into the bathroom, and slammed his head against the tile wall. When ex-bouncer Eddie Mannix pulled the two apart, Mayer screamed, "You're finished, Gilbert. I'll destroy you if it costs me a million dollars" (Fountain, 131). Eleanor Boardman, who witnessed the entire event, escorted Gilbert away before he could do any more damage.

Louis B. Mayer kept his promise. Gilbert appeared in a series of bad films, including *His Glorious Night*. He tried to get out of his contract with MGM, but Mayer wouldn't allow it. Greta Garbo, years after their relationship ended, insisted that he appear opposite her in *Queen Christina* (1933). Although Gilbert and Garbo's silent collaborations—*Love, Flesh and the Devil* and *A Woman of Affairs*—were widely successful, *Queen Christina* did not revive his career.

Knowing that his career was over, Gilbert drank increasingly and plummeted into ill health. He was thirty-six years old when he died in 1936 of heart failure. Whether Gilbert's voice was the cause of his failure in the talkies, he went down in history as the silent film actor with the laughably high-pitched, effeminate voice and was mocked in plays and films for years to come.

In contrast to Gilbert's failure, Greta Garbo made a seamless transition into talking pictures. Garbo, who trained at the renowned Swedish theater school Dramatiska Teatern, began making films in her native Sweden. When she traveled to the United States with director Mauritz Stiller, she did not speak English. However, this did not stop her from making silent pictures. Garbo's first few silent films, *Torrent* (1926) and *Flesh and the Devil* (1926) were smash hits with audiences. She became known for her luminous eyes, extraordinary sex appeal, and ability to push the sensors. But could Garbo talk?

When asked about making talking films, Garbo responded, "If they want me to talk I'll talk. I'd love to act in a talking picture when they are better, but the ones I have seen are awful. It's no fun to look at a shadow and somewhere out of the theatre a voice is coming" ("The Hollywood Hermit," 137). By the time Garbo made a talking picture, the quality of sound had greatly improved since such early talkies as *The Jazz Singer*. Leading up to her first foray into sound in Eugene O'Neill's *Anna Christie* (1930), Greta Garbo and others at MGM were nervous about her how her voice would sound on the recording. Fortunately, Garbo's voice had a rich, deep quality that resonated well in motion pictures. Director Fred Niblo referred to Garbo as "blonde with a 'brunette voice,'" alluding to its darker, deeper quality (Swenson, 217). Her illustrious voice intensified her image as a mysterious exotic foreigner in Hollywood.

In *Anna Christie*, Garbo plays Anna, a destitute woman seeking help from her long-lost father. Spoken with a Swedish accent, Garbo's first words in the film are "Give me a whiskey—ginger ale on the side. And, don't be stingy baby [*Anna Christie*]." The bartender, Larry, responds, "Well, shall I serve it in a pail [*Anna Christie*]?" Garbo's voice reflects Anna Christie's pain and resignation from life. Yet before she speaks a word, one can see from the way Garbo carries herself and the listless look in her eyes that this woman experienced a life of disappointment and suffering.

Anna Christie opened in New York on March 14, 1929. *Variety* reported, "Garbo talks OK" (quoted in Swenson, 219). The film, marketed by MGM with the tagline "Garbo Talks," set first-week ($109,286), second-week ($92,100), and third-week ($76,727) box-office records. With ticket prices in 1929 ranging from 25¢ to $1.50 (average price of

35 to 75¢) and the country still reeling from Black Tuesday, the success of the film was even more extraordinary (Swenson, 225). The Academy of Motion Picture Arts and Sciences nominated Greta Garbo for her performances in *Anna Christie* and *Romance* for 1929/1930, but Garbo lost to Norma Shearer in *The Divorcee*.

In the following years, Garbo remained one of Metro-Goldwyn-Mayer's highest-paid stars. The public's fascination with Garbo grew steadily after the addition of sound, as did Garbo's attempts to elude the press. "Miss Garbo . . . is a shrinking violet when it comes to being interviewed," reported the *New York Times* ("The Hollywood Hermit," 137). She refused to give interviews and went to great lengths to avoid the press. However, this mysterious behavior only fueled the public's interest in Garbo. Her reputation as a recluse even played out in her films. In *Grand Hotel* (1932), Garbo plays a Russian ballerina disenchanted with fame and the constraints of her career. One night, she refuses to go onstage and utters the line, "I want to be alone [*Grand Hotel*]." This phrase remained closely associated with Garbo for the rest of her life.

Greta Garbo's costar in *Grand Hotel*, the legendary John Barrymore, was another actor who made a successful transition into talking pictures. In the theatrical tradition of his father, Maurice Barrymore, and mother, Georgie Drew Barrymore, John Barrymore joined his siblings Ethel and Lionel on the stage. Even though John exhibited early issues with alcohol and failed to show up for performances, he had a quality about him that critics and audiences adored. It was clear that he had something extraordinary. In 1922, Barrymore gave one of the most highly acclaimed theatrical portrayals of Hamlet in the history of the American theater. After *Hamlet*, bored with the monotony of theatrical runs, Barrymore gave up the theater and moved to California to make movies.

When Barrymore began making movies, Hollywood was still producing silent films. His first films included *Dr. Jekyll and Mr. Hyde* (1920), *The Sea Beast* (1926), and *Don Juan* (1926). With his theater experience and vocal training in preparation for *Hamlet*, no one doubted that Barrymore would fare well in talking pictures. Barrymore's first appearance in a talking film was his reading of *Henry VI* in Warner Bros.' *The Show of Shows* (1929), followed by his first feature, *General Crack* (1930). The addition of sound did not slow his career. Over the next decade, he appeared in more than thirty films often alongside notable actresses such as Joan Crawford, Greta Garbo, and Katharine Hepburn. However, like John Gilbert, Barrymore's demons led him to drink.

John Barrymore's lifetime affliction with alcoholism finally caught up with him and resulted his early death in 1942 at the age of sixty. Barrymore, known as "The Great Profile", became a legendary figure for his work in silent and sound pictures. When Barrymore received a star on the Hollywood Walk of Fame in 1940, theater owner Sid Grauman shoved Barrymore's famous profile into the wet cement next to it. After immortalizing his face on the sidewalk, Barrymore retorted, "I feel like the face of the bathroom floor" ("Great Profile Set in Cement," 63).

The introduction of sound was a turning point in filmmaking that made or broke the careers of film actors in that era. Silent actors whose voices lacked a certain quality, such as John Gilbert, fell from the height of fame and success to obscurity almost instantly. In contrast, actors with exceptional voices such as Greta Garbo and John Barrymore flourished in talking pictures. These actors were able to excel in a medium that was unexplored. The significance of the artistic achievements of early sound movies and the actors in them is reinforced by the fact that seventy years later people are still watching *The Jazz Singer*, *Dinner at Eight*, and *Anna Christie*. These films became part of movie history and the foundation on which modern filmmaking was built.

Works Cited

Anna Christie. MGM, 1930.

Fountain, Leatrice Gilbert. *Dark Star: The Untold Story of the Meteoric Rise and Fall of the Legendary Silent Screen Star John Gilbert.* New York: St. Martins, 1985.

Grand Hotel. MGM, 1932.

"Great Profile Set in Cement." *Life*, 30 Sept. 1940:63.

Hall, Mordaunt. "The Screen." *New York Times* [New York], 7 Oct. 1927:24.

"Hamlet." *Theatre Magazine*, Jan. 1923:22.

"The Hollywood Hermit." *New York Times* [New York], 24 Mar. 1929:137.

The Jazz Singer. Warner Bros., 1927.

Moore, Colleen. *Silent Star.* Garden City: Doubleday & Company, 1968.

Swenson, Karen. *Greta Garbo: A Life Apart.* New York: Scribner, 1997.

The Importance of Being Harpo: Why Marx Matters

Abigail Adams

"Name one of the Marx Brothers."

Most people would answer, "Groucho." Naturally, the wise-cracking front-man of the famous family comes to mind first, with Harpo a close second.

A lot of people think of Harpo Marx as a kind of idiot clown—in fact, many still believe that he was mute. You wouldn't think of Harpo as a historical figure or someone who had any important effect on society in general. Except for the oddity of having been a male harpist, Harpo isn't seen as a particularly important person.

It is a surprise, then, to learn of the real Harpo—the social, friendly, active, groundbreaking, and, above all, interesting person he really was. If success, to you, means success in show business, then all the Marx Brothers made it. If it means success in life, Harpo clearly stands apart.

If you had met Harpo as a child, he probably would have seemed like the last person you would expect to succeed in show business. Harpo was the second-born in his family, a philosophical daydreamer with an easygoing personality that allowed him to accept all the unusual—and sometimes astonishing—experiences that life had in store for him.

Harpo was the first American entertainer to appear in Russia after the USSR was officially recognized by FDR in 1933, and he smuggled papers into the United States on his way back. He became a member of the Algonquin Round Table, despite his near illiteracy, and was welcome on Alexander Woollcott's private island, as well as the Hearst Ranch and the Vanderbilt mansion. He annoyed his neighbor Rachmaninoff, forcing the pianist to move, but was fond of the unbalanced musical genius Oscar Levant, despite the fact that Oscar had come to his house for dinner one evening and stayed for over a year.

Harpo once worked as a piano player in a whorehouse and was once thrown out of a casino in Monte Carlo. He played golf, badminton, croquet, and other such civilized games; but he wouldn't say no to a frantic game of around-the-table ping-pong with his brothers, if only to make his mother smile. Harpo knew Irving Berlin, George and Ira Gershwin, George Bernard Shaw, Somerset Maugham, Robert Benchley, Dorothy Parker, and Ethel Barrymore. He knew gangsters, con men, writers, movie stars, and millionaires.

Harpo was born Adolph Marx in the year 1888. It was an exciting time to be alive. The next few decades would see many changes in technology. Radios would be in every home and eventually talking pictures in the cinemas. Despite this, the threat of indigence was very real. There was no financial safety net for those who fell behind, but those who could ride the wave of prosperity would do well in the coming century. There were no guarantees, only opportunities.

The Marx Brothers started out in an apartment on East Ninety-Third Street in New York City, in a poor Jewish neighborhood. It was their mother, Minnie, who was determined to put her entire family in show business. Her role model was the boys' Uncle Al. Al Shean was one-half of the popular vaudeville team of Gallagher and Shean. Uncle Al wasn't doing too badly by the standards of the day or compared to Minnie's family who were struggling financially. Minnie's husband, whom everyone called Frenchie, was a tailor, but not a very good one. Most of his customers were friends of the family. He had a remarkable talent for cooking, but even though everyone else knew this, he somehow never realized it himself.

The boys' grandfather would sit in the corner in the little apartment and read aloud from the Torah or tell stories in German. Leonard, the oldest of the five boys, was too restless to listen, but the old man had a rapt audience in young Adolph. This boy was by no means stupid, though he would not go far in school. Harpo actually left school during his second try at the second grade. He had been thrown out of the window repeatedly by bullies, and one day, at the age of eight, he decided not to go back to class.

Leonard left school at the age of twelve and was already a dyed-in-the-wool juvenile delinquent. It was his personality more than anything else. Chico tried to teach Harpo everything he knew, but fortunately for the younger brother, most of this instruction went over his head. Harpo simply did not have his brother's scheming nature.

We'll never know how much growing up in poverty influenced the brothers later in life. Certainly they all had their quirks about money. Groucho refused to check his hat in restaurants because he didn't want to tip to get it back. Chico's lifelong gambling addiction more than once had his brothers in court freezing his assets on his behalf. When they were children, they spent their days stealing, trading, borrowing, and begging. Chico was especially talented at making deals, but even he wasn't always lucky; and when the chips were down, anything handy was sacrificed to the cause. Even the watch Harpo received on his bar mitzvah was not-so-mysteriously stolen and pawned. Harpo never held a grudge against Chico. They all did what they could to survive. If one of the brothers managed to steal coal for the oven, and another to beg scraps from the butcher, then Frenchie could fix dinner. For many families of the era, this was the bottom line.

The Marxes didn't have a patent on difficult childhoods. Most of the entertainers of the era grew up poor. Al Jolson was a Russian immigrant. George Burns grew up not far from Harpo, and their families shared similar circumstances. Eddie Cantor was an orphan at the age of three. He was raised by his grandmother in a tenement basement, and he entertained people on the sidewalks for pennies. There were exceptions to the general rule, of course. Fanny Brice came from a family that was considered well-to-do at the time, and Jack Benny was often teased by other entertainers for having grown up middle class. For many, though, show business represented a way out of poverty, as well as a way for the poorly educated to avoid a life of menial work. Even so, there was nothing glamorous about small-time vaudeville. Traveling performers were often treated badly or with indifference by the general public. They slept in barns or in vermin-infested beds in fleabag hotels. They sweltered in the summer and froze in the winter. There was a stigma attached to being an entertainer as opposed to someone who "worked" for a living. It wasn't considered respectable to be a song-and-dance man, though this contempt is incomprehensible now. Vaudevillians put up with these things, knowing all the while that only a few of them would make it to the top.

Unlike other entertainers such as Al Jolson and George Burns, Harpo Marx did not show an early inclination to pursue show business. However, not to succeed would be to defy the formidable Minnie, so succeed he did. Minnie was the original stage mother and the driving force behind both the family and the act. It was Minnie's idea that each of her sons play an instrument. When the family acquired a piano, Chico was given the task of learning to play it. A guitar was procured for Groucho, and when the opportunity presented itself to get a harp into the act, Minnie couldn't resist it, and Harpo taught himself to play the harp. Minnie was a good manager, taking every opportunity to "class up" the act using as little money as possible. The harp itself brought in an extra $5 a month when it was introduced into the act. After subtracting the $4 monthly payments, the net profit was a dollar a month. Harpo was dragged into the act before the harp was purchased because his mother had gotten a good deal on a set of four boys' suits and at the time had only three boys on stage—Groucho, Gummo, and another boy named Lou Levy. Harpo eventually made the decision not to talk on stage after a critic commented that his pantomime was great, but the effect was ruined when he spoke.

Ever since starting work with his brothers in vaudeville, Harpo's family was the one major constant in his life. Most people who met the Marxes had to take them or leave them as a whole since Harpo's generally complacent personality seemed to fly out the window when he was around his brothers. In fact, no one could have been more different from the everyday Harpo than Harpo himself was when he was onstage. Having been brought up from street urchins into the equally rough-and-tumble world of vaudeville, the brothers had little idea of how to behave in polite society. At times, they might have seemed more suited for a society of orangutans. Fortunately for them, they didn't much care how they appeared to others. There was nothing the brothers enjoyed more than poking fun at high society. *A Night at the Opera* is the most famous example of this, but the theme runs through all their movies. Typically, Margaret Dumont, as a wealthy matron, would play the foil to Groucho's moth-eaten con man character, who was always scheming to be invited into the upper-crust of her society. Harpo and Chico would show up as transients and steal everything that wasn't nailed down. Destruction and chaos ensued. This formula was successful on stage and screen, though in reality, it was Harpo who was accepted into polite society. Despite their differences, the brothers were expert at performing together, as they had done since childhood. It was only when they were together that they were truly unmanageable. One Marx was difficult; four were a tornado.

The Cocoanuts was the first Marx Brothers film. It starred Groucho, Chico, Harpo, and Zeppo, and was adapted from the brothers' established stage show of the same name. This gave the brothers an unusual amount of control over what happened on the set, and they proceeded to take gleeful advantage of the situation by driving directors Robert Florey and Joseph Santley completely up the wall. Chico was the worst of the group, always running off to phone a bookie or a girlfriend. Producer Walter Wanger solved this problem by having phones installed in the jail cells that were used as set dressing in the movie and then assigning one cell to each of the brothers. That helped keep them together during filming, but it didn't curb off-set pranks. The continuous changes made to the dialogue were another problem. It seems that the famous Marx creativity had a way of interfering with productivity. There was simply no way to curb their exhausting enthusiasm.

It wasn't easy to make a movie in those days, even with more cooperative actors. "Talkies" were a recent invention and had technology all their own. After 1927 when Al Jolson starred in *The Jazz Singer*, the first full-length movie with sound, silent movies were suddenly outdated; and many silent film stars' careers ended, it seemed, overnight. Movies, for a while, ceased to be about acting. Sound was the new star.

At first, technical problems were a major issue. There was as yet no way to put the soundtrack on the film, so one machine was used for the film and another for the sound. That meant that when the movie was shown, the sound didn't always match up with the film. The large hot lights that were used in filming silents didn't work well for sound movies either. They made such a loud buzzing noise that they had to be moved into soundproof booths and were eventually replaced by quieter lights as the technology advanced.

Microphones were placed around the set in parts of the scenery, and actors were required to stay near them while delivering lines, unnaturally limiting their movement and range of expression. It would be an understatement to say the actors were unhappy about this. The later invention of boom microphones helped normalize the situation.

Despite the drawbacks, there was no going back to the way things were before. If you were an actor, you had to talk. Except for Harpo, who quickly became known as the only star of talking movies who didn't talk. Some people, it seems, are destined for success.

All the brothers were groomed for show business, but Groucho may have been the only one who really cared. Born Julius Henry Marx in 1890, Groucho was a wisecracking, intelligent egotist who craved attention, but the pressure to be the "star" of the family was intense. In later years, Groucho retreated into cynicism and bitterness. His circle of friends became smaller until it contained only those who were with him in the beginning, in vaudeville.

In many ways, Hollywood during the time the Marx Brothers were movie stars was not much different than Hollywood today. Marriages typically lasted as long as it took the ink to dry on the license. Alcohol abuse was prevalent. Depression was a problem for those whose self-esteem was perpetually low. Even the accolades of the crowds could not convince all celebrities of their worth. Stars often cultivated friendships with the expectation of receiving career-boosting benefits before the relationships ran out of steam. People making millions lived beyond their means in order to impress other millionaires who were doing the same.

How did Harpo avoid the curse of fame? His beginnings were no different than many others. He was not overtly religious; neither did he have strict moral training. Certainly he should have been just as susceptible to the pitfalls of celebrity as anyone else.

Harpo's philosophy was "live and let live." He didn't try to "fix" people or their personal problems because he didn't see people as problems needing to be solved, and he never avoided people just because their behavior was strange. It would have been hypocritical if he had. He accepted all sorts of personality quirks in others—phobias, superstitions, temper tantrums—and others returned the courtesy by accepting his unpredictable high spirits. Harpo wasn't critical and didn't compare people to one another. He didn't try to make Groucho quieter or Chico less reckless. He let things happen instead of trying to *make* things happen. Harpo was rarely unhappy because he didn't expect life to be any different than it was.

Everyone who knew Harpo could count on one thing—they knew he would be the same Harpo no matter how long it had been since they'd seen him last. They knew he would still be generous and forgiving, wild and unpredictable, always adding to his impressive but motley collection of friends. Once rated a friend by Harpo, one was always a friend, despite any changes that might occur later in life. That's how people knew they could trust him, and they were right.

Harpo was married only once, to a woman named Susan Fleming. They adopted four children and never divorced. Harpo died September 28, 1964, in Los Angeles of complications from heart surgery. He was seventy-five years old. His wishes were that his remains be cremated and his ashes sprinkled into the sand trap at the seventh hole of the Rancho Mirage golf course. I have no proof this was actually done. On the other hand, I have no doubt it was. It would have taken a close friend to do it, but for a person like Harpo, there was no shortage of those.

Maybe Harpo will never come to mind first when people think of the Marx Brothers. It doesn't really matter; he never cared much about being first. Harpo only cared to live in the present, not longing for the past or worrying about the future. Movie actors and musical performers aren't exactly rare these days, but people who know how to live in the moment are in very short supply.

Perhaps this nation of glamour worshipers doesn't know what has been lost. Maybe in order to know that, you have to know what you had in the first place.

Bibliography

Alicoate, Jack. "The New Entertainment Vitamin, 1928-1929—Fox Movietone, Paramount, MGM, United Artists, THE QUEEN KELLY FIASCO, Universal, Independent Producers." Online 1911 Encyclopedia Britannica. http://encyclopedia.jrank.org/articles/pages/2086/The-New-Entertainment-Vitamin-1928-1929.html (accessed March 3, 2010).

Barber, Rowland, and Harpo Marx. *Harpo Speaks!* New York: Bernard Geis Associates, 1961.

Burns, George. *All My Best Friends*. New York: G. P. Putnam's Sons, 1989.

"Harpo Marx (1888-1964): Find A Grave Memorial." Find a Grave: Millions of Cemetery Records. http://www.findagrave.com/cgi-bin/fg.cgi?page=gr&GRid=679 (accessed January 18, 2010).

Kenrick, John. "Funny Girl Debunked—Fanny Brice Facts." Musicals101.com—The Cyber Encyclopedia of Musicals. http://www.musicals101.com/brice.htm (accessed January 29, 2010).

_____. "Al Jolson Biography—Part I." Musicals101.com—The Cyber Encyclopedia of Musicals. http://www.musicals101.com/jolsonbio.htm (accessed January 29, 2010).

Marsden, Les. "Harpo Marx (Adolph/Arthur)—The Marx Brothers." Chico, Harpo, Groucho, Gummo, Zeppo—The Marx Brothers. http://www.marx-brothers.org/biography/harpo.htm (accessed January 18, 2010).

Samit, Benji. "Harpo: A Dossier—*NY Times* Clippings." BenjiSamit.com. http://www.benjisamit.com/harpo/2.htm (accessed January 28, 2010).

The Cocoanuts (The Marx Brothers). Film. Directed by Robert Florey. Universal City, CA: MCA Universal, 1995.

"The Eddie Cantor Appreciation Society." The Eddie Cantor Appreciation Society. http://www.eddiecantor.com/bio.html (accessed January 29, 2010).

Mae West:
A Woman of Experience

Cinzi Lavin

It is 1900, and at the Theatre Royale in Brooklyn, New York, a seven-year-old Mae West calmly struts out on the stage. The daughter of a corset model and a prizefighter, she has performed in several variety shows and is already a highly skilled singer, dancer, and all-around entertainer. This performance, a charity benefit for the Elks Club, finds her preparing to sing a song called "Movin' Day" before an intimidatingly large crowd. However, upon reaching center stage and hearing the orchestra strike up her introduction, the child stamps her foot and begins crying—then yelling. She is shouting for the spotlight, which was not being employed for her number. The amused audience made an outcry for the stage manager to do so, and having her demand satisfied, she began her performance. Not only did she receive thunderous applause from the admiring crowd that day, but she was also given a gold medal.[1]

Mae West was, beyond doubt, a star born for success. With an immense amount of innate talent and the strong support of her family, she was ensured of a promising career. However, her courage in asserting herself—as the above story illustrates—and her unwavering faith in her own artistic judgment are the elements that made her a larger-than-life celebrity. That her professional career was played out on both the boards and on the silver screen was a testament to her versatility, her ambition, and her drive to offer the world a taste of her unconventional and controversial spin on sex and relationships. To be sure, she wanted to entertain; but in the tradition of the greatest of entertainers, she also wanted to make people think, to challenge their beliefs, to make them laugh at themselves and find entertainment in the often ridiculous world around them.

Bemused by the repression of her time, she strove to inject a little lighthearted bawdiness into the conscience of the hypocritical American public. She was practical enough to use whatever mediums would reach the most people, whatever venues would guarantee the widest fame. Thus, she made the transition from Vaudevillian to Hollywood actress.

It might come as a surprise to learn that Mae West was initially cold to the idea of starring in films. As a seasoned professional in the Vaudeville circuit who had made a name for herself (which some uttered in whispers), she had little interest in the fledgling movie industry. By 1928, she had already been jailed for obscenity charges for her play *Sex* and had made a huge Broadway success with another of her plays, *Diamond Lil*. Both fame and infamy were hers in the glow of the footlights, so there would have been little reason for her to consider a cinematic career during the early days of film.

There are other factors to consider as well. According to biographer Maurice Leonard,

the movies had made an impact on the public, but to
vaudevillians they were not regarded as an attractive source
of income. Movie people were looked down upon, considered
even less meritorious than burlesque performers.[2]

In addition, Mae was hardly the prim adolescent that defined the
earliest "type" for leading ladies in film, nor did she possess the anemic
figure that constituted the physical norm for the part. Curvaceous, full,
and overtly sensual, her physique was impossible to ignore; and no
costumer on earth could have made her appear willowy on camera.

Beyond this, the notion of films as an enduring art-form was yet to
be established; they were more often than not considered a novelty, one
which sometimes drew so little attention that live acts—including Mae
West—were hired by cinemas in order to ensure full houses between
showings.[3]

Finally, it bears noting that Holly Wood, as it was then known, was
a farming suburb of Los Angeles, itself a "sleepy Southern California
city" according to a screenwriter of the time.[4] "This Hollywood would
not have attracted Mae," writes Maurice Leonard, adding, "Hollywood
was provincial, the big money was to be made on Broadway and thus
Broadway remained Mae's target."[5]

However, as time passed and the First World War broke out, the
American public turned to the cinema as never before to escape the grim
realities of life. It could be said that WWI made Hollywood—turned it
into the dream factory that kept the world at bay, at least for a while.
It suddenly became apparent to actors and Vaudevillians that movies
could showcase their talent on a grand scale and introduce them to vast
audiences nationwide.

> Theatrical artists reappraised their situation as they began to
> realize that greater fame could be achieved from one movie
> than from an entire life spent on the boards. Mary Pickford,
> "America's Sweetheart," was now the highest paid woman
> in the world. Both Charlie Chaplin and Douglas Fairbanks
> had already become millionaires. The Talmadge sisters were
> national figures, as were Gloria Swanson, Harold Lloyd, and
> Tom Mix.[6]

And so Mae accepted a part—a mere character role—in the 1932
George Raft vehicle *Night After Night*. Hollywood and Mae proved to
be a curious concoction. She quickly formed a great dislike for movie

people, whom (according to Leonard) she considered "fey, talentless, and unreliable."[7] Furthermore, she did not like the film's director Archie Mayo:

> That he knew a great deal about films cut no ice with Mae: she thought he had had no theatrical experience. In reality, he had not come to the Coast and entered films until 1915, after stage experience in the East . . . . He was experienced in comedy but his style owed much to the slapstick of the silent era, a school to which the wise-cracking Mae owed nothing.[8]

In order to get her bearings in a new environment, the ever-professional Mae came to the set days before her scheduled shooting and sat, quietly observing how the magic of film worked. She quickly saw that she would have to tone down her stage persona—that in this new medium, less was more. According to Leonard,

> many theatrical actresses had made themselves ridiculous by playing to the camera as broadly as they played in theatres. The result was a grotesque pantomime.[9]

Most jarring, perhaps, was Mae's realization that her comic timing—a rare and invaluable talent honed by decades of stage experience—would have to be recalibrated if it were to work in the cinematic genre.[10] The problem, of course, was that there was no pause for audience reaction—because there *was* no audience, at least not at the time of filming. To further complicate matters, she would have to use her intuition (rather than gauging the response of a live audience, as in the theatre) to guide her in her delivery during a scene.

Taking matters squarely into her own hands as she had done ever since playing the "Baby Vamp" as a child in New York variety shows, "she insisted, impertinently, that all scenes with which she was involved had to be shot her way."[11]

This intransigent attitude brought matters swiftly to a head when she and director Mayo disagreed over her opening scene in the film.[12] In it, she enters a nightclub wearing a conspicuous display of diamond jewelry. She gives her fur to the coat-check girl, who remarks, "Goodness, what lovely diamonds!" to which Mae replies with the now-famous line, "Goodness had nothing to do with it, dearie."

"I knew it was a great line, that it would break up the audience," Mae later told writer William Scott Eyman. "It had to be protected with footage. There was a big row about that. Mayo wanted to cut away."[13] Mae, for her part, instinctively knew that there needed to be time for the audience to absorb and respond to the line with their laughter. The essence of the art of entertainment—and in this case, Mae's forte, comedy—was what her experience dictated she had to preserve at all costs. Indeed, in viewing many films of the time, it is not uncommon to see a hysterically funny line followed immediately by an abrupt cut to another scene. The effect on the natural reaction of the viewer is dampening. *Were we supposed to be amused?* Surely that is the one question with which no comedian ever wants a crowd to struggle.

Mae suggested that the camera follow her as she ascended a staircase after delivering the line, allowing the audience the opportunity to react. Mayo disagreed, countering that it was a waste of time. The two were at loggerheads, both adamantly insisting the scene be shot their way, and production on the film ground to a halt.

After intervention by a studio executive who realized that of the two, Mae (a bit-part player) was the greater force with which to be reckoned than Mayo, the director, the filming continued—shot according to her plan. However, Mayo was privately assured by the studio that if it did not work, the staircase footage could be cut.[14]

Of course, the scene worked perfectly as Mae intended it. In fact, her expertise in adapting to film became more and more evident. She was allowed to rewrite her lines. "The one-liners of which she became undisputed mistress," says Leonard, "were an innovation dreamed up to suit the movies. She had rarely used them on stage and admitted as much to *Premier* magazine."[15]

"For the pictures I had to write wisecracks," said Mae. "I figured the only way to get material over was to punch it across with funny lines. I mean, in the films, they wouldn't let me sit on a man's lap. And I've been on more laps than a napkin."[16]

Night After Night opened in New York in October of 1932, and Mae West's film debut was met with wild acclaim. "See, I was right," said Mae of her filming suggestions. "I've always known what's best for me."[17]

Meanwhile, film critics couldn't get enough of the sight of Mae on camera. Leonard Hall of *Photoplay* wrote:

> Blonde, buxom, rowdy Mae—slithering across the screen in a
> spangled, sausage-skin gown! Yanking our eyes from Georgie
> Raft and Connie Cummings! Battling for the scene with that
> magnificent, veteran trouper, Alison Skipworth! I dare say

that the theatre has never sent Hollywood a more fascinating,
spectacular and useful figure than Bounding Mae West, queen
of the big-hearted, bad girls of show business.[18]

Raft, the star of the show, amiably quipped, "Mae West stole
everything but the cameras."[19]

While this is true, more illuminating observations than that have
been made about Mae's first work in film. For instance, it has been
noted that Mae does very little in the film, having barely more than two
scenes in the entire picture, but that her impact is formidable:

> Without Mae *Night After Night* would be undistinguished—it
> is only remembered today as the film which introduced Mae
> West to the Screen.[20]

Some critics assert that Mae's greatest achievement (which could
be said for her entire career, both stage and screen) is in having created
a new type of female film character. Bringing humor to the "deadly
serious matter of sex," as Maurice Leonard writes, she "banished forever
the concept of the sinister vamp."[21] Theda Bara, the silent-film actress,
was as openly sexual as Mae, but fashioned herself as a predator. Mae
didn't have to try that hard. The mating game was a source of fun and
amusement that she felt confident she would win—again and again.
She could afford to joke around while fooling around, exercising her wit
along with her sex-appeal.

Her landmark artistic transition from stage to screen in *Night After
Night* also merits comment:

> In a way Mayo's directorial lack of imagination works in Mae's
> favour. In the "Goodness" scene the camera does little more
> than frame the picture, creating a proscenium arch, and this
> enables Mae to use the set as a stage. The whole sketch,
> including her sashay out of frame, is essentially vaudeville.[22]

Recognizing her newfound success for what it was and abandoning
her plans to return to New York, Mae settled into a posh Hollywood
apartment and went on to accustom herself to the profitable venue that
was moviemaking. She took notice of the practicalities that went into a
successful film, and by securing the services of Ernest Haller (who had
done a spectacular job of lighting her in *Night After Night*), she assured
herself of looking good on camera in her subsequent movies.

And subsequent movies there were, many written by Mae herself. Her resume now boasted the word "scriptwriter" besides the word "playwright." In 1933 she appeared in two films, *She Done Him Wrong* (which Mae wrote and which was nominated for an Academy Award for Best Picture) and *I'm No Angel*.

To say that she had taken Hollywood by storm would be an understatement, especially considering that the scandal caused by her provocative characters in *She Done Him Wrong* and *I'm No Angel* forced Hollywood studios to establish the Motion Picture Production Code, which regulated the content of movies. In an ironic twist of fate, the creation of the MPPC drove Mae to rely even *more* heavily on double-entendres in order to get her lines past the censors. Her trick worked, and thus one of her trademark gimmicks became famous.

But Hollywood already owed a lot to Mae. *She Done Him Wrong* was wildly popular (starring a young Cary Grant that Mae had instantly recognized as star material and cast opposite herself), but *I'm No Angel* was even more successful, premiering in New York to an unparalleled 180,000 people.[23]

> By the end of the year the two films combined had earned over a million dollars net profit for Paramount . . . . She was a phenomenon, the most sought-after star in the industry. As far as Paramount were concerned she could do no wrong. She had not only saved the company from bankruptcy but had restored optimism.[24]

I'm No Angel—her third work in Hollywood—is considered Mae's finest film. That she could comprehend and refine the skills necessary to make a great movie having worked so short a time in the genre is an astonishing feat. The picture is brimming with great laughs, many Mae's funniest and most memorable lines ever. Still, she remains true to her roots as a theatre entertainer. Says biographer Leonard, "In vaudevillian fashion the film's impact is immediate, hitting the audience between the eyes and leaving it clamouring for more."[25]

Mae West would go on to make twelve films in all, and the lavish Hollywood apartment she had chosen to live in as a newcomer to California would become the sanctuary in which she died forty-eight years later. She would make some good movies, among them *Belle of the Nineties* (1934) and *My Little Chickadee* (1940) in which she shared the camera with fellow former-Vaudevillian W. C. Fields. She would make some bad movies, such as *Myra Breckinridge* (1970) and *Sextette* (1978), the latter of which she starred in as an eighty-five-year-old caricature of herself.

Not content with having conquered stage and screen, she would go on to perform on radio and television, write several books (including a best-selling autobiography), and even make rock-and-roll record albums.

Beyond the scores of lovers she would have over the years, her experiences with everyday individuals would shape her outlook on life and her belief in treating everyone as equals. Her bold support of women's liberation, civil rights, and gay rights would put her decades before her time.

Indeed, for Mae West, life was all about experience.

But at the fateful point in her career when she traded footlights for footage, Mae West committed herself to delivering her message to the broadest audience possible. Says writer Eric Braun, "She had struck a blow for honesty in sexual expression that is still echoing around the world today, and she had done it all with supreme good humour."[26] Writes Maurice Leonard, "Mae was thirty years ahead of . . . the feminist revolution of the 1960s. Yet her message was not shrill; some things, she realized, were better delivered tongue-in-cheek." [27]

While the venerable humorist Will Rogers, referring to Mae's advent in Hollywood, figured she "had to come out here to teach the other girls how to speak their lines,"[28] British novelist Hugh Walpole wrote, "Only Charlie Chaplin and Mae West in Hollywood dare to directly attack with their mockery the fraying morals and manners of a dreary world."[29] Vaudeville may have taught Mae her trade, but Hollywood immortalized her. She could do more for less on stage but could do less for more on film, and as we can still plainly see, a little of Mae West goes a long way.

Endnotes

[1]   Maurice Leonard, *Mae West: Empress of Sex* (New York: Carol Publishing Group, 1992), 15-16

[2]   Ibid., 35

[3]   Ibid., 36

[4]   Ibid.

[5]   Ibid.

[6]   Ibid., 49

[7]   Ibid., 109

[8]   Ibid., 108

[9]   Ibid., 108-109
[10] Ibid., 109
[11] Ibid.
[12] Ibid.
[13] Ibid.
[14] Ibid., 110
[15] Ibid., 110-111
[16] Ibid., 111
[17] Ibid.
[18] Ibid., 112
[19] Ibid.
[20] Ibid.
[21] Ibid., 112-113
[22] Ibid., 113
[23] Ibid., 136
[24] Ibid., 136-137
[25] Ibid., 137
[26] Ibid.
[27] Ibid.
[28] Ibid.
[29] Ibid.

Bibliography

Goin' To Town, DVD. Directed by Alexander Hall. 1935, Universal City, CA: Glamour Collection, 2006.

Go West Young Man, DVD. Directed by Henry Hathaway. 1935, Universal City, CA: Glamour Collection, 2006.

I'm No Angel, DVD. Directed by Wesley Ruggles. 1933, Universal City, CA: Glamour Collection, 2006.

Leider, Emily Wortis. *Becoming Mae West*. New York: Farrar, Straus & Giroux, 1997.

Leonard, Maurice. *Mae West: Empress of Sex*. New York: Carol Publishing Group, 1992.

Louvish, Simon. *Mae West: It Ain't No Sin*. New York: St. Martin's Press/ Thomas Dunne Books, 2006.

Night After Night, DVD. Directed by Archie Mayo. 1932, Universal City, CA: Glamour Collection, 2006.

162-2

More than Major Strasser: Conrad Veidt

Jan Merlin and William Russo

He dealt with upheavals in his personal and professional life. Sound movies must have been a minor issue when one's head has a bounty, threatened by Nazis because of marrying Jewish women and managing to perform with icy charm and confidence on film.

Conrad Veidt, who some claimed he denied being Semitic himself—the quintessential Nazi villain of propaganda movies in the 1940s—facetiously told a reporter, "No, I was not born with a monocle in my eye." His innate guarded sense of privacy guided his modest reply, "What use is there for a biography of myself? I'm just a movie actor." He dismissed his importance to the burgeoning art of film at the height of the silent movie era and his ties to F. W. Murnau and German Expressionism. As to his reticence and laconic demeanor, in contrast to the hellfire of the soul he presented in characters, Conrad Veidt protested, perhaps too much, "I wish, naturally, to prevent the possibility that someone may write an accidental, superficial, incomplete, and perhaps untrue picture of me." Was he even then acting the role of a self-deprecating man?

No more challenging gauntlet could be tossed down for biographers.

Born in Berlin in 1893, Veidt's theatrical interest seemed at odds with his father's sense of propriety, but in the years before the Great War, the first praise the boy received in a school play hooked him forever. Conrad found himself dropping out of school and loitering near theaters where he could absorb the atmosphere. Flamboyance did not escape Conny, and he behaved and dressed conspicuously to win attention. An audition was arranged with the noted theatrical director, Max Reinhardt, who saw talent oozing from the pretentious youth. Hardly yet leading man material, the director first signed him to year's contract. The youngster was given bit parts and walk-ons to play while learning the art of his new profession at the Deutsches Theater.

The engagement was cut short in 1916 by the war, but contracting jaundice earned Conny a medical discharge and a chance to travel with a theater unit to entertain German soldiers. He was assigned better roles and more important parts to play. During most of 1917 and 1918, he worked under Reinhardt's direction and honed his ability as a quick study, later an advantage in talking films. Impulsively, he married a Jewish girl, Augusta Holl, only to be divorced the next year. When the war was over, at the start of 1919, he starred in a little-known work called *The Coral*. He gave poetry readings that year as well, a one-man show that was meant to titillate the growing audience of female admirers with his *Poems of Ecstasy* show.

In latter years Veidt recalled his early stage work: "I was never a villain on the stage. I always played strong, sympathetic types. My first stage role with a speaking part, believe it or not, was as a priest. It wasn't until I began acting in films that the producers and directors saw me primarily as a bizarre villain. I was happy and content to play either 'the good guy' or 'the bad guy' as they say in American slang, as long as the role and the screenplay called for plenty of dramatic conflict and emotional expression."

The lure of film work arrived in earnest during 1919; Veidt realized the money was worth the time, though he regarded movies as a cheap form of entertainment and not true art. The actor used his own savings to form Veidtfilme, directing himself in a couple of productions. He disliked being in short scenes out of sequence from a script; it was so unlike doing performances on a stage from beginning to end where the growth of any character was played into a dark mass of a hushed audience beyond a separating proscenium. Playing for handfuls of motion picture crews would never be as satisfying to the actor, despite a salary each day that equaled what he earned in theater for a month. He retained his ties to stage so long as he could. In those primitive days, filming was concluded when the sun went down; and once shooting was over, he hurried back to work in the nightly dramas at the Deutsches Theater where he'd rapidly become a popular draw. It was there he met F. W. Murnau with whom he formed a professional partnership.

Murnau would make a number of movies with Conrad as his lead actor, including a turn in a Teutonic version of *Dr. Jekyll and Mr. Hyde* (*Der Januskopf*). It was one of those turning points in which the public responded to Veidt's darker performances. He relished character roles that lit a passion in his heart, playing the likes of Admiral Nelson, Frederic Chopin, or Paganini. Accents were not essential in a silent picture. His startling and hypnotic looks carried the plot and drew audiences. As for Conny, he declared his feeling about movies and his approach to acting, "I think the motion picture industry is a stupid business and I despise acting the scenes in short snatches, one at a time. I hate this film work. I am disgusted with myself. On the stage I could never play a part unless I felt it with all my heart and soul."

Richard Oswald of *Oswaldfilme* was also impressed by Conrad Veidt's striking looks on the stage and promised to create a European sensation of him. He offered Veidt an outrageous role that would shock the audience and perhaps inspire cultural and legal change. In May of 1919, the film, *Different from Others*, was released in Berlin. It flew in the face of Paragraph 175, a German statute outlawing homosexual behavior. Featuring a gay man facing blackmail who turns the tables on his tormentor, it presented a sympathetic parade of victimized men in society's bad graces throughout history and ended in tragic suicide for Conrad's role as Paul Korner in Oswald's film. As the groundbreaking movie never saw release in the United States during Veidt's lifetime, the lack of publicity may have allowed his American cinema career to flourish without complaint.

By 1920, a second role was to transcend the Atlantic Ocean, and Veidt became a name known to America. He played Cesare, the somnambulist, a figure of deadly fantasy in Robert Wiene's Expressionistic horror film *The Cabinet of Dr. Caligari*. According to some cinephiles, that film changed movies overall and especially altered the future of Conrad Veidt and perhaps his thinking too: "No matter what roles I play, I can't seem to get *Caligari* out of my system." He yearned to play a variety of off-beat characters, those that epitomized the tormented soul, on the verge of damnation. In short order, he gave searing portrays of *Ivan the Terrible* and *Rasputin*.

One characteristic part from 1924 was another film with Robert Wiene called *The Hands of Orlac*, the concert pianist whose hands are amputated in a train crash; but he is given new hands—those of a murderer, whose hands had a mind of their own. He described these roles as "mostly mental," though he wished he could play the adventure hero. Conny's star was rising, and in 1923 Conny married a wealthy Jewish heiress, Felicitas Radke. They were happy to welcome a daughter in 1925, whom they named Viola, but were later divorced, and Felicitas took the child to reside in Switzerland.

John Barrymore recognized Conny's brilliance and wanted him to play the foil in *The Beloved Rogue*. The star wrote to Veidt, insisting that the picture could not be made without "one of the most talented men in the film world." Whatever the Great Profile wanted, he was given, and Veidt donned the powdered wig to play Louis XI. It meant traveling to Hollywood at the peak of the silent era. In Germany there was a sense that their greatest film star had sold out. Stage actors were in huge demand by motion picture productions for speaking English beautifully; British and authentic European accents and manners were a decided asset. Once in his new environment, Veidt met a cadre of other German film talent that had immigrated to the sunny world of movie magic. He was pleased to encounter a more recent young protégé of Reinhardt, the winsome Luise Rainer, poised to gather two Oscars in a row.

Of course, Joseph Von Sternberg and Marlene Dietrich were also delighted to have him join them in America. Dietrich had once auditioned for Max Reinhardt's theater company but was turned away. She became a chorus girl and did minor roles onstage and in German films until *The Blue Angel* rocketed her to stardom. Veidt, tall and imperious, was eager to conquer the movie business with bigger budgets and bigger studios. He believed himself ready for Hollywood success and noted: "Nothing seems to come up to your expectations. But nothing I had heard about Hollywood was enough." The tinseled glamorous world of film-land was a heady place to enter.

Running Universal was a fellow German named Carl Laemmle, who knew how to make his new visitors to America feel at home. He matched Veidt with one of his most successful directors, Paul Leni. It was in *Waxworks*, directed by Leni, that Veidt had played the sinister *Ivan the Terrible*, winning accolades. Comparisons to Lon Chaney were raised, and that was high praise indeed, especially since Universal Studios wanted a rival to MGM's leading character actor. So for $1,500 per week, with a German-speaking director, Veidt was ready for his close-up, and Leni readied himself to direct *The Man Who Laughs*.

The motion picture forced Veidt to wear prosthetic teeth and keep his mouth in a hideous wide grin. In the story, the character's mouth had been sliced open as a punishment, to make him appear to be a laughing gargoyle. It was the kind of challenge Veidt was ready to tackle, taking hours of painful practice to maintain the expression. A variation of his character appeared on a wall at Steeplechase Park on Coney Island, announcing "The Funny Place." Veidt's grotesque image was used years later for comic book creator Bob Kane when he wanted a foil for Batman, his caped crusader. Since then, Veidt's characterization influenced the famous image of the Joker, played over the years by actors like Cesar Romero, Jack Nicholson, and Heath Ledger.

With fame and fortune in his grasp, Conny was ready for a third picture for Universal named *The Magician*. During its filming, something terrified him. As the actor later explained, "In the middle of my third Hollywood picture *The Magician*, the earthquake hit Hollywood. Not the real earthquake. Just the talkies." But for Veidt, the talkies represented an end to his Hollywood career. He knew his limited English and his classical, if not stereotypical, German accent would limit the roles he could play in American cinema. He feared he would never speak English without an accent and figured his selection of film roles would shrink to caricatures. It was a heart-breaking and disappointing situation. He wanted to return to Germany and pick up his film career there. He quoted Shakespeare to explain his desire to walk away from Hollywood: "I am but a poor player that struts and frets his hour on the stage."

Universal Studios had no such reservations about the quality of Veidt's performances when they moved into the sound world where speaking English, in an American style, was in order. The executives had optioned the best role for Veidt from the Broadway stage. They wanted Conrad to play what could be his most sinister and bizarre role yet: Count Dracula. Another candidate was Lon Chaney, whose health gave out, leaving Veidt the prime choice as an established film star for the part. The foreign actor who'd originated the role on Broadway was unknown and had an even more peculiar accent. His name was Bela Lugosi.

To sweeten the deal of casting Conrad Veidt as Dracula, the studio intended in 1929 to have Paul Leni direct the picture, reuniting the old professional associates for their biggest blockbuster. Then, to complicate matters and send the most negative augur of all to the reluctant Veidt, Leni contracted blood poisoning from an abscessed tooth and died unexpectedly. Conny had already made his decision, and this was the sign he needed. Conrad Veidt refused to do the role that would have guaranteed him screen immortality. He chose to return to Germany in 1930 and pick up his acting career where he had left it in his homeland.

Alas, Germany was undergoing a radical change. Veidt performed in Germany's first talkie, but in 1933 he decided it best he and his third wife, Ilona Prager, move elsewhere. As she was Jewish, his official papers

"He's just like any other man, only more so": On Humphrey Bogart's Journey from Broadway Stage Journeyman to Hollywood Screen Immortality

Ben Bergin

You don't learn a damned thing working in pictures.[1]
—Humphrey Bogart, August 21, 1956

It is of some irony that the man most notorious in Hollywood history for playing caustic, cynical tough guys, creator of the "Rat Pack," and for whom the process of lingering over a hard drink or cigarette is named, should have initially forged his career playing parts perhaps a little closer to home—what he himself referred to as "White Pants Willies" roles or—as Elia Kazan, assistant director on *Chrysalis* with Bogie in 1932, more articulately put it—"patent leather parlor sheiks";[2] privileged and forgettable juvenile leads, foppish romantic seconds who, for all his distaste, mirrored the existence of his wealthy roots and upbringing. Discovering that Bogie may well have been the first

---

[1]   *Look 20*, prod William Atwood
[2]   Thompson, 12

man to utter "Anyone for tennis?" (despite his claims that the actual line in question was "It's forty-love outside. Would anybody care to watch?"[3]—a line that defies all the boundaries of probability by actually being worse) on a Broadway stage is rather like having the curtain pulled back on the *Wizard of Oz*, but certainly those characters would not have been unfamiliar to him.

Humphrey DeForest Bogart is one of the most mythologised characters in Hollywood history; as plentiful as the rumours that he was born on the final Christmas of the nineteenth century, that he acquired a scar chasing down an escaped prisoner during World War One, that his slight lisp was the result of a botched surgery, are the rumours that these rumours were, in fact, rumours, deliberately planted by Warner Bros. to enhance his air of mystique. What is certain, however, is that the privileged son of a New York Upper West Side surgeon and his extremely successful commercial artist wife got his first taste of show business as an infant, modeling for his mother. A far cry from Sam Spade indeed, but then his family had him destined for studying medicine at Yale. However, young Humphrey did not blend well with the private school system and, after being expelled, he joined the navy for the final days of the War, and after drifting from one employment to the next, it was left to the Bogarts' neighbours to offer him a job. Fortunately said neighbours were producer William A. Brady, actress Grace Gears, and children Bill Jr. and Alice. Alice in particular seems to have taken a shine to the young Humphrey and convinced her father to give him an office job and subsequently, in 1920, the position of company manager for the tour of *The Ruined Lady*. This was a job that Bogart applied himself to with both the professionalism and wit that were to become such hallmarks of his image and that lent him a great deal of success on the tour until the final night of the run. Bogart was amazed by the indolent lifestyle of the performers in comparison to the rigour of his own and constantly teased actor Neil Hamilton upon the theme. Come the last show Hamilton decided to give the lippy young manager a taste of his own medicine and told Bogart to take his place on stage for the night, a challenge that Bogart could hardly back down from. Despite shaking with nerves and writhing in terror as one actor (in character) "got angry"[4] with him, a dramatic spark had been lit; and with spectacular disregard for racial accuracy, Alice subsequently got him a one-line role as a Japanese butler in a piece called *Drifting*, a play that Alan Dale of *The*

3   Benchley, 30.
4   Benchley, 25.

New York American described—in what may be the most spectacular, if utterly incomprehensible, piece of dramatic criticism in print history—as "strangely protuberant,"[5] though any critique of Bogart's contribution is sadly lost to history. Fortunately, the redoubtable Mr. Dale was on hand to note Bogie's "trenchant bad acting"[6] for his next role in *Swifty*, though as the new-found actor's first question to director John Cromwell was as to whether he should face the audience or his fellow cast members, it seems as though he had more pressing matters to deal with than a mesmerising performance. Interestingly, while this naiveté may seem cute or even laughable, it does, in fact, hint at the naturalism that would not only make Bogart stand out on stage years later but would also ease his transition from the two thousand seat theatres of Broadway to the meticulous close-ups of Hollywood.

While he may have been acting the fop on stage, beyond the curtain he was already forging the reputation that would define him. After the second act of *Meet The Wife* (for by the early twenties he was steadily working in the theatre), he removed his greasepaint, changed into his suit, and went home, a not unusual set of actions had he not been a key player in act three, leaving the rest of the cast, including Mary Boland, to improvise wildly around his absence. This lack of professionalism may seem uncharacteristic, but his reaction upon being questioned the next day by the stage manager—i.e., punching him in the mouth—is somehow charmingly more apt for the man most would come to know initially as an on-screen gangster.

His Hollywood debut would not come until 1929, in a Warner Bros. short entitled *Broadway's Like That*, and though some copies survive, their sound does not. It is of some small irony then that it was the addition of sound to film that would initially open the door for Bogart to the movie studios. By 1930 silent stars such as John Gilbert were beginning to disappear, their voice recordings either not matching their silent on-screen persona, or simply bad, and the studios were searching for new talent to replace them. That year Fox was seeking a lead in their picture *The Man Who Came Back*, and fortunately for Bogart his brother-in-law Stuart Rose was working for Fox in New York as eastern story editor. Rose convinced his boss, Al Lewis, to allow Humphrey to audition, conceding that while his theatrical reviews were, at best, mixed, his consistent stage work proved he had vocal ability to match his acting skills. Lewis conceded. Bogart made his way to Tenth Avenue,

---

5   Ibid.

6   Ibid.

and Lewis described the test as "magnificent,"[7] offering the actor a substantial salary of $750 per week.

The most common reason for many New York stage actors to head to Hollywood at that time was, of course, the Depression. Fame and fortune beckoned for both serious actors, whose purses were being squeezed on the boards of Broadway, but also for anyone who was attracted to the glamour and money that Los Angeles studios could offer. For all his critical maulings, Bogart's professionalism stood out. In a career spanning eighty-one films he was never late; never showed up without utter command of his lines; and, possibly most tellingly, he would rehearse not only until he was ready but until all the other actors were too, marking him out from other, more selfish, performers, like Sinatra and Brando (though Bogart himself qualified that when it came to singing, his friend Sinatra was a consummate professional, and he respected the trail-blazing Brando)—a trait that may well have been a result of his grounding in theatrical companies rather than having been initiated in front of the camera. His longevity in the theatre would have helped him to stand out from the young hopefuls, and even the harshest critiques he received helped to harden him and give him an edge that would serve him well.

The Depression, however, was affecting studios as well as actors; and he lost the part in *The Man Who Came Back*, lacking the box-office clout to land the lead for a big studio. Of course, the notoriously forthright Bogart didn't help himself when, asking if his golfing party could play through the slower foursome in front, he was challenged with "Who the hell do you think you are?" His response "My name is Humphrey Bogart; I work at Fox. What are you doing playing a gentleman's game at a gentlemen's club?" might have carried more weight had it not unwittingly been directed at the then vice president of Fox. He made six movies, each of decreasing artistry, the only one of any note being *Up The River* which launched both the film career of Spencer Tracy and a lifelong friendship between the two men. While he briefly returned to Hollywood in 1932 for Columbia, he was loaned to Warner Bros., where he played tenth-billing in bad films; he spent the first half of the decade primarily in New York and primarily on stage. Indeed, the only movie of any significance would be *Three On A Match* featuring Bette Davis where, for the first time, Bogart played a criminal (in this case a mugger/enforcer) rather than a now-ageing ingenue. The theatre, however, still had him playing romantic juveniles, a pattern that would continue until

---

[7]   Benchley, 44.

May 1934 when, in one of the most significant moments of Bogart's life, director Arthur Hopkins would see him in the otherwise forgettable *Invitation To Murder*. To everyone's astonishment Hopkins offered him the role of killer Duke Mantee in Hopkins's new project titled *Petrified Forest*, a role completely at odds with anything anyone had seen Bogart do before and an almost unthinkable departure from his previous body of work. Hopkins explained, "[Bogart was an actor] I never much admired. An antiquated juvenile . . . in white pants swinging a tennis racquet . . . as far from a cold-blooded killer as one could get. But the voice persisted . . . and the voice was Mantee's."[8]

The casting was inspired and the performance a revelation. With his (real, not made up) two days' stubble, a brutal self-inflicted hair cut, and pallid skin achieved by denying himself sunlight to achieve the affect of time spent in prison, Bogart literally drew gasps from his audience every time he walked onto the stage. Both his physical appearance and his performance brought immediate comparisons with John Dillinger, very much in the public eye at that time, and an intoxicating mix of glamour and danger. The play, which opened at the Broadhurst Theatre on January 7, 1935, was a hit and in particular the performances of English star, Leslie Howard, and Bogart, whose work critic Brooks Atkinson in *The New York Times* described as "the best of his career."[9] However, the run ended on the say-so of Howard, whose stardom was such that he refused to be replaced by an understudy when he no longer wanted to continue. While this must have been initially galling for Bogart (though not, perhaps, as galling as for Howard's understudy), it proved to be one of the most fortuitous occurrences of his professional life. The play had garnered enough notoriety for Warner Bros. to take it on, though Bogart—despite his rave reviews—was once again left out in the cold. Only Howard of the original leads would be recreating his role for the cameras, the studio preferring the tried-and-tested Edward G. Robinson for the role of "Duke" rather than an actor whose previous experiences with them had been distinctly unimpressive. When a despondent Bogie told Howard, however, the Brit was outraged and sent Jack Warner the now-infamous telegram: "No Bogart, no deal. L. H." Once again, the sway held by the Oscar-nominated star proved final, and Bogart's gratitude was such that seventeen years later he would name his daughter Leslie Howard Bogart in honour of his friend. As with the play, the film was a success, Bogart so well received that he was given equal top-billing with

---

8   Meyer, 49.
9   Sperber and Lax, 46.

Howard and a five-year contract with Warner Bros. starting at $550/week and rising to $1,750, which he signed in January of 1936. It seemed as though Bogie the movie star had finally arrived.

He had signed a significant contract with a major studio, he and then-wife Mary had bought a house on Horn Avenue, Los Angeles, and thanks to *Petrified Forest* he seemed to have finally made it in film. However, while his work for Warner Bros. was steady and well-paid, he could not get past the studio's image of him as a hoodlum. For all that he may have been raised a gentleman, abhorred bad language in front of a lady, enjoyed fine scotch and played chess daily, he was as typecast as shallow a villain as it was possible to be. In his first two years under contract he was involved in twelve films, eight of which saw him playing a criminal and in two of which he and Edward G. Robinson killed each other. Throughout the two following years he made seventeen pictures, playing a gangster of some sort in eleven and dying in nine. Despite a passionate and sexually charged performance in the excellent *Dark Victory* with Bette Davis, Jack Warner simply did not see romantic potential in Bogart—some far cry from New York only a couple of years previously when he could *only* get cast in sybaritic, weak, romantic roles. Legend, of course, lays the responsibility for the fresh wind in the sails of

Bogart's career at the hands of the unfortunate George Raft who turned down the roles of Rick, in *Casablanca*, and Sam Spade in *The Maltese Falcon* (allegedly Raft believed that working with unproven director John Huston would ruin his career, rather bringing to mind the record companies who wouldn't sign the Beatles. The more one reads about Raft, the sorrier a figure he becomes), roles that would forge Bogie's lasting and iconic status in Hollywood history. First, however, came *High Sierra* and a role that would finally bring the depth and complexity to a career that had been marked and weighted by the shallowness of its parts. Raft turned the role down *twice* (he didn't want to play a character who died), as did Paul Muni, with Cagney, Robinson, and Garfield also rejecting the character of Roy "Mad Dog" Earle, a criminal on the run. Bogart, though, brought sympathy and an underlying softness to a character who was innately hard-bitten and tough. The relationships he formed with Ida Lupino's Marie and Joan Leslie's Velma proved that not only could he handle romance, but that he had a unique ability to merge it with the gangster genre, as well as demonstrating the mix that would become his hallmark of gangster and gentleman. *The Maltese Falcon* followed; the movie not only cemented Bogart as a leading man but also established a director-actor relationship that would define the noir genre as well as a friendship that would last until the end; with Spencer Tracy too fraught with grief, it was left to Huston to read the eulogy at Bogie's funeral in 1957: "He regarded the somewhat gaudy figure of Bogart, the star, with amused cynicism; Bogart, the actor, he held in deep respect."[10] *Casablanca*—which, as well as being Bogart's most iconic performance, is held by many to be the greatest movie of all time—brought him his first Oscar nomination, though thanks to the notoriously violent jealousy of his third wife Mayo "Slugger" Methot he claimed he never saw the film. While Methot may have come across as borderline psychotic (let's be honest, the nickname doesn't help), as Bogie pointed out, there aren't many people who *wouldn't* be jealous of Ingrid Bergman; "if Ingrid stopped to look at you, you'd got sex appeal!"[11] It would be Huston—again—who would finally direct him to victory at the Academy Awards for *The African Queen*, beating out some stellar competition in Montgomery Clift's *A Place In The Sun* and Marlon Brando's Stanley in *A Streetcar Named Desire*. Brando's performance was to usher in a new style of acting on both stage and screen with Stanivslasky's "Method" becoming the standard, and Hollywood had

---

[10]   Thompson, 120.

[11]   Ibid., 57.

moved on; grubby sleeveless vests and craps had replaced tuxedos and roulette, elegant wit with raw inarticulate emotion. Bogart respected Brando but less so the new style: "The audience is ahead of you . . . . If a guy points a gun at you, they don't need to see your face twitching, they know you're afraid."[12] However, Bogart seemed to have found an inner peace that had been lacking in his private life almost his entire existence. Legend has him accusing Ingrid Bergman after she had married director Roberto Rossellini, "You used to be a great star, and what are you now?" and receiving Bergman's caustic response "a happy woman." While he would continue to make movies until his death (indeed, he believed that doing so helped him stay healthy), he appeared to have found contentment off-screen with his final wife, Lauren Bacall, and their children. Many people, factors, coincidences, and chances came together in order to turn the privileged Upper West Side child into an actor and to transfer his forgettable stage contributions into a film career as, oft-quoted, beloved and revered as any in Hollywood history. While Bogie the man himself was something of a mystery, caught between the rumours spun by the studio he worked for, his on-screen image and a complex—if old-fashioned—man at heart, he may have claimed to have missed the stage: "In theatre I worked at eight, was through by eleven; all the rest of the night and the next day to play and catch up with my drinking . . . . Working in pictures is for the birds."[13] However, his heart was very much in Hollywood. On August 21, 1956, a mere four months before his unexpected death, he allowed a collection of six young would-be actors into his home to interview him, including Janet Lake, Gerry Gaylor, Bob Benevedes, Tom Laughlin, Jerry Frank, and Dennis Hopper. He also permitted the conversation to be recorded.[14] Perhaps the final insight as to his transition should be left up to him.

Frank: Why did you move to Hollywood?
HB: There was more money out here.
Benevedes: What gratification do you get from working in the movies? Don't you miss the applause you get on stage?
HB: I have a charming wife, two beautiful kids, a gorgeous home, and a yacht—and I've had the applause. But I'll be damned if I know why I work so hard . . . . Sinatra and I were talking about it the other day . . . . Working is therapy, I guess . . . . This is a

12 Duchovnay.
13 Ibid., 17.
14 *Look 20*, prod. William Atwood.

bad town to be out of work in. After a week or so of not working, you're so bored you don't know what the hell to do.

Like his most famous creation, Rick Blaine, Bogie may have loved to play the cynic who only had his eye on his bank balance; but the truth is, like Rick, he was in it for love.

Bibliography

Media

Look 20, "Bogart on Hollywood: An Old Pro Tells Some Young Hopefuls How To Make Good In The Movie World," Aug. 21, 1956. Prod. William Atwood.

Literature

Benchley, Nathaniel. *Humphrey Bogart. New York:* The NY Times Company, 1981.

Duchovnay, Geralt. *Humphrey Bogart—A Bio-Bibliography*. Westport, CT: Greenwood Press, 1999.

Meyers, Jeffrey. *Bogart: A Life in Hollywood*. London: Andre Deutsch Ltd, 1997.

Sperber, A. M., and Eric Lax. *Bogart*. New York: William Morrow and Co, 1997.

Thompson, David. *Humphrey Bogart*. New York: Faber and Faber Inc. 2009.

Carry On, Sherlock Holmes: Stage to Screen and Back Again

William Russo and Jan Merlin

Though many actors made the transition from stage to screen, few roles gave the opportunity for dozens of actors to play the same part in silent films, in sound movies, on theater stages, and on television and radio. A recent count tally listed over seventy admiring actors having played variations on the most elementary of these iconic characters, Sherlock Holmes, in over two hundred storylines.

Created by Dr. Arthur Conan Doyle in 1887 with a novella titled *A Study in Scarlet*, Holmes became a sensation in print as a consulting detective making deduction through cold logic. The hailed books and short stories would not wind down until before the close of the First World War; "His Last Bow" had a setting around 1916, when Conan Doyle's literary topic interests shifted elsewhere. The writer was never fond of Holmes, though that protagonist was based on a former medical professor, Dr. Joseph Bell, for whom Doyle had worked as a clerk while at Edinburgh Royal Infirmary. Doyle had tried to dispatch the detective at least once, killing him off in "The Final Problem" in 1893—but Holmes was not so easy to kill in print. Once he hit the stage, he was immortal.

Actually, Doyle first thought of writing Holmes for the stage. Another man had done a play, *Under The Clock*, using his invented detective, and there was rumor that a second play about Holmes by someone else was in the works. Doyle managed to interest a few important English actors, but soon found that he'd lose total control over the project. Each star found fault with the role or various scenes and demanded changes. The hopeful playwright may have disliked Sherlock Holmes, but couldn't betray his own masterpiece. Over the years, his stage version was getting nowhere; and by the turn of the century, the resolute Doyle began to waver. He was ready to capitulate.

In the late 1890s, Doyle met an American visitor to London, Charles Frohman, who suggested he contact an established talented American actor and playwright, known as William Gillette. The friend was sent the entire collection of Holmes stories and expressed a wish to collaborate on a play script. It was a peculiar arrangement the two made, since neither ever met. They wrote their separate treatments, fashioning them together back and forth with overseas telegrams, putting together a play for Gillette to do. Both men were middle aged when Sherlock Holmes made his American stage debut, William being younger than Conan by six years and considering himself perfect for the role of the wildly popular fictional detective. The intrigued actor came up with the notion of wearing a deerstalker hat on stage, which he'd seen depicted in earlier illustrations of the short stories character in *Strand Magazine*.

Gillette first appeared onstage as Holmes in 1899 at the age of forty-six at the Garrick Theatre, where he did the show for six months with more than 250 performances.

Gillette had stumbled upon a gold mine. He took the play on the road and established the epitome of the classic Holmes persona, including cape and mannerisms with pipe and violin. For thirty years he parlayed his stern, taciturn, and laconic behavior into a mold for anyone else daring to attempt a portrayal. Gillette wanted Holmes to have a romantic interest of sorts, and Doyle consented to whatever he asked for the character. In essence, Gillette borrowed references and plot ideas from several known stories and wove them into his own play conception, drawing upon the Doyle characters and plotlines, substituting Billy, a young pageboy, rather than having Mrs. Hudson at 221b Baker Street.

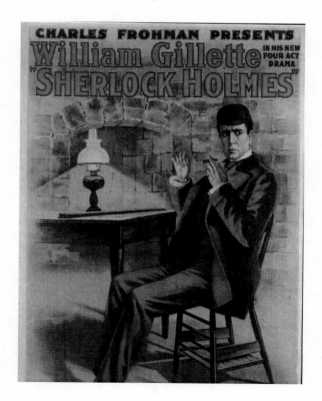

In 1916, after having performed Holmes regularly since the play's debut, Gillette brought his portrayal to the silent screen for posterity. This didn't end his involvement with the detective role. He was to make periodical appearances on the Broadway stage as Holmes, often by public demand. In 1905 he came back for another stint over six months, perhaps inspiring the first movie short version of Holmes (out of Denmark, now lost). At the end of 1910 Gillette came back with another revival and innumerable shows. In 1915 he appeared at the Empire Theatre. This didn't end his involvement with the detective role. He returned as Sherlock in 1928 for a month of shows, and again in January of 1930, at age seventy-seven, to reprise his act.

In between those theatrical appearances, the image of Holmes was taking on a younger look in the cinema. From 1921 through 1923 a series of short subject films, based rather closely on the published stories, began to appear. Nearly every Conan Doyle short story was filmed. The only omissions were the novellas like *A Study in Scarlet* and *Hound of the Baskervilles*. The silent actor named Eille Norwood, at age sixty, took on the role of Holmes in every short subject film. Today many of these lost gems are only available on DVD in England, and many others have not been seen for generations.

In 1922 John Barrymore took on the young Holmes as a smitten college student at Cambridge with his friend John Watson (Roland Young) and grew in the second half of the film to be a more recognizable Holmes, whose encounters with the evil Moriarty permeate his youth to adulthood. The role neither interested Barrymore nor audiences, though the lost film for years grew in its mythic mystery. Once discovered and restored in the 1970s, it was merely a curio, though critics speculated that sound would have provided Barrymore with more of a challenge and given audiences more to savor.

At a physical age that the literary Holmes had long since retired to Sussex to keep bees, William Gillette brought back his spry but decidedly ancient Sherlock. Audiences saw the legendary Gillette as Holmes, but the detective role had been taken to the talking films in 1929. When Conan Doyle died in July of 1930, Clive Brook stepped into the first sound movie version of *The Return of Sherlock Holmes*. Clive Brook had begun his career on the English stage in 1918 after the Great War, but his youthful matinee idol looks whisked him to the silent screen, and later to Hollywood, the mecca for all theatrical people. But this early sound picture was done at the Astoria Studios in Queens, New York, scarcely depicting London at all. And there was a writing credit for Conan Doyle on this film about the murder of Watson's future son-in-law.

In the early 1930s well-known Broadway actor/director named Robert Rendel became Holmes on film for another version of *The Hound of the Baskervilles*. Chosen for his ability to handle dialogue, his Holmes has generally been lost for decades, but segments discovered have not disclosed a classic, for his acting was said to be less than elementary.

When Raymond Massey took on the sleuth role, tackling the case of *The Speckled Band*, released in the United States in late 1931, it was Massey's first talking film, and his training on the London stage transcended the sound issues of the early days. He returned regularly to stage work, playing Abe Lincoln on film after his theater success with that role. His theatrical voice and ponderous tones made Massey's Sherlock an intimidating figure. He was modern, witty, and handled the pipe in clenched teeth while mixing chemicals.

Alas, Raymond Massey, like a Moriarty victim, was mysteriously replaced, despite good reviews, within the year by Clive Brook, whose earlier portrayal had won earnest and diehard fans. *Sherlock Holmes* of 1932 was considered a far more superior film than the first talking Holmes tale, mainly due to Brook's comfort and the technological improvements in cinema. Once again, Moriarty reared his ugly presence, giving Holmes and Watson (Reginald Owen) fits.

When Clive Brook returned to the character in 1932, he discovered that Moriarty had taken on all the attributes of a Chicago gangster during Prohibition. Though many felt the updating of Holmes stories was sacrilege, the Brook version did just that, making Holmes more like Elliot Ness. But then, the true screw turned. Reginald Owen, (age forty-five) born the year Holmes made his first literary appearance, made a magical transformation. He went from filming in the role of Watson in the summer of 1932 to six months later enacting Holmes himself in the winter. Yes, Reginald Owen suddenly appeared as Sherlock Holmes in the talky version of *A Study in Scarlet*. If audiences were not befuddled already, this film had Holmes and Watson living at 221-a Baker Street. Apparently the old digs were being redecorated. Mrs. Hudson was nowhere to be found, and Owen had hoped to become the new face of the franchise. His other memorable role a few years later was to fill in for the ill Lionel Barrymore when he played Ebenezer Scrooge in 1937's version of *A Christmas Carol*.

British filmmakers still did not turn to Basil Rathbone, the inimitable actor from South Africa, who could play a Russian count, tormenting Garbo in *Anna Karenina*, for the next Holmes. Instead, they turned in 1931 to Arthur Wontner who signed up to do five films as Sherlock, nearly all using plot ideas from the canon stories. Some are available today, like *Murder at the Baskervilles* and Sherlock Holmes's *Fatal Hour*, *The Triumph of Sherlock Holmes* (based on *The Valley of Fear*), and *The Sign of Four*; still unavailable for modern viewers is *Sherlock Holmes and The Missing Rembrandt*. Moriarty is the man behind each plot of these potboilers, even dragging Holmes from retirement in Sussex. Into his sixties by the end of the series in 1937, the American stage had been cleared from a Hollywood production of the first rank from Twentieth Century Fox when they picked Rathbone to do *Hound of the Baskervilles* for early release in 1939. The early success required Rathbone and Nigel Bruce reprising their respective roles for a version of the Gillette play for the big screen.

Over at Universal, Roy William Neill, a fellow Brit and Holmes aficionado, managed to set up a modern series in 1942, with Holmes now fighting for the Allies. It was the end of the grand era of Rathbone's career as nemesis to Zorro. He signed on with Universal, and that meant a steady diet of low-budget horror films, like a version of Poe's *The Black Cat*, but as always, the role of Holmes did offer character actors a chance to play the lead. Rathbone went for the most productive period of his career, establishing his reputation for all time as the quintessential Sherlock.

Basil Rathbone had made a career at Warner Bros. of playing villains against some of the great adventure stars, like Errol Flynn and Tyrone Power, where he could bedevil Greta Garbo. The first appearance as Sherlock had ended with Holmes at the Baskerville estate calling out to Watson for "the needle." This shocking display of anti-heroic addiction often ended on the cutting room floor. When Rathbone had an opportunity to play, once again, a heroic figure in *The Adventures of Sherlock Holmes*, based on the old Gillette play, he found himself instantly regarded as the epitome of a classic version.

A worse fate befell him. Poverty Row studio, Universal, took up the franchise and gave him a dozen more appearances, including one buffoonish cameo in Olsen and Johnson's lowbrow *Crazy House*. When the character was updated to contemporary 1940s, the studio argued that it increased the pace of the stories and appealed to young audiences. Rathbone went along with Nigel Bruce as Watson. Rathbone went on to do a dozen more, usually three per year, with increasingly smaller budgets and weirder hairdos for Rathbone.

Passed over to play the pageboy Billy in Mrs. Hudson's employ for the Rathbone version of *The Adventures of Sherlock*, child star Frankie Thomas was busy with other projects in 1939; but as a standard freelance actor now in his mid-teens, he could have easily played the role of Billy. Having cut his teeth playing Bonita Granville's sleuthing boyfriend in the Nancy Drew series, he was ripe for a role in his favorite reading material, the Holmes stories.

Frankie's family were Broadway theater professionals, part of a clique that dominated social strata in Hollywood of the era. Through his father and mother, youthful Frankie met Basil Rathbone, the emerging Holmes of the film world. The coveted role of Billy went to Terry Kilburn, a native British boy who had picked up the mantle of Freddie Bartholomew. Nevertheless, Frankie loved the Holmes stories and read all avidly. He later, as an adult, when out of Hollywood's limelight, wrote a series of novels that featured Holmes and Watson in new adventures. His titles, over a dozen, are still in print. He disliked the Bruce portrayal of Watson intensely and would alter that in his own books, but always favored the actor he saw frequently on the studio lot, Basil Rathbone.

If Rathbone had felt overloaded with the role, he did not show it openly. He went on in 1945 to do a radio series with his sidekick, Nigel Bruce, playing Holmes and Watson in a series of original adventures. The brains behind the franchise was Roy William Neill, who cleverly integrated issues and problems from "His Last Bow" to "The Dancing Men" and "The Musgrave Ritual" and other tales into modern versions, even to the point of referring to the untold tale of the "Giant Rat of Sumatra." Yet when the director/producer died suddenly in early 1946 while on vacation in England, Rathbone bailed out of the series.

Moreover, he left Hollywood entirely for almost six years, bemoaning the curse of typecasting.

Rathbone toured the country in a series of plays and evenings, barnstorming through Canada and meeting an adoring public who constantly reminded him of Holmes. When his latest wife, Ouida Bergere, fancying his need to return to the role, despite his protests actually wrote in the same vein as Gillette, a new play about Sherlock, Rathbone relented. She had written dozens of silent films and put together a pastiche geared to Rathbone who was now in his sixties. Who better to play the role than to have Basil Rathbone return as Holmes on Broadway? And in 1953, he did. As a promotion for the role he had made famous, Rathbone actually did a live television show, playing Holmes in "The Adventure of the Black Baronet" in late May. Nigel Bruce was on vacation in Mexico and did not reprise Watson.

Rathbone was above criticism on his depiction of Holmes, but the play written for him by his wife ran in late October for only three performances. Yet Rathbone was motivated. He approached NBC-TV for the chance to portray Holmes again for a new generation on the new mode of entertainment that swept the nation in those Cold War days of the 1950s. But a man in his sixties seemed unlikely to be a television draw, according to executives at the peacock network. On top of that, Rathbone's former comrade, Nigel Bruce, so active in the years after the Universal franchise, had suddenly died of a heart attack and could not rejoin him. At this point Rathbone surrendered the ghost of playing Sherlock for all time, though wherever he went, he was always recognized as the great consulting detective. He died in 1967.

A British series was underway in the fifties, making some half-dozen episodes with British actor Alan Wheatley as Holmes. He later received American fame when he played the Sheriff of Nottingham against the stalwart Richard Greene's *Robin Hood* on a British series that transferred well to the United States. Wheatley's Holmes never made to the States and remains a lost performance. Within a few years by 1954, Ronald Howard, the son of Leslie Howard, was cast as the sleuth. The British series was filmed in France and not shown in England until recently. Only one episode of the thirty-seven produced was based on one of the old stories ("The Red Headed League"). Only a few well-known names dotted the casts of guest actors. Paulette Goddard and Delphine Seyrig were damsels in distress for Howard's Holmes.

Peter Cushing tackled the Hammer version of *Hound of the Baskervilles*, with his costar Christopher Lee playing Henry Baskerville in 1959. In 1968 British television was treated to sixteen episodes based on the sacred canon of the Doyle stories, with Peter Cushing giving a performance as the master detective. It had been the first attempt since the 1920s to give the stories faithful adaptation, but it was not the last effort.

Patrick Macnee, the Avenger of television with Diana Rigg, played Holmes finally in 1996 in a television movie entitled *The Case of the Temporal Nexus*; but earlier he had been Watson twice: once in 1991 in *Sherlock Holmes and the Leading Lady*, with Christopher Lee as the detective, and he first played Watson in 1976 with Roger Moore, fresh off James Bond, as the consulting detective in *Sherlock Holmes in New York*.

Christopher Lee had the distinction of actually playing Sherlock Holmes in 1962 in a story about Moriarty and a deadly necklace. He later limned Sherlock's smarter brother Mycroft in Billy Wilder's sexual satire *The Private Life of Sherlock Holmes* in which the detective and Watson were more than buddies.

Jeremy Brett played Dr. Watson on stage in Los Angeles, opposite another stalwart Sherlock Holmes version provided by Charlton Heston in *Crucifer of Blood*, based on *Sign of Four*. Heston later went on to do the television movie version without Brett. In the early 1990s, Jeremy Brett and his Watson, Edward Hardwicke, went on the London stage for two weeks, playing out again the William Gillette chestnut, *The Adventures of Sherlock Holmes*. It was a hot ticket for those who could attend the standing-room-only performances.

When Jeremy Brett tackled Holmes in 1984, he had a twofold goal. One was to become the best Holmes on record and, second, to film all the short stories and novellas. Brett had an obsession with the similarities between him and the character, and was unable to escape him away from the Granada Studios sets in England. As he shot episodes of stories in no particular order, the series almost attained its goal by the early 1990s. Joan Wilson who produced the shows died in 1985, throwing the star into grief and depression as she was also his wife. Brett, suffering a heart condition, soon succumbed in 1995 at age sixty-one, leaving the glossy productions a dozen stories short of fulfilling his dream. If anyone had made a dent in the legendary depiction of Rathbone, it was clearly Jeremy Brett.

During the highly praised Brett series, shown on PBS in the United States, several amusing coincidences occurred. Alan Howard (cousin of an earlier Sherlock, Ronald Howard) made one appearance as a stiff aristocrat who retained Holmes's service in the case of "The Priory School." Later, a young boyish actor played a jockey impersonating

Lady Beatrice Falder in the episode entitled "Shoscombe Old Place." The actor's early role in a Sherlock Holmes episode may well have been a harbinger of later work in a Holmes story; in 2009, the dapper star Jude Law was cast as the young Dr. John Watson in the Robert Downey version of *Sherlock Holmes.*

Even in the latest 2009 *Star Trek* movie, Holmes is quoted by Spock (Zachary Quinto) to the befuddlement of his fellow crewmembers, though Spock and Captain Kirk have always been variations on Holmes and Watson. To name all the actors who have tackled the Holmes role, both in satire and seriously, would be daunting. Every actor who is tall, imperious, and difficult to cast as a hero finds Holmes an attractive role. Those who have played stalwart heroes all too often (Stewart Granger, Roger Moore, Charlton Heston, Michael Caine) found the role a refreshing change of pace. Stage actors like John Wood and Nicol Williamson have played the role on Broadway and on film.

Whether the latest height-challenged incarnation of Holmes by Robert Downey Jr. will follow the lead of Rathbone and Brett is unclear. *Variety*'s critic predicted that productions of the former Sherlocks will never be matched by Downey's quasi-superhero version, but there is a slight chance that in twenty years, the aging iron man of movies may take his Holmes to the stage in the hoary latest revival of William Gillette's old chestnut. Fans of Holmes should carry on for a few more decades to see how the latest incarnation in the lifetime of Sherlock Holmes plays out.

SUGGESTED READING

Doyle, Sir Arthur Conan, Leslie S. Klinger, and John Lecarre. *The New Annotated Sherlock Holmes*. Norton, 2004.

Haining, Peter. *The Television Sherlock Holmes*, published with Granada Television. Virgin Books, 1991.

Park, Orlando. *The Sherlock Holmes Encyclopedia*. Avenel, 1985.

Wexler, Bruce. *The Mysterious World of Sherlock Holmes: The Illustrated Guide to the Famous Cases, Infamous Adversaries, and Ingenious Methods of the Great Detective*. Running Press, 2008.

Harold Lloyd: Horatio Alger in Straw Hat and Horn-Rims

Maurizio Giammarco

Perhaps the most singular image that comes to mind for most viewers when they think of Harold Lloyd is that of a young bespectacled man dangling precariously from the arms of a collapsing clock high above street level in his classic film *Safety Last* (1923). The image is an indelible one. It occurs at the climax of an ingeniously-crafted plot that features Lloyd as a country boy who leaves his hometown of Great Bend to find fortune and acclaim in the big city, for once he acquires both, his sweetheart promises to marry him.

But in another important respect, that iconic shot from *Safety Last*, along with its storyline, reveal something else, something deeper: the indomitable qualities that would come to be associated with Harold Lloyd, the man as well as the artist—determination, energy, courage, inventiveness. For both his life and career were filled with a series of rich, compelling contrasts: As a child, he witnessed the divorce of his parents, and yet, from all accounts, he maintained a spirit of optimism and resiliency that informed both his character and his work; as a teenager, he experienced economic deprivation but as an adult eventually became one of the wealthiest personalities in Hollywood; as a young actor struggling to achieve success, first, on the stage, then, later, on the screen, he became one of the most successful comedic actors during the Silent Age of film; as an ardent supporter of the theater, he dismissed the new medium of motion pictures but then went on to become one of the silent screen's most accomplished inventive filmmakers.

Perhaps the most revealing contrast regarding Harold Lloyd's career was that although he achieved extraordinary professional success as a comedic actor and director, he did not earn the same distinction as artist in the world of comedy; for at that time, and for far too long afterwards, he was overshadowed by the two legendary figures of that world: Charlie Chaplin and Buster Keaton.

But one of the many ironies at work during this period was that Lloyd actually made more films than Chaplin and Keaton combined, and drew more audiences to the box office than his more recognizable rivals. Another is that Lloyd, similar to Chaplin and Keaton, was attentive to comic detail, investing considerable time and energy to developing gags and complications of plot, crucial to the success of his films, from the one-reelers to the full-length features. Furthermore, Lloyd displayed acrobatic skills; and in this regard, he compares with Keaton in the daredevil stunts he continually performed in his efforts to win the heart of the girl. But not only that: Lloyd was considered a gifted actor who played comedic roles rather his being a natural comedian, and this distinction enabled him to create more multifaceted characters, both playful and poignant. In this respect, then, he could mirror Chaplin's expressiveness. And from a business perspective, Lloyd shares another similarity with Chaplin in that he obtained ownership rights to his films; thus, the two savvy comedians enjoyed a far more comfortable lifestyle than Keaton.

If, then, his work is seen as brilliant, why was it underrated, even neglected at times, throughout film history? Because according to Kevin Brownlow, "the vagaries of access introduced latter-day audiences to Lloyd via the wrong films, and denied them the right ones. From 1915 to 1919, he made scores of comedies that, like the Chaplin films made for Keystone in 1914, were no more of ephemeral value. They were indeed 'mechanical,' and, while they had legions of fans, have not stood the test of time" (11).

Brownlow observes that Lloyd, as both a performer and as a director, developed slowly; unlike Chaplin, whose initial efforts already began to show signs of brilliance as early as 1915, Lloyd did not emerge with his own distinctive style until 1919. Those early films, available for home movie use for years, suggest that Lloyd, at that early stage of his career, was not exceptional. It is with the later shorts and features that his brilliance becomes evident. And Lloyd—an honest, attentive evaluator of his own work—would make that distinction as well, for he was careful to discriminate between the quality of his later films with that of the early slapstick one-reelers.

After his early varied attempts to create characters such as Willie Work and Lonesome Luke, inspired in large measure by Chaplin, Lloyd believed that his career began in earnest with the arrival of his most memorable persona: the Glass Character, the ordinary-looking man who wore a straw hat and horn-rims and who made his appearance in a one-reel picture called *Over the Fence* (1917). Through this character, Lloyd displayed the bright disposition and resiliency of spirit that were attributable to Lloyd himself, qualities that audiences came to recognize and embrace. And as he developed this persona, Lloyd matured as a filmmaker as well. As one example, with successes such as *Grandma's Boy* (1922), he was integral in bringing about the advent of the "feature-length" film. With the arrival, then, of the Glass Character, the silent feature films that followed would constitute Harold Lloyd's finest work.

*

Harold Clayton Lloyd was born in the small town of Burchard, Nebraska, on April 20, 1893. According to Jeffrey Vance and Suzanne Lloyd, his stage career began at the age of thirteen when he met an actor named John Lane Connor, a young leading actor with the Burwood Stock Company, who became a mentor to Lloyd, got him various juvenile parts in plays, and helped develop the young man's acting technique (18). And although he had none of Chaplin's or Keaton's Vaudeville training, Lloyd revealed a natural talent that enabled him to make the most dangerous tumbles and falls seem effortless. Athletic and rigorous, he could fall from a window as effectively as he could scale a wall; consequently, this natural talent would become one of the signature trademarks of his acting career, for example, in the "thrill" film comedies he would later make. In 1912, after his parents divorced, Lloyd (along with Gaylord, his older brother), moved with his father to San Diego, where, in a fortuitous meeting of luck and circumstance, he reunited with Connor, joined his acting troupe, and performed regularly in various San Diego stock companies. That same year, though, his father's business collapsed; and so Lloyd and his brother moved with their father again, this time to Los Angeles, where the motion picture industry existed, albeit in its early stages, for New York was still the nation's film capital.

Desperately seeking employment, Lloyd found work in Los Angeles in 1913, finding roles primarily as an extra at the Universal Manufacturing Company for $3 a day, using his knowledge of makeup techniques to sneak past the studio guard, disguised as a regular extra (Vance and Lloyd, 19-20). This experience was one that Lloyd would later recreate in his one reel-comedy *Hey There* (1918). Unlike Chaplin and Keaton, Lloyd, during this period, found only the most meager of roles, such as a "Hottentot" in *The Patchwork Girl of Oz* (1914). But it was at this time, working as an extra, that he met, and made friends with, another struggling, ambitious young actor, Hal Roach, one who would have a formative impact on Lloyd and his career.

Roach soon came upon a small inheritance, assembled his own production company, and shortly thereafter both he and Lloyd created Willie Work, a character imitative of Charlie Chaplin. In 1914, Chaplin had emerged as the leading figure of film comedy with his indelible portrait of the Little Tramp character, and so for many struggling comedians, imitation became the sincerest form of flattery, an approach they hoped would ensure them success. But the character of Willie Work was neither amusing nor the comedies featuring him commercially viable.

Despite this disappointment, Roach's production company had started to become successful, as both Roach and Lloyd developed another character, "Lonesome Luke," a Chaplin-inspired bumbler involved in knockabout chases. Lloyd described his new character in this way: "The cunning thought behind all this, you will observe, was to reverse the Chaplin outfit [of The Little Tramp]. All his clothes were too large, mine all too small. My shoes were funny, but different; my mustache funny, but different" (92). Made between 1915 and 1917, the Lonesome Luke films were popular with audiences, but for Jeffrey Vance and Suzanne Lloyd, they displayed none of the characteristics of the persona Lloyd would best be known for, or the depth and subtlety of acting that went along with it (23).

And Lloyd, ever the astute observer of his own work, came to that recognition as well one evening when he and Bebe Daniels, an actress with whom he worked extensively, attended the cinema to see one of their Lonesome Luke comedies. As the eponymous character appeared on screen, a boy sitting next to Lloyd remarked, "Oh, here's that fellow who tries to do like Chaplin." That moment was seminal to Lloyd, for in his words, "I wasn't going on forever being a third-rate imitator of anybody, even a genius like Chaplin" (110). After that night, Lloyd persuaded Roach and the studio he worked for to abandon Lonesome Luke and move in a different direction, for as Lloyd observed:

> I had the feeling, and rightly so, that I would never get farther with Lonesome Luke than I had, because underneath it all, he was a comedy character and couldn't possibly rise to the heights that Chaplin had. And while you didn't try directly to imitate Chaplin, Luke was a character that belonged to that category (19).

Sometime in 1917, Lloyd did indeed move in a new direction, one that would become the most fruitful of his career; for it was at this time that "the kid with glasses" was invented or, as he always came to be identified in the film credits, "the Boy."

*

By 1918, the Glass Character would become the persona for which Harold Lloyd would ultimately be celebrated. In reflecting upon his creation, the comic actor and director seized upon the essence that defined "the Boy": his ordinariness. As Lloyd himself observed, "funnier things happen in life to an ordinary boy than to a Lonesome Luke" (102). Unlike Chaplin's or Keaton's personas—perennial misfits who, even when they succeeded, never truly became part of society—Lloyd's "kid with glasses" was a young earnest, determined boy from modest roots whose defining mission was "to make good"—and to do so with a smile. In short, the Glass Character was Everyman. Toward this end, Lloyd drew upon a simple prop that enabled him to achieve that ordinary man quality: glasses.

> While my character was not a comic character in appearance I donned the glasses to make him instantly recognizable. They were not a gimmick. They were a trademark the same as Chaplin's derby and cane. But my glasses gave a character besides. Someone with glasses is generally thought to be studious and an erudite person to a degree, a kind of person who doesn't fight or engage in violence, but I did, so my glasses belied my appearance. The audience could put me in a situation in their mind, but I could be just the opposite to what was supposed. So the glasses not only had an identifying characteristic but also a comedy characteristic (19).

To find the "trademark" glasses that would come to define his character, Lloyd experimented with different styles and sizes before settling on tortoiseshell horn-rims while the frames were without lens so that no glare would appear from the studio lights. A crucial reason why Lloyd decided on tortoiseshell horn-rims was because many young men of the day wore them, and so, for him, the glasses became synonymous with youth. Historian Joseph L. Burneni attests to this point, describing the enthusiasm of consumer-oriented college students eager to buy the Lloyd-like frames after seeing them featured in the comedian's films (2). Furthermore, Lloyd never permitted his gag men to create gags about his glasses:

> I never used my glasses to draw special attention to them. They were like my nose, my mouth, my eyes. They were something that was part of me. I never took my glasses off. I don't think my audiences ever saw a picture of Harold Lloyd without his glasses. If I was to play a Civil War soldier (*Grandma's Boy*, 1922), I had my glasses adapted to give the feeling of a century ago. So, when I played football, people didn't give a thought to it that I wore my glasses. Even when I went in swimming, I had my glasses on. When I was in bed, I had them on too. People accepted the glasses as part of my

screwball type of character. There was a scene in one of my pictures (*The Freshman*, 1925) where people were stepping on my face, and generally giving me a going over. The audience didn't stop and think, "Oh, his glasses will be broken!" They just didn't think of my glasses as separate from my own personality (144-45).

The Glass Character evolved slowly from the Lonesome Luke figure that audiences were accustomed to seeing. But once the transition occurred, beginning with the 1919 one-reel *Just Neighbors*, it also involved a change in acting style. For although there would be many moments when Lloyd would still rely upon the broad slapstick comedy of his earlier films, the Glass Character was more gentle, kind, and clever in nature; therefore, the acting became more realistic, more nuanced, in which "the Boy" exhibited subtle facial expressions of annoyance as well as delight. Thus, earlier comedies of thrills and slapstick evolved into comedies with a developing storyline in which the leading girl became a foil for "the kid with glasses."

These one-reel comedies featuring the Glass Character were so successful that it naturally led to the production of a series of equally successful two-reel comedies, the first one entitled *Bumping into*

Broadway (1919). This evolution from one-reel to two-reel comedies and, eventually, feature length films, gave Lloyd the opportunity to deepen and enrich his comic persona and the hilarious scenarios he would find himself embroiled in. Toward this end, Lloyd, once a man of the stage, invested ever greater time, care, and expense in his films: he was attentive to the use of inter-titles—clever and amusing in themselves—that were woven throughout the respective storylines; he increased the number of gag men on his productions in an attempt to discover new story angles and gags in crafting well-constructed plots that were credible as they were funny; and he was one of the earliest filmmakers to use previewing, showing a rough cut of a film to an unsuspecting audience and gauging their reaction, as a means of developing his timing and pacing in his films (despite a tragic accident in1919 involving a prop bomb that caused him to be hospitalized for eight months, in which he suffered severe burns to his face and body, and lost part of his right thumb, finger, and palm).

*

In 1924 Harold Lloyd wrote of the necessity of avoiding the same theme and type of film: "It is our intention to mix up the type of offering we will present. That has been our policy in the past, and it has worked out highly satisfactorily. For no matter how great the appeal of a player, he cannot go on forever giving his public the same kind of picture, release after release" (1). These words revealed the growing sophistication and maturity of Lloyd's screen comedy, which found its most brilliant realization in those films now regarded to be his best—and which can stand alongside those of Chaplin's and Keaton's: *Grandma's Boy* (1922), *The Freshman* (1925), *The Kid Brother* (1927), and, of course, *Safety Last* (1923), considered by many to be his masterpiece. In illustrating his observations on comedy, Lloyd's screen persona did not function as a single repetitive note, but, rather, as variations on a theme. In this respect, the Glass Character was less a character than a comic attitude, be it the coward of *Grandma's Boy*, the unsophisticated newcomer of *The Freshman*, the timid mountain boy of *The Kid Brother*, or the resilient young man of *Safety Last*; the essence of Harold Lloyd's screen persona—optimism, ambition, ingenuity, and determination—was always apparent.

And the essence of that persona would continue into a new profoundly different period in film history, for in 1927, the silent era of motion pictures, for all intents and purposes, came to an end with the arrival of *The Jazz Singer*. No longer was the focus on the visual, but on the aural as well. Initially, Lloyd, like Chaplin, was ambivalent about this transition; but according to Tom Dardis, in early 1929, 89 percent of films then in release contained either sound effects or dialogue (208). Thus, the emergence and growing popularity of pictures that talked presented challenges for many stars of the silent era. Lloyd clearly understood that the appeal of his films featuring "the kid with glasses" was visual, gag related, kinetic. Furthermore, he opposed the use of a ready-made scenario, preferring instead to work with his stable of gag writers, testing any number of ideas during filming before deciding on those he considered best; now, though, with the arrival of sound, a script became essential.

Nevertheless, like the intrepid, adventurous character he portrayed on screen, Lloyd plunged into sound films with *Welcome Danger* in 1929. He shot, and even previewed, *Welcome Danger* as a silent film before deciding it needed to be a sound film. And although it did not reflect his best work, audience members were so curious to hear "the Boy" speak that they made *Welcome Danger* Lloyd's most profitable film. Under his own supervision, he made five more sound films in the 1930s: *Feet First* (1930), *Movie Crazy* (1932), *The Cat's Paw* (1934), *The Milky Way* (1936), and *Professor Beware* (1938).

Of all these films, many consider *Movie Crazy* and *The Milky Way* to be the best. Critic Richard Schickel argues that "the film [*Movie Crazy*] as a whole was the most successful approximation of his silent film style that Lloyd made after the coming of sound, and it continues to rank among the best movies about movies—comedy subdivision—that Hollywood ever turned out" (205). As for *The Milky Way*, Lloyd worked with Leo McCarey, an enormously popular director during the 1930s and was one of the figures responsible for establishing a new distinctive form of comedy, now known as screwball, in which the style is essentially verbal, not physical. Lloyd played the leading role, but the success of the film derived in large measure from the ensemble acting of a gifted supporting cast with impeccable timing (a standard feature of screwball comedies). Still, Lloyd garnered his best reviews of the decade for *The Milky Way*, and according to Schickel, his career may have lasted even longer had he performed in more films of this type (211).

From the era of silent movies to the age of talking pictures, Harold Lloyd developed in his best films an indelible comic persona who also became an archetype of American decency and normality. Like all Americans, the "kid with glasses" was eager to succeed and could, at times, become aggressive in his competitive quest for success. But in recognizing the essence of his character, viewers acknowledged those qualities of decency and determination that they saw in—or wished to believe about—themselves. In this regard, "the Boy" on the silver screen became a mirror for themselves and for the 1920s, a decade steeped in its own set of powerful contrasts—wealth and poverty, industry and agrarianism, Americans and immigrants, loss and hope. In striving to achieve success in their everyday lives, people sought to display those very qualities the Glass Character exhibited time and again on screen. In doing so, they personified the Horatio Alger myth; and in Harold Lloyd, they had found its most engaging, optimistic representative.

Works Cited

Brownlow, Kevin. Introduction. *Harold Lloyd Master Comedian*. Jeffrey Vance and Suzanne Lloyd. New York: Harry N. Abrams Incorporated, 2002. 10-15.

Burneni, Joseph. "Looking Back: An Illustrated History of the American Ophthalmic Industry." (1994) quoted in D'Agostino, Annette M. "Harold Lloyd: The Glasses." *The Lloyd Herald* 3:2 (1998):2.

Cahn, William. *Harold Lloyd's World of Comedy*. New York: Duell, Sloan, and Pearce, 1964.

Dardis, Thomas. *Harold Lloyd: The Man on the Clock*. New York: Viking Press, 1983.

Lloyd, Harold, and Wesley W. Stout. *An American Comedy*. New York: Longmans, Green and Co., 1928.

Lloyd, Harold. "Comedy Development." *On Lloyd*. Harold Lloyd-Actors and Actresses, n.d. Web. 25 June 2010.
<http://www.filmreference.com/actors-and-actresses-Le-Ma/Lloyd-Harold.html>.

Lloyd, Harold. Interview. Columbia University Oral History Research Office. Transcript. Jan. 1959:19.

Lloyd, Harold. "The Autobiography of Harold Lloyd." *Photoplay*. June 1924:110.

Lloyd, Harold. "The Funny Side of Life." *Films and Filming*. January 1964:19.

Schickel, Richard. *Harold Lloyd: The Shape of Laughter*. Boston: New York Graphic Society Ltd., 1974.

Vance, Jeffrey, and Suzanne Lloyd. *Harold Lloyd Master Comedian*. New York: Harry N. Abrams, Incorporated, 2002.

Anything But Silent: The Film Legacies of Charlie Chaplin and Buster Keaton

Matthew Bowerman

Onde of film's greatest stories was forged in duet:

April 16, 1889—December 25, 1977
October 4, 1895—February 1, 1966

These dates mark the respective lives of Charles Chaplin and Buster Keaton, considered by historians, educators, fans, and film scholars to be two of the most prolific revolutionaries in the history of cinema.

Courage. Imagination. Risk.
The spirited belief in the everyman.
A relentless pursuit of perfection in the art form.
An acute sense of humor amidst the wreckage and
dysfunction of the world.
Unwavering drive to tell a poignant, vulnerable story.

This is the combined legacy of Buster Keaton and Charlie Chaplin, kid-vaudeville performers turned legends through the lens of the movie camera. How did these two comets, bred of similar backgrounds, follow such startling parallel courses across the landscape of a fledgling art form that revolutionized entertainment in this country and, subsequently, worldwide? How did the transition from silent film to the age of the talkies inform each of their lives and careers? Do film lessons of this bygone era, as seen through their respective visions and work, still resonate in the technology of today?

As they were raised in a time of profound hardship, the early nineteenth century offered little for those without political affluence, capitol, or the proper pedigree from which to make their way in an uncertain world; but it was the lure of vibrant characters, song, dance and the spectacle of the laughing audience that drew these two boys into their new habitats—the stage. The music halls and vaudeville circuit of the 1920s, both in the United States and Europe, promised fantasy and escapism for a public burdened by war, depression, poverty, and hostile political factions.

Both children had parents who found their financial livelihood as performers in the circuits, carving their own established journeys, gaining some reputation and fame as accomplished comedy and musical acts, taking the children along for performances. As the stories go, the boys were in the various parent acts, and then they *became* the acts themselves. History and myth followed after that, weaving hilarious tales of adolescent assertiveness and early-age comic genius that would chart funny-bone futures for each of these promising tiny clowns.

The documented evidence suggests a wonderful anecdote about the five-year-old Charlie taking over for his ailing mother, Lily, during a performance at the Aldershot Canteen (Weissman, 2009, 27). His performance, following her loss of voice onstage, humiliated her and spurred Charlie to action when she walked off, performing a rendition of "Jack Jones" for the rugged and unpredictable crowd. He would embody her mannerisms and take the crowd through her downfall onstage while they choked on their laughter and flooded the stage with coins. Much like his later work in *The Kid*, *City Lights*, *The Pawnshop*, *The Tramp*, and *The New Janitor*, Charlie had identified a vulnerable human moment to characterize. He would take the audience through the despair of a broken character while making them laugh. It was this performance of his mother's, however, as Charlie explains in his biography, that changed his life and set him on a new path of storytelling, which would be a throughline on much of his future artistry. "When the fates deal in human destiny, they heed neither pity nor justice. Thus they dealt with Mother. She never regained her voice, and as autumn turns to winter, so our circumstances turned from bad to worse" (Chaplin, 1964, 19).

A continual theme, Charlie would consistently explore the damaged female heroine in all her seasons, as well as the connected natures of pathos and catharsis, the tragic hero always one step behind, emotionally and socially fragile, just barely winning out in the end, but never without paying a price. From these early moments he would begin to explore every minute aspect of mime, pantomime, and mimicry, crafting hundreds of characters, becoming a master of props and situational humor, linking the majority of his work and his audiences to the fact that he was playing real human beings that everyone could identify and, therefore, laugh with or at. His subsequent training found him onstage and backstage wherever his mother, and later his brother, could get him in. From the "Eight Lancanshire Lads" he explored his dance and musical sides touring and honing his footwork (McDonald et al., 1973, 17). Acrobatics, singing, dancing, stories, jokes, physical comedy, impersonations were practiced along the way; he tried it all and spent his time studying the art of becoming someone else. Charlie was fashioning a style and brand of humor all his own, and while initially based on stock bits of his predecessors, he began exploring humanity in his work in a way that had not really been explored before, moving beyond stereotype and one-dimensional caricature. While it would be still some time before Fred Karno, Mack Sennett, and the birth of "The Tramp" in 1914's *Kid Auto Races At Venice*, the child Charlie Chaplin Jr. had been reborn as the star of a thousand characters. Joseph (Frank or Francis) Keaton, known affectionately as "Buster," debuted professionally in 1899 in "The Three Keatons," a vaudeville trio performance act featuring his mother on music, his father as the principal storyteller/narrator/straight-man, and Buster as the foil for his father's physical slapstick and all-around manhandling.

While legend says that Buster was performing much closer to infancy, the reality simply acknowledges that Buster's life was informed as a direct result of living in a vaudeville environment from an extremely early age. While Chaplin loved the idea of stage and being a witness to his mother's at-home and onstage performance persona, he stumbled onto a unique opportunity, which created a life for him. But Keaton was literally conceived in the midst of the traveling troupes of his parents, and performing was almost a guarantee by association. One could say that in bearing such a great appreciation and love of his mother's stage life, Charlie found a natural preponderance for all things theatrical, and Keaton was plugged into the pulse of this world before he even realized he was wearing make-up and a beard.

This Keaton act and the on-the-job training it afforded was imprinted on Buster from childhood through his early adult life, as he worked with his parents for many years. They helped to train him, to refine his technique, and exposed him to other professionals of the company who also engaged in his training along the way. As they grew and gained notoriety, Buster's family had a reputation as having a second headline act, but one of the funniest and toughest acts anywhere. Much as he earned his nickname "Buster"—Keaton declares in the 1958 Columbia University "Reminiscences of Buster Keaton" that Harry Houdini gave him the nickname "Buster" when he fell down a flight of stairs as an infant, survived undamaged, and was noted for "taking a buster" (Columbia University 2000). Buster remained a "do it the rough way" performer dedicated to creating a physical style of work as a physical comedic actor that had audiences laughing and gasping at the same time. He would imitate and shadow his father onstage, mocking and pulling audience's focus, and then become the human rag doll at the hands of his father. "The funny thing about our act," declared Buster after his final toss Tuesday, "is that Dad gets the worst of it, although I'm the one who apparently receives the bruises . . . . The secret is in landing limp and breaking the fall with a foot or a hand. It's a knack. I started so young that landing right is second nature with me. Several times I'd have been killed if I hadn't been able to land like a cat. Imitators of our act don't last long, because they can't stand the treatment" (*Detroit News*).

Buster's comedy training, coming from years of honing through the vaudeville experience of his parents, left room for danger in his work and gave the audience a new type of hero to cheer: one who was emotionless and unafraid of risks and physical feats of daring. Eventually he understood his calling as a solo artist and left the act to redefine himself and his training under the tutelage of film mogul Roscoe "Fatty" Arbuckle; but by this point his stoic, unemotional, and stony look of indifference had stuck, earning him "stone face" as a moniker and a way of navigating his emerging presence onscreen.

The 1900s gave birth to film and the screen careers of Chaplin and Keaton, both masters of physical comedy, adept at becoming anyone. Humanity, in all its dysfunctions and hilarity, was their canvas, and they both painted with a deft brush. The flashy, balletic presence and magnetic charm of Chaplin made him one of the first big comic film stars, something he cherished, cultivated, and was nearly destroyed by, while Keaton's work lived on the periphery, as his was a world without emotion, but not without substance. It was this darker intellectual world that also led Keaton through his collapsed marriage and alcoholism, while Chaplin's access to women, publicity, and huge sums of money contributed to his questionable female relationships and consistent pattern of divorces. The comic desperation that both performers portrayed so clearly onscreen was the same anguish and burden both men struggled with throughout their careers. Chaplin was responsible for writing, directing, and starring in over forty-seven films between 1915 and 1967, while Keaton was involved in thirty-nine films between 1917 and 1965. They easily held roles in over 250 combined films, with multiple guest spots, walk-ons, and television appearances during their careers.

It is with confidence that one could say that no two performers were as skilled as these two during or since with regard to the levels of technique, grace, natural skill, imagination, daring, understanding of the craft, musicality, and willingness to create laughter above all else. They worked to please; they worked for the laughs and were masters at creating ingenious ways in which to evoke that hard to capture essence of funny. They were loved and misunderstood, hounded and harassed, worshipped and systematically dismantled by press, politicians, spurned lovers and a world that could not fully accept the scope and breadth of their genius. When the world changed, and entertainment with it, both Keaton and Chaplin struggled to find their new place in a celluloid universe that they had helped to create and define as an art form.

In *Film Daily*, March 4, 1927, Thomas Edison proclaimed,

> I don't think the talking movie picture will ever be successful
> in the United States. Americans prefer silent drama. They
> are accustomed to the moving picture as it is and they will
> never get enthusiastic over any voices being mingled in it.
> Yes, there will be novelty to it for a little while, but the glitter
> will soon wear off and the movie fans will cry for silence or a
> little orchestra music . . . . We are wasting our time going on
> with this project. (Louvish, 2009, 226)

When the sound came, it hit with a deafening roar as studios, actors,
producers, and directors all scrambled to understand and implement the
materials and transitions into their films. For Keaton and Chaplin—who
for so long had explored the grace, vulnerability, and poignancy of the
human spirit through silence—found themselves with an unspoken
question. To talk or not to talk? After all, the age of talkies also marked
a paradigm shift in the way people viewed film entertainment and
comedy specifically. These men, moving into this new age, had created
characters and led lives within artistically solitary worlds, filled with
stoic indifference, marital indiscretions, addictions, and pain, victims
of the film society they helped to engender, often exhibiting the deep
bruises of their darker natures through the bright smile or stony stare.

For Keaton he would go on to work in language-dubbing shorts, go head to head over creative control with MGM, and wander through a series of relationships with Educational Pictures and Columbia, achieving financial success for companies but ultimately losing his way through alcohol and marital instability. He stuck with sound and worked for the rest of his career, fairly consistently, in the medium that, in some ways, took the provocative power of his "stone face" character. It wasn't until closer to the mid-1940s that he grounded his life again and used his strengths as a storyteller and his previous reputation to mount a significant comeback through various guest appearances, film walk-ons, and fairly successful television programs. Keaton knew he might love the silent world, but he understood that he could make sound work for him creatively if he had to bend that way. Chaplin, a cynic of the sound era, was apt to fight and did not see sound as a viable option for his work. "Dreams do not speak" (Louvish, 226). Chaplin believed The Tramp would die if he talked, and so he stepped from his pathos lens and adjusted his political lens, setting sight on the Third Reich in *The Great Dictator*, striving to carry his pantomime and comedy into a new genre that would honor the requirements of sound while also maintaining the integrity of what he did so well. It was the first time he spoke on screen, and it proved to be a far more political move than an artistic one. Chaplin became so embroiled over U.S.-German relations that it did not matter if he spoke or not in public as long as his film characters spoke out for whatever the government wanted him to advocate for. As an artist with powerful connections and a striking flair for the dramatic, his use of voice became his message in support of war against Germany and a call to arms against Jewish persecution.

As he became more political, he became more dangerous to the U.S. government, and it was this track that ultimately led to his undoing and government-imposed exile from the United States; whereas Keaton continued to pursue his craft in the 1940s and 1950s as a film actor and writer, still floundered in quasi-obscurity, never as creative or known as during his heyday.

Chaplin's politics and interest in women proved to nearly destroy his career and reputation worldwide. *Limelight*, his last film made in the United States, was practically shut down, its distribution cancelled, and it wasn't until 1972 when he returned to the United States to receive his Lifetime Achievement Award that he was given the welcome that the "Little Tramp" had hoped for. Martin Sieff, in a 2008 review of the book *Chaplin: A Life*, wrote, "Chaplin was not just 'big,' he was gigantic. In 1915, he burst onto a war-torn world bringing it the gift of comedy, laughter and relief while it was tearing itself apart through the First World War. Over the next 25 years, through the Great Depression and the rise of Hitler, he stayed on the job. It is doubtful any individual has ever given more entertainment, pleasure and relief to so many human beings when they needed it the most."

Richard Corliss, in *Time* magazine, said of Keaton:

> Watch his beautiful, compact body as it pirouettes or pretzels in tortured permutations or, even more elegantly, stands in repose as everything goes crazy around it. Watch his mind as it contemplates a hostile universe whose violent whims Buster understands, withstands and, miraculously, tames. Watch his camera taking his picture (Keaton directed or supervised all his best films); it is as cool as the star it captured in its glass.

The medium was still in its infancy; comics were pioneering the craft of making people laugh at moving images. Keaton, it turns out, knew it all—intuitively.

A porkpie hat, the flick of a cane, the whirling somersault into a handstand, and the twitch of a mustache—the symbols iconic and eternal in a society constantly earmarked by change and progress in fast forward. Film and the ingenuity packed into its evolution were driven by their creativity and work ethics; modern comedians from Red Skelton to Chevy Chase credit their physical work to watching Keaton and Chaplin films. Modern-day physical comic superstars like Jim Carrey and Will Farrell have found inspiration in these timeless classics, and directors like Stephen Spielberg and Woody Allen still recognize these architects as creating what is now modern film.

In an interview for *The New Yorker* and Penelope Gilliatt, Woody Allen, when asked to compare the two giants, gives both artists equal weight: "*City Lights* and *The Gold Rush* and *The Navigator* and *The General* are the four great comedies, aren't they?" (Kobel 207, 59). So how do they survive? How in an age of cell phone and Twitter, credit card, and e-mail, do these heroic clowns still draw a paying audience, one who connects with these distant and presumably outdated throwbacks out of touch with a global material world?

How do Chaplin and Keaton still find favor in the tumult of today and have hundreds of thousands of fans? When film is forged now with mega-budgets, green screen, digital imaging, and drawn-out shoots with hit-and-miss performances, what is eternal about these films and their silent magicians? Is it because they give us hope in the everyman hero who will survive no matter how many lumps he has to take? Do they find their way into a simpler, cleaner sense of laughter and funny that was born long before dirty jokes and college frat-party toilet humor? What is idyllic and poetic, dangerous, and wonderful about them? It has to be more than the fact that this was a fledgling art form; after all, Harold Lloyd, Raymond Griffith, Mabel Normand, Constance Talmadge, and Max Davidson all worked hard and created very funny films.

Why these two, who were so similar in so many ways? To this day the international jury is still out on which is 'better,' and I suggest there is no trial to be had. T. Dan Callahan, in his 2002 Senses of Cinema website, explains it well: "There is no pressing reason to choose between them, any more than there is a reason to choose between Fred Astaire and Gene Kelly." They were mirror images of one another's genius and creativity, a silent duo exploring two separate, but equally compelling, aspects of human nature, partners in forging a new destiny for film, each wracked by their demons, each memorialized for the joy they have brought millions. "I never thought we'd come to this," Keaton says to Chaplin in *Limelight* (Chaplin, 1952), both of them past their prime, irrelevant in sound, longing for youth and silence (Callahan, 2002, 1). This Chaplin film, in a brilliant bit of casting, sets the two friends together, frame by frame, as they piece film history together, both struggling to accept and reclaim what was lost to them through the ravages of time.

Even in old age, when so much timing and fluidity of motion had left the body, there was perfection in their combined emotional vulnerability and openness to working off one another. The film has them tied to one another in life and death, just as they are inextricably bound in film history and myth. Their skills and natural abilities are legendary and something still not seen on the screen to this day. None have worked harder or cultivated a more varied body of work than these two in the history of comic film.

Whether embracing or shunning sound in the footnote of history, they set a world in motion through their comedic archetypal identities and created a reason for laughter in dark times, made just as relevant in today's turbulent world. We still need heroes and clowns to remind us of what is important in the world as human beings—as people. And it is perfectly okay to be able to laugh at them and with them. After all, Buster and Charlie did it every day of their lives, and they created a magical, multi-layered world from which to do it:

> They had understood the language they were speaking. They
> had invented a syntax of the eye, a grammar of pure kinesis,

and except for the costumes and cars and quaint furniture in
the background, none of it could possibly grow old. It was
thought translated into action, human will expressing itself
through the human body, and therefore it was for all time . . . .
They were like poems, like the renderings of dreams, like
some intricate choreography of the spirit (Auster, 2002).

Bibliography

Auster, Paul. *The Book of Illusions*. New York: Henry Holt, 2002.
Blesh, Rudi. *Keaton*. New York: Macmillan Publishing Co., 1966.
Buster Keaton Memorial Museum. 2010. "Life of the Great Stone-Face."
    www.busterkeatonmusuem.happywebsite.biz (accessed March 25,
    2010).
Callahan, Daniel. *Senses of Cinema: Buster Keaton*. 2002. http://archive.
    sensesofcinema.com/contents/directors/02/keaton.html   (accessed
    March 25, 2010).
Chaplin, Charles. *My Autobiography*. New York: Penguin Books, 1964.
Columbia University Board of Trustees. 2000. "Buster Keaton on
    Comedy and Making Movies." New York. http://www.fathom.com/
    course/10701030 (accessed March 25, 2010).
Columbia University. 2000. "The Reminiscences of Buster Keaton."
    Interview from 1958. In the Collection of the Columbia University
    Oral History Research Office. New York. http://www.fathom.com/
    course/10701030/session2.html (accessed March 25, 2010).
Corliss, Richard. "That Old Feeling: Fatty and Buster." New York: *Time*
    magazine. 2001.
Detroit News. "Part 1: A Vaudeville Childhood." Dec. 4, 1914. www.
    busterkeaton.com/bio1.htm. (accessed March 25, 2010).
Ebert, Roger, editor. *Roger Ebert's Book of Film*. New York: The Ebert
    Company, Ltd., 1997.
Harris, Mark. *Pictures at a Revolution: Five Movies and the Birth of the New
    Hollywood*. New York: The Penguin Press, 2008.
Keaton, Buster, and Charlie Samuels. *My Wonderful World of Slapstick*.
    New York: Doubleday, 1960.
Kobel, Peter. *Silent Movies: The Birth of Film and the Triumph of Movie
    Culture*. New York: Little Brown & Company, 2007.
Louvish, Simon. *Chaplin: The Tramp's Odyssey*. New York: St. Martin's
    Press. 2009.

Maslan, Laurence, and Michael Kantor. *Make 'Em Laugh: The Funny Business of America*. New York: Hachette Books Publishing, 2008.

McDonald, Gerard, ed., Michael Conway, and Mark Ricci. *The Films of Charlie Chaplin*. New Jersey: The Citadel Press, 1973.

Mitchell, Glenn. *The Chaplin Encyclopedia*. London: B. T. Batsford Ltd., 1997.

Owen, Harold H. Jr., et al. *The Motion Picture and the Teaching of English*. New York: Meredith Publishing Company, 1965.

Sanders, James. *The Celluloid Skyline: New York and the Movies*. New York: Alfred Knopf Publishing, 2001.

Sklar, Robert. *Film—An International History of the Medium*. New York: Harry N. Abrams Inc., 1993.

Stevens, George Jr. *The Great MovieMakers of Hollywood's Golden Age at the AFI*. New York: Alfred Knopf Publishing, 2006.

Tobias, Patricia Elliot and David B. Pearson. 2009-2010. "Buster Keaton: The Buster Keaton Myths." http://www.busterkeaton.com/bookshelf.htm (accessed March 25, 2010).

Weissman, Stephen. *Chaplin: A Life*. New York: Arcade Publishing, 2008.

The Jean Arthur Discovery Plan

Erik Christian Hanson

Juggling three women at once is no small feat:

Babe is a playful and independent reporter who marches to her own drum. She's been preoccupied lately duping Longfellow Deeds so she can earn a month's vacation with pay.

Then there's Clarissa, secretary for the newly appointed Senator Jefferson Smith. Despite the fact that everyone calls her Saunders (her last name), she, in her heart of hearts, would swoon if someone found her first name beautiful. She's bright, vulnerable, and sarcastic. While she's expressed her frustration over keeping Smith away from anything that smells of politics, she firmly believes, if Mr. Paine's (her boss) promises come to fruition, that she may be working in the White House someday.

Last but not least is Connie. She's a sweet young woman who works for the government, but she has the following strikes against her that the other women don't: she's engaged to a bureaucrat who has nothing resembling a personality, she's a stickler about morning schedules, and she's prone to bouts of wailing.

The difficulty in choosing one to be with, and for how long, is that they all bring something unique to the table. They don't nag me to stay longer, and they don't place any kind of demands on me. Tiring of them, any of them, has not occurred yet, and it remains a mystery to me why. The easy part in choosing one is that they travel by mail, in the form of a DVD, and they're all fictitious.

The women, who have been occupying my time of late, are all screen creations of the same woman: the undervalued Jean Arthur.

In 1930, director John Cromwell told Jean Arthur "she would never make it in Hollywood" (quoted in Oller, 61). Never. Make. It. In. Hollywood. If you've seen her work, you know how preposterous this suggestion seems. And yet, a year later, the woman who would eventually have her name above title in the films of Frank Capra, George Stevens, and Howard Hawks took Cromwell's advice and quit the profession as she was granted her release from Paramount. Eight years of work in silent films and talkies behind her, Jean returned to New York. The *Motion Picture Almanac* confirmed her departure from the business when it listed her name as "no longer in motion pictures" (Oller, 66).

After relocating to New York, Arthur began building her confidence on Broadway with roles in *Lysistrata*, *Foreign Affairs*, *The Man Who Reclaimed His Head*, and *The Curtain Rises*, for what she referred to as "the happiest years of my life" (Oller, 73). A positive critical reception made Hollywood take note; so much so that Arthur was lured back to Hollywood by Harry Cohn, the confirmed "son of a bitch" who ran Columbia Pictures. Even though she announced her plans to stay on Broadway because "they let me act" (Oller, 74), she signed a five-year contract that allowed her to have her cake and eat it too. She would be employed for as many as four films a year and could return to Broadway once a year, based on a clause she incorporated into her contract.

But the rug would shortly be pulled out from under her, though, since Cohn's promise to put her "only in big-time productions" (Oller, 78) proved hollow and failed to materialize—hardly surprising given Cohn's "son of a bitch" reputation. The broken promise, which seemed to demoralize an actress who was salivating for a chance to star in a vehicle that would illuminate her skill-set, would not be the career-killer it was presumed to be. Enter the importance of Frank Capra.

When *Mr. Deeds Goes To Town* was a week into production without the role of Babe Bennett cast, Frank Capra found himself desperate for an actress. Coming across dailies of Arthur in a scene from the film *Whirlpool*, Capra cast her immediately. Her voice was part of what contributed to Capra's interest. "Low, husky—at times it broke pleasingly into the higher octaves like a thousand tinkling bells" (Capra quoted in DiBattista, 149). The fact that her voice helped make her career was surprising, even to Arthur.

Years prior, after suffering as the ingénue or western heroine in silent films, the arrival of sound would transform her career. Little did she know it, though. Sound, which was predicted to be nothing more than a fad, and a fleeting one at that, proved to have staying power. This presented a dilemma for silent film actors because they "were now panicking at the thought that their untrained voices would be judged unworthy and their talkie careers pronounced dead on arrival" (Oller, 51). Jean was among those panicking. After doing a voice test for Paramount Pictures, Jean reacted overdramatically, commenting that it sounded like a "foghorn" (Oller, 52). However one describes it, foghorn or not, it is fair to claim that that "beloved cashmere croak, possibly the most distinctive voice of any Golden Era actress" (Atkinson, 2), was Jean's meal ticket.

So there it was—her big chance, cast in a Frank Capra film alongside Gary Cooper. A role worthy of her talent finally arrived, and she was going to knock it out of the park, much to the dismay of Harry Cohn. When Capra made his decision to cast her, Cohn referred to her as a "has-been" (McBride, 343) and expressed that he didn't care much for her voice or face. "D'ja see *her* face? Half of it's angel, and the other half horse" (quoted in Oller, 84). Objections from the "son of a bitch" aside, Capra would come up with a solution that will be noted later.

Meeting Babe Bennett in her first scene says it all. While her editor exhausts himself by tossing out ideas about Deeds (the man who's just inherited millions) for his staff to consider, Babe stands in a corner, engrossed with a piece of rope. She's listening, and she's not. She carries the confidence of a reporter who's been down this road before, and panic, desperate panic, regarding a story angle isn't in her makeup. When she gets a moment alone with her editor, her interest in a Deeds story only increases when she's promised a month's vacation with pay.

Her early outings with Deeds give her everything a reporter could dream of. When her editor asks about an evening out on the town with Deeds, Babe dryly replies that she was "the world's sweetest ingénue." Cognizant of it or not, Arthur had to get sweet satisfaction at being able to deliver that line in a Capra film, a line that mocks the role of ingénue, a role she was all too familiar with (and tired of) in her early films. While Babe comes across as a reporter devoid of feelings, Deeds's purity slowly melts her cynical exterior, and it is what eventually makes her fall for him. This was a deliberate choice on Capra's part to have a heroine "whose hardened exterior serves as protective covering for her basic tenderness" (Capra quoted in McBride, 163). To see Arthur handling a phone conversation where Cooper's character tells her that "you've made up for all the fakes I've met" showcases what she can do with her face, not just her legendary voice. She internalizes that moment for the world to see, hangs up the phone, and starts ranting about whether Deeds is the biggest imbecile or the grandest man alive. His compliment shakes her to the core, and it's evident immediately that she's fallen for him and wished she hadn't. Arthur nails it. "With an adroitness scarcely imaginable a few years earlier, she manages an utterly convincing transformation from cynic to romantic over the course of the film" (Oller, 85).

When Deeds remains mum during his insanity trial, it's Babe (and Babe only) who can get the man to speak. On the stand, Arthur pours her heart out to explain why the supposedly insane man, Deeds, won't defend himself. Deeds has been hurt by everyone in town, especially her. She shares how she got closer to him so she could laugh louder and divulges, with tears of irony, that it's a "fitting climax to my sense of humor." Deeds, relatively lifeless for a majority of the scene, gets resuscitated, not by Babe defending him, but by the simple fact that she—put on the spot, mind you—declares her love for him. Deeds's head turns at Babe's confession, and you know, right then and there, that he's going to finally make a case for himself. Considering the impression we get when we meet Babe in her workplace to the one we form of her in court, Arthur's transformation is worth noting. Capra marveled about her performance, stating that "some actresses could have played the cynical part, while others could have done the romantic ending. But no one could have done them both as well as Jean" (Oller, 86).

A few years later, Capra and Arthur would be reunited in *Mr. Smith Goes to Washington*. Like she did in *Deeds*, Arthur shows her acting chops as the cynical romantic, this time secretary to a new and wide-eyed senator. Upset with her assignment as nurse to a senator, an "honorary stooge," Saunders finds her sole motivation for cooperating is the promise of future rewards, specifically a job working in the White House if her boss, Senator Paine, gets his way. To up the ante as a retort to her remark about her eyes being " big green dollar marks," Paine offers her a handsome bonus to assure her compliance in keeping Senator Smith (played by James Stewart) away from anything political.

In the early stages of the film, Arthur's character mocks the man she's supposed to monitor; she refers to him as Daniel Boone and wonders whether he's "animal, vegetable, or mineral." But as time goes on, as the political machine attempts to annihilate Jefferson Smith's goodness,

Saunders finds herself falling for the man, a boy in a man's world, whose ideals will not waver in the face of adversity. Reminiscent of her role in *Deeds*, Arthur plays the female convert who will end up serving as the cheerleader for the jaded Smith. As John Oller, author of *The Actress Nobody Knew*, confirms,

> She is both the agent of the unsuspecting hero's ultimate triumph and the buffer Capra has set up between the almost unbearably naïve protagonist and the presumably more skeptical audience. For if the world-weary Saunders can be converted to Smith's cause, then we will be convinced as well. (115)

The highlight of the film and her career takes place at Press Club Restaurant. Saunders's concern over Smith reaches its boiling point when her boss's daughter, Susan, plans to wine and dine him so he'll miss what's being heard in the Senate that day—a deficiency bill that will ruin his dreams of building a camp for boys. While Smith's out on the town, Saunders drowns her sorrows out with her friend from the press, Diz, at Press Club. In a haze induced by alcohol and guilt, Saunders is forced to come to terms with the feelings she has for Smith, a man she wants to understand, a man who believes people should view the world as if they "just came out of a tunnel." Acting mother-like in the beginning of the scene, Saunders immediately catches herself in a vulnerable moment, clearly something she's not used to or likes the taste of, and asks Diz, "Say, who started this?" Arthur puts on an acting clinic in this scene hopping from her remorse about Smith being toyed with and how she won't be "party to no murder," to proposing to her friend Diz, to offering Diz the chance to back out and reject her marriage proposal because her first name is Clarissa, to testing whether her name is as beautiful as her boss's daughter (the object of Smith's affection), to quitting her job the moment they leave the restaurant, bonus or no bonus; the emotions Arthur evokes from one second to the next—concern, shame, vulnerability, rage, discomfort, and hope—are astounding. When asked about the scene, Capra said, "I defy any other actress to play that scene" (Oller, 116). Commended for its oblique tone, Howard Hawks (who later directed Jean in *Only Angels Have Wings*) and Capra "delighted in the comic indirectness by which Saunders declares her love for Smith by proposing to Diz" (DiBattista, 155). Amid the praise, Arthur, known to be never satisfied with herself, humbly offered "it's all there in the words" (Oller, 116). The words are good, but it's

Arthur that makes them sing. Her long glare at Diz before she proposes, her hiccup, her ethereal daze when she describes that it was like sending Smith off to school for the very first time, her self-conscious plea for Diz to tell her that her name is beautiful, her forgetting that she proposed to Diz, and her aggressive rant about how she "won't take it, see" make a well-written scene a classic embedded forever in the minds of those who have been fortunate enough to witness it.

Nothing like the characters she played for Capra, Arthur's role in George Stevens's *The More the Merrier* had *Variety* refer to it as "undoubtedly the best screen role of her career" (Oller, 141). In the film, Arthur plays Connie Milligan, a repressed young woman engaged to a rarely seen bureaucrat. As a gesture of her patriotism during wartime, Connie sublets half of her apartment to Mr. Dingle, an elderly and calculating gentleman who keeps the fact that he's a millionaire a secret. When Dingle rents out half of his room without Connie's approval to Joe Carter, an inventor (played by Joel McCrea), chaos ensues. Dingle's scheming ways only intensify when he tries to pair Connie up with the inventor. The kindling has been thrown on the fire, and the audience has to wait and see whether sparks will fly between the attention-starved Connie and the handsome inventor. Maria DiBattista, author of *Fast-Talking Dames*, offers her insights on the burgeoning romance between the characters on screen:

> Arthur uses her voice to give nonverbal expression both to Miss Milligan's easily flabbergasted idealism and to her flustered sexuality. Stevens knows just how to play up and off her talent for befuddlement in the love scene he stages with Joe on the steps of Connie's apartment building. (150)

Stevens milks everything he can out of his cast, utilizing a talent for making the immaterial much more important and entertaining than it should be. While the scene on the steps is worth a rental, the concluding moments of the film, in particular Arthur's performance, are unforgettable. The final scene of the film has Arthur "executing a virtuoso turn on what the female voice can say without words" (DiBattista, 150).

Roles in films of famed directors. Terrific performances. But who knows about Jean Arthur? Who ranks her among the greats?

One must pause here and wonder how the Motion Picture Academy of Arts and Sciences overlooked Arthur's contribution, mainly that of Babe, Connie, and Saunders to the world of cinema. How does

Hollywood neglect to appreciate an actress of this magnitude, an actress frequently heralded for her talent?

For starters, the press didn't care for her. Inserting a no-publicity clause into your contract will do that. Even though her clause was a by-product of her shyness, other didn't see it that way. "To the Hollywood press, this was an act of monumental hubris" (Oller, 102). An enigma to the press, Arthur would share that she had a similar sensibility to that of Greta Garbo. "Her seclusion. Her refusal to talk for publication. Her belief that only her work is important to her public. I feel that way, too" (quoted in Oller, 92).

Besides infuriating the Hollywood press, she was, as others would claim, impossible to work with. Fits of crying, whining, or vomiting seemed to be par for the course in working with her. After she finished filming a scene, she would run to her dressing room immediately to hide. Capra remarked, "Never have I seen a performer plagued with such a chronic case of stage jitters" (Oller, 86). The jitters, stemming from her own insecurity, would be confirmed by two of her most prominent leading men: Gary Cooper and Cary Grant. Cooper would go on record later with his method for dealing with her during the filming of *Mr. Deeds Goes to Town*. Method used: he simply turned a deaf ear to her self-created problems. A close friend of Arthur's, Roddy McDowall, would shed light on the most effective way to lure his insecure friend to the set. "You had to break it to her softly, gently. You'd talk about how 'it's a lovely day, oh Jean, by the way if you're ready . . .'" (Oller, 86). While McDowall's advice may have worked for some, Capra offered his take on how to direct Arthur. "Kick her in the ass" (McBride, 343)!

Aside from kicking Arthur in the derriere, Capra would employ two techniques that quelled her insecurities during production. Counteracting Harry Cohn's concerns over Arthur's supposedly half-horse, half-angel veneer, Capra solved the issue "by making sure his cameraman Joe Walker always shot the actress with her best face forward" (Oller, 85). The second technique Capra focused on was how to film close-ups with his timorous actress. Known for delivering stellar performances in master shots (with all the actors present in the shot), Arthur had tremendous difficulty with close-ups since, often times, a script supervisor would be the one reading lines to her off camera instead of an actor that was present in the master. Annoyed that she couldn't duplicate the confidence she had during the master shot, Capra came up with a plan to combat her worries. He relied on a control button that would play the soundtrack from the master shot, just as she was about to perform for her close-up. "So in her mind she was actually working with all the actors just the way she had in the master shot" (Capra Jr. quoted in *Mr. Smith*). Impossible to work with or not, it's clear it didn't matter to Capra since he tried to accommodate her in any way that he could.

At the time of her passing, Leonard Maltin, renowned film critic, told the world that they "deserve to discover Jean Arthur" (quoted in Oller, 287). Deserving to discover Jean Arthur is too casual of a plea to swallow. The notion that you deserve something presupposes that you've waited patiently and/or earned the right to discover Ms. Arthur. Film lover or not, you *should* discover her and *need* to. Your life will be enriched for doing so.

As far as discoveries go, we need to express our gratitude to the director who made us aware, on a global scale, of her existence. We owe it to Mr. Capra for stumbling across those dailies of a woman nobody thought would amount to anything. We owe it to Mr. Capra for casting Arthur when Harry Cohn, a known tyrant, objected to it. We owe it to Mr. Capra for accepting and dealing with her insecurity as a performer (which was no affectation). We owe it to Mr. Capra for creating a technique (on the set of *Mr. Smith Goes to Washington*) that made his actress comfortable when it came time for her close-up. We owe it to Mr. Capra for filming her with her best face forward. We owe it to Mr. Capra for dragging Ms. Arthur out of her dressing rooms when it was time to film and allowing her to run back to that room after the scene was finished. We owe it to Mr. Capra for knowing that she would deliver once she was in front of the screen, regardless of the fact that her co-stars found her difficult to work with.

Regarded by Capra as his favorite actress, George Stevens would come to share the same sentiment. George Stevens Jr. confirmed that his father "felt that Jean Arthur was the greatest actress he had ever worked with" (Oller, 138). Perhaps the highest praise, the praise that should only increase your need to discover her, comes from Charles Champlin, American film critic and writer:

> No other actress in the Hollywood galaxy was even remotely like Jean Arthur . . . . She was a kind of educational force in a way that neither she nor Capra nor anyone else may have thought about consciously. Perhaps to her own generation, but certainly to those of us who were coming on stream a bit later, she was a revelation. (Oller, 288)

Revelation or not, the question must be posed: do we judge the person or the artist? If you judge the person, you'll find a shy, insecure, and reclusive woman who didn't cater to the Hollywood machine. If you judge the artist, you'll find a woman that gave us layered performances, after fighting bouts of nausea, that stay in your mind forever.

A discovery plan for Jean Arthur, if you've made it this far, is below:

1. Read John Oller's biography, the only one written about her, *The Actress Nobody Knew*.
2. Go to the website for Turner Classic Movies. Type in her name and find out when her next film is playing. Ask TCM to notify you by e-mail with a reminder, so you will not miss it when it airs.
3. Rent or purchase *Mr. Deeds Goes to Town*, *Mr. Smith Goes to Washington*, and *The More the Merrier*. Watch the "morning schedule" scene in *The More the Merrier* and see how Connie sucks you right in. Watch the scene in *Mr. Deeds Goes to Town* where Babe attempts to convince Longfellow Deeds, the man

she worked so hard to crucify for a story and paid vacation, to defend himself, and she'll nab your heart. Watch the scene where Saunders proposes to Diz in *Mr. Smith Goes to Washington*, the scene Howard Hawks called "one of the best love scenes that I've ever seen in a picture. That was a beautifully-done thing" (Oller, 116). Watch those films and tell me how, how it's possible, that she was nominated for only one (as Connie in *The More the Merrier*) of those performances. The Motion Picture Academy of Arts and Sciences should be ashamed of themselves for not granting her an Honorary Oscar.

If you find yourself committed to the discovery plan and have a hard time choosing which woman to hold on to, Babe, Connie, or Saunders, don't say that I didn't warn you. Juggling three fictitious women is harder than you think and should be experienced in moderation. Jean Arthur can be blamed for that.

Bibliography

Atkinson, Michael. "Jean Therapy." *Village Voice*. 9 May 2000. 15 Aug. 2009. http://www.villagevoice.com/2000-05-09/film/jean-therapy/.

DiBattista, Maria. *Fast-Talking Dames*. New Haven: Yale University Press, 2001.

McBride, Joseph. *Frank Capra: The Catastrophe of Success*. New York: Simon and Schuster, 1992.

Mr. Smith Goes to Washington. Directed by Frank Capra. Performed by James Stewart, Jean Arthur, Claude Rains, and Thomas Mitchell. DVD commentary. Columbia Pictures, 1939.

Oller, John. *The Actress Nobody Knew*. New York: Proscenium Publishers, 1997.

CHARLES WAGENHEIM
WW-6000-46

Charles Wagenheim: He Never Met a Character He Couldn't Play!

Kal Wagenheim

As a child, living in Newark, New Jersey, I was told that we had "a famous actor" who was a relative: Cousin Charlie!

I am not a scholar or an expert on Hollywood film history, but Charles Wagenheim was the first cousin of my father, Harold Wagenheim. I met Charlie years ago when I was in my thirties (I am now seventy-four years old) and can supply a few anecdotes that may be of interest. I will combine these with information about Charlie that is available on the Internet.

* * *

The little fellow we called "Cousin Charlie" was born in Newark, New Jersey, on February 21, 1896, the son of immigrants who came to America around 1890 from Riga, a port town in Latvia, which had a large German-origin population.

I was told that he got his start in acting in the Yiddish theatre on Manhattan's Lower East Side, where he worked together with Paul Muni, who later rose to superstardom. Family members told me that Charlie followed Muni out to Hollywood and that Muni helped connect him to the film world.

Also, I heard that, at one point, both Charlie and Muni separated from their respective wives and lived together for about six months (a precursor to *The Odd Couple!*), but Charlie did return to his spouse and lived with her for many years.

* * *

Gary Brumburgh, in a biographical sketch on www.imdb.com, wrote the following about my cousin, Charles Wagenheim:

> In a career comprised of hundreds upon hundreds of minor character parts on stage, film and TV, Charlie was initially drawn to acting to counterbalance an acute case of shyness. Wounded in World War I, he was compensated for an education by the government and chose to study dramatics at the American Academy of Dramatic Arts in New York, graduating in 1923. After touring with a Shakespearean company, Charlie appeared in a host of Broadway plays, several of them written, directed and/or produced by the prolific George Abbott, including *A Holy Terror* (1925), *Four Walls* (1927) and *Ringside* (1928). Following his stage role in *Schoolhouse on the Lot* (1938), Wagenheim turned indefinitely to Hollywood where his dark, graveside manner, baggy-eyed scowl, thick and unruly mustache and lowlife countenance proved ideal for a number of genres, particularly crimers and westerns.
>
> He scored well when Alfred Hitchcock chose him to play the assassin in *Foreign Correspondent* (1940), a great thriller starring Joel McCrea and Laraine Day. He went on to enact a number of seedy, unappetizing roles (tramps, drunks, thieves) over the years but never found the one juicy part that could have put him in the top character ranks. Usually billed tenth or lower, he was more atmospheric filler than anything else as his various cabbies, waiters, deputies, clerks, morgue attendants, junkmen, etc., will attest. Some of his better delineated roles came with *Two Girls on Broadway* (1940); *Charlie Chan at the Wax Museum* (1940); *Half Way to Shanghai* (1942); the cliffhangers *Don Winslow of the Navy* (1942) and *Raiders of Ghost City* (1944); *The House on 92nd Street* (1945); *A Lady Without Passport* (1950); *Beneath*

the 12-Mile Reef (1953); and *Canyon Crossroads* (1955). One of his more promising cronies came in his role as The Runt in *Meet Boston Blackie* (1941), which started Chester Morris in the popular 40s "B" series as the thief-cum-crimefighter, but the sidekick role was subsequently taken over by George E. Stone.

Of his latter filming, Wagenheim was cast in the very small but tense and pivotal role of the thief who breaks into the storefront in which the Frank family is hiding above in *The Diary of Anne Frank* (1959). TV took up much of his time in later years and he kept fairly busy throughout the 60s and 70s. Wagenheim played the recurring role of Halligan on *Gunsmoke* (1967-1975) and performed until the very end on such shows as *All in the Family* and *Baretta*. On March 6, 1979, the 83-year-old Wagenheim was bludgeoned to death in his Hollywood apartment after he was surprised coming home from grocery shopping during an act of robbery. By sheer horrific coincidence, elderly character actor Victor Kilian, of *Mary Hartman, Mary Hartman* fame, was beaten to death by burglars in his Los Angeles—area apartment.

*   *   *

The Broadway theatre website www.ibdb.com also has a bit of information about his work in theatre: *American Holiday*, where he played Ike (February 21, 1936—March 1936); *Twentieth Century*, a comedy, where he played the Photographer (December 29, 1932—May 20, 1933); and *East of Broadway*, a comedy written by Charles Wagenheim, which had a very short run (January 26, 1932—February 1932).

*   *   *

I recall one afternoon, watching TV on a small black-and-white set, when a Charlie Chan film came on. The credits rolling down the screen at the start of the film showed his name. I called out to my great-grandmother, and we sat there, eagerly awaiting the moment when Charlie would appear. At one point, Charlie Chan received a phone call from someone who told him that "bad things" were happening at an apartment not far away. Charlie goes there with his Number One Son, who always looked scared to death. They entered and found the apartment empty. Number One Son went over to a closet, opened the door, and who fell out? Charlie! He was on the screen for perhaps two seconds. But it was a day's pay!

Another time, friends of mine and I went to the Cameo Movie Theatre on Elizabeth Avenue in Newark, and they were showing an installment of *Don Winslow of the Navy*. At one point, we see Don Winslow, the hero, seated in the back of a cab that is heading down a steep hill in San Francisco. The camera shifts to the driver, a little evil-looking fellow with a moustache. "It's Cousin Charlie!" I whispered loudly to my buddies. They knew all about him. Suddenly Charlie lets loose of the wheel, turns, and tries to strangle Don Winslow, as the cab hurtles down a steep San Francisco street. While everyone else in the theatre was yelling and rooting for Don Winslow, my pals and I were yelling, "Get him, Charlie!"

Around 1978, when I was in my late thirties, I flew out to Los Angeles to visit my father, who had moved out there years earlier. My father told me how to contact Charlie (they remained in occasional touch), and I called him. Charlie picked me up in his car. He was much older than me, and I was impressed to note that while I needed eyeglasses to drive a car, Charlie was fine without them. He explained that his wife, Lillian, a psychologist, years earlier had purchased a small apartment house; they lived in one unit and rented out the rest. Charlie then took me to lunch at a restaurant owned by his good friend Alan Hale Jr., the star of *Gilligan's Island*.

In early March 1979, my father called me from Los Angeles with the sad news that Charlie was dead. He explained that Lillian had suffered a stroke and was confined to their apartment. A woman had been hired to help her. Charlie came back from food shopping, entered his apartment, and surprised the woman who was in the process of going through drawers and stealing articles. Charlie began yelling at her, asking her what she was doing. Apparently the woman panicked and hit Charlie with an object that killed him. I never found out what happened to Charlie's invalid wife.

* * *

Below are details of Charlie's film and television work spanning 1929 to 1979—more than two hundred roles (source: www.imdb.com)—followed by his stage appearances from 1925 to 1938 (source: www.ibdb.com):

Gunsmoke: Return to Dodge (1987) (TV) (dedicatee: in memory of)
All in the Family . . . . Bum (1 episode, 1979)
    —The Return of Stephanie's Father (1979) TV episode . . . . Bum
What's Happening!! . . . . Lefty (1 episode, 1979)
    —The Thomas Treasure (1979) TV episode . . . . Lefty
How the West Was Won (1978) TV mini-series . . . . Las Mesas citizen
Mad Bull (1977) (TV) . . . . Panhandler
. . . aka The Agressor (UK)
Baretta . . . . Eddie / . . . (5 episodes, 1975-1977)
    —Make the Sun Shine (1977) TV episode . . . . Howell
    —Playin' Police (1977) TV episode . . . . Eddie
    —Guns and Brothers (1977) TV episode . . . . Eddie
    —Shoes (1976) TV episode . . . . Attendant
    —Ragtime Billy Peaches (1975) TV episode . . . . Old Man
Ark II . . . . *Old Slave* (1 episode, 1976)
    —The Slaves (1976) TV episode . . . . Old Slave
The Missouri Breaks (1976) . . . . Freighter
McNaughton's Daughter (1976) (TV)
. . . aka Try to Catch a Saint
Three for the Road (1 episode, 1975)
    —Odyssey in Jeans (1975) TV episode
Harry O . . . . Hal Gordon (1 episode, 1975)
    —Silent Kill (1975) TV episode . . . . Hal Gordon
Gunsmoke . . . . Joshua Halligan . . . (29 episodes, 1966-1975)
. . . a.k.a. Gun Law (UK)
. . . a.k.a. Marshal Dillon (USA: rerun title)
    —The Fires of Ignorance (1975) TV episode . . . . Joshua Halligan
    —The Disciple (1974) TV episode . . . . Joshua Halligan
    —Like Old Times (1974) TV episode . . . . Joshua Halligan
    —Kitty's Love Affair (1973) TV episode . . . . Joshua Halligan
    —Talbot (1973) TV episode . . . . Joshua Halligan
    (24 more)
The New Land (1 episode, 1974)
    —The Word Is: Celebration (1974) TV episode
The Six Million Dollar Man . . . . Farmer (1 episode, 1974)
    —Nuclear Alert (1974) TV episode (uncredited) . . . . Farmer
The Magician . . . . Johnny McVey (1 episode, 1974)
    —The Illusion of the Deadly Conglomerate (1974) TV episode . . . .
Johnny McVey
Kojak . . . . Hepplewhite (1 episode, 1973)
    —Girl in the River (1973) TV episode . . . . Hepplewhite

The Streets of San Francisco . . . . Skid Row Bum (1 episode, 1973)
—Legion of the Lost (1973) TV episode . . . . Skid Row Bum
The Doris Day Show . . . . Edgar / . . . (4 episodes, 1970-1972)
—Jimmy the Gent (1972) TV episode . . . . Mr. Jenkins
—Who's Got the Trenchcoat? (1972) TV episode . . . . Milt Schnitzer
—Mr. and Mrs. Raffles (1971) TV episode (as Charlie Wagenheim) . . . . Pop Genson
—Buck's Portrait (1970) TV episode . . . . Edgar
Bonanza . . . . Donovan / . . . (4 episodes, 1959-1972)
. . . a.k.a. "Ponderosa" (USA: rerun title)
—Riot (1972) TV episode . . . . Donovan
—The Code (1966) TV episode . . . . Felger
—Breed of Violence (1960) TV episode . . . . Trager
—Mr. Henry Comstock (1959) TV episode . . . . Pike
Alias Smith and Jones . . . . Bartender (1 episode, 1971)
—The McCreedy Bust (1971) TV episode . . . . Bartender
Ironside . . . . Gas Station Attendant (1 episode, 1971)
. . . a.k.a. The Raymond Burr Show (USA: syndication title)
—From Hrûska, with Love (1971) TV episode . . . . Gas Station Attendant
Adam-12 . . . . Bill Barlow (1 episode, 1970)
—Log 135: Arson (1970) TV episode . . . . Bill Barlow
The Baby Maker (1970) (uncredited) . . . . Toy Shop Owner
Lancer . . . . William (1 episode, 1970)
—Splinter Group (1970) TV episode . . . . William
The Bold Ones: The Lawyers . . . . Hotel Clerk (1 episode, 1970)
. . . a.k.a. The Lawyers
—Point of Honor (1970) TV episode . . . . Hotel Clerk
Hello, Dolly! (1969) (uncredited) . . . . Pushcart man
Hail, Hero! (1969) . . . . Painter #1
Mannix . . . . Danny Boyle (1 episode, 1968)
—You Can Get Killed Out There (1968) TV episode (as Charlie Wagenheim) . . . . Danny Boyle
To Die in Paris (1968) (TV) . . . . Trusty
Cimarron Strip . . . . Elderly Prospector (1 episode, 1967)
—The Hunted (1967) TV episode . . . . Elderly Prospector
A Guide for the Married Man (1967) (uncredited) . . . . Man in Steam Room
The Big Valley . . . . Baggage Man / . . . (3 episodes, 1965-1967)
—Cage of Eagles (1967) TV episode . . . . Storekeeper

—Tunnel of Gold (1966) TV episode . . . . Clerk

—The Murdered Party (1965) TV episode . . . . Baggage Man

The Wild Wild West . . . . Shukie Summers / . . . (2 episodes, 1966-1967)

—The Night of the Bogus Bandits (1967) TV episode . . . . Vance Rawlinson

—The Night of the Flaming Ghost (1966) TV episode (uncredited) . . . . Shukie Summers

Felony Squad (1 episode, 1967)

—The Strangler (1967) TV episode

Archive Footage:

Disneyland

—A Tiger Walks: Part 2 (1966) TV episode (uncredited) . . . . Man Yelling News

—A Tiger Walks: Part 1 (1966) TV episode (uncredited) . . . . Man Yelling News

The Fugitive . . . . Fisherman (1 episode, 1966)

—Right in the Middle of the Season (1966) TV episode . . . . Fisherman

Run Buddy Run . . . . LarWilry (1 episode, 1966)

—Win Place and Die (1966) TV episode . . . . LarWilry

The Rounders . . . . Charlie Brown (1 episode, 1966)

—It's the Noble Thing to Do (1966) TV episode . . . . Charlie Brown

Follow Me, Boys! (1966) (uncredited) . . . . Charlie, Court Bailiff

Run for Your Life . . . . The Hobo (1 episode, 1965)

—A Girl Named Sorrow (1965) TV episode . . . . The Hobo

Honey West . . . . Desk Clerk (1 episode, 1965)

—A Neat Little Package (1965) TV episode . . . . Desk Clerk

The Cincinnati Kid (1965) (uncredited) . . . . Old man

Cat Ballou (1965) (uncredited) . . . . James

The Addams Family . . . . Mr. Boswell (1 episode, 1965)

—Thing Is Missing (1965) TV episode . . . . Mr. Boswell

Ben Casey (3 episodes, 1962-1964)

—For Jimmy, the Best of Everything (1964) TV episode

—My Enemy Is a Bright Green Sparrow (1963) TV episode

—For the Ladybug, One Dozen Roses (1962) TV episode

A Tiger Walks (1964) (uncredited) . . . . Man yelling news

The Virginian . . . . Piney (1 episode, 1963)

. . . a.k.a. The Men from Shiloh (USA: new title)

—The Judgment (1963) TV episode . . . . Piney

Beauty and the Beast (1962) . . . . Mario
Lonely Are the Brave (1962) (uncredited) . . . . Convict
Checkmate . . . . Okie (1 episode, 1961)
      —Juan Moreno's Body (1961) TV episode . . . . Okie
The Life and Legend of Wyatt Earp . . . . Spangenberg (1 episode, 1961)
. . . a.k.a. "Wyatt Earp"
      —Hiding Behind a Star (1961) TV episode . . . . Spangenberg
The Police Dog Story (1961) . . . . Firebug
The Untouchables (1 episode, 1961)
      —Augie "The Banker" Ciamino (1961) TV episode (uncredited)
Tallahassee 7000 . . . . Korck (1 episode)
      —The Alibi (?) TV episode . . . . Korck
Surfside 6 . . . . Little Man (1 episode, 1960)
      —The Clown (1960) TV episode . . . . Little Man
One Foot in Hell (1960) (uncredited) . . . . Banker
. . . a.k.a. The Last Man
Inherit the Wind (1960) (uncredited) . . . . Hotel Clerk
The Story of Ruth (1960) (uncredited) . . . . Ruth's father
Tightrope . . . . Roy (1 episode, 1960)
      —The Penthouse Story (1960) TV episode . . . . Roy
Overland Trail . . . . Barfly (1 episode, 1960)
. . . a.k.a. Overland Stage
      —Vigilantes of Montana (1960) TV episode . . . . Barfly
Peter Gunn . . . . George Markle / . . . (2 episodes, 1960)
      —The Murder Clause (1960) TV episode . . . . George Markle
      —The Hunt (1960) TV episode . . . . The Tramp
Mr. Lucky . . . . Charles Van Halsington III (1 episode, 1960)
      —The Brain Picker (1960) TV episode . . . . Charles Van Halsington
      III
Not for Hire . . . . Moki (1 episode, 1960)
      —Big Man (1960) TV episode . . . . Moki
The Donna Reed Show . . . . Vendor (1 episode, 1960)
      —The Free Soul (1960) TV episode . . . . Vendor
The Lawless Years . . . . Freddie the Dripple / . . . (2 episodes, 1959)
      —The Sonny Rosen Story (1959) TV episode . . . . Louis the Gimp
      —Framed (1959) TV episode . . . . Freddie the Dripple
Alfred Hitchcock Presents . . . . Henlein (1 episode, 1959)
      —Specialty of the House (1959) TV episode . . . . Henlein
The Diary of Anne Frank (1959) (uncredited) . . . . Sneak thief
The Lineup (1 episode, 1959)
. . . a.k.a. "San Francisco Beat"

—The Garmen Millingham Case (1959) TV episode
The Tunnel of Love (1958) . . . . Day Motel Man
Damn Yankees! (1958) (uncredited) . . . . Bit Role
. . . a.k.a. What Lola Wants (UK)
Tales of Wells Fargo . . . . Quinn (1 episode, 1958)
     —The Manuscript (1958) TV episode . . . . Quinn
Colgate Theatre (1 episode, 1958)
     —Adventures of a Model (1958) TV episode
Zorro . . . . Pasqual (1 episode, 1958)
     —The Cross of the Andes (1958) TV episode (uncredited) . . . .
Pasqual
Toughest Gun in Tombstone (1958) . . . . Pete Beasley
Meet McGraw (1 episode, 1958)
. . . a.k.a. The Adventures of McGraw (USA: new title)
     —The Diamond (1958) TV episode
The Restless Gun . . . . Old Timer / . . . (2 episodes, 1958)
     —Hornitas Town (1958) TV episode . . . . Old Timer
     —Hang and Be Damned (1958) TV episode . . . . Prospector
Lonelyhearts (1958) . . . . Joe
. . . a.k.a. Miss Lonelyheart
The Power of the Resurrection (1958) . . . . Merchant
. . . a.k.a. The Passion and the Power of the Christ (USA: video title)
Leave It to Beaver . . . . Painter (1 episode, 1957)
     —The Clubhouse (1957) TV episode . . . . Painter
Sergeant Preston of the Yukon . . . . Jake Peary (1 episode, 1957)
     —Ghost Mine (1957) TV episode . . . . Jake Peary
Harbor Command (1 episode, 1957)
     —The Bag (1957) TV episode
This Could Be the Night (1957) (uncredited) . . . . Mike
The Lone Ranger . . . . Griff Peters (1 episode, 1957)
     —Breaking Point (1957) TV episode . . . . Griff Peters
The Bob Cummings Show (1 episode, 1957)
. . . a.k.a. Love That Bob! (USA: rerun title)
     —Eleven Angry Women (1957) TV episode (as Charles
Waggenheim)
The Gray Ghost . . . . Trainor (1 episode, 1957)
     —The Missing Colonel (1957) TV episode . . . . Trainor
Crusader . . . . Charlie Sanso (1 episode, 1956)
     —The Counterfeiters (1956) TV episode . . . . Charlie Sanso
The Adventures of Jim Bowie . . . . Pierre Jobert (1 episode, 1956)
     —The Ghost of Jean Battoo (1956) TV episode . . . . Pierre Jobert

Science Fiction Theatre . . . . Ed Gorman / . . . (2 episodes, 1955-1956)
   —The Miracle of Dr. Dove (1956) TV episode . . . . Ed Gorman
   —The Strange Dr. Lorenz (1955) TV episode . . . . Everett
Schlitz Playhouse of Stars . . . . Charlie Duckwater / . . . (2 episodes, 1955-1956)
. . . a.k.a. Herald Playhouse (USA: syndication title)
. . . a.k.a. Schlitz Playhouse (USA: new title)
. . . a.k.a. The Playhouse (USA: syndication title)
   —Pattern for Pursuit (1956) TV episode . . . . Charlie Duckwater
   —The Unlighted Road (1955) TV episode . . . . Roy Montana
Blackjack Ketchum, Desperado (1956) (uncredited) . . . . Jerry Carson
The Killer Is Loose (1956) (uncredited) . . . . Clothing Store Owner
Kismet (1955) (uncredited) . . . . Beggar
Celebrity Playhouse (1 episode, 1955)
   —Day of the Trial (1955) TV episode
The Prodigal (1955) . . . . Zubeir
Canyon Crossroads (1955) . . . . Pete Barnwell
Sign of the Pagan (1954) (uncredited) . . . . Palace Messenger
Bengal Brigade (1954) (uncredited) . . . . Headman
. . . a.k.a. Bengal Rifles (UK)
Suddenly (1954) (uncredited) . . . . Iz Kaplan, gas station operator
Executive Suite (1954) (uncredited) . . . . Luigi Cassoni
The Boy from Oklahoma (1954) (uncredited) . . . . Hymie, the Timekeeper
Beneath the 12-Mile Reef (1953) (uncredited) . . . . Paul
The Veils of Bagdad (1953) . . . . Bedouin spy
Vicki (1953) (uncredited) . . . . Seedy Movie House Patron
Loose in London (1953) (uncredited) . . . . Pierre
The Girl Next Door (1953) (uncredited) . . . . Junkman
Death Valley Days (1 episode, 1953)
. . . a.k.a. Call of the West (USA: syndication title)
. . . a.k.a. The Pioneers (USA: syndication title)
. . . a.k.a. Trails West (USA: syndication title)
. . . a.k.a. Western Star Theater (USA: syndication title)
   —The Bell of San Gabriel (1953) TV episode
Salome (1953) (uncredited) . . . . Simon
. . . a.k.a. Salome: The Dance of the Seven Veils (USA)
Tangier Incident (1953) (uncredited)
Boston Blackie (3 episodes, 1952-1953)
   —The Gunman (1953) TV episode
   —Death Does a Rumba (1953) TV episode
   —So Was Goliath (1952) TV episode

Something for the Birds (1952) (uncredited) . . . . Cab Driver
The Miracle of Our Lady of Fatima (1952) (uncredited) . . . . Villager
. . . a.k.a. Miracle of Fatima (UK)
The Story of Will Rogers (1952) (uncredited) . . . . Sam
Lure of the Wilderness (1952) (uncredited) . . . . Townsman
The Sniper (1952) (uncredited) . . . . Mr. Alpine
The Captive City (1952) (uncredited) . . . . Phone Man
Aladdin and His Lamp (1952) (uncredited) . . . . Old Arab
Street Bandits (1951) . . . . Gus Betts, slot machine maker
. . . a.k.a. Flight from Fury (USA)
The Big Night (1951) (uncredited) . . . . Barfly
A *Streetcar Named Desire* (1951) (uncredited) . . . . Passerby
Jim Thorpe—All-American (1951) (uncredited) . . . . Briggs
. . . a.k.a. Man of Bronze (UK)
The Tall Target (1951) (uncredited) . . . . Telegraph Clerk
Mask of the Avenger (1951) (uncredited) . . . . Townsman
House on Telegraph Hill (1951) . . . . Man at Accident
Pier 23 (1951) . . . . Lefty, the policy man (second episode)
. . . a.k.a. Flesh and Leather (USA: TV title)
Inside Straight (1951) (uncredited) . . . . Tomson's Secretary
Three Guys Named Mike (1951) (uncredited) . . . . Irate Man
The Company She Keeps (1951) (uncredited) . . . . *Pete*
Double Deal (1950) (uncredited) . . . . Bus Driver
The Goldbergs (1950) (uncredited) . . . . Painter
. . . a.k.a. Molly
Dial 1119 (1950) (uncredited) . . . . Man on Street
. . . a.k.a. The Violent Hour (UK)
Three Secrets (1950) (uncredited)
A *Lady without Passport* (1950) . . . . Ramon Santez
Mystery Street (1950) (uncredited) . . . . Baggage Clerk
. . . a.k.a. Murder at Harvard
Three Little Words (1950) (uncredited) . . . . Johnny the waiter
Motor Patrol (1950) . . . . Bud Haynes
The Reformer and the Redhead (1950) (uncredited) . . . . Zoo Attendant
The Yellow Cab Man (1950) (uncredited) . . . . Drunk
Key to the City (1950) (uncredited) . . . . Drunk
*Samson and Delilah (*1949) (uncredited) . . . . Townsman
. . . a.k.a. Cecil B. DeMille's Samson and Delilah (UK: complete title)
    (USA: complete title)
Scene of the Crime (1949) (uncredited) . . . . Nervous witness
The Great Sinner (1949) (uncredited) . . . . Gambler with ring
Criss Cross (1949) (uncredited) . . . . Waiter

The Set-Up (1949) (uncredited) . . . . Hamburger Man
A Woman's Secret (1949) (uncredited) . . . . Algerian Piano Player
I Cheated the Law (1949) . . . . Al Markham
Siren of Atlantis (1949) . . . . Doctor
Joan of Arc (1948) (uncredited) . . . . Calot (a taxpayer)
The Gallant Blade (1948) (uncredited) . . . . Bit
Cry of the City (1948) (uncredited) . . . . Counterman
Bodyguard (1948) (uncredited) . . . . Dr. Briller, Optometrist
Man-Eater of Kumaon (1948) . . . . Panwah's Father
River Lady (1948) (uncredited) . . . . Man
The Miracle of the Bells (1948) (uncredited) . . . . Mr. Kummer
Scudda Hoo! Scudda Hay! (1948) (uncredited) . . . . Joe the Barber
. . . a.k.a. Summer Lightning (UK)
Man from Texas (1948) . . . . Arthur (bank cashier)
Alias a Gentleman (1948) (uncredited) . . . . Con
Pirates of Monterey (1947) . . . . Juan
Merton of the Movies (1947) (uncredited) . . . . Employment Man
The Corpse Came C.O.D. (1947) (uncredited) . . . . Claude
Monsieur Verdoux (1947) (uncredited) . . . . Bank Manager's Friend
Time Out of Mind (1947) (uncredited) . . . . Jim
Lighthouse (1947) . . . . Quimby, insurance adjustor
The Brute Man (1946) (uncredited) . . . . Pawnbroker
. . . a.k.a. The Brute
The Dark Corner (1946) (uncredited) . . . . The Real Fred Foss
The Hoodlum Saint (1946) (uncredited) . . . . Mr. Cohn
Night Editor (1946) (uncredited) . . . . Phillips
. . . a.k.a. The Trespasser (UK)
House of Horrors (1946) (uncredited) . . . . Walter, the printer
. . . a.k.a. Joan Medford Is Missing (UK)
Tangier (1946) (uncredited) . . . . Hadji
From This Day Forward (1946) (uncredited) . . . . Hoffman
Whistle Stop (1946) (uncredited) . . . . Deputy
Colonel Effingham's Raid (1946) (uncredited) . . . . Man at Town
    Meeting
. . . a.k.a. Man of the Hour (UK)
The Spiral Staircase (1945) (uncredited) . . . . Desk Clerk
The House on 92nd Street (1945) . . . . Gus Huzmann
Easy to Look At (1945) (uncredited) . . . . Louie
Within These Walls (1945) (uncredited) . . . . Convict Joseph Ciesak
The Jungle Captive (1945) . . . . Fred, first morgue attendant
. . . a.k.a. Wild Jungle Captive (USA: reissue title)

Captain Eddie (1945) (uncredited) . . . . Workman

Dangerous Partners (1945) (uncredited) . . . . Little Man at Lunch Counter

The Scarlet Clue (1945) (uncredited) . . . . Rausch

Boston Blackie Booked on Suspicion (1945) (uncredited) . . . . Mr. Sobel
. . . a.k.a. Booked on Suspicion (UK)

The Last Installment (1945) (uncredited) . . . . First Bartender
. . . a.k.a. A Crime Does Not Pay Subject: The Last Installment (USA: series title)

Counter-Attack (1945) (uncredited) . . . . Tashkin
. . . a.k.a. One Against Seven (UK) (USA: working title)

Salome Where She Danced (1945) (uncredited) . . . . Telegrapher

Strange Illusion (1945) (uncredited) . . . . Tom, Armstrong's Assistant

A Song to Remember (1945) (uncredited) . . . . Waiter

House of Frankenstein (1944) (uncredited) . . . . Jailer

Sergeant Mike (1944) (uncredited) . . . . Hall

Storm over Lisbon (1944) (unconfirmed) . . . . Frustrated Man
. . . a.k.a. Inside the Underworld (USA: reissue title)

An American Romance (1944) (uncredited) . . . . Shoe Salesman

Summer Storm (1944) (uncredited)

Raiders of Ghost City (1944) . . . . Hugo Metzger, alias Abel Rackerby (Chs. 8-9)

The Black Parachute (1944) (uncredited) . . . . Kurt VanDan

The Whistler (1944) (uncredited) . . . . Man at Flophouse

Ali Baba and the Forty Thieves (1944) (uncredited) . . . . Barber

The Song of Bernadette (1943) (uncredited) . . . . Water Thief Sent to Jail
. . . a.k.a. Franz Werfel's The Song of Bernadette (USA: complete title)

Calling Dr. Death (1943) . . . . Coroner

Frontier Badmen (1943) (uncredited) . . . . Melvin

Appointment in Berlin (1943) (uncredited) . . . . Hoffman, the Florist

I Escaped from the Gestapo (1943) (as Charles Waggenheim) . . . . Hart
. . . a.k.a. No Escape (UK)

Don Winslow of the Coast Guard (1943) . . . . Mussanti

Dr. Renault's Secret (1942) (uncredited) . . . . Jacques, a detective

The Daring Young Man (1942) (uncredited) . . . . Fritz

Sin Town (1942) . . . ."Dry-Hole"

Half Way to Shanghai (1942) . . . . Jonathan Peale

Blondie for Victory (1942) (uncredited) . . . . Sugar Hoarder
. . . a.k.a. Troubles Through Billets (UK)

Mystery of Marie Roget (1942) (uncredited) . . . . Subordinate to Prefect
. . . a.k.a. Phantom of Paris

Fingers at the Window (1942) . . . . Fred F. Bixley
Mississippi Gambler (1942) (uncredited) . . . . Collins
. . . a.k.a. Danger on the River (USA: TV title)
Babes on Broadway (1941) (uncredited) . . . . Reed's Composer
Paris Calling (1941) (uncredited) . . . . French Waiter
. . . a.k.a. Paris Bombshell (USA: reissue title)
The Get-Away (1941) . . . . Hutch/Hoodlum in Montage
. . . a.k.a. The Getaway (USA)
They Dare Not Love (1941) (uncredited) . . . . Valet
Out of Darkness (1941) (uncredited) . . . . Traitorous Assistant Editor
. . . a.k.a. John Nesbitt's Passing Parade: Out of Darkness (USA: series title)
. . . a.k.a. Voice of Liberty
The Penalty (1941) (uncredited) . . . . Taxi Driver
Meet Boston Blackie (1941) . . . . The Runt
Respect the Law (1941) (uncredited) . . . . Johnson's Secretary
. . . a.k.a. Crime Does Not Pay No. 33: Respect the Law (USA: series title)
Dark Streets of Cairo (1940) (uncredited) . . . . Dumiel, the captive jeweller
Sky Murder (1940) (uncredited) . . . . Ricoro, Flight Attendant
Charlie Chan at the Wax Museum (1940) . . . . Willie Fern
He Stayed for Breakfast (1940) (uncredited) . . . . Timid waiter
Buyer Beware (1940) (uncredited) . . . . Doctor
. . . a.k.a. Crime Does Not Pay No. 30: Buyer Beware (USA: series title)
Foreign Correspondent (1940) . . . . Assassin
I Love You Again (1940) (uncredited) . . . . Malavinksy (fingerprint man)
Sporting Blood (1940) (uncredited) . . . . Man at Race Track
. . . a.k.a. Sterling Metal (USA: TV title)
Andy Hardy Meets Debutante (1940) (uncredited) . . . . Waiter
Two Girls on Broadway (1940) . . . . Harry, Bartell's Assistant
. . . a.k.a. Choose Your Partner (UK)
Jack Pot (1940) (uncredited) . . . . Cigar Stand Proprietor
. . . a.k.a. Crime Does Not Pay No. 28: Jack Pot (USA: series title)
Pound Foolish (1940)
. . . a.k.a. Crime Does Not Pay No. 26: Pound Foolish (USA: series title)
Know Your Money (1940) (uncredited) . . . . Brand, the Printer
. . . a.k.a. Crime Does Not Pay No. 27: Know Your Money (USA: series title)
Jezebel (1938) (uncredited) . . . . Customer

The Smiling Lieutenant (1931) (uncredited) . . . . Arresting Officer
Gentlemen of the Press (1929) (uncredited) . . . . Bit Part
The Trial of Mary Dugan (1929) (uncredited) . . . . Court Stenographer

* * *

Charles Wagenheim Appearances in Broadway Productions:

Schoolhouse on the Lot (Original, Play, Comedy)
    Performer: Charles Wagenheim (Sam)
    Mar. 22, 1938—May 1938
The Drums Begin (Original, Play, Drama)
    Performer: Charles Wagenheim (Kammerich)
    Nov. 24, 1933—Dec. 1933
Ringside (Original, Play)
    Performer: Charles Wagenheim (Joe)
    Aug. 29, 1928—Sep. 1928
Four Walls (Original, Play)
    Performer: Charles Wagenheim (Herman)
    Sep. 19, 1927—Jan. 1928
The Devil to Pay (Original, Play, Drama)
    Performer: Charles Wagenheim (Mijpel)
    Dec. 3, 1925—Dec. 1925
A Holy Terror (Original, Play)
    Performer: Charles Wagenheim (Bill Chapman)
    Sep. 28, 1925—Oct. 1925
Blind Alleys (Original, Play, Drama)
    Performer: Charles Wagenheim (Michael Osky)
    8 Performances, November 1924

Heaven Will Protect the Working Girl: Marie Dressler

Jon Steinhagen

Iris in: 1927. Our Heroine, despondent, sits at an old table covered by cheap oilcloth. She hasn't anything else to occupy her mind than her troubles on this dreary night.

Close-up: She catches a glimpse of her reflection in the window—big and tall, jowls dripping off her square, nearly masculine face. She is pushing sixty. Her hair is thinning. She looks exhausted.

Dissolve to: Flashback of happier times: footlights, applause, greasepaint, flowers in her dressing room, a twelve-piece orchestra vamping until she's ready.

Dissolve to: The Present: Our Heroine squishes a cockroach. It's been four years since she's had work on Broadway, nearly ten since she stood before a motion picture camera. If people remember her at all, they assume she's dead.

Medium shot: Our Heroine gets up, goes to the window, and pulls down the shade to hide her reflection. She notices how grimy the shade is. She has been contemplating the life of a housekeeper. Now, as the shade snaps, our Heroine gets a good glimpse of the possibilities the window has to offer: one jump and it would all be over.

Cut to: The telephone rings, stopping our Heroine from opening the window.

Our Heroine is Leila Marie Koerber, a Canadian-born comedienne who went under the handle "Marie Dressler" her entire professional career. In her prime, she was a tall full-figured, striking woman who fit in with the major headliners of the late nineteenth century: Lillian Russell and May Irwin. But Marie's prime was long gone by 1927, the time of my imagined silent film scenario regarding her desperate hours. Contemporary leading ladies were going without corsets, had their hair bobbed, rarely wore dresses with floor-length hemlines, and certainly didn't wish to be "buxom." Marie Dressler was not a flapper. She was, however, a trouper, having come up through light opera and vaudeville to a series of appearances in Broadway extravaganzas. Nearing thirty, she played a month as Dottie Dimple in the 1897 farce *Courted into Court*; but once attaining her thirties, she enjoyed longer runs and more prominent roles, such as Viola Alum in the 1899 musical-fantasy-spectacular *The Man in the Moon*, which gave her six months of employment before the century turned. By Christmas 1900, she played the eponymous role in the musical comedy *Miss Prinnt*, although she left the production halfway through its run to pursue another premiere role. Her appearances in musicals were always comic, and the musicals themselves tended to lean towards farces and burlesques, particularly *The King's Carnival* in 1901, which closed the 1900-1901 season, picking up again for another month of healthy business in September 1901. For the first decade of the twentieth century, Dressler piled up comic roles with cartoon names: Lady Oblivion (*The Hall of Fame*, 1902), Ex-Queen Tarantula (*King Highball*, 1902), Philopena Schnitz (*Higgledy-Piggledy*, 1904), Tilly Buttin (*The College Widower*, 1905), Matilda Grabfelder (*Twiddle-Twaddle*, 1906), and Gladys De Vine (*The Boy and the Girl*, 1909). She wasn't playing characters; she was playing caricatures. It was during this period that she reportedly endured a six-year marriage and, sadly, gave birth to a child who died in infancy. Two elements of this busy decade would be echoed in her talking pictures, *Chasing Rainbows* (actors traveling all over the country with a hit show) and *Emma* (in which she revives a child thought to be stillborn), which will be discussed later.

After this accumulation of grand nonsense, Dressler achieved her greatest stage success portraying another Tilly, this time spelled "Tillie," in *Tillie's Nightmare*. This musical comedy opened in May 1910, and

Dressler played Tillie Blobbs—a not very attractive name no matter how you approach it. She received rave notices for her comic turns throughout the show, particularly a hilarious drunk routine, which she would recycle again in her later films. Dressler was also a capable pianist, and she had a hit with the song "Heaven Will Protect the Working Girl," a novelty written for her by the prolific but wholly forgotten composer A. Baldwin Sloane and lyricist Edgar Smith. Dressler accompanied herself on the piano while singing the song, and it was composer Sloane's biggest hit. Dressler parlayed her success for a solid year and a half; *Tillie's Nightmare* closed in December 1911, leaving Dressler at liberty to pursue other projects.

Her most ambitious presentation was *Marie Dressler's All Star Gambol*, which had a limited run of eight performances in the spring of 1913. A revue "special," Dressler not only romped about in sketches and musical numbers, but also (according to the program) took responsibility for the scenic design, the costume design, the libretto duties, and the staging. She must have exhausted herself, if this litany of creativity is to be believed. Songwriters Sloane and Smith returned to provide her with a song they no doubt hoped would be a follow-up success to "Heaven Will Protect the Working Girl": "A Great Big Girl Like Me."

"A Great Big Girl Like Me." Indeed. Dressler had no vanity about her age and weight, at least in public. By the time her *All Star Gambol* rang down its final curtain, Dressler was facing her forty-fifth birthday, but she knew her height (she reportedly stood five feet seven inches), weight (I've never run across an account of her weight, but then a lady never tells, correct?), and homely looks kept her in business. "Homely" really isn't a fair or accurate way to characterize Dressler's looks; to my eyes, her face is lively and well defined, albeit somewhat on the square side. She was a *handsome* woman, and while she knew her features were sliding southward as each year rolled by, she never lost a certain vitality in her face; indeed, many have commented on how *active* her face is: it is a strong face backed by intelligence and talent.

Just the thing for silent pictures.

In 1914, she was hired by fellow Canadian Mack Sennett to star in his biggest gamble thus far: a full-length comedy, *Tillie's Punctured Romance*. Released during the Christmas season of 1914, *Tillie's Punctured Romance* released silent comedy from its usual two-reel format and made history. Aside from Dressler's star turn on a variation of her Tillie Blobbs's character (she's renamed Tillie Banks for the film, no doubt because she stands to inherit a great deal of money), the film offers Charlie Chaplin in the male lead as a handsome villain, the beautiful

Mabel Normand as Chaplin's real romantic interest, and a smorgasbord of Sennett's familiars: bumpkins, con artists, a high-society affair turned upside down, a chase, and the Keystone Kops making a mess of everything. Dressler stomps her way through the action, raw and vulgar, giving as much as she gets. The comedy in *Tillie* is typical of the era: countless slaps, kicks to the posterior, and pratfalls. By the end of the picture, Dressler is in an automobile perched precariously on the end of a pier; of *course*, she's got to end up in the water, and she does. The Kops crash into her, sending the auto into the drink, and for a moment your heart stops because you're never really sure in silent comedy if Sennett provided a stunt dummy for the shot or sent Dressler tumbling off with the auto. Either way, she survived.

What's interesting about the film is its conclusion, which shows the con artist (Chaplin) getting his comeuppance, but only *after* the two leading ladies—both of whom have been used by him—join forces. It's immensely satisfying to see Norman and Dressler—beauty and the beast—end up as friends, united by their common loathing of one bad man. In some ways, this "girls teaming up against the men" notion finds its way into several of Dressler's pre-Code films, as we'll see.

The success of *Tillie's Punctured Romance* informed a few Tillie sequels: *Tillie's Tomato Surprise* (1915) and *Tillie Wakes Up* (1917), in which Dressler returned as Tillie, surnamed Banks in the former and Tinkelpaw in the latter. Between the two sequels, she returned to Broadway to direct and appear in a play called *A Mix-Up*, which did business for four months until closing in March 1915, and to appear in the 1916 revue *The Century Girl*, a six-month success that closed at the end of the 1916-1917 season. With the country at war, Dressler gave up her stage work to appear in four more films during 1917-18, took a vocal and prominent position during a stage labor strike, and then . . .

Nothing.

Her pro-union labor stance dropped the black veil of blackball on her stage career. Her film career, spotty as it was, dried up. She was fifty. She had nothing coming in. For nearly two years, she had nothing to do except look at her scrapbook. Stage work came again in the form of a musical revue, *The Passing Show of 1921* (sixth months of work, closing in late May 1921), and the musical *The Dancing Girl* (four months of work from January to May 1923). These were routine gigs, not starring vehicles. At this point, she was being hired as a novelty, recognized mostly as a has-been, the Big Funny Lady who played Tillie. And then . . .

Seemingly endless nothing.

Which brings us back to Our Heroine in 1927, going from the contemplation of housework to a contemplation of suicide until her telephone rings, and she's saved.

Dressler was always kind, considerate, and generous to young talent, a characteristic evident in her stance during the Chorus Girls Strike in 1917, but of salvaging value in 1927, when screenwriter Frances Marion (1888-1973) called Dressler for a film at MGM. Marion, twenty years younger than Dressler, had remembered her elder's kindnesses during her journeyman years in the film industry; and she had since risen to become one of Hollywood's most powerful, productive, and creative women second only (if not equal to) June Mathis. Marion had a hot comic property on her hands: *The Callahans and the Murphys*, and she immediately thought of Dressler for the role of Mrs. Callahan. Marion had convinced M-G-M mogul Irving Thalberg to green light Dressler, further suggesting she be paired with contract comedienne Polly Moran (1883-1952) as Mrs. Murphy. The hitch was finding Dressler, if she was still alive. In one of those coincidences that appear to have come from a publicist's pen (and might have, if Dressler hadn't insisted—later—that it was true), Marion finally tracked Dressler down on the very night the latter was planning to plummet from her window.

The Callahans and the Murphys was released in June 1927 and, by all reports, was an outstanding success, thanks to the clowning of the two leading ladies, who shared a history of silent film slapstick and work with Sennett. Like Dressler, Moran had been considered a beauty in her heyday, back in the era of the Gibson Girl, but by 1927 had matured into a short plump lady with a cowcatcher smile. While often considered a foil to Dressler, Moran—a Chicago native—was more of a countermatch, a counterpoint; theirs was a complimentary pairing that would become more evident in their talking pictures. *The Callahans and the Murphys*, however, was too successful for its own good: evidently, its reliance on (and vivid depiction of) Irish stereotypes drew and hue and cry from the Irish community; and the picture was yanked from distribution soon after its release. And we can't enjoy it or condemn it today: the film is lost.

Despite the momentary success of *The Callahans and the Murphys*, life wasn't all velvet for Dressler; nor was she assured of a "comeback." M-G-M did not offer her a contract, but she was able to fish around for further work in films, mostly in supporting roles: *The Joy Girl*, for Fox, was released in September 1927, and *Breakfast at Sunrise* for First National later that year, where she played a queen. It was during this time that Warner Bros. was introducing their Vitaphone process, and by October 1927 *The Jazz Singer* made film moguls sit up and pay attention to talking pictures once and for all. By 1928, all Hollywood was sound crazy; but Dressler made three more silent films, two for M-G-M, *Bringing Up Father* and *The Patsy*. The latter was directed by King Vidor for Marion Davies's (read: William Randolph Hearst's) production unit. It's a charming comedy, with Davies in a Cinderella role: as Pat Harrington, she is the ignored member of the family; her sister gets all the new clothes and all the consideration. Pat is in love with her sister's boyfriend, but he barely notices she's alive. Dressler was cast as Davies's selfish mother, and when she's in the same frame as Davies, Dressler gets our attention. Funny and sweet as Davies is, one can't help being constantly aware of Dressler's *presence*: not just her size and shape, but her technique. *The Patsy* was released in April 1928 while most of the major studios were preparing for sound, but Dressler was "talking" long before her first talking picture, and by that I mean one can mentally *hear* her at times: halfway through the picture, Pat has managed to make her sister's boyfriend notice her, and they share a first kiss in the front seat of his roadster. Dressler, catching sight of this through the kitchen window, throws open the window and, with a wind-up like a pitcher prepping a curve ball, shouts "PAT!!!" No title card necessary. We've heard it; we've imagined the voice. *The Patsy* was popular, and Dressler seemed to have found a market for herself as harridans or battleaxes. *Funny* harridans and battleaxes, mind you—selfish as Ma Harrington is, there's nothing quite so alarming, or comic, as seeing Dressler getting ready for a country club dinner dance. We see her petite beautiful daughters flitting about in their undergarments, and then we cut to Dressler's bedroom, where she's being cinched into her corset by her husband. Moments later, the three ladies are primping themselves in front of the same floor-length mirror—and the daughters can't compete with their mother's immensity.

And still no contract.

Dressler survived the remainder of the 1920s and the dawn of sound by doing supporting work, but it was becoming clear to moviegoers that whatever the quality of the picture, Dressler would always stand out. Her role as Aunt Ethel in the god-awful *The Vagabond Lover* is, perhaps, the only reason to watch the thing. Produced by the newly-formed RKO in 1929 as a showcase of sorts for radio and record crooner-bandleader Rudy Vallee, *The Vagabond Lover* is . . . well, dismal. But audiences liked Dressler, and she found herself paired with Polly Moran again in a two-reeler, *Dangerous Females*. By the time Dressler played "herself" in M-G-M's all-talking, all-singing, all-dancing parade of stars *The Hollywood Revue of 1929*, her career path at M-G-M was pretty much set. Aside from the lost silent and the two-reeler, Dressler was paired with Moran in seven films: *The Hollywood Revue of 1929*, *Chasing Rainbows*, *The Girl Said No*, *Caught Short*, *Reducing*, *Politics*, and *Prosperity*. They were good together, obviously; if audiences hadn't particularly cared for Dressler and Moran, a bulk of their films wouldn't have been made.

Moran was fifteen years Dressler's junior, and in their pairings she's often given the more energetic roles that require pratfalls and gags: particularly, in *Chasing Rainbows* she gets a powerful blast of water in the face when Dressler breaks a dressing room sink; in *Reducing*, she gets (among other things) dumped into a mud bath and locked in a sauna. She gets a face full of fountain pen ink in *Reducing* and a face full of soot in *Politics*. Her characters are usually a little arrogant and ambitious, whereas Dressler's characters are usually earthy and wise. No matter who you are and what you think of yourself, Dressler always has your number. Of the Dressler-Moran films, 1930's *Caught Short* is lost to us (well, the soundtrack exists, but no image), *Politics* is the best, and *Prosperity* is the one that needs to make a reappearance thanks to its timely story regarding bond fraud and the salvation of a bank. We'll return to *Politics* in a moment.

1930 was the banner year for Dressler's total rehabilitation. In February, M-G-M released two vehicles that featured Dressler in supporting roles: the routine backstager *Chasing Rainbows* and the not-so-routine *Anna Christie*, ballyhooed at the time as Greta Garbo's first talking picture and based on Eugene O'Neill's drama. Dressler has the essentially minor role of Marthy, a boozy river hag who is friends with Anna's father. Dressler shares Garbo's arrival scene, and the rest is history. I've seen only two actors who can draw one's attention away from Garbo: John Barrymore in *Grand Hotel* (1932) and Marie Dressler in *Anna Christie*. Dressler isn't trying to steal the scene; there's no undue mugging or scene-pulling tricks. She's just *authentic*. Her gin-soaked worldliness comes off just as real as her overweight trouper in *Chasing Rainbows*. In this film, she once again is a woman who's got everyone else's number—she can spot a phony a mile away, and she wastes no time letting the phony know she's onto him or her. She also gets to perform a song written especially for her by Gus Edwards in the "working girl" vein of her heyday: early in the film, Dressler entertains her fellow train passengers with the song "Poor But Honest." Her face changes with each lyric as she tugs and fiddles with her ratty fox cape and awful hat, and while she growls more than sings, it's three minutes of an old school performer who has your attention and won't let it go. She polishes off the song in a single take, and we wish she was the main character. Sadly for *Chasing Rainbows*, all of its two-color Technicolor sequences are lost, meaning we're deprived of four musical numbers, one of which is another Dressler song.

M-G-M kept her busy after the double whammy of comedy and drama in her February releases: April found her and Moran supporting William Haines in *The Girl Said No*, May found her supporting Lillian Gish in *One Romantic Night* and paired again with Moran in the lost *Caught Short*, August found her essaying a *grande dame* role opposite Norma Shearer in the screen adaptation of Rachel Crothers's hit play *Let Us Be Gay*, and November found her in *Min and Bill*.

Seven releases in ten months, but not in any specific stereotype, unless that stereotype can be called tough old broad. Her characterization of Min Divot, proprietor of a run-down dockside hotel and bar, teamed her up with Wallace Beery and won her the Oscar for Best Actress, which she picked up the day after her sixty-third birthday. Min, in a way, is an extrapolation of Marthy: a run-down, aging Mother Earth. Min, however, is sacrificial (although she goes to great lengths to hide her selflessness)—she wants the best for the orphan she's cared for all her life to the point where she breaks off all future contact because it means the orphan can head in the right direction without looking back or risking being sucked back into the seamy, hardscrabble dockside life. *Min and Bill* is short on humor, as even Dressler and Beery's famous destruction of a room as they go after each other is more worrisome than comic. Regardless, in the space of a year, Marie Dressler had made an effortless transition from silence to sound, had shared the screen with some of Hollywood's biggest names (Garbo, Haines, Gish), enjoyed successful partnerships (Moran and Beery), and snagged an Oscar.

She had seven more films to go.

While not often discussed as a typical pre-Code actress, I think Dressler holds a unique place in pre-Code film as an extension or maturation of the liberated ladies portrayed by the younger actresses and beauties of the time. She often embodies older women who have survived on their wits and moral codes, living, in some respects, outside the traditional fringe of wives and mothers, as can be seen in *Let Us Be Gay* (as a society matron who gives parties partly to amuse herself and partly to control the lives of others), *Min and Bill* (Min runs the hotel, peddles bootleg liquor, shaves the men, and what exactly IS her relationship with Bill?), and in all of her last seven films. Particularly in her films with Polly Moran, she plays a woman who has to correct the errors of men; in *Reducing*, she learns that her niece is pregnant and steamrolls into the responsible fellow's apartment to shame him into marriage; in *Prosperity*, she comes out of retirement to clean up the mess her son and sister-in-law have made of the family bank; in *Politics*, she is a housekeeper who finds herself a mayoral candidate. This last is a fantastic reimagining of *Lysistrata*: Dressler is housekeeper to Moran's politically ambitious shrew, but after a neighbor's daughter is killed by mob violence at a local speakeasy, she starts asking some pretty tough questions *of* the current mayor who is, of course, in the pocket of the racketeers. Dressler's concern as a citizen is so passionate that the ladies of the town immediately make her run for mayor, even though Dressler dissembles, claiming she has no head for politics, and besides, she's got her canning to do. What follows is a seriocomic reversal of types when the local women, under Dressler's urging, withdraw their wifely duties from bed, parlor, and kitchen, reducing the local men to childish, incompetent fools. It's a small town experiment in feminism that, in the end, doesn't compromise its vision in order to restore order and harmony. Had *Politics* been made just five years later, after Hollywood voluntarily let its artistic license be muffled by the demands of the Production Code, one can only imagine that Hattie Burns would not only *not* wind up as mayor, but we'd be insulted by vignettes of smug husbands magnanimously "taking back" their wives. Fortunately, *Politics* was released in July of 1931, and Hattie not only triumphs over the racketeers but she becomes mayor, too—and presides over her own daughter's wedding. *Politics* was also one of the top moneymaking films of 1931. As was Dressler's prior release, *Reducing*.

An amazing reversal of fortune for Dressler, who five short years before had been moments from taking a tumble out a window. To top it off, she was voted the most popular box office star for three years running; and after *Politics* she garnered her second Oscar nomination (but not an Oscar) for *Emma*, which was released on New Year's Day of 1932 and—in this author's opinion—is Dressler's best film and the role for which she deserved the Oscar, the one in which she utters a line that might have been her own motto: when asked by another character what she will do once she leaves the family for whom she has been caring for twenty years, she says, "Same as I always do. Work. Work's good for me."

Sometime after filming *Prosperity*, which was released in November 1932, her energy began to flag. She was diagnosed with cancer, although rumor has it that her diagnosis was kept from her by M-G-M head Louis B. Mayer. Mayer, at least, was sensitive enough not to keep his biggest box office draw (over Shearer, Crawford, and Garbo, no less!) going like a workhorse—there was an eleven-month gap between *Emma* and

Prosperity. Mayer encouraged Dressler to rest up, to take vacations, but my feeling is Dressler wasn't fooled. Just as her characters always seemed to smell a phony, no doubt Dressler sensed the full scope of her condition. She rested. She waited. When she could work, she worked.

Her last films were released in August 1933: *Tugboat Annie*, *Dinner At Eight*, and *Christopher Bean*. *Tugboat Annie* reunited her with Wallace Beery (who had gone on to win an Oscar for himself in 1931's *The Champ*) and saw her play, once again, an extrapolation of Marthy and Min Divot, only this time Dressler is indeed married to Beery, and the story is not quite as grim as that of *Min and Bill*. Sick as she was, an extended sequence where she becomes progressively drunk at a party (because she's trying to keep Beery off the sauce, and drinks his cocktails before he can) is a riot and harkens back to her famous drunk routine in *Tillie's Nightmare* twenty-three years prior. *Tugboat Annie* turned out to be the most profitable film of 1933.

She received top billing in the all-star *Dinner At Eight* (above John Barrymore, she was that popular), and as Carlotta Vance, the aging actress who's seen better times, she is honest and authentic: when her character remembers her prime as a Broadway headliner with suppers at Delmonico's and snow in Central Park, you'd swear Dressler wrote her own monologue if it wasn't for the fact that the film is based on George S. Kaufman and Edna Ferber's play of the same name. To the end, Dressler is without vanity, as she constantly acknowledges her battleship figure and her bulldog jowls; but she is also wise to pretenders, sharing a parting shot with the impossibly young Jean Harlow.

Marie Dressler "retired" to Santa Barbara and finally succumbed to cancer on July 28, 1934, the same month Hollywood succumbed to censorship pressures and obeyed the Code. Sadly, only two of her films—*Anna Christie* and *Dinner At Eight*—are commercially available, and *Tillie's Punctured Romance* tends to find its way into bargain collection of silent slapstick on budget labels. Fortunately, the new trend of on-demand DVD has provided fans and the curious a chance to reacquaint themselves with Dressler, making *The Patsy*, *The Divine Lady*, *The Hollywood Revue of 1929*, *Chasing Rainbows*, *The Girl Said No*, *Let Us Be Gay*, *Min and Bill*, *Reducing*, *Politics*, *Emma*, and *Tugboat Annie* available; but they all are worthy of re-release. This was a woman who faced down Death to enjoy a second life as a beloved movie star, although one might wonder if her later success in films made her nostalgic for the "good old days" when she trod the boards, when fans waited for her at the stage door, when the applause continued to wash over the theater even after the final curtain rang down. However she felt, she appears to us in her pre-Code films as a warm, caring, unselfish, smart, funny, and—above all—*human* being who makes you think that you wouldn't mind it at all if she was your granny, your aunt, or your mother. Or just someone you know. Whether or not her career receives the full rehabilitation it deserves, only time, interest, and commerce can tell.

But Heaven will protect the working girl.

Bibliography

Bordman, Gerald. *American Musical Theatre: A Chronicle*. 2nd edition. New York: Oxford University Press, 1992.

Biographical information and theatrical chronology were culled from the Internet Movie Database (imdb.com), the Internet Broadway Database (ibdb.com), and the Turner Classic Movies website (tcm.com).

22

Talkers, Fast and Smooth: Lee Tracy and Warren William

Jon Steinhagen

Two men,
born at opposite extremes of America,
polarized in temperament,
as physically unlike as two physically unlike things can be,
and possessing vocal chops as dissimilar as one can be,
one an oboe in need of a new reed,
the other a cello played with a bow of silk.

Two men,
whose professional handles were made up of two first names,
(or, depending on how you look at it, two last names).

Two men,
whose Hollywood output is best appreciated
during a specific period of the Depression
and the development of talking pictures
—a period referred to as "pre-Code"—
a time when rogues could be, and often were, film heroes.

Lee Tracy and Warren William:
Hollywood's charming ne'er-do-wells of the pre-Code era
—one leading us to the sunshine,
the other preferring to brood in the shadows—
and both enormously adept at seducing us.

•

Warren William was the elder, born in Aitkin, Minnesota, on December 2, 1894. His full name was Warren William Krech, which one hopes doesn't rhyme with "wretch" (but it probably does), son of Freeman and Frances. Perhaps the stark chilliness of Minnesota's winters was infused in young Krech's blood; even when tackling a straightforward role of seduction, Warren William the screen actor seems a little withdrawn from his romantic prey, as if at a remove because he's more interested in the effect his love-making is having rather than the actual sensation he's deriving from the love-making. Whatever emotional restraints he inherited from his native state, William grew to be what every actor who wasn't always wanted to be: talk, dark, and handsome. His angled moustache gave him a suave, sophisticated countenance, one equally at home in old Europe or in modern Manhattan, while his dark locks remained pomaded in a carefully swept-back gloss, emphasizing his broad angular forehead and Romanesque nose. To my eyes, he resembles a cross between John Barrymore and Mischa Auer, but lacking the penetrating gaze of the former and the sometimes pop-eyed, drowned Chihuahua "ethnic" look of the latter. If nothing else, Warren William looked like a Leading Man, albeit one from stock.

Less than four years later, on April 14, 1898, William Lee Tracy was born in Atlanta, Georgia, and perhaps the warmer climate made him naturally antsy and restless, just as William's northerly childhood made him naturally cool and reserved. Regardless, the red-headed Tracy did his bit in the Great War as a second lieutenant and promptly, upon his return stateside, gave up his plans to pursue electrical engineering and headed for Broadway. Like William, his looks are stock, although Tracy would never be considered of the standard Leading Man mold. Tracy's face was round and somewhat cherubic, a peach dumpling of a face with a little pursed mouth. If William reminded you of Barrymore, Tracy reminded you of the guy who sold Barrymore his shoes. Seeing William, you figured this guy was either going to passionately embrace the heroine at some point during the evening or try to force himself on her; with Tracy, you figured he was there for comic relief, or at least be a pain in the neck.

In their movies of the pre-Code era, they were often both (lover-rapist, comic-annoyance), but they could and did surprise us, too. Tracy is both heartless and empathetic to John Barrymore in *Dinner At Eight* (1933), a "small" role for him; but he is usually snappy and sappy, favoring heavy doses of the snap (1932's *The Strange Love of Molly Louvain* and *Blessed Event*, 1933's *Bombshell*). Tracy's and William's appeal and finesse seems to stem, in part, from their artistry in teetering between façade and feeling, realism and romance. Nowhere else is this better illustrated in William's career than in the opening scene of *Beauty and the Boss*, Warner Bros.'s 1932 adaptation of *The Church Mouse* (a popular Europe-cum-Broadway play). William is the fast-paced, progressive, dashing Baron Josef von Ullrich, head of an enormous European bank who is distracted by the arousing attributes of his inefficient but seductive stenographer. For the first half of the sequence, he makes some rather atrocious, chauvinistic remarks about "pretty women" in general, behaving like a martinet who has only just discovered something called Lust; when he finally fires the girl, the regal, pseudo-prudish act is dropped, and he beckons her to return, to have a seat—he doesn't complain now that she's crossing her legs. Wordlessly, he gives her a cigarette from his expensive cigarette case, lights it for her, and then pours her a liqueur. During this, he is all smiles and bedroom eyes—Little Red Riding Hood, meet the wolf. William sustains the seductive act until it's time to get back to work, whereupon he's the rigid bluestocking once again, and we didn't see the transition, the character sleight of hand.

The majority of William's portrayals from the period 1931-33 give plenty of freight to similar Jekyll-Hyde shadings. Tracy, too, moves effortlessly between two different realms: a machinegun delivery designed to stun opponents and lovers alike into silence and submission, and a soft-spoken sentimentality that sounds like apple pie, home, and hearth. Tracy's examples are too numerous to mention here; but his definitive turn as "Space" Hanlon in *Bombshell*—alternately razzing, pestering, bolstering, promoting, and sweet-talking Jean Harlow (in my opinion, his perfect match)—shows how well he could effect that sudden, startling switch from goof to goo.

Tracy and William startle us at how fast they can switch modes, rather like dropping a phonograph needle on different spots of a record, but they also raise some questions:

- Which of these modes (stuffy/sexy, clown/hero) is the real mode?
- Which "character" is the put-on, the ruse?
- Who *are* these guys, really?
- And where did they come from?

Well, aside from Minnesota and Atlanta, they came from The Stage. The Great White Way. Broadway.

1923 was a banner year for "William Krech": he got married and made a few silent films. His wife, Helen, remained by his side for the next twenty-five years; motion pictures, however, didn't give him much pleasure at first. Appearing in *The Town That Forgot God* and *Plunder* (the latter a fifteen-episode Pearl White serial), Mr. Krech dropped his last name and, as Warren William, spent nearly an entire decade in Manhattan before moving back West for good in 1931. In February of 1924, he appeared in *The Wonderful Visit* in the role of Sir John Gotch, KBE, a handle that reeks of High British. Just shy of thirty, William made his debut as one of those stiff-upper-lip fellows whose every thought is dipped in sherry and wrapped in a Union Jack. He had a knack for playing "up," taking on many mature roles during his Broadway stint, his height, profile, and somewhat heavy-lidded gaze lending him the *gravitas* favored in such roles. His characters from 1924 to 1928 sound every bit as fustian as they look: George Cadwalader (*Expressing Willie*, 1924—now *there's* a title for you!), Keith Reddington (*Nocturne*, 1925), Gerald Fay (*Twelve Miles Out*, 1925-26), Dr. Achilles Swain (*Paradise*, 1927-28), and Captain Leslie (*Sign of the Leopard*, 1928-29), to name a few. I name a few because not one of these titles means anything to anybody these days. They were quickly forgotten dramas and comedies, never revived and only of historical interest to—well, people like myself, I suppose, who want to track the rise of a particular actor (if such a litany of trifles can be truly called a "rise"). Of the eighteen stage productions William appeared in between February 1924 and June 1931, very few could even be called successes—*Twelve Miles Out, Let Us Be Gay* (1929), and *The Vinegar Tree* (his final Broadway credit) are the only ventures to run six months or more. For the most part, William starred in short-lived productions, but while he didn't have luck enough to land a unique, career-defining characterization (as Lee Tracy did, as we'll see), he *did* manage to stay employed. He enjoyed four premieres in 1925 alone, including a turn as Johannes Rosmer for thirty performances in The Stagers' May 1925 production of Ibsen's *Rosmersholm*. Here we might find some sort of indication as to how William the Broadway Actor was used to greatest effect, as Ibsen's brooding, haunted thinker, accused of abandoning one set of ideals (two, really, political *and* domestic), ending a suicide. But Rosmer is not the "star" part in *Rosmersholm*. Rebecca is, and William's Rebecca was Margaret Wycherly, a loonily wistful old school actress who would go on to spell a variety of imbalanced matriarchal roles in several films of the 1930's and 1940's. William was good enough to get away with Ibsen, but not good enough to make any of his premiere roles his own. When Rachel Crothers's *Let Us Be Gay* was filmed by M-G-M in 1930, his role was given to Rod la Rocque, and yet it might have made a solid film debut for William had the cards been stacked in his favor. Even when William's final stage play, Paul Osborne's *The Vinegar Tree*, was filmed in 1933, his role went to Conway Tearle. You see where I'm going with this: these are roles for men with pomaded hair or pencil-thin mustaches. These parts could be played by anybody with the requisite attributes.

Warren William, prior to Hollywood, was a stalwart, reliable leading man, believable in authority roles, consumed lovers, philandering husbands chastened by adventurous wives, and schemers. Broadway gave him plenty of experience but no artistic gelatin; his ability to combine all of these attributes into one role would not be fully realized until his Hollywood years. Broadway established him as a commodity but not a Name—the sometimes thin fare of the era meant his talents, too, were spread too thin.

Not so Lee Tracy. He saw five Broadway premieres between February 1924 and his first trip to Hollywood in 1929, three of which were huge hits, the last affording him a Name as well as a Type. In February 1924 (the same wintry month that Warren William was making his stage debut in the short-lived *The Wonderful Visit*), Tracy lucked into a long run: George Kelly's comedy *The Show-Off*, which ran out the rest of the 1923-24 season and played the entire next season, finally shutting down in June 1925. In it, Tracy had the supporting role of Joe, the leading lady's brother who spends much of his time dithering in the cellar, fooling around with "raddio." Joe's purpose is to barb an occasional deflation towards the title character, Aubrey Piper, the fast-talking, obnoxious, toupee-wearing salesman whose ongoing pointless gab alienates the family into which he wishes to ingratiate himself. It is sometimes erroneously thought that Tracy originated the role of Aubrey on Broadway: he did not, but the error is understandable—if you read the play today, it's difficult not to envision Tracy as the motor-mouth Aubrey. Twenty-five years later, after his film career what pretty much over, Tracy would indeed get a crack at Aubrey for twenty-one performances at the Arena Stage in New York City. And he'd be great.

Regardless, being in a hit is being in a hit, and Tracy was employable thereafter. Unfortunately, his next two Broadway outings (*The Book of Charm*, 1925, and *Glory Hallelujah*, 1926) were forgettable comedies that rehearsed longer than they ran (in the latter, Tracy had the thankless role of "Clerk"). He lucked out again, however, as the song-and-dance man Roy Lane in *Broadway*, one of those epic slices of hard-boiled "realism" co-authored by George Abbott and offering the public a supposedly honest look at bootleggers, gangsters, chorus girls, and what it's like "backstage." Not a musical, but offering a template for the countless early talkie musicals of 1929-30, *Broadway* employed Tracy for a solid eighteen months. He was indeed making up for lost time on his two prior misfires. Less than six months after closing *Broadway* in February 1928, Tracy made an even bigger splash as Chicago reporter Hildy Johnson in *The Front Page*.

Hildy Johnson did more to define Lee Tracy as "Lee Tracy" than any other role. True, the film version from 1931 deprives us of Tracy and offers instead Pat O'Brien, but Hildy Johnson—the original Hildy Johnson—was everything Lee Tracy had promised to be, and more. Fast-talking, manipulative, crafty, and a way of slinging a telephone that appears more Art than Function, Tracy landed as Johnson and made talent scouts realize that here was a unique actor, not necessarily a unique role. Tracy didn't just speak fast, he *thought* fast; and after eight months of the Chicago newsroom, he was making a few pictures for Fox.

Tracy's film debut happened with the forgotten (and rarely, if ever, screened) *Big Time* in 1929, opposite Mae Clarke, another pre-Code honey whose career has gone undeservedly underappraised and underpraised. His films from 1929 to 30 are unseen and unlamented, although he does offer a one-off stint as The Buzzard in the talkie adaptation of Molnar's *Liliom* in 1930, long before the source was given a carousel waltz and an eight-minute soliloquy for its antihero as *Carousel*. Tracy honored his Fox contract and hastily beat it back to Broadway, where he enjoyed a modest success in Howard Lindsay and Betrand Robinson's *Oh, Promise Me* (for a tidy 145 performances) and Norman Krasna's *Louder, Please*, directed by his *Broadway* alum George Abbott and featuring the controversial Louise Brooks fresh of her association with G. W. Pabst. These appearances kept him busy from November 1930 through January 1932, but not busy enough to keep him satisfied, and it was back to Hollywood for good. Or for then.

While I could spend a long, long, long time going over William's and Tracy's many original and striking performances in the pre-Code films they made, I'm going to touch on two that, to me, marked their successful transition from Broadway stardom to film stardom. I'll give seniority to Warren William and *Under 18* (I've seen it billed as both *Under 18* and *Under Eighteen*, but have chosen to refer to it by its numerical title, in keeping with the film's lurid and misleading trailer). While *Under 18* is not William's screen debut (that would be 1931's *Honor of the Family*), I believe it sets up what we can expect from him at his juiciest. This isn't to say William has the leading role in the film. On the contrary, he appears in only two sequences. Directed by Archie Mayo and produced by Warner Bros.'s First National, *Under 18* was filmed in late 1931 and released as a sort of New Year's appetizer on January 2, 1932. Essentially, Marian Marsh plays a girl from the tenements who sees her older sister's marriage for love to a pool-playing, abusive bum head straight for the divorce courts. Trying to help scrape up the $200 her sister needs to pay her shady divorce lawyer, Our Heroine at once denounces the ideal of marriage for love to her delivery truck-driving fiancé and heads off to the stupendously appointed penthouse apartment of a Broadway producer for the money, knowing that he will want flesh for cash.

Just this basic summary sounds lurid enough without the salacious title of *Under 18*, which is a confusing title anyway. We're to assume, from the title, that Marian Marsh is a minor, and yet her age is never specified during the film (she's supposed to be younger than her sister, Anita Page), and questions about statutory rape or Marsh's status as jailbait are never addressed. One begins to suspect *Under 18* must be referring to Marsh's dress size.

At any rate, it's all rather business-as-usual in terms of plot until Marsh, who works as a modiste at a downtown salon, models a fur coat for the girlfriend of fabulously wealthy producer Raymond Harding, played by friend William. We first see him in profile (naturally), idly leafing through a magazine with a bored look on his face (just another mink), bored until the fetching Ms. Marsh opens the mink she's modeling—all she's got on is a slip. William sees this and takes a sudden interest in the purchase. Soon enough, the girlfriend is off in a fitting room, and William is sending a clerk out for Marsh's lunch (a cheese sandwich and a Coke). William is evidently so cultured and refined that he needs "Coke" explained to him, and Marsh obliges with "Coca-Cola." Marsh dithers on whether or not she should have the 5¢ Coke or the 10¢ Coke, and William naturally insists she get the 10¢ Coke (what's more expensive must be the best). He all but drools on her as she cools herself in front of an electric fan, and on his way out, he instructs her to turn to him for "anything at all." The next day, he sends orchids to Marsh's mother, which has the same effect as sending Baccarat crystal to a lunchwagon—it's astounding not because it's fancy but because it's ludicrous.

We don't see William again until Marsh—with nowhere to turn for the $200 needed for her sister's severance from her brute of a husband—takes the long elevator ride of doom to William's massive Art Deco apartment, where an orgy of sorts is taking place in William's rooftop pool (as someone remarked to me upon seeing this setup, "Gee, I'd hate to live underneath all *that*!"). Marsh is ferried through the hedonism by William's all-too-knowing butler, and it takes William a moment or two to remember who she is. The lovely thing about William's rogue Harding (named, perhaps, with a wink towards the philandering twenty-ninth president Warren G.?) is that it's clear that he feigns remembering Marsh, his interest triggered more by his appraisal of her body than his words. He then utters one of the ultimate bits of brass in pre-Code dialogue: "Why don't you take off your clothes and stay awhile?" This guy is so smooth his come-ons sound as harmless as invitations to tea. Don't worry (if you *were*): Ms. Marsh's virtue remains intact.

Under 18's progress, from the start, is a rather routine affair until the arrival of Warren William. His poise, elegance, money, and *voice* (after all, folks, the Talkies are supposed to *talk*) present a smoother, cleaner world where, until then, it was living room weddings, Irish landladies putting out the garbage, front stoops, delivery trucks, and a view of the New York skyline from Marsh's fire escape, where she sleeps in order to take the edge off the summer heat. William's world is spacious, airy (even when overpopulated by faceless extras diving for bracelets discarded into pools), huge rooms, sliding panels (William's "study" not only has a wardrobe large enough to live in, there's also a concealed bar that's to die for), and grand pianos. You want to live where Williams lives, even viewing the setup with contemporary eyes. William's character came to represent the society that, most of the time, was invisible to us working-class slobs, up there in the clouds—and when the gods come down, it's as if they're bored by their constant splendor, and corruption of innocence is its only bromide.

Lee Tracy, however, is a working-class slob, albeit one with brains, brass, and bravado. Aside from his four Fox appearances at the dawn of sound, I feel Tracy truly makes his debut with *The Strange Love of Molly Louvain*, another Warner Bros.—First National talker based on an unpublished play by Maureen Dallas Watkins, author of the perennial pleaser *Chicago*. Molly Louvain, however, doesn't murder anybody to get her name in the headlines. She doesn't have to: she's the marvelous Ann Dvorak (steps away from her ahead-of-its-time portrayal of a society woman on a rapid elevator to Hell in *Three On a Match* later in 1932), and men want to sleep with her. One, in fact, has: ten seconds after the titles, it's clear to all that the man with whom she is walking has clearly deflowered her. But this is a happy time for Molly—until she realizes she's been dumped (the father and fiancé-to-be is a son of the rich). That's okay—there's a stocking salesman who wants her (for sex) and a bellboy as well (for love). She winds up running away with the stocking salesman who takes no time to turn to a life of petty crime; she meets up with the bellboy while she works as a dance hall hostess (he's now a student). Circumstances (and the movies) being what they are, Molly and the kid wind up as unwitting accomplices to her husband's heist of a car, which leads to a shoot-out and the death of a cop. Molly ankles it with the kid; she sneaks into a public restroom at dawn with two bottles of peroxide and emerges as Jean Harlow. Some disguise. She and the boy pass themselves off as a married couple and rent a room.

We're at least thirty minutes into the film and, like *Under 18*, we feel as though we've seen this before—at least we think we've seen all these elements somewhere before, just not mixed up together into one movie.

And then, the telephone rings; the door opens; and Lee Tracy breezes in, barely acknowledges Molly and her boyfriend, and takes the phone call. Evidently, it's the only telephone in the building, and he made a prior arrangement with a previous tenant that he could come and go as he pleases, as he's a reporter. Tracy answers the telephone with a flourish, this being the era of the candlestick model, wherein the receiver hung from the telephone stalk. Tracy flips the receiver into the air, catches it, and starts firing off his mouth. We're breathless, and so are Molly and her fake husband. Where is that voice coming from? Part buzz saw and part "raspberry," Tracy's voice is unique, as if he not only refused to have his adenoids out but asked for extra adenoids to be put in. But Tracy's rapid-fire repartee is no less smooth than Warren William's warm round deep rumblings: this is a guy who thinks a mile a minute, and his mouth is just trying to keep up with it. It's Hildy Johnson, folks, fresh from the Chicago newsroom. And the trick with the telephone? Possibly straight from the play, not to mention Tracy's way of ending a call, turning "Right!" into a two-syllable word (difficult to approximate on paper, the closest I can get is "RYE-eeet!"). No sooner is he off the telephone than he's sizing up Molly, sending the kid out for groceries, and the fun begins. He's got a line for everything, and an improvised way of meeting all needs (a little music? Just open the window and call down to the radio shop owner across the street to turn up the volume on the model he's selling on the sidewalk).

What follows is more or less as you would expect. Somewhere along the way, Tracy (playing "Scotty"; he has snappier names than the urban William) falls in love with Molly, despite some scuffling over the word "tramp," and it's not exactly plausible that Tracy can't figure out the Molly the police and the reporters (i.e., him) want is the same Molly he's trying to make.

It doesn't matter. What William and Tracy do to sensationalist talkies like *Under 18* and *The Strange Love of Molly Louvain* is *enliven* them, make us sit up, and take notice. It's significant that their characters in these early career entries show up late in the action yet grip us until the end. It's almost as if by way of an introduction: here are Broadway stars of a certain caliber and experience who use their disparate gifts (a voice like a nest of wasps, a profile like Barrymore elongated) to grab us with fast patter or smooth talk, promising lives of adventure and improvisation (Tracy) or sex and luxury (William). Tracy gets the girl because he's not just one step ahead of the other guys in the story; he's a full three city blocks ahead, thumbing his nose at them, to boot. William may or may not get the girl; in fact, he often doesn't in his grasping roles where his smooth talk, command, and hauteur are ramped up to give us ultimate roguery (*Skyscraper Souls*, *Employee's Entrance*, *The Match King*, *The Mind Reader*—outstanding movies all, but covered extensively elsewhere). Until a story concludes, however, you can bet the heroine will be fascinated by him because, like Tracy, he offers something our ordinary lives cannot offer—or at least the *possibility* of something less than ordinary.

By the time Breen and his Code enforcement clamped down on Hollywood on July 1, 1934, Tracy and William were being disseminated into the mainstream, Tracy suffering the ultimate punishment for his public sins by having his entire role removed from *Viva Villa* and thereafter consigned to Poverty Row studios and programmers, William embarking upon a steady stream of one-note roles (he's either suave or sordid from 1934 on, never both) that are neither challenging nor interesting. He's at his most wooden and invisible when stuffed into historical or noble roles (Caesar in *Cleopatra*, for example) and gives off a faint odor of B-list talent when subjugated to series roles that others either did better at before him (society detective Philo Vance) or will be remembered for in the future (the Perry Mason series). William never returned to the stage, but he never had to endure television either. He gamely rolled out his smooth deep pear-shaped tones in movie after movie, tinkering at his "labor-saving devices" at home, causing no scandals, and not minding that his glory roles from 1931 to 1934 were long behind him when he died at age fifty-three in 1948 from multiple myeloma.

Lee Tracy, on the other hand, continued to booze it up after M-G-M cancelled his contract (and his entire *Viva Villa* performance) secondary to his public urination onto a brace of Mexican soldiers in 1934. A string of programmers followed, and before long he returned to the stage, hoping to recapture the success he had in the 1920s. It didn't happen. *Bright Star* opened and closed in October 1935; *Every Man For Himself* likewise made a flash in the pan in December 1940. His theatrical endeavors after that were mostly relegated to stock or special events, like the aforementioned revival of *The Show-Off* with Tracy in the role he was meant to play, but of special interest is his ten-performance star turn as hoofer Harry Van in Robert Sherwood's *Idiot's Delight*, staged in limited-run revival at City Center. His co-star was Ruth Chatterton, another scion of pre-Code stardom, and one's mouth waters at the concept—not to mention what it must have been like backstage with Chatterton and Tracy regaling the no-names in the supporting roles with tales of the Warners, Paramount, and M-G-M backlots.

Tracy outlived William by twenty years, and those twenty years were not without their momentary blips of glory. 1960 saw him in the plum supporting role of a dying President in Gore Vidal's *The Best Man*, a fine portrayal preserved in the 1964 film version, for which he also received an Oscar nomination for Best Supporting Actor. He made a last stab at Broadway success in the four-performance flop *Minor Miracle* by Al Morgan, co-starring with old Broadway and Talkie cronies Dennis King and Pert Kelton. An occasional television role brought his career (and life) to a close in 1968, at the age of seventy.

Their legacy died out, somewhat. One could say that the suave charmer of questionable motives character was, in some ways, absorbed by the Rock Hudson of the 1950s (I'm thinking of *Magnificent Obsession* and *Giant* in particular), but there are few actors I've seen who've been able to capture William's duality of predator and potentate, killer and king. As for Tracy's nervy reporters and promoters, for a while it seemed another actor named Tracy (of the Spencer variety, new to M-G-M in 1935) tried to fill Lee's shoes (I think of Spencer Tracy in *Libeled Lady* or as Clark Gable's wisecracking sidekicks in *San Francisco*, *Test Pilot*, and *Boom Town*, although I don't think Lee Tracy would've been at home in the more fisticuffs roles).

They're gone, but—as time passes—their glory roles become available on home video, even if a bulk of them are only available as on-demand DVD purchases. In the 1990s, when the studios were raiding their vaults for VHS and laser disc reissues, these titles were on the market, but today they're hard to find. And this is a shame. Where else can you be entertained by two actors who, at first glance, were complete opposites but followed career paths that started around the same time (1924) and reached their apex of stardom at the height of the Depression, before the Code's hammer fell and movies began lying to us?

Lee Tracy and Warren William—as their dual proper names suggest—showed us the full ranges of their characters, that people can be good and bad, suave and smarmy, conniving and honest, angels and devils, complex people who enliven every story, every situation, as if to suggest, "You won't know what to expect next, really."

And that's why we come back to the movies again and again, right? RYE-eeet!

Bibliography

Sources

Books

Doherty, Thomas. *Pre-Code Hollywood: Sex, Immorality, and Insurrection in American Cinema, 1930-1934.* New York: Columbia University Press, 1999.

LaSalle, Mick. *Dangerous Men: Pre-Code Hollywood and the Birth of the Modern Man.* New York: St. Martin's Press, 2002.

On-line

Biographical information and theatrical chronologies were culled from the Internet Movie Database (imdb.com), the Internet Broadway Database (ibdb.com), and the Turner Classic Movies website (tcm.com).

Eddie Quillan: A Study in Versatility

Susanne Robertson

"Longevity" is defined in the *Merriam-Webster* dictionary as a great duration of life or a long continuance of career. The fact of the matter is that in order to achieve longevity, whether in life or career, it is necessary to change and grow, in other words, to evolve. This evolution provides a solid foundation for establishing endurance in the face of personal or professional challenges. In the entertainment industry durability can be a particularly elusive quality to achieve given the vicissitudes of the field. A performer who enjoys a particularly long and successful career is generally regarded as being outside the norm. Performers in this illustrious group are admired and commended for their resiliency. Edward "Eddie" Quillan (1907-1990), an American actor, is a perfect example. His professional life began as a child on the vaudeville stages, progressed to silent films and talkies, and continued through the age of television into the 1980s. His filmography reads like a compendium of American entertainment history. After over one hundred films and two hundred television appearances, Eddie Quillan has emerged as one of America's finest and most recognized character actors.

Eddie was born in Philadelphia, Pennsylvania on March 31, 1907, into a family of vaudeville entertainers. His father, Joseph Quillan (1884-1952), and his mother, Sarah (1885-1969), had a theatrical career as troupers in their native Scotland. After marrying and coming to this country, they continued to be actively involved on the stage. Mr. and Mrs.

Quillan were highly regarded performers and were contracted players in the most prestigious of the "big time" vaudeville franchises.[1]

Vaudeville, a theatrical genre of variety entertainment, sometimes referred to as the heart of American show business, flourished in North America from the early 1880s until the early 1930s. The usual date given for the birth of the form is October 24, 1881, when Tony Pastor, a circus ringmaster turned theatre manager, staged the first bill of self-proclaimed "clean" vaudeville in New York City. His intent was to provide respectability to the genre, hoping to draw a potential audience from the middle class and also making the form more consistent with the Progressive Era's interests in education and self-improvement. B. F. Keith took the next step, starting in Boston, where he built an empire of theaters, which E. F. Albee managed to great success. Circuits such as those managed by Keith-Albee enabled a chain of allied vaudeville houses to contract acts for regional and national tours. One of the biggest circuits was Martin Beck's Orpheum Circuit of which the Quillans were a part. This circuit was incorporated in 1919 and brought together forty-five (45) theaters in thirty-six (36) cities throughout the United States and Canada.[2]

The three most common levels of vaudeville contracts were "small time" (lower-paying contracts for frequent performances in converted theatres), "medium time" (moderate wages for two performances each day in legitimate theaters), and "big time" (possible pay of several thousand dollars per week in large theaters patronized by the middle- and upper-middle class). As performers in the "big time," the Quillans rose in celebrity and established a regional and national following. They worked their way into better working conditions and the best pay of the contract players. This was the ideal situation for the family and ensured their financial security in a volatile and fickle business.

During World War I, in 1917, Joseph Quillan wrote a vaudeville skit called *The Rising Generation.* Eddie made his debut at the age of seven performing with his three brothers (Buster, John, and Joe) and one of his sisters (Marie) as part of this act, singing, dancing, telling jokes, and playing musical instruments. Their father travelled with the boys, usually during the summer months, and managed the act.[3] Edward

1   S. D. Trav, *No Applause—Just Throw Money: The Book That Made Vaudeville Famous* (New York: Faber and Faber, 2005), 158.

2   http://en.wikipedia.org/wiki/Vaudeville, 1-3.

3   Joe Collura, "Eddie Quillan: Mr. Personality," *Classic Images*, April 1987, issue 142, 29.

toured together with his eight siblings throughout the United States. In an interview with Michael Ankerich in July 1988, Eddie described his early life on the road:

> We played most of the places we were allowed to play as children. Because of the authorities, we couldn't play everywhere. We could never get into New York because the Gerry Society was so strict."[4]

The Gerry Society was founded in the late 1800s by lawyer Elbridge Thomas Gerry for the purpose of protecting minors from exploitation in the workplace.

Eddie went on to describe a typical vaudeville day:

> I would get up around 11:00 a.m., and we would do the show at 2:00 p.m. Then we had another evening show, usually two, so that made three performances a day. We would finish about 11:00 p.m., and then, after we got our makeup off, would go to a restaurant to get something to eat. So it was 1:00 a.m. or so before we went to bed.[5]

Occasionally the family was on the road while school was in session. During these times the Quillan children received their education through the New York Professional Children's School, which was by correspondence. By the time he was in his teens, Quillan was a consummate performer—a triple threat—singing, dancing, and acting. In addition he played the saxophone and appeared as a stand-up comic.

While growing up in vaudeville, Eddie was a fan of motion pictures. His favorite actors were the Western players: Tom Mix, Eddie Polo, and Harry Carey. He admired the comedic genius of Charlie Chaplin. Eddie had no desire at this time to become a movie actor. His mother is actually credited with planting the idea in his mind. The story goes that on one occasion while the family was performing in Chicago the children had individual portraits taken. When his mother, Sarah, looked at publicity photos, she expressed the idea that Eddie ought to be in pictures, which made him start to consider the possibility.

---

[4]   Michael G. Ankerich, *Broken Silence, Conversations with 23 Silent Film Stars* (Jefferson, NC: McFarland & Company, 1993), 250.

[5]   Ibid.

After ten years in theatre the Quillans settled on the West Coast. In 1922, while performing in Los Angeles, Joseph Quillan started to investigate the possibility of a movie career for his children. He had been following the development of the film industry quite closely. The art of motion pictures grew into maturity during this age of silent films, and Joseph Quillan was ready to take advantage of this especially where his talented children were concerned.

Joseph made the rounds of many studios at first with no apparent success. Finally, he applied to Mack Sennett's Keystone Studio. Sennett (1880-1960), known in these days as the King of Comedy, was a Canadian-born Academy Award—winning director who was regarded as the inventor of slapstick comedy in film.[6] Quillan's application was accepted, and Edward and his four (4) siblings were given an audition. While watching the film tests, Eddie and his brothers were horrified and thinking the result terrible walked out. However, when Sennett watched the screen test, he was so impressed with Eddie that he went so far as hiring a private detective to find him.[7] At the time the family was touring throughout California as part of the Orpheum Circuit. When Sennett finally located him, Eddie was informed that he was the only one of the family to be accepted by the studio. Sennett signed him to a contract in 1922. Quillan's first film appearance was in the 1922 comedy short *Up and At 'Em*.[8]

A unique opportunity presented itself to Quillan in 1924 when he had an encounter with a stranded motorist. Quillan stopped to help a driver change a flat tire. Come to find out, the driver worked for Cecil B. DeMille and was so grateful to be rescued from his predicament that he arranged for Edward to take a screen test. Edward was subsequently signed to play a small part in the film *Should Husbands Marry?*[9] This connection with DeMille would prove to be fortuitous a few years later.

In 1925 Sennett signed Eddie for a one-picture deal: *The Love Sundae* (1926) opposite actress Alice Day. After the preview the picture was sent back to Pathé in New York so the studio heads could have a chance to examine Eddie's potential.[10] This company was founded in 1896 as

---

[6]   http://en.wikipedia.org/wiki/Mack_Sennett, 1.

[7]   Cedric Osmond, Birmingham, ed. *Stars of the Screen, 1931: A Volume of Biographies of Contemporary Actors and Actresses Engaged in photoplay throughout the World* (London: H. Joseph, 1930), 110.

[8]   http://www.answers.com/topic/eddie_quillan, 1.

[9]   http://www.cyranos.ch/sp.quil-e.htm, 1.

[10]   Ankerich, 251.

the Societe Pathé Frères by brothers Charles, Emile, Theophile, and Jacques Pathé in Paris, France. Expanding into the American market during the first part of the twentieth century Pathé, became the largest film equipment and production company in the world as well as a major producer of phonograph records.[11] Negotiations were begun, and Eddie was signed to a long-term contract with Sennett.

The relationship started smoothly enough but soured over the next few months. The first of two major disputes Eddie had with Sennett centered on his salary. Mr. Quillan thought Eddie was not earning enough from his contract, and he was upset with Sennett for covering up what he thought was a rather high cost of living in Hollywood. Sennett had promised that the cost of living would be not greater in California than in Pennsylvania—definitely a spurious claim. Quillan told Sennett that Eddie was going to have to earn more money or else he would sue. Sennett countered with the fact that he couldn't sue because Eddie was under contract. Finally under threat that Mr. Quillan would pack up and go back east with his talented son in tow, Sennett gave in and raised Eddie's salary from $65 a week to $175.[12] Things quieted down for a while.

[11]   http://en.wikipedia.org/wiki/Pathe, 1.

[12]   Ankerich, 251.

His next ten (10) film appearances were all comedy shorts that were vehicles for Day. During the course of the next three years, 1925-1928, Edward would go on to make nearly twenty (20) two-reelers with Sennett. He would spend much of the remaining years of the 1920s in comedy shorts featuring actresses Ruth Taylor and Madeline Hurlock.[13]

At first, Sennett tried to turn Quillan into a new Harry Langdon. Langdon (1884-1944), an American comedian, appeared in vaudeville, silent films, and talkies. He became a major star at Sennett's Keystone Studios. At the height of his film career he was considered one of the four (4) best comics of the silent film era along with Charlie Chaplin, Harold Lloyd, and Buster Keaton. His character was that of a childlike man with an innocent understanding of the world. He was a first-class pantomime whose classic expression consisted of the "dead pan," a weak smile, and owlish blink. Invariably he always appeared forlorn when

---

[13]   http://en.wikipedia.org/wiki/eddie_quillan, 1.

confronted with misfortunes—usually the domestic kind.[14] Quillan, being highly energetic, sharply comedic, and ever-smiling, did not fit this mold. Instead, he went on to establish himself quite successfully in lighthearted roles.

The next conflict with Sennett resulted in Eddie breaking his contract. The situation involved the script for one of Eddie's two-reel comedies, *Pass the Dumplings* (1926). When Eddie received the three-page outline of the story, there was something that he thought was a bit risqué. He felt it was out of character for his comedic role. Eddie went to Sennett and told him that he refused to play the particular scene the way it had been written. Mr. Quillan got involved and told Sennett basically that he didn't need a comedian to get a laugh with a dirty joke. Sennett was adamant and wouldn't budge this time. He ordered Eddie to do the scene. Eddie said he would do it but this would be the last picture he would do for him. When the picture was finished, he walked out, and that was the end of his career with Sennett.[15]

Quillan began to freelance. He starred in the comedy *A Little Bit of Everything* (1928), notable because it featured his siblings Marie, Joseph, and John in starring roles.[16] During this year, also, Cecil B. DeMille personally chose Eddie to add some comedic touches to *The Godless Girl*, which otherwise was a serious film dealing with high school atheist clubs and the treatment of teenage delinquents. Eddie was interested in playing the lead and auditioned for the part. The role he was subsequently offered was not a large one and was initially turned down by his father. After much negotiation, DeMille finally asked his screenwriter, Jeanie MacPherson, to extend the part to span the entire script. Once she accepted and the script was revised, Eddie accepted the part.[17] The film, as conceived and shot by DeMille, was a silent film, which began its principal photography in January of 1928 and was initially finished by early summer. During the actual filming of the picture Eddie, with his comedic strut and famous double take, continued to impress DeMille, who allowed him to improvise his own scenes. The practice was very rare in those days and almost nonexistent for DeMille, who liked full control. In October, with the popularity of talkies sweeping the country, Pathé executives called for the adding of dialogue to a number of sequences and for Fritz Feld to direct them.

---

[14]   *New York Times*, obituary, December 23, 1944, 18.

[15]   Ankerich, 251.

[16]   Wiki/eddie_quillan, 1.

[17]   Collura, 29.

This movie was Eddie's first feature-length film and a definite turning point in his career.[18]

During the time *The Godless Girl* went from being a silent movie to one with talking sequences, Eddie was cast in *Show Folks* (1928), a movie about a Broadway dancer who finds love and fame aided by the right dancing partner (Lina Basquette). Carole Lombard had a small role in the film as well. Eddie also was involved in the film *Geraldine* (1929), a story about a romantic triangle involving a lawyer, a tutor (Quillan), and a beautiful student (Marion Nixon). Both films contained some dialogue that ran throughout the pictures.[19] Silent films formed the majority of features produced in both 1927 and 1928.

Show Folks can be considered Quillan's first major screen credit and enjoyed modest success. The film had a talking sequence directed by a stage director brought in from New York to the West Coast especially for the sequence that involved Quillan and Lombard. Eddie has this to say about the scene:

> In the scene, Carole Lombard had just left me, and I was very upset, pacing up and down the floor. The director was telling me how the scene should be recorded. I disagreed and asked him if he had seen the other scenes of the picture. He said he had, and I asked him why he was asking me to play the part that wasn't my character at all. I told him I wasn't changing it just because we were talking. And I didn't. That was the only time I ran into a problem with a director coming in and directing only one segment of a picture.[20]

While Eddie was in the middle of filming *Show Folks*, DeMille left Pathé and joined MGM. Consequently Eddie's contract with DeMille was transferred to Pathé Studios. He was signed to a long-term contract at which point he began to be offered roles that were increasingly varied.

Nosy Neighbors (1929), a good-natured comedy, directed by Paul Bern, came out a few months after *The Godless Girl* and was essentially a non-talkie with only a few audible lines thrown in for effect. The film is notable because it featured most of the Quillan clan as inheritors of a Southern plantation and the unwilling participants in a hillbilly feud.

---

18   Ankerich, 253.

19   Collura, 29.

20   Ankerich, 253.

His sister Marie, who would eventually begin a film career of her own, appeared opposite her brother in the film. This was the last time Eddie would work professionally with his mother and father.[21]

Silent film actors traditionally emphasized body language and facial expression so that the audience could understand the emotions involved in the screen portrayal. Many times this style resulted in overacting and the overall effect melodramatic. By the midtwenties, however, many American silent films had adopted a more naturalistic acting style.[22] Eddie, with his low-key approach and subtlety of expression, adapted well to this style. This fact would allow him to segue into talkies with minimum difficulty.

Commercialization of sound cinema began in the United States in the mid- to late 1920s. The first feature film originally presented as a talkie was *The Jazz Singer*, released in October 1927. The motion picture was a tremendous box office success, due in no small part to Al Jolson who was already one of America's biggest stars. The gross earnings totaled $2.2 million in the United States and abroad. This was a turning point for the film industry proving that sound technology was worth the investment.[23]

By the early thirties talkies were a global phenomena. In the United States they helped secure Hollywood's position as one of the world's most powerful cultural commercial systems. While the introduction of sound led to a boom in the movie industry, it had an adverse effect on the employability of many Hollywood actors of the time. Those without stage experience were regarded negatively by the studios. Those whose heavy accents or unpleasant speaking voices had been concealed in the silent era were particularly at risk. Audiences now began to look at certain silent-era stars as old-fashioned, their style outmoded. Many of the new medium's biggest stars came from vaudeville and musical theater such as Jolson, Cantor, MacDonald, the Marx Brothers, Cagney, and Joan Blondell.[24] Eddie, as an established character actor, was on the cutting edge of the new industry and was primed to succeed.

Eddie made his all-talkie debut in *The Sophomore* (1929), with Sally O'Neill. Because of his stage experience and vocal training Eddie made an easy transition into sound. He claimed he had few reservations about it and didn't need to change his style because that was the way

---

[21]   Collura, 29-30.

[22]   http://en.wikipedia.org/wiki/silent_film, 2-3.

[23]   http://en.wikipedia.org/wiki/sound_film, 1, 7.

[24]   Wiki/sound_film, 15.

he worked. Eddie did feel that the sound technicians could be a bit unnerving. He has this to say:

> The sound men were the ones who were the gods in those days. They were in a place that looked like a big ice box. We would do a scene, and everybody would look toward that big green monster. The door would open, and we would hear, "No good for sound," and then we'd have to do it over again until it was right.[25]

One of his first talkies, *Big Money* (1930), was one of his favorite films. The story concerned a brokerage house messenger who gets mixed up with gamblers and a murder. Eddie felt the role stretched him not just as a comedian but as a serious actor.[26]

On January 29, 1931, RKO Pictures gained control of the Pathé Exchange, which included Pathé's Culver City studio and all its contract players. Afterwards known as RKO Pathé, it functioned for a short time as a separate entity within the greater RKO Corporation. Then in 1932, in an effort to curb financial losses, David O. Selznick, production chief, merged RKO Radio and RKO Pathé into a singular unit. Although extensive layoffs and salary cuts occurred during the Selznick regime, Eddie Quillan remained on the payroll and for a while continued to be seen in some of that studio's few money-making productions of the very early thirties.

Eddie remained a popular leading and secondary actor throughout the sound film era. He became a favorite in supporting roles throughout the 1930s and 1940s. He appeared in such outstanding films as 1932's *Girl Crazy*, in which he plays the hero and sings the popular Gershwin ballad "But Not For Me." More often than not, however, Quillan alternated between starring in inexpensive features and being cast in supporting parts, mostly through loan-out deals with bigger studios, particularly Paramount and MGM.[27]

The role for which Eddie is probably best known is Tommy Elison, the most endearing and tragic character of the ill-fated crew, in the movie, *Mutiny on the Bounty* (MGM, 1935). This film starred Clark Gable, Charles Laughton, and Franchot Tone. Eddie said of working with Gable:

25   Ankerich, 254.
26   Ibid., 255.
27   Collura, 29.

> There have been a lot of idols, but to me, Clark Gable was the greatest. Not only did the women like him, but the men liked him also. He had a great following with men. He was down-to-earth and was all man. Working with him was a lot of fun. I liked him tremendously.[28]

Eddie's overall performance was very well received in the Unites States. He received the Box Office Blue Ribbon Award and the Screen Actors Guild Award. It was the first time that SAG had given the award to an actor in a supporting role.[29] Eddie had the good fortune to work with many excellent directors, but his favorite was Frank Lloyd, who like his parents was born in Scotland. Lloyd had purchased the rights to *Mutiny on the Bounty* hoping to play Captain Bligh himself. He settled into his director role quite easily and created a classic.

During this period Eddie was panned by critics only once when he was cast as master sleuth Ellery Queen in *The Mandarin Mystery* (1937). Critics felt casting Quillan was a fatal mistake. Although the film contained the original structure of the book, *The Chinese Orange Mystery*, the general consensus of film reviewers was that the script was played for laughs, and childish acting by Quillan and ineffective direction by Ralph Staub brought the first series of Ellery Queen films to a halt. A heavily edited version for television was subsequently developed but experienced no more success than the film.[30]

John Ford next cast Eddie in *Young Mr. Lincoln* (1939), as Adam Clay, a boy accused of murder, who, along with his brother, Matt, is defended by an affable new attorney (Henry Fonda as Lincoln) and saved from hanging. Eddie had this to say about Ford:

> Some directors would do things to upset you so that they'd get the desired feeling they wanted for a particular scene. In John Ford's case, it was a very deliberate thing. Generally a low-key person, he had a way of manipulating people without coming right out and verbally attacking them, although he could do that too.[31]

---

[28]   Ankerich, 255.

[29]   Collura, 30.

[30]   http://www.rediscovery.us/ellery/movies.html, 2.

[31]   Collura, 30.

Eddie felt that working with Henry Fonda was a joy. He was lucky enough to have the opportunity to do it once more in John Ford's 1940's film adaptation of the John Steinbeck novel, *The Grapes of Wrath* playing the role of Connie Rivers, a radio mechanic.[32] One other notable dramatic performance of this time for Eddie was in David Selznick's *Made for Each Other* (1939). He starred along with Carole Lombard and James Stewart. *Weekly Variety* called him "superb as the daring aviator who brings serum to dying child."[33]

Eddie spent a good part of the 1940s at Universal. Quillan's appealing personality was seen in "B" musicals, comedies, and even serials during the 1940s. So-called B movies identified a film intended for distribution as the less-publicized bottom half of a double feature. Early "B" movies were often part of a series in which the star repeatedly played the same character. Almost always shorter than the top-billed films they were paired with, many had running times of seventy (70) minutes or less.[34] A decided break for Eddie from these films was the unique opportunity of performing in the film *It Ain't Hay* (1943) opposite the comedic duo Abbott and Costello.[35]

Following World War II, Hollywood cut back on its output of films. Eddie found himself less in demand by the studios. Discouraged at playing simple roles such as bellhops and soda jerks, Quillan continued for a short time in motion pictures until *Sensation Hunters* (1946), when his film career waned. Leaving the industry entirely, he owned and operated a bowling alley in El Monte for a period of time.[36]

In 1948 Columbia Pictures producer Jules White managed to lure him back to movies, teaming him together with veteran movie comic Wally Vernon for a series of comedy short subjects. From 1948 through 1956 Eddie co-starred with Vernon in a series of sixteen (16) two-reel comedies, which highlighted the physical dexterity of both men. White accentuated extreme physical comedy in these films, and Vernon and Quillan made a good team, as they were particularly suited to slapstick.[37]

During his film career Eddie worked with the screen's greatest stars. Along with the actors previously mentioned, he worked with Spencer

32   http://movies.msn.com/celebrities/celebrity-biography/eddie-quillan/, 1.
33   Collura, 30.
34   http://en.wikipedia.org/wiki/Pathe, 1.
35   Movies.msn.com, 1.
36   Collura, 31.
37   Collura, 31-2.

Tracy in *Big City* (1937), John Wayne in *Allegheny Uprising* (1939), Marlene Dietrich in *The Flame of New Orleans* (1941), and Robert Mitchum in *Follow the Band* (1943).[38]

Quillan was also engaged for smaller parts in the following decades. One notable appearance was his role of Sandy in the 1954 Vincente Minnelli musical *Brigadoon*, starring Gene Kelly, Van Johnson, and Cyd Charisse. Eddie would work with Doris Day and James Garner in *Move over Darling* (1963). Quillan also appeared in the role of Mr. Cassidy in the 1969 Gene Kelly film adaptation of *Hello, Dolly!* starring Barbra Streisand, Walter Matthau, and featuring Louis Armstrong. Eddie worked off and on in films throughout the sixties and occasionally into the seventies. Fluff roles also came his way with *The Ghost and Mr. Chicken* (1965), *Angel in My Pocket* (1969), and *How to Frame a Figg* (1971).[39]

In addition to his film work in the fifties, Eddie began to work in television when he was offered the chance to work with Jackie Cooper in *The People's Choice*. Once beginning his television career, Eddie would appear in over two hundred (200) television programs. He had roles in a multitude of TV series: *I Love Lucy*, *The Jack Benny Show*, *Perry Mason*, *Daniel Boone*, *The Man from U.N.C.L.E.*, *The Addams Family*, *The Wild, Wild West*, *Andy Griffith*, and *Petticoat Junction*.[40]

His brother, Joe, was a well-known comedy writer in radio and television, known for his contributions to the *Our Miss Brooks* radio and TV show. It was through Joe that Eddie met Hal Kanter who would cast him years later in his first recurring role in a network series, *Valentine's Day*, starring Tony Franciosa.[41] In 1968, Kanter made Eddie a series regular in *Julia*, starring Diahann Carroll.

In the 1970s Quillan made guest appearances on such television series as *Mannix*, *Chico and the Man*, *Baretta*, *Lucas Tanner*, and *Police Story*. After meeting and befriending actor and director Michael Landon, he played numerous bit roles in the television series *Little House on the Prairie*. During this decade he was seen rarely in the movies. His last movie was *The Strongest Man in the World* (1975).

Quillan remained active into the 1980s on television. He appeared in *Moonlighting* and *The A Team*. He was also seen in the Landon-directed

---

[38]   Ankerich, 255.

[39]   Collura, 31.

[40]   Ankerich, 256.

[41]   Collura, 31.

series *Highway to Heaven* and *Father Murphy*. He made his last television appearance in a 1987 episode of the crime-mystery series *Matlock*.[42]

In his retirement years, Eddie continued to lead an active life enjoying golf, bowling, and swimming. A lifelong bachelor, he lived in North Hollywood with his two sisters, Peggy and Roseanne. He became a favorite interview subject for film historians thanks to his congeniality and the clarity of his recall. He was pleased that his films were being shown in film revivals and on television and thrilled to be remembered by the younger generation who kept his desk filled with letters. Eddie said, "It's probably because the movies we made then were so much better than those of today."[43] When asked about the Golden Days of Hollywood (1930-1955), he cites the family atmosphere that was generated between contract players and the camaraderie of those working in the major studios. He thought the closest he had experienced it in television had been on the Hal Kanter, Michael Landon, and Robert Blake shows.[44]

Cancer claimed his life in July 1990. His *Los Angeles Times* obituary published July 25, 1990, describes him as an "actor who played young heroes and boys next door" in some of Hollywood's most memorable motion pictures. He was interred at the San Fernando Mission Cemetery in Mission Hills, Los Angeles, California.[45]

By today's standards the fact that Eddie Quillan worked so successfully in the entertainment industry for over sixty years is truly amazing. Longevity is a quality to be sought and rarely attained. The emphasis on craft rather than stardom or financial gain has slowly diminished over the course of time. However, one fact remains constant. A passion for the art is essential for endurance. Looking back over Eddie's career, we see many reasons for his success—some personal, some professional—but over it all is this passion for his craft. In the course of an interview he was asked, as he was on many occasions, for the secret to his professional longevity, Eddie answered,

I love my work, and I will stay with it as long as I am able.[46]

[42]   Ibid.
[43]   Ankerich, 257.
[44]   Collura, 31.
[45]   Strassel, Stephanie. "Eddie Quillan—Acting Career Spanned 60 Years," *Los Angeles Times*, July 24, 1990. Issue CIX, 20:1.
[46]   Ken D. Jones, Arthur F. McClure, and Alfred E. Twomey, *More Character People* (New Jersey: Citadel Press, 1984), 17-19.

Bibliography

Books

Ankerich, Michael G. *Broken Silence, Conversations with 23 Film Stars.* North Carolina: McFarland & Company, 1993.

Birmingham, Cedric Osmond, ed. *Stars of the Screen, 1931: A Volume of Biographies of Contemporary Actors and Actresses Engaged in Photoplay throughout the World.* London: H. Joseph, 1930.

Crafton, Donald. *The Talkies: American Cinema's Transition to Sound (1926-1931).* New York: Scribner's Sons, 1997.

Cullen, F., F. Hackman, and D. McNeilly. "Vaudeville History" in *Vaudeville, Old and New: An Encyclopedia of Variety Performers in America.* xi-xxxi. London: Routledge, 2007.

Jones, Ken D., Arthur F. McClure, and Alfred E. Twomey. *More Character People.* New Jersey: Citadel Press, 1984.

Magill, Frank N. *Magill's Cinema Annual 1992. A Survey of the Films of 1991.* CA: Salem Press, 1992.

McClure, Arthur F., Alfred E. and Twomey. *The Versatiles: A Study of Supporting Character Actors and Actresses in the American Motion Picture, 1930-1955.* New Jersey: A. S. Barnes, 1969.

Mitchell, Glenn. *A-Z of Silent Film Comedy, an Illustrated Companion.* London: B. T. Batsford Limited, 1998.

Parkinson, David. *History of Film.* New York: Thames & Hudson, 1995.

Tosches, Nick. *Where Dead Voices Gather.* Boston: Back Bay Books, 2002.

Trav, S. D. *No Applause—Just Throw Money. The Book That Made Vaudeville Famous.* New York: Faber & Faber, 2005.

Articles

Ankerich, Michael F. "Reel Stars: A Double Take with Eddie Quillan," *Classic Images.* April 1989. Issue 170, pp. 8, 10.

Collura, Joe. "Eddie Quillan: Mr. Personality," *Classic Images.* April 1987. Issue 142, pp. 29-31.

"Eddie Quillan," *Motion Picture World.* September 10, 1927, p. 93.

"Eddie Quillan, Actor, 83." *New York Times.* July 25, 1990, p. 18:1.

Magliozzi, Ronal S., and Charles L. Turner. "Witnessing the development of independent film culture in New York: An Interview with Charles Turner." *Film History Journal.* Bloomington, Indiana: Indiana University Press, 2000. Volume 12, Number 1, pp. 72-91.

Strassel, Stephanie. "Eddie Quillan—Acting Career Spanned 60 Years," *Los Angeles Times*. July 24, 1990. Issue CIX, p. 20:1.

Internet Websites

http://en.wikipedia.org/wiki/Eddie_Quillan
http://en.wikipedia.org/wiki/Mack_Sennett
http://en.wikipedia.org/wiki/Pathe
http://en.wikipedia.org/wiki/silent_film
http://en.wikipedia.org/wiki/sound_film
http://en.wikipedia.org/wiki/vaudeville
www.film.virtual_history.com/person.php?personid=960
www.movies.msn.com/celebrities/celebrity-biography/eddie_quillan
www.printable.pro.imdb.com/name/nm0703600/bio
www.answers.com/topic/eddie_quillan
www.cyranos.ch/spquil-e.htm
www.hollywood.com/celebrity/192582/Eddie_Quillan
ww.imdb.com/name/nm0703600
www.imdb.com/name/nm0703600/publicity
www.nytimes.com/1990/07/25
obituaries/eddie_quillan-actor-83-html?pagewanted=1
www.rediscovery.us/ellery/movies.html

Filmography*

Title	Year	Role
A Love Sundae	1926	
The Ghost of Folly	1926	
Puppy Lovetime	1926	Eddie
Alice Be Good	1926	
Her Actor Friend	1926	
The Perils of Petersboro	1926	
Should Husbands Marry?	1926	
Hesitating Horses	1926	
Kitty from Killarney	1926	
Pass the Dumplings	1927	
The Plumbers' Daughter	1927	
Catalina, Here I Come	1927	Eddie
The College Kiddo	1927	
The Golf Nut	1927	
For Sale, a Bungalow	1927	
Ain't Nature Grand	1927	

The Bull Fighter	1927	
Red Hot Bullets	1927	
Love in a Police Station	1927	
A Little Bit of Everything	1928	Eddie Quillan and Family
Show Folks	1928	Eddie Kehoe
Geraldine	1929	Eddie Able
Noisy Neighbors	1929	Eddie Van Revel
The Godless Girl	1929	Samuel "Bozo" Johnson—The Goat
The Sophomore	1929	Joe Collins
Night Work	1930	Willie
Big Money	1930	Eddie
Stout Hears and Willing Hands	*1931*	
Sweepstakes	1931	Bud Doyle
The Tip-Off	1931	Thomas "Tommy" Jordan
The Big Shot	1931	Ray Smith
Girl Crazy	1932	Danny Churchill
Strictly Personal	1933	Andy
Broadway to Hollywood	1933	Ted Hackett III
Meet the Baron	1933	Dock Extra
Hollywood Party	1934	Bob Benson
Gridiron Flash	1934	Thomas Burke
Mutiny on the Bounty	1935	Ellison
The Gentleman from Louisiana	1935	Tod Mason
The Mandarin Mystery	1936	Ellery Queen
London by Night	1937	Bill Hawkins
Big City	1937	Mike Edwards
Swing, Sister, Swing	1938	Chuck "Satchel Lips" Peters
Made for Each Other	1939	Conway
The Family Next Door	1939	Sammy
The Flying Irishman	1939	Henry Corrigan
Young Mr. Lincoln	1939	Adam Clay
Hawaiian Nights	1939	Ray Peters
Allegheny Uprising	1939	Will Anderson
The Grapes of Wrath	1940	Connie Rivers
La Conga Nights	1940	Titus Endover
Margie	1940	Joe
Dancing on a Dime	1940	Jack Norcross
Dark Street of Cairo	1940	Jerry Jones
Where Did You Get That Girl?	1941	Joe Olsen
Six Lessons from Madame	1941	Skat
The Flame of New Orleans	1941	Third Sailor

Too Many Blondes	1941	Wally Pelton
Flying Blind	1941	Riley
Kid Glove Killer	1942	Eddie Wright
Priorities on Parade	1942	"Sticks"
It Ain't Hay	1943	Harry the Horse
Follow the Band	1943	Marvin Howe
Alaska Highway	1943	Pompadour "Shorty" Jones
Melody Parade	1943	Jimmy Tracey
Here Comes Kelly	1943	James Aloysius "Jimmy" Kelly
Hi ya, Sailor	1943	Corky Mills
The Imposter	1944	Cochery
Hi, Good Lookin'!	1944	Dynamo Carson
This Is the Life	1944	Gus
Slightly Terrific	1944	Charlie Young
Twilight on the Prairie	1944	Phil
Dixie Jamoboree	1944	Jeff Calhoun
Moonlight and Cactus	1944	Stubby Lamont Jr.
Dark Mountain	1944	Willis Dinsmore
The Mystery of the Riverboat	1944	Jug Jenks
Jungle Queen	1944	Chuck Kelly
Song of the Sarong	1945	Tony Romans
Jungle Raiders	1945	Joe Riley
Sensation Hunters	1945	Ray Lawson
A Guy Could Change	1946	George Cummings
A-Hunting They Did Go	1948	
Crabbin' In The Cabin	1948	
Parlor, Bedroom and Wrath	1948	
Let Down Your Aerial	1949	Eddie
Sideshow	1950	Big Top
House About It	1950	Eddie
He Flew the Shrew	1951	Eddie
Fun on the Run	1951	
A Fool and His Honey	1952	Eddie
Heebie Gee-Gees	1952	Eddie
Stop, Look, and Listen	1952	
He Popped His Pistol	1953	
Doggie in the Bedroom	1954	
Brigadoon	1954	Sandy
His Pest Friend	1955	Eddie
Nobody's Home	1955	Eddie
He Took A Powder	1955	Eddie

Come on Seven	1956	Eddie
Richard Diamond	1957	1 episode—Mel Jones
The Bob Cummings Show	1958	1 episode—"Bob in Orbit," Sergeant
The Texan	1959	1 episode—"The Smiling Loser," Slick Parker
Law of the Plainsman	1959	1 episode—Horace Arnold
The Alaskans	1959	1 episode—"Contest at Gold Bottom," Kid Johns
77 Sunset Strip	1960	1 episode—"The One That Got Away," Inspector Ferguson
The Real McCoys	1958-	0 2 episodes—"The Talk of the Town"/"The Honeymoon," Bellboy
The Dennis O'Keefe Show	1960	1 episode—"Send This Boy to Camp," George Martin
Lock Up	1960	1 episode—"Top Secret," Switzer
The Jack Benny Program	1961	1 episode—"Jack Goes to Las Vegas"
Surfside 6	1961	1 episode—"Little Mister Kelly," Chuck
Death Valley Days	1961	2 episodes—"Trial by Feat," Hill Benehy/"Gamle with Death," Job
87th Precinct	1961	1 episode—"The Modus Man," Blinky Smith
Mister Ed	1961	1 episode—"Ed the Hero," Photographer
Hennessey	1962	1 episode—"Close Enough for Jazz," Ticket Taker
Pete and Gladys	1962	1 episode—"The Chocolate Cake Caper," Lennie
My Three Sons	1962	1 episode—"The Kibitzers," Mr. Hewlitt
Checkmate	1962	1 episode—"Side by Side," Willie the Barber
The Lucy Show	1962	1 episode—Vincent
Bonanza	1962	1 episode—"Ride the Wind," Danny Culp
The Rifleman	1962	2 episodes—"Conflict"/"Mark's Rifle," Angus Evans
Who's Got the Action?	1962	1 episode—Dingo, the Telephone Repairman
McHale's Navy	1963	1 episode—"One of Our Engines Is Missing," Sailor
Papa's Delicate Condition	1963	
Come Blow Your Horn	1963	Elevator Boy
Summer Magic	1963	Mailman
Promises! Promises!	1963	Bartender
Hazel	1963	1 episode—"You Ain't Fully Dressed Without a Smile"
Gunfight at Comanche Creek	1963	Steven's House Desk Clerk
Glynis	1963	1 episode—"The Pros and Cons," Eddie
Take Her, She's Mine	1963	Gateman
Move Over, Darling	1963	Bellboy
Viva Las Vegas	1964	Master of Ceremonies
Petticoat Junction	1964-4	2 episodes—"The Genghis KIeane Story," Mort/"Spur Line," Dick
Advance to the Rear	1964	Sergeant Smitty
No Time for Sergeants	1964	1 episode—"The Permanent Recruit," Cook

The Bill Dana Show	1964	1 episode—"Laughing Gas"
Valentine's Day	1964	2 episodes—"Fraudulent Female"/"The Life You Save Is Yours." Grover Cleveland Fipple
Burke's Law	1964-5	2 episodes—"Who Killed Mother Goose?"/"Who Killed ½ of Glory Lee?" Amos Burke, Secret Agent
Zebra in the Kitchen	1965	
The Bounty Killer	1965	Pianist
Vacation Playhouse	1965	1 episode—"Cap'n Ahab," Emcee
The Andy Griffith Show	1965	1 episode—"The Taylors in Hollywood," Bell Hop
The Ghost and Mr. Chicken	1966	Elevator Operator
The Addams Family	1964-6	5 episodes—"The Addams Policy"/"Morticia, The Decorator", Joe Digby/"Gomez, the People's Choice," Clyde Arbogast/"Crisis in the Addams Family," Horace Beesley/"Gomez, the Politician," George Bass
Frankie and Johnny	1968	Cashier
Perry Mason	1961-6	3 episodes—"The Case of the Misguided Model," agent/"The Case of The Captains' Coins," Photographer/"The Case of the Cowardly Lion," Bookkeeper Keller
The Man from U.N.C.L.E.	1967	1 episode—"The Yo-Ho-Ho and a Bottle of Rum Affair," Scotty MacPherson
Batman	1967	1 episode—"Batman's Anniversary," Newsie
It's About Time	1967	1 episode—"To Sign or Not To Sign," McAllister
Eight on the Lam	1967	Car Dealer
A Guide for the Married Man	1967	Cologne Salesman
Cimarron Strip	1967	1 episode—"Till the End of Night," Guard
The Big Valley	1967	1 episode—"Night of the Executioner," Hotel Clerk
Wicked Dreams of Paula Schultz	1968	Man on Bicycle
Gomer Pyle, U.S.M.C.	1967-8	2 episodes—"Goodbye, Dolly," Bill/"Lou-Ann Poovie Sings No More"
Did You Hear the One About The Traveling Saleslady	1968	Salesman
The Good Guys	1968	1 episode—Episode no. 1/5, Man
The Guns of Will Sonnett	1967-9	3 episodes—"Trail's End"/"A Difference of Opinion," Desk Clerk/"And a Killing Rode Into Town—Hotel Desk Clerk

The Wild, Wild West	1967-9	2 episodes—"The Night of the Sabatini Death," Snidley/"The Night of the Cut Throats," Hogan
The Virginian	1969	1 episode—"The Girl in the Shadows," Edmunds
Angel in My Pocket	1969	Reverend Beckwith
Hello, Dolly!	1969	Mr. Cassidy
Daniel Boone	1966-70	5 episodes—"Nobless Oblige," Proprietor/"Then Who Will They Hang from the Yardarm if Willy Gets Away," Mr. Stokey/"The Enchanted Gun," Higgens/"First in War, First in Peace," Inn Landlord/"The Accused," Ephraim Smith
Over-the Hill Gang Rides Again	1970	Silver Dollar Bartender
How to Frame a Figg	1971	Old Man
Love American Style	1971	1 episode—"Love and Formula 26B"/"Love and the Loud Mouth"/"Love and the Penal Code"
Me and the Chimp	1972	1 episode—Mike's Day with Buttons
Adam-12	1972	1 episode—"The Tip," TJ
Columbo	1972	1 episode—"Short Fuse," Ferguson
The Jimmy Stewart Show	1972	1 episode—"Song of the Jailbird," Burglar
The F.B.I.	1972	1 episode—"The Deadly Species," Amos Wick
Now You See Him Now You Don't	1972	Charlie, School Custodian
The Judge and Jake Wyler	1972	Billy Lambert
Incident on a Dark Street	1973	Security Guard
She Lives!	1973	Janitor
Griff	1973	1 episode—"All the Lonely People," Tompkins
Hitchhike	1974	Counterman
Here's Lucy	1970-4	2 episodes—"Lucy Fights the System," Mr. Jackson/"Lucy, the Part-Time Wife," Cab Driver
Melvin Purvis G-Man	1974	Hotel Clerk
Gunsmoke	1971-4	2 episodes—"The Tarnished Badge"/"Lynott," Barkeep
The Strongest Man in the World	1975	Mr. Willoughby
Mannix	1973-5	2 episodes—"Search for a Dead Man," Willie/"To Quote a Dead Man," Informant Hobo
Lucas Tanner	1974-5	3 episodes—"One to One"/"Shattered"/"Pay the Two Dollars," Mr. Krebbs
Harry and Maggie	1975	Max Lovechild
The Streets of San Francisco	1975	1 episode—"Runaway," Timkins

Chico and the Man	1977	1 episode—"The Black Tie Blues," Bum
The Banana Company	1977	Sebring
Police Woman	1977	1 episode—"Merry Christmas," Waldo
Mad Bull	1977	Rafferty
Mr. Too Little	1977	Concessionaire
Baretta	1978	1 episode—"Why Me?"
The Darker Side of Terror	1979	Watchman
Kaz	1979	1 episode—"The Avenging Angel"
ABC Afterschool Specials	1979	1 episode—"A Special Gift"
The Jeffersons	1980	1 episode—"The Loan," Guard
For the Love of It	1980	
Here's Boomer	1982	1 episode—"Flatfoots," Arthur
Father Murphy	1982	1 episode—"John Michael Murphy, RIP," Grizzly
Little House on the Prairie	1977-80	7 episodes—"For the Love of Blanche—Buffalo Bill Days of Sunshine, Days of Shadow, Part I," Old Timer/ "The In-Laws," Kavendish/"The Return of Mr. Edwards," Shorty/"Someone Please Love Me," Gargan (2 more)
Hardcastle and McCormick	1985	1 episode—Surprise on Seagull Beach
Hell Town	1985	Smitty
Hell Town	1985	7 episodes—"One Ball"/"The One Called Daisy"/"Stumpy Boy"/ "I Will Abide"/"Fast Louie," Poco Loco (2 more)
Moonlighting	1985	1 episode—"In God We Strongly Suspect," Abbie
Highway to Heaven	1984-8	3 episodes—"Basinger's New York," Bart/"Tramp"/ "Highway to Heaven, Part 1-2," Clyde
The A Team	1986	1 episode—"The Grey Team," Old Man
Matlock	1987	1 episode—"The Author," David Sears

*http://www.imdb.com/name/nm0703600/

Fred Astaire: The Perfect Leap from Stage to Screen

Howard Oboler

Fred Astaire is a name that will always be synonymous with grace, elegance, charm, and, of course, dance. Although he is first and foremost remembered as one the greatest dancers of all time, he was also a highly accomplished choreographer, singer, and actor. His notable career on the stage and subsequent success in Hollywood films encompassed a total of seventy-six years! In studying how Fred Astaire became both a stage and film legend, one should first understand the role his parents played in fostering his dancing and singing skills and those of his older sister, Adele.

Fred Astaire was born in 1899 to Johanna and Frederic Austerlitz in Omaha, Nebraska. Mr. Austerlitz worked in Omaha at a brewery after emigrating from Austria in 1892. Johanna Austerlitz was of German ancestry but born in the United States. When the Austerlitz children revealed a natural talent for dancing and singing, they were given formal training and their mother began to dream about their becoming a vaudeville team. Her dream became more of a reality in 1904 when Mr. Austerlitz lost his job and she decided to move to New York City with the goal of launching a show business career for Fred and Adele. Although Fred Astaire never spoke disparagingly about his parents, one might assume that his mother had something in common with the strong-willed stage mother of June Havoc and Gypsy Rose Lee. Like her, Johanna Austerlitz was determined that her two talented children would succeed in show business. The surname "Astaire" was given to the Austerlitz children by their parents in 1905 when Fred and Adele were taking dancing and singing lessons that focused on their developing a vaudeville act. Their teacher suggested the name change because he thought Austerlitz was an unsuitable name for the stage. Astaire was derived from L'Astaire—a family surname. Apart from seemingly an elegant modification of "Austerlitz," the name "Astaire" summons up visions of the moon (i.e., the moon goddess Astarte) and stars. In light of the high level of success the Astaires were to achieve, a more apt surname could not have been chosen.

Fred and Adele's first vaudeville act finally came into being and was called "Juvenile Artists Presenting an Electric Musical Toe-Dancing Novelty." It debuted in 1911 in Keyport, New Jersey, where the brother-and-sister team was well-received by the local newspaper critic. It is interesting to note that in his first appearance on stage, the preteen Fred Astaire wore a top hat and tails—an outfit that was to become his signature look in films. Indeed, Astaire became so closely identified with wearing formal attire in his films that a song "Top Hat, White Tie and Tails" was specifically written for him by Irving Berlin for the 1936 film *Top Hat.*

With the aid of their father's salesmanship and the unique nature of their act, the Astaire children began to enjoy vaudeville bookings in major cities throughout the United States. However, because the older Adele had grown almost three inches taller than Fred, and in order to abide by the child labor laws in effect, the Astaire team was obliged to take a two-year break from appearing on the vaudeville circuit. Albeit they did not perform before audiences for nearly two years, Fred and Adele nevertheless continued to enhance their dancing skills; tap dancing, the tango, the waltz, and other popular ballroom dances were incorporated into their act. Given their past record of success on the vaudeville circuit and the more sophisticated nature of their revised dance routines, the now-adult Astaires were finally offered the opportunity to make their debut on the Broadway stage in the 1917 patriotic revue *Over the Top.* This was followed by *The Passing Show of 1918, For Goodness Sake* (1922), and then by two memorable George and Ira Gershwin book musicals, *Lady be Good* (1924) and *Funny Face* (1927). The last three shows also gave Fred and Adele Astaire the opportunity to appear in the subsequent London stage productions. Their first appearance on the London stage was in 1923 when their

Broadway hit *For Goodness Sake* was successfully transferred across the Atlantic with the new title "Stop Flirting."

Fred and Adele Astaire essentially performed on stage as serio-comedic dancers. Even when they weren't cast in the roles of brother and sister, their dances together rarely, if ever, had any amorous overtones. Thus, romantic ballads like "'S Wonderful" from *Funny Face* were usually performed by Adele with the show's other male lead or by Astaire with a dance partner other than Adele. In some instances, a romantic dance number would not be performed by either of the Astaires (e.g., "Dancing in the Dark" was performed by Tilly Losch as a solo in *The Band Wagon*).

By the late twenties, the Astaires had not only won the hearts of critics and theatergoers on both sides of the Atlantic but Fred Astaire was also acknowledged to be one of the world's greatest tap dancers. Although Fred's dancing skill now outshone that of his sister Adele, she still drew audience and critical acclaim because he fashioned the team's choreography to ensure that Adele was given equal attention. Many dance historians who have charted Fred Astaire's career consider Adele to be the best partner he ever had. Not only was she a marvelous dancer but her long slim legs, striking dark eyes, and bright smile added immeasurably to her overall stage presence. It is interesting to note that while Fred and Adele Astaire were perfectly matched on-stage, their offstage personalities clearly differed. Specifically, Adele was open, flirty, fun-loving, and known to have a saucy tongue. Fred, on the other hand, was private and reserved and always made an effort to keep his personal life away from the eyes of the press.

After *Funny Face* completed its run, the Astaires were summoned to Hollywood by Paramount studios for a screen test. However, despite their success on the stage, they were not considered suitable for films. Undaunted, they returned to Broadway and appeared with Marilyn Miller in the 1930 musical *Smiles*. This was followed by one of their biggest hits, *The Band Wagon*, a revue with music and lyrics by Dietz and Schwartz. The show's score included the incomparable "Dancing in the Dark" and "I Love Louisa." The comedians, Frank Morgan and Helen Broderick, and the ballet dancer, Tilly Losch, were also featured in this landmark musical.

Unfortunately, *The Band Wagon* would prove to be the last time that Fred and Adele Astaire would appear together. They split as a team in 1932 when Adele married an English nobleman, Lord Charles Cavendish, and chose to retire from the musical stage. Adele had become somewhat bored with performing on the stage, and the lure of joining the ranks of the British aristocracy became more enticing to her than the world of the theater. The closest Adele Astaire came to returning to the world of musical entertainment occurred in 1937. At that time, she started filming a movie in England with Maurice Chevalier and the English musical stage star Jack Buchanan. However, she considered her performance to be unsatisfactory and withdrew after two days of filming. One may assume that Adele's freedom from the rigors of professional dancing for five years and the lack of her brother as a dance partner strongly contributed to her decision. Adele Astaire was not about to risk incurring her brother's ridicule or jeopardize her highly regarded professional reputation.

While Astaire had to adjust to the trauma of losing the dance partner with whom he was so comfortable and closely identified, he was now also free of the limitations imposed by dancing with his sister. Specifically, he could now pursue a more romantic pairing with a new dance partner. In 1932, he did just that when he appeared on the Broadway and London stage with Claire Luce in *Gay Divorce*. Ms. Luce was an attractive, sexy blonde who later acted in straight plays. The music and lyrics were by Cole Porter, and the highlight of the show was the "Night and Day" dance sequence for which Astaire created the choreography. The popularity of this legendary song and the romantic dance Astaire and Luce performed to its strains are cited as the key reasons for the show achieving a respectable run of 248 performances since it did not receive enthusiastic reviews. More importantly, *Gay Divorce* marked Astaire's last appearance on the stage because Hollywood ultimately became more artistically and financially rewarding for him than Broadway.

By 1933, the Great Depression had the United States and the rest of world firmly in its grip. Even though the theatre, and particularly theatrical musicals, provided the American public with an opportunity to forget its cares for a few hours, the theatre had two obvious drawbacks: it was a relatively expensive source of escape, and it was generally based in large cities. Movies, on the other hand, offered a more viable opportunity for escape because they were less expensive to attend, and movie theatres existed in countless locales throughout the United States. With the advent of talking pictures, movie studios were constantly seeking new talent, particularly singers and dancers. Consequently, Astaire was again requested to come to Hollywood for a screen test. This time it was at the behest of David O. Selznick who was then the head of RKO Pictures.

Surprisingly, Fred Astaire's second screen test proved to be disappointing; and it, like the first he made several years earlier with his sister, has been lost for posterity. However, there is the following written record of Selznick's reaction to Astaire's second test: "I am uncertain about the man, but I feel, in spite of his enormous ears and bad chin line, that his charm is so tremendous that it comes through even on this wretched test. And I would be perfectly willing to go ahead with him." Clearly, Selznick recognized that Astaire's looks were a detriment to his screen presence but that his overwhelming charm readily compensated for his physical shortcomings. The impact of Astaire's charm on the screen is succinctly captured by Audrey Hepburn's response to the question as to whether Astaire was good-looking: "I think so, because charm is the best-looking thing in the world, isn't it?"

Notwithstanding the less-than-enthusiastic response by Selznick, RKO decided to place Astaire under contract. Given the strong demand for dancing and singing talent to perform in the highly popular movie musicals of the thirties, placing Astaire under contract was not surprising. However, before using him in an RKO motion picture, the studio loaned him to MGM to appear in the 1933 film *Dancing Lady*, which starred Joan Crawford and Clark Gable. *Dancing Lady* was Astaire's film debut, and while Crawford was an inadequate dance partner, Astaire succeeded admirably playing himself in a brief role. Although the film proved to be a box office hit, when Astaire returned to RKO Pictures, the studio was still unwilling to give him a starring role. As a result, in his next film, *Flying Down to Rio*, he received secondary billing alongside his new dance partner, Ginger Rogers. The film starred the Latin beauty Dolores Del Rio and Gene Raymond as her love interest. It premiered at the Radio City Music Hall where it enjoyed a record-breaking three-week run; it was also a huge success upon its release nationwide. Film reviewers were very much taken with Astaire's screen presence in contrast to the lukewarm response of Selznick and other RKO studio executives to Astaire's aforementioned second screen test. The film is well remembered for its wonderful score, which included "Flying Down to Rio," "Orchids in the Moonlight," and, more importantly, "La Carioca." The latter provided Astaire and Rogers with the opportunity to perform a superb dance number in this their first screen pairing. In some of their later films, they would again perform a similar grandiose dance sequence. To wit: "The Continental" in *The Gay Divorcee* and "The Piccolino" in *Top Hat*. "The Continental" was written by Con Conrad and Herb Magidson and was the first song to win a Best Song Oscar when this Academy Award category was first established in 1934. "The Piccolino" was composed by Irving Berlin. Astaire and Rogers's performance of these two majestic dance numbers served to entrance movie audiences and critics alike.

The qualms RKO executives may initially have had about Astaire's looks on screen were soon forgotten given the financial success of *Flying Down to Rio*. Indeed, the studio was now looking for another property in which to pair Astaire and Rogers. However, Astaire was adamant about not wanting to become linked to a dance partner. While he was willing to make a future film with Ginger Rogers, he was against the idea of their becoming a movie team. He believed an exclusive dance partnership imposed too many constraints on his choreographic freedom, and he also felt he was still overcoming the negative aspects of his partnership with his sister Adele. In spite of his desire for more artistic freedom as a dancer in films, the highly enthusiastic public response to the Astaire-Rogers duo, coupled with RKO executive pressure, made Astaire relent. Thus, in 1934, they made their second film together, *The Gay Divorcee*. It was based on the Cole Porter musical *Gay Divorce*, in which Astaire made his last stage appearance. The title was changed from "divorce" to "divorcee" to accommodate the censorship laws that were then strongly enforced. Specifically, a divorce could not be promoted as a happy event. The word "gay," on the other hand, meant light-hearted at that time, and its use in the film title was therefore not a cause for censorship concern. After seeing Astaire and Rogers dance and fall in love to the strains of "Night and Day," moviegoers were hooked; they too fell in love but with the screen duo of Astaire and Rogers! Although Astaire had been highly resistant to being paired with another dancer, he could not ignore the fact that his partnership with Rogers had catapulted both to stardom. Further, Astaire, but not Rogers, was now contracted to receive a percentage of the gross profits from the films he made for RKO. Starting with *Flying Down to Rio* in 1933 and ending with *The Story of Irene and Vernon Castle* in 1939, Astaire and Rogers made nine black-and-white films together under the RKO banner; six of these ranked among RKO's biggest moneymakers at that time and are credited with helping the studio survive the Great Depression. They also made Astaire a wealthy man.

During the six-year period of the Astaire-Rogers partnership at RKO, Astaire made only one film, *A Damsel in Distress* (1937), in which he appeared without Rogers. This film was made at Astaire's request because he was still concerned about being tied to a specific dance partner. In this case, Joan Fontaine was chosen to play the dancing object of his affection. Needless to say, Fontaine's dancing ability was non-existent; but Astaire, as always, compensated for his partner's shortcomings. He was also greatly helped by George Burns and Gracie Allen, his brilliant comic sidekicks, and the memorable score by the Gershwins, which included "A Foggy Day in London Town" and "Nice Work if You Can Get It." The performances of these songs by Astaire were two of the film's highlights. During the same time period, Rogers appeared in a number of well-received films without Astaire or any other dance partner. These included *In Person*, *Stage Door*, *Having Wonderful Time*, and *Vivacious Lady*. Astaire and Rogers were reunited by MGM in 1949 when they starred in their first Technicolor musical *The Barkleys of Broadway*. Despite being a critical and box office success, the film was the tenth and last time Astaire and Rogers would appear in a motion picture together. Neither performer wanted to recapture the past because each had successfully moved on since their split ten years earlier—Astaire to a wealth of different dancing partners and Rogers to a variety of starring roles in major film comedies and dramas. Rogers's only venture into a musical without Astaire was in the misconceived film version of the groundbreaking Moss Hart show *Lady in the Dark* (1944). The movie unwisely eliminated most of the sophisticated Kurt Weill—Ira Gershwin Broadway score, and thereby left Rogers with little opportunity to either dance or sing.

What is it that made the screen team of Astaire and Rogers work so well? In response to that question, Katharine Hepburn is famously reported to have said, "He gives her class and she gives him sex." That may be true, but there are a number of other factors that account for Astaire and Rogers dominating film musicals in the thirties. For one, each performer was a triple threat. Both could not only dance, but they could also sing and act. Although Rogers could not match Astaire's dancing and singing talent, she clearly outshone him as an actor, and even won a Best Actress Oscar in 1940 for her role in *Kitty Foyle*. None of the other performers in musical films at that time offered the triple skills evinced by Rogers and Astaire. For example, the popular musical comedy team of Dick Powell and Ruby Keeler would sing together, but Powell was never called upon to dance with Keeler in any of the seven movies in which they appeared. Other dancers in the films of that era (e.g., Eleanor Powell, Bill Robinson, Ray Bolger, etc.) didn't have permanent partners and were basically solo tap dancers whose dancing skills weren't as wide ranging as those of Astaire or Rogers. Consequently, during the thirties, Astaire and Rogers reigned supreme as a film musical team.

Secondly, many of the greatest American popular composers for the theater (e.g., Kern, Gershwin, Porter, and Berlin) were chosen to write the scores for the Astaire and Rogers films.

Whether Astaire would sing the Oscar-winning "The Way You Look Tonight" to Rogers, or the pair danced to the strains of "Let's Face the Music and Dance," all their films contained one or more now classic songs. How could a depression-weary public not find itself captivated by a film that contained a song such as "Isn't This a Lovely Day?" "Cheek to Cheek," "A Fine Romance," "Change Partners," or "They Can't Take That Away From Me"? Admittedly, the fine music and lyrics of these glorious songs readily earned them a distinctive place in the annals of popular songdom, but their initial performance by Astaire also accounts for their success. While Astaire's voice did not have the range and beauty of a Bing Crosby or a Russ Columbo, his elegant singing style, smooth delivery, and great diction enabled him to leave his personal stamp on all the songs he sang. Astaire's singing provided the perfect introduction to the dance numbers with Rogers that usually followed. Oscar Levant considered Astaire to be "the best singer of songs the movie world ever knew." Though one may question Levant's exalted evaluation of Astaire's singing, we must still acknowledge that Astaire's fine vocal ability was a decided asset that made him the outstanding singer/dancer of his day. Rogers was rarely given the opportunity to sing a song by herself, but in those instances where she did sing alone (e.g., "They All Laughed" in RKO's 1937 *Shall We Dance*), the result was completely satisfying.

Another factor that contributed to Astaire's and Rogers's screen success was the choreographic responsibility Astaire requested and was given. In the ten films he made with Ginger Rogers, Astaire created the choreography for almost all the dance numbers. He was often assisted by the choreographer Hermes Pan. By having control over the film's choreography, Astaire was able to present himself at his best in dance solos, and in dances with Rogers, to their mutual advantage—particularly since Rogers's dancing skills were less formidable than those of Astaire. Besides creating his own choreography, Astaire was also a perfectionist who would rehearse the dance numbers he created for weeks or months to ensure that his and Rogers's performance came across as graceful and natural no matter how complicated the choreography. The result of their lengthy rehearsal periods is reflected in their dazzling dancing together. In those instances where Astaire did a solo number in his films with Rogers (e.g., "Top Hat, White Tie and Tails"), his extensive preparation once again led the movie audience to find Astaire's dancing easy and fluid as opposed to arduous. That, indeed, was Astaire's primary goal as a dancer in films.

In addition to creating the choreography for many of his films, Astaire is also credited with introducing the photographic concept of filming a dance routine in a single shot. As a result, the dances in the Astaire-Rogers musicals become self-contained entities with no interspersed cross cutting or zoom shots to distract from the overall movement of the dancers themselves. Filmgoers could thus view and appreciate Astaire's and Rogers's entire body in motion as opposed to just their dancing feet. Given this visual perspective, members of the audience could readily imagine themselves dancing in Astaire's or Rogers's place. Such happy fantasizing only served to heighten the popularity of their films. Astaire's approach was in sharp contrast to the elaborate aerial shots and other photographic wizardry that typify the musical sequences in the films Busby Berkeley directed during the same period in movie musical history.

We thus come to realize that Fred Astaire's successful move from stage to screen was the result of several factors: the ability to not only dance but also to sing and act; a wide range of superb popular songs to dance to and/or to sing; choreography created by Astaire that made his dance sequences unique and sometimes awesome; intensive rehearsing of his dance numbers prior to actual filming; the novel photographing of those dance sequences to capture the dancer's full body in motion, and, most significantly, being paired at the outset of his film career with the ideal dance partner: Ginger Rogers!

Throughout the thirties and until the early forties, Astaire was unrivaled in films as its leading male dancer. Whether he performed solo numbers or danced with a partner, there was no one else who was his equal. However, Fred Astaire's premier position was finally challenged in 1942 when Gene Kelly made his movie debut in *For Me and My Gal*, which starred Judy Garland. Kelly had appeared in minor roles in Broadway musicals during the late thirties but in 1940 made a major impact as Joey Evans, the anti-hero of the Rodgers and Hart musical *Pal Joey*. His historic performance in that role led Hollywood to come calling, and Kelly's screen career was launched. Like Astaire, Kelly was a superb dancer, a very capable singer, and a good actor; but unlike Astaire, Kelly also brought sexual charisma to his screen roles.

As far as Astaire and Kelly appearing together in a film, this occurred only twice. The first time was when the two sang and danced to the Gershwin song "The Babbitt and the Bromide," in the 1946 film *Ziegfeld Follies*. In a way, this song recaptured the past for Astaire since he and his sister Adele introduced it twenty years earlier in the stage musical *Funny Face*. The second pairing of Astaire and Kelly was in the 1976 M-G-M documentary *That's Entertainment, Part 2*. In it, they performed several song-and-dance numbers as an introduction to various scenes from historic M-G-M musicals.

While the two men shared a common set of performing talents, they did indeed differ. Astaire was a better singer than Kelly, while Kelly was a better romantic actor than Astaire and, as previously noted, radiated more sex appeal. If we focus on their dancing skills, Kelly was more acrobatic and athletic than Astaire, while Astaire brought a greater sense of elegance to his dancing. Gene Kelly reflected more of the working-class, common man in the roles he played as opposed to the upper-class image imparted by the often tuxedo-clad Astaire. Despite their differences, Hollywood accommodated these brilliant dancers simultaneously for fifteen years, and so did the film-going public. They were even somewhat interchangeable. When Gene Kelly was unable to appear in *Easter Parade* (1948) because of a physical injury, he was replaced by Fred Astaire. This memorable film provided Astaire with both Judy Garland and Ann Miller as his dancing partners.

Perhaps the ultimate means for comparing Astaire and Kelly would have been if Kelly had danced with Ginger Rogers. He did not; however, a comparison we can make is to view Astaire dancing with

Rita Hayworth in *You'll Never Get Rich* (1941) and *You Were Never Lovelier* (1942) versus Kelly dancing with her in *Cover Girl* (1944). Since Rita Hayworth's looks and dance style are more akin to those of Ginger Rogers than other dance partners Astaire and Kelly shared (e.g., Cyd Charisse, Vera-Ellen, and Leslie Caron), using Rita Hayworth as a basis of comparison is feasible. Of course, we all have our individual opinions and preferences, but the consensus appears to be that Astaire and Kelly come off as dancing equals rather than one being superior to the other.

A positive result of the Astaire-Kelly competition was that it fostered creativity. Many of the films in which each appeared are noteworthy because of their special effects and innovative dance routines. For example, Gene Kelly's captivating dance sequence with Jerry, the cartoon mouse, in *Anchors Aweigh* (1946) and his fabulous splashy dance cum umbrella in *Singin' in the Rain* (1952) are two classic moments in movie musical history. Not to be outdone, Astaire danced with a hat-rack in *Royal Wedding* (1951), and of greater renown in the aforementioned film, Astaire danced on the walls and ceiling of his hotel room. Through the magic of film technology and the ability of the hotel room set to rotate, Astaire appeared to defy gravity. He made movie audiences gasp in disbelief and wonder whether the fleet-footed Astaire had truly overcome the forces of nature! Astaire and Kelly also covered new territory in their routines with their respective dance partners. The extended ballet sequence performed by Kelly and Leslie Caron at the conclusion of *An American in Paris* (1951) and "The Girl Hunt" ballet danced by Astaire and Cyd Charisse in *The Band Wagon* (1953) are prime examples of landmark dance numbers in musical films.

A significant difference that does separate Astaire from Kelly as performers in films is the fact that Kelly never had a long-term dance partner as did Astaire with Rogers. The closest Kelly came to being linked to a dance partner was Judy Garland with whom he made three films: *For Me and My Gal* (1942), *The Pirate* (1948), and *Summer Stock* (1950). As a result of Kelly not having a long-term association with another screen performer, his name stands alone in the annals of musical films while Astaire is, and will always be, inescapably tied to Rogers.

As Fred Astaire fans well know, after he and Ginger Rogers split as a team, he appeared in films with a myriad of other dance partners (e.g., Eleanor Powell, Rita Hayworth, Judy Garland, Vera-Ellen, Lucille Bremer, Jane Powell, Ann Miller, Leslie Caron, Audrey Hepburn, and Cyd Charisse); but he never allowed himself to again become inexorably linked to another performer. In fact, he never appeared in more than two films with any of the aforementioned performers. Clearly, some of the women with whom he danced had particular dance skills that matched his own. For example, Eleanor Powell's tap dancing artistry or Cyd Charisse's balletic ability enabled Astaire to create dance routines that remain unequalled to this day. Has any tap-dance number in films ever reached the peak achieved by Astaire and Eleanor Powell's astonishing dance to "Begin the Beguine" in *Broadway Melody of 1940*? Although she could not match either Powell or Charisse in their respective areas of dance expertise, no one other than Ginger Rogers could perform as capably in as many varied areas of dance as she could with Astaire. Also, apart from their bodies blending so expertly on the dance floor, Astaire and Rogers were able to bring a level of credibility to the silly plots that characterize most of their films together. We believe that the attractive, earthy, and wise-cracking characters Rogers usually played could succumb to Astaire's charm and seductive dancing. In contrast, the many other women with whom Astaire danced never meshed as well romantically as Rogers did with him. Rita Hayworth, for example, was a superb dancing partner in the two films they made together, but it was hard to accept Fred Astaire as her love interest off the dance floor.

The sultry love goddess of the World War II years would later be more appropriately matched with the likes of Glenn Ford in *Gilda* and Gene Kelly in *Cover Girl*.

In light of their strong and highly successful professional bond, one may wonder whether Astaire and Rogers connected off-screen as well. The answer to that query is no. When Astaire and Rogers made their first film together in 1933, Astaire was already married to Phyllis Potter, with whom he would have two children: Fred Jr. and Ava Astaire McKenzie. Their happy marriage lasted until Phyllis's death from lung cancer in 1954 at the age of forty-six. Rumor has it, however, that Phyllis Astaire was jealous of Ginger Rogers and preferred that Astaire and Rogers's physical contact on film be basically restricted to dancing. As a result, Astaire may hug or put his arm around Rogers in their movies together, but they never engaged in lip-to-lip kissing. The lack of a strong display of physical affection didn't lessen the believability of their romantic interest in one another because they effectively expressed their love through their dance routines. As previously noted, Rogers was an excellent actress, and her facial expressions during her dance numbers with Astaire serve to complement the emotions she so capably expresses with her body. A romantic kiss might not only seem redundant but also less powerful than the romantic messages conveyed during their dances together. After his wife's death, Astaire waited twenty-six years before marrying his second wife, Robyn Smith, a jockey who was forty-five years younger than he. Whether he had any serious romantic interest in Ginger Rogers during the long period before he remarried is unknown but unlikely. Hollywood gossip magazines and newspapers would surely have pounced on such a newsworthy item.

After he completed filming *Funny Face* and *Silk Stockings* in 1957, Astaire decided to retire from dancing in musical films and focus on acting instead. He was then fifty-eight years old and, in the course of his twenty-five-year film career, had appeared in thirty musical films. His first venture into a non-musical was the highly acclaimed nuclear war drama *On the Beach* (1959). He also gave a note-worthy performance years later in *The Towering Inferno* (1974) for which he received a Best Supporting Actor Oscar nomination. Astaire did, nevertheless, make another major movie musical during this later period in his career. It was in 1968 when he appeared in *Finian's Rainbow* as the titular Irish rascal in search of the pot of gold at the end of the rainbow. Despite its success on Broadway, its brilliant score by Burton Lane and E. Y. Harburg, and its being directed by Francis Ford Coppola, the film was a box office flop.

Although Astaire chose to no longer perform as a dancer in films, he did not abandon his dancing career. He decided to dance on television where he proved that his dancing skills had in no way diminished. During the period 1958-1968, Astaire appeared in four Emmy Award-winning television specials that featured Barrie Chase as his dance partner. Ms. Chase was a highly skilled dancer and a wonderful match for Astaire. There was talk that Chase and Astaire were amorously involved during the period they performed together. If so, their affair only served to heighten the intensity of their romantic dance duets. Astaire's first TV special, "An Evening with Fred Astaire," won nine Emmy Awards including Best Single Performance by an Actor, but this recognition still didn't provide the impetus for him to return to the world of Hollywood musicals.

Fred Astaire died in 1987 at the age of eighty-eight. In this review of his glorious career on the stage and screen, numerous theatrical works, films, and dancing partners have been identified as major elements that contributed to his fame and success. However, if one was to single out a key factor that enabled Fred Astaire to make the perfect leap from stage to screen, credit must ultimately be given to Ginger Rogers. Perhaps the fact that she, like Astaire, was the product of a driven stage mother who orchestrated her career made Astaire and Rogers kindred spirits destined to succeed together professionally. We can only wonder whether Astaire's transition to motion pictures would have been as immediately successful if he had been initially paired with a dance partner other than Rogers. Of course, given his extraordinary talent, creativity, determination, and on-screen charm, Fred Astaire couldn't possibly fail to eventually make his mark in the world of movies; Ginger Rogers, however, clearly expedited the transitional process. Fortunately, we have their legacy of ten films to watch, enjoy, and appreciate how two greatly talented human beings complemented each other to their mutual advantage. Further, all the films that comprise Astaire's long and successful screen career are available for purchase or rental. As a result, we will always be able to enjoy the dance numbers and the songs that made him a legend. Neither we nor Astaire's family could ask for a better present.

Clearly, Johanna Austerlitz's mission in life was accomplished!

Reference Quotes

P.5: "I am uncertain about the man." Epstein, p.19.
P.5: "I think so, because charm." Ibid., p.33.
P.8: "He gives her class." Ibid., p.88.

BIBLIOGRAPHY

Croce, Arlene. *The Fred Astaire and Ginger Rogers Book*. New York: Galahad Books, 1974.

Epstein, Joseph. *Fred Astaire*. New Haven & London: Yale University Press, 2008.

Green, Stanley. *Encyclopedia of the Musical Theatre*. Cambridge, MA: Da Capo Press, 1976.

_____. *The World of Musical Comedy*. Cambridge, MA: Da Capo Press, 1980.

Shipman, David. *The Great Movie Stars—The Golden Years*. New York: Crown Publishers, 1970.

Astaire, Adele. Wikipedia. http://en.wikipedia.org/wiki/Adele_Astaire 2009 Sep. 09.

Astaire, Fred. Wikipedia. http://en.wikipedia.org/wiki/Fred_Astaire 2009 Sep. 09.

Eddie Cantor: From Rags to Riches

Helaine Feldman

Known as the "Apostle of Pep" and "Banjo Eyes" on stage and "Poonelo" at home (the name referred to a dog with huge brown eyes once on a bill with Eddie in vaudeville, which his wife said reminded her of him), Eddie Cantor was called by biographer Herbert G. Goldman "the most forgotten star of the twentieth century." This could be because not much of his work has been saved—there are few records of vaudeville and Broadway performances, his films never became classics, his TV shows were not in syndication, his style might today be considered "corny," and much of his work was done in blackface, which now is considered politically incorrect. Nevertheless, Cantor was a major star in all media—from vaudeville to Broadway, films, radio, recordings, and TV—and one of the first millionaire entertainers.

Yet this "star" could have been a hoodlum, could have spent time in jail as many of his childhood friends did, had fate not intervened and set him on another course. "I grew up on the sidewalks of New York, with an occasional fall into the gutter," he wrote in his 1928 autobiography, *My Life Is In Your Hands*.

Born Isidore Itzkowitz on the Lower East Side of New York City on January 31, 1892, young Izzy was orphaned early and raised by his maternal grandmother, Esther Lazarowitz Kantrowitz. Esther supported her young grandson in various ways—taking in sewing and running an unlicensed employment agency for Polish immigrant girls who desperately needed to find work. When she enrolled her young grandson in school, she mistakenly gave him her name, "Kantrowitz," instead of his, "Itzkowitz"; and the registrar shortened it to Kanter. Without parents, without much money even for food, and with his grandmother always struggling to provide for the two of them, young Izzy took to the streets. He fought (he had to in order to survive), and he stole (also a means of survival that gave him status so that he wouldn't be picked on by the bigger boys). In fact, in one of his fights, he was cracked in the head with a rock and sustained a scar in the middle of his forehead that remained throughout his life. He found out early on, however, that he had other talents—he was funny, he could recite, and he liked the attention that this brought him. He also was in constant motion—perhaps hyperactive before there was a name for this condition and drugs to treat it.

Fast forward a couple of years and the Educational Alliance created a program to get East Side youngsters out of the city during the summer months and into the country for fresh air and a more wholesome environment. Izzy was a perfect candidate to spend two weeks at the Alliance Camp in Cold Spring, New York, forty-five minutes north of the city. It was at camp that he began entertaining—telling stories and singing, much to the delight of the other campers and the directors, as well. He was so popular that his stay at camp was extended for another two weeks and, eventually, for the entire summer at what later became known as Surprise Lake Camp. It was here that he actually honed his raw talent.

In the city, he was on his own and running wild most of the time. He dropped out of school in 1905 at the age of thirteen. Having more time to hang around, Izzy found his way to one of the other neighborhood schools where he became smitten with one of the girls on the basketball team. The girl, Ida Tobias, was then fourteen and the daughter of a successful businessman. It was Ida who changed his name to Eddie, because she thought it was cute. Needless to say, Ida's parents were not pleased to meet Eddie and tried for many years to end the relationship. It was at this time, too, that Eddie discovered the theatre and went whenever he could—mostly sneaking in. Eddie was scrawny, had broken teeth (from yet another fight), and that large scar in the middle of his forehead. He didn't seem a likely candidate for a career in show business.

Nevertheless, one of his friends suggested that they team up and try to earn some money entertaining at clubs, weddings, and bar mitzvahs. It worked for a while, but soon his friend found a job and quit the act. Eddie continued to consider himself an actor. He entered an amateur night at a local vaudeville theatre, billing himself as an impersonator, and won first prize. The year was 1908; he was now a professional—and he was hooked. His first job in commercial show business was in a burlesque show called *Indian Maidens*. The show played one-night stands in Pennsylvania, West Virginia, and surroundings for about six weeks. After returning to New York, Eddie and a friend went to Coney Island to get summer jobs as singing waiters. The pianist who accompanied them was Jimmy Durante, who became his show business partner for a while and remained a lifelong friend.

Eddie needed money if he was to court Ida properly and so held a variety of non–show business jobs, but Ida realized that his heart was in show business, and she encouraged him to pursue this path. Eddie, now calling himself a dialectician, began making the rounds of bookers and producers and changed his name to Cantor. Surprisingly, he began finding work in vaudeville. The *Utica* (NY) *Daily Press* reviewed his act, saying, "Eddie Cantor, a comedian, had some good talk and some good songs which he handled so well that there was not a dull moment in the fifteen minutes he used."

Joseph M. Schenck of the People's Vaudeville Company—a small time chain whose other officers included Nicholas Schenck, Adolph Zukor, and Marcus Loew, all future movie moguls—caught Eddie's act and booked him for several dates. This was when Eddie started using charcoal to give his face some character and also to give himself a different look so it would appear as though he had a whole new act at other bookings. Wiping off the lines, he discovered blackface. According to Herbert Goldman's book, "Blackface had been a staple of show business for more than eighty years by the time Eddie Cantor donned burnt cork, presumably at the Lyric Theatre in Hoboken, around June 1911."

Next Eddie was hired to appear with an act called "Bedini and Arthur." He started out as a gofer but soon added comedy bits. This was his first appearance in top-lined vaudeville. The act was billed "Bedini & Arthur—Assisted by Eddie Cantor." It was here that he created his stage persona: clapping his hands, rolling his eyes, and walking quickly from side to side on stage. Eddie stayed with the act for two years until he met Gus Edwards, who was producing kids' vaudeville acts called *Kid Kabaret*. Here he met and worked with George Jessel, who became another lifelong friend. Eddie was now earning a regular salary, and so on Valentine's Day 1913, he proposed to Ida, who readily accepted. They were married on June 9, 1914.

Next up—still in vaudeville, was the Orpheum Circuit, working with Jessel and Will Rogers. Here he also came to the attention of Al

Jolson, whom he was imitating as part of his act. He formed several other vaudeville acts and continued traveling. It was when he was performing as "Cantor and (Al) Lee" and playing at the Orpheum Theatre in Los Angeles that Earl Carroll was in the audience. Carroll recommended Eddie to producer Oliver Morosco, who offered Eddie, but not Al Lee, a part in a play called *Canary Cottage*. The money was not great, but it was going to be coming to Broadway. *Canary Cottage* became Eddie's first role in a real musical comedy. It was Morosco who dubbed him "the Apostle of Pep." Eddie stole the show. One thing led to another, and Eddie's next career move was to appear in the new edition of Ziegfeld's *Midnight Frolic*, the after-theatre revue presented by Florenz Ziegfeld on the roof of the New Amsterdam Theatre. Billed as "A New Nut," Eddie debuted in the *Midnight Frolic* on October 13, 1916. He told jokes, sang, played the banjo, and wowed the audience. He never came to Broadway with *Canary Cottage*, instead performing in the *Midnight Frolic* for twenty-seven consecutive weeks continuing to improve his soon-to-become trademark delivery. He sang songs while prancing up and down across the stage, clapping his hands, rolling his eyes, and exiting with a wave of his handkerchief.

Eddie's popularity did not go unnoticed by Florenz Ziegfeld, who soon moved him up to the *Follies*. He debuted in the *Ziegfeld Follies of 1917*, appearing alongside Fanny Brice, W. C. Fields, Will Rogers, and Bert Williams. (He certainly had come a long way from New York's Lower East Side.) The show opened at the New Amsterdam Theatre on June 12, 1917, and played until September 15, 1917. The reviews were glowing: The *New York Evening Telegram*: "Mr. Cantor . . . is new to the *Follies*, and won the warmest welcome of the evening in clever singing patter and dancing." The *New York World*: "A comparatively new singing comedian, Eddie Cantor, who descended from the *Frolic* on the roof, made one of the hits of the night." The *New York Tribune*: "Cantor is a blackface comedian who possesses the comic spirit and knows what to do with a song."

Eddie was back for the *Ziegfeld Follies of 1918* and now known as one of Broadway's top comedians. He developed a father/son relationship with Ziegfeld, which, unfortunately, became severely strained in 1919 when Eddie sided with the fledgling actors' union (Actors' Equity Association) in a dispute with the producers. Ziegfeld asked Eddie why he was doing that to him. According to Cantor's son-in-law, Mike Baker (married to Marilyn Cantor, the fourth of Eddie's five daughters), Eddie said, "I am not doing this to you. I am doing this for all the actors out there who have no representation." Although the *Follies* continued to run despite the strike, Ziegfeld became reluctant to honor a promise to Eddie to develop a book show especially for him.

In the interim, Eddie worked for other producers, including the Shuberts. In 1920, the Shuberts gave him star billing above the title in a Broadway revue entitled *The Midnight Rounders*. This show played for seventy weeks along the Shubert Circuit. Then came another Shubert revue, *Make it Snappy*. By the time this show closed, Eddie was tired of revues, disillusioned with the Shuberts, and wanted to do a musical with a story. Ziegfeld, who had been following his success, finally called him. They met, reconciled, and it was announced that Eddie Cantor had signed a long-term contract and would return to the *Follies*. The contract also stipulated that Eddie would star in a Broadway book show by the end of the year.

Coincidentally, Eddie played golf regularly at New York's Van Cortlandt Park with a lyricist named Joseph McCarthy who conceived the idea for a show in which Cantor would play a golf caddy at a country club. He brought the idea to Ziegfeld, and soon after, the show *Kid Boots* was ready. *Kid Boots* opened on Broadway at the Earl Carroll Theatre on December 13, 1923. The *New York Commercial* wrote:, "It is a whale of a musical comedy which Flo Ziegfeld is presenting at the Earl Carroll Theatre, and it is Eddie Cantor who is the 'whole show.'" The *New York Times* said, "For it is Eddie Cantor, seeming a bit more fervent and wide-eyed than he ever has before, who makes *Kid Boots* what it is." Cantor was already a star; *Kid Boots* made him a celebrity, wrote Herbert Goldman.

Kid Boots was Eddie's first book musical. The cast included Mary Eaton, a dancer who had appeared on Broadway in several shows, including the *Ziegfeld Follies*. Mary's contract was negotiated by her father, and he insisted that Mary—who, by this time, had achieved a degree of stardom—be listed as a costar. But Eddie refused. They finally agreed to the wording: Eddie Cantor in *Kid Boots* with Mary Eaton. The show ran on Broadway for fourteen months before going on the road, had over one thousand performances, and a top ticket price of $16.50, a new high for Broadway at that time.

Mary's sister, Doris Eaton, also an alumna of the *Ziegfeld Follies*, wrote in her book *The Days We Danced*, published in 2003: "I don't think Cantor ever got over sharing the marquee with Mary, and while he was publicly kind to her, he never showed any personal warmth or friendliness to her or any of the Eatons. Years later when he wrote about *Kid Boots* in his memoir, he never even mentioned Mary's name. Gratuitously, in his curtain speeches, he would often say, 'Kid Boots is a sweet and simple show. Mary Eaton is sweet and I am simple.'"

Meanwhile, Paramount had bought the film rights to the show from Ziegfeld and signed Eddie to play the lead. Of course, it was to be a silent film, and the show was a musical, but Paramount forged ahead nevertheless. The picture was to be shot during the summer in order not to interfere with Eddie's stage work, and Clara Bow was signed to be the female lead. The movie opened in 1926, and the New York Times said Eddie seemed "to be just as much at home before the camera as he is on the stage." Eddie had actually appeared in several early experimental films, most notably Widow at the Races in 1913, but Kid Boots was his first starring role in a feature film.

His next film was Special Delivery in 1927, his second and last silent vehicle. The cast of Special Delivery included William Powell and was directed by William Goodrich, a.k.a. Roscoe (Fatty) Arbuckle, now working behind-the-camera following a well-known scandal that had ended his acting career.

Motion pictures changed forever in 1927 with the opening of The Jazz Singer, the first feature-length motion picture with synchronized dialogue sequences. In other words, "talkies" had arrived. Both Eddie and his friend George Jessel had been considered for the lead role, but it went instead to Al Jolson.

In 1927, Eddie was back on Broadway in the Ziegfeld Follies. Although Flo Ziegfeld would not allow him to appear in full-length films, he managed to appear in several shorts for Paramount, which had a studio on the East Coast so that Broadway and vaudeville names could appear in films. Paramount, according to Leonard Maltin in his book The Great Movie Shorts, had the biggest lineup of top names of any studio during the early 1930s. Eddie appeared for Paramount in That Party in Person, Ziegfeld Midnight Frolic, The Cockeyed News, Getting a Ticket, Glorifying the American Girl, and Insurance. Glorifying the American Girl, produced by Florenz Ziegfeld and released by Paramount in 1929, was basically a film glorifying the Ziegfeld Follies. The cast was headed by Mary Eaton (of Kid Boots) and featured cameos by many Follies stars, including Helen Morgan, Rudy Vallee, and Eddie Cantor. This pre-Code movie was notable for being the first talkie to use the word "damn" and also for its very revealing costumes, similar to those in the Broadway Follies. Insurance lifted one of Eddie's vaudeville skits directly on to the screen. "The short is probably a faithful recreation of one of Cantor's vaudeville routines and, as such, is a valuable record of what it must have been like to see a headliner at the Palace," wrote Maltin.

In 1928, Eddie starred in another book show on Broadway for Ziegfeld—*Whoopee*. It was a resounding hit. The score included "Makin' Whoopee," which became one of Eddie's signature tunes, as well as "Love Me Or Leave Me," popularized by Ruth Etting. Brooks Atkinson, writing in the *New York Times*, said, "Mr. Cantor has never been so enjoyable a comedian. From the blackface singer of mammy songs . . . he has developed in *Whoopee* into a versatile and completely entertaining comic."

As he was the toast of vaudeville, Eddie was now the toast of Broadway, and the poor boy from New York's Lower East Side was now a millionaire many times over. This prompted an announcement on May 8, 1929, that Eddie was retiring from the stage when his contract with Ziegfeld expired. "I love the theatre," he said, "and now that I am a millionaire, why should I tie myself down to time schedules and be prevented from following my own inclinations? For instance, I haven't yet seen one of my daughters—I have five—graduate from school." What was not mentioned in the announcement was the fact that Paramount wanted him to remake *Kid Boots*—with sound. Ziegfeld squelched that project, however, because he had a deal pending with Sam Goldwyn for sound picture rights to *Whoopee*. But everything changed in October 1929. The stock market crashed, and Eddie, like many others, was wiped out financially and was back, on paper at least, to the poverty he had known as a child.

Whoopee closed on Broadway on November 23, 1929, and Eddie was ready for the next step in his career and working to rebuild his bank account. He and his family left Broadway for Hollywood to bring *Whoopee* to the screen. "Working in pictures I could make in six weeks what I'd made in a year—important to a guy who'd recently lost his shirt," Eddie said in his book *Take My Life*, published in 1957.

Whoopee was the first of seven movie musicals he made in the 1930s. *Whoopee* (1930) was filmed in two-color Technicolor and based on the 1928 Broadway show. The film was produced by Florenz Ziegfeld and Samuel Goldwyn. Future stars Betty Grable, Ann Sothern, and Virginia Bruce appeared uncredited as "Goldwyn Girls." The film also launched the Hollywood career of choreographer Busby Berkeley. Outstanding was Eddie's rendition of the song "Makin' Whoopee."

Whoopee was followed in 1931 by *Palmy Days*, for which Eddie was also credited as a writer as well as star. Once again, it was produced by Samuel Goldwyn and choreographed by Busby Berkeley, who also made a cameo appearance. George Raft and Charlotte Greenwood were also in the film. *Palmy Days* was released in late September 1931 and was the beneficiary of a massive publicity campaign to overcome any bad financial effects on the film industry due to the Great Depression. The film was successful both due to Eddie's appearance and to the scantily clad chorus girls. In 1931, too, Eddie debuted on radio, and from that time until 1954, he was a regular and one of the most popular stars on this medium.

In 1932, Eddie starred in *The Kid From Spain* for Samuel Goldwyn. The cast included Robert Young, Noah Beery, J. Carrol Naish, and, playing himself, Sidney Franklin, the American matador. *The Kid From Spain* opened at the Palace Theatre on November 17, 1932, inaugurating a straight picture policy, thus sounding the official death knell for vaudeville. Reviews were good, as was business, since Eddie took the opportunity to talk about the film on his radio shows. Herbert Goldman writes that after the release of the film and its popularity, "Cantor was now the number one star of radio and one of the nation's leading film stars. This conquest of the two leading media of the day, added to his reputation from the stage, made Eddie Cantor probably the top star in the world." He was also "the top money earner in show business."

Eddie's next film was *Roman Scandals*, a 1933 black-and-white musical starring Eddie with Gloria Stuart, Edward Arnold, and Ruth Etting, who had made her Broadway debut in the *Ziegfeld Follies of 1927* and appeared again with Eddie on Broadway in *Whoopee*. Busby Berkeley was back as choreographer, and the Goldwyn Girls, now scantily clad as slave girls, included Lucille Ball and Paulette Goddard.

In the early 1930s in Hollywood, *The Wizard of Oz* was a very hot property. The book, written by L. Frank Baum, had arrived in bookstores in 1900 as *The Wonderful Wizard of Oz* and was well received by children, adults, and critics. The story was developed into a stage play, which opened in 1902, and came to New York the following year. Between its original company, second company, and other touring productions, *Oz* played throughout the United States for seven seasons. Baum died in 1919, and in 1924, Baum's son sold the property to Chadwick Pictures. The only thing memorable about the film that followed was that Oliver Hardy, before he began his partnership with Stan Laurel, appeared as a farmhand, disguised as a Tin Man. Later editions of *Oz* were also aired on the radio. By 1933, when movies had sound, MGM became interested in the story, but Baum's son wanted to work with Samuel Goldwyn. So after months of negotiations, Goldwyn paid $40,000 for screen rights and announced the picture in late summer 1933 as a Technicolor vehicle for Eddie Cantor, Goldwyn's biggest star since having appeared in several successful musicals for him. Cantor was to play the Scarecrow despite the fact that Fred A. Stone who had played the Scarecrow in the 1902 musical was closely identified with the role. But in December 1933, Goldwyn tabled the picture and, instead, cast Cantor in *Kid Millions*. MGM finally wound up making *The Wizard of Oz* in 1939, with Ray Bolger as the Scarecrow.

Kid Millions (1934), produced by Samuel Goldwyn, about a Brooklyn Boy (Cantor) who inherits a fortune from his archeologist father but has to go to Egypt to claim it, had a cast including Ann Sothern (graduated from her Goldwyn Girl days to now get billing), Ethel Merman, and George Murphy. The film's "ice cream fantasy sequence" was Goldwyn's first attempt at film with three-strip Technicolor. Lucille Ball and Paulette Goddard repeat as Goldwyn Girls.

Strike Me Pink was released in 1936. In this film, Eddie plays a mild-mannered manager of an amusement park beset by mobsters. Ethel Merman is back, along with Brian Donlevy and William Frawley (pre-*I Love Lucy* days). Eddie also brought along some of his radio family for the film, including Harry Einstein as the befuddled Greek, Parkyakarkus, and Sidney Fields (pre-Abbott & Costello films in the fifties).

This was Eddie's last film for Samuel Goldwyn. It is vintage Cantor. In most of the Goldwyn films Eddie played characters named Eddie: Eddie Simpson (*Palmy Days*), Eddie Williams (*The Kid from Spain*), Eddie a.k.a. Oedipus (*Roman Scandals*), Eddie Simpson Jr. (*Kid Millions*), and Eddie Pink (*Strike Me Pink*). All the films feature Eddie in a series of adventures, unlikely situations, and locales—and all are successful. Eddie is the focus of the film despite being surrounded by a bevy of Busby Berkeley dancing beauties. Throughout, Eddie remains Eddie, dancing around, clapping his hands, and rolling his eyes. And audiences love it. He has created a persona, much the way Charlie Chaplin and Buster Keaton created personas. Writer Donald W. McCaffrey says, "With the exception of the Marx Brothers team no other comedian has brought from the stage to the screen so much of the vigor of vaudeville and the musical comedy as Eddie Cantor. A stand-up comic with the skills of a song-and-dance man, he possessed the charisma to dominate a theatre or film skit."

In 1937, Eddie starred in *Ali Baba Goes to Town*, his first film for Twentieth Century Fox. It was produced by Darryl F. Zanuck. The cast included Gypsy Rose Lee, using her real name, Louise Hovick, as her stage name; John Carradine; Roland Young; and Tony Martin.

But times were changing; audiences were becoming more sophisticated and increasingly found Eddie's films "old-fashioned." He continued to be a major star on radio, however. When his contract with Twentieth Century Fox ended, Eddie wrote a letter to *Variety*, saying,

> Darryl Zanuck and I disagreed over my next story. I felt, and still feel, that it is time to get away from the formula pictures I have been making. It is important at this time to make a big musical, where I can play "Eddie Cantor" for a change.
>
> Despite the fact that *Ali Baba Goes to Town* will gross $2 million, it is my contention that one who has been successful in the theatre, as in my particular case, will be successful on the screen. I want to sing and I want to play something else besides an insipid character which the audience does not believe.
>
> The disagreement with Zanuck was, believe me, a friendly one. At the present time, negotiations have been opened up between two studios and myself, so that maybe, before you go to press, I will know my future plans for the screen.

Metro Goldwyn Mayer and RKO were the studios in question, and Eddie agreed to make pictures for both.

He did *Forty Little Mothers* for MGM in 1940. Busby Berkeley directed this film, with a cast including Judith Anderson, Ralph Morgan, Bonita Granville, and, in an uncredited bit, eighteen-year-old Veronica Lake.

After this film, Eddie had another project in mind. For years, he had hoped to bring *Three Men on a Horse*, a play by John Cecil Holm and George Abbott, to either stage or screen. When things didn't work out for a screen version, Eddie decided to produce it for the Broadway stage despite the fact he was now much too old for the part. It was retitled *Banjo Eyes* and opened on Broadway on December 25, 1941. It was Eddie's final Broadway show.

Eddie went back to Hollywood to do *Thank Your Lucky Stars* for Warner Bros. in 1943. This is a World War II fundraiser, with a cast also including Dennis Morgan, Joan Leslie, Edward Everett Horton, S. Z. Sakall, and Dinah Shore, whom he had introduced on his radio show. The slim plot involves theatre producers staging a wartime charity program only to have the production taken over by their egotistical star, Eddie Cantor, playing himself. Meanwhile, an aspiring singer, Morgan, and his songwriter girlfriend, Leslie, conspire to get into the charity program by replacing Cantor with their look-alike friend, tour bus driver Joe Simpson, also played by Cantor, in a dual role. Many Warner Bros. stars performed in musical numbers as themselves, including several not known as singers. This film features the only screen musical numbers ever done by Bette Davis, Errol Flynn, Olivia de Havilland, and Ida Lupino. Each was paid a $50,000 fee for their appearance, which was then donated to the Hollywood Canteen, a club offering free food, dancing, and entertainment to servicemen. John Garfield and Bette Davis were the driving forces behind the Hollywood Canteen and Garfield, along with Humphrey Bogart, made a cameo appearance in the film. Bette Davis's rendition of "They're Either Too Young Or Too Old" is a highlight of the film. Ticket sales combined with the donated salaries from the performers raised more than $2 million for the Hollywood Canteen.

Eddie's next film was *Show Business* for RKO in 1944. The cast also included George Murphy (before he became a U.S. Senator), Joan Davis, Nancy Kelly, and Constance Moore. Eddie played Eddie Martin in this story of a vaudeville act. No stretch for Eddie.

In *Hollywood Canteen*, the film Eddie makes for Warners in 1945, Eddie played himself as an act appearing at the Canteen. The film also starred Joan Leslie, Robert Hutton, and Dane Clark. Clearly, Eddie Cantor's career as a film actor was nearing its end.

If You Knew Susie in 1948 was Eddie's last film and teamed him once again with Joan Davis.

By the late 1940s, Eddie's film career was over although in 1952 he had a cameo role in *The Story of Will Rogers*, the biopic about his long-time friend. He was now more an institution than a major star although one more challenge remained: television.

Eddie was just as successful on TV as he had been in vaudeville, theatre, radio, and on screen, although he was in his late fifties when this phase of his career began. An article in *Variety* said, "Cantor, who has been a standout in every facet of show business from his childhood vaudeville start with Gus Edwards, through legit, silent films, talkers, radio and now TV, once again gave double-play proof that talent and basic entertainment values can sell in any and every medium."

His first contract was to do twelve variety shows a year beginning in the fall of 1950. George Rosen of *Variety* wrote that the *Colgate Comedy Hour* "established Cantor, a veteran of forty years as a luminary in all phases of the entertainment industry as a TV natural." Jack Gould of the *New York Times* said the "ageless Eddie was the exuberant trouper of tradition, singing, wise-cracking, dancing and thoroughly enjoying himself . . . . He is TV's undisputed new hit." And Ben Gross of the *Daily News* said, "He is the dynamic comedian that he was in the days of the *Ziegfeld Follies*. He sings, he dances, he acts with cyclonic energy. One must see him to appreciate what he puts into his work."

In between shows, Eddie continued a vigorous schedule of public appearances, talks, one-man shows, guest shots on radio, and charity work. But the TV show, along with these other activities, was taxing his strength and affecting his health. Mike Baker tells the story that when Eddie had a heart attack during his performance on the *Colgate Comedy Hour*, he finished the show sitting down and then went by ambulance to the hospital where he was surrounded on the gurney by doctors, aides, and tubes of all kinds. He called for daughter Margie to lean down close to him and whispered, "Do you get the picture? We just won First Prize in the Rose Bowl Parade."

Nevertheless, he was focused on a new project: bringing *The Eddie Cantor Story* to the screen. Eddie was not in the film, although he appears as an audience member in the last scene watching Eddie Cantor, played by Keefe Brasselle, singing. The film, released in 1953, was not successful.

Eddie's health continued to decline during the late fifties and into the sixties. His film career was over, radio was dead, and he no longer had the strength for regular TV. There were frequent hospitalizations, several heart attacks, and prostate and gall bladder problems. Nevertheless, he honored a commitment to record his old songs for RCA. The last recording was completed in June 1957. Then in the early sixties, according to Mike Baker, he did his final performances, recording a five-minute radio show called *Ask Eddie Cantor*, for twenty-six weeks from his home in Palm Springs. It was autobiographical and aired for twenty-six weeks on more than six hundred stations. Sadly, Eddie Cantor's long career was now over.

Eddie died at home on October 10, 1964.

Eddie Cantor was a popular and beloved entertainer for more than half a century. But he was more than that. He was a fighter and defender of the rights of his fellow performers; he was a mentor to young performers—Bobby Breen, Deanna Durbin, Dinah Shore, and Eddie Fisher, among others. Eddie also introduced Thelma Carpenter, a black singer, on his radio show. The sponsor, at the time, said he wanted her off the show. Eddie's response was "If she goes, I go."

In 1919, when Actors' Equity Association, the fledgling union of stage actors, went on strike to gain recognition by the producers in order to improve the wages and working conditions of actors, Eddie defied his mentor—and employer—Florenz Ziegfeld to side with the actors. The breach in their relationship lasted far longer than the strike, but Eddie took a stand and later served on the Equity governing Council.

In 1933, when Hollywood film actors formed a union—the Screen Actors Guild—Eddie lent his support and celebrity to that organization and became its first National President.

In 1937, radio actors organized into the American Federation of Radio Artists (AFRA), and once again Eddie was at the forefront of the organizing effort and became the union's first President. The Board Room at the New York office of AFTRA (the "T" for television was added in 1952) is named in his honor.

Eddie was also a great humanitarian. He earned a fortune during his career, and he *raised* a fortune for many charities and Jewish organizations. Mike Baker notes that when President Franklin Roosevelt asked Eddie to help raise money to fight polio by reaching out to the nation's wealthiest, Eddie responded by saying almost every one of the millions of Americans could afford a dime, so let's have a march of dimes and raise even more money. The President went on radio to announce the campaign and gave credit to "my friend Eddie Cantor for suggesting the March of Dimes." Eddie was a tireless fundraiser for Bonds for Israel and the United Jewish Appeal, among other groups, and was National President of the Heart Fund. He also coined the slogan "Drive carefully. We love our children." During World War II, he supported and entertained the Allied troops abroad and entertained frequently at the Hollywood Canteen at home. Never forgetting his summers spent at Surprise Lake Camp, he offered assistance throughout his life and served on the Board of Directors for many years.

So while his star may have dimmed during the years since his death, many of the organizations he helped and supported continue and remain strong to this day.

Bibliography

Cantor, Eddie (as told to David Freedman). *My Life is in Your Hands*. The Curtis Publishing Company: New York, 1928.

Cantor, Eddie, with Jane Kesner Ardmore, *Take My Life*. Doubleday & Company: New York, 1957.

Fricke, John, and Jonathan Shirshekan. *The Wizard of Oz, An Illustrated Companion to The Timeless Movie Classic*. Fall River Press: New York, 2009.

Goldman, Herbert G., *Banjo Eyes*. Oxford University Press: New York, 1997.

Henderson, Mary C., and Alexis Greene. *The Story of 42nd Street*. Back Stage Books: New York, 2008.

Maltin, Leonard. *The Great Movie Shorts*. Crown Publishers, New York, 1972.

Travis, Doris Eaton (with Joseph and Charles Eaton as told to J. R. Morris). Marquand Books: Seattle, 2003.

Starring as the Cadet: Frankie Thomas on Broadway and in Hollywood

William Russo

In July of 2005, under a pleasant bougainvillea-covered pergola in the patio of former *Tom Corbett Space Cadet* co-star and close friend Jan Merlin, Frankie Thomas recorded sessions over several days of rambling discussions about his career, the motion picture studio system, and many other issues concerning his theatrical family. His mop of golden hair had become tarnished, but still unruly, one of the few artifacts of his childhood stardom. His face was a tanned expanse of wizened skin, but he was elfin and energetic. A chain smoker, he never inhaled. Yet a discreet smoker's cough interrupted his words regularly.

When I gave my gift to Frankie, an autographed letter he apparently wrote in answer to some fan in 1939 during the time he was working at *Metro*, he looked puzzled. Studying the memorabilia, he declared, "That's Dad's signature." He thought about it, musing, "Evidently this [was sent] to me at *Metro*. It was forwarded from *Metro* to our home address. That is my father's autograph. Seldom did I see any fan mail. For instance, there were ten thousand fan letters to us during the *Tom Corbett* show, but we never heard about it. It was to the studio's advantage to keep letters from us because we'd want more money if we heard about it."

Frankie recalled how studio personnel usually answered fan mail. "I was working on *Nancy Drew and the Hidden Staircase*, shortly before they released the third one. That letter never went to the studio workers. At the studios, I knew the two people, assigned to me and to Bonnie [Bonita Granville], who handled mail. I could have walked over to their office and found out, but never did." He never explained the oddity of his father responding to fans as if he were his eighteen-year-old son. Frankie didn't seem puzzled that his parents kept this harmless letter from him. His family worked in concert, deferring to one another's career. We asked him about his beginnings.

The parents of the Golden Child of Broadway and Hollywood were established married stage actors billed as Frank M. Thomas and Mona Bruns. Frankie was born into the legitimate theater surroundings of New York just as sound and film joined together during the Great Depression to create the improved entertainment of the twentieth century. The only child of the two working thespians resembled a beautiful blue-eyed cherub. Naturally, he would be first brought on stage by his mother as a baby in a scene of a play she did, and inevitably became a polished young stage actor, which led to film work. When Hollywood hired him, he was given juvenile roles in movies for eight years, appearing in fifteen films.

Since the transition from silent to sound pictures brought new focus on filming stage plays heavy with dialogue, Frankie proved unique as a transplant from the Broadway stage. During our interviews, conducted less than a year before his death in 2006, Frankie stated there were only a handful of child actors who made it big in films of the 1930s, and he was among them. No other boy of thirteen years of age or less had gone to Hollywood as a result of his own Broadway success. Not Mickey, Dickie, Jackie, or Freddie. Only Frankie.

Frankie Thomas didn't make another movie after 1942.

First impressions deceived many who met Master Thomas Jr., and his actor parents may have contributed to his age confusion. In the year he triumphed on Broadway in *Wednesday's Child*, he was a sensitive thirteen-year-old charmer with a mop of curly light blond hair. Everyone thought him to be two or three years younger than his actual age, though he behaved off screen much older than he looked, having a surprising maturity, controlled manner and attitude, which was part of the young actor's facade. That year, the *New York Times* published an interview in which readers were left with the notion that Frankie was a genius on the order of Einstein. The *Times* writer was amazed Frankie was in the first year of high school! Yet Frankie was then the normal age for that grade level. He had been playing ten years old both on stage and in films.

To the New York reporter in 1934, Frankie gushed, "I was born to the stage, to be an actor. I never wanted to be anything else. I never will want to be anything else. It's in my blood, I guess." As the witness wrote on December 9, 1934, about the budding young star, Frankie then let out a heavy sigh, indicating how much "the miniature artist [is] in love with his art." The teenager then included his parents for the article by blowing his mother and father a kiss and tossing his blond mane; it was pure show business.

Unlike other child actors, Frankie never retained his boyish repertoire of gestures or body language. As he matured, he tried to play his roles like a young leading man; he was down-to-earth, without frills or exaggerations. He exemplified a no-nonsense style of acting, more akin to Spencer Tracy's dictum of learning the lines and not falling over the set furniture. Seventy years after his first major media interview, Frankie disparaged the "Method" style of brooding contemplation. He dismissed any idea that he was "intuitive" when performing. He was simply a professional.

According to his parents, relatives of yet more actors, the Thomas clan was like the Barrymores or Booths. Frankie wasn't born in a wardrobe trunk, but he certainly spent plenty of time napping on a dressing room shelf while his parents trod the boards. According to their report to the *New York Times* in 1934, "He went on the road when he was two weeks old. He made his stage debut as a squirming infant, at the ripe age of nine months. He had a speaking part with several robust lines at the age of five. A veteran trouper, he had appeared on Broadway at nine. He starred last season in *Wednesday's Child* and went to Hollywood for the screen version . . . . He has been at school for less than three years, but is already in the first year of high school. He has not the faintest idea, and cares less, about his IQ rating. He does not mention football. Last week he was studying Hamlet's soliloquy."

Frankie's education was cutting-edge apprenticeship. PCS, as known by those in the business, was the Professional Children's School, an academy for young performers, especially those whose parents were often on the road, working in touring plays. It also allowed the children to act in road shows and continue their education. The *Times* joked that it ensured "the actor who has 'been on stage all of his life' the ability to sign an Equity contract with something more intelligent than an X, but also proves a boon to any Broadway producer who, through some playwright's vagary, finds that it is absolutely necessary to assemble a handful of child actors in a hurry." By the early 1930s the New York-based school listed an enrollment of 230 child performers, taught by a faculty of 14. Most of the faculty devoted their teaching strictly to correspondence work.

When Philip Dunning was casting his play *Remember the Day*, requiring a large cast of children, he went first and foremost to *PCS* where he knew the best performers could be found. Their backgrounds, training, and orientation to the rigors of show business made these children ideal performers. "They were as proud of their scholarship as they were of their professional eminence and they told me about the school. They sent their lessons in daily and received their instruction by correspondence. When *Remember the Day* came along I knew that it could be cast. All we had to do was visit the school and have a talk with the principal. It was like selecting Rhodes scholars."

Frankie spoke highly of this educational experience. "Mother and Dad put me in a school called the *Professional Children's School*. The kids who worked in the business all went there. A whole batch went there, even Milton Berle. It was not to start me in the business, but it was supposed to be a very good school. So Mom came over to pick me up from *PCS*."

Frequently, Mona Bruns attended a casting call with her son in tow. Frankie recalled one occasion, "It was for a thing called *Carry Nation*. She went in and the room was filled with older women. That's what they wanted, the women who went around with Carry Nation." Frankie spent most time with his mother, observing the traditional process of casting, rehearsing, and learning every nuance. He absorbed the many details of stagecraft. He recounted how "I was standing at the door, and my mother went up to Blanche Yurka who later played Madame DeFarge in the movie *Tale of Two Cities*. She was one of the finest interpreters of Ibsen. She was tall like a Viking and was a notable stage director. She said to my mother, 'Well, Mona, we have nothing for you. These women are all much older than you.' Blanche looked over to me and said, 'But I can use the kid.' And that was my first job. Out of the blue." Frankie admitted, however, "At that time they were writing a lot of parts for children, boys and girls." His mother may well have known that Frankie was a natural and let Blanche Yurka "discover" him.

The boy was prepared to be a star. For those meeting him as a pint-sized thespian, shuttling between custody of his two worlds, Hollywood and Broadway, the child displayed a disarming sense of democracy. "Call me Frankie. Everyone does," he announced to the press in 1934. Trained at the knees of his guardian parents, the threesome clung together throughout the rest of the twentieth century, first debating whether Frankie's official stage debut was to take place in Syracuse or Buffalo. He was able to "reel off names of repertory companies, supporting players, tank towns, train trips." His father added, "Many a night he slept on the shelf in our dressing room." Frankie chimed in, "I do my best sleeping on Pullmans. I sleep better on trains than anywheres."

Playing a small role on Broadway during October and November of 1932 was an auspicious debut for the boy. Though not a great hit, *Carry Nation* presented him along with some future stars of Hollywood. In the cast were Josh Logan, Mildred Natwick, Myron McCormack, and James Stewart. Frankie worked mostly with adults, and his interplay with other children was often confined to sharing the stage. Yet Frankie liked to say his entrance into theatre and acting was an accident, "You'd think a fellow whose mother and father were in the business, and an aunt and uncle, would be put in the business, but I started in by mistake." He sometimes added, "*Carry Nation* was the first part I went out for," indicating it was perhaps a calculated effort to win a role from Blanche Yurka. As for his continuing education, Frank noted dismissively, "The children's school did it all by correspondence."

Two more Broadway roles were given him in 1933. "I went into a show that made a star out of Burgess Meredith." He referred to *Lil Old Boy*, in April of the year. He followed this part with another in October. "We did *Thunder on the Left*, which didn't do too well, but *Wednesday's Child* was a hit. It was the finest role ever written for a kid." Frankie was ready for the biggest role of his adolescent life. "I liked every bit of the work. I come back to Mother and Dad as the reason. They were pros. They saw to it I was the same way."

That marvelous opportunity came early for Frankie. "They say it's the most difficult juvenile part ever written. It's a great part." The plot told of the emotional turmoil of a young boy whose parents divorce and shunt him off to military school as the adults start new lives, without the encumbrance of a child to remind them of the past. As *Bobby*, Frankie would make his performance stand out on the stage. He denied that he had any intuitive understanding of the boy's plight, but in 1934 he told newspaper reporters, "It's awfully hard to memorize things you don't understand. I was kept in after school one day because I couldn't memorize two verses from *Ancient Mariner*, but I was able to memorize eighty-four pages of *Wednesday's Child* in four days."

Decades later Frankie said, "The play opened to rather good notices," which still gave the long-retired actor a great deal of pleasure and reason to be proud. The play ran just fifty-six performances in early 1934, but an *RKO* studio executive happened to attend the play one night. "I got to Hollywood because *RKO* bought the film rights to *Wednesday's Child*, only after they got me under contract. They said they would do it only if they could get the boy."

Studios in those days were usually leery of coping with parents or guardians of professional children, but in the case of Master Frankie, his parents were themselves well-regarded stage actors. They were not treated in the same fashion as the typical interfering family members dealt with by Hollywood; the Thomas acting family was a package deal. "When they signed me for *Wednesday's Child*, Dad negotiated the contract. In the first draft, they said neither of my parents would be on the set. They had some bad experiences with parents. They anticipated some problems, but Dad knocked that provision out. After a few weeks, they had a part written in for Dad and Mother played the original nurse, a small role."

In one of its more catty reports from the era, the *New York Times* gave a somewhat bemused different account in September of 1934 of the filming of *Wednesday's Child*: "The young star is causing the studio some concern. He has ideas about how the picture should be made and who should be in it and is quite noisy in mentioning them. *RKO* cast one of its contract players in the role of his mother and he rebelled so strongly against anyone but his own mother, Mona Bruns who was in the New York production, playing the part that she was placed in the picture. Now, studio officials say, he is working on a job for his father."

Leaving the electricity of live audiences on Broadway for the closed sets of the studio system was no problem for Frankie. He was surprised by a sense of excitement that was palpable at *RKO*. "Energy, something undefined. I remember that when I was doing *Wednesday's Child*, there was this odd feeling, something in the air, and I went to this grip, and asked what's everybody so excited about? 'Oh, we're bringing in a big one tonight. Astaire and Rogers.' There will be something that you sense. You don't know what the hell it is. Not at other places. It was more prevalent at *RKO*. I was there at the depths of the Depression . . . and I can't say I felt it anywhere else, but because I was a little kid."

Frankie enjoyed the hard work and long hours as he recreated his role, this time with ebullient Edward Arnold playing his father. "In those days of good featured players, I used to know all the people in the cast, right down to the smallest role. If you came from one studio to another, you might stay there." He didn't mind the late hours, having performed in legit theatres. "I was only supposed to work so many hours. We went over and over. That was a lot of rules laid by someone who didn't know what we were doing."

As for his debut, Frankie could not heap enough praise on the work he did. "Well, they made the picture, which was reasonably successful. Eddie Arnold played the father. And then I went back to New York to do a play. It was a very happy time. Then I came back to California to do a picture, and back to New York to do a play. And it was just great." So long as he had the stimulation of the two worlds of performing, he seemed like the luckiest child on earth. "I loved the business. And I loved listening to old character actors tell stories about that romantic time. We made so many good pictures in the 1920s. By 1931 the majority of American people could find their entertainment only for 25¢ in the local movie house. They'd go several times a week. This was their dream world. This is what they wanted to be."

Back to Broadway in October of 1934, Frankie took on a role in *The First Legion*, "which was successful, had an all male cast, and had a wonderful cast, including Johnny Litel, who later played Bonnie Granville's father in the Nancy Drew movies." Also in the cast was Charles Coburn, soon to be off to Hollywood where he'd portray a series of elderly gentlemen. *The First Legion* ran into the New Year with over one hundred performances, but Frankie was back to Hollywood shortly after to film his second motion picture, *Dog of Flanders*. Frankie had extra leverage as a free-lancer. He'd come to the notice of "a fellow at *Metro* called Irving Thalberg, the Boy Genius. Thalberg was very conscious of art. He would buy things, and convince Metro to buy things that weren't commercial. My god, he did it often."

For the first few years of his career, there could be no greater angel of support than Thalberg. "He seemed to be looking out for roles for me," contended Frankie. "We were shooting *Dog of Flanders*. It's my second picture. All of a sudden the production stops, and Mother was with me on the set. She was always with me. We were taken out to this limousine. We didn't know what the hell was going on. We were off to Culver City and went through the main gate without a stop. We were ushered in to this large room. Even at my age I knew that there was something big going on. There were five brains there. They took a look at me. And someone said, I think it was Mayer, 'No, he's too strong. Women won't cry for him.' And Thalberg said, 'But I saw him play a boy in a wheelchair on stage. Mayer said, 'No, no woman's gonna feel sorry for him.' And I was ushered out."

Of the men sitting in the room besides Thalberg and Mayer were David O. Selznick and George Cukor. The film under consideration was already one of the biggest and most prestigious of the *Metro* years: *David Copperfield*. Casting had become contentious, as Mayer wanted Jackie Cooper for the lead role, but was dissuaded because he was simply too American and too well-known for the part. Thalberg felt Frankie, less known, could act well enough to carry it off. Others were not so sure. Frankie's acting had a big deficiency. "Crying for me was the most difficult. Not for others. I got nothing on stage but these big parts of crying. I would pray. My mother used to speak to me about concentration, but it was still very hard. It was hard. When I broke down in movies in big close-ups they'd put stuff in my eyes, especially for me."

Loss of this important role made considerable impact upon Frankie and his sense of pride. "Three days later, *Variety* had a headline that *Metro* signs an Australian boy actor, Freddie Bartholomew, for the role in *David Copperfield*." Frankie still seemed to feel resentment after seventy years' passage, not considering that perhaps his American accent had been most at fault, as it had been for Jackie. By September of 1936, Thalberg's frail health gave out, and as for Frankie, the boy's most ardent supporter at *Metro* was gone. It was a severe loss that could not be underestimated. "Every time that a boy's part came up at *Metro*, Thalberg called for me." Now those calls would never come.

While unchallenging studio roles were offered, Frankie took advantage of a chance to return to the stage in New York to perform in a play called *Remember the Day*, about a schoolteacher and memories of her students. Frankie rode the lengthy train ride back to New York to step into the key role. "I had Broadway to fall back on." It also provided him with something he savored. "I played with my father. I have told the story quite often because it's a favorite. The producer was this wonderful man named Phillip Dunning. He had written this great play, a big hit. He went to my father and said this part wasn't very much, but will you do it with him. Well, my father honed this part, and the director left him alone to do it, and finally, by the time we opened at the *National Theatre*, it was a jewel of a part. And when the opening night came, the producers from *RKO* were there because I had done a couple of pictures for them . . . . I don't know what the President of *RKO PICTURES* thought of my performance, but he signed Dad to a seven-year contract. And that's how we came out here to live."

Frankie's devotion to his father and mother was unbounded. To play with his father "was my biggest thrill on Broadway." He added, "Dad was quite a prominent leading man in his day. If I had an idol, and this may sound corny if I did, it was my father." Without Frankie's success as a child star, his acting parents would not have had a renewed career as character actors. For decades afterward, Frank M. Thomas and Mona Bruns were fixtures on television and radio shows. They owed renewed acting careers to their son and the doors he opened. When first they came to Hollywood, Frankie reminisced, "We were living on the outskirts of Burbank about a mile and half from *Warners*. We could drive out about a few blocks to Riverside Drive and there was nothing but orange groves as far as you could see. The little house is now gone, taken by the freeway."

When Frankie returned to Hollywood in 1937, he did a popular *Universal Studio* serial for Saturday afternoons at the movies. *Tim Tyler's Luck* might have been fun, working with elephants and chimps; but it was as a step towards making young Thomas a teenage idol, without a contractual commitment to any studio. Though Thalberg was gone, Frankie received a call from a producer at *Metro*. They were recasting a potentially lucrative series. "Ann Rutherford was there." But when Frankie stood next to the actress, he was clearly shorter. "The producer said, 'You know maybe it would be funny if the boy were shorter than his sister.' And indeed, they hired Mickey Rooney for the role of Andy Hardy." Frankie insisted there was no competition among the child stars of the day. "The best one got the role. The others did a better job than I would have done."

Broadway beckoned again in the fall of 1936. Producers had cast the famous Mauch Twins, Billy and Bobby, to do a role in *Seen But Not Heard*. The boys had played *Penrod and Sam* in a series of movies, but they were about to be cast as the twins opposite Errol Flynn in the Warner Bros. epic, *The Prince and The Pauper*.

As the Mauch boys were unable to do the play, Frankie stepped in happily. Though it meant he must be flown back to New York to save time, he was more than delighted with the chance to appear for a change of pace role, far different from his usual "sweet" boys of the movies. The trip required five stops by airplane, over sixteen hours of flying, to get back to Broadway in the age before jet travel. He would appear this time with a young thirteen-year-old actress named Anne Baxter who would become a star in pictures during the next decade. Frankie insisted, "By that time, the rush of movies was too much. We were doing one after another."

Frankie and his parents made the decision to remain living in California for the foreseeable future, even if Frankie lost doing another New York stage role. "Broadway and Hollywood was a job, like being an electrician. There wasn't all this interest in the behind the scenes. I have got to be in makeup, I have to know my lines." Frankie eschewed the glamour of it all, and even went so far as to castigate the studios for failing now and then. "There was no perfection at the studios. They missed on the boy who grew up to be a millionaire producer, what's his name. Missed on three pictures." He meant Gene Reynolds, who replaced Frankie at the end of the *Boys Town* film as its new mayor. The Industry had put their faith in another boy, and Frankie, by the end of 1938, was nearing the end of his golden run in movies.

Frankie wanted more challenging roles from the studios hiring him. "I don't think *Metro* was more well-oiled than *RKO*, but *Universal* was more slapdash. They were grabbing on to what's left. We did something with Eddie Horton and Mary Boland. The producer comes to me and says you're going to be great playing this kid, and raised by millionaire parents. I said I don't want to play that part. I want to play the head of the gang. He said, 'Well, Kid, okay.' And they got Jackie Searle to play the other part. They would never have done that at *Metro*."

Frankie grew tired of the typecasting, but the system had assigned him the role of goody-two-shoes. He was never to be offered rebellious, unreasonable, or more dramatic roles. He could have resigned himself to the mission Hollywood gave him, yet knew he could have done better.

"I never wanted to be an ordinary kid. My career, my personal career, was to me the most wonderful thing in the world. Listening to those great stories of character actors. There's an old saying that the inside story, that's the one that's interesting. And I just lived on that. After a while I got thinking that I was part of those stories, and that was my fun time. Other kids were out playing football, and that kind of stuff, but I was perfectly happy." It was a refrain he often voiced, but there grew in him a highly apathetic view of his movie work. Of *Boys Town*, he said simply, "It was a good picture. Some big ones that I did, I didn't think that, but that's neither here nor there." He was not overly ecstatic when *Metro* gave him the call to do *Boys Town*. He shrugged. "Gee, I had a job." Though Frankie's acting style was unadorned and honest, it was of the older school, and he had lost his edge.

There were no more trips to Broadway, where he received accolades and stimulation. Now, after his fourth picture, there seemed to be just more similar roles. He represented, in his stalwart quiet demeanor, something that struck casting directors and studios as the typical military cadet. He had a conservative and safe disposition, at least on the surface. His discontent with his stature in Hollywood was keeping him from signing a term contract with any studio. He was a curious misfit long before it became fashionable. Frankie avoided the party circuit that most of the other young stars joined. He claimed he wasn't musical enough for the Mickey Rooney gang. They all played instruments and had Gene Krupa ambitions. Frankie was more aloof, partly because he was a New York actor in a California orange grove, or perhaps because of deeper issues. He'd always had an adult perspective, all in the name of professionalism, but it certainly didn't help him to fit in with his contemporaries. His father bought a boat, and he often went sailing with him in Santa Monica Bay. Mona and her husband and son spent many contented hours playing bridge with friends. Frankie wasn't particularly interested in popular sports, but did like tennis and took lessons from Charlie Chaplin's personal trainer, and sports celebrity, Big Bill Tilden. "Tennis was my main form of recreation."

Studios grew more reluctant to give Frankie a call in his latter-teens. Whether he became completely disillusioned or not, he knew something was up. "I was freelancing and doing one picture at *Metro* and another at *Paramount*." Frankie had sunk to accepting a cameo in a lesser Humphrey Bogart movie, *Invisible Stripes*. Was it punishment to be dropped from featured player to something akin to a walk-on?

In 1939, he had a date with Judy Garland, and they went to one of the famous Sunset Boulevard clubs. Entering, Judy nudged Frankie in distress to point out that Louis B. Mayer was seated at a table on the other side of the lounge. She insisted they stop by Mr. Mayer and exchange some sort of pleasant greeting. Her reason was simple: they had to prove to Mr. Mayer that they had not been out drinking. The *Lion of Metro* expected his youthful role models to present squeaky-clean public images. Frankie knew they had to pay their respects, and they soon left the place.

Frankie related far better to older professionals than to his own acting peers. He reported going out on the town with character actors like Henry Hull, fascinated by the man's tales of backstage shenanigans. Perhaps one of his rare exceptions, he made friends with Bonita Granville. She and Frankie worked in four *Nancy Drew* movies together, with Frankie playing her boyfriend *Ned Nickerson*. "Bonnie and I did the Drews. Actually, they put Bonnie in *Angels Wash Their Faces* because they wanted to see us together."

Nearing his twentieth birthday, Frankie returned to Broadway for a last time, playing the title character in *Your Loving Son*. It was an unmitigated disaster, lasting three performances. Instead of following a pattern of success, feeling renewed by stage work, the experience had turned to ashes. He had to go back to Hollywood and continue doing stock teenage roles, such as a budding test pilot in a low-budget production of *Flying Cadets*. He also faced the ignominious role of a cadet in *The Dead End Kids At Military School*. Then, after playing yet another military school cadet with Ginger Rogers in the notable 1942 feature *The Major and the Minor*, one of the biggest films of year, the twenty-two-year-old actor entered the Merchant Marine service during World War II. He limited discussions about his brief service aboard each of three cargo ships in the North Atlantic, embroidering somewhat about what was fearsome but without incident. Unlike many of his compatriots in Hollywood, he opted not to be involved with the USO.

When the war ended, the family trio moved back east, where they found work in radio soap operas. Bridge games with friends were always favorite amusements, and Frankie tried his hand at writing novels. The family rented an apartment to live in on the West side of Manhattan in New York City, spending weekends in a small farmhouse they owned in New Jersey. The daily trade papers printed an item about *Rockhill Radio Productions*, which was searching for a youthful All-American Boy to head up their proposed live sci-fi television and radio venture *Tom Corbett, Space Cadet*. That office was mobbed by hordes of young actors seeking work. Frankie managed to get an appointment to be seen in the summer of 1950, and was matched up with two New York actors,

Jan Merlin and Al Markim, who were by then set to do co-starring cadet roles. Frankie was immediately hired and given the series lead.

Having passed his thirtieth birthday, he was a star again, appearing as teenaged *Tom Corbett* on live television and radio where his training as a stage actor under pressure came across. He could quickly memorize pages of dialogue overnight; *Corbett* was to be his final acting role, the one he most treasured. He played the stalwart, heroic Tom for six years. (Jan had deserted the show after three seasons to play "heavies" in Hollywood.)

When the innovative series ended, Frankie gave up his acting career entirely, claiming nothing could ever top that heroic role. He never tired of making appearances as *Tom Corbett* at festivals and kept his original uniform for the rest of his life. In the following years, he took up teaching bridge and authored a column about the game. In his spare time, he completed a dozen novels, printed here and abroad, about the intellectual Holmes, whose cases were easily and cleverly solved and left him greatly unsatisfied.

Twenty years later, Frankie and his aged parents moved back to Hollywood. They had a circle of acquaintances from show business there and settled down to a happy retirement. Frankie took up golf, and continued to teach bridge classes and write his columns and books. His father died in 1989 at the age of 101.

The next year, Jan Merlin and Frankie discovered they lived near one another, and took up their old friendship again. The two men and their wives attended the Newark, New Jersey, *Old Time Radio Convention* in 1993, where they performed one of their radio scripts of the sci-fi series with members of the old cast and crew. His mother lived on until her one hundredth birthday.

Frankie had faithfully visited her; like the cadets he played, he was steadfast, loyal, pleasant, and hid his deep sadness with sudden bouts with alcohol. He struggled to keep sober and seemed to be able to do so; he and Jan continued to make appearances together. Frankie always wore his fading uniform at those events, but he was visibly fading himself. Travel became almost impossible. Changing flights on cross-country trips was more than a challenge. At age eighty-four, it was becoming too painful for him to turn down any invitation, but he could not continue to appear for his fans.

The Golden Boy of Hollywood and Broadway made certain we knew that he wished to be buried in that ancient space cadet outfit, and his wish was carried out in May of 2006.

His show's favorite phrase is engraved upon the bronze marker of his grave, set alongside those of his mother and father amid the trimmed green lawns of the Hollywood Forest Lawn Cemetery overlooking Warner Bros. Studio:

Spaceman's Luck!

Katharine Hepburn On Stage

Judy Samelson

INTRODUCTION

In 1999, the American Film Institute released another of its famous lists. This one was dubbed the Top 50 Greatest American Film Legends. Divided evenly among male and female stars, Humphrey Bogart topped the list of men, while Katharine Hepburn stood alongside him—as she had, valiantly, on the deck of *The African Queen*—at the head of the distaff group. While lists of this sort usually spark heated debate among those of us who adore the movies and stars of the period now referred to as classic Hollywood, it would be difficult to deny Bogie and Kate their head-of-the-class designation. Both got their start kicking around the regional and Broadway theatre scene before they ventured out to Hollywood where they carved out careers that elevated them to iconic status. Bogart, sadly, died far too young, though if anything his legend increased in the years following his death and continues to this day. Hepburn, conversely, lived a very long life. She was ninety-six when she passed on June 29, 2003—though, as one postmortem tribute allowed, I don't have to believe it if I don't want to—and for over sixty of those years she was never far from the consciousness of the American public.

Over the course of her long and sublime career, Hepburn was often quoted on the subject of the movies. She loved them. She loved being an audience, and she loved making them. "What is better than a good movie?" she once inquired rhetorically of writer Lee Israel in a late-sixties interview for *Esquire*. The process of making pictures, she said, was easy, and it was fun. And as the ever-pragmatic Yankee told Dick Cavett in their legendary 1973 chat, it was also well paid.

But the stage was trickier. Where moviemaking was tailor-made for Hepburn, the theatre, she admitted to Cavett, could be torment. Where moviemaking suited her internal clock, allowing her to rise in the predawn hours, as was her wont, the theatre imposed late nights and demanded stamina. Because of the discipline and sheer energy required to play eight shows a week—vitality that she had in abundance but that she also acknowledged was not as easy to maintain on stage as it looked—Hepburn often likened appearing in a play to a jail sentence.

Still, throughout her career, Hepburn frequently left the Hollywood sunshine, which wreaked havoc on her freckled complexion, and moviemaking, which transformed her from unknown to national treasure, to voluntarily incarcerate herself on stage. It could be argued (by someone other than me, of course) that Hepburn's theatrical career never quite equaled the luminous four-time Oscar-winning one she built on the screen. But I would suggest that in the boldness of its reach, the former was not so far removed from the latter. A theatrical career that stretched to encompass plays by Philip Barry, Shakespeare, and Shaw—even a Broadway musical—bore more than a passing resemblance to a film career that leapt from screwball comedy to high adventure in the wilds of Africa to Eugene O'Neill and Euripides. Regardless of the arena, her penchant for taking risks and making intriguing and unexpected choices—her determination to embrace artistic challenge—seems to have been marked on Hepburn's DNA.

For the young Hepburn and her contemporaries, the theatre in the late twenties and thirties was the training ground where they honed their burgeoning skills. It was also a point of departure: recognition in the theatre bought a ticket to the West Coast and, for many, movie stardom. With the noted exception of Hepburn's *On Golden Pond* co-star Henry Fonda, most never returned to the stage—or if they did, it was for an occasional dip in the pool. But as a 2009 exhibition of her theatrical papers revealed, no one dove off the deep end quite so often, so vigorously, or so adventurously as Katharine Hepburn.

—**Judy Samelson**

Credit: The following article originally appeared on Playbill.com in July 2009. © 2009 PLAYBILL®. An edited version is reprinted here. Used with permission.

Katharine Hepburn On Stage
By Judy Samelson
July 6, 2009

I have admired Katharine Hepburn (oh, all right, I've been a fan) since . . . well, I'll only say that nine Presidents have occupied the White House since she insinuated herself into my then-young consciousness. Not only was her work compelling but in her independence, forthrightness, sense of adventure and fairness and loyalty, her personal life seemed to offer a design for living that was particularly enticing to a 13-year-old girl. Decades later, Hepburn's power to captivate—even now, six years after her death at 96 on June 29, 2003—lives on. So, when my editor asked me to cover "Katharine Hepburn: In Her Own Files"—the exhibition of the actress' theatrical papers on view through Oct. 10 at The New York Public Library for the Performing Arts—I jumped at the assignment.

In 2004, the trustees of Hepburn's estate donated to the Academy of Motion Pictures Arts and Sciences' Margaret Herrick Library in Los Angeles what the library has called the largest presentation of material documenting a film career they have ever received from a single performer. Subsequently, in October 2007, the actress' estate donated the papers covering her stage career to The New York Public Library for the Performing Arts. When one considers the fact that Katharine Hepburn juggled a successful film and stage career by practically commuting between Los Angeles and New York (a given now, but not the done thing in her day), the bi-coastal division of this array of professional and personal material takes on a pleasing symmetry. The Hepburn theatrical papers are housed in the library's Billy Rose Division, and it is from this vast collection that the library's executive director Jacqueline Z. Davis and curator of exhibitions Barbara Cohen-Stratyner developed the current exhibition.

"Katharine Hepburn: In Her Own Files" allows fans a privileged peek—via letters, telegrams, journals, photos, etc.—into the support Hepburn received from friends and teachers, the diligence and good humor with which she approached her work and the personal satisfaction she seems to have derived from it. The exhibition encompasses the broad sweep of Hepburn's stage career from its earliest days in college theatrics to her final appearances on Broadway. Items in frames line the walls of the Vincent Astor Gallery, while other more fragile pieces are displayed in glass cases in the center of the space. Enlarged images of Hepburn in various stage roles hang banner-style from the ceiling. In one corner of the gallery there is a flat-screen TV on which excerpts from videotaped talks given by friends and colleagues at the library in 2008 are played in a loop. Finally, since even an exhibition designed to spotlight her work in the theatre could not completely ignore the movies that made her an icon, Hepburn's film years are also represented with photos and ephemera from the library's general collections.

It may come as a surprise to some to discover that Katharine Hepburn had a globetrotting theatrical career that took her from fresh-out-of-college appearances in stock companies to Broadway, from the West End to the American Shakespeare Festival Theatre in Stratford, CT—even as far as Australia with The Old Vic Company. She was one of the few stars born in that era of glittering Hollywood legends of the 1930s to return repeatedly to the stage. As she told Dick Cavett in a 1973 interview, she had a theatre clause built into her film contracts from the very start, giving her control over her career and enabling her to leave Hollywood and tread the boards periodically. Something else she said during that legendary interview revealed an unexpected insecurity but also a determination to triumph over it. "I was so tormented in the theatre," she told Cavett. "It frightened me so that I thought I must come back and overcome that. And it took me my whole life."

That life in the theatre encompassed everything from untraditional ingénues (*The Warrior's Husband*) to musical grande dames (*Coco*)—from Philip Barry to Enid Bagnold to George Bernard Shaw to William Shakespeare. The trajectory wasn't always upward. The Hepburn career resembled the stomach-churning ups and downs of an E-ticket ride on more than one occasion. In 1934, after having won the first of her record four Oscars for what was only her third role in pictures (*Morning Glory*), Hepburn starred on Broadway in *The Lake* for producer-director Jed Harris and was famously cut down by Dorothy Parker's scathing critique that her performance ran the gamut of emotions from A to B. What could have leveled a lesser person only served to fuel her fire and her career would ultimately render Parker's potshot obsolete, as Hepburn excelled in exploring and conveying all manner of emotion in the roles she took on.

What follows, then, is a walking tour of "Katharine Hepburn: In Her Own Files"—a fan's-eye view of this fascinating exhibition of the theatrical papers of the Great Kate.

THE EARLY YEARS, BROADWAY & HOLLYWOOD

Bryn Mawr

- From 1925 to 1928 Hepburn attended Bryn Mawr, the women's college on Philadelphia's Main Line, and during that time became active in student theatrics. Among the first items displayed in the gallery are Hepburn's map of the college campus and a program for *The Truth About Blayds*, a 1928 production in which she had the male role of Oliver Blayds Conway.

A young actress of possibilities

- The years between her college graduation and Broadway are documented with a program from *The Czarina*, in which Hepburn appeared for Edwin Knopf's Baltimore stock company in 1928, a photograph of Hepburn in *The Big Pond*, a play that opened in Great Neck (Hepburn was fired after one night, something that would happen more than once in her early stage career), as well as an Actors' Equity contract, dated Aug. 26, 1928, for a play called *Night Hostess*, where her part is described as "a night hostess and understudy as assigned" for a salary of $50. Many sources list *Night Hostess* as her Broadway debut; however, Hepburn always maintained that she got a better job in New York and left the play before it arrived on Broadway in September 1928.
- Following these items is a 1928 letter of introduction from writer-director David Wallace to director-producer George C. Tyler, in which he writes: "I want to introduce you to Katherine [*sic*] Hepburn, a young actress of possibilities . . . . She's had a variety of experience including summer stock and she played for Arthur Hopkins in *These Days*."
- A *Playbill* from *These Days* (Cort Theatre, November 1928) represents Hepburn's Broadway debut. Also displayed are her "sides" from the play. Sides are the pages from the playscript that contain only an actor's lines, stage directions and cues. Each of the sides is stamped on the front with the act and scene and with the name "Veronica," Hepburn's role in the play.
- Her next Broadway appearance came in *Art and Mrs. Bottle* (Maxine Elliot's Theatre, Nov. 18, 1930-December 1930), starring Jane Cowl. Hepburn was hired for the play, then fired and then rehired. In her autobiography "Me," she wrote of Cowl's generosity—helping

with her makeup, softening her look—and Cowl's encouragement is evident in the displayed opening night telegram to the young actress. It reads, simply: "Be a good girl and act pretty."

- A fan letter reads: "Naturally, Jane Cowl was the drawing card but for all her kerchief flutters my eyes kept going back to the silent unknown, her back to the audience. No tricks to steal the scene, but what concentration! So when I got home I put the check mark after the name, a memo to me to watch this one, she's going to be someone." Next to the letter is a cast list from an *Art and Mrs. Bottle* program. The list sports a tiny check mark next to Hepburn's name.

- After *Art and Mrs. Bottle* Hepburn joined The New York Players, a summer stock company run by Milton Stiefel. Stiefel, one of her early supporters, was the first to offer her leading roles and she appeared in a number of plays with his company, including *Let Us Be Gay*. Displayed next to a Christmas card from Stieflel is a program from that 1932 production at the Comstock-Cheney Theatre, later to become Stiefel's Ivoryton Playhouse.

A star is born

- A group of photos, including a banner hanging above, feature Hepburn in full Amazon regalia tussling with Colin-Keith Johnston in her next Broadway outing, Julian F. Thompson's *The Warrior's Husband* (Morosco Theatre, March 11, 1932-May 1932). Hepburn played Antiope to Johnston's Theseus and intrigued audiences from the moment she stepped onto the stage, leaping down a narrow flight of stairs with a stag over her shoulder.

RKO and the movies

- The good notices Hepburn received for *The Warrior's Husband* led to a screen test that brought her to the attention of director George Cukor, who became a lifelong colleague and friend; producer David O. Selznick; and RKO. In the span of one year in Hollywood, she was introduced in her first film, *A Bill of Divorcement*, starring John Barrymore and Billie Burke and directed by George Cukor; billed over the title in her second, *Christopher Strong*, about an aviatrix's doomed love affair; won the first of four career Oscars in her third, *Morning Glory*, co-starring with Adolphe Menjou and Douglas Fairbanks Jr.; and followed that with one of her most beloved performances as

Jo March in the George Cukor-directed *Little Women*. Hollywood stardom brought with it press coverage in movie magazines, such as the copies of *Picture Play* and *Modern Screen* displayed here alongside studio publicity portraits taken by the famed star photographer Ernest A. Bachrach.

The Lake

• Now a bona fide movie star, Hepburn planned a return to Broadway in the Jed Harris production of *The Lake*. Displayed are a series of telegrams between Harris and Hepburn concerning the production. Harris—whose Broadway credits as either producer or director included *The Royal Family*, *The Front Page* and *Our Town*—was a talented but difficult, some would say sadistic, man. He had a notorious reputation for either bedding or belittling his stars—or both. Laurence Olivier was said to have based his Richard III on him, and Playbill's former senior editor Louis Botto once told me that George S. Kaufman, who worked with Harris on *The Front Page* and *The Royal Family*, had such disdain for Harris that he once said when he died, Kaufman wanted to have his ashes thrown in Jed Harris' face. Harris' behavior with Hepburn did nothing to alter his tyrannical reputation. However, the telegrams on display were all written in April 1933, when Harris was still in the courting stage and Hepburn was still receptive. He wanted her to star not only in *The Lake* but also in *The Green Bay Tree*.

• One telegram, dated April 20, 1933, mentions Hepburn's good friend Laura Harding:

> "Dear Katie—Laura Harding is in my office reading *The Lake* which I want you to do after *The Green Bay Tree* STOP After she gets through it I'm going to have her call you up and tell you in great detail what my ideas about these things are STOP Your telegrams are so long and loving I wish you'd send me lots more STOP Love and wonderful personal regards. Jed."

• Hepburn passed on *The Green Bay Tree*—and nearly drowned in *The Lake*. The play opened at the Martin Beck Theatre on Dec. 26, 1933, and closed in February 1934. In her autobiography she wrote of the contentiousness during rehearsals, and the warning she received from Helen Hayes ("Don't let Jed direct you. He will destroy your confidence."). During rehearsals Harris fired the director, Tony

Miner, and criticized Hepburn's every move, thereby confirming Hayes' prediction. Why he did this to his star remains a mystery. Harris insisted on keeping the play open. Even as a flop, Hepburn was a draw. But there were some bright spots. Hepburn kept a fan letter from this period that is displayed next to the Harris telegrams. It reads: *"The Lake* is the only Broadway play I have ever attended. I don't usually allow myself such luxuries, but I couldn't resist seeing you."

THEATRE GUILD

• Hepburn's association with the Theatre Guild, co-founded by Lawrence Langner, Theresa Helburn and Armina Marshall, began in the late '20s. In 1936-37, she toured in the Guild production of *Jane Eyre*, represented in the exhibition by two striking Vandamm Studio images. One of the banners hanging from the ceiling shows Hepburn in costume as the title character and the other pictures the star decidedly out of costume, sitting cross-legged on the floor of the stage set with the play's crew—in her usual trousers, cigarette in hand. The play had a successful tour but Hepburn didn't think it was the right vehicle for her return to the New York stage. The experience of *The Lake* had made her skittish, not only for herself but also for the coffers of the Guild. If she were going to tackle Broadway again, she had to come back in the right vehicle.

• That vehicle arrived in the form of Philip Barry's *The Philadelphia Story*, which opened at Broadway's Shubert Theatre on March 28, 1939, and ran for a year. Prior to her involvement in the play, Hepburn's film career had been in a slump, and the Theatre Guild and Phillip Barry had not had a discernible hit in a while. Tracy Lord changed that for all of them: Hepburn and the play were a great success. The exhibition features a framed souvenir program from *The Philadelphia Story* as well as a color photo of Hepburn (as Tracy) in designer Valentina's stunning white gown and red coat. Also included is a telegram from her old Bryn Mawr schoolmate Margaret Barker. Barker, a Group Theatre actress and instructor, befriended Hepburn when they attended Bryn Mawr and in her correspondence uses their college nicknames: Beanie and Kaydiddle. The telegram, dated March 28, 1939, reads: "Dear Kaydiddle—I hear you're finally playin' the fiddle and over the moon. Love and rare wishes Beanie Barker."

Hepburn's reply is framed alongside the telegram:

April 8, 1939

"What a wonderful wire. And wasn't it lucky that the fiddle wasn't out of tune. I'm only sorry that you weren't with me. Thank you a thousand times. Love, Kate."

- After the Broadway run and before she took *The Philadelphia Story* on tour, Hepburn, with the film rights in her pocket, returned to Los Angeles and to a new studio: Metro-Goldwyn-Mayer. She had her pick of co-star and director and made what is now considered one of the most elegant romantic comedies ever to have emerged from Hollywood. The film is represented by a framed copy of Hepburn's *LIFE* magazine cover (Aug. 6, 1941) as well as a *Picturegoer* cover of her and James Stewart locked in a moonlit embrace.

- Hepburn reunited with the Theatre Guild and Philip Barry for *Without Love*, which opened at the St. James Theatre on November 10, 1942. There are photos of her and co-star Elliot Nugent onstage and a souvenir book from the play. Another small photo shows Hepburn in one of Valentina's costumes for her in the play alongside a notebook page on which Hepburn sketched the dress in pencil and wrote, "Color powder blue, skirt simply floated, made of strips of gray, rose, white and powder blue . . . I don't know whether it was organdy or starched chiffon, but it sure was heavenly." *Without Love* ran for three months, closing in February 1943. If lightning didn't exactly strike twice for the collaborators, it did give Hepburn another opportunity to transfer a play to the screen, this time as a vehicle for her third pairing with Spencer Tracy in 1945.

SHAKESPEARE

Perhaps the most intriguing items in the exhibition relate to Hepburn's Shakespearean roles because they allow us to witness her process, via detailed notes and sketches, and the input she received from various colleagues. Virtually all of these productions are represented in some fashion in the exhibition.

As You Like It

On Jan. 26, 1950, Hepburn opened at the Cort Theatre in *As You Like It*, produced by the Theatre Guild. Lawrence Langner had challenged her to tackle the role of Rosalind saying that if she didn't do it, she would be considered limited.

- Vandamm Studio photos show her with William Prince as Orlando, and an enlarged photo taken by Ellen Darby presents a terrific, if somewhat incongruous, image of Hepburn and Prince onstage in costume. Taken during rehearsals, Prince is seated and Hepburn is standing in cape and tights with a script and the ubiquitous cigarette.

- In the glass case, there's an opening night gift signed by the Guild's Theresa Helburn, Lawrence Langner and Armina Marshall inscribed, in part:

  > January 26, 1950—
  > Let no face be kept in mind
  > But the fair of Rosalind
  > —to our Kate with love
  > Terry
  > Lawrence
  > Armina

- Some examples of congratulatory notes Hepburn received on opening night are shown below. As was her habit, she wrote her responses at the bottom of the telegrams.

  > ANITA LOOS: "January 26, 1950—Love to you. Congratulations to Shakespeare."

  > Hepburn's reply: "That was a mighty cute wire. I don't know how the old boy would feel, but it made me very proud. See you soon. Affect."

  > JAMES CAGNEY: "January 27, 1950—Dear Kate: The gang convined [*sic*] last night and we heard all the good news of the play . . . . Want you to know that all the Cagneys are pulling for the greatest hit in your entire career. We think your [*sic*] great."

  > Hepburn's reply: "Dear Jim: Thought for a while the Irishers were going 2 have 2 come back and fight my battles."

  > JOHN FORD: "January 26, 1950—Get in there and pitch Tutz."

  > Hepburn's reply: "Dear Jack: Thank u 4 ur wire on opening nite. It's very classical but I'm sure u intended it 2 be. I think that that is an old Eng. word as it very likely may be on 2nd thought. How I adored '*She Wore a Yellow Ribbon*.'"

- There is also a letter from Constance Collier. Collier, who appeared with Hepburn in the 1937 film *Stage Door*, was a classical actress and had played all of Shakespeare's great women. She was also an acting coach and worked with Hepburn on this production as well as on Shaw's *The Millionairess*, in which Hepburn appeared in 1952. Their professional relationship blossomed into a close friendship. Below is an excerpt from Collier's letter. (The "Michael" referred to is the play's director Michael Benthall.)

January 28, 1950

My dear, dear Kate,

I have lived again in the glories of the theatre in its highest sense. Shakespeare, you and Michael have refreshed and renewed me. I have been for a long time like a scorched garden waiting for a shower and it came with our association. But beyond the theatre I know I have made a beloved friend for the rest of my life . . . . You will never know how much I admire you as a person besides being the very great artist you are.

- A framed telegram dated Dec. 4, 1950, wishes Hepburn well on the Los Angeles opening of the tour. Signed by the "MGM Studio Drivers," it reads: "Sincere good wishes for a grand opening and a long, successful run."
- Like other great theatre stars of her generation and before—The Lunts, Katharine Cornell—Katharine Hepburn embraced the theatrical tradition of touring. The *As You Like It* tour produced a journal in which she seemingly recorded every detail—from the population of the towns she played in to the interstate routes taken to get there, to the hotel accommodations. The journal on display is open to a page that presents a fascinating look into life on the road with Katharine Hepburn. In this particular entry, she wrote about her arrest for speeding while on her way from Tulsa, OK, to the tour's next stop in Wichita, KS. (The "Charles" referred to is Charles Newhill, her longtime driver and friend.) An excerpt reads:

". . . Halfway from Tulsa—about sixty-five miles—in Blackwell, Okla. Charles and I were arrested for speeding. A handsome and extremely irritating and drawling Oklahoman drew alongside when we were going seventy in a sixty-five mile an hour zone with the road straight and flat as a pancake.

He pulled us over and took about a half hour to get out of his
and get to ours, 'You are under arrest.' 'What the hell for?' I
said. He said, 'Speeding—follow me." I said, "Just a minute
officer—we are trying to get to Wichita in time to do a play."
"You should have left earlier," he said calmly looking at me.

[After following the cop to a lawyer's office, she continues:]

They gave me an inquiring look and I said, "I have been
arrested by this moron," turning to the policeman who was
then coming to the door. I stood there in a seething rage and
so did Charles . . . . They cannot find a judge or justice of the
peace. I said that I was sorry I did not have a week to take
off and . . . if I ever found an Oklahoma car in Connecticut I
would flatten all the tires. In the meantime, Cox kept calling
to find someone to judge us. I paced to make the cop nervous
and backed into a gas stove, singing my coat.

The Old Vic Tour

In 1955 (from mid-May to mid-November), Hepburn toured Australia
with Robert Helpmann and The Old Vic Company, performing in *The
Merchant of Venice*, *The Taming of the Shrew* and *Measure for Measure*.

• Photos of Hepburn and Helpmann, a Dolgov costume sketch of
Hepburn as Katharina in *The Taming of the Shrew* and a prompt script
from *The Merchant of Venice* represent the tour.

The American Shakespeare Festival Theatre

In the summer of 1957, Hepburn appeared in *The Merchant of Venice*
and *Much Ado About Nothing* for John Houseman and Jack Landau's third
season of the American Shakespeare Festival Theatre in Stratford, CT.
She returned to the company in the summer of 1960 to appear in *Twelfth
Night* and *Antony and Cleopatra*.

• There is a prompt script from the production of *Much Ado About
Nothing* alongside a legal pad with Hepburn's notes and sketch of
the set.
• Hepburn's appearance in *Antony and Cleopatra* prompted letters of
guidance (with corresponding illustration) from modernist furniture

designer Terence Robsjohn-Gibbings ("Gibby"). Two of his letters are displayed. In one (dated February 2, 1960) he advised, "Instead of manicuring or bathing, you might be posing for a portrait to be subsequently carved on one of your temples. This would give you a nice opportunity to wear royal clothes and crown." And in another (dated November 11, 1959) he counseled that her Cleopatra must remain modern in costume and approach, writing that "Katharine Cornell's Cleopatra looked like a Westchester matron in a hostess gown" and that Vivien Leigh's was "fancy dress in the Albert Hall." Hepburn's Cleopatra, he wrote, "With all your energy and full of the wild satirical humor of Alexandria" must be "barbaric, pagan, splendid."

- A fascinating notebook that she kept while preparing for *Antony and Cleopatra*, shows densely-packed pages, in Hepburn's hand, divided into two columns dissecting each scene and character, each entrance and exit, a breakdown of the mood and atmosphere of each scene. She kept these notebooks for other productions as well.

SHAW

- In 1952 Hepburn starred in George Bernard Shaw's *The Millionairess* in England (presented by Hugh "Binky" Beaumont's H.M. Tennent Ltd.) and later in the year on Broadway at the Shubert Theatre (produced by the Theatre Guild in association with Beaumont). The play co-starred Robert Helpmann and Cyril Ritchard and was directed by Michael Benthall. On display is a letter from Lawrence Langner to Hepburn, in which he wrote of the Theatre Guild's efforts to obtain Shaw's permission to do the play and described a humorous encounter with the great GBS. The letter is dated June 25, 1950, and reads, in part:

Armina and I had a wonderful visit with George Bernard Shaw and talked about *The Millionairess*. The following dialogue may amuse you:

Armina: She's a very good athlete.

GBS: *(not hearing correctly)* I know she's a good actress. I mean can she—is she strong?

Armina: Is she strong? Why she gets up and plays tennis every morning. She's one of the most athletic girls I know. She's terrific.

GBS: Then I think it's dangerous for her to play the part.

LL: (getting a word in edgeways) Why?

GBS: Dangerous for the actor she's doing the Judo with. She'll probably kill him.

LL: Oh, no, GBS. She's a very tender-hearted girl. She wouldn't kill another actor.

- Another telegram—from Benthall and Beaumont—reads: "Cyril Ritchard eager to play Adrian STOP We feel this good idea in spite of height. Has personality and great vitality"—to which Hepburn queried at the foot of the telegram: "Lovely. But how could I Judo him?"
- The strenuous performance she was giving in *The Millionairess* caused Hepburn to experience extreme vocal problems. Prior to the Broadway opening in October 1952, she lost her voice almost entirely and, as she wrote in her autobiography, she was desperate to find someone who could help. She had studied with a number of teachers over the years, but most helpful to her during this period was a man named Alfred Dixon. Dixon's typewritten exercises, titled "Tonal Shades," are displayed next to a chart labeled "Tones, Sound and Shades," illustrating symbols corresponding to different tonal shades. Hepburn apparently did her homework because beside these are her meticulous handwritten notes interpreting these lessons. All of these notes were kept in and are displayed alongside a leather portfolio with the initials ST (presumably, for Spencer Tracy).

COCO

- In 2008, the library hosted a series of talks under the banner "Remembering Kate." Each talk was devoted to a different area of Hepburn's stage career. The talks were recorded and video excerpts appear on a television screen in the gallery. Among the friends and colleagues who read from Hepburn's papers were Sam Waterston and Zoe Caldwell, whose focus was on her appearance in her first and only stage musical, *Coco*.

- On December 18, 1969, Hepburn opened at Broadway's Mark Hellinger Theatre in the Alan Jay Lerner-André Previn musical about pioneering French fashion designer Gabrielle Chanel. She played in it until the summer of 1970, but at the start, it seemed that she thought the project would not be right for her. Lerner, however, was determined to get her, as evidenced by the correspondence that passed between them. In an excerpt from one of Lerner's letters, written to her from the Hotel Plaza Athenee on September 16, 1967, Waterston read:

  > Believe me when I tell you that never in my entire professional life have I ever wanted anyone to play any role in anything I have ever written as much as I want you to play Coco. If you allow me I will prove it to you by doing anything and everything within the bounds of artistic, legal, economic and social reason to make it possible for you to do it conveniently, happily and comfortably.

  Hepburn's reply, read by Zoe Caldwell:

  > I am doing two things virtually at the same time [presumably, this was a reference to the two films in which she starred back to back—*The Lion in Winter* and *The Madwoman of Chaillot*] and I do not enjoy working this way. I'm an all-for-one sort of person. I'm convinced that any deal between us is impossible and this is why . . . You have done a wonderful job and there are many people who could do it brilliantly. I offer you no time, no freedom. I just don't want to be tied up at my age. And this is a proper attitude . . . . Frankly, I'm not sure that I will ever act again . . . . I'm sorry if I led you on. I should have stated my position more clearly to begin with. I felt I had. Affectionately, Kate.

- Hepburn loved to sketch and paint. On display is one of the notebooks she kept during *Coco* rehearsals, open to a page in which she painted herself in costume as the Countess Aurelia from her 1969 film *The Madwoman of Chaillot*.
- Work on *Coco* proceeded with Hepburn signing on but insisting that they hire a director experienced in musical theatre ("I don't want expensive chaos," she wrote in one letter read by Caldwell) and concerned that Lerner would not be ready in time for the start

of rehearsals. In an effort to ease Hepburn's concerns, Lerner, in a letter read by Waterston, declared emphatically (and humorously): "Barring crippling illness, atomic war, planetary collision—or your wishes—rehearsals will begin in November. And that's that. Period."

- Hepburn gave a speech from the stage of the Hellinger after a performance on May 8, 1970. She was asked by actor Keir Dullea to request a moment of silence in memory of the four students shot by the National Guard earlier that week on the campus of Kent State University in Ohio. Her speech, as read by Caldwell, said, in part:

> A few days ago four kids were shot and killed in Kent State College, Ohio. Now you may call them rebels or rabble-rousers or anything you name. Nevertheless they were our kids and our responsibility. Our generation is responsible and we must take time to pause and reflect and do something. You can pray, but we must think—and together—for if we don't, we are lost. The mayor joins with me and the rest of the cast in asking you to stay for a few minutes silence . . . . If any of you wishes to leave you are free to do so. But if you do leave, I know you will still think about it.

- Hepburn left *Coco* before the end of the Broadway run to film *The Trojan Women*. Beseeching her to stay, members of the orchestra signed a petition that hangs next to a library note card labeled, "The Beloved of the Backstage":

> Dear Miss Hepburn
> Mademoiselle, you can't quit—You can't!
> Why not?
> Because we want to work for you.
> The *Coco* Orchestra

- Hepburn's emotional curtain speech, delivered at her final performance in the musical, is read movingly by Zoe Caldwell in the video excerpt:

> When I started rehearsal I was very, very frightened. And all these people that you see in the back of me really gave me the faith to go on. Then there was the terror of the opening night and for some wonderful reason, for me, you people gave

me a feeling that you believed that I could do it. I've lived a very fortunate life because I had a father and a mother who believed in me. I had brothers and sisters who believed in me and a few friends who have believed in me. And I hope that you learn a lesson that I have learned. That is . . . I love you and you love me.

At the start of her career, Hepburn glibly stated that she didn't want to be an actress; she just wanted to be famous. She also said: "I'm a personality as well as an actress. Show me an actress who isn't a personality and you'll show me a woman who isn't a star." But to anyone giving this exhibition even a cursory glance, her commitment to her own excellence and to that of any project in which she was involved—her seemingly inexhaustible curiosity in the clothes, the sets, the movement, the voice—indicates a more thoughtful and deeper desire. Famous? Yes. A star? Certainly. But what lies beneath and what her fans are now being treated to is a self-portrait of someone who took her art—her life's work—very seriously.

One of Miss H's most celebrated film roles was that of Josephine March in *Little Women*. Early in the picture, Jo enters the home of her newfound friend Laurie and upon seeing the grandness before her exclaims, "Christopher Columbus! What richness!" Try to resist the urge to blurt out the same when you enter "Katharine Hepburn: In Her Own Files." It won't be easy.

Billie Burke:
A Blithe Spirit Forever

Val Sherman

Introduction

Is it at all surprising that the daughter of a successful clown would walk the stages of Broadway and have an enduring career in motion pictures, beginning with silent films and lasting for forty-five years? Perhaps the person who would have been most astonished by this is the woman herself, Billie Burke. Not only did performing originally hold no appeal for her, but after she was a success on Broadway, Billie reflected that "I was not an ambitious girl. I had not hankered for fame or visualized myself as accomplishing great things."[1] In light of this sentiment, as expressed in her autobiography, *With a Feather on My Nose*, it is all the more impressive that Billie Burke still delights viewers, and will forever be associated with one of the most enduring films ever produced.

Born in Washington, D.C. on August 7, 1884, Billie's father, William Ethelbert Burke, was a professional clown who had performed with Barnum & Bailey's circus.[2] Her mother, Blanche Hodkinson,

---

[1]   Billie Burke, with Cameron Shipp, *With a Feather on My Nose* (New York: Appleton-Century-Crofts Inc., 1949), 83.

[2]   In addition to 1884, sources cite 1885 and 1886 as the year in which Billie Burke was born. In her memoirs, Billie avoids mentioning the date. Grant Hayter-Menzies, author of *Mrs. Ziegfeld: The Public and Private Lives of*

was descended from a distinguished New Orleans family that had significant wealth prior to the Civil War. As Billie's father toured the country, she spent her early years in Washington, D.C. with her mother and grandmother, a stately woman of impeccable manners. Facing financial hardships on tour, her father moved the family to London, when Billie was eight. Her father established *Billy Burke's Barnum & Great London Songsters* and performed throughout Europe and Russia, often accompanied by Billie, while her mother assumed the role of tour manager. It was after moving to London that Billie was formally baptized in Westminster Abbey and received her full name, "Mary William Ethelbert Appleton Burke."[3]

In spite of her husband's strong objections, which were based upon Billie's shy and reserved nature, Blanche was determined that her daughter become an actress, opera singer, or dancer. She intended that Billie not just perform, but become an artist of significant reputation. Blanche managed Billie's formal training in the arts, and at fourteen she began singing in musical revues in small English towns. This led to performing at the London Pavilion, where she earned £10 a week. In retrospect, Billie did not view Blanche as a typical stage mother, trying to vicariously live through her daughter's success. Instead, she attributes her mother's determination to a realistic perception that the arts presented one of the few paths for a woman to achieve legitimate

---

Billie Burke, and Richard and Paulette Ziegfeld, coauthors of *The Ziegfeld Touch: The Life and Times of Florenz Ziegfeld, Jr.*, all had direct access to and conversations with Patricia Burke, Billie and Florenz Ziegfeld Jr.'s daughter, in the writing of their respective works. Patricia also wrote the forward to *The Ziegfeld Touch*. In both of these sources, Billie's date of birth is given as August 7, 1884. Grant Hayter-Menzies, *Mrs. Ziegfeld: The Public and Private Lives of Billie Burke* (Jefferson, North Carolina: McFarland & Company Inc. Publishers, 2009), 14. Richard Ziegfeld and Paulette Ziegfeld, *The Ziegfeld Touch: The Life and Times of Florenz Ziegfeld, Jr.* (New York: Henry N. Abrams Inc. Publishers, 1993), 55.

[3]   For details on the origins of Billie's name, see Burke, *Feather*, 12-13; Billie Burke, with Cameron Shipp, *With Powder on My Nose* (New York: Coward-McCann Inc., 1959), 11; and Hayter-Menzies, *Mrs. Ziegfeld*, 15.

recognition,[4] combined with Blanche's own romantic idealism.[5] As Billie presents the information, it does not seem that she is trying to excuse or justify her mother's intentions. She offers her views on this subject in a direct, straightforward manner. Throughout her mother's life, Billie and Blanche possessed a unique bond. Blanche continued to reside with her daughter, even after Billie married; and Billie extensively relied on her mother's advice and support, both in professional and personal matters. Blanche clearly was a woman of strong-will. If Blanche ever had any theatrical aspirations, Billie made no specific mention of them. In the foreword to *The Ziegfeld Touch*, Billie's daughter, Patricia, however, viewed her "Gramma Burke" as a "thwarted actress."[6] Even allowing for Billie's desire to present her mother in the best possible light, it doesn't diminish their close relationship, or the pivotal role Blanche played in creating the path, which Billie was destined to follow.

Early Career in London

Significant turning points in Billie's career came as a result of her association with four men: Charles Frohman, Charles Hawtrey, Florenz Ziegfeld, Jr., and George Cukor. It was the first of these men who transformed Billie from a pretty voice in musical reviews to a leading lady on Broadway. An American, like Billie, Frohman's greatest influence on her career wouldn't come for a few years; however, in 1903, he was co-producing a new show in London, *The School Girl*. Billie was eighteen years old. She had a small part, including one song, "Mamie, I Have a Little Canoe." It was the most popular number in the production, and Billie became an immediate audience sensation. *The School Girl* ran for two years, solidifying the young star's popularity. Her picture postcard was prominently displayed everywhere, beside those of royalty and other celebrated actresses. Billie had clearly arrived.

---

4   Entertainment was an increasingly significant means of employment for women in the post-Civil War industrialized United States, as the desire for leisure activities increased. Between 1890 and 1910, the number of women working in entertainment increased from 4,652 to 15,436, as indicated by census responses. Albert Auster, *Actresses and Suffragists: Women in the American Theater, 1890-1910* (New York: Praeger Publishers, 1984), 31.

5   Burke, *Feather*, 23.

6   Patricia Ziegfeld Stephenson, foreword to *The Ziegfeld Touch: The Life and Times of Florenz Ziegfeld, Jr.*, by Richard Ziegfeld and Paulette Ziegfeld (New York: Henry N. Abrams Inc. Publishers, 1993), 6.

Charles Frohman was a producer who also served as an artist's manager. In the first two decades of the twentieth century, the esteemed list of actors whose careers were transformed under his guidance includes Maude Adams, John Drew, Ethel Barrymore, and May Robson. He built and owned the Empire Theatre and operated five others.[7] His enduring friendship with J. M. Barrie was responsible for the extraordinary success of Maude Adams, who starred in the stage adaptation of *Peter Pan*, which Frohman produced, along with Barrie's other plays. Frohman was literally a star-maker, scouting both actors and productions to transport across the Atlantic in one direction or another. A hit in New York appeared in London the following season. A star on the British stage was introduced to New York audiences, as in Billie's case. He found plays for his actors; and they continued to perform in his productions each season, either in New York, London, or on tour. As today, the relationship between theatre in New York and London was firmly established and regularly reported by the New York press, demonstrating its significance as popular art and entertainment.

When Frohman made plans to bring *The School Girl* to New York, he was not prepared to offer Billie the number for which she became famous. Instead, it was given to one of the leading ladies in the show, who was under his management. He offered Billie a less impressive role and stood firm, over her pleadings to repeat her success in New York. Choosing to remain in London, she appeared in musical comedies on a steady basis.

Before his death on October 6, 1906, Billie's father was able to see all that his daughter had accomplished and how unlike she was from the quiet, bashful girl she was as a child. Billie accepted that she was an actress by trade. She was eager to work, and though she accepted roles, which she may have thought were not necessarily furthering her career, she was developing a more discerning attitude towards the work she desired. While appearing in the musical *The Belle of Mayfair* in 1906, she was noticed by Charles Hawtrey. Hawtrey was both an actor and theatre owner/manager. Billie was not interested in continuing to appear in musical comedies and showcases, and Hawtrey realized her potential for straight comedy. He offered her the lead opposite himself in *Mr. George*, which opened in 1907. Billie credits Hawtrey with teaching her the craft of comic timing and delivery.[8] She learned to play to her fellow

---

7   Brooks Atkinson, *Broadway*, rev. ed. (New York: Macmillan Publishing Co. Inc., 1974), 42, 43.

8   Burke, *Feather*, 41.

actors on stage and not to the audience, as she did in musicals. Though *Mr. George* was not a success, it did not diminish Billie's enthusiasm. She felt the play was a wonderful opportunity to display her talents and finally believed that she was entitled to consider herself an actress. "I was an actress on the stage—a comedienne, at last."[9] Her appeal seemed to be limitless, and she was given the honor of being presented to King Edward and Queen Alexandra. Americans, at least in New York, were becoming familiar with Billie, as the press covered her success, shrewdly anticipating her eventual return home.

Billie found herself positioned between the two men responsible for her early career: Frohman and Hawtrey. Hawtrey wanted Billie to appear in his next play, *Mrs. Ponderberry's Past*. At the same time, Frohman approached Billie to star in a British play he was bringing to New York, *My Wife*. Not only was Billie loyal to Hawtrey for all that she had accomplished under his training, but she was not neglectful of how she was treated when Frohman transferred *The School Girl* to New York. Frohman, understanding her connection to Hawtrey, left the offer open. When *Mrs. Ponderberry's Past* closed for the summer, Billie agreed to take the part in *My Wife*, and the press welcomed her imminent debut on Broadway:

> Mr. Frohman is confident that Billie Burke, who will be (John) Drew's leading woman next season, will greatly please New Yorkers. Miss Burke herself is delighted with the prospect of playing in her native land, where, up to the present, she has had a great success in London.[10]

The notice also attested to Frohman's influence and reputation. So in August of 1907, Billie and her mother set sail for New York, with *My Wife* scheduled to open and an astonishing salary of $500 a week.

A Star in New York

American theatre in the 1900s was undergoing the strains of growth, as it broke away from nineteenth-century conventions. At the end of the nineteenth century, audiences were happily content with plays, which

---

9   Ibid., 42.
10 "Vaudeville Chase All Over Europe." *New York Times*, http://query.nytimes. com/gst/abstract.html?res=9C06E6D71E30E233A2575AC0A9609C94669 7D6CF (June 9, 1907).

relied upon familiar genres: the comedy of manners, the melodrama, the social climber, and even that of the tragic Indian.[11] Playwrights, whether responding to popular taste or out of their own complacency, were not writing new works that challenged the accepted fare. Geographically another change took place as theatres began to make their way uptown to Times Square from the area centered around Fourteenth Street.

Twentieth-century audiences were slowly becoming more discerning, specifically as they were introduced to the plays of George Bernard Shaw and Henrik Ibsen.[12] These authors presented a new alternative for both theatergoers and playwrights, weaving together realism, complex characters and social commentary. While people lined up for each newly imported work by Shaw in the early 1900s, American playwrights continued to write what was familiar and resisted exploring new themes and any potential controversy.

My Wife succeeded as pure entertainment. Adapted from a French play, it is an amusing farce about a young ward, Trixie, played by Burke, who unintentionally becomes enamored with her guardian, while waiting for her intended true love to return from Morocco. Starring John Drew—one of the most esteemed actors of the period, and uncle to Lionel, Ethel, and John Barrymore—*My Wife* arrived on Broadway to an already receptive audience. Despite an enthusiastic notice from the *New York Times* for the play, the review was somewhat tepid in its opinion of Billie, saying that she was "wholly pleasant, though in no way remarkable."[13] However, audiences responded markedly different and immediately took her to their hearts, as they did in London.

The competition that season was particularly strong. In addition to *My Wife*, Frohman presented six other plays, including shows for Maude Adams, Ethel Barrymore, and Mary Boland. David Belasco gambled on a new star in *The Warrens of Virginia*: Mary Pickford. Theatergoers with more diverse tastes welcomed an adaptation of Dostoevski's *Crime and Punishment* and *Rosmersholm* by Ibsen. 1907 was also the year Florenz Ziegfeld, Jr. produced the first *Ziegfeld Follies*.

Frohman attended to all aspects of Billie's career, and along with Blanche, they freely gave their assent or disapproval to the details of her

---

[11] Ethan Mordden, *The American Theatre* (New York: Oxford University Press, 1981), 25.

[12] Ibid., 32.

[13] "Drew has Success in 'My Wife' at Empire." *New York Times*, http://query. nytimes.com/gst/abstract.html?res=9F03E4D8163EE233A25752C0A96F9C 946697D6CF&scp=1&sq=%22billie+burke%22&st=p (September 1, 1907).

personal life, as well. For Billie, life was as carefree off stage as it was on stage. She was introduced and welcomed by New York society. Billie's salary of $500 per week paid for previously unknown extravagances for both herself and her mother. This extended not only to their lives in New York, but also when Billie toured, always accompanied by Blanche. Of special significance at this time was a deep friendship she developed with Mark Twain. Billie's success and reputation extended beyond New York City. She entered popular speech as the term *to billieburke* took hold, meaning, "to act adorably."[14] When *My Wife* toured, department stores carried a line of curly hair extensions and dresses modeled after her.[15] Reviews, however, were still less enthusiastic than Billie's mass appeal. Burke maintained this view throughout her career, that while critics found her gracious and pleasant, they could not account for why audiences embraced her so strongly.[16] Billie's next role in *Love Watches* in 1908 provided them with the opportunity to reassess their earlier opinions.

A domestic comedy about a wife during her first year of marriage, Billie considered *Love Watches* "the best play I was ever in."[17] And the critics agreed. She went from being a popular audience favorite to a legitimate stage star. Beneath the headline in the *New York Times* review it proclaims, "Billie Burke, Very Charming, and Now a Star, wins Great Favor in Attractive Role."[18] Among the platitudes contained in the review is the opening line "Miss Billie Burke came into stardom at the Lyceum Theatre last evening,"[19] and later finds that *Love Watches* "is delightfully played, Miss Burke passing from the leading lady stage to that of star, with signs of developing talent, an improved method, and no end of appealing charm."[20] After 172 performances lasting nearly two

[14] Patricia Ziegfeld, *The Ziegfelds' Girl: Confessions of An Abnormally Happy Childhood* (Boston: Little, Brown and Company, 1964), 19. "Who's Who This Week in Pictures," *New York Times*, http://select.nytimes.com/gst/abstract.html?res=FB0810F7385513738DDDA00894D8415B828FF1D3 (October 9, 1932).

[15] Burke, *Feather*, 77.

[16] Ibid., 75, 76.

[17] Ibid., 85.

[18] "A Dainty Comedy at the Lyceum," *New York Times*, http://query.nytimes.com/gst/abstract.html?res=9D00E0DD133EE233A2575BC2A96E9C946997D6CF (August 28, 1908).

[19] Ibid.

[20] Ibid.

years, Frohman transferred the play to London and except for Billie, he recast it with British actors. Regrettably, the response was not the same as in New York, and the play did not appeal to the critics.

Disappointed, but undeterred, Billie and her mother returned to New York; and Billie purchased a house on thirty-five acres of land in Hastings-on-Hudson, New York, which Blanche immediately set about renovating. Named Burkeley Crest, it would become a second home for Billie and Ziegfeld, after their marriage. Their other residence was the Ansonia apartment building on New York's Upper West Side.

Though Billie originally may not have been ambitious for fame and stardom, she did not accept what was offered without question or a fight, when necessary. Billie was still earning $500 per week, the same amount as when she appeared in *My Wife*. Learning that the Shuberts were offering stars under contract greater salaries, Burke approached Frohman. As she relates the exchange, Frohman, in his straightforward manner, told her what he was going to do. Her salary was not going to change; however, he would place $1,000 per week into bonds for her. In addition, she would now receive 10 percent of the gross box office receipts from her shows, also to be placed in an account.[21] These amounts would become her family's salvation in times to come.

Billie's career continued in a succession of comedies, with the exception of *The Land of Promise*, all produced by Frohman.[22] Her roles were younger variations of her later films roles, as if she were now playing the daughter to those women. She portrayed ingénues with light, frothy bon mots slipping off her tongue, who were exquisitely dressed, delightful in social settings, and accompanied by the handsomest of men to the most elegant of parties.

One of these plays, *The Mind-the-Paint Girl*, affected Billie significantly. It was also her "most important."[23] *Paint Girl* reflected the continuing evolution of theatre, since the beginning of the century. A growing number of playwrights and actors were no longer interested in pure escapism, but were attracted to works that had a stronger sense of relevancy and were concerned with contemporary issues and attitudes. This demanded that characters become more complex, deeply layered,

---

21   Burke, *Feather*, 100.

22   Between 1910 and 1914, Burke starred in *Mrs. Dot* (1910), *Suzanne* (1910), *The Philosopher in the Apple Orchard* (1911), *The Runaway* (1911), *The Mind-the-Paint Girl* (1912), *The Amazons* (1913), *The Land of Promise* (1913), and *Jerry* (1914).

23   Burke, *Feather*, 114.

and driven by conflicting motivations, in all, more psychologically developed. This approach was not only observed in dramas. Writers such as Booth Tarkington and Harry Leon Wilson introduced a larger dimension of realism into their comedies, as well.

Presented in New York in 1912, *The Mind-the-Paint Girl* had previously been unsuccessful in London. Frohman still believed it would appeal to an American audience. He attributed this in part to Sir Arthur Wing Pinero, one of Britain's foremost playwrights. The protagonist, Lily, is an actress pursued by men of reputation and noble lineage. If the peerage is next to godliness, an actress is one step away from total debasement. The play, while a comedy, is a critique of English society and social mores. Directed by Dion Boucicault, it awoken in Billie a sense that she could achieve more than she had up to now. Working with Boucicault made Billie aware of acting as a craft, which required challenging roles in order to grow dramatically. Proclaiming as part of the headline, "Miss Burke is Splendid—By Long Odds the Best Thing She Has Done,"[24] the *New York Times* went on to reinforce Billie's own impressions:

> And in this act (the third) Miss Billie Burke, having previously distinguished herself by the most varied and alluring exhibition of comedy acting which she has yet given, made a truly splendid revelation of emotional powers hitherto unsuspected.
>
> It is possible to congratulate her most heartily on this performance, which from start to finish is suggestive of an understanding of the character, a grasp of its meaning, and a very varied and admirable technical proficiency in conveying its various moods.[25]

Paint Girl had a successful engagement of 136 performances, her longest run since *Love Watch*. There was a brief tour, which included the National Theatre in Washington DC, where President and Mrs. Woodrow Wilson attended a performance.[26]

---

[24] "Latest Pinero Play Seen At The Lyceum," *New York Times*, http://query. nytimes.com/gst/abstract.html?res=9406E7D9113AE633A25753C1A96F9 C946396D6CF (September 10, 1912).

[25] Ibid.

[26] "Wilsons at a Theatre," *New York Times*, http://query.nytimes.com/gst/ abstract.html?res=9400EFDF1F3AE633A2575AC0A9659C946296D6CF

After this new experience and approach to acting, Billie Burke wanted to continue to assert herself and take greater risks on the stage. Charles Frohman did not have anything comparable to *Paint Girl* to offer Billie, and instead she went into *The Amazons*. Despite being written by the same playwright, Sir Arthur Wing Pinero, *The Amazons* was a retread of all the actress's earlier roles. Though Frohman was not outright dismissive of Billie's desire to expand her range, he believed that "great successes are made by the masses, not the classes."[27] According to him, the adoration that an audience felt for a star was not dependant on the choice of material. Frohman was more successful in assessing an actor's potential than he was in his selection of plays, which disproved his perception that popularity always drove the box office.[28] With the exception of *Paint Girl*, all the shows in which Billie performed from 1910 through 1914 had rather brief runs in New York.[29] Despite this, Billie's popularity did not suffer. In an assessment of Broadway's leading ladies of 1913, the *New York Times* listed Billie first among celebrated young actresses, including Laurette Taylor.[30]

Mrs. Ziegfeld

A chance encounter on the evening of December 31, 1913, had an unforeseen effect on Billie's personal and professional life. She was appearing in Somerset Maugham's play *The Land of Promise*, and together they went to a costume party at the Sixty Club rather late in the evening. According to Billie, she had never met Florenz Ziegfeld, Jr. prior to this evening. The circumstances surrounding their courtship were tempestuous and dramatic. Ziegfeld had been divorced for close to one year from the actress-singer Anna Held, to whom he was wed by common law for sixteen years.[31] At the time he was involved with Lillian Lorraine, a star of the *Follies*. His reputation for women was well-known in society circles and throughout the theatre community.

(March 9, 1913).

27 Mordden, *The American Theatre*, 32.

28 Atkinson, *Broadway*, 43.

29 Burke, *Feather*, 263-265.

30 "The Rising Generation," *New York Times*, http://query.nytimes.com/gst/abstract.html?res=9C02EED9113BE633A25754C0A96F9C946296D6CF (September 7, 1913).

31 Eve Golden, *Anna Held and the Birth of Ziegfeld's Broadway* (Lexington, Kentucky: The University Press of Kentucky, 2000), 81, 161.

Billie, herself, was fully aware of his notoriety. However, the attraction was instantaneous and deeply intense. As Billie states with such heartfelt honesty, "But even if I had known then precisely what tortures and frustrations were in store for me during the next eighteen years because of this man, I should have kept right on falling in love."[32]

Ziegfeld courted not only Billie, but her mother as well. Blanche found him gracious and charming, enjoying the attention Ziegfeld showed her, which included gifts and trips to the theatre for just the two of them. Not everyone welcomed Ziegfeld's attention. Frohman was adamantly opposed to the union and insisted that Ziegfeld would ruin Burke's career. Billie tried to objectively weigh her options and devotions to these two men, curiously reminiscent of a prior decision she had to make early in her career when Frohman approached her while she was acting opposite Charles Hawtrey in London. Except this time, Billie was forced to conclude just how much she loved Ziegfeld and if she could walk away from the romance. In between matinee and evening performances of *Jerry*, Billie married Ziegfeld in New Jersey on Saturday, April 11, 1914. When it was reported in the *New York Times* two days later, it appeared on the front page.[33] Billie never saw Charles Frohman again. He was in Europe when she married and only returned to New York once in the subsequent year before drowning in the sinking of the *Lusitania* on May 7, 1915.

After her marriage, Burke was no longer the darling of the Frohman office. Almost out of spite, she was sent on tour with *Jerry*, which consisted entirely of brief and one-night engagements. Out of this, however, came Billie's first encounter with silent motion pictures. As a legitimate stage star, she had not eclipsed the attention of the film industry. At the end of the tour in Los Angeles, various producers approached her, and news of their interest reached the Frohman office. The reaction was swift, and she was informed that if she were to sign to appear in films, she would not be cast during the following season. When Billie returned to New York, she felt that she had to make a difficult choice regarding her career. Her relationship with the Frohman office had clearly changed, especially after the death of Charles Frohman. The current management was not interested in furthering her career, and Burke was not content to become merely an appendage of Ziegfeld, either as wife or society dilettante. Billie severed her relationship with the Frohman company,

---

[32]   Burke, *Feather*, 120.

[33]   "Billie Burke Weds," *New York Times*, http://query.nytimes.com/gst/abstract.htm l?res=9D02E5DE153DE733A25750C1A9629C946596D6CF (April 13, 1914).

allowed Ziegfeld to serve as her manager, and made her first motion picture in Hollywood for Thomas H. Ince for a salary of $10,000 per week.[34]

By now, motion pictures were proving to be a viable competitor to the stage for audiences. Silent film producers actively tried to showcase Broadway actors, and beginning with early silent films, they often had notable actors repeat their stage performances. Two innovations, which enabled film to be more competitive, were length and price.[35] Silent films had advanced beyond short one-reels and now were comprised of multiple reels, two, three, and up to five. This allowed film to tell a complete narrative story. Also, as the cost of admission rose, film became more of a middle-class attraction, as compared to early silent films, which appealed to a distinctively lower class. By 1914, the cost of a motion picture ticket in New York was $1, comparable to Broadway.[36] World War I also had a profound effect on the film industry. For the first time, U.S. film production surpassed that of Europe, where it virtually ceased during the war. This increased the demand for American films, both domestically and abroad, allowing it to become the dominant global film producer and distributor.

Billie temporarily relocated to Los Angeles for *Peggy* in October 1915, just months after getting married. Before completion of the film, Thomas Ince offered her a five-year contract. Billie was certain that her stage work and training would have allowed her to become one of the first true motion picture stars and that she could have successfully made the transition when sound was first introduced, roughly a decade later.[37] Burke acknowledges the wrenching decision she had to make—between career and marriage—and in the end, as we know, she chose her marriage.

Though Billie turned down Ince's offer of a contract, she did make sixteen silent films, beginning with *Peggy*, which was released in 1916 and continuing through 1921. Predominantly they were made in New York. The *New York Times* review of *Peggy* confirms Billie's assessment of the opportunities that working in silent film would have afforded her, "Billie Burke and the movies are kindred spirits . . . . The Titian-haired

34   Burke, *Feather*, 169.
35   David Bordwell, Janet Staiger, and Kristin Thompson, *The Classical Hollywood Cinema: Film Style and Mode of Production to 1960* (New York: Columbia University Press, 1985), 133.
36   Ibid.
37   Burke, *Feather*, 170-171.

actress romped through an unusually entertaining picture with all the camera knowledge and assurances of a screen veteran."[38] Billie balanced her stage and screen work with the demands of her marriage. Ziegfeld's indiscretions were a constant concern, and Billie acknowledged early on that, "I was destined to be jealous of the entire *Follies* chorus as well as the *Follies* star list for the rest of my married life."[39] On a much more life-affirming note, Billie gave birth to her daughter, Patricia, on October 23, 1916, who was pampered, praised, loved, and disciplined by both of her parents despite any professional obligations.

Motion pictures did not offer the excitement of appearing before an audience, and in an interview with the *New York Times* after the opening of *A Marriage of Convenience* in 1918, Billie announced that she was planning to build her own theatre.[40] Having a theatre would allow her to offer a season, where she determined her roles and productions. As for the movies, Burke offered a rather dim perspective:

> The movies? Well, of course, they're not like the stage, are they? Not that they don't do plenty of things for you that the stage does not—they get you everywhere, and bring you letters from all ends of the earth. But they're rather—well, demoralizing . . . . They pay well, of course, but they are also tiring. They leave no time for anything else. I don't care much about them. The only good one I ever did was the first one, "Peggy." . . . But only one thing will make me happy, and that is to own a theatre. It is wonderful to have your own theatre—you can do so many things. Special matinées, you know, and all that sort of thing. Just wait.[41]

Billie's comments came just two years after *Peggy* and long before she began acting in film full-time, with the occasional performance on stage. Her view of film did soften in later years. However, when she gave the interview, it didn't matter to audiences which medium

---

38   "Miss Burke's 'Peggy' Seen on the Screen," *New York Times*, http://query. nytimes.com/gst/abstract.html?res=9907E4DA1E38E633A25754C1A9679 C946796D6CF (January 17, 1916).

39   Burke, *Feather*, 174.

40   "Minute Visits in the Wings," *New York Times*, http://query.nytimes.com/ gst/abstract.html?res=9902E6DC103BEE3ABC4D53DFB3668383609ED E (May 5, 1918).

41   Ibid.

she preferred. She was voted Queen of the Movies in 1922 during a weeklong charity event in New York on behalf of the Association for Improving Conditions of the Poor.[42] In reality, though the physical theatre never did materialize, Billie did not stop performing, primarily in plays produced by Ziegfeld.

Billie was in Baltimore on tour with *Intimate Strangers* by Booth Tarkington when Blanche died on February 7, 1922, at Burkeley Crest. When her health had declined due to complications from diabetes and she could no longer climb steps, Billie and Flo provided Blanche with her own house at Burkeley Crest, where she was attended to by a cook and two nurses.

For some time, Billie had felt restricted by the plays Ziegfeld produced, just as she had in Frohman's productions. Her notices were good, but the runs largely short. When Gilbert Miller offered Billie the opportunity to star in Ferenc Molnar's *The Swan*, she was confident that the production would provide her the chance to reclaim her identity on stage.[43] Billie had no doubts as to whether she should accept the role. Ziegfeld's opinion was rather different. Flo did not take kindly to competition, criticism, or intervention from outsiders. He felt threatened by another producer providing his wife with the acclaim and success at which he failed. Despite Burke's adamant objections, in the end, she acquiesced and rejected the offer, which went to Eva Le Gallienne; and her performance in *The Swan* greatly contributed to her rising career.

The Swan is another example of how Billie's relationship with Ziegfeld shaped her professional choices. Billie is clear in her belief that jealousy is what fueled Ziegfeld's uncompromising stance, even though he later realized the error in his judgment.[44] Grant Hayter-Menzies suggests a different assessment in *Mrs. Ziegfeld*. According to his position, Flo may have wanted to spare Billie's feelings and protect her from having to acknowledge that she was better suited to play the mother.[45] At the time

[42] "Billie Burke Votes Queen of the Movies" *New York Times*, http://query.nytimes.com/gst/abstract.html?res=9904E6D8163BE533A25753C1A9639C946395D6CF (May 10, 1922).

[43] Gilbert Miller was the son of actor/producer Henry Miller, Burke's costar in *Marriage of Convenience* in 1918. Actress Ruth Chatterton virtually served as co-producer of the production. Burke, *Feather*, 192.

[44] Burke, *Feather*, 206.

[45] Grant Hayter-Menzies, *Mrs. Ziegfeld: The Public and Private Lives of Billie Burke* (Jefferson, North Carolina: McFarland & Company Inc. Publishers,

Miller offered her the role, Burke was no longer an ingénue, but would have been thirty-seven when the production went into rehearsal in 1923.[46] Eva Le Gallienne, in her early twenties, was the appropriate age for the lead. While legitimate, producers have various reasons for the casting decisions they make, and Miller had his. It would be presumptuous to know what motivated him to offer Burke a role intended for one much younger. The stage is built upon a fantasy, which requires audiences to suspend belief and accept the artifice of the performance unfolding upon the stage. Audiences are tolerant and forgiving, especially with respect to stars. Ziegfeld was a man of enormous drive and lived without restrictions. The grandeur of his *Follies* is as much a comment upon his unlimited imagination, as it is upon the audience's receptiveness to such extravagance. Ziegfeld's supposed concern in this manner appears to be dramatically uncharacteristic. Here was a man who, despite his unquestioned devotion to his wife, still carried on a personal life with other women, which severely impacted her. It seems more accurate, and consistent with his character, to accept that Billie's triumph in another producer's play would be a personal defeat for Ziegfeld, in spite of his love and generosity for his wife.[47]

Burke's life was slowly overshadowed by Ziegfeld's opulence, both in his productions and lifestyle. She no longer appeared in a new show each theatrical season, as in prior years. However, she found unparalleled joy in being a mother and clearly enjoyed the comforts of her lifestyle. Unfortunately, in addition to Ziegfeld's attraction to other women, Billie had to contend with his excessive gambling, especially as they began spending considerable amounts of time outside of New York in Palm Beach. Billie was not aware of the extent of her husband's financial speculation on Wall Street, and following the Stock Market Crash in 1929, Ziegfeld was penniless, losing $1 million and hugely in debt.[48] She would not realize the extent of his losses for some time. Combined with the money that Frohman had begun putting away for Billie, her savings were estimated at $500,000, all of which she gave to Ziegfeld.

2009), 106.

[46] Ibid., 107.

[47] Ziegfeld's devotion to Billie was never in question. According to his publicist, Bernard Sobel, "I believe that there was one transcending love that superseded all other passing flare-ups of the affections and that was his [Ziegfeld's] love for Billie." Bernard Sobel, *Broadway Heartbeat, Memoirs of a Press Agent* (New York: Hermitage House, 1953), 122.

[48] Burke, *Feather*, 222.

Both emotionally and financially, Ziegfeld was unable to function as before. Billie was aware that it was her responsibility to provide for her family and that work was the only option available.

If Billie's marriage can be said to have been the bridge between her stage career and her film career, which was about to begin in earnest, *The Truth Game* in 1930 served as a transition between her roles in both media. Billie, recognizing that she was no longer an ingénue, accepted a supporting role designed for a character actress. While she was pleased with the part, she needed the work, given Ziegfeld's financial losses. This was the first time she was not the female lead and recognized the shift. Despite her extensive work in comedy up to this point, she saw this part as presenting unwelcome challenges. "Oh, that sad and bewildering moment when you must turn the corner and try to be funny! This was when I turned the corner. It was an imposing corner for me, because I have had to try and be funny ever since."[49] Billie's loss of stage innocence, or more accurately, an honest acceptance of her own stage presence, was particularly difficult to accept; but she did face it and was received as enthusiastically as before. As Brooks Atkinson, then chief drama critic for the *New York Times*, concluded, "Miss Burke is sunny and spirited, bobbing lightly through the minor treacheries of a trade-edition comedy—and very pleasant to see and hear."[50] The character's personality and Burke's portrayal was a precursor to the light, fluttery woman, which would become Billie's trademark persona on screen. Producers now began to consider Billie for character roles.

[49] Ibid., 219.

[50] J. Brooks Atkinson, "The Play," *New York Times*, http://select.nytimes.com/gst/abstract.html?res=F10C15FC3B5E13778DDDA00A94DA415B808FF1D3&scp=5&sq=%22the%20truth%20game%22%20burke&st=cse (December 29, 1930).

A Career in Hollywood

Ziegfeld was still plagued by poor health, even as he continued to work, and the responsibility to support her family was Billie's major concern. Despite not wanting to be separated from Flo, Burke's next play was in California, *The Vinegar Tree*, co-produced by David Belasco. The play was presented in Los Angeles and San Francisco. While in Los Angeles, George Cukor attended a performance and offered Billie the part of Katherine Hepburn's mother in *A Bill of Divorcement* (1932), with John Barrymore as her husband. For the second time, Hollywood called; and for the second time, Billie accepted. However, this time, without knowing it, motion pictures would become her milieu for connecting with an audience, with only occasional forays back to the theatre.

Before production began, Billie was able to return to New York and care for Flo. He accompanied her back to Los Angeles and was admitted to the hospital, as she began work on *A Bill of Divorcement*.

Though he was beginning to recover, before the completion of principal photography, Ziegfeld died on July 22, 1932.[51]

In retrospect, Billie believed that she should have returned to New York and the stage.[52] However, work presented itself in Los Angeles, her daughter felt at home in California, and Flo had left substantial debts following his death. After *A Bill of Divorcement*, Billie began work on *Christopher Strong* (1933), again starring Katharine Hepburn and directed by Dorothy Arzner, the pioneering female film director.

Billie was reunited with director George Cukor on her following film, *Dinner at Eight* (1933), and created the onscreen persona for which she is most associated. To viewers, her performance appeared effortless. In a sense, Billie made a return to the beginning of her career and her training under Charles Hawtrey. Just as Hawtrey acknowledged her affinity for comedy, the studio system also identified her greatest strength lay in this genre of popular entertainment. Billie perfected the charmingly self-obsessed woman whose own perception of reality exists to the exasperation of her family. She appears to glide in and out of her scenes, as if she were actually floating several inches off the ground, never anchored to anything but her own concerns. In truth, this bubbly, carefree creation was anything but the real Billie, who purposefully and with determination provided for her daughter and herself, following the death of Ziegfeld. As with her stage career, film audiences may have mistakenly assumed the woman onscreen was a reflection of the woman off screen. As Bernard Sobel, the long-time publicist for both Ziegfeld and Billie, recounted, "The world has based its estimate of her character on her roles, never having the opportunity to judge her wisdom and depth of feeling."[53]

Burke appeared in sixty-five sound films opposite the most popular stars of the period, including Margaret Sullivan (*Only Yesterday*, 1933), Ginger Rogers (*Finishing School*, 1934; *The Barkleys of Broadway*, 1949, also starring Fred Astaire), Spencer Tracy and Elizabeth Taylor (*Father of the Bride*, 1950; *Father's Little Dividend*, 1951, both directed by Vincente

---

[51]   Billie received the call to come to the hospital while she was doing a screen test opposite Walter Pidgeon, who was being considered for the film (Burke, *Feather*, 239.) Years later, Pidgeon would portray Florenz Ziegfeld, Jr. in the motion picture musical version of *Funny Girl* about Fanny Brice, who became a star in the *Follies*.

[52]   Burke, *Feather*, 251.

[53]   Bernard Sobel, *Broadway Heartbeat, Memoirs of a Press Agent* (New York: Hermitage House, 1953), 114.

Minnelli), Bette Davis (*The Man Who Came to Dinner*, 1942), and Cary Grant in the first of the three *Topper* films she made (*Topper*, 1937; *Topper Takes a Trip*, 1939; and *Topper Returns*, 1941). She was nominated for a Best Supporting Actress for *Merrily We Live* (1938), a comedy reminiscent of *My Man Godrey* and starring Constance Bennett, who appeared in the first two *Topper* films. Dorothy Arzner directed Billie in three films (*Christopher Strong*, 1933, opposite Katherine Hepburn; *Craig's Wife*, 1936, with Rosalind Russell; and *The Bride Wore Red*, 1937, starring Joan Crawford and Franchot Tone). Billie was offered a contract with Metro-Goldwyn-Mayer, when *The Great Ziegfeld* was made in 1936.[54]

Of all her films, and the one for which she has achieved iconic stature, *The Wizard of Oz* (1939) affectionately remained her favorite.[55] Glinda the Good Witch of the North possessed a quality, which Billie associated with the characters she portrayed on stage.[56] MGM's most successful character actresses under contract were all considered for the part, including Fanny Brice. There was mutual agreement in casting

54   Burke, *Feather*, 250.

55   Ibid., 258.

56   Ibid.

Billie.[57] Her Glinda would play well with audiences, and also opposite Margaret Hamilton's Wicked Witch of West.[58]

Billie's last films are notable for her mature, dramatic performances in *The Young Philadelphians* (1959) starring Paul Newman and *Sergeant Rutledge* (1960), directed by John Ford. Her final film was the cameo-laden motion picture *Pepe* in 1961. Throughout her film career, Billie appeared on radio and repeatedly on television. She had her own radio show, running from 1943 through 1946, and in 1955 starred in a television production of *Arsenic and Old Lace* opposite Helen Hayes. What was to be Billie's return to Broadway in early 1959 never materialized. She had been performing alongside Eva Le Gallienne and Una Merkel in a play, *Listen to the Mocking Bird*, by Edward Chodorov. However, the play was plagued by several problems and closed in Boston during its out-of-town tryout. Unfortunately, this was Billie's last theatrical performance.

Family was always at the heart of Billie's life. Patricia and her husband, William Stephenson, lived directly next door. After they married, Billie had deeded them land from the property of her Brentwood home, which she had purchased in 1939. A loving grandmother, Billie found immense joy from her relationships with her four grandchildren, who lived just over the garden gate. Billie Burke died on May 14, 1970, in Los Angeles, where she still lived next door to her daughter and son-in-law.

If Billie had returned to New York following Ziegfeld's death, there is sufficient reason to believe she could have achieved the lasting fame and recognition for her work in the theatre, which she desired. Is portraying Glinda and ensuring a place in popular culture forever adequate compensation? No one will ever know. Nor can it be said with any certainty that had she remained in the theatre, she would have reached the rarefied heights and legendary status as an Eva LeGallienne or Lynn Fontaine. What can be said is that Billie Burke had a personal life and professional career, which suggests a lavish stage or screen production on its own. Though she regretted that her film roles were largely the same, and often indistinguishable from one another, they possess a distinctive quality, a *Billie Burkeness* about them, which only she could

---

[57]   Aljean Harmetz, *The Making of The Wizard of Oz* (New York: Alfred A. Knopf, 1977), 127.

[58]   Burke was paid $766.67 a week. Judy Garland received $500.00 per week (Harmetz, 133-134). In comparison, Burke's salary for *Peggy* in 1915 was $10,000 per week. Several factors contributed to this discrepancy, significantly the Depression and the studio system's tight reign over salaries.

have delivered. The combination of voice, poise, and a firm belief in the logic of the illogical could not have been possible by any other talent. Despite her desire to remain on the stage, she has achieved iconic status as Glinda, something that would have been incomprehensible to the young girl who never intended to be a performer at all and in the early days of her career lacked ambition. While the theatre may have been Billie Burke's spiritual and artistic home, forever she will live, beautiful and ageless, with a trill in her voice, *somewhere over the rainbow* in the wonderful land of Oz.

BIBLIOGRAPHY

Atkinson, Brooks, *Broadway*. rev. ed. New York: Macmillan Publishing Co. Inc., 1974.

Auster, Albert. *Actresses and Suffragists: Women in the American Theater, 1890-1910*. New York: Praeger Publishers, 1984.

Bordwell, David, Janet Staiger, and Kristin Thompson. *The Classical Hollywood Cinema: Film Style and Mode of Production to 1960*. New York: Columbia University Press, 1995.

Burke, Billie with Cameron Shipp. *With A Feather On My Nose*. New York: Appleton-Century-Crofts, 1949.

_____. *With Powder on My Nose*. New York: Coward-McCann, 1959.

Fischer, Lucy. *American Cinema of the 1920s: Themes and Variations*. New Brunswick, New Jersey: Rutgers University Press, 2009.

Golden, Eve. *Anna Held and the Birth of Ziegfeld's Broadway*. Lexington, Kentucky: The University Press of Kentucky, 2000.

Harmetz, Aljean. *The Making of the Wizard of Oz*. New York: Alfred A. Knopf, 1977.

Hayter-Menzies, Grant. *Mrs. Ziegfeld: The Public and Private Lives of Billie Burke*. Jefferson, North Carolina: McFarland & Company Inc. Publishers, 2009.

Mordden, Ethan. *The American Theatre*. New York: Oxford University Press, 1981.

Nissen, Axel. *Actresses of a Certain Character: Forty Familiar Hollywood Faces from the Thirties to the Fifties*. Jefferson, North Carolina: McFarland & Company Inc. Publishers, 2007.

Schatz, Thomas. *The Genius of the System: Hollywood Filmmaking in the Studio Era*, 1st ed. New York: Pantheon Books, 1988.

Sobel, Bernard. *Broadway Heartbeat: Memoirs of a Press Agent*. New York: Hermitage House, 1953.

Ziegfeld, Patricia. Introduction to *The Ziegfeld Touch: The Life and Times of Florenz Ziegfeld, Jr.*, by and Richard Ziegfeld and Paulette Ziegfeld, 6. New York: Harry N. Abrams Inc. Publishers, 1993.

—————. *The Ziegfeld's Girl: Confessions of An Abnormally Happy Childhood*. Boston: Little Brown and Company, 1964.

Ziegfeld, Richard, and Paulette Ziegfeld. *The Ziegfeld Touch: The Life and Times of Florenz Ziegfeld, Jr.* New York: Harry N. Abrams Inc. Publishers, 1993.

BURNS & ALLEN
in Paramount Pictures

Double Act:
George Burns and Gracie Allen

Lauren Milberger

A young man, about twenty-eight, walks into a luncheonette called Wiennig and Sberbers, on Forty-Fifth Street in New York City. It's an actors' hang out; the entire Vaudeville crowd spend their time there. It's 1922, and the young man is an out-of-work Vaudevillian actor, so poor he finds himself using the free hot water and the ketchup to make soup. He's handsome, Jewish, with a little make-up on his collar to remind the folks he's an actor, that he's one of them. His hair is thinning, but he's not yet ready for a toupee (Burns, 1988). He wears a loud checkered suit and slowly puffs on a cigar that, since it's the early twenty century, he's allowed to smoke inside (Clements and Weber, 1996). Every once in a while he writes a few jokes down on a piece of paper in badly spelled handwriting and off-center lines, mostly because, like most East Side tenement kids, he never finished school, but also because he is something they wouldn't discover for decades later: dyslexic. While his lack of reading skills means he can't spell to save his life, it makes him good at something else: listening. And so he sits in a corner booth and just listens. He listens to the owners and the crowds, and he doesn't listen for jokes, not in the standard way, but in a way he calls "comedy of inference"—the funny things of everyday life, the comedy of "nothing," the way people are just funny and don't even know it (Burns, 1955).

He takes another puff off his cigar, slowly revealing the gold tooth he wears to impress people, but which only makes him look more like a

Vaudeville wannabe than a real actor (Clements and Weber, 1996). And he waits, because this man needs a partner. In Vaudeville, a performer almost always needs a partner in an act, someone to bounce things off, to dance with, to do animal acts or acrobatics with, or just someone to feed the seal. And this kid has done it all, done every act and used every stage name, just to be in show business—because he wants it that bad. And yet, as much as the kid wants it—to be a Big Time hoofer at the Palace, the Mecca and dream of any Vaudeville performer—he's still nothing but Small Time. He's Small Time because deep down inside he fears being anything else. He's Small Time because he doubts his own abilities—so much so that his last job was just doing imitations of other people's acts, while his own original jokes ate a hole in his pocket. But the kid's luck is about to change; it's about to walk through the door (Burns, 1988).

A young girl, who looks about nineteen but is closer to twenty-nine, with dark long black curls, pale Irish skin, and two different-colored eyes—one blue and one hazel—enters the restaurant (Burns, 1988; Freeman, 2008). She walks timidly into the place, yet with a sense of strength and self-assurance, even though she's been out of work for a year—her first encounter with unemployment after years of steady work. She's hungry and just as desperate as the young man, although she may be more desperate for food than for a good act (Burns, 1988; Clements and Weber, 1996).

Finally, the kid, the handsome Jewish man with the gold tooth, eyes the girl and calls her over, standing as she approaches, as all gentlemen would for a lady. She takes a deep breath and walks toward him. The man is George Burns, and the woman is Gracie Allen and together they will change the face of comedy, through nearly every form of entertainment the twentieth century has to offer.

BEGINNINGS

George Burns and Gracie Allen couldn't have come from more different backgrounds; yet they somehow found each other to form one of the most successful boy/girl acts in comedy, Vaudeville, and radio history—while managing to fall in love along the way. Burns, born Nathan Birnbaum in January of 1896, Jewish and poor in the Lower East Side of New York, came from the humblest of backgrounds. The ninth of twelve children of immigrant parents, Dorothy and Louis Birnbaum, George lived with his family in what could only be described as a Jewish slum. The entire family crammed themselves into a small tenement apartment, and after his father died in 1903, in the influenza epidemic, young Nathan had to work odd jobs to help keep food on the table (Burns, 1980). Burns, known as Nattie to his friends, would later change his name from Nathan Birnbaum to something less Jewish, a name that fit better on a marquee or a business card—a move that was not uncommon in that era (Burns, 1988). In a time when most hotels, businesses, and country clubs discriminated against blacks, Jews, and actors, splitting the difference only worked in Burns's favor. Burns would say he changed his name every time he changed his act (also a common practice) because his acts were so bad it was the only way he could get booked again in the same theater (Burns, 1988). Although this may be true, odds are that a major contribution to Burns's name change was the anti-Semitic climate he found himself in.

Still, Burns wasn't kidding when he said that all he needed was a change of name and a new act to keep performing in show-business, a.k.a. Vaudeville—even if it was a bad act. During Vaudeville's heyday, almost every town had a theater; and the bigger cities like Chicago, New York City, and San Francisco had several. By the time a performer could get booked in the same theater a second time, the odds of being remembered were slim, affording bad acts like Burns the ability to keep working. Further, since most acts were booked out of New York, oftentimes the first time the theater manager saw an act would be the day it performed (Burns, 1988). Later, when Burns reached almost eighty years in show business, one of his most famous comic lines was "new talent has no place to stink." Burns lamented the loss of opportunity, previously provided by the prevalence of theaters and long-distance booking, to make mistakes and learn. This was something George Burns, in his early years, was in great need of—that was, until he met Gracie Allen.

While George was born on one coast, Gracie was born on another. Grace Ethel Cecile Rosalie Allen was born in San Francisco, California, a year before George, according to census records—a fact she would never reveal to anyone, including her own husband. Burns went to his own grave, almost forty years later, never knowing his wife's true age. He assumed Gracie was five years younger than he was, while the world thought she was nearly ten years younger, and it wasn't until records from the 1900 census were revealed that her true age was known. Also discovered recently was Gracie's high school year book, which puts her graduation year as 1914, at the age of nineteen (Freeman, 2008).

So while young Nattie Birnbaum dreamed of show business, singing on street corners for spare change and entering dancing contests, Gracie

Allen was born into a show business family. Her mother, Margaret Allen, taught dance lessons; and her father, George Allen, was a song-and-dance man who primarily worked up and down the East Coast. Gracie made her first appearance on stage when she was only three years old, and by the time she was a teenager, she was performing professionally with her sisters in a very successful Irish dance act called The Four Colleens. Unfortunately, by that time, Gracie's father had left his family to fend for themselves, abandoning his wife and five children. Her father's departure must have been the hardest on little Gracie, who was the youngest of the Allen children. When her father finally tried to reconnect with his daughter thirty odd years later, after Gracie had become a star—surprising her backstage at the Palace Theater—her only remark on the encounter was "He had nothing to say to me when I was growing up, and I had nothing to say to him now" (Burns, 1988, 17).

About the only thing Burns and Allen did have in common was that they both grew up in single parent homes. The shared loss of their fathers during their youth may have been an experience that, consciously or not, bonded George and Gracie, and shaped the people they would become.

When George first met Gracie, he had just ended his latest song-and-dance act. Although George had written a few of his own lines, the act, which was called "Two Broadway Thieves," consisted mostly of George and his partner doing imitations of other people's acts (Burns, 1988). After twenty years in show business, George Burns was still toeing the line, always putting together an act that was safe, that kept him working, and this last act the safest of them all. George had no interest in taking a risk on new material, because if his act failed, he could be fired or "given back his pictures" (Burns, 1988). Like actors today, Vaudeville actors had eight-by-ten pictures of themselves. In Vaudeville, however, the pictures were not used to get jobs; they were given to the theater owner once a job was secure to display in the lobby. When an act was fired, the owner literally gave the performers back their pictures, hence the common euphemism (Burns, 1988). George wanted to play it safe, so he wouldn't be given back his pictures.

When George and Gracie met, it was the first time in George's life that he wasn't looking for a dance act, which was ironic since both of them had primarily been dancers up to that point. This time around, Burns had decided to do what was known as a "talking act," a boy/girl flirtation act, very popular in the day, often referred to as a "street corner" act. It required no sets and usually consisted of a girl and a boy meeting on a street corner (really just a bare stage and a curtain) and flirting in a comic patter. This was a safe act for Burns, because he didn't have to use his own jokes. He could use dialogue he had put together from joke books—material that was already tested and sure to land with an audience (Burns, 1988). Gracie had her own act, written by her then-famous boyfriend, Benny Ryan, who was a very successful singer/dancer/songwriter/actor (his most famous song was "M.I.S.S.I.S.S.P.P.I."). Ryan was everything George wasn't and almost everything George wanted to be. But Gracie hadn't performed her own act for a year, because the act required a very expensive set, which she could no longer afford, after her previous partner had shipped the set to the wrong theater (Clements and Weber, 1996). After about twelve months of no work, during which she took classes in stenography, which she hated, and begrudgingly accepted money from her sisters back home, Gracie had had enough—she had to return to performing again. Since George's act had the cheapest scenery (none), the duo agreed to do George's new act and not Gracie's old act. But Burns and Allen did not start out this act in the roles the world would come to know them in. In this act, George would be the comedian, and Gracie would be the straight woman (Burns, 1988).

THE ACT

In private, George was known as the funniest of his friends, even leaving his best friend, comic legend Jack Benny, in stitches. Therefore, it seemed logical to Burns that he be the comedian and Gracie be his straight woman—Gracie would feed George the set-ups for his punch lines. But on stage, the act flopped. At their first performance at the Hill Street Theater in Newark, New Jersey, the audience wasn't laughing at George. They were laughing at Gracie. Off stage, Gracie had a bird-like voice that seemed to rise an octave when she was on stage—a natural comic device that made the audience laugh at her set-ups—while George's jokes were welcomed with nothing but dead silence. The audience loved Gracie, not just for her voice but also for the earnestness and truthfulness in which she spoke (Burns, 1988). In the future, it would be one of the factors that helped Burns and Allen stand out from a crowd of similar acts. As the days and weeks went on, George started to give Gracie more and more of the funny lines, until, he jokes, she was the entire act (Burns, 1988). Burns claims he started to change their respective roles on stage intermediately after their first performance and right before the second show later that day, but reviews of the day suggest that it took at least a year for Burns to put pride aside completely and let Gracie be the star (Clements and Weber, 1996). Once he did, however, Burns and Allen soared to the heights of their profession, and soon George's "lack of involvement" in the act became a running joke. At one point during their Vaudeville act, Burns would take a carpet out on stage and lie down on it (Burns, 1988). Later, Burns started smoking cigars on stage, which helped with his comic timing. The cigar soon became one of George's signatures in the act, because, as he would later quip, "I began smoking my cigar on stage—mainly so I'd have something to do while Gracie did the act" (Burns, 1988, 49). Cigar smoking became so much his signature that when Burns passed away he was buried with three cigars in his pocket (Krebs, 1996).

~

Gracie: Smartness runs in my family. When I went to school I was so smart my teacher was in my class for five years (Burns, 1978, 57).

~

The more successful Burns and Allen became, the more new material Burns wrote into the act. And the more material he wrote, the bolder he got, and more original. George would say he started out with all kinds of jokes for Gracie, including sarcastic jokes and mean jokes. Certain jokes coming out of her mouth just didn't fly with audiences, but the dumb jokes did (Burns, 1988). Soon Burns and Allen's act resembled something along the lines of what was known at the time as a "Dumb Dora" act, a dumb woman and an all-knowing man. But what made Burns and Allen's act different from the typical Dumb Dora act of the day was that the character of Gracie Allen, at her core, wasn't dumb at all. She just had her own sense of logic. In fact, Gracie herself would say her character was very smart. And while Dumb Dora acts of the day were misogynistic, with the superior man and the nitwit woman, Gracie was not put upon by George, the man. George was put upon by her and her "illogical logic," as George called it (Burns, 1988). Gracie was always the dominant character in the duo, so much so that even though George Burns (and later he and his writers) wrote everything that Gracie said, Burns's own character in the public consciousness was that of the untalented husband, boyfriend, or partner of the talented Ms. Allen. The character of Gracie Allen is the founding mother of such modern comic characters as Rose Nylund (*Golden Girls*) and Phoebe Buffet (*Friends*). Burns and Allen established the template for what has become a seminal character in popular comedy.

~

Gracie: Where do you keep your money?
George: In a bank
Gracie: What percent do you get?
George: Four percent?
Gracie: Ha. I get eight.
George: You get eight?
Gracie: Yup. I keep it in two banks.
(Burns, 1988, 48)

~

Another factor that didn't make Gracie just another example of discrimination toward women was the combination of the way Burns wrote her and the way Gracie delivered the lines. Burns and Allen were a perfect match. Burns took Gracie's comedy from the "comedy of inference" that his mother taught him and which he had learned from observing life (Burns, 1955). It was new and exciting, and it got Burns and Allen noticed. Soon George was incorporating singing and dancing into the act, in between the jokes. George says this was very bold of him at the time (Burns, 1988; Clements and Weber, 1994), although records of the day suggest Gracie's fiancé, Benny Ryan, was already doing something very similar with his act, Ryan and Lee, also a Dumb Dora act (Clements and Weber, 1996). Even if this is true, it was Burns and Allen that made the incorporation of song-and-dance inventive, which may be why today no one has heard of Ryan and Lee.

~

George: I'll take you home if you'll give me a kiss.
Gracie: All right. If you take me home, I'll give you a kiss.
George: Wait a second. Is your mother home?
Gracie: Sure she is, but my father won't let you kiss my mother.
(Burns, 1988, pp. 51-52)

~

LOVE GETS IN THE WAY

George said the audience fell in love with Gracie at first sound, but it took a little bit longer than that for George to admit his feelings to Gracie and even himself (Burns, 1988). After all, Gracie was engaged, and any complication that might break up the Burns and Allen act meant good-bye to the only success George had ever had as a performer. Burns was in love with two women—show business and Gracie—and he was going to have to make a choice, even if it meant losing one or both in the process. It seemed apparent to everyone but Gracie how George felt about her. Mary Kelly, Gracie's roommate and long-time friend of the couple, former girlfriend of Jack Benny, and co-star on their radio show for a short time, said,

> It was obvious from the very first that he was head over heels in love with Gracie. He waited on her hand and foot. Half the time she didn't know at what theater they were playing. George did everything but carry her there. Once a week they'd go dancing at a night club. As they grew to know each other

better, they would have dinner together every night—but Gracie was very strict about paying her check, unless George had invited her. (Clements and Weber, 1996, 14)

George was besotted—and once he had the courage to tell Gracie and Gracie finally believed him, it still wasn't an easy road to the altar. Gracie rejected George at every pass by fooling herself into thinking that he was only joking, and all the time professing her devotion to Benny Ryan. Finally, a few days before Christmas, George threw down the gauntlet—an ultimatum: marry him or end the act. For a man whose life was show business, it may have been the boldest move of George's life up to that point. Then, just when it looked like Gracie would indeed marry Benny Ryan instead of George, Gracie called George at three in the morning on Christmas Eve and agreed to marry him. To her death, Gracie still wore the same cheap wedding band on her marriage finger. The loving marriage they built was a long way from their first impressions of each other the night they met backstage—the evening before they met to talk about the act over lunch at Wiennig and Sberbers (Burns, 1988). Burns felt that Gracie "acted uppity and tossed her long black curls from her shoulders" (Clements and Weber, 1996, 8). While Gracie felt George "acted outrageously conceited over a split week engagement in a five-a-day[59] grind house . . . and used out of date slang" (Clements and Weber, 1996, 8). They were married in Cleveland on January 7, 1926, and they never looked back.

~

Gracie: It seems like only yesterday that my mother tripped him as we walked down the aisle.

George: I guess your family didn't approve.

Gracie: Oh, sure they did. In fact, they applauded her when she did it. But, I want everyone to know one thing. I was courted by the youngest, handsomest, most charming, most sought after star in show business.

George: Thank you, very much.

Gracie: But I still married George anyway, because I love him.

Burns and Allen Radio Show, 1934-1950 (Burns, 1988, 71)

---

[59] "Five-a-day" refers to the number of shows. The more shows, the smaller the Time, the less prestigious. Big-Time performers only had to do two-a-day (Burns, 1988).

IN WITH THE NEW, OUT WITH THE OLD

By the late 1920s Burns and Allen could only be described as "megastars" in Vaudeville playing the Big Time houses, including the Palace on Broadway (Burns, 1988). But Vaudeville was dying, and there wasn't anything Burns and Allen could do about it. When talking pictures were first introduced in the late 1920s, they weren't just the century's new toy—they had a darker side. Affectionately referred to as the monster that ate acts, talking pictures were either career launching points or destroyers of people's livelihoods, all in the name of progress. In Vaudeville, performers could tour for years with the same act; jugglers, acrobats, animal acts, strippers, they could almost spend an entire lifetime roaming the country and Canada with seemingly the same act (American Masters, 1997). With so many Vaudeville houses crisscrossing the nation, not to mention different circuits and Times (Small, Medium, and Big), it wasn't just a name that the audience was likely to forget; it was the entire act. With film, once an act was committed to celluloid, it could travel the country faster than any one act was physically able to. What's more, if you liked an act, and remembered it, you didn't have to wait years to see it again—all you had to do was put down money and see the same thing the next day—and for a cheaper price than you would pay to see it on stage (American Masters, 1997).

For Burns and Allen, the transition into film was easy—they were a talking act, perfect for talking pictures. They were also an act used to writing new material, new jokes (Burns, 1988). Comedy is a format that lives and dies not just by its audience's reaction but also by the goings of the times. For acts like Jack Benny, Burns and Allen, or Bob Hope changing material had become old hat. Of course, on stage, they did not have to change their material as often as they would have before recorded sound film (and later television and radio), but nonetheless, changing material was not as alien for them as it would have been to other performers. In addition, comedians like Benny, Hope, and Burns and Allen were fairly young during this era; they were in their twenties and thirties. By contrast, older performers, who may have been doing the same act all their lives, would have found it more difficult to adapt. With the stock market crash of 1929 following soon after the introduction of talking pictures, many performers who could not make the transition to the new talking medium died penniless and alone. Even Mary Kelly, George and Gracie's friend, who Burns and Allen tried to help when Vaudeville was no more, turned to alcohol and by 1941 had died in her sleep at the age of forty-seven (Burns, 1988).

There really is no official end date to Vaudeville; it faded away gradually. But many see the symbolic end of Vaudeville as May of 1935 when the Palace Theater in New York City gave its last full Vaudeville bill or "two a day" show. That summer, the Palace was playing talking pictures instead, with an occasional Vaudeville act thrown in. Soon after, the Palace was done with Vaudeville for good (S.D., n.d.). By that time, Burns and Allen had already found another way to make a living.

~

George: You're too smart for one girl.
Gracie: I'm more than one. My mother has a picture of me when I was two.

Lambchops, 1929

~

TALKING PICTURES

In film, George and Gracie started out doing shorts—smaller vignettes very similar to their stage act. In fact, their first short, *Lambchops*, presented in 1929 by Vitaphone (a subsidiary of Warner Bros. Pictures

Incorporated) was almost word-for-word their stage act reenacted in a studio. The only change in the piece was their acknowledgment of the camera. This breaking of the fourth wall seemed almost natural for Burns, since George made wry looks and pauses to the audience during the act on stage. For Gracie, it was newer, as she had never taken her eyes off George on stage, making their act as real as possible for her—it seemed that all she was doing was having a perfectly normal conversation. Gracie Allen was perhaps the first real method actor. If she had to eat breakfast or darn a sock, Gracie never cheated. She always did any task as if she was doing it in real life. She didn't understand why one wouldn't (Burns, 1988).

For this new medium George added a different entrance and exit. George felt that the way actors enter the "stage" and the way they exit it was one of the most important components in an act (Burns, 1998). George and Gracie entered the frame looking around and under things until George finally found what they were looking for: the audience. George asked Gracie to say hello to the audience, which she did; and then they went directly into their routine, followed by a brief song and dance. At the end of the short, George looked at his watch and said that they were done, but Gracie points out that the audience is still out there, so the couple goes into an additional patter that finally leads to George shooing Gracie off camera as the end credits fall. George later said people told him that breaking the fourth wall was avant-garde for the time period, but George just thought it was funny. In a subsequent short the shooing became "Say good-bye, Gracie" to which Gracie would answer good-bye, a sign-off that would follow George and Gracie all the way through radio and television, where it became "Say good-night, Gracie." One of the most persistent myths in show business history is that Gracie would always answer George with "Say good-night, Gracie" (Burns, 1988). This line perhaps conveyed the essence of Gracie's persona, but there is no recorded history to suggest the line was ever uttered by Gracie herself. George confirms this in Gracie's biography, which he wrote. Soon, the breaking of the fourth wall became a signature for the couple. They extended the device further when they reached television, making George a narrator for the show, speaking directly to the audience frequently throughout each episode (Burns, 1988).

~

George: Gracie, do you like to love?
Gracie: No.

George: Well, what do you like?

Gracie: Lamb chops.

George: Lamb chops. How many lamb chops can you eat?

Gracie: Four.

George: You mean, a little girl like you can eat four lamb chops alone?

Gracie: No, silly not alone. But with potatoes, I could.

Lambchops, 1929 (Burns, 1988, 72)

~

Between 1930 and 1932, Burns and Allen made several shorts under the Paramount banner (Burns, 1988). After their first short, George wrote more story-oriented scripts, although the plots fairly simplistic and the scripts were peppered with many of the same or similar jokes they had used on stage. George was able to use the word play and banter that had made the couple famous in Vaudeville with great ease, still depicting Gracie as the cute little dimwit and George as the exasperated man who was forced to deal with her. Once Burns and Allen graduated from shorts to features, they continued playing versions of their stage personas, sometimes changing nothing but the last names. At first, Burns and Allen were mostly relegated to second banana comic side stories. It wasn't until they became popular on the radio that their film career really went into full swing, with appearances in such pictures as *The Big Broadcast* series, an ensemble-based series that capitalized on the popularity of Burns and Allen and other radio stars such as Jack Benny. Still their appearances were small, for George felt that if the audience saw too much of Burns and Allen, they would grow tired of them (Clements and Weber, 1996). Later, Burns and Allen were able to headline a few films by themselves (*Here Comes Cookie* and *Love in Bloom*), in addition to appearing in another ensemble comic series known as the "College" series (*College Humor, College Holiday*, and *College Swing*). Near the end of their film career, they appeared with such legends as Fred Astaire (*Damsel in Distress*) and Eleanor Powell and Robert Young (*Honolulu*). Gracie even starred in two movies on her own, *The Gracie Allen Murder Mystery* and *Mr. and Mrs. North*, and she also appeared in a cameo in *Two Girls and a Sailor*. Watching *Mr. and Mrs. North* is a rare treat, as it is the only time Gracie Allen plays a character that is not "Gracie Allen" or even named "Gracie" to begin with. Although based on a very popular play at the time about a husband and his semi-daft wife who solve murders (ala Nick and Nora in *The Thin Man* series), the character of Mrs. North is in no way as mixed-up as the character of

Gracie Allen and may, in fact, be the closest thing to presenting a "real" Gracie Allen on screen rather than the character of Gracie Allen she became so closely associated with.

~

Mr. Miller: What's the big idea busting in like this? Where have you lived all your life?
Gracie: Well I don't know, I haven't died yet.

The Big Broadcast of 1936

~

YOU AIN'T HEARD NOTHIN' YET

It wasn't just the invention of talking pictures that led to the extinction of Vaudeville. The popular theory is that as soon as Al Jolson uttered the infamous phrase, "You ain't heard nothin' yet," in the first talking picture, *The Jazz Singer*, the death watch was started on Vaudeville. But no historical event is caused by just one action; there is always more than one contributing factor. George Burns offers up the theory that the Vaudeville houses, burlesque, and the stock companies all could have survived if it wasn't for rise of one thing: radio. Strippers, animal acts, jugglers, any sight-based act was finished in show business with the popularity of radio (Burns, 1988). It wasn't just the novelty of talking entertainment, as with Talkies; it was the proximity radio provided. For the first time in America, people didn't have to leave their homes for professional entertainment. And now Americans who couldn't afford to go see a Vaudeville show were hearing performers they had only read about in the newspapers. George Burns recalls a time near the end of Vaudeville where the owners of the theater that Burns and Allen were playing in held the curtain for a half hour so the audience could listen to *Amos and Andy*, out of fear that the audience wouldn't come out for the show if they had to miss their favorite radio program (Burns, 1988). This was almost fifty years before any home recording devices, decades before cassette tapes, VCRs, DVDs, Tivo, or streaming; and there was no such thing as a rerun. If you missed a radio show, that was it.

Radio was a revolutionary idea at the time it appeared. Rumors of the sound being harmful to one's hearing or that the radio could catch fire or blow up didn't deter people from tuning in. Considering similar fears about the dangers of today's technology—from warnings that iPod ear buds are harmful to our ears or that cell phone use causes cancer—the fears of radio seem par for the course. Today nothing seems to deter the human race from our fascination, and even obsession, with the latest technological innovations—and radio wasn't any different.

Radio was a medium where Burns and Allen could thrive. Radio was perfect for music and comedy acts, since all that was needed was a voice at the other end of the microphone. At first, radio consisted of only farm reports and, later, big bands like Guy Lombardo and his "Royal Canadians." But soon radio began to include performers like Vaudeville and Ziegfeld Follies star Eddie Cantor doing comedy on the air. Within a few years, radio was dominated by talking performers. The airwaves were filled with dramas, soaps, plays, and the start of what would become the sitcom on TV: half-hour comedies (invented by the great Jack Benny) (Burns, 1988). Most comedy shows started at first more like Vaudeville sketch acts with the characters doing a series of comedy vignettes strung together by a loose story arc, and interspersed with musical acts and an announcer to hock goods for whatever company was sponsoring the show.

Sponsorship was a pervasive feature of radio. A show was not called simply the George Burns and Gracie Allen Show; it was called *The Spam Show with George Burns and Gracie Allen, Maxwell Coffee Time with George Burns and Gracie Allen, The Philco Radio Time Show with Bing Crosby, The Kraft Music Hall with Eddie Cantor*, and so on. In fact, sponsorship was the only way a show could get on the air. Without a sponsor, there wouldn't be any money to pay the cast and crew. In Vaudeville, ads were displayed across the back curtain for all to see, but radio was a talking medium, and so the first commercial was invented. Commercials weren't just inserted in between shows or during breaks between acts as they are today; they were incorporated within the action of the show. Oftentimes, commercials would spring up out of nowhere as an announcer would suddenly launch into a litany about how much he loved: insert product here. In this way, radio changed the landscape of American pop culture and the advertising industry. The saturation of sponsorship we experience today, with place names such as The American Airlines Theater, The Cadillac Winter Garden Theater, and Citi (Citi Bank) Field in New York, as well as ever-increasing product placements in films and TV, really isn't anything new. Arts and commerce have had a symbiotic relationship for centuries, even if today's society thinks it is a new invention.

~

Gracie: My sister Bessie just had a brand-new baby.
George: Boy or girl?
Gracie: I don't know, and I can't wait to get home and find out if I'm an
     aunt or an uncle. (Burns, 1978, 63)

~

THE VAUDEVILLE TRADITION

George Burns and Gracie Allen were known as character comedians, a tradition that stems from Vaudeville itself. Performers came on stage with their own names—unlike in the legitimate theater, where actors could disappear behind characters and plots. In Vaudeville, even if performers were playing put-on characters, they used their own names, making it harder to hide and easier for the audience to blur the line between fact and fiction. This line became almost translucent with the invention of talking pictures and later with radio and television. When acts like Burns and Allen moved from Vaudeville to talking pictures, and from there to radio and then television, they tended to be surrounded by other actors who took on new characters with each performance, while people like George and Gracie consistently played the same screen/ stage personas. Later, on television and radio, the boundary between real and fictional identities became virtually invisible. George and Gracie played Vaudeville performers named George Burns and Gracie Allen, with the same best friends; the same address; and, at a certain point, their own son, Ronnie, playing their fictional son, also named Ronnie Burns. Of course, even from the beginning Burns and Allen had been using the names of their real life relatives in their act. Thus, it made sense that much of Burns and Allen's audience felt that George and Gracie the performers were, in fact, the same people as George Burns and Gracie Allen the characters (Burns, 1988). Interestingly, after years of being nominated but never winning the Emmy Award for Best Actress in a Comedy Series, one year Gracie Allen was nominated in the Best Performance in a Variety Show category, pitting her against actors who were playing themselves, as many seemed to think Gracie was (Gracie lost to Dinah Shore; Whipp, 2009).

~

George: A funny thing happened to my mother in Cleveland.
Gracie: I thought you we're born in Buffalo. (Burns, 1978, 63)

~

Vaudeville was still in the public consciousness late into the 1960s and the early 1970s, since at that time many members of the Vaudeville generation were still living. Today, however, Vaudevillian traditions seem less familiar. Character comedians like Burns and Allen are one such tradition; this type of role has become far less common over the decades. Exceptions exist, however, such as Stephen Colbert, Sarah Silverman, and Larry David, all of whom are comics playing characters with their own names but with distinct comic personas separate from their real life identities (Whipp, 2009). Perhaps the purest incarnation of the character comedian today would be Stephen Colbert, the star of *The Colbert Report*. Using his own name, Colbert lampoons left-wing news pundits. Colbert developed his bombastic pundit character on

Comedy Central's *The Daily Show*, before receiving his own show, also on Comedy Central. Like Gracie Allen, Colbert plays an exaggerated character for comic effect while using his own name and many of his own personal details to talk about himself on the air. Of course, it is a lot easier for today's audience to discern the difference between Stephen Colbert the person and Stephen Colbert the character, because Colbert widely admits off-air that his show is a parody, appearing in interviews as himself. And even though he was almost unknown to most of his current audience before *The Daily Show*, thanks to recorded film it is well-known that Stephen Colbert had played other characters before he took on his current television persona. By contrast, Gracie Allen only appeared once on film as a character other than her eponymous persona and almost never gave interviews as herself. This perpetrated the myth among the public that Gracie Allen the character and Gracie Allen the person were one and the same. Gracie felt she was giving the public what they wanted, and she never felt she was interesting enough for audiences to care about her and not the character (Burns, 1988). Whether Gracie knew what she was doing or not, it may have been her own insecurities that allowed the most famous woman of her generation to have some sense of privacy.

George and Gracie moved to television in 1950, with *The George Burns and Gracie Allen Show*, transferring the same structure from their latter years in radio (i.e., their sitcom years). It is at this point that we can more clearly see parallels between Burns and Allen and comedians such as Larry David and Sarah Silverman. Unlike Colbert, David and Silverman have adapted their on-stage or public personas to situation-type comedies, where they engage in fictional scenarios alongside other actors playing other characters, but also including actors from their real lives playing fictional versions of themselves. For example, when Larry David, the co-creator and writer of *Seinfeld*, acts in a scene alongside Jerry Seinfeld, also co-creator and star of the television series *Seinfeld*, in some outlandish situation on David's HBO series *Curb Your Enthusiasm*, it must provide the audience with a very similar experience to when George Burns and Gracie Allen played alongside fellow comedian and best friend Jack Benny. One might think that these comedians' personas are so outlandish that no one could believe they were really like that. But Sarah Silverman, who very often has played her comic persona on television talks shows, says that in real life, and even on film sets, most people expect her to be as crass as her character on *The Sarah Silverman Program* (Whipp, 2009). People felt the same way about Burns and Allen, assuming that they were just like their stage/screen personas.

FAME

Gracie Allen was a public figure almost all her adult life. By the time of Gracie's retirement in 1958, generations of people had no idea what it was like to not see or hear Gracie Allen on stage or once a week in their living rooms; she had been with them through Vaudeville, movies, seventeen years of radio, and eight years of television. Gracie was so famous that she was her own cottage industry. She had an advice column (written by George and his writers), card games, paper dolls, and coffee cans; and she appeared in countless magazine advertisements not just for her own sponsors but for other products as well. Before Gracie Allen, there was no such thing as a guest star. She was the first actor to appear on other shows to promote her own. She was also the first to do countless stunts for self-promotion, including running for President, leading a media-hyped search for her "missing" brother, and playing a "one-finger concerto" at Carnegie Hall.

Burns and Allen even made it to Europe, appearing live on stage in London and on British radio, and having their American radio show translated into French (Burns, 1988). The National Safety Council used Gracie as their spokesperson with the slogan "Don't be a Gracie." Gracie was, in fact, the most famous woman of her time; and although Lucille Ball is remembered as the "Queen of Comedy," Lucy is, in fact, only second to Gracie Allen, the "First Lady of Radio" and the "Nitwit of the Network." Gracie was the most famous woman in comedy for forty-odd years (Burns, 1988). In addition, Gracie's catchphrases are still a part of the American vernacular, even if no one remembers anymore where they came from. "Oh, George Porgie," "There you go again," and "I bet you say that to all the girls" are but three examples of catchphrases that swept the nation with Gracie's popularity (Burns, 1988).

Gracie was so famous it was hard for her to go out in public because she was often mobbed for autographs—both her voice and her face gave her away. Decades before any stalker laws, good-hearted Americans would walk up to the Burns and Allen's home in Beverly Hills and expect to be invited in for tea (Burns, 1988). America had invited George and Gracie into their homes for twenty-five years, and so they saw them as family. If Gracie Allen were alive today, she would be followed by paparazzi at every turn and perhaps would not have been able to keep her real persona so secret from the public.

AND SO IT GOES

By 1958, Gracie Allen had had enough of show business and announced her retirement during her televisions show's eighth season. For Gracie, it was a long time coming. She had expressed to George for years her desire to retire—even as early as 1935, Gracie was quoted, in a rare interview as herself, that if she had the money, she wouldn't work (*New York World-Telegraph*, August 30, 1932). Show business was a love, but still only a job for Gracie, while for George it was his love and his passion. It was hard to say where his love for show business ended and his love for Gracie began (Burns, 1988). Knowing this, Gracie, for the love of her husband, stayed in show business as long a she could, until an ailing heart made it impossible for her to continue. After suffering many small heart attacks and being put on medication, Gracie Allen was done being Gracie Allen. She told no one of why she was retiring, and only a few select family members and friends knew the true reason. In fact, George himself didn't even know how serious her heart condition was. His family felt the news would devastate George, and so they did not tell him—or maybe, George did know, but just didn't want to face the fact Gracie was dying (Biography, 1996).

TO BEGIN AGAIN

The joke was that Gracie Allen was the talent and George was just the guy feeding her the funny lines. Even though he wrote the words she said, and even though he was a very successful producer at the time, George Burns had very little confidence in himself after Gracie retired (Burns, 1988). At first, the audience didn't accept George as a solo performer; and after Gracie passed away in 1964, it didn't look like they ever would. But George Burns is a great example of perseverance. He stands as an example of how to live one's life—to never give up. Just when he thought he was done for in show business, ten years after he lost his beloved Gracie, while he was mourning the loss of his best friend Jack Benny, it all changed in an instant. George went from has-been comic to Oscar-winning humorist when he took the part originally meant for Jack Benny in the film adaptation of Neil Simon's *The Sunshine Boys*. From then on audiences flocked to see George perform. He wasn't doing anything different, still telling the same jokes and singing the same songs, but now the world had finally caught up with him (Burns, 1980, 1978). A far cry from the unsure boy of twenty-eight Gracie Allen had met all those years ago, George Burns died a man of one hundred years, living and dying on his own terms, confident, doing what he loved and living to the age he said he would (Krebs, 1996).

~

Gracie: My brother was held up by two men last night.
George: Your brother?
Gracie: Yes.
George: Was held up by two men?
Gracie: Yes.
George: By two men?
Gracie: Yes, my poor dear brother was held up last night by two men.
George: Where?
Gracie: All the way home. (Burns, 1988, 72)

~

LEGACY

The last of the Vaudevillians may have come and gone, but the comedy tradition they left behind still remains with us today. Bob Hope once said, "When Vaudeville died, television was the box they put it in" (Library of Congress). From television to film to the Internet, Burns and Allen continue to live on in our society, whether the world knows it or not. Comedy owes a great deal to Burns and Allen and the Vaudevillians that time has forgotten.

Bibliography

American Masters: Vaudeville. PBS. Nov. 26, 1997.
Burns, George. *I Love Her That's Why*. Simon and Shuster. 1955.
_____. *Living It Up: Or They Still Love Me in Altonia*. G. P. Putnam's Sons. 1978.
_____. *The Third Time Around*. G. P. Putnam's Sons. 1980.
_____. *Gracie: A Love Story*. G. P. Putnam's Sons. 1988.
Clements, Cynthia, and Sandra Weber. *George Burns & Gracie Allen: A Bio-Bibliography*. Greenwood Press. 1996.
Whipp, Gleen. "Role Play: Me, Myself, Not I." *Variety*. Aug. 20, 2009.
Krebs, Albin. "George Burns, Straight Man And Ageless Wit, Dies at 100." *New York Times*. Mar. 10, 1996, obituary section.

Britt, George. "Gracie Allen Succeeds in Being Funny Only When She's Natural, Team Agrees." *New York World-Telegram.* Aug. 30, 1932.

Freeman, John. 2008. Western Neighborhood Project: Preserving the History of San Francisco, "Gracie Allen: Jul. 26, 1895-Aug. 27, 1964." http://www.outsidelands.org/gracie-allen.php (accessed on Mar. 26, 2010).

S. D., Trav. New York City Info, "Times Square Vaudeville." http://www.timessquare.com/New_York_City/Times_Square_NYC/Times_Square_Vaudeville (accessed on Mar. 25, 2010).

Library of Congress, "Bob Hope and American Variety." http://www.loc.gov/exhibits/bobhope (accessed on Feb. 21, 2010).

The Perfect Fool: Ed Wynn the American Clown

Michael D. Jackson

"Comics are people who say things funny-clowns do funny things while wearing funny clothes." This is Ed Wynn talking about comedy while reporters scribble away on note pads. He said this often, for he was certainly the expert. Ed Wynn spent his entire adult life in show business playing one character: Ed Wynn. Oh, his name would be changed in the program from show to show—sometimes he was Chuckles, sometimes Simon, sometimes the Fire Chief. One very important time he was called Uncle Albert. For the most part, if we go by his own definition, Ed Wynn was both comic and clown. He wore funny clothes and was adept at physical comedy. His standard costume usually consisted of a strange jacket of bright colors and bold patterns—perhaps a vivid plaid with a white fur collar that buttoned horizontally. He wore round glasses of the type popular in the 1920s (most notably on silent film comedian Harold Lloyd), painted his eyebrows in happy arches, and wore lipstick. From under some sort of little funny hat, his hair stuck out like Bozo the Clown. His voice twittered and cracked like an adolescent boy, and he laughed with little high-pitched pops and hoots, routinely covering his mouth in faux embarrassment with this fingers. Ed Wynn, above all, was a story teller. Ed's impossible stories were vehicles for his many puns and comical turns of phrase or lead-ins to his songs or demonstrations of his latest invention, which was always ridiculous, but seemed completely necessary to him. His career had ups and downs, but he sustained that original Ed Wynn character to the end of his life. He started in Vaudeville and was on the very first bill at the famed Palace Theater in 1913. He transitioned to Broadway where he appeared in sixteen shows up through World War II. He was one of the first Broadway comedians to enter television with his own variety show in 1949 while also popping up in movies from time to time. Through the 1950s and 1960s he made more serious appearances in dramatic roles for television movies and series—surprising everyone with his ability to become a character other than "Ed Wynn." The last chapter of his life found him a regular company player in films made by Walt Disney, culminating in the role of Uncle Albert in *Mary Poppins*, which made him, above all other accomplishments, immortal. The longevity of this entertainer is what is so amazing about Ed Wynn today. How many single character clowns managed such a career? A handful of his kind can be counted: Bert Lahr, the Marx Brothers, Jimmy Durante, and Abbot and Costello, for example. These were people who made a career on a single character and even a very limited bag of tricks, but they grew into the American consciousness and were familiar friends ready to make the world laugh through war and depression. Their ability to continually entertain through decades in all mediums of show business was their magical gift, and Ed Wynn personified this all-American brand of clown.

What made Ed Wynn tick is difficult to say. Very little is known, even from his own family, as to what exactly went on in his mind. From all accounts it would seem that he only thought about his act and devising new routines for his shows. However, he was a husband and father and grandfather. His son, Keenan Wynn, became a notable character man of stage and screen (sharing it a few times with his dad in several Disney films). His grandson is Ned Wynn, former bit player in beach party films turned writer (he was raised by his mother and stepfather Van Johnson). Ed met his wife, Hilda, in Vaudeville—her father was actor Frank Keenan. This was an all show business, all the time, family.

Frank Keenan was a method actor before anyone was a method actor. He would thoroughly research a role, reading up on everything about the character, time, and place of the play and filled his script with notes. It was this kind of research to build a character that made him the standout star of the drama *Todd of the Times*. This was a man who went to Boston College at a time when actors didn't do such things. Frank Keenan's method predated Stanislavski, which made him the polar opposite of his son-in-law Ed Wynn. In fact, Frank didn't think much of Ed because he was a comic. Also, he didn't approve of the marriage to his daughter Hilda because Ed was Jewish and Frank's family was staunch Catholic. For years, Frank Keenan shut Ed and Hilda out of his life until the three found themselves playing Chicago and staying at the Sherman House Hotel at the same time. Ed and Hilda walked into the elevator and found themselves face to face with Frank Keenan. When Frank turned his back on them—making Hilda cry—Ed took a stand: "This is silly, you know! I'm your son-in-law, and nothing can change that." This confrontation turned the tide, and Frank Keenan changed his attitude towards the couple completely. Regardless of the reconciliation, Frank Keenan didn't think Ed's act was dignified. Ed's son, Keenan Wynn, referred to his grandfather as a "furniture actor," because he needed the furniture to prop himself up or he'd fall over drunk. Born in Iowa in 1858, Frank Keenan acted in serious plays his entire life, producing and appearing in his own "Frank Keenan Players" productions on tour and on Broadway through 1928.

Ed and Hildy had son, Keenan, in 1916. In the last part of the 1950s, Keenan felt that he needed to purge his soul and write a book about his life. He called it *Ed Wynn's Son* and chronicled how he had tried all his life to become his own person and not live in the shadow of his father. He made the strong point that because he was raised in the topsy-turvy world of show business he grew up late emotionally. Ironically, though, he thought his son Ned would have it better; Ed Wynn's firstborn grandson wrote a similar book about his crazy Hollywood upbringing. This book shows that history repeated itself—Keenan Wynn was as distant and uninvolved a father as was Ed Wynn.

When he decided to write his book, Keenan called his father to tell him of his plans. Ed's reaction, after thinking about the idea, was to ask, "Will there be some laughs?" Keenan returned that he didn't think the family was always so funny. Ed asked Keenan to make sure to write about his fourth birthday party. "We had a wonderful party." Keenan stated that to the best of his ability, he wanted to tell the whole truth of his life as Ed Wynn's son. Ed was worried that the book would only be one sided.

Not many equate Keenan Wynn with Ed Wynn at all. The two are so completely different physically and as performers that it is hard to believe they are related. Keenan may have thought he lived in his father's shadow, but he had his own lifelong successful career. He started in summer stock, moved on to Broadway, and by the early 1940s was making films for MGM. He worked steadily in television and films until his death in 1986, usually playing a grouchy comic villain. If Ed Wynn had raised an emotionally damaged son, he had at least raised a fine actor who found great success. In Ed Wynn's terms, he had done his job.

Born Isaiah Edwin Leopold to a hat manufacturer in Philadelphia, Ed was always joking around to get attention. When Ed was seven years old, the family went to see a show at the Walnut Street Theater, which changed his life. From then on all he could talk about was wanting to go into show business. On family trips to Atlantic City, Ed would spend his time on the boardwalk entertaining idle spectators. After a few summers of this, he became known as the clown of the beach. His father, of course, didn't want to hear anything of the kind. He wanted his son to go into the family hat business.

After one too many times playing hooky to sneak into vaudeville matinees, Ed's father told him he had to cut out the comedy. Ed was in high school then, and he felt he'd had enough education and decided to run away. His father disinherited him, temporarily. This was 1900, and a local newspaper gave a mention of the episode, announcing that Ed "had decided to give up all claims on his father's wealth and would devote the rest of his life to theatricals as playwright and actor."

The father felt having an actor in the family was a disgrace, so Ed decided to change his name. "You can't do that," exclaimed his dad. "If you make it, nobody will know you're my son." Ed did go into the family business for a short time when a branch office was set up in Boston. Eventually, Ed decided to sell off his stock and make a break for New York with the proceeds. From the stock of hats, he saved a floppy panama hat, which became his first prop and character-defining costume piece. In 1902, when Ed arrived in New York, he met Jack Lewis and George Whiting playing the piano and singing in a dive on West Forty-Third Street run by the prize fighter Kid McCoy. As Ed tells it, "Lewis took me for a rich man's son who would make good pickings. I told him I was an actor looking for a partner. We joined up, and he lived off me for weeks, with neither of us working. My dear mother was very thoughtful, so we never wanted for money."

They worked up an act called "The Rah! Rah! Boys." Ed played a college freshman and Jack Lewis a sophomore. They got their first chance to try out the act on stage thanks to Jim Corbett, a regular Ed knew from Kid McCoy's who was the Emcee for a benefit show at the West End Theater on 125th Street. The boys crashed the stage door by telling the doorman they were related to Corbett. Once inside, Corbett agreed to let them go on as the crowd was pretty tough. They were introduced as "a celebrated comedy team from California." Wynn and Lewis skipped out onto the stage in their college uniforms and sang, "Rah, rah, rah! Who pays the bills? Ma and Pa!" Looking back on this, Ed would comment, "That joke killed vaudeville." Lewis had a bulldog on a chain, and Ed would wave a cap gun around, punctuating the patter with the repeated cry of "Grape-nuts!" From all reports, the audience ate this up. Just like it would happen in a movie, there was an agent in the audience of this particular benefit show—Joe Shea, a booker of Vaudeville acts. He went back stage after the performance to meet the famous Lewis and Wynn from California. He offered them $200 a week if they would open the Colonial Theater the following day. They nabbed the offer and spent the next two years touring as the "Rah! Rah! Boys."

To go from being absolutely unknown and unemployed to scoring a major vaudeville contract overnight was more than a boost of confidence. "I had an attack of the biggest head you ever saw." How could it be otherwise? By 1912, Ed was earning $300 a week billed as "the boy with the funny hat."

Ed was playing the Orpheum Theater, Winnipeg, when he met his wife-to-be, Hilda, on the same bill. He was playing a sketch called "Joy and Gloom" with Edmond Russon. Hilda was playing in her father's act, a one-act drama called *Man to Man*. Hilda was eighteen, and according to Ed, "she was the cutest thing in girls I ever saw."

Ed played the first bill of the new Palace Theater in New York in 1913 and the following year married Hilda. The Palace Theater quickly became the pinnacle of vaudeville. Following the Palace engagement, Ed and Hilda toured in vaudeville for ten years, Ed folding and wearing his funny hat in funny ways and playing in sketches dripping with one-liners, before returning to the Palace Theater in a sketch he wrote called, "The King's Jester." This was a costume piece about a clown's attempts to bring a smile to the face of a melancholy monarch. When he played the same sketch at the Orpheum Theater in Brooklyn, it was on the same bill as Anna Held, producer Florenz Ziegfeld's former wife and star of his *Follies*. Ed was such a big hit that a Ziegfeld talent scout invited him to see Ziegfeld personally. Turns out, Ziegfeld had seen Ed's act before, realizing, "I know you. I've seen you with that hat."

"Mr. Ziegfeld, I swear I'll throw it away and never use it again."

Ed was held to his promise and signed for the *Follies of 1914*. With his induction into the New York "Big Time," Ed could buy a house on Long Island, keep an apartment in the city, and start a family. Keenan Wynn was born while Ed was appearing in *The Passing Show of 1916*, Ed's first time as top-billed star of a Broadway revue. Just in case the baby was born while Ed was on stage, the orchestra was prepared to give him the news. In the middle of the Saturday matinee on July 27, the band broke off and launched into a new song: Gus Kahn's "Pretty Baby." Ed stopped cold and ran over to the conductor to receive the message. "My wife has just had a baby. I'm the daddy of a baby boy!" he announced to the audience as they cheered.

The pregnancy had been hard on Hilda, and she vowed never to have another child. Her life as an actress was over, and she took on the role of mother and mistress of a gigantic mansion on Long Island called Wyngate. While Ed was busy working on Broadway, becoming a multimillionaire (by the time Keenan was nine, Ed was worth $3 million), Hilda was busy furnishing the mansion with grand pianos, handmade furniture, silver, and mink. Their neighbors were George M. Cohan, Richard Barthelmess, William Gaxton, Hedda Hopper, Sam Harris, and everyone connected to Broadway who wanted to raise kids. The first four years of Keenan's life seemed to be very happy, but then Hilda started to retreat into silence and became morbidly depressed. Keenan's fourth birthday party, which was a big affair where the Who's Who of Broadway were in attendance, marked in Ed's mind the last time the family was truly happy. Hilda slipped into sickness, and Ed worked constantly in one Broadway show after the next as well as toured all of them across the country.

While in the *Gaieties* at a salary of $1,700 a week, Ed was the highest-paid entertainer on Broadway in 1919. The show was a hit and had a guaranteed tour for a year. Most actors didn't live as well as Ed Wynn. In 1919 there was no limit to the number of weeks of unpaid rehearsal an actor had to give to a show. A producer could call the whole show off the day before it opened, and the cast would be out of luck penniless. A show could close on the road and leave the actors stranded out of town. The poor treatment of the troupers came to a head that year, and the actors went on strike one rainy day in August. Two thousand actors marched from Columbus Circle down Broadway, chanting, "No more pay. Just fair play!" Ed was paid well, so he could have stayed out of the strike. But he believed that all theatre people should be unionized and protected, so he walked off the show to march with the other actors. Instead of giving performances in the theaters, the actors gave them in the streets to explain the strike to the public. That historic day, twenty-one Broadway shows closed at once.

Ed paraded in the picket lines on Broadway, stood on soapboxes making speeches at street corners, enlisted new recruits for the strikers among stars who were his friends. Some friendships broke up as not everyone agreed with the union—especially producers like Sam Harris and George M. Cohan. One speech given by Ed was so emotional that some of the bystanders picked him up and carried him down the street on their shoulders. When news came that the union had won the strike, Ed and Hilda got in the car and drove around the neighborhood honking the horn and spreading the news of victory.

When the strike began, the Equity treasury was rather low, so the actors threw a benefit show at the Lexington Avenue Opera House. Ed's contribution started from a seat in the house. He climbed up onto the stage and announced that Judge Lyndon had served him with an injunction that ordered him not to appear in the show. Under the circumstances he would not be able to perform his act, which would have consisted of—and then he went about performing the whole act by showing the audience what they wouldn't be seeing.

However, the ramifications of the strike caused Ed to be blacklisted by the Managers' Protective Association. They swore that Ed Wynn would never work on Broadway as long as he lived. Ed had no choice but to go it alone and decided to write, produce, and star in his own show. He sat himself down at the piano and started writing songs. He hired actors from side shows and circuses to avoid the problems with blacklisted actors. The show was *Ed Wynn's Carnival*. Financed on a shoestring, Ed mortgaged the house, and Hilda pawned the jewels to raise the capital needed to produce the show. They rented what they could from costume storage on the cheap. Once he had an idea of the costumes and sets he could use, Ed wrote sketches to fit them. All of this was fine, but Ed still needed a theater. B. C. Whitney, a manager from Detroit who hadn't joined the Protective Association, had ambitions of using Ed Wynn's talents. The two met by accident while Ed was waiting to try to see Ziegfeld in the hopes of booking a theater. After Ed told Whitney all about his show, Whitney happily agreed to help out, and they tried out the show in Philadelphia and then were able to move it to the New Amsterdam on Forty-Second Street. The manager was Abe Erlanger, and he hated the Shuberts, so he gave Ed Wynn the crown jewel of Broadway houses to be sure they noticed.

Equity, indebted to Ed, bought every seat on the first night. Ziegfeld sat in the first row. At the end of the last act and multiple curtain calls, Ziegfeld turned to one of his regular directors, Ned Wayburn, and demanded, "Why don't you give me finales like that?" After the Broadway run, the show toured for a year. Money talks, and so Ed's enemies couldn't hold a grudge for long. His next shows would be scheduled into the George M. Cohan Theater for *The Perfect Fool* and Charles Dillingham's Theater for *The Grab Bag*.

Historian Ethan Mordden notes, "When we consider the components of the twenties show, whether musical comedy, operetta, or revue, we find only one that was absolutely crucial right from the dawn of the first age [of the musical]: the star comic." The star comic of the 1920s and into the 1930s didn't mean any actor playing a comic role, but a particular comic personality whose individual character and style drew the public to the show. This quality was found in the likes of W. C. Fields, Eddie Cantor, Joe Cook, the Marx Brothers, Fanny Brice, Bert Lahr, Jimmy Durante, and Ed Wynn—all people who also went on to make their mark in the movies. Not many of these people, however, got to recreate their Broadway performances in the movies. Joe Cook, for example, seemed to always get Bert Lahr's stage roles in the film versions. In a few cases, these comedians did get to go along for the film versions. Eddie Cantor was able to recreate his starring role in *Whoopee*. *The Coconuts* and *Animal Crackers* couldn't have been made without the Marx Brothers. Jimmy Durante got to do *Jumbo* (albeit twenty-five years later), and Ed Wynn got to play "Crickets" in the film version of *Manhattan Mary* (1927) though the title was changed to *Follow the Leader* (1930).

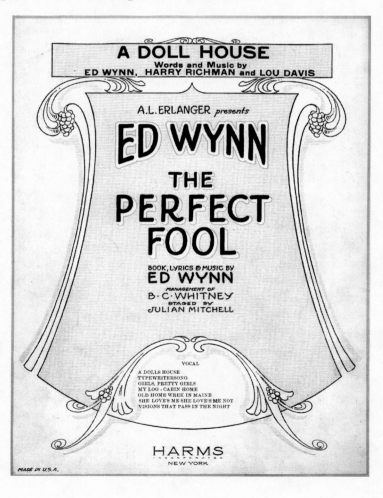

The Perfect Fool (1921) was not only Ed's next big hit on Broadway, but it was a title that stuck to him, and he was noted as being "the perfect fool" the rest of his career. This was another do-it-yourself show, and Ed made a million dollars on it. The title for the show came to Ed when he was outside the New Amsterdam one day and saw a woman trying to buy two tickets only to find the show was sold out. The woman told the box office clerk that she wanted the tickets for her anniversary—she and her husband loved Ed Wynn, saying, "We think he's the perfect fool." Ed filed it away for future use and told the clerk to sell the woman two house seats, and that was the last he heard of her.

During the run of *The Perfect Fool*, Ed thought he'd try out the new medium of radio. He performed routines in a two-hour broadcast, but only a limited number of people heard it in those early days of radio in 1922. When the technology progressed and nearly every household had a radio, Ed would become famous to all those who never saw him on the stage as "The Fire Chief" on his weekly half-hour comedy show.

In *The Grab Bag* (1924), Ed perfected his lisp, the simper, the lunatic inventions, and his final persona that he would stick with for the rest of his career. One gag involved an inch-long harmonica, which Ed demonstrated in the first act. "I shall now oblige you, I hope, with a musical solo." After blowing a little tune, the harmonica got lost inside his mouth, and it seemed as though he had swallowed it. For the rest of the show, he'd stand by the wings and give a nervous cough. An out-of-sight stagehand simultaneously blew on a full-size harmonica, which seemed to emanate from Ed's stomach. The ongoing gag was a riot throughout the show.

The popular composing team of DeSylva, Brown, and Henderson wrote Ed's next vehicle, *Manhattan Mary* (1927). This was the same year of the team's biggest hit, *Good News*, so Ed couldn't have asked for better company. The show was produced by George White, who was trying to recreate the success of Ziegfeld's *Sally*, which had starred Marilyn Miller and Leon Errol (Joe Cook nabbed Errol's role for the film). Elizabeth Hines played the title character in a typical rags-to-riches story interrupted by shenanigans from Ed Wynn. Songs included "Broadway [the Heart of the World]" and the dance sensation "The Five Step." Hines wasn't working out during previews, and so White brought in Ona Munson to replace her. Munson had made her debut in George Whites *Scandals* in 1919 and would work steadily on Broadway through the 1930s.

Ed's first Depression-era show was *Simple Simon* (1930). Even produced by Ziegfeld with a Rodgers and Hart score, the show bombed. Still, the production ran a year including four months on Broadway, tour dates, and a month return to Broadway before finally closing. The show combined Mother Goose fantasy with Coney Island foolery. Starting the show in a modern Coney Island setting, Ed, as Simon, runs a news stand. All the key characters showed up for introductions, and then Ed found himself in Storybook Land with the key characters transformed into Mother Goose people. This was nothing more than a zany world for Ed to run in and out of, introducing his gadgets and delivering his puns. Critic Robert Benchley suggested the jokes dated back to the Civil War, calling it, "a series of some of the highest-pensioned gags in the GAR."

STRAIGHT MAN: Business is looking up.
WYNN: It has to; it's flat on its back.

But if the show received lousy notices, Ed still won out, pleasing his fans with his usual brand of humor. Also, this is the show where Ruth Etting introduced "Ten Cents a Dance," which became one of her signatures. Etting got the part when the original actress, Lee Morse, went on a drinking binge and could hardly stand up, much less sing. Ziegfeld fired her and brought in *Follies* star Etting with only three days to go before the New York opening.

"Ten Cents a Dance," though having nothing to do with the plot, marked the introduction of one of Ed's most famous inventions—famous because he would keep using it the rest of his career. Ruth Etting sang the song perched on top of a piano on a bicycle. After some patter, Ed would peddle the piano around the stage as Etting sang the tune. What exactly was the audience to make of this? Here was a dramatic torch song about a taxi dancer—both beautiful and sad—and there was Ed Wynn the clown driving her around on this bicycle/piano contraption, disrupting any sense of mood the song might have achieved. This made the song a vaudeville turn rather than a story song, but it didn't seem to matter—the novelty won over, and Etting still had a hit song to keep in her back pocket for years to come. The routine can be seen performed with Dinah Shore on Ed's TV variety show, this time with the more generic "Shine on Harvest Moon."

DINAH SHORE: Can you accompany me on this?
ED: On this piano I can accompany you anywhere.
DINAH: (*after hopping on the piano*) I made it. Follow that cab!
　　(*Ed plays the piano a bit*)
DINAH: Ed, I had no idea you played the piano so well.
ED: I've only been playing for five days.

DINAH: Five days?!

ED: That's right. The first time I played was after I hurt my hand five days ago. Do you remember how the doctor bandaged my hand? Well, that's when it all started. I said, "Doctor, when this bandage comes off will I be able to play the piano?" And he said yes. That's all I know. Dinah, would you sing "Shine on Harvest Moon"?

DINAH: I'd love to, Ed.

ED: Oh good, I'd love to hear you sing that song.
    (*Ed folds his arms and waits for Dinah to sing. Dinah waits for Ed to give her the intro on the piano.*)

DINAH: Ed, aren't you going to play it?

ED: Oh yes, I'm not doing anything. What key?

DINAH: Oh . . . two flats.

ED: If I have the key I can play in any flat.

Then, laughing at his own joke, they launch into the number. The routine is finished off with a rendition of "Tea for Two" as Ed peddles the piano off stage into the wings, and the curtain falls. Ed recreated the routine on Walt Disney's TV show on an episode devoted to the *Golden Horseshoe Revue*, a wild west variety show, which famously played at Disneyland for decades. The show was the perfect kind to include the antics of Ed Wynn, so in this way, a small part of *Simple Simon* has been preserved.

The following season Ed opened in *The Laugh Parade* (1931) with a score by Harry Warren, who would make a bigger splash writing for the Warner Bros. musicals thereafter. Although the show represented more of the same, it was Ed's biggest hit of the decade. During most of the show's run, Ed did double duty appearing in his radio show, *The Fire Chief*, for Texaco, although at first the sponsor wasn't convinced that Ed Wynn would go over as purely an aural entertainer. So they sent their top advertising man down to "listen" to *The Laugh Parade* by sitting in a box seat with his back to the show. Apparently Ed passed the test because the radio show became very popular.

Ed's inventions were particularly outlandish in *The Laugh Parade*. He introduced a brown derby hat with a removable brim so that the wearer could tip his hat in the winter and not catch cold and demonstrated a bed for trapping bed bugs. His jokes came in the usual manner: Just before launching into a juggling routine, he said to the conductor, "Just play something in a jugular vein." He repeated the piano on bicycle routine, presented his own version of "Punch and Judy," and got mixed up with an acrobatic act. Critic John Mason Brown of the *New York Evening Post* said that Ed Wynn was "the only master of his own special brand of nonsense, a comic law unto himself." Ed Wynn insinuated himself into scenarios where he otherwise didn't belong, commenting, participating, and disrupting to comic affect. This was his basic formula, regardless of the title of the show, plot, or songs.

Former strike enemies, The Shuberts, wanted to cash in on Ed as well and put him up at their prize theatre, The Wintergarden, in *Hooray for What* for Christmas 1937. Strangely, for an Ed Wynn vehicle, the show had something to say about serious contemporary issues. Wynn, as Chuckles the horticulturist, invents a gas to kill worms in his apple orchard:

> ED: Dancing worms you know, because they love to go into the big apple.

The important turn of events is that Chuckles finds the gas can kill humans.

> ED: This gas will revive the dead. I've got a big offer from the Republican Party.

The discovery sparks an arm's race among the powers of Europe, all trying to steal Chuckles's formula. A lady spy manages to copy down the formula with the aid of a hand mirror. However, thanks to the mirror, she copies it down backwards, thereby creating laughing gas instead of killing gas. This accident causes the world to be one of brotherly love.

ED: Generally speaking, diplomats are generally speaking.

This timely musical, not out of sync with a lot of the theatre going on during the Great Depression and the war in Europe, played on the daily news for material. In a year when Japan had captured the Chinese capitol of Peiping and Shanghai, Franco blockaded every Loyalist port in Spain, Italy withdrew from the League of Nations, the Spanish bombarded Barcelona and Hitler took over Austria, Ed Wynn could comment on stage, "The trouble with the world is that Italy's in Ethiopia, Japan is in China and Germany is in Austria. Nobody stay's home!"

Although choreographer Agness de Mille contributed a stark "Hero Ballet," the musical was hardly sober; for Ed cavorted with acrobats, trained dogs, and made smoke come out of his ears. Still, the Harold Arlen/Yip Harburg score (their first collaboration on a book musical) stuck to the topicality of the show. Their patriotic offering, "God's Country," said,

> Hi there, chappie,
> Look over the seas and be happy.
> We've got no Mussolini,
> Got no Mosely.
> We've got Popeye
> And Gypsy Rose Lee.

This song strangely shows up with slightly revised lyrics in the Mickey Rooney/Judy Garland film *Babes in Arms*.

By 1940, the Broadway revue as it had been established in the 1920s was practically dead, and *Boys and Girls Together* would be Ed's last real success in the genre. The idea for the show came when a group of Yale boys stopped Ed in a hotel lobby and asked him when he was going to do another show. *Hooray for What* had seemed like it would be Ed's last revue, but this run-in from a group of young fans inspired Ed to get back to work and write a new show. He engaged Sammy Fain to compose the score with Jack Yellen and Irving Kahal writing the lyrics. Ed wrote most of the sketches with help from Pat C. Flick. None other than Irene Sharaff designed the costumes, and the great Hans

Spielac did the orchestrations with input from Russell Bennett and Don Walker—Broadway legends one and all. Ed produced, wrote, directed, and starred. But then, outside of three Broadway productions, this had always been the case.

Not more than a series of sketches and songs vaguely connected by the idea of young people in love, Ed would act as Emcee and generally happen to entangle himself with the supporting performers who presumably had no prior plans of including a clown in their act. The bicycle routine was resurrected with Jane Pickens perched on top singing, "You Can't Put Catsup on the Moon." The show played from October 1940 to March 1941 and then went on tour. Almost immediately after, Ed began work on what would turn out to be his last Broadway appearance, for his brand of comedian no longer had a place on Broadway. The new comedian would not necessarily be the star anymore. He would be integrated into the plot, become an actual character with individual traits particular to the story. He would not turn to the audience and crack a joke simply to get a laugh. His comedy would come out of being a part of a situation, and his humor would be natural and humanistic. He would be *Oklahoma!*'s Ali Hakim, *Can-Can*'s Boris, or *The Pajama Game*'s Hines. Stars were still important, but they would now play characters in musicals with a deeper sense of purpose. This was not Ed Wynn. So off to television he went to invade the new medium's variety show—a half hour version of televised vaudeville.

Ed spent the majority of World War II entertaining the troops, and when the war came to an end, television started to emerge as a viable new form of entertainment. Ed had so far only worked in films sporadically, just as the other Broadway clowns had. There was, it seemed, a limited place for Durante, Cantor, Lahr, Brice, and others in movie musicals. The Marx Brothers fared better with their successful series of films at Paramount and then MGM, but by the 1940s even their act was fading out—each brother going out on his own to play personal appearances and cameos, with Groucho finding a new career as game show host. Ed Wynn, for a short time, was able to recycle his stage career on his own TV show.

What makes *The Ed Wynn Show* so great is that it is a way of getting a fair idea of what happened in all those faded Broadway shows. The *Oklahoma!s*, *South Pacifics*, *Pajama Games* and *Guys and Dolls* can all be experienced today; for they belong to a group of classic musicals that are continually revived, and any good actor who can sing it can effectively play a role. The *Grab Bags*, *Perfect Fools*, and *Laugh Parades* are lost; and even if they weren't, who would play Ed Wynn today? Nathan Lane? *The Ed Wynn Show* preserved an era of Broadway that can only be cobbled together from the great Broadway comedians' recycled routines in movies and TV variety shows. However, Ed didn't just go back to old routines, but he also updated his act to be relevant to a contemporary audience. He knew he was being seen on a twelve-inch black-and-white screen rather than a lavish colorful stage show.

> ED: You're going to see a musical spectacle and a dramatic spectacle. And if you've watched enough television that's what you need—a pair of spectacles.

> ED: You know it pays to advertise. And as long as my sponsor pays I'll advertise.

> GARRY MOORE (Radio Host): Ed, I'd like to get into television.

> ED: I think you should get into television. I think television is rapidly replacing entertainment.

> ED: I can't wait to get to France because I have a cousin in Paris and a nephew in Niece. Jokes like I've just said will eventually bring back . . . some other form of entertainment.

In 1951, Walt Disney's *Alice in Wonderland* was released, and Ed provided the voice and the likeness for the Mad Hatter. His performance is one of the big delights of the film, and the tea party scene is one of the most successful in a film that otherwise received a cold shoulder from the public. At the time, this film was only part of the decline of Ed's career, rather than evidence of a fresh new career in films that would come. In the 1960s, with the film's rerelease and even a television showing, *Alice in Wonderland* grew to be as loved as any of the classic Disney-animated features, and the Mad Hatter now stands out as one of the cherished Ed Wynn performances.

After his variety show expired, Ed embarked on a new career as television special guest. During this time he was forced to shed his clownish costumes and painted face. He had to become a real person to survive. He did not have to shed the Ed Wynn charm, which was totally genuine, but "The Perfect Fool" had to go. 1956 was a turning point due to two important projects. Keenan and José Ferrer talked Ed into appearing in a small part in a movie Ferrer was directing called *The Great Man*. Ed played Ed Beaseley, the owner of a Christian radio station. He was nominated for a Golden Globe Award for the role. Next, Keenan was coaching Ed through the role of "Army" in a *Playhouse 90* TV movie *Requiem for a Heavyweight*. Ed was clearly out of his element—this wasn't just a small featured role, and he couldn't rely on any of his old bag of tricks. Moreover, the show was filmed live, like a play. Because of his insecurities in playing the manager of a prize fighter (Jack Palance), he kept joking around and goofing his lines. He nearly got himself fired, but Jack Palance said he would quit if Ed Wynn was let go. When the filming began, Ed was ready and completely in character.

In *Requiem for a Heavyweight* Ed is thoughtful and real—no lisp and no "Hoo hoo" laugh. His head bobs as he's listening—a nervous habit? His line readings are natural, and he relates to others well, playing off them. In fact, he is actually more real in it than Jack Palance or Keenan Wynn, who seem to be trying too hard to be characters. There is one moment when he delivers a line the way "The Perfect Fool" might do it: "If that was an inch short, you'd smoke your nose [hoo]." Still, in this solemn persona, Ed seems sad—his mouth closed tightly as if to control the tears. He is completely connected to the material. Knowing Ed Wynn's career to this point, he gives a fascinating, even amazing, performance. Rod Serling was impressed and would use Ed again in episodes of his *Twilight Zone* series.

Requiem for a Heavyweight launched a new and very productive chapter in Ed Wynn's career, mixing television and film roles. For playing Mr. Dussell in *The Diary of Anne Frank*, Ed received an Academy Award nomination. But then, he was back on TV playing the grandfather in a remake of *Meet Me in St. Louis*. The Disney Studio became Ed's new home for the remainder of his days, starting with *The Absent Minded Professor* as well as the sequel *Son of Flubber*. These two films were a family affair as Keenan was featured as the villain Alonzo Hawk, and even grandson Ned has a small part in each film. Ed plays none other than the Fire Chief, a novel reprise of his former radio character.

Babes in Toyland gave Ed the opportunity to return to his traditional clowning as the adaptation of the operetta from 1903 had plenty of room for Ed's inventions, jokes, and even the kind of costume he might have worn in *Simple Simon*. Walt Disney regularly used his TV show to promote his upcoming projects. In fact, he was criticized more than once for turning his episodes into one-hour movie trailers. Actually, the Disney TV show was designed to advertise and pay for Disneyland itself. Thus, *Disneyland* was the name of the show for the first several seasons. The name would change over the years to *Walt Disney Presents*, *The Wonderful World of Color*, and *The Wonderful World of Disney*. On a 1961 episode of *The Wonderful World of Color*, Walt Disney takes the TV audience on a backstage tour of the *Babes in Toyland* sets. The subject of the episode is the wrap party for the film. After we get a glimpse of the last shot on the production schedule, Walt and Annette host a party with all the cast members and crew. Co-star Tommy Kirk is there watching Ed Wynn do a turn as Ed Wynn and then presents him with a "Mousker"—a gold statue of Mickey honoring the celebrated comedian's sixty years in show business. Kirk remembered working with Ed Wynn as great fun, saying, "I thought he was delightful and so did everyone else. You couldn't *not* like him. He was completely crazy, and he was just as crazy *off* screen as he was on. But it was all, of course, an act."

For all its inconsistencies, *Babes in Toyland* is a cute film with some excellent bits of comic business, good dancing, and a great cast. The critics didn't go for it, but it has become a Christmas time favorite for children. One day Ed Wynn came up to Kirk at the studio and asked him, "Tommy, listen, have you seen *Babes in Toyland?*" Kirk replied that he had, and Wynn returned, "I hear it isn't very good." Kirk felt sad to hear Ed Wynn say that, for working with him on the film had been such a good experience. He thought to himself, "I don't think it is either, Ed." But he didn't say it out loud; he was embarrassed and very sad for Ed Wynn and himself. The studio's disappointment in the film was not directed at Ed Wynn or Tommy Kirk, for each would go on to make many more films for Disney.

The big film, though not the biggest role, was *Mary Poppins*. This was the great culmination of all of Walt Disney's experience rolled into one film. Ed played Uncle Albert, a man who can't stop laughing. Once he gets going, he floats about on the ceiling and can't get down. The Sherman Brothers gave Ed the delightful "I Love to Laugh" to sing, and the sequence allowed him to deliver his corny old-fashioned Jokes: "I know a man with a wooden leg named Smith." The role was tailor made for him, and so he is perfection in it. The monumental popularity of the film and its status as one of the great children's classics means that Ed Wynn is continually introduced to new generations. Children today may never know anything about "The Perfect Fool" or "The Fire Chief," but they know who Uncle Albert is.

After Uncle Albert, nothing really compares. Ed made a welcome addition in small roles to the casts of *Those Calloways*, *That Darn Cat*, assorted television appearances, and his final film, released after his death, *The Gnome-Mobile*. During these last years, beyond three marriages, Ed had reduced his life from the grand Wyngate on Long Island to a small apartment on the corner of Beverly Glen and Wilshire in Little Holmby, the neighboring village to Beverly Hills. Now, in his seventies, he had simplified his life into an economic package. He could look back on his life and be proud that he was acknowledged for successfully adapting with the changing times. He conquered the great popular form of entertainment, vaudeville; climbed the ladder to the top of Broadway stardom; won over the radio audience; and was a television pioneer. Then, as unlikely as it seemed, he succeeded in dramatic roles as well as staying true to his gift as a comedian in the movies—all along working with the greatest talents in all these mediums.

Ned Wynn observed, "I wonder if I have ever known a more graceful man than Ed Wynn. Massively egocentric, ponderous, and pedantic, nonetheless, in him all the beauty of fame and fortune had become quintessential." Ned found his grandfather to be gentle and kind. Keenan found his father's personality too dominating—a man who talked more than he listened. Neither son nor grandson was ever able to feel that they really knew Ed Wynn. He was a kind of walking caricature, and he was devoted to his audience above all. Even Ed himself once said to his son, "To tell you the truth, Keenan, I never wanted to be a real person." He may have lived up to that wish, but there must have been more underneath the funny costume and painted face. We will never know. We will only take joy in his antics as the Mad Hatter and

Uncle Albert—two career-defining characters preserved for generations to come. Keenan Wynn summed up his father as living "in a dream world of his own creating, in which the reality was his will to succeed. It was a world as quaint as a nursery tale, where the babies came out of cabbages, toilets didn't exist, and there was nothing as disturbing as passion or prejudice. Nobody ever got a belly ache, only a 'stomach distress.'"

Although Ed Wynn may live on in his film appearances, his stage origins are lost, save for the remnants we can glean from the Museum of Radio and Television. His contribution to American popular entertainment should not be forgotten, for he was an original, a leader in his field on stage and off. He was beloved by a public that stuck with him to the end, and yet he could be relevant enough to enchant new generations. His brand of comedy, which is associated with his many great comic peers with whom he shared the dawn of Twentieth Century show business, continues on in TV variety shows like *America's Got Talent* and *Saturday Night Live*. He informs the comedy delivered from stage stars like Nathan Lane and Bill Irwin. He has insinuated himself into a place that allows for Billy Crystal and Robin Williams. There is a spirit that lives on, which we can all identify with as "I love to laugh!"

Bibliography

Atkinson, Brooks. *Broadway*. New York: The Macmillan Company, 1970.

"Ed Wynn." *Internet Broadway Database*. Online. The Broadway League. 23 Jun. 2009.

"Ed Wynn." *Internet Movie Database*. Online. IMDb.com Inc., 23 Jun. 2009.

Green, Stanley. *Broadway Musicals of the '30s*. New York: Da Capo Press Inc., 1971.

Lahr, John. *Notes on a Cowardly Lion*. New York: Alfred A. Knopf, 1969.

Maltin, Leonard. *The Disney Films*. New York: Hyperion, 1973.

Minton, Kevin. "Sex, Lies and Disney Tape." *Filmfax*. Apr/May 1993: 67-71.

Morden, Ethen. *Beautiful Mornin': The Broadway Musical in the 1940s*. New York: Oxford Unversity Press, 1999.

——————. *Make Believe: The Broadway Musical in the 1920s*. New York: Oxford University Press, 1997.

——————. *Sing For Your Supper: The Broadway Musical in the 1930s*. New York: Oxford University Press, 2005.

Wynn, Keenan. *Ed Wynn's Son*. New York: Doubleday and Company Inc., 1959.

Wynn, Ned. *We Will Always Live in Beverly Hills*. New York: William Morrow and Company Inc., 1990.

Valley, Richard. "Just an Average Joe (Hardy): An Interview with Tommy Kirk." *Scarlet Street*. Spring 1993:60-69.

Films Referenced

The Absent Minded Professor. Robert Stevenson, Director. Walt Disney Productions. , 1961.

Alice in Wonderland. Clyde Geronimi, Wilfred Jackson, Hamilton Luske, Directors. Walt Disney Productions, 1951.

Babes in Toyland. Jack Donohue, Director. Walt Disney Productions, 1961.

The Diary of Anne Frank. George Stevens, Director. Twentieth Century Fox, 1959.

Follow the Leader. Norman Taurog, Director. Paramount Pictures, 1930.

The Gnome-Mobile. Robert Stevenson, Director. Walt Disney Productions, 1967.

Mary Poppins. Robert Stevenson, Director. Walt Disney Productions, 1964.

That Darn Cat. Robert Stevenson, Director. Walt Disney Productions, 1965.

Those Calloways. Norman Tokar, Director. Walt Disney Productions, 1965.

Son of Flubber. Robert Stevenson, Director. Walt Disney Productions, 1963.

Television Programs Referenced

"Backstage Party." *Walt Disney's Wonderful World of Color*. By Larry Clemmons. Jack Donohue, Hamilton Luske, Directors. 17 Dec. 1961.

The Ed Wynn Show. 6 episodes. CBS. 22 Sept. 1949-15 Jun. 1950.

"Golden Horseshoe Revue." *Walt Disney's Wonderful World of Color*. By Larry Clemmons. Ron Miller, Director. 23 Sep. 1962.

Meet Me in St. Louis. By Irving Brecher. George Schaefer, Director. 26 Apr. 1959.

"One for the Angels." *The Twilight Zone*. By Rod Sterling. Robert Parrish, Director. CBS. 9 Oct. 1959.

"Requiem for a Heavyweight." *Playhouse 90*. By Rod Sterling. Ralph Nelson, Director. CBS. 11 Oct. 1956.

This is Your Life. Axel Gruenberg, Director. Host Ralph Edwards. NBC. 1 Oct. 1952.

A Cinemactor's Forgotten Theatrical Resume: Spencer Tracy On Stage

James Fisher

Spencer Tracy is well-known as the outstanding American cinema actor of his generation. Little has been written about Tracy's theatrical roots, where he shaped the remarkable naturalism he demonstrated in his more than seventy films. He acted in every sort of motion picture genre available within the Hollywood system, and he moved easily from serious drama to light comedy. Unlike his contemporaries who demonstrated similar versatility, Tracy moved through these forms without a radical transformation of his physical persona, but through the revelation of a unique facet of his intellectual and emotional personality. During the 1920s he fell under the influence of a few theatrical giants (including George M. Cohan and Ethel Barrymore) and served as a journeyman actor touring in stock productions with occasional performances on Broadway. Hard-won stage stardom led to his film acting, but it is clear that the theatre had provided Tracy with the techniques and training he carried into his singular cinematic career.

In the late 1920s, when silent films vanished and "talkies" arrived, movie moguls pirated plays, actors, and artisans from the theatre. Although stage actors had often appeared on screen during silent movie days, the demand was significantly increased after 1927, when Al Jolson first declaimed, in the *Jazz Singer*, "You ain't heard nothin' yet!" It has become traditional to argue that the most versatile actors come from the stage. Of the outstanding screen actors of the first generation of sound—Humphrey Bogart, James Cagney, Edward G. Robinson, Paul Muni and others—all had significant stage experience.

One such stage-to-film actor, regarded by many critics and peers as perhaps the finest American cinemactor, Spencer Tracy (1900-1967), made over seventy feature films between 1930 and 1967. Tracy became the thinking man's—and woman's—tough guy. In serious and often socially conscious dramas such as *Bad Day at Black Rock* (1955) and *Judgment at Nuremberg* (1961), he embodied the lone man required to courageously stand up for truth, decency, and compassion when cowardice or compromise might instead make his path a smoother one. Tracy demonstrated a remarkable skill, effortlessly shuttling back and forth between comedy and drama, easily dominating both genres with a simplicity and human resonance that brings the viewer close to his characters. He acted in literally every sort of motion picture genre available within the Hollywood system. And unlike his few contemporaries who demonstrated similar versatility, he moved through these forms without a radical transformation of his physical persona, but instead through the revelation of a unique facet of his intellectual and emotional personality. Of the stars who emerged in the 1930s, Tracy possessed a cinematic dexterity that could only be challenged by a Cagney, a Davis, a Hepburn, or a Garbo.

What in Spencer Tracy's own life experiences prepared him to enact such a diverse array of characters and situations with such mastery of technique and versatility? It is not easy to know, for Tracy himself was little help to biographers or critics of his cinematic achievement. Few major film stars of the golden age of Hollywood were as reluctant as Tracy to speak of his work or to become involved in matters of self-promotion. He rebuffed reporters and interviewers, generally refused to seriously analyze his acting techniques in any public forum, and avoided virtually all public functions and honors particularly after World War II. As he once put it, "Write anything you want about me. Make up something. Hell, I don't care" (Halliwell, 685). In the rare and inevitably brief interviews he reluctantly granted, Tracy is often frank about his own failings, which included a life-long struggle with alcoholism, and he is either unduly modest about his work or impatient and jocular when discussing it. Near the end of his career, in April 1961, he offered a typically tongue-in-cheek reply to *Los Angeles Mirror* reporter Erskine Johnson's question about Tracy's method: "It's never been very demanding. It doesn't require much brainwork. Acting is not the noblest profession in the world, but there are things lower than acting. Not many, mind you—but politicians give you something to look down on from time to time."

Katharine Hepburn has often claimed that "Spencer always thought that acting was a rather silly way for a man to make a living" (Halliwell, 685), but accepting the portrait of a reluctant actor who simply does his job without fuss or nonsense is far too simple. The eloquence and simplicity of Tracy's work demonstrates a level of thoughtfulness and thoroughness of interpretation, detail, and character development that could only result from an actor who took his job very seriously. Before he stepped before a camera, Tracy had thoroughly analyzed the character and distilled this web of complexities into essences. He once advised a young actor—Burt Reynolds—to never let anyone catch him acting. It is clearly impossible to ever catch Tracy at it—he just exists on screen as a total human being acting and reacting naturally. In some comments to reporter Don Alpert published in the *Los Angeles Times* in November 1961, Tracy provided a hint about his acting style: "I'm Spencer Tracy with some deference to the character. When a person says he's an actor—he's a personality. The whole idea is to show your personality." A month later, Phyllis Battelle quoted Tracy in the *Los Angeles Times* as saying that "the only thing an actor has to offer a director and finally an audience is his instinct. That's all." In his final interview, given to Roy Newquist on the set of *Guess Who's Coming to Dinner* (1967), Tracy again stated the actor's art in the simplest of terms: "What any good actor does is crawl into the part he's playing and play it as completely as he can. He catches the character and is that character consistently" (151).

Many aspects of Tracy's prowess as a screen actor must certainly be attributed to his little-known years as a stage actor. Although he returned only once to the theatre after becoming a leading player in film in 1930, Tracy's experience as a journeyman stage actor during the 1920s offers a vivid picture of the development of his art as well as a portrayal of a lively era of the American stage. An examination of Tracy's stage work, long obscured by his screen triumphs, proves the point that the stage gave him everything that he used so effectively on screen. His acting career truly began while he was a student at Wisconsin's Ripon College, where he became an active member of the dramatic society and played a leading role in their 1921 production of *The Truth* by Clyde Fitch. The campus newspaper critic felt that Tracy "proved himself a consistent and unusually strong actor in this most difficult straight part. His steadiness, his reserve strength and suppressed emotion were a pleasant surprise to all who heard him as Warder" ("Commencement Play"). When the play was repeated in early 1922, the campus reviewer stressed that "Spencer

Tracy deserves special mention. His quiet manner of portraying the deceived husband was characterized by such an air of strong reserved force as to be quite remarkable" ("Campus Players"). Tracy had another success at Ripon in *The Valiant* by Halsworthy Hall, in which, as a convict, he played "an unusual character in which the soul of a man is disclosed as courageous even until death. He acts the part of an actor, and in the last moments when Joe meets the girl, his realism is more than could be expected of an amateur" ("Exceptional Staff").

Having found his niche at Ripon, Tracy decided to leave after barely a year to pursue his newfound passion in New York, enrolling at the American Academy of Dramatic Art (AADA) on 2 April 1922. He and his roommate Pat O'Brien had very little money but found the theatrical life of New York exhilarating. Broadway was at the time enjoying a peak of diverse creative activity. However, work was tough to find for a novice actor, and as Tracy himself later recalled, "there were times when my pants were so thin, I could sit on a dime and know if it was heads or tails" (Halliwell, 685). In the summer, he appeared in some stock productions including *Her Wedding Guest* and continued his acting studies.

While still a student at the AADA, Tracy made his Broadway debut in November 1922 when he stepped into a bit role as a robot in the prestigious Theatre Guild production of Karel Capek's expressionistic melodrama *R.U.R.*, which had opened at the Garrick Theatre the previous month. The play is set on a mysterious island where entrepreneur Harry Domin (Basil Sydney) and a corps of scientists manufacture humanoids—robots—designed without a free will to do the manual toil of humanity. Having played God, however, Domin is shocked to discover that his robots have developed their own will and have taken over the world. The *New York Times* (10 October 1922) felt that "in the intelligence of its writing, the novelty of its action and the provocative nature of its mood *R.U.R.* sustains the high traditions of the Theatre Guild." Arthur Hornblow in *Theatre Magazine* (December 1922) considered it "an outrageously fine melodrama." Tracy joined the cast without a single rehearsal, being told by the stage manager to do what the other robots were doing. He also managed to wangle a robot role for O'Brien, and the two young actors (on their salary of $15 a week) ate a little better and enjoyed the reflected glory stemming from their minor participation in one of the major theatrical events of the year. *R.U.R.* ran for 184 performances, was directed by Philip Moeller and Agnes Morgan from a translation by Paul Selver and Nigel Playfair, with scenic design by Lee Simonson.[2] It is a classic example of the expressionistic movement in theatre, which garnered much international attention between the end of World War I and the middle of the 1920s. As a result of the play, "robot" became a household word.

Following *R.U.R.*, Tracy spent the summer of 1923 appearing in several stock productions—including *The Man Who Came Back*, *Getting Gertie's Garter*, and *Lawful Larceny*—for the Wood Players under the guidance of Leonard Wood Jr. in Fall River, Massachusetts, and White Plains, New York. He made $40 a week with the Wood Company and met his future wife, Louise Treadwell, who was also in the company. In the fall of 1923, Tracy joined the Repertory Theatre of Cincinnati, under the direction of Stuart Walker, for several productions, including *The Gypsy Trail* and *Seventeen*. These stock productions were all standard entertainments of the time, forerunners of the light comedies and melodramas that would fill movie screens a decade later. Many of Tracy's films, particularly during the 1930s, are similar in content and style to these plays, and dramatists of these minor productions would also contribute screenplays to many of his earliest movies.

Tracy completed his intense training at the AADA in March 1923 and embarked on seven rough-and-tumble years as an actor in a multitude of stock companies and, occasionally, on Broadway. There is no doubt that it was a difficult and often frustrating existence, but it was also a graduate course in the school of theatrical hard knocks. With the emergence of Eugene O'Neill and a few other innovative dramatists shortly after World War I, the New York stage began to develop in quality. Quantity had existed in the American theatre for much longer—and even a beginning actor like Tracy could find fairly regular work within the complicated tangle of stock companies throughout the country. The smallest of towns had a theatre that might play host to a touring stock company or vaudeville bill from one week to the next, and the actor without a recognizable name could make a living. However, he had to work hard for his money and lived a gypsy life—a few weeks here, a few weeks there—knocking about the theatrical circuits.

What seemed to be a confirming stroke of good luck came when within weeks after finishing at the AADA, Tracy landed a small role in distinguished producer Arthur Hopkins's lavish Broadway production of Zoe Akins's play, *A Royal Fandango*, directed by Hopkins, with scene design by Robert Edmond Jones. *Fandango* opened at the Plymouth Theatre on 12 November 1923; its plot involved an unhappily married European princess, Amelia (Ethel Barrymore), who falls in love with a naive matador, Chucho (Jose Alessandro).[3] The lovers are never able to be alone until they retreat to the matador's castle in Spain. Her inattentive husband, Prince Peter (Cyril Keightley), pursues her when he discovers that she has run off. The princess is moved by her husband's newfound ardor and returns home with him, leaving Chucho kissing a flower Amelia has dropped on her hasty departure. This potboiler is hardly more than a footnote in the distinguished stage career of Barrymore, and, except for Tracy's appearance in a bit role, it would otherwise hold little interest. In later years, Tracy became good friends with Barrymore when he was a star at MGM, and the elderly Barrymore was ending her career as a respected movie character actress. Unfortunately, Tracy never made a film with Barrymore, although he did make several with her brother, Lionel (whom he had seen and admired in *The Claw* on stage while a student at the AADA). Tracy's salary was less than $100 a week, but he did receive some good advice from the star. In her autobiography, Barrymore recalled the encounter with Tracy: "He had one line to say, and I saw that he was very nervous, so I said to him, 'Relax. That's all you have to do—just relax. It'll be the same in a hundred years.' . . . He has been relaxing with notable success for twenty-five of those hundred years" (250). The cast of *Fandango* also included Edward G. Robinson in a small role. Tracy and he became good friends but never acted together again, and their only subsequent connection is that Robinson took over two movie roles from an ailing Tracy in the 1960s: *Cheyenne Autumn* and *The Cincinnati Kid*. Playwright Akins had several stage successes in her career, most particularly *Declassé* (1919), but *Fandango* was certainly not among her outstanding efforts. Although Heywood Broun in the *New York World* felt that "Shaw himself has seldom written more shrewdly and entertainingly of woman the pursuer," most reviews were only modestly respectful of what the *New York Times* (13 November 1923) described as "a very light fandango."

After the failure of *A Royal Fandango*, with a mere twenty-four performances, Tracy joined stock companies in Elizabeth, New Jersey, in December 1923, and Winnipeg, Canada, in January and February 1924. He also appeared with the W. H. Wright Company in Pittsburgh in April 1924 and Grand Rapids in June 1924, where he became friends with actress Selena Royle, who advised Tracy and helped him to get ahead as an actor. Royle later played a supporting role in Tracy's 1947 movie *Cass Timberlane*. Tracy joined a stock company at the Montauk Theatre in Brooklyn from September 1924 through the spring of 1925, followed by a return engagement in Grand Rapids and then a season with Frank McCoy's Trent Theatre Stock Company in Trenton, New Jersey, during the fall of 1925. For McCoy he appeared in productions including *The Best People*, *The Song and Dance Man*, *The Back Slapper*,

Shipwrecked, Chicken Feed, Buddies, Wedding Bells, Quincy Adams Sawyer, and *The Family Upstairs*. Also during the fall of 1925, Tracy acted in a tryout tour of *The Sheepman*, an Earl Booth production, but the play closed before reaching Broadway. During the spring and summer of 1926, he again worked with the W. H. Wright Company in Grand Rapids before returning to New York.

Upon returning to Broadway, Tracy landed the role of Jimmy Wilkes in Margaret Vernon's *Yellow*, produced by the era's foremost theatrical impresario, playwright, composer, and actor George M. Cohan. Opening on 21 September 1926 at New York's National Theatre for a successful run of 135 performances, the production was directed by John Meehan under Cohan's watchful eye.[4] The melodramatic plot involves Val Parker (Chester Morris), a wastrel who abandons his live-in girlfriend Daisy (Shirley Wade) to marry into respectability through his relationship with Polly (Selena Royle). When he discovers Daisy is pregnant, he offers her $5,000 through an intermediary, his pal Jack (Hale Hamilton). Daisy is irate and rejects it, turning to prostitution to support herself. Val's marriage is unhappy; he longs to return to Daisy, and when he does, she shoots him. Val lives, but Daisy eventually dies; and when his former treatment of her becomes public, he is run out of town. One critic described Tracy's character as "an uncouth but genuine bank clerk" (Hornblow, 1926), but the general critical assessment was clearly stated by the *New York Times* (22 Sep. 1926), whose critic felt that

> the stress in this new play is laid upon incident rather than character, and the play as a whole is a straggling and strangely muddled piece—a play which contains several scenes that are quite engrossing, but which proceeds with so little regard to form that ultimately it eludes its audience almost completely.

Yellow was a modest Broadway success but did little to enhance the career of producer Cohan, who, since the 1890s, had been the wunderkind of the New York stage. Cohan's genial comedies and musicals remained popular well into the 1920s, although his plays became passé after World War I when the American theatre's cutting edge became the dramas of playwrights such as Eugene O'Neill, Robert Sherwood, Susan Glaspell, Maxwell Anderson, and Elmer Rice. However, the professional and personal influence of Cohan upon Tracy was significant; and throughout the remainder of his life, Tracy would offer nothing but praise for Cohan. John McCabe, a Cohan biographer, has suggested that "Tracy's acting derived essentially from Cohan" (215), and as late as 1940 writers like Hollywood columnist Sidney Skolsky pointed to Cohan mannerisms in Tracy's performances. It is certainly true that Cohan encouraged Tracy's instinctive naturalness and relaxation, traits already in evidence in his earliest performances at Ripon. Little visual evidence of Cohan's acting survives, but in his 1932 film *The Phantom President*, co-starring Claudette Colbert and Jimmy Durante, an aging Cohan displays a breezy charm and naturalism not at all unlike that evident in Tracy's comic performances.

One example of Cohan's interest in Tracy is demonstrated by an often repeated anecdote: During the preparations for *Yellow*, Cohan interrupted rehearsal one day. While he walked slowly from the back of the theatre to the stage, Tracy, struggling to grasp his characterization, assumed he was about to be fired. Instead, Cohan called Tracy the finest young actor he had ever seen. Tracy's natural instincts for comedy grew under Cohan's guidance. His first feature film, *Up the River* (1930), displays his impressive comedic skill—in fact, Tracy's acting is the only aspect of this primitive early talkie that holds a viewer's attention today. Better demonstrations of his comic flair can be found in *Me and My Gal* (1932), *Libeled Lady* (1936), *Riffraff* (1936), the Tracy-Hepburn comedies, *Father of the Bride* (1950), and in the beleaguered and ultimately avaricious old police captain of *It's a Mad, Mad, Mad, Mad World* (1963). *Father of the Bride* offers a particularly masterful comic performance—Tracy provides a symphony of varied reactions to the little indignities, fears, and uncertainties surrounding the marriage of his daughter and the accompanying circus of putting on an elaborate wedding circa 1950. In *Woman of the Year* (1942), the first of the Tracy-Hepburn films, he is the definitive "regular guy," enduring a relationship with a woman too caught up in her career to have time for a real marriage. He loves her and tolerates her thoughtlessness until he senses that he must compel her to see their mutual dilemma. When she finally understands that she has gone too far, she attempts to prove her love with a demonstration of domestic prowess by making breakfast—despite the fact that she has none of the requisite skills. As she slowly demolishes the kitchen, he quietly watches her with equal parts bemusement, horror, and loving understanding. With hardly a word, his reactions build to a comic aura and reality around a slapstick scene belonging more to Laurel and Hardy than to romantic comedy.

Perhaps Tracy's comedic brilliance is best observed in the inevitable comic touches he added to even the most serious roles. For example, in the otherwise grim *Judgment at Nuremberg* (the *Schindler's List* of 1961),

Tracy, as the venerable Judge Dan Haywood, plays a brief scene at a bratwurst stand where he encounters a young German woman. They exchange friendly smiles, and he builds his reactions to suggest that the old jurist thinks he's being flirted with. As the young woman coyly departs, she purrs a few words in German that he does not comprehend. He asks the cashier to translate and learns that the woman said, "Goodbye, Grandpa." Tracy's deflated reaction is priceless, and only an actor of his consummate style would dare contribute such a moment to a characterization otherwise requiring the utmost gravity and sincerity. However, such moments of an individual momentarily suffering one of life's absurdities makes him recognizably human—and more real; he is one of us. These humanizing comic touches are undoubtedly an outgrowth of Tracy's internship with Cohan. And it is very likely that his charming Irish rogue-politician in *The Last Hurrah* (1958) is something of a homage to Cohan, for the performance is marked by the easy Gaelic blarney and twinkling eyes found in surviving film footage of Cohan. Cohan later lamented Tracy's switch from stage to screen, but they continued as friends for the remainder of Cohan's life. When Tracy's pal James Cagney was preparing to play Cohan in *Yankee Doodle Dandy* (1942), he turned to Tracy for reminiscences. Tracy's final interview, conducted by Roy Newquist on the set of *Guess Who's Coming to Dinner* (1967), includes warm remarks from Tracy about the influence of his old theatrical mentor. Surely Tracy's gifts were as much instinctive as they were learned, but Cohan's contribution to Tracy's technique is incalculable.

For his part, Cohan was so impressed with Tracy's natural abilities that he wrote his next play, *The Baby Cyclone*, with Tracy in mind for a leading role. Following the closing of *Yellow*, Cohan had wanted Tracy to appear in his new musical comedy, *The Merry Malones*, but Tracy instead joined the road company of the William A. Brady production of *Ned McCobb's Daughter*, which played in Chicago and elsewhere in early 1927. From April to June of 1927, he rejoined the W. H. Wright Company at the Faurot Opera House in Lima, Ohio, for a season, costarring with his wife, Louise. Ads in the Lima newspaper heralded "a season of high-class stock, presented by a permanent company of distinguished New York players in great plays at small prices" (Spencer Tracy clipping file). The Tracys acted in *Laff That Off*, *The Patsy*, *The First Year*, *Smilin' Through*, *The Family Upstairs*, *The Best People*, *Chicken Feed*, *The Cat and the Canary*, *The Alarm Clock*, *Applesauce*, and *The Whole Town's Talking*. Tracy returned to New York to appear on Broadway in *Cyclone* while Louise abandoned her acting career for family concerns.

The Baby Cyclone opened on 12 September 1927 at New York's Henry Miller Theatre for 187 performances, written and produced by Cohan, with nominal direction by Sam Forrest under Cohan's supervision.[5] During the rehearsals, Cohan reportedly told Tracy to "act less."[6] The "Baby Cyclone" of the title is actually a Pekingese dog belonging to a young couple, Gene and Jessie Hurley (Tracy, Nan Sunderland). Gene is annoyed by Jessie's preoccupation with the dog and sells it for $5 to a woman he meets in the street. This leads to a fight with Jessie that involves the interference of a stranger, Meadows (Grant Mitchell), who takes her home with him. When Gene arrives to straighten out matters, he encounters Lydia (Natalie Moorehead), Meadow's fiancée, who happens to be the woman to whom Gene has sold the dog. There is a considerable farcical dispute over ownership of the dog, but finally Gene and Jessie come to agreement and return home. This airy bit of comic fluff—the sort of theatre that subsequently disappeared with the rise of radio and television situation comedies—was as well received as any Cohan product of the era. It ran a season on Broadway and then had a long life on stock stages throughout the country. Typically, a Cohan play provided ripe roles for actors, as the critics noted. Richard Dana Skinner in *Life* lauded: "Spencer Tracy's masterly delineation is . . . quite the best piece of acting of its kind I have seen in many months. He is not only convincingly at ease at all times, but the variety and sincerity of his facial expressions add sumptuously to the force of every line." The *New York Times* (13 September 1927) praised the entire package: "It all was projected through crisp, racy dialogue and with the aid of two first-rate performances, those of Grant Mitchell, looking a little more benign than ever, as the broker, and Spencer Tracy, as the excitable husband."

Following the closing of *The Baby Cyclone*, Tracy went into the road company of Cohan's *Whispering Friends* during the spring of 1928, taking over the lead from William Harrigan. This tour ended Cohan and Tracy's professional association, as Cohan's career largely declined after the mid-1920s, with the exception of a few stunning returns to acting in plays by others, most notably Eugene O'Neill's *Ah, Wilderness!* in 1933 and the Rodgers and Hart musical *I'd Rather Be Right* in 1936. After the end of his work with Cohan, Tracy nearly played the lead in the Broadway production of *Gods of Lightning*, but the role subsequently went to Charles Bickford. Following this, he appeared in rapid succession in three Broadway failures, and another production that failed to make it to Broadway, along with a brief engagement in stock in Baltimore.

While working in Baltimore, Tracy was signed for the leading role of Richard Banks in Warren F. Lawrence's play *Conflict*, directed by Edward

Clarke Lilley, with scene design by P. Dodd Ackerman.[7] The play opened at New York's Fulton Theatre on 6 March 1929. It focuses on Richard Banks (Tracy), a dull clerk, who is drafted into World War I and attains the status of hero in the air corps and is awarded many decorations. Upon his return home after the war, his inflated ego leads him to marry a local rich girl who had no use for him before the celebrity surrounding his war-time heroism. However, when he is unable to attain the level of success in civilian life that he had in the military, Banks's marriage falls apart. Ultimately, he finds some success as a commercial pilot and a newfound humility. Robert Littel in the *New York Post* described Tracy's character as "unattractive, baffled, conceited, self-mistrusting, unhappy and completely maladjusted," adding that he

> comes to life more than the play warrants through the natural, capable acting of Spencer Tracy, a young man with a sure touch and an ability to concentrate on the character he is trying to create. With good opportunity, Mr. Tracy ought to be heard from more emphatically in the future.

Brooks Atkinson in the *New York Times* (24 March 1929) noted that Tracy "gives, without the slightest trace of ostentation, an astonishingly thorough exposition of the leading character, Richard Banks . . . . Mr. Tracy acts it with so sincere a restraint that at first sight you may not fully appreciate its completeness."

Tracy was hired for the role in *Conflict* after one of the leading players, Clark Gable, bowed out. In Hollywood, Tracy and Gable would co-star in three highly successful films: *San Francisco* (1936), *Test Pilot* (1938), and *Boom Town* (1940)—all involving men of action in the same mold as Tracy's *Conflict* character. Familiar character actor Frank McHugh, who would later make a mark in Warner Bros. films of the 1930s, had a role in the play, and he later appeared with Tracy in *The Last Hurrah*. The cast also included two other character actors who later appeared in films with distinction: Albert Dekker and Edward Arnold. Tracy's understudy for the production was a young actor named Clifford Odets, who also had a bit role in the play. Odets later abandoned his acting career to become one of the most acclaimed American dramatists of the 1930s and, later, a screenwriter. Tracy missed none of the fifty-two performances of *Conflict*, so Odets never had an opportunity to play Banks, and the two never worked together on a film. Publicity for *Conflict* in the *New York Times* featured Tracy prominently (including an excellent portrait sketch) in advance of the play's opening, and it is clear he was being promoted as a new stage star. However, the play's failure slowed Tracy's path toward stardom.

Despite the good reviews for Tracy's acting and respectful comment on the play itself, *Conflict* failed. Once again, Tracy was out of a job and turned to Selena Royle, who helped him to get some stock work in Providence, Rhode Island.[8] He lost the job there because, as he later explained it, the producer felt he lacked the requisite sex appeal to be a matinee idol. It was at this point that Tracy seriously considered abandoning his acting career, but his wife, Louise, insisted that he continue.

Following his time in Providence, Tracy was cast in a featured role in John McGowan's drama *Nigger Rich*, presented by legendary producer Lee Shubert.[9] Written and directed by McGowan, the production featured scenic designs by Rollo Wayne, and the plot was about a bumptious one-time war hero, Mike Kelly (Eric Dressler). Kelly loafs around a servicemen's club living off the good will of his cronies, including Gunny Jones (Richard Taber) and Eddie Perkins (Tracy). When he makes a quick killing on a horse race, Kelly roughly abandons his pals for a life among the elite. Ultimately, however, he is revealed as little more than a small-time chiseler. His life in ruins, he makes amends by signing his insurance policy over to his old buddies before committing suicide.

This comic-melodramatic potboiler, which underwent a number of title changes before returning to the distasteful one insisted on by the author, included the following statement in the program: "There is no Negro element in this play. The title, *Nigger Rich*, is an expression indicating sudden acquisition of wealth by a squanderer." The play's title had generated some controversy, as reported widely in New York newspapers, and when producer Shubert changed the title to *True Colors*, McGowan wrote a letter to him via the *New York Telegram*, stating,

> Your letter to me stating that you have had objections made to you by several societies against the use of the title *Nigger Rich* does not seem to me sufficient ground for relinquishing what to me is the proper and fitting title. In as much as the play does not touch on any racial problem, I see no reason for the change, and if you insist on calling it *True Colors*, I would prefer that you withdraw it from production.

Shubert reluctantly relented, perhaps realizing that the play stood little chance of making it anyway. It underwent some significant script repair after a poorly received opening night, but it was not enough to save the production. It also did little to boost Tracy's career, despite the fact that he personally received excellent notices, which was becoming typical. Robert Littel in the *New York Evening World* captured the general critical sentiment of *Nigger Rich*, calling it

> a rather stiff-jointed comedy that churned water without getting any—where far too much of the time, but that was also briefly illuminated by some extremely funny lines, not a few of which were in the mouth of Spencer Tracy, more of whose easy acting and accurate, well-pitched vernacular I would like to have seen and heard.

Other critics similarly praised Tracy's acting. Burns Mantle wrote in the *New York Daily News* that he was "one of the most satisfying of the younger naturalists of the theater." John Anderson in the *New York Evening Journal* felt that "'Mr. Tracy portrays quietly and with great force, another such sullen soldier as he played last year in *Conflict*." Gilbert Seldes in the *New York Graphic* "was impressed with Spencer Tracy's thoughtful idea of a good simple sergeant." And Brooks Atkinson stated in the *New York Times* (21 September 1929) that "both Eric Dressler and Spencer Tracy, who have appeared in similar parts before, charge their acting full of vitality that is significant in character. They bristle with talent as much as they do with life." However, they were uniformly negative about the play itself, and it closed after only eleven performances at the Royal Theatre. After the quick closing of *Nigger Rich*, Tracy quickly joined the tryout tour of Owen Davis's *Dread*, with stops for performances in Washington, Brooklyn, and other cities. Produced by George M. Cohan's ex-producing partner, Sam H. Harris, the play also featured Madge Evans, George Meeker, Mane Haynes, Frank Shannon, and Miriam Doyle. Despite the talent involved, *Dread* folded before it could reach Broadway. On 3 December 1929, Tracy stepped into the leading role in Hugh Stange's play *Veneer*, a new drama that was struggling to hang on at New York's Sam H. Harris Theatre, despite a spate of mediocre reviews, as exemplified by the *New York Times* (24 November 1929), whose critic noted that it was "a singularly disturbing tale of romantic idealism in conflict with the brittleness of reality." *Veneer*, which had opened on 12 November, was produced by Harry L. Cort and Charles H. Abramson, with settings by Yellenti.[10] The melodramatic plot focuses on a young woman, Ailie Smith (Joanna Roos), a confirmed naive romantic, who has the tendency to view life as she wishes it would be instead of as it is. She falls under the spell of Charlie Riggs (Henry Hull), a confirmed womanizer, who convinces her to live with him without the bonds of matrimony. Once they are living together, Ailie begins to see that Riggs is nothing but a crass opportunist. She learns that she is pregnant, however; and when Riggs hears about it, he deserts her. After a time, he hits bottom and contritely returns to Ailie only to discover that he is too late; she has killed herself. Tracy took over for Hull, a distinguished character actor on stage and screen. Hull later played the roles of Dave Morris in *Boys Town* (1938) and Bennett in *Stanley and Livingstone* (1939), both with Tracy. Adding Tracy to the cast of *Veneer* was no help to the box office, however, and the play closed after thirty-one performances. Undoubtedly feeling frustrated with his poor luck on Broadway, Tracy signed on for a short run of the play in Chicago. *Veneer* probably added little to Tracy's abilities as a stage actor—he had already developed skills as an actor well beyond those required to handle a stock role in a standard melodrama. He would play a few wasters and scoundrels like Riggs in films, most notably during his years as a leading player at Fox, where he acted in numerous potboilers similar to *Veneer*.

One can easily imagine that Tracy might well have felt his hopes for stage success were doomed by the end of 1929, but a major turning point was on the horizon. Fledgling producer Herman Shumlin signed an initially reluctant Tracy for a role in John Wexley's three-act drama *The Last Mile*, under the direction of Chester Erskine, with scene design by Henry Dreyfus, at New York's Sam H. Harris Theatre.[11] Wexley's play was based in part on a playlet published in 1929 in *American Mercury* called "The Law Takes Its Toll,"' by Robert Blake, a death row prisoner. When it opened on 13 February 1930, the play and especially Tracy's electrifying performance were hailed by critics. *The Last Mile* is set in the death house of Oklahoma's Keystone State Penitentiary where tension is high as inmates await their end. Following the execution of Richard Walters (James Bell), it is Eddie Werner's (George Leach) turn. As he is served his last meal, a guard is overpowered and killed by some of the prisoners. John "Killer" Mears (Tracy), a ruthless hardened criminal and powerful force among the inmates, leads a prison uprising in which two other officials are slain. Ultimately, the uprising is put down; and order returns to the penitentiary after Mears, convinced of the failure of the rebellion, gives himself up and is gunned down.

Rough language, gritty and hard-hitting naturalism, highly-charged action, and a realistic look at the darkest side of prison life led some critics to worry about the impact of *The Last Mile* on its audience. It is interesting to wonder how Tracy, a Catholic, would have responded to the review by J. J. R. in *Catholic World*: "To the religious sense of a Catholic it is revolting.... Of the bad art of this play we offer criticism; against its blasphemy, an outspoken protest." Most reviews were enthusiastic, however, and it was immediately apparent that Tracy had arrived. Some critics, like Ralph Barton in *Life*, recognized the ensemble nature of the play:

> The seven convicts in The Last Mile, perfectly played by Howard Phillips, James Bell, Hale Norcross, Ernest Whitman George Leach, Don Costello and Spencer Tracy deserve a special medal for a tour de force. Their most difficult scenes are played while each man is locked in his cell, facing the audience. These actors cannot see each other, they can only hear each other's voices, but their team work is perfect.

However, it was Tracy's performance that engendered the most enthusiasm. John Hutchins in *Theatre Arts Monthly* felt that "the haunting dejection of the condemned man in the first act is succeeded by the relentless fury and drive of Spencer Tracy's portrayal of Killer Mears," and *Theatre Magazine* stated that "all the parts—there are no women in the cast—are expertly performed, especially that of John Mears, the killer, invested by Spencer Tracy with an admirable poise and desperate courage." It was Richard Dana Skinner's assessment in *Commonweal* that was most universally noted: "Spencer Tracy puts the final seal on his qualifications as one of our best and most versatile young actors." Another young actor who later gained considerable recognition as a distinguished stage director, Harold Clurman, saw a performance and called Tracy "the straight goods . . . He looked as if he could take over and demolish the jail." Although the opening night performance of *The Last Mile* drew an enthusiastic response, it was not without incident, as Tracy recalled years later:

> I was supposed to grab the guard to get the keys to unlock the cell, but that night the keys flew into the footlights. So I choked the guard a little more, grabbed his gun, and said, "Now get those keys, you son-of-a-bitch!" The poor guy crawled down and got the keys and afterward, when I saw the marks on his neck, I realized I'd really choked him. He was damn near dead. (Newquist, 146)

In films, Tracy subsequently played several hardened criminals. Tracy played a prisoner in his first feature film; and in his second, the forgotten classic *Quick Millions* (1931), he played a gangster. The next year, on loan-out to Warner Bros., he have one of the earliest strong hints of his cinematic potential in *20,000 Years in Sing Sing*, directed by Michael Curtiz, which opened on 24 December 1932.[12] *Sing Sing* was originally intended as a vehicle for James Cagney, who was at the time in the midst of one of his periodic battles with his studio for more money and better scripts. Based on Sing Sing Warden Lewis E. Lawes's memoirs, *Life and Death in Sing Sing* (1928), the film was perceived in its time to be a starkly realistic portrait of life in America's penal system, much as *The Last Mile* was. Curtiz, who later directed such Warner Bros. classics as *Yankee Doodle Dandy* and *Casablanca* (1943), made use of a bleak semi-documentary style to capture a plausible image of the netherworld of life behind bars.

20,000 Years in Sing Sing was one of the earliest Warner Bros. films to provide the gritty streetwise naturalism that became typical of their product in the 1930s. In this film, a cocky hood, Tom Connors (Tracy), goes to jail, where he angrily resists conforming to the rigid rules and regulations there. He tries to high-hand Warden Long (Arthur Byron), and they become locked in a battle of wills. When Tom is put in solitary confinement, he finally relents and becomes a model prisoner, struggling to maintain his cockiness while also playing by the rules. His unscrupulous lawyer, Finn (Louis Calhern), who is supposedly working to get Tom out, is actually conspiring to keep him in so that he can seduce Tom's girlfriend, Fay (Bette Davis). When Fay is seriously injured in a car crash caused by Finn, Tom receives a twenty-four-hour leave from the understanding Warden Long to visit her. While Tom is with her, Finn shows up and attempts to intimidate Fay ("a trouble-making broad"). He is stunned to find Tom there to defend her. There is a fierce fistfight as a cop, who has tailed Tom from the train station, attempts to get into the locked apartment. Fay, fearing for Tom's safety, fatally shoots Finn. Tom leaves via the window, as the cop breaks down the door to discover Fay alone in bed with Finn's corpse. The cop assumes Tom has murdered Finn and reports this to Long, who takes considerable heat from other law enforcement officials and the press for releasing Tom. Although he plans taking it on the lam, Tom finally returns to prison because he has given his word to Long ("I'll come back—even if it means the chair, I'll come back.") Tom claims he has killed Finn and is sentenced to die in the electric chair, but Fay, still recovering from her injuries, arrives at the prison on the day of Tom's execution to convince

Long that she is the one who killed Finn. But Tom, wanting to protect Fay and "do something decent with my life," makes her leave as he prepares to face his sentence. As they part, Tom tries to express his feelings, "And remember, Fay, I love you more than—" Fay tearfully replies, "Yeah, I know, Tommy, more than life." The inevitability of the film's ending mirrors the inevitable defeat of Mears and his fellow prisoners in *The Last Mile*.

With the solid popular success of *The Last Mile*, Tracy became one of the most talked-about actors on the New York stage.[13] Inevitably, Hollywood studios became interested in both the play and Tracy, as he later remembered:

> *The Last Mile* was my real smash hit, and while I was in it I made tests for all the studios—Universal, MGM, Fox, Warners. Nobody ever said a word—they never even called to tell me I was lousy. In those days they loaded you with makeup for a screen test. I wasn't exactly pretty, anyway, so I probably ended up looking like a gargoyle. They most likely threw the film in the ashcan, but I didn't care very much because I never thought I'd be a movie actor; I had no ambition in that direction and was perfectly happy on the stage. (Newquist 145)

Despite Tracy's seemingly casual disinterest in the cinema, the movies did call again. In June 1930, while still appearing in *The Last Mile*, he made two short subjects for Warner Bros.-Vitaphone, *Taxi Talks* and *The Tough Guy*.[14] Not long before the release of these shorts, director John Ford, who had only recently made the transition from directing silents to talkies, saw a performance of *The Last Mile*. He later recalled that Tracy's natural but vital acting led him to see the play again, and with some difficulty he convinced Fox Studios to permit him to hire Tracy for a leading role in *Up the River*. On 6 May 1930, Tracy signed a Fox contract for one picture and began his thirty-seven-year career in Hollywood.

Ford had originally intended to make a serious, realistic portrait of life behind bars, in the manner of *The Last Mile*; but when MGM scooped him by releasing *The Big House* (1930), he realized that he would have to make some serious changes. Ford decided to convert *Up the River* into a comic satire of the prison genre, and he might well have been surprised to find that Tracy, whom he had seen only as the intense Killer Mears, was as comfortable in farcical comedy as he had been in heavy drama. When the film was released on 12 October 1930, both the movie and Tracy received excellent notices. *Variety* noted that it was "Tracy's first talker, and he easily makes the screen grade." The popularity of *Up the River* led to a five-year leading player contract for Tracy at Fox, where he remained until 1935, when he signed with MGM for what was ultimately a twenty-year stint, after which he worked as an independent star.

Following Tracy's debut in films, there were periodic attempts to lure him back to the stage. He flirted with the notion on several occasions, particularly when his screen fortunes seemed to be in decline. During late 1941 and early 1942, not long after he received his first significantly negative reviews for a film performance in *Dr. Jekyll and Mr. Hyde* (1941), playwright Paul Osborn corresponded with Tracy about the possibility of his appearing in *The Innocent Voyage*, which Osborn had based on Richard Hughes's novel *A High Wind in Jamaica*. Osborn—whose diverse theatrical works included *On Borrowed Time* (1938), *Mornings at Seven* (1939), and *A Bell for Adano* (1944)—had planned to visit Tracy in California in December 1941 after sending Tracy two acts of the play. Tracy wired Osborn: "Think script beautiful job. Sure it can be truly fine play. Frankly have some concern about dialect."[15] Tracy was also concerned that the plans MGM had for him would not permit a significant break for a stage play. When Osborn's schedule prevented his trip west to see Tracy, he persisted in a long letter dated 12 December 1941, in which he enclosed a third act of the play. Despite the social uncertainties at the start of America's involvement in World War II, Osborn suggested that Dwight Wiman, who had produced some of his earlier plays, might be interested in producing the play with Tracy in the lead. Osborn also had hopes of securing the talents of the up-and-coming director Joshua Logan, and wrote to Tracy of Logan's enthusiasm, noting that "he is brilliant on script as I have learned to my advantage. He is very excited about this play and you have been so long in his mind as the best actor in America that he seems the one." War news continued to create a sense of uncertainty about the project, and Osborn wrote to Tracy on 27 December 1941 to say he was continuing to improve the script, but that the play would probably not get produced before the fall of 1942. Tracy's hesitation about signing on for the play and his busy schedule at MGM, along with the problems of getting the play produced during wartime, are acknowledged by Osborn, who amusingly writes that Tracy should not assume that

> this letter is a tame acceptance on my part of a refusal on
> yours. I intend to do everything I can to get you to play the

part—but the thing at the moment seems to be to let it rest and not rush or worry you about it. I will, however, while talking peace to you in Washington, bomb you in Hawaii if I get the chance.

Osborn also noted that he would keep watch for other plays that might interest Tracy, suggesting that "if I can't get you for mine at least I'll try to rope you in for somebody else." Tracy, clearly touched by Osborn's good-humored persistence, responded by letter to Osborn on 2 January 1942 that he was "glad that you are going to continue working on the play. I shall be there [New York] February first, and I sincerely hope that you will continue to bomb me." Osborn did, but by the fall of 1942 Tracy wrote that "I am afraid the chances of doing your play, much as I would like to, are about nil." Osborn reluctantly pressed on without Tracy, and *The Innocent Voyage* was produced on Broadway unsuccessfully in 1943. Ever persistent, Osborn also sought Tracy in 1947 for his play *The Bridge*, but Tracy was again obliged to decline.

Thoughts of a return to the stage persisted with Tracy, despite the fact that he had not been able to arrange to appear in the Osborn play. Shortly after the release of *A Guy Named Joe* in 1943, Eugene O'Neill came into the picture. Tracy had apparently expressed interest in returning to the stage in an O'Neill play, and in a letter on 31 December 1943 to producer Lawrence Langner, O'Neill writes of his interest in Tracy's work:

I'd sure like to meet Tracy, because I admire him, but this is no time, as I know he'd be the first to understand. Too much is on our necks. *The Great God Brown* might be a good bet for him—to play Brown, of course. He'd be fine in the first part, before Dion's death, and fine in the last part. The trouble is—for a star—that a lot of the best of the play is Dion's. *Strange Interlude* is Nina's play—always has been here and in Europe. You can't get away from it. That's the way it's written. I can't see Tracy in *Marco*, either—nor see a *Marco* revival except with music to give it a fresh angle. My best bet for Tracy would be *Lazarus Laughed*. Now give heed to this and reread it carefully in the light of what that play has to say to-day. "Die exultantly that life may live," etc. "There is no death" (spiritually) etc. Also think of the light thrown on different facets of the psychology of dictators in Tiberius and Caligula. Hitler doing this little dance in triumph after the fall

of France is very like my Caligula. Think it over. You might
also get Tracy to read it with this idea in mind. (548)

But there would be no O'Neill revival for Tracy, which is unfortunate since Tracy's Irish temperament and understanding of alcoholic urges undoubtedly made him a potentially prime actor for O'Neill's later plays.

During World War II, Tracy appeared at army camps and hospitals, and on 10 and 11 February 1944 he appeared live on stage to narrate Aaron Copland's "Lincoln Portrait" for two performances with the Los Angeles Philharmonic conducted by Alfred Wallenstein. Shortly afterward, his long-awaited return to the stage finally came when he agreed to star in Robert E. Sherwood's play *The Rugged Path* in a production of the Playwrights' Company, directed by Garson Kanin, with settings and lighting by Jo Mielziner.[16] The drama opened on 10 November 1945 at New York's Plymouth Theatre and provided Tracy with a strong character in a play that was otherwise an overblown and didactic exploration of many wartime issues. Tracy received enthusiastic reviews, as typified by Ward Morehouse's comments in the *New York Sun*:

> Tracy, in the role of a restless, liberal-minded editor who goes to war for the peace of his soul and the justification of his faith, gives a solid, under-playing performance in a role that is never an easy one. The character of Morey Vinion is given to speech-making and fluency of phrase, and Tracy's naturalness in certain trying moments is indeed a tribute to his ingrained skill as an actor. He went westward years ago after his triumph in *The Last Mile*. He returns apparently unharmed by stardom of the screen.

Morey Vinion (Tracy), a disillusioned foreign correspondent at the outset of World War II, is losing his faith in his country and in himself. Sensing none of the fighting spirit of America's forefathers in those around him, Vinion engages his own private war with his conservative superiors on his newspaper. When he publishes an editorial promoting aid to Russia, his brilliant young assistant, Hartnick (Rex Williams), architect of the editorial, is fired. More disillusioned than ever, Vinion quits the paper and joins the Navy. Ultimately, he ends up as the sole survivor of a Navy destroyer. Washed up on a small Philippine island, he continues his fight against aggression with a band of Filipino patriots until he is killed in a battle with the Japanese. Vinion is posthumously awarded the Congressional Medal of Honor, but his wife (Martha Sleeper) sends it to the Filipino freedom fighters as a tribute to their struggle.

From the start, *The Rugged Path* was a troubled experience for most of the creative talents involved. The program reported that the cast and production staff included fourteen World War II veterans, including director Garson Kanin, and Tracy was initially enthusiastic. However, he became increasingly dissatisfied with the play during its out-of-town tryouts. Prior to the Broadway opening, performances were scheduled in Providence, Washington, and Boston; and during these tryouts, Tracy developed a troubling case of stage fright due, in large part, to a loss of confidence in the play. He resigned in Boston, but after some persuasion by Kanin and Sherwood, who also elicited the support of Tracy's longtime co-star and companion Katharine Hepburn, Tracy agreed to continue. He missed several performances during the Boston run, announced as the result of a sinus infection. The play finally opened in New York where Tracy received generally rapturous reviews, although most critics found significant fault with the play.[17] Stark Young in the *New Republic* felt that "Mr. Tracy, in a very poorly written part, taking it as a whole, throughout the play did good work and delivered with sporting fortitude things that at times must have made him sick." According to most critics, Tracy was "ideally cast" (*Newsweek*) and, being in nearly every scene, gives the production an authority, which is not evident in the action and dialogue. Whether he is telling off his bosses for their ostrich-like complacence or addressing a ragged company before he is clipped by a Jap bullet, he floods scenes with energy and emotional meaning. It is good to see him acting on the stage again. It would be better had he a more effective chunk of the theatre (Barnes).

John Mason Brown in the *Saturday Review* provided the most eloquent critical assessment of Tracy's performance:

> Spencer Tracy is, of course, a player of uncommon ability. A cliché of New York dramatic criticism, always repeated as if it were not moss-covered, is that Hollywood spoils legitimate actors. Mr. Tracy should give this bromide a burial indecent in its haste. He remains on the stage as a fine a player as he was fifteen years ago when as Killer Mears in *The Last Mile* he unhinged the vertebrae of local theatre goers. In fact, he remains the same actor his films have again and again shown him to be. He is as male as an old Bull Durham and as likable

as a cop who has had a good Christmas. He is boyish and adult, all in one smile or breath, and as honest as the year's longest day. As an actor he is incapable of shaming because so palpably he takes personal possession of every word he is given to speak. When it comes to making a quiet line audible, few players are his equal. He does not have to raise his voice to quicken our interest. The truth is that his performance is in itself enough to ease the path of Mr. Sherwood's play, and make that path travel-worthy.

And Rosamund Gilder in *Theatre Arts Monthly* wondered what the theatre had lost when Tracy devoted himself to films:

> He is still a fine actor; whether he might be now a great one had the theatre been able to hold him, is an insoluble question. He has power, breadth, sincerity, simplicity—all invaluable assets. His whole body, massive as it is, is imbued with his thought, so that his back is often as expressive as his lined and rugged countenance. He is able to give the highest value to moments of tension, to silences which in the hands of a good actor are more forceful than words.

Although he stayed with the production long enough for his son John to fly to New York to see him perform, an increasingly dissatisfied Tracy left the cast after eighty-one performances. Tracy never returned to live theatre again, but there is little doubt that the stage had provided him with the techniques and experiences he carried into his singular cinematic career.

Notes

[1] Tracy's versatility is demonstrated by the fact that he appeared with distinction in dramas of social significance (*Fury*, *Bad Day at Black Rock*, *Judgment at Nuremberg*), romantic comedies (*Man's Castle*, *Woman of the Year*, *Adam's Rib*), farces (*Libeled Lady*, *It's a Mad, Mad, Mad, Mad World*), gangster pictures (*Quick Millions*, *20,000 Years in Sing Sing*), adventures (*Captains Courageous*, *Northwest Passage*), drawing room dramas (*Keeper of the Flame*, *Edward, My Son*), screen biographies (*Stanley and Livingstone*, *Edison, the Man*), westerns (*The Sea of Grass*, *Broken Lance*), film noir (*The People Against O'Hara*), and even a horror movie (*Dr. Jekyll and Mr. Hyde*) and a couple of musical comedies (*Bottoms Up*, *Marie Galante*).

2   The cast of *R.U.R.* included Basil Sydney (Harry Domin), Kathlene MacDonnell (Helena Glory), Henry Travers (Mr. Busman), William Devrereux (Dr. Gal1), Moffat Johnson (Dr. Hallelmeir), John Anthony (Mr. Fabry), Louis Calvert (Mr. Alquist), Helen Westley (Nana), Mary Bonestell (A Robotess), Myrtland La Verre (A Robot), John Rutherford (Radius), Mary Hone (Helena), and John Roche (Primus).

3   The cast of *A Royal Fandango* included Cyril Keightley (Prince Peter), Ethel Barrymore (Princess Amelia), Teddy Jones (Prince Michael), Charles Eaton (Prince Alexander), Lorna Volare (Princess Titania), Virginia Chauvenet (Lady Lucy Rabid), Harold Webster (Mr. Wright), Denise Corday (Henriette), Walter Howe (Parrish), Drake DeKay (Arthur), Jose Alessandro (Chucho Panez), Beverly Sitgreaves (Ampero), Edward G. Robinson (Pascual), Aileen Poe (Pilar), Frank Antiseri (Skelly), and Spencer Tracy (Holt).

4   The cast of *Yellow* included Joseph Guthrie (Hotel Porter), Chester Morris (Val Parker), Jose Rivas (Hotel Waiter), Selena Royle (Polly), Hale Hamilton (Jack Crompton), Marjorie Wood (Jen Wilkes), Shirley Warde (Daisy Lingard), Spencer Tracy (Jimmy Wilkes), Frank Kingdon (Thomas W. Sayre), Jane Wheatley (Mrs. Sayre), Richard Freeman (Pau1), Daniel Pennell (Donaldson), Eva Cassanova (Carrie Williams), Martin Malloy (Welles), Harry Bannister (Inspector Graney), H. Paul Ducet (Louis), Mary Meehan (Cigarette Girl), Walter Hale (Page Boy), Helen Macks (Check Girl), Frank Burbeck (An Old Roue), and Paul Hanson (Policeman).

5   The cast of *The Baby Cyclone* included Joseph Holicky (Evans), Agnes Gildea (Crandall), Nan Sunderland (Jessie Hurley), Grant Mitchell (Joseph Meadows), John T. Doyle (Dr. Hearn), Spencer Tracy (Gene Hurley), Natalie Moorehead (Lydia Webster), Charles F. McCarthy (Cassidy), Joseph Allen (Kellogg), William Morris (Robert Webster), Georgia Caine (Mrs. Robert Webster), Oliver Putnam (Edwards), Doris Freeman (Maid), and Barlowe Borland (McCracken).

6   While playing in the Boston tryout of *The Baby Cyclone* in August 1927, Tracy exited the theatre to discover a huge crowd gathered on the Boston Common demonstrating over the execution of Sacco and Vanzetti.

7   The cast of *Conflict* included Edward Arnold (Roger Winship), George Meeker (Chet Touteen), Peggy Allenby (Ruth Winship), Lois Arnold (A Maid), Dennie Moore (Mary Bishop), Spencer Tracy (Richard Banks), Charles Scott (A Barman), Seth Arnold (Lieutenant "Pop" Touso), Frank Mc Hugh (Sergeant "Chink" Burt), Joseph Boland (Lieutenant Scott), David Mann (Lieutenant Anderson), Jack Mead (Lieutenant Williams) Albert von Dekker (Baron Von Mueller), Jack Bennett (A Bartender), and Mabel Allyn (Daisy Hall).

[8]   Royle landed a contract with MGM in the late 1940s and appeared with Tracy in *Cass Timberlane* (1947).

[9]   The cast of *Nigger Rich* included Roderick Maybee (Denning), Spencer Tracy (Eddie Perkins), Don Beddoe (Blake), Adelaide Hibbard (Mrs. Mason), Elvia Enders (Helen Page), Eric Dressler (Mike Kelly), John A. Butler (Joe Burns), Helen Flint (Nina Welman), Franklyn Fox (Ray Cole), Richard Taber (Gunny Jones), Rikel Kent (Martin), William Lemuels (Tucker), and Gene West (Gates).

[10]   The cast of *Veneer* included Ruth Hunter (Ethel), Harold Waldridge (Pete), Jeanne Greene (Maysie Bedell), John Kane (Skeets), Henry Hull (Charlie Riggs), Edith Shayne (Ms. Gordon), William Roselle (George Lawrence), Marion Grant (A Girl), Joanna Roos (Ailie Smith), Robert Sinclair (A Student), Ranald Savery (A Young Man), Jack C. Connolly (Callahan), and Richard H. Wang (Ling).

[11]   The cast of *The Last Mile* included Howard Phillips (Fred Mayor), James Bell (Richard Walters), Hale Norcross ("Red" Kirby), Ernest Whitman (Vincent Jackson), George Leach (Eddie Werner), Don Costello (Drake), Spencer Tracy (John "Killer" Mears), Herbert Haywood (O'Flaherty), Orville Harris (Peddie), Ralph Theadore (Principal Keeper Callahan), Richard Abbott (Harris), Joseph Spurin-Calleia (Tom D'Amaro), Henry O'Neill (Father O'Connors), Clarence Chase (Evangelist), Bruce Macfarlane (Frost), and Albert West (Brooks).

[12]   The cast of *20,000 Years in Sing Sing* included Spencer Tracy (Tom Connors), Bette Davis (Fay), Lyle Talbot (Bud), Arthur Byron (Warden Long), Grant Mitchell (Dr. Ames), Warren Hymer (Hype), Louis Calhern (Finn), Sheila Terry (Billie), Edward J. McNamara (Chief of Guards), Spencer Charters (Daniels), Sam Godfrey (Reporter), Nella Walker (Mrs. Long), Harold Humber (Tony), William LeMaire (Black Jack), Arthur Hoyt (Dr. Meeker), and George Pat Collins (Mike).

[13]   Another screen great, Clark Gable, also played Killer Mears on stage, in the West Coast production. It provided him with an important early career break, just as it had with Tracy. *The Last Mile* was first filmed in 1932 by World Wide Studios, with Preston Foster in the Tracy role; and a low-budget remake in 1959, produced by United Artists, featured Mickey Rooney in Tracy's part.

[14]   Tracy may have appeared in a third Short for Warner Bros.-Vitaphone, *The Strong Arm*, but this has proven impossible to verify.

[15]   All correspondence between Spencer Tracy and Paul Osborn is preserved in the Paul Osborn papers, at the State Historical Society of Wisconsin in Milwaukee.

[16] The cast of *The Rugged Path* included Spencer Tracy (Morey Vinion), Martha Sleeper (Harriet Vinion), Clinton Sundberg (George Bowsmith), Lawrence Fletcher (Leggatt Burt), Henry Lascoe (Charlie), Ralph Cullinan (Pete Kenneally), Nick Dennis (Fred), Rex Williams (Gil Hartnick), Jan Sterling (Edith Bowsmith), Theodore Leavitt (Firth), Paul Alberts (Albok), Sandy Campbell (Dix), Lynn Shubert (Stapler), Sam Sweet (Kavanagh), Howard Ferguson (Doctor), William Sands (Costanzo), David Stone (Guffey), Gordon Nelson (Hal Fleury), Clay Clement (Colonel Rainsford), Vito Christi (Gregorio Felizzrdo), Robin Taylor (Catalino), Kay Loring (Hazel), Emory Richardson (Jamieson), and Ernest Woodward (Major General MacGlorn).

[17] The author of *The Rugged Path*, Robert E. Sherwood—best known for his earlier plays *The Road to Rome*, *The Petrified Forest*, *Idiot's Delight* (for which he won the Pulitzer Prize), *Abe Lincoln in Illinois*, and *There Shall Be No Night*—wrote very little drama following the closing of *The Rugged Path*. During World War II, Sherwood had largely abandoned his theatrical career to work as a speechwriter for President Franklin Roosevelt.

Works Cited

N.B. Unless otherwise specified all reviews cited in this article may be found in the Clipping Files of the Wisconsin Center for Film and Theatre Research in Madison.

Alpert, Don "Tracy: There Are No Kicks in Acting." *Los Angeles Times*, 18 Nov. 1962: n pag.

Anderson, John. "Nigger Rich at Royale." *New York Evening Journal*, 21 Sep. 1929: n pag.

Atkinson, Brooks, *New York Times*, 24 Mar. 1929: X1.

_____. "The Play." *New York Times*, 21. Sep. l929: n. pag.

Barnes, Howard. *New York Herald Tribune*, 12 Nov. 1945: n pag.

Barrymore, Ethel. *Memories*. New York: Harper, 1955.

Barton, Ralph. "Theatre." *Life*, 6 June 1930. 18.

Battelle, Phyllis, "Spencer Tracy Says Actors Are Unloved." *Los Angeles Times*, 18 Dec. 1962: n pag.

Brown, Heywood. *New York World*, 13 Nov. 1923: n pag.

Brown, John Mason. *Saturday Review*, 24 Nov. 1945: 20.

"Campus Players Again Make Hit with the Truth." *Ripon College Days*, 17 Jan.1922:1.

Clurman, Harold. "The New York Actor: The Truth about Us in Our Stars." *New York*, 11 Feb. 1974:38.

"Exceptional Staff Will Stage Drama." *Ripon College Days*, 25 Oct. 1921:3.

Gilder, Rosamond. *Theatre Arts Monthly*, Jan. 1946: 9.

Halliwell, Leslie. *Halliwell's Filmgoer's Companion*. New York: Scribner, 1988.

Honblow, Arthur. *Theatre Magazine*, Dec. 1922:375.

_____. *Theatre Magazine*, Nov. 1926:66.

Hutchens, John. *Theatre Arts Monthly*, Apr. 1930:278-280.

Johnson, Erskine. "Spencer Tracy Says He Acts Less Nowadays." *Los Angeles Mirror*, 29 Apr. 1961:3.

Littel, Robert. *New York Evening Post*, 24 Mar. 1929: n pag.

_____. *New York Evening World*, 21 Sep. 1929: n pag.

Mantle, Burns. "Review." *New York Daily News*, 21 Sep. 1929:n pag.

McCabe John. *George M. Cohan: The Man Who Owned Broadway*. Garden City, NY: Doubleday, 1973.

McGowan, John. Letter. *New York Telegram* 14 Sep, 1929: n pag.

Morehouse, Ward. *New York Sun* 12 Nov, 1945: n pag.

New York Times 10 Oct. 1922: 16.

_____. 13 Nov. 1923:25.

_____. 22 Sep. 1926:30.

_____. 13 Sep. 1927:37.

_____. 24 Nov. 1929: X1.

Newquist. Roy. *A Special Kind of Magic*. New York: Rand, 1967.

Newsweek, 19 Nov. 1945:84-85.

O'Neill, Eugene. *Selected Letter of Eugene O'Neill*. Edited by Travis Bogard and Jackson R. Bryer. New Haven: Yale UP, 1988.

R., J. J. "The Last Mile." *Catholic World*, May 1930:214.

Seldes, Gilbert. "Nigger Rich." *New York Graphic*, 21 Sep. 1929: n pag.

Skinner, Richard Dana. *Commonweal* 9 Apr. 1930:25.

_____. *Life*, 6 Oct. 1927:21.

Spencer Tracy Clipping File. Milwaukee Public Library. Milwaukee, WI.

Theatre Magazine. Apr. 1930: n pag.

Variety, 22 Oct. 1930: n pag.

Young, Stark. New Republic 26 Nov. 1945:711.

(This article originally appeared in *New England Theatre Journal*
Volume 6 1995. Reprinted with permission.)

Go Into Your Dance:
Al Jolson, Ruby Keeler,
and the Evolution of the
Early Hollywood Musical

James Fisher

On the evening of January 19, 1971, a sixty-one-year-old grandmother glided down a pink-hued staircase on the stage of Broadway's 46th Street Theatre. She received a thunderous, prolonged ovation eclipsed moments later by an even more enthusiastic response when, with a chorus of bright-eyed juveniles, she performed a precise and vigorous tap dance to Vincent Youmans's "I Want to Be Happy" in the hit revival of the 1925 musical, *No, No, Nanette*. Astonishingly, that grandmother had last appeared on a Broadway stage forty-two years before, when she performed a similar tap routine to George and Ira Gershwin's "Liza" in *Show Girl* (1929), on a few nights serenaded from the audience by her then-husband, Al Jolson (1885?-1950).

This remarkable "comeback" by Ruby Keeler (1910-1993) mirrored that of Jolson, the vaunted "World's Greatest Entertainer," who, like Keeler, experienced a career resurgence late in life following the release of an enormously successful film biography, *The Jolson Story* (1946), for which the sixty-something Jolson provided vocals. A second hit film, *Jolson Sings Again* (1949), followed, and Jolson reemerged as a top flight entertainer on radio, records, and the live stage, like Keeler receiving ovations before audiences of moviegoers and fans from several generations prior to showings of *Jolson Sings Again*—and, more notably, before American troops in Asia during the Korean War, a commitment to American service personnel he had developed entertaining in every conflict since the Spanish-American War. That Jolson's stage career had begun in the 1890s mattered as little to him as to Keeler when she blithely disregarded the years when she scored her autumnal triumph in *No, No, Nanette*.

Parallels in the careers of Jolson and Keeler are numerous and the most significant may be found in their individual and joint contributions to the birth of sound film musicals, contributions meriting a fuller appreciation. Jolson and Keeler emerged a full generation apart on vaudeville stages and Broadway, as did many film musical stars at the dawn of sound. The fact of vaudeville and Broadway's importance as a wellspring of classic American cinema is seldom explored by film critics and historians who, it seems, are comparatively unschooled in or dismissive of American theatre history. Theatre-trained actors dominated movie screens even during the silent period (where else would actors have come from?) and there was a virtual stampede of stage actors and vaudevillians to Hollywood when the "talkies" arrived, as the necessity for vocally adept actors became all too obvious. The transition from silent to sound movies is a well-worn topic in film histories and popular culture—who, for example, can forget the hilarious high-pitched whine emanating from Jean Hagen's silent movie goddess attempting her first "talkie" in *Singin' in the Rain* (1952)? Accounts of silent stars with heavy foreign accents or voices ill-suited to their screen images who lost their careers in the transition have been repeated (and exaggerated) with frequency. At the same time, the constructive impact of theatre performers to early sound films—and most especially to the first screen musicals—is too often overlooked or undervalued.

From the early to mid-1920s through the rising and falling fortunes of musicals between the two Warner Bros.-made milestones of early screen musicals, *The Jazz Singer* (1927) and *42nd Street* (1933), the impact of theatre actors is significant, and the source of both strengths and weaknesses in the evolution of screen musicals of the first five years of sound. Many early movie musicals were adapted from stage hits or written directly for the screen by veteran Broadway composers, lyricists, and librettists, but it can be argued that musicals are most profoundly indebted to stage performers, and it may be more than a coincidence that two of them were not only from Broadway, but were under contract to the same Hollywood studio and married. Jolson and Keeler both possess confirmed berths in the annals of film history, but it is also true that the nature of their contributions is often misunderstood, as much of the first few years of sound are misunderstood. The couple co-starred only once, in *Go Into Your Dance* (1935), a Warner Bros. backstage musical, and this entertaining, fast-paced, wisecracking programmer both demonstrates the strengths and weaknesses of early screen musicals and marks the true end of the first, and least appreciated, phase of the sound era.

The evolution of sound and Jolson's involvement in it are far more complicated stories than the common version that describes the great Jolson turning from a stage career to elevate new technologies into the sophisticated film medium of today. There is truth in this, but exploration into sound film had begun decades earlier, and Jolson's flirtation with film was also not new. Before the great successes of *The Jazz Singer* and its follow-up film, *The Singing Fool* (1928), won audiences to sound films, Jolson had actually appeared twice on screen, although the physical evidence of both appearances is lost. In *The Honeymoon Express*, his 1913 stage musical produced by the Shubert Brothers, the first act ended with a filmed automobile chase with Jolson, as his perennial blackface stage character, Gus, driving an automobile full of his fellow cast members. As the silent footage ended with the car racing toward the camera, the screen rose and Jolson and his fellow players in the car rolled onstage exactly as they appeared at the conclusion of the filmed chase. Several critics reviewing the show remarked on the effectiveness of this innovative bit, but unfortunately the footage is lost. Jolson later signed to star in a 1923 D. W. Griffith film tentatively titled *Black Magic* (alternative titles: *Mammy's Boy* or *Black and White*), but after shooting for a few days, Jolson, who was cast as a young white lawyer disguised as a black man to solve a murder, saw the raw footage shot and was so dissatisfied that he withdrew from the production and immediately sailed for Europe to avoid being compelled to complete the film. Griffith sued Jolson unsuccessfully, the film was scrapped, and the footage made has been lost.

For most film historians, Jolson's only real significance is his involvement with *The Jazz Singer*, but only as a conduit for the birth of sound. It could be argued that his contributions were more varied, but perversely his salesmanship of sound through the power of his personality and singular singing voice did not really begin sound. Experimentation had begun decades earlier, dating back to the very beginnings of cinema in the 1880s, with Thomas A. Edison attempting to merge motion pictures with sound recordings. Failing to devise an adequate process of sound synchronization, Edison gave up for many years while others in Europe and the U.S. continued experimentation. As early as 1900, the first public viewing of a projected sound process took place and Edison tried again in the 1910s to perfect a process, but the true breakthroughs came with sound on film processes explored by several inventors in the early 1920s, including Lee De Forest (Phonofilm) and Ted Case (Movietone). Despite the superior quality of these processes, and their demonstrated worth in sound short subjects De Forest and Case produced, the Hollywood studios seemed mostly disinterested, undoubtedly because so much was invested in silent films, which had reached the pinnacle of artistic achievement and commercial success by the mid-1920s. Warner Bros., which in the mid-1920s was an insignificant studio on the brink of bankruptcy, became interested in sound as a means of survival and gaining a stronger foothold within the Hollywood system.

Despite the obviously superior quality of the sound on film processes pioneered by De Forest and Case, Warner Bros. chose a synchronized sound process in which silent film elements were projected in synchronization with sound recorded on large discs. This process, Vitaphone, was tried out with a series of sound shorts shown in New York City in 1926, including *A Plantation Act*, which featured Jolson onstage at New York's Metropolitan Theatre, appearing in his characteristic blackface and performing three songs associated with his stage career, "When the Red, Red Robin Comes Bob-Bob-Bobbin' Along," "April Showers," and "Rock-a-Bye Your Baby With a Dixie Melody," and including a few spoken remarks. Much has been made by cinema historians of Jolson's seemingly spontaneous dialogue in *The Jazz Singer*, which he may or may not have ad-libbed, but he had already applied these skills on film in *A Plantation Act*, where, again, they may or may not have been pre-planned. This film and its sound discs were lost for seventy years and only recently found and reassembled to provide evidence. *A Plantation Act* is available to be seen on a lavish three-disc DVD release of *The Jazz Singer*, and is a fortunate survivor of the Vitaphone era. In many cases with Vitaphone movies, film and sound were easily separated; in some cases, the film footage exists, but the sound discs are lost—in other cases, just the reverse. And, sadly, in some cases, neither appears to exist.

Along with *A Plantation Act* and other Vitaphone shorts, Warner Bros. released the full-length Vitaphone feature *Don Juan* (1926) starring John Barrymore, with a synchronized musical score recorded by a symphony orchestra and sound effects, but without spoken dialogue. This is certainly an odd choice, especially given Barrymore's stature as a dramatic actor renowned for performing Shakespeare, but *Don Juan* provides evidence that the studio remained tentative about the value of talk (or, for that matter, singing) on film, or considered it a mere novelty to be left to sound shorts like *A Plantation Act*. It is also possible that they believed audiences preferred actors in pantomimic silence, truly a singular art form, or that there was a lack of confidence about adding sound recording of dialogue which meant that actors had to be situated very close to immobile microphones and cameras stuck in sound proof booths so as not to be heard on the sound recording. The question of what the audience wanted from sound technology was still unanswered as Warner Bros. approached Jolson to appear in *The Jazz Singer*.

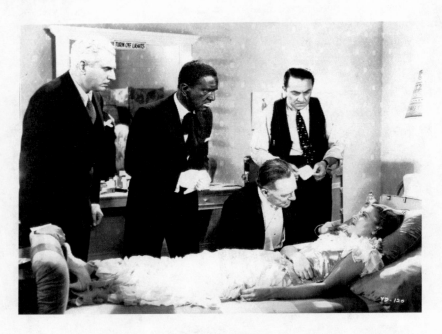

Whatever doubts or fears Warner Bros. may have had about the viability of sound and confusion as to how to apply it, they plunged ahead with *The Jazz Singer*. The film was based on what had been a popular 1925 Broadway play (without music) by Samson Raphaelson, but the question of who might star in a screen version remained a concern—and music might well have been omitted had the star been a non-musical actor. On Broadway, George Jessel played the role of "jazz singer" Jakie Rabinowitz, caught between his love of the popular stage and his orthodox father's insistence that he become a Jewish cantor, but Jessel proved troublesome in negotiating salary for the film. Warner Bros. briefly considered stage comedian and singer Eddie Cantor before turning to Jolson, who wisely took Warner Bros. stock in partial payment for his services. Jessel and Cantor both made early talkies in the wake of the success of *The Jazz Singer*, as did many stage stars, and Cantor became a major film star beginning in 1930 in a series of films for producer Samuel Goldwyn. Jessel had little success on screen, as did many stage stars who tried the "talkies" in Jolson's immediate wake between 1928 and 1933. Like many early sound stars, Jolson, Jessel, and Cantor were all stage veterans whose talents had been honed in vaudeville and musical comedy, and it is clear from critical response to *The Jazz Singer* that audiences received the film (and Jolson's performance in the sound sequences) much as they might if viewing live theatre. Mordaunt Hall, writing in the *New York Times*, confirms this:

> Mr. Jolson's persuasive vocal efforts were received with rousing applause. In fact, not since the first presentation of Vitaphone features, more than a year ago at the same playhouse, has anything like the ovation been heard in a picture theatre. And when the film came to an end Mr. Jolson himself expressed his sincere appreciation of the Vitaphoned film, declaring that he was so happy that he could not stop the tears.[1]

And writing in *Film Spectator*, Welford Beaton noted that *The Jazz Singer* "definitely establishes the fact that talking pictures are imminent. [. . .] There is one scene in *The Jazz Singer* that conclusively sounds the knell of the silent picture: that showing Jolson at the piano, playing idly and talking to his mother. It is one of the most beautiful scenes I have ever seen on a screen."[2]

---

[1]   Mordaunt Hall, "Review," *New York Times* (October 7, 1927):24.
[2]   Welford Beaton, "Review," *Film Spectator* (February 4, 1928): 7.

Jolson's success in *The Jazz Singer* and *The Singing Fool* inspired other stage stars to make Vitaphone appearances at Warner Bros., including musical, vaudeville, and night club entertainers Fanny Brice, Sophie Tucker, Harry Richman, Marilyn Miller, and Frank Fay, as well as dramatic actors such as Barrymore and George Arliss, among others. Most had scant success since some were almost exclusively known only by New York audiences and others were not well-served by their first (and in some cases, only) vehicles, many of which were still primitive in their use of sound and stagey since directors faced problems of moving heavy and noisy cameras while filming sound sequences. One of the first following Jolson's twin triumphs in *The Jazz Singer* and *The Singing Fool* was Brice's partial-"talkie" *My Man* (1928), now considered lost (although sound discs survive), and her second all-talking film, *Be Yourself!* (1930), produced by Joseph M. Schenck, which is a decidedly weak, slapdash effort (Brice also appeared to little effect in Paramount's short subject, *Night Club*, in 1929, a lost film). Despite footage of Brice used in Warner Bros.'s *The Man from Blankley's*, starring Barrymore, Brice did not appear in a major film again until she played herself in an extended cameo in MGM's *The Great Ziegfeld* (1936), and she ultimately appeared in only two additional films, MGM's *Everybody Sing* (1938) and *Ziegfeld Follies* (1945). Sophie Tucker suffered a similar fate in her Warner Bros./Vitaphone screen debut in *Honky Tonk* (1929) which, like

Brice's *My Man*, is lost (again, sound discs survive, but the film footage is missing). Tucker did not appear in another film until she played character roles as Judy Garland's mother in MGM's *Broadway Melody of 1938* and *Thoroughbreds Don't Cry*, both made and released eight years later in 1937. All of Tucker's few remaining screen appearances were cameos as herself. Harry Richman failed to launch a film career in *Puttin' on the Ritz* (1930) and Frank Fay similarly found no traction in the all-star *The Show of Shows* (1929) and a few weak Vitaphone efforts. Marilyn Miller fared somewhat better when she appeared ably in three films, *Sally* (1929), *Sunny* (1930), and *Her Majesty, Love* (1931), but all were only modest successes that failed to match her stage popularity (and failed to generate enough box office magic to justify her high salary demands). Miller's early death ended any hope that she might co-star on screen with Fred Astaire, with whom she had appeared on Broadway in the musical *Smiles* (1930).

Only non-musical actors Barrymore and Arliss developed substantial film careers, somewhat inexplicably in the case of Arliss, who was then over sixty-years-old (and looked much older), decidedly un-photogenic, and heavily made up in the style of silent film actors in an obvious attempt to hide his age. Arliss's sound film debut, *Disraeli* (1929), was marketed as a cultural event: a distinguished stage actor (which he certainly was)—in one of his greatest stage roles. Arliss proved adept in a wide range of characterizations, often of historical or literary figures, and often taken from his stage successes. He won an Academy Award for *Disraeli* and appeared in eighteen additional films, most successful, before he retired in 1937. Barrymore became a major star in the first decade of sound, even as his health declined as a result of longtime alcoholism. Despite what Jolson must ultimately have felt was a disappointing and frustrating screen career, he had more longevity on screen than most of his peers.

It is obvious that Jolson was the reason sound films—particularly musicals—successfully captured the attention of the movie-going public. *The Jazz Singer* (1927), the film typically credited as "the first sound film" and with rendering silent films passé, was a hit due to Jolson's presence. The significance of this unique movie—and Jolson's performance—is undeniable. What is less known is that despite Warner Bros.'s "supreme triumph" (as advertisements touted) with *The Jazz Singer*, Jolson's follow-up film, *The Singing Fool* (1928), far exceeded the commercial success of *The Jazz Singer* and obliterated any lingering doubts or resistance to sound in Hollywood and with the public (only Charlie Chaplin held out—making silent features through 1936 with *Modern Times*). In fact, within months of the release of *The Singing Fool*, silent films were quite simply obsolete and any still in production revised plans to include sound sequences. To have succeeded in turning the tide against silent films this decisively (by early 1929 virtually all released features were "talkies") required a star of Jolson's magnitude to sell it.

However, audiences did not care about the particular process—the only factors that seemed to matter were the novelty of sound itself and, in the case of these first Vitaphone features, the presence of Jolson. Critics frequently deride or dismiss Jolson's screen work, finding his "over-the-top" personality and limited acting skills, a problem made worse by the primitive qualities of early "talkies": cheap production values, cliché-ridden scripts, stilted dialogue, sentimental songs, and, in Jolson's case (and those of a few of his contemporaries), the employment of the shameful tradition of blackface. It is true that Jolson is no screen actor in the manner it was soon understood, but screen acting at the beginning of sound was virgin territory. Jolson's larger-than-life theatrical talents did not suit the new medium's close range eye, yet it was potent enough to demonstrate the value of sound films. Audiences quickly embraced not only more youthful stars—Jolson was in his early 40s when he made *The Jazz Singer*—but, increasingly, actors with more natural, understated styles. By the time Jolson played his final screen roles in 1939, he had toned down the stagey qualities and overly emotive acting evident in his first few films. This adjustment also finally doomed his movie career in leading roles since his greatness rested to a significant extent on a titanic persona that clearly belonged in a live theatre. Those who had seen Jolson perform in legitimate theatres consistently insisted that the Jolson of films and recordings is a pale shadow of what they experienced in person from "The World's Greatest Entertainer."

When Jolson appeared on Warner Bros. stages to shoot *The Jazz Singer*, he was already a legend. He had dominated the popular stage and phenomenally successful tours of his Broadway shows continually for over fifteen years, following a decade-long rise from vaudeville obscurity to Lew Dockstader's Minstrels. During Jolson's time with Dockstader, reviewers increasingly noted that he outshined the titular head of the troupe; for example, a critic writing in the *Columbus (Ohio) Evening Dispatch* in 1909 enthused that Jolson "almost breaks the speed limit in one of the best features of the big show. [. . .] his creation of wit and melody was one of the parts of the show put in late in the evening, so as to leave a pleasant taste in the mouth."[3]

Within little more than a year, Jolson left Dockstader and signed on with the Shubert Brothers, major producers of light musical entertainments, who added him to the cast of their Winter Garden Theatre musical revue *La Belle Paree* (1911). Once again, Jolson outshined the show's star, in this case, comedienne Stella Mayhew, performing in blackface and contributing broad comedy and songs. Within a few months, Jolson appeared in another Shubert show, *Vera Violetta* (1911), this time stealing the thunder of French chanteuse Gaby Deslys. That same year, Jolson began a recording career that racked up a remarkable eighty hit records by 1928, and his face was a consistent presence on sheet music covers. In subsequent Shubert musicals, Jolson's use of blackface morphed into the aforementioned recurring character, Gus, a dervish of comedy and song, in a series of loosely-constructed musicals in which Gus typically resolved the romantic problems of the "white" characters and burst into song for no apparent reason, as was typical of stage musicals of the time. In fact, the shows were so thinly constructed that Jolson took to stopping in mid-performance to ask the audience if they would prefer him or the rest of the show. The inevitable response led to now legendary one-man concerts and Jolson's subsequent Shubert shows were similarly claptrap affairs permitting the star free range, including *The Whirl of Society* (1912), *The Honeymoon Express* (1913), *Dancing Around* (1914), *Robinson Crusoe, Jr.* (1916), *Sinbad* (1918), *Bombo* (1921), and *Big Boy* (1925). All were long-running Broadway hits and

---

3   C. W. R., "In and Out of the Theatres," *Columbus Evening Dispatch* (November 16, 1909): 14.

even more successful on extended tours across the United States. Jolson was touring in *Big Boy* when he took a hiatus to appear in *The Jazz Singer*, after which he essentially abandoned the stage until 1931 to film, in rapid succession, four more Warner Bros. musicals: the aforementioned *The Singing Fool*, *Say It With Songs* (1929), *Mammy* (1930), and a screen adaptation of *Big Boy* (1930).

Jolson remains a problematic figure—his aggressive personality was an acquired taste for many and his rise on screen was meteoric and his fall was, in many respects, cruel and probably unavoidable. More than any other performer, he exemplifies the primitive early days of movie musicals, and also more than others he paid the greatest price for being a sound film pioneer. He appeared unprotected in raw, primitive efforts that exploited but did not adequately showcase or enhance his true talents. By the time the technology and the quality of production improved, his screen career was in steep decline. He brought his broad stage techniques to a medium more responsive to subtlety, a style that audiences, even the most die-hard Jolson fans, came to favor. Since his death in 1950, Jolson's problematic use of blackface, a device that rightly has come to be seen as a demeaning racial stereotype, undermines appreciation of the positive elements of his talents and the importance of his achievements. Jolson's intentions, however innocent, have not spared him from being perceived as an icon of bigotry. By the standards of his time, and even our own, Jolson was certainly not a bigot. It was well-known among black performers in Hollywood that the Jolson home was singular in welcoming them and Jolson contributed enormous sums of money to charitable organizations of all sorts, particularly those stressing brotherhood among races and creeds. Cultural and film critics continue to present Jolson's name as a synonym for racism, perhaps because he was the last truly great performer to employ blackface—and his blackface performances, unlike those of his stage contemporaries, are preserved for posterity in these early sound films, even though it must be pointed out that virtually every movie musical performer from the dawn of sound well into the 1950s appeared, at some point, in blackface, including such major stars as Fred Astaire, Bing Crosby, Shirley Temple, Mickey Rooney, Judy Garland, Eddie Cantor, and Ethel Merman, among many others.

Regarding blackface, Jolson was only a latter-day exemplar of a well-worn theatrical tradition. Blackface minstrelsy existed at least as early as 1828, nearly one hundred years before Jolson appeared on screen in blackface in *The Jazz Singer*. Thomas D. "Daddy" Rice is most often credited with introducing the practice of white actors appearing in blackface in his "Jump Jim Crow" song and dance, which gained such widespread popularity that it inspired many imitators and the birth of minstrel shows, not to mention providing a name for the laws of the pre-Civil Rights American South. By the 1840s, minstrel shows were the most pervasive and lucrative forms of popular entertainment throughout the U.S. (and Europe)—and continued to be so well into the twentieth century. In short, Jolson did not invent this racist stage convention (which, it could be argued, is also an homage, however odious from a contemporary standpoint, to African American contributions to music and culture), and that he was just one of numerous entertainers, white and black, who exploited racial and ethnic stereotypes in a range of entertainment forms, including minstrel shows, burlesque, vaudeville, radio and television, and movies.

It is also the case that once he appeared on screen, Jolson both capitalized on his fame as a blackface entertainer and tried to escape it. In all but one of his films, blackface is restricted to "on-stage" sequences—that is, his appearance in blackface is only seen in show-within-the-film scenes in which Jolson plays a Jolsonesque entertainer preparing to go on stage or performing. It was a stage "mask," one which Jolson was never able to fully abandon, even when the tradition had long since become outmoded and other performers gave it up. The one film in which he completely avoided blackface, *Hallelujah, I'm a Bum* (1933), arguably his best screen performance (made for United Artists, not Warner Bros.), failed dismally at the box office and, as such, a logical assumption emerged that the omission of blackface (which, for his audience, seemed to mean the omission of Jolson's true stage persona) was the reason for its failure. Jolson appeared in blackface for the entirety of his earlier film, *Big Boy* (except for a brief finale as himself), recreating his stage character, Gus. This oddity of a film does not really work, especially so since Jolson shares the screen with actual black actors, but it is an historically interesting document of Jolson's stage career. It, too, did not do particularly well at the box office, a paradox leaving movie makers to consider that the best Jolson was a moderate use of blackface. After *Hallelujah, I'm a Bum* blackface was featured in at least one sequence of all of Jolson's remaining films with the exception of a cameo appearance in Twentieth Century-Fox's *Hollywood Cavalcade* (1939). These films include the final three made for Warner Bros., *Wonder Bar* (1934), the aforementioned *Go Into Your Dance*, and *The Singing Kid* (1936), as well as two features for Twentieth Century-Fox—*Rose of Washington Square* and *Swanee River*, both released in 1939, as well as a cameo in Warner Bros.'s lavish film biography of George Gershwin, *Rhapsody in Blue* (1945), in which Jolson played himself. This last is revealing in that Jolson appears in blackface in an off-stage scene showing him at a dressing table prior to a performance taking a telephone call. The makeup is clearly intended to hide Jolson's age; nearing sixty at this time—or possibly older (he was born in Seredzius, Lithuania, and the exact year of his birth is unknown, though most historians estimate the year as 1885 or 1886)—maintaining the illusion of Jolson at the height of his early Broadway career was the obvious goal.

Back up to the immediate aftermath of *The Jazz Singer*, the runaway success of the partial "talkie" *The Singing Fool*, which remained, somewhat remarkably, the highest grossing Hollywood film for a decade, until Walt Disney's *Snow White and the Seven Dwarfs* (1938) and David O. Selznick's *Gone With the Wind* (1939), is without question one of Jolson's weakest films, a comparatively poor effort (at least as evidenced by surviving prints in deplorable condition) far less effective or affecting than *The Jazz Singer*. The film's success undoubtedly resulted from its timing—*The Jazz Singer* had generated much publicity, pro and con, regarding sound, and any film that had followed—particularly starring *The Jazz Singer's* star—would have inevitably succeeded. A promising opening sequence featuring a long tracking shot following patrons entering a speakeasy leads to revealing Jolson in the guise of a waiter. Jolson's character, Al Stone, aspires to be a songwriter and is played for a fool by a gold-digging chorine who marries him and gives birth to a baby before leaving him for another man, taking the beloved child with her. When the child becomes ill and dies, Al is inconsolable, but survives by going back on stage to sing his lullaby to the child, "Sonny Boy." The song, which became a major hit, is undeniably mawkish, as is the film itself, but 1928 audiences were apparently moved to the point that *The Singing Fool* became the first sound-era blockbuster. Once again, Jolson's presence and sound (though *The Singing Fool* was a partial "talkie" like *The Jazz Singer*) proved briefly unbeatable, perhaps because few sound films had yet to make it to the screen, despite increased audience interest (the first all-"talkie" released that year, *The Lights of New York*, was also a hit for Warner Bros.).

Within less than a year, Jolson followed *The Singing Fool* with the "all-talking, all-singing" *Say It With Songs*, which barely made a profit despite Jolson's presence (and that of Davey Lee, the same child actor who had played "Sonny Boy," and a new mawkish song, "Little Pal," following the "Sonny Boy" model), and both *Mammy* and *Big Boy*, released the following year (1930), were only moderate successes. The problems manifested themselves early—Jolson's age and limited screen acting ability, overly sentimental plots, the slow pacing of early sound films in general, and the use of blackface cost Jolson his short-lived screen dominance. His moment as a box office champion was spectacular and brief, and he was unable to recover it until 1946 when a highly fictional screen biography, *The Jolson Story* (1946), did so well at the box office that a sequel (rare for an A-picture in that era) was called for, resulting in *Jolson Sings Again*. These two films featured Jolson's newly-recorded vocals of vintage tunes, many from his early Warner Bros. films, lip-synched by actor Larry Parks, who portrays Jolson. In the last four years of his life, Jolson was not only back on top in films, but also in radio and recordings, a remarkable "comeback" by any standard.

In 1930, as Jolson's screen stardom suddenly declined, he could not imagine such a future. Jolson, who felt Warner Bros. had let him down via poor scripts and production values, left Hollywood to return to Broadway in a Shubert-produced musical, *The Wonder Bar* (1931). He must have been distressed to find only moderate success in his Broadway return, although more receptive audiences responded to *The Wonder Bar* tour during much of 1931-32. Jolson returned to Hollywood for *Hallelujah, I'm a Bum*, a unique nearly sung—through Depression-era tale in which he played Bumper, a hobo residing in New York's Central Park espousing the virtues of poverty as a means to a footloose existence. Featuring an original score by Richard Rodgers and Lorenz Hart, the film, now regarded as an experimental classic of the early sound era, flopped at the box office despite excellent reviews for the film itself and for Jolson's performance. It was, however, a harbinger of changes to film musicals in general, with its far more fluid movements, breaking away from the "proscenium arch" aspect of so many 1927-1933 musicals.

Chastened by the flop of *Hallelujah, I'm a Bum*, Jolson returned to Warner Bros., where much had changed in the years since *Big Boy*. Despite the setbacks of Jolson's lukewarm return to the stage and the failure of *Hallelujah, I'm a Bum*, Warner Bros. signed Jolson to a three-picture deal. The films would be *Wonder Bar*, *Go Into Your Dance*, and *The Singing Kid*, for which he was paid the then astronomical price of $60,000 per picture and ten percent of the gross exceeding $800,000. The last of these films, *The Singing Kid*, is an entertaining film on a modest scale, with Jolson's character, Al Jackson, a reversal on his reckless *Go Into Your Dance* character. In *The Singing Kid*, Jolson plays a generous and loyal Broadway star two-timed by a gold-digging wife and their lawyer, a revelation that sends him into a depression and a psychosomatic loss of his voice. To recuperate, he goes to the country where he is charmed by a little girl (Sibyl Jason) and her aunt (Beverly Roberts) who, ultimately, restores his confidence, an act demonstrated when he successfully returns to the stage. *Wonder Bar* (1934) was the only one of Jolson's new deal that could truly be said to be a "special" picture.

Wonder Bar is given a first-class production, and its story is a musical imitation of *Grand Hotel* (1932), rival studio MGM's blockbuster starring Greta Garbo, John and Lionel Barrymore, Wallace Beery, and Joan Crawford. Like the MGM film, *Wonder Bar*, which was inspired by *The Wonder Bar*, Jolson's Broadway musical, features several Warner Bros. stars along with Jolson, including Dick Powell, Ricardo Cortez, Kay Francis, and Dolores Del Rio, along with a stable of Warner Bros. most iconic character actors, most notably Louise Fazenda, Guy Kibbee, Ruth Donnelly, and Hugh Herbert as two pixilated couples of middle-aged American Midwesterners on the loose in Paris. Jolson plays Al Wonder, a Parisian nightclub owner and star, who becomes entangled in the turbulent lives of his employees and the club's patrons. The film, which was completed shortly before the censorious Hollywood Production Code was enforced, features a range of incidents and characters that within a year would become taboo, such as when Jolson, on the bandstand as club patrons dance, notices two overtly effeminate men dancing together and proclaims "Boys will be boys!" Adulterous characters (male and female), professional gigolos, prostitutes, a suicide, and even a murder that goes unpunished are key ingredients in the film.

The visual elements of *Wonder Bar* are lavish by any standard (although most of the film is set in various spaces in the nightclub) and the Dubin and Warren score features two excellent songs, "Don't Say Goodnight" and "Why Do I Dream Those Dreams?" (oddly, neither of these is sung by Jolson). Busby Berkeley's choreography of Jolson's big number, "Goin' to Heaven on a Mule," is clearly intended to be the standout element, situated near the end of the film, but it ranks as one of the most racist sequences in any film of the time. This story song—ostensibly part of the nightclub floor show—features Jolson as a black farm hand singing to a little girl of an all-black Heaven where watermelons tap dance, pork chops grow on trees, and dice games are played with the Emperor Jones. Clearly intended as a musical comedy homage to Marc Connelly's Pulitzer Prize-winning 1930 fable/play *The Green Pastures*, which translates Bible stories into a "black" idiom, the sequence also gives a satiric nod to Eugene O'Neill's 1920 drama *The Emperor Jones* and all manner of minstrel show imagery. Above all, the number is meant to celebrate (with tongue in cheek) Jolson's association with blackface minstrelsy, but its ludicrous indulgence in grossly stereotypical imagery severely mars a film that otherwise features what is arguably Jolson's best acting performance in a leading role prior to *Go Into Your Dance*.

As previously noted, Jolson's career, and that of his wife Ruby Keeler, had many parallels—and if he could be considered to have ushered in sound films, Keeler could well be regarded as the conduit through which the next era of sound musicals triumphed. Her Warner Bros. films are clearly less diverse than Jolson's. Following *42nd Street*, in which she rose to prominence, Keeler appeared, in rapid succession, in three other similar backstage musicals, *Gold Diggers of 1933* (1933), *Footlight Parade* (1933), and *Dames* (1934), all of which paired her with Dick Powell, as did two romantic musicals away from the backstage setting, *Flirtation Walk* (1934) and *Shipmates Forever* (1935), after which she appeared with Jolson in *Go Into Your Dance*. Keeler's final two Warner Bros. films were *Colleen* (1936), which again teamed her with Powell, and *Ready, Willing and Able* (1937), which cast her opposite the lackluster Ross Alexander. Her screen persona was typically the girl-next-door and more or less naïve as the plot's circumstances demanded. Busby Berkeley choreographed the production numbers and she was usually featured in an at least a couple of these in each movie she made, with a few of the numbers, like the title song of *42nd Street*, emerging as Berkeley classics. These include "The Shadow Waltz" from *Gold Diggers of 1933*, "Shanghai Lil" and "By a Waterfall" from *Footlight Parade*, and most especially "I Only Have Eyes for You" from *Dames*, in which Powell, singing the song on a subway, begins to see Keeler's image in place of the girls in advertisements on the wall. The number explodes into a mass of moving, shifting Keeler faces in Berkeley's kaleidoscopic style. Ultimately, a mob of female dancers dressed and wigged to resemble Keeler replace the images, with Keeler herself strategically placed in the foreground of every shot. Among the most characteristic of Berkeley's choreographic achievements, it also demonstrates that Keeler was, between 1933 and 1937, his muse.

The Berkeley-style musical techniques and new stars like Keeler were two important developments among the considerable changes musical films were facing when Jolson returned to Warner Bros. in 1934. A glut of stagey film musicals, many taken from old-fashioned stage shows of the 1910s and 1920s, released between *The Jazz Singer* and 1933 by Warner Bros., and other major studios, had turned movie audiences against musicals of what might be described as the Vitaphone era. The synchronized sound process had given way to sound on film by 1933, and the conventions of Vitaphone-era musicals also had to change.

Hallelujah, I'm a Bum was one of several experiments to shake loose of those earlier techniques and Warner Bros., the pioneer of movie musicals, succeeded where *Hallelujah, I'm a Bum* had not, by bringing the form back to life with the surprise hit musical *42nd Street*, a new prototype for screen musicals propelled to success, in part, by the presence of a new star, Ruby Keeler.

42nd Street, which benefited greatly from a contemporary and comparatively realistic backstage story following the creation of a new Broadway musical, as well as the inventive choreography of Busby Berkeley, made Keeler a top Warner Bros. star. She had made a mark as a featured dancer on Broadway in the Gershwin musical, *Show Girl*, and she arrived on screen in *42nd Street* best known as the much younger wife of Warner Bros.'s greatest star, Jolson—undoubtedly, the role of Peggy Sawyer, the innocent chorine who saves the show, went to Keeler because of her relationship to Jolson. Playing a naïve young chorus girl elevated to stardom by circumstance, Keeler seemed, in many respects, to be acting on screen her own story, and audiences were certainly aware of the connection.

Keeler's career as a hoofer began in childhood despite the inability of her poor Irish Catholic family to pay for dancing lessons. Fortunately, a dance teacher at Keeler's school noticed her potential and offered free lessons. The teacher also arranged an audition for dance director Julian Mitchell, but she was only thirteen-years-old and the law required Broadway chorus girls to be at least sixteen. Keeler lied about her age and Mitchell added her to the chorus of George M. Cohan's musical, *The Rise of Rosie O'Reilly* (1923).[4] The show followed Cohan's well-honed formula for many of his 1920s musicals, a formula not unlike that of Keeler's Warner Bros. musicals, with a focus on a spunky character's climb out of poverty to success and romance. *The Rise of Rosie O'Reilly* featured such songs as "A Ring to the Name of Rosie" and "Born and Bred in Brooklyn," and stressed the Irish heritage of its author, not to mention that of its youngest chorus member. Keeler's apprenticeship in this show, which ran for several months, led to a job at the El Fay "speakeasy" run by Texas Guinan. Broadway producer Charles B. Dillingham spotted Keeler in the chorus there (as did gangster Johnny Costello, who became enamored of her) and he cast Keeler in a small role in the musical comedy *Bye, Bye, Bonnie* (1927). Conveniently cast as a character named "Ruby," Keeler was given a specialty dance spot

---

4   The cast also included Margaret Dumont, soon to be the beloved stage and screen foil for The Marx Brothers.

in "Tampico Tap," which led to similar assignments in the short-lived musical *Lucky* (1927) and the far more successful *Sidewalks of New York* (1927) before she landed a featured role as Dixie Dugan in *Show Girl*, with a cast including Jimmy Durante (with his vaudeville partners Eddie Jackson and Lou Clayton) in his Broadway debut playing a Durante-esque character named Snozzle. The cast also included Eddie Foy, Jr., Nick Lucas, and Frank McHugh as Keeler's love interest. McHugh, like Keeler, would soon become a fixture of the classic 1930s Warner Bros. musicals.

Show Girl opened on July 2, 1929 for 111 performances, and was a typically lavish Florenz Ziegfeld, Jr. production designed by Joseph Urban and directed by playwright William Anthony McGuire, with choreography by Bobby Connolly, who became a part of the Warner Bros. musical staff in the 1930s. George Gershwin wrote the score, with lyrics by his brother, Ira, and additional lyrics by Gus Kahn, Thomas Malie, Sidney Skolsky, W. H. Farrell, and Durante, who contributed his own specialty material (including his perennials, "Can Broadway Do Without Me?" "Jimmy, The Well-Dressed Man", and "So I Ups to Him"). The Gershwins' contributions included one unqualified hit, "Liza," during which Jolson, who was in the process of wooing Keeler, stood up in the audience to sing it to her while she danced. This story has several variations—in *The Jolson Story* this event is recreated as a spontaneous act on opening night when Keeler (fictionalized as Julie Benson in the film) becomes too nervous to continue and Jolson sings to calm her nerves. No such affliction struck Keeler in reality—and she herself later claimed that she thought it inappropriate of Jolson to have sung to her from the audience, but the truth seems to be that this was a pre-arranged bit of business and Jolson did it nightly for at least two weeks during the show's run, much to the delight of audience members who took it as a spontaneous act. Regardless of the truth, Jolson and Keeler were subsequently wed in an explosion of publicity, all of which subsequently led to Keeler's screen career, a direct result of Jolson's dominance at Warner Bros. in the period.

Keeler left Broadway's *Show Girl* to accompany Jolson to Hollywood where, prior to *42nd Street*, she appeared in a couple of short subjects, most notably *Ruby Keeler* (1929), a mini-profile, and she is glimpsed in newsreel footage with Jolson interpolated into the film *Show Girl in Hollywood* (1930), but otherwise she was a virtual unknown to movie audiences as anything other than Mrs. Al Jolson. *The Jolson Story* depicts Keeler as a reluctant film star—a woman more interested in creating a family than in a career, but Keeler seems to have embraced her screen stardom, at least initially. *42nd Street* launched her into a series of highly popular musicals cut from the same cloth, often co-starring her with Dick Powell, who had played her juvenile love interest in *42nd Street*. Several of these films—*Gold Diggers of 1933*, *Footlight Parade*, *Dames*, and *Ready, Willing and Able*, as well as the aforementioned *Go Into Your Dance*—feature backstage settings with Keeler playing naïve and/or true blue young chorines, although a few Keeler-Powell pairings abandoned backstage plots to try different settings, as in *Flirtation Walk*, *Shipmates Forever*, and *Colleen*, but Keeler's character remained fundamentally unchanged in all of them—although there is an imperceptible reduction of naiveté. Given her background, the real Keeler could hardly have been as naïve as her screen image, but her mild-mannered persona seems to have been genuine—and the implication that she sought family life over career is validated by her post-Jolson life. As was typical of most musicals of the 1920s and 1930s, both on stage and screen, plot and characters were little more than excuses for a song, dance, or specialty routine, and exploitation of the performer's patented persona, whether true or false in regard to the performer's actual personality, was typical. The fiction reflected reality and the reality began to match the fiction—even as a grandmother starring in *No, No, Nanette*, Keeler retained her screen image playing a sweet-natured, squeaky-clean aunt raising an adventurous niece and tap-dancing a little on the side.

With one exception, all of Keeler's Warner Bros. films featured songs by Al Dubin and Harry Warren, the impressively prolific songwriting team, who consistently supplied at least a couple of hit songs for each Warner Bros. musical post-1933. The exception among Keeler's films, *Ready, Willing and Able*, featured songs by Johnny Mercer and Richard Whiting, most notably the classic "Too Marvelous for Words," which was employed as a production number for Keeler and Broadway dancer Lee Dixon, both of whom danced on the keys of an enormous typewriter. Despite a hit song, *Ready, Willing and Able* failed to excite movie audiences, perhaps because Keeler was partnered with the uninspiring (and essentially non-musical) Ross Alexander instead of Powell. The decided lack of chemistry in this new romantic pairing and the shrinking popularity of Warner Bros. musicals in general during the late 1930s led to a decline in Keeler's career. There is also reason to suspect that Jolson's dissatisfaction with his Warner Bros. vehicles may have hastened Keeler's departure. Neither made another Warner Bros. film after 1937, until Jolson returned briefly to film his cameo in *Rhapsody in Blue* during World War II (and after the end of the Jolson-Keeler marriage). As for

Keeler, she freelanced with little success. When Katharine Hepburn famously turned down a role in RKO's *Mother Carey's Chickens* (1938), a film she considered so inferior that she felt compelled to buy her way out of her long-term RKO contract, Keeler was offered the part of Kitty Carey, daughter of Fay Bainter's Mother Carey, in a wan dramatization of Kate Douglas Wiggin's novel of a poor widow and her daughters in a turn-of-the-century small town. For Keeler, the film provided her first non-musical role and she gives a credible performance, but it did not lead to other dramatic opportunities.

More importantly, during this period, the Jolson-Keeler marriage unraveled and by 1939 they were separated. Wishing to save the marriage, Jolson somehow managed to convince Keeler to join the cast of his new stage musical, *Hold On to Your Hats* (1940), presumably in hopes that working together might lead to reconciliation. This proved a savvy public relations maneuver, since the break-up of the Jolson-Keeler marriage—which had been a long one by Hollywood standards—generated considerable publicity. Keeler dutifully participated in the out-of-town tryouts for the show and her co-starring credit is featured on early editions of sheet music of the show's songs. However, she had no interest in reconciliation and backstage tensions mounted. She left the cast before the Broadway opening, and in a statement demonstrating the naiveté typical of her screen persona, Keeler told the press, "When I agreed to appear in Al's show, I thought we could work together as friends." Dancer Eunice Healy replaced Keeler in a cast also including Martha Raye, Bert "The Mad Russian" Gordon, Margaret Irving, and Jinx Falkenburg, and *Hold On to Your Hats* opened on Broadway on September 11, 1940 for a solid 158-performance run and rhapsodic reviews for Jolson's Broadway return. A divorce was finalized in late 1940 and Keeler appeared only one more time in a screen musical, playing a dancer in Columbia Pictures's *Sweetheart of the Campus* (1941), a B-picture directed by Edward Dmytryk in which she played a nightclub hoofer with minimal dialogue and a couple of brisk dance routines accompanied by Ozzie Nelson's orchestra. Keeler married businessman John Lowe that same year and retired from show business to raise a family for thirty years before returning to Broadway in triumph for *No, No, Nanette* in 1971, much as Jolson had triumphed via *The Jolson Story* near the end of his life.

Ultimately, the influence of these two singular entertainers can be best gauged in their sole co-starring film, *Go Into Your Dance*, a typical Warner Bros. musical of the era, and a result of their individual contributions to the development of screen musicals in the early sound era. *Go Into Your Dance* (known as *Casino de Paree* in its European release) features Jolson and Keeler in well-crafted variations of their established screen personas. Whatever their individual acting talents—or lack of same—both had achieved relative ease with their established personas and the demands of the camera by the time they appeared in this film at the apex of their individual careers. Under the guidance of Warner Bros. contract director Archie Mayo, Jolson gives one of his breeziest and most commanding performances as Al Howard. In a majority of his post-*The Jazz Singer* films, Jolson is named Al; surnames change, but Al is eternal—perhaps Warner Bros. assumed audiences would not accept him under any other name or perhaps it is simply a recognition that Jolson was bigger than any role he could ever play. Al Howard is a charmingly feckless Broadway star with a reckless penchant for running out on shows to play the horses and carouse. Keeler plays Dorothy Wayne, a loyal, sweet-natured, feisty Irish American chorine drawn somewhat unwillingly into Howard's orbit, much as Keeler was drawn into Jolson's world in the late 1920s.

When *Go Into Your Dance* went into production, fan magazines and columnists generated rumors concerning the state of Jolson's value as a film star. According to these reports, Jolson was given the starring role only due to Keeler's insistence and her willingness to co-star (she was then at the height of her screen popularity) which, presumably, would assure success. This rumor has persisted, making its way into Jolson biographies, but the suggestion that her popularity exceeded his at this or any point in the 1930s has little genuine merit, not least because *Wonder Bar*, released only shortly before, was one of the most commercially successful films of the year. Jolson may not have been able to claim sole credit for *Wonder Bar's* popularity, but his value to the studio remained high. Despite past missteps, including the maudlin *Say It With Songs*, which tried too hard to repeat the successful formula of *The Singing Fool*, and the box office failure of UA's *Hallelujah, I'm a Bum*, Jolson's stock remained relatively high even if the studio could not seem to create a definitive vehicle for him (*The Singing Fool* seemed to provide that formula, but the thudding failure of *Say It With Songs*, which followed the formula, almost immediately suggested otherwise). Jolson himself expressed concern with the quality of his post-*The Singing Fool* and pre-*Wonder Bar* vehicles, but his films consistently made money, if not as spectacularly as they had for *The Jazz Singer* and *The Singing Fool*. Most likely, Warner Bros. may have felt that a Jolson and Keeler team would guarantee a major success, certainly a reasonably assumption, and that they wanted to keep the couple happy.

Another fact that refutes the rumor is that Keeler's billing never equaled Jolson's, even in *Go Into Your Dance*. His on-screen billing appears before and as large as the title (Keeler's follows the title in smaller print) and existing trailers for the film stress his presence above all else, with the first-time pairing of the Jolsons as the next most important selling point. In addition, Jolson's role seems tailor-made for him and the film seems at least as much his vehicle as Keeler's, perhaps more so, and in production values the equivalent of any film she made (it should be pointed out that Keeler was never the sole star of any movie—often her films such as *42nd Street*, *Gold Diggers of 1933*, and *Footlight Parade* also featured a host of popular Warner Bros. stars and featured players). In truth, the Keeler films at Warner Bros. were as successful as they were for two reasons: (1) the appealing pairing of Keeler with Dick Powell and (2) Busby Berkeley's choreography for the great Dubin and Warren songs. *Go Into Your Dance* is also clearly an attempt to bring a new twist to the formula of Warner Bros. musicals, merging characteristics of backstage musicals in the new *42nd Street* style with the gritty realism of Warner Bros. gangster films. In *Go Into Your Dance*, the merging of gangster and backstage musical elements is appealing for many reasons, and the mix of melodrama with popular music and brisk comedy provided both Jolson and Keeler with a strong showcase.

The *Go Into Your Dance* screenplay by Earl Baldwin, was adapted from a novel by Bradford Ropes, author of *42nd Street* and several other novels brought to the screen by Warner Bros., and it begins when a committee of angry producers bans Al's future appearances on Broadway (a twist on *42nd Street*, which begins with a hubbub over the start of a musical, instead of a closing). Al has walked out on a hit show once again, throwing cast and crew out of work in the midst of the Great Depression. Al's protective sister Molly, played with diamond-hard toughness by Glenda Farrell, is aware of Al's instability, but rushes to his defense. The producers are impressed by Molly's loyalty, but are unbending—Al is banned from Broadway. Molly tracks Al to Caliente, sobers him up, and tries unsuccessfully to convince him to reform. Al seems cavalier in his reaction to the banning, but in truth he simply refuses to let Molly know the truth—he is shaken by the news. The dialogue between Al and Molly—and for much of the film—is laced with Broadway slang of the era, which Jolson and Farrell handle briskly, allowing the brother-and-sister affection/antagonism to filter through.

Molly's reformation plan includes a plot to partner Al with Dorothy, her old chum from her chorus days, in an act for a Chicago nightclub. Molly hopes to save Al's career and believes straight-arrow Dorothy will have a positive influence on her errant brother. Dorothy resists the plan, even though she is grateful to Molly for past kindnesses. Molly is finally persuasive and convinces the reluctant Dorothy to try with Al. Oddly enough, in *Go Into Your Dance*, Jolson and Keeler, neither of whom are actors in the strictest sense, work most effectively in non-musical scenes, especially so at this point in the plot as Dorothy attempts to convince Al to form a stage partnership. They exchange wisecracks, with Dorothy attempting to match his braggadocio by claiming she can dance in any style. To prove her point, she rolls back the carpet as Al accompanies her on the piano, joking and playing a range of musical styles as Dorothy gamely demonstrates her dancing skills. It proves the most charming scene in the film and a scene like it was interpolated in Jolson's last stage musical, *Hold on to Your Hats*, five years later. Keeler left the show during its out-of-town tryouts, but one of her few performances in the show was captured in a newspaper photograph with a beaming Jolson watching Keeler dancing, much like the aforementioned scene in *Go Into Your Dance*.

Some dialogue scenes are also largely effective, although in the more melodramatic moments certain lines verge on the mawkish, as when Al confesses his love for Dorothy following a shooting:

> AL: I love ya.
>
> DOROTHY: To think I had to get shot to hear you say that.[5]

Jolson handles this moment with sensitivity, which make it more affecting than might be expected. Later in the same scene some "show must go on" clichés emerge:

> STAGE MANAGER: Mr. Howard, Second Act, Mr. Howard. What'll we do?
>
> AL: There is no second act.
>
> STAGE MANAGER: You mean you're not going on?
>
> AL: I'm not going on.

---

[5]   This dialogue is transcribed directly from the release print of *Go Into Your Dance* (1935).

DOROTHY: Al?

AL: Yes, honey.

DOROTHY: You've got to go on. Why . . . why, it's everything you've struggled for. It's a big hit. And I'm all right.

AL: What does a hit mean to me now. I want to stay here with you.

DOCTOR: Better do as she asks, Mr. Howard. There isn't a thing you can do here now.

DOROTHY (to Al): Please, for my sake.

AL: All right, Dotsy.[6]

The first exchange appears in the surviving release print of the film, but is not present in the final script—and significant differences are found in the second exchange as well. The latter scene appears in the script as follows:

ASSISTANT MANAGER: (timidly) Mr. Howard—everybody's waiting for the second act. What do we do?

AL: (without looking around) Forget it—forget it!

DOROTHY: (weakly, reaching up a shakey hand for Al) Al—(Al immediately crouches down beside her.)

AL: Yes, honey . . .

DOROTHY: Go on out there—Al.—You've got to—they're waiting.

AL: What I've got to do is stay right here.—I love you—nothing else counts.

---

[6] Ibid.

DOROTHY: (gratefully, happily) No, Al . . . Go on out—do the finale.

AL: (choking) Finale nothing! What do I care about the show! I want to be just with you, kid—I've never realized till now how much you've really meant to me—

DOROTHY: (smiling up at him—weakly) But you've got a hit, Al—and you're going to make me happy if you see it through! For my sake—won't you please do it?

DOCTOR: She means it, Mr. Howard—and she's right. (Al stares up at the Doctor) The best thing you can do for her is what she asks. (patting Al's shoulder) Go back and finish the show.

AL: No—no!

DOROTHY: (pulling Al close to her) Please, Al—I want you to.

AL: (choking) All right, baby—for you! (rising slowly) Better get her to the hospital, hunh [sic]?

DOCTOR: (shaking head) She'll be better right here . . . . I've sent for instruments in my car.

AL: (to Dorothy) I'll be right back, kid.—Stick with us! (He has difficulty making the door, but is taken in the firm grip of a hard-boiled electrician, who helps Al out.)[7]

Whether or not the improvements were ad-libbed on the set during rehearsals or, more likely, were part of last minute rewrites, remains unclear. There are other differences between the lengthier script (which shows evidence of its novelistic origins) and the shorter, tighter release print. For example, Molly is called "Sadie" in the script and the title is typed as *Casino de Paree* (its European title), although it is crossed out and replaced by *Go into Your Dance*, probably as a result of Dubin and Warren submitting a song by that name. The existing version of the film

---

[7]   Earl Baldwin. *Casino de Paree*. Adaptation and Screen Play. Scene 254, pp. 134-135.

has some rough editing, suggesting post-filming cuts to shorten it or to remove redundancies or, perhaps, to take out jokes and bits of business that failed to please in previews. Surviving trailers include different shots of the scenes that appear in the film—at one point, Jolson is seen in a window dressed in a bathrobe singing the title song, but no such scene is included in the film.

Following the first encounter between Al and Dorothy, they are seen scoring a success in Chicago in the elaborate "About a Quarter to Nine" number and all goes well until Molly brings a wealthy gangster, known only as The Duke (played by Barton MacLane), to see a performance in hopes that Al can secure financial backing to open a Broadway nightclub. In essence, he hopes to become his own producer to get around the Broadway banishment. The Duke agrees to provide the support if, in exchange, Al will find a featured spot in the show for his ex-singer wife, Luana Wells, played by legendary torch singer Helen Morgan. Luana is eager to make a show business comeback, but unbeknownst to The Duke, Luana is attracted to Al. He initially responds favorably, unaware that she is The Duke's wife until Molly wises him up.

As the film proceeds, another complication arises when Dorothy recognizes that she has fallen in love with Al. Her secret and unrequited feelings lead to a painful decision to withdraw from the act. She informs Molly, who manages to persuade her to stick it out in the act until Al can pull off the New York opening, an ambitious plan involving ripping the seats out of a legitimate Broadway theatre to reinvent it as a nightclub offering a show, dancing, and dinner for an affordable price. Al works intensely to pull the club and the show together, but he struggles to keep the persistent Luana at bay. He is finally forced to tell her, in no uncertain terms, that he will have nothing to do with her romantically, leading Luana to ominously vow revenge. A further crisis occurs when Molly is falsely accused of murdering one of The Duke's partners and Al is compelled to risk the bankroll from The Duke to get her out of jail. Unexpectedly, Molly disappears and on opening night it seems that her bail—which represents a bond to be posted with Actors' Equity—is forfeit. As a result, the Equity officer refuses to let the show open and Al is in the sad process of informing the cast mere minutes before curtain time when word comes that Molly has returned and proven her innocence. The bail is released and the show goes on.

Many typical musicals of the period might end on such a positive note, but *Go Into Your Dance* shifts from a romantic musical to a melodrama in the tradition of Warner Bros. gangster movies as the vengeful Luana tells

The Duke that Al has lost the money. Infuriated, The Duke impulsively sends two gunmen to even the score before he hears a radio broadcast of Al's show opening. He tries to call the gunmen before it is too late, but cannot reach them or Al, who he attempts to call on the backstage telephone. Following the ending of the show's first act, which features an elaborate production number, "She a Latin from Manhattan," Al and Dorothy step into the alley outside the stage door, where Dorothy spots the gunmen taking aim at Al. She protectively steps in front of him and is shot, as the previous dialogue excerpt demonstrates. In the ensuing panic, Al carries Dorothy back to the dressing room and, as a doctor is summoned, Al realizes the depth of his feelings for Dorothy. As indicated in the fast-paced climax in the dialogue previously examined, Al tells Dorothy he loves her and refuses to continue the show while the doctor tends her wounds. Dorothy insists that Al go on, so he reluctantly returns to the stage and sings the title song. When Al takes a bow and rushes back to the dressing room the doctor informs him that Dorothy will survive. She encourages him to go back onstage for an encore of "About a Quarter to Nine," which he joyfully performs as Dorothy listens from the dressing room.

Go Into Your Dance, like so many of the best Warner Bros. musicals in the post-*42nd Street* era, is enlivened by brash, wisecracking dialogue, a rapid pace (especially so in the climax, with each frame filled with continual motion), a standout Dubin and Warren score (including "About a Quarter to Nine" and "She's a Latin from Manhattan," both of which became Jolson standards), and in this case an uncommonly strong supporting cast. The haunting Morgan, in her best screen appearance aside from her roles in Rouben Mamoulian's early musical drama *Applause* (1929) and James Whale's classic *Show Boat* (1936), sings the torchy "The Little Things You Used to Do," but it is unfortunate that she and Jolson do not sing together. Theatre and film buffs viewing the film today will surely ache to see them perform a medley of the 1920s standards they made famous, and despite her fine acting, Morgan is unfortunately wasted. The cast also features comedienne Patsy Kelly, who continually reappears in a running gag as a down-on-her-luck vaudevillian, Irma "Toledo" Knight, attempting to convince Jolson to put her in his act. Kelly and Keeler have no scenes together, but thirty-six years later Kelly co-starred with Keeler in the Broadway revival of *No, No, Nanette*, playing Keeler's feisty Irish maid, Pauline. Keeler won kudos for her ageless tap dancing and Kelly netted a Tony Award for her vintage clowning, including an hilariously arthritic dance during which she shouted "Eat your heart out!" to an amused Keeler. Among the rest,

Farrell and MacLane give expert supporting performances, as do Akim Tamiroff, Arthur Treacher, Ward Bond, Phil Regan, Sharon Lynne, and Joyce Compton in brief roles, and Dubin and Warren themselves are glimpsed briefly in a rehearsal scene.

As for the stars, despite the significant age differences and somewhat incompatible performance styles, there is an undeniable chemistry between Jolson and Keeler. Musically, they are front and center in the major production numbers, "About a Quarter to Nine" and "She's a Latin From Manhattan," the two Dubin and Warren standards to emerge from the score. Entertainingly staged in the Busby Berkeley style, these numbers were choreographed by Bobby Connolly, Keeler's Broadway dance director from *Show Girl*. Elaborate and entertaining, these sequences otherwise fall short of the Berkeley standard while aping the scope of a typical Berkeley number, despite the fact that Connolly received a "Best Choreography" Academy Award nomination for "She's a Latin from Manhattan," one of four nominations he received in his career.

The "About a Quarter to Nine" number is, however, rather more effective, and is especially informative regarding the partnership of the Jolsons. It exemplifies Warner Bros.'s attempt to offer the Jolson-Keeler team as a challenge to RKO's blockbuster duo, Fred Astaire and Ginger Rogers, then at the pinnacle of a partnership that ultimately reaped nine films in the 1930s and an encore in 1949. The studios typically imitated success in this way, usually less effectively, and Warner Bros. were uncommonly shameless in this regard, despite the fact that the studio led the way in gangster pictures and, at this point in time, backstage musicals. In this attempt to siphon off some Astaire-Rogers glory, Warner Bros. is blatant: in "About a Quarter to Nine," Jolson appears in white tie and tails *ala* Astaire, while for part of the long number Keeler is dressed in a high fashion white gown very like those typically worn by Rogers. As with Astaire and Rogers, Keeler dances on polished, mirrored floors with a large chorus of male dancers, also in white tie and tails, while Jolson sings. The number is effective, but the problem with presenting Jolson and Keeler as a team is most evident in this number. Jolson was a singer and comedian, Keeler a dancer—when they are together in a musical sequence their individual skills do not mesh, obliging them to perform much of the long number mostly separately, with the limited impact of Jolson serenading Keeler (reminiscent of his singing "Liza" to Keeler from the audience during the run of *Show Girl*), who dances with the chorus, an anonymous partner (in "She's a Latin from Manhattan"), or solo. "About a Quarter to Nine" ends with Jolson and Keeler side-by-side floating into the heavens, but there is none of the glorious romantic merging typical of an Astaire-Rogers number, despite the effectiveness of their individual contributions.

The score of *Go Into Your Dance* features one interpolation—Jolson sings "Celito Lindo" in Spanish in a scene in which Al Howard is on a bender in Mexico and, once again, Jolson reaps a strong moment from a stage device he often employed. On Broadway, he frequently performed in various languages, learning the songs phonetically, to the great amusement of his audiences (he also parodied grand opera—and a variation of this parody is included in *Mammy*). In the film *Wonder Bar*, Jolson sang "Ochi chyornye" ("Dark Eyes") in Russian and often worked Yiddish into even the best-known songs—especially for comic effect. Other Dubin and Warren songs included "A Good Old-Fashioned Cocktail," which featured Keeler and a female chorus in a small nightclub setting early in the film, and Jolson's solo, "Mammy, I'll Sing About You," also performed in this early nightclub scene. The nightclub's master of ceremonies introduces Al to sing, and although this is a "mammy" song, Jolson does not perform it in blackface. Apparently, this resulted from a change of plan during the shooting of the scene, since still photographs survive of this scene with Jolson, wearing the same double-breasted suit, in blackface. What exactly precipitated this change is unknown—perhaps simply the fact that given the circumstances of the scene there was no plausible means for Jolson to get into blackface, not that plausibility was a hallmark of musical sequences in films of this era.

Returning to the subject of blackface, other than the film's fast-paced conclusion, in which he sings "Go Into Your Dance" and a reprise of "About a Quarter to Nine" in blackface, Jolson is only seen in it briefly in a short "minstrel show" fantasy in the middle of the six-minute-long "About a Quarter to Nine" production number. It seems likely that to use blackface in "Mammy, I'll Sing About You" seemed too much, even for Jolson admirers. Certainly by 1935, the minstrel tradition was essentially over and the blackface stage mask had run its course as changing racial attitudes made it an undeniable symbol of "Jim Crow" racism. The question the Warner Bros. seemed to skirt was whether or not the audience would accept Jolson without blackface, but *Go Into Your Dance* seems to suggest ambivalence about it. Blackface is used in Jolson's final Warner Bros. feature, *The Singing Kid*, the following year. His best number, teamed with Cab Calloway, "I Love to Sing-a," eschews it, although this song follows an opening prologue medley in which Jolson is seen in character singing bits of songs from his most famous shows and films (including *Go Into Your Dance*), some providing glimpses of him in blackface. Blackface is also used in an on-stage scene, again with Calloway, for "Save Me, Sister," a mock gospel number. Even more telling is an amusing sequence in which The Rhythm Boys, a musical quartet, try to prevent Jolson from singing "My Mammy" and other songs of the kind. The sequence ends with Jolson and the Rhythm Boys singing on a street corner as a car passes and splashes mud in their faces, transforming them all into blackface singers despite their attempt to stop it. A decade later, when Columbia Pictures made *The Jolson Story*, the issue of blackface was somewhat resolved by including it in the early scenes as Jolson appears in Dockstader's Minstrels and as he scores his first stage successes. Once past that point in his life, however, blackface disappears from the film. It is even less seen in *Jolson Sings Again*, only glimpsed in some clips from *The Jolson Story* interpolated into the film. Jolson's "comeback" via the popularity of *The Jolson Story* was based almost exclusively on his mellow vocals in updated arrangements of the greatest songs associated with him—blackface no longer had any currency with audiences except as history.

In *Go Into Your Dance*, Jolson and Keeler emerge as a viable screen team despite the hurdles, with his brashness and larger-than-life persona complemented by her youthful sweetness and more reactive acting. Jolson's style is always of the "in your face" variety, even in a more toned-down variety in his later Warner Bros. films. For contemporary audiences, his style does not always wear well—such a boldly presentational approach is now only typical of the snarkiest, self-reverential comedies made by Jim Carrey, Will Ferrell, and other comedians. Keeler, on the other hand, can hardly be said to act at all. Critics found her charmingly amateurish and rarely denied her appeal. What would have been the point? Audiences clearly embraced her as she was and it is undoubtedly the case that her popularity and enduring fame result from her lack of formal acting skills which left only her naturalness. The roles she played were surely a gloss of her own persona, in the way that Jolson's brashness was a reflection of his hard-driving personality, and her freedom from affectation is pleasing. In 1971, when Keeler returned to Broadway in *No, No, Nanette*, she essentially played a senior version of the same character and audiences found it equally appealing—with one critic noting that she seemed to be someone's mom playing a role in the PTA show—except when she danced, when a fierce professionalism emerged.

Go Into Your Dance was the only teaming of Jolson and Keeler in a feature film, altogether they also appeared together, albeit briefly, in a

Warner Bros. short, *A Day at Santa Anita* (1937), where they are seen (in Technicolor) watching the races with other film stars of the era. They also performed together on radio, but the only surviving broadcast is a *Lux Radio Theatre* adaptation of Arthur Hopkins and George Manker Watters's hit 1927 play, *Burlesque*. Originally aired on June 15, 1936, when *Go Into Your Dance* was still fresh in the memories of movie fans hoping for another Jolson-Keeler teaming, this audio performance is on a par with *Go Into Your Dance*, providing them similar characters. Jolson plays an unstable performer and Keeler loyally provides him with the needed stability. The two leading characters of *Burlesque*, played in the Broadway production by Hal Skelly and Barbara Stanwyck (a young Oscar Levant, Jolson's radio sidekick in the late 1940s, was also in the cast), are Skid, a dissolute burlesque comic, and Bonny, his stage partner and girlfriend. *Burlesque* would have been a solid screen vehicle for Jolson and Keeler, as amply demonstrated in this broadcast. Both give entertaining, well-interpreted performances in an hour-long adaptation hosted by Cecil B. DeMille, with Jolson singing two interpolated numbers from his songbook, "Toot, Toot, Tootsie" (accompanied by Keeler's tap-dancing) and "Is It True What They Say About Dixie?" as well as one encore, "A Pretty Girl Is Like a Melody," sung during sign-off banter with DeMille. Why Warner Bros. did not pursue *Burlesque* as a screen option for the Jolsons is unclear, but it is likely that the Jolsons dissatisfaction with the studio leading to their departure in 1937 was the reason. The surviving recording of *Burlesque*, which is commercially available on compact disc and in excellent audio condition, is a revealing complement to *Go Into Your Dance*.

Go Into Your Dance opened at New York's Capitol Theatre on May 2, 1935 before going into wide release. Critics and audiences reacted favorably, with reviewers emphasizing the effectiveness of the Jolson-Keeler partnership. *Time* magazine's critic applauded the "good-humored backstage musicomedy," adding that "the two most notable ingredients are Ruby Keeler's legs and Al Jolson's mother complex."[8] Andre Sennwald, reviewing for the *New York Times*, went further, stressing Jolson's "enthusiastic presence" as the aspect that

> pulls the picture into the safety zone of musical entertainment.
> When he is absent from the screen one's attention is likely
> to stray, even in the face of Miss Keeler's nimble dancing.
> But when he opens up with "A Latin From Manhattan" and

---

8   "The New Pictures," *Time* (April 29, 1935): 56.

"About a Quarter to Nine," which are among the seven songs written for the piece by Harry Warren and Al Dubin, one must give way to the pleasurable realization that Mr. Jolson's in his minstrel heaven and all's right with the world.[9]

Variety's critic shared Sennwald's perspective, pointing out that *Go Into Your Dance*

has much to recommend it as a lavishly produced, vigorously directed and agreeably entertaining musical picture. Besides everything else it has Al Jolson in top form, plus a nifty set of songs, and Jolson to sing 'em. Along with Jolson this time, and for the first time his screen partner is the missus, Ruby Keeler—a romantic touch that should mean considerable at the gate.[10]

Another assessment, this one from *Film Weekly*, again stressed Jolson's centrality to the movie's overall effectiveness:

Jolson may black his face, and he may sing a Mammy song, and he may get outrageously sentimental now and then, but few will gainsay that he is a grand entertainer. He breezes through this picture as though he were enjoying a holiday instead of working extremely hard.[11]

Despite the solid success of *Go Into Your Dance* and *The Singing Kid* the following year, Jolson terminated his contract with Warner Bros. on May 20, 1937, insisting that Keeler do the same, an insistence that it may be presumed did not help their crumbling marriage. In Jolson's case, he never again appeared as the leading star in a film and Keeler only completed two more features, the aforementioned *Mother Carey's Chickens* (1938) and *Sweetheart of the Campus* (1941), both in which she played secondary roles.

Jolson had ushered in sound when it was most in need of a singular figure of surpassing popularity and talent and Keeler emerged just as musicals films at the end of the brief and primitive Vitaphone era

9   Andre Sennwald, "Review," *New York Times* (May 4, 1935): 17.
10   Bige, "Review," *Variety* (May 8, 1935): 16.
11   John Gammie, "What—And What Not—To See," *Film Weekly* (August 23, 1935): n.p.

required new faces and talents for a screen form coming into its maturity. These two stars of the early sound era—joined at the time by marriage and intersecting careers—exemplify the strengths and weaknesses of sound film, musicals on screen, stage traditions as they influenced the screen, and the cult of personality that has remained a foundation of the definitive performance art medium of the 20th and 21st centuries.

Acting Naturally On Stage and Screen: Spencer Tracy's Enduring Legacy

Brenda Loew

Prologue

All Spence had to do was walk on the stage and you knew he belonged there . . . . He dominated it. It's difficult to be natural on stage, but it's the only place where Spence was completely natural.[1]
—Selena Royle,[2] leading lady, W. H. Wright Company,
Grand Rapids, Michigan, and early champion of
Spencer Tracy[3]

$\mathbb{S}$pencer Tracy,[4] one of the most legendary American film actors of all time, earned a reputation for performing naturally both on stage and

---

[1] Words used to describe Tracy's acting style include natural, naturalism, naturalist, naturally, naturalness (Fisher 1995).

[2] Royle later appeared with Tracy in the role of Louise Wargate in Sinclair Lewis's *Cass Timberlane* (MGM, 1947).

[3] Alison King, *Spencer Tracy* (New York: Crescent Books, 1992), 13.

[4] b. April 5, 1900—d. June 10, 1967. Tracy appeared in seventy-four films from 1930 to 1967. In 1999, the American Film Institute ranked Tracy ninth among the Greatest Male Stars of All Time.

screen[5]—a peerless distinction essential for understanding the entirety of Tracy's enduring legacy. Whether acting before a live audience or through the lens of a camera, Spencer Tracy's natural performance style connected with the public in a unique way. For five decades, his bond with audiences was nothing less than magical. Tracy's naturalism[6] made him believable playing rare, difficult, and offbeat roles as well as the "normal, average guy who was nobody in particular."[7] During Tracy's motion picture career, "he was hailed as one of the greatest screen actors of his time by some of the other great actors of the day.[8] Nightclub comics of the Golden Age era impersonated superstars like Humphrey Bogart, Clark Gable, and James Cagney—but not Spencer Tracy."[9] Cagney, who modeled his 1938 Rocky Sullivan character in *Angels with Dirty Faces* (Warner Bros.) "on a hophead and a pimp with four girls in his string"[10]

---

[5]   Tracy said that he deliberately violated existing stage tricks of expression in favor of the naturalness of the screen when he made his theatrical debut in the Theatre Guild production, *R.U.R.* (*Hartford Courant*, 1933, D3).

[6]   At the turn of the twentieth century, the theatrical style called naturalism was the new rage. Naturalism, compared to older styles of theatre, for example, Shakespeare, was defined as performances creating a perfect illusion of reality reflecting the way real people spoke—a style attempting to recreate reality by seeking complete identification with the role (ECONOMICexpert.com). Actors delivered their lines with psychological intention as if from conversation reflecting life. Naturalistic actors tried to speak lines as if normal, everyday speech . . . . The illusion of emotional depth was created by using pauses and hesitations (Riis, 2004). Natural acting centered on the individual, distinctions of personality. Audience viewed players as actual people with distinguishing personalities. Actors became models for individual lifestyles. By their naturalistic acting in roles that replicated contemporary life, the public identified with them: exemplars and metaphors of modern life (Benjamin McArthur, *Actors and American Culture, 1880-1920* [Philadelphia: Temple University Press, 1984]).

[7]   Martha Nochimson, "Chapter 5 Katharine Hepburn and Spencer Tracy," in *Screen Couple Chemistry: The Power of 2*, ed. Martha Nochimson (Austin, TX: University of Texas Press, 2002), 189.

[8]   Nancy Reagan often compared Walter Houston to Spencer Tracy. But John Houston pointed out, "Spencer Tracy was always Spencer Tracy" (Laurence Grobel, *The Houstons* [New York: Avon Books, 1989], 189).

[9]   King, *Spencer Tracy*, 1.

[10] James Cagney, *Cagney by Cagney* (New York: Doubleday & Company, 1976), back cover.

remarked, "I'm easy to imitate but you never saw anyone imitate Spencer Tracy. It's because there's nothing to imitate except his genius and that can't be mimicked.[11] You can't mimic reserve and control[12] very well."[13] "He makes you believe what he is playing," Humphrey Bogart said of Tracy. "You don't see the mechanism working, the wheels turning."[14]

The naturalness Spencer Tracy projected from the stage in his pre-Hollywood theatre work during the 1920s[15] greatly contributed to the naturalism he brought to the talkies during Hollywood's Golden Age. To be sure, Spencer Tracy was born with an instinctive genius of knowing how to "just do it"—but he also learned some of it along the way.[16]

---

[11]   Garson Kanin, *Tracy and Hepburn: An Intimate Memoir* (New York: Bantam Books Inc., 1972), 244.

[12]   To act a role with restraint is to underplay. William Gillette (1853-1937) specialized by underplaying his parts, gaining the audience's attention by his very calm. "He seems to be doing nothing, but he is doing many things," said drama critic Norman Hapgood, "making a hundred subdued movements of his frame or head or face to reflect every change in the situation." George Arliss (1868-1946) remarked that movie acting had to be natural: "I had always believed that for the movies acting must be exaggerated, but I saw in this one flash that restraint was the chief thing that the actor must learn in transferring his art from the stage to the screen." Sincerity, restraint, the appearance of not acting at all proved the most effective movie acting techniques (McArthur, *Actors and American Culture, 1880-1920*, 174,206).

[13]   John McCabe, *Cagney* (New York: Carroll & Graf, 1999), 356.

[14]   Martin F. Nolan, "No one has replaced Spencer Tracy as the master of believability. The actor's actor," *The Boston Globe*, April 5, 2000, A 19.

[15]   Andersen calls Tracy's performances on Broadway and in "countless" stock productions "forgettable" (86). Interestingly enough, the critics would later also call "forgettable" many of the pre-code Fox Films Tracy appeared in during the early 1930s. Well-researched essays detailing Tracy's performances during his years at Fox are found in *Spencer Tracy, Fox Film Actor: The Pre-Code Legacy of a Hollywood Legend* published by New England Vintage Film Society Incorporated. Brenda Loew, Editor.

[16]   Nineteen years after Tracy's death, an analysis of his acting style as either innate or learned was considered moot by some (Leslie Bennetts, "Artists pay tribute to Spencer Tracy," newyorktimes.com, March 4, 1986. http://www.nytimes.com/1986/03/04/movies/artists-pay-tribute-to-spencer-tracy.html).

Act I

Tracy's Artless and Aimless Youth

Both Bogart and I were wastrels . . . . Spencer Tracy was also one.
—Lauren Bacall[17]

Milwaukee-born Spencer Bonaventure Tracy, whose middle name means "good adventure," was an underachieving, difficult, and gifted child. When he was seven years old, he ran away from home, seeking adventure. "That was the beginning of the wanderlust, I suppose," admitted Tracy.[18] Often truant from school, he got into many fights. "I just couldn't get interested in books. They bored me . . . . For the sake of my mother, who was very intent on making something out of me that would do credit to her colonial ancestors I tried spasmodically to be interested. I managed to stagger along from grade to grade, just getting by on passing grades and an occasional ability to kid the teachers along."[19]

On the other hand, Spencer Tracy was also a Boy Scout and an altar boy. Competitive, he played baseball and boxed. He hated to lose. The future Hollywood icon held a job as a lamplighter, lighting fifty gas street lights nightly and polishing their globes for $3.50 a week. He attended fifteen different schools, including St. Rosa's Parochial School in Milwaukee and six high schools, before earning a diploma at age twenty.[20]

Spencer Tracy displayed a special interest in movies as a young teenager.[21] Tracy loved silent films. One reason he admitted he

17 Laurence Grobel, *The Houstons* (New York: Avon Books, 1989), 369.

18 Spencer Tracy, "Spencer Tracy labels his career 'Hitch Hiking to Hollywood'; Opens own story in days when he attended 15 or 18 schools," *Hartford Courant*, February 14, 1937, D1.

19 Tracy, "Spencer Tracy labels his career 'Hitch Hiking to Hollywood,'" D1.

20 King, *Spencer Tracy*, 9.
Kristen Gilpatrick, *Famous Wisconsin Film Stars* (Oregon, WI: Badger Books Inc., 2002), 12-13.
Christopher Andersen, *An Affair to Remember The Remarkable Love Story of Katharine Hepburn and Spencer Tracy* (New York: Avon, 1997), 96.

21 According to Davidson, the only reason Spencer went to school "was because of the beatings and threats from his father, and tearful entreaties of his mother" (Davidson, *Spencer Tracy, Tragic Idol* [New York: E. P. Dutton, 1987], 18).

attended school was to learn how to read subtitles in silent movies.[22] His older brother Carroll, who later became Spencer's business manager and confidant, recalled in an Associated Press story (March 1, 1951) that Spencer watched Bronco Billy Anderson's westerns so many times he fell asleep in the theatre. When Carroll woke him, "Spencer told me, 'That's what I'm going to be: an actor.'"[23] "He would put on live shows based on the films he had seen in the basement of the house . . . . Spencer both wrote and performed in these shows . . . . Several ended in fights as the young customers . . . who had paid one cent to watch, rioted, complaining about the quality of the scripts . . .[24] and over the fact that Spencer always cast himself in the lead[25] hogging most of the good parts for himself."[26] Despite Spencer's instinctive natural talent, no precedent existed in the Tracy family for a career in show business.

[22]   Andersen, *An Affair to Remember*, 91.
       Jane Ellen Wayne, *The Leading Men of MGM* (USA: Da Capo Press, 2006), 206.
[23]   Gilpatrick, *Famous Wisconsin Film Stars*, 13.
[24]   King, *Spencer Tracy*, 9.
[25]   Andersen, *An Affair to Remember*, 93.
[26]   Bill Davidson, *Spencer Tracy, Tragic Idol*, 17.

During World War I, seeing the chance to go places and do things, Spencer Tracy left school and joined the U.S. Navy with his Marquette Academy friend, William J. (actor) "Pat" O'Brien.[27] "We'd known one another since grammar school and we'd always pretty much liked to do the same things . . . . But it never occurred to either of us to figure out what we might do if we ever got out of the Navy."[28] During two years of cleaning ships and standing watch at the Norfolk Naval Yard in Virginia, Tracy realized he "had to get his life in order."[29] Tracy's father, who managed a trucking company, encouraged Spencer to join him in that business—or become a priest. But after being discharged in 1919, Tracy enrolled in the Northwestern Military and Naval Academy at Lake Geneva, Wisconsin, where he met Kenneth Edgers, a cultured, sophisticated boy from Seattle. Edgers profoundly influenced Spencer's life. Edgers would be entering Ripon College, one of the most prestigious colleges in the Midwest, and Spencer decided to follow his friend and go there too.[30]

[27]   Donald Deschner, *The Films of Spencer Tracy* (New York: Cadillac Publishing Co. Inc., 1968), 34.

[28]   Tracy, "Spencer Tracy labels his career 'Hitch Hiking to Hollywood,'" D1.

[29]   King, *Spencer Tracy*, 10.

[30]   King, *Spencer Tracy*, 10.
      Davidson, *Spencer Tracy, Tragic Idol*, 22.
      Andersen, *An Affair to Remember*, 96.

Act II

Tracy Discovers His Vocation at Ripon College, A Nurturing Environment

In the first two decades of the twentieth century dramatic training was divided between the traditional and the new, stock companies and acting schools. Success on the stage was not measured by technical knowledge but by the degree to which the player could establish that magical relationship between himself and the audience. No course of study, no academic degree could confer what in the final reckoning is a gift.[31]

Spencer Tracy, a member of the class of 1924, attended Ripon College from February 1921 to April 1922. "One thing my two years in college did for me, it gave me an aim in life. Up to that time I had no particular idea what I wanted to do. I was just sort of drifting around, waiting for something to happen or trying to stir up a little synthetic excitement."[32]

A premed student, he planned to become a doctor—a plastic surgeon. But something happened that made him change his mind: Tracy was recruited to join Ripon's Eastern Debate Team. As Tracy later told it, Professor Boody, an instructor in the English department, approached him. "'I want you to join debate,' he told me one day. 'Me?' said I ungrammatically. 'Yes, I think you'd make a good debater. You like to argue about other things; let's see how you can argue from a platform'" (Ripon College Archives). "It was just a step from the debating team to school dramatics. Again, it was Professor Boody who encouraged me, but it didn't take much urging this time. The idea was growing stronger and stronger in my head that I wanted to be an actor; that I'd always wanted to be an actor but had only just realized it."[33]

---

[31]   McArthur, *Actors and American Culture, 1880-1920*, 103-104.

[32]   Spencer Tracy, "College debating team gave Spencer Tracy to the theatre; Popular movie star traces arduous climb to his first hit," *Hartford Courant*, February 21, 1937, D3.

[33]   Tracy, "College debating team gave Spencer Tracy to the theatre," D3.

So Tracy gave speaking on the theatrical stage a try. Ripon's drama society, Mask and Wig, was run by Professor J. Clark Graham.[34] In March, 1921, Graham reported "a certain decisiveness, a clipped firmness of expression indicating poise, self-control and confidence" in Tracy's speech. "I was impressed and invited him to try out for our next play."[35] Tracy[36] was nervous and in a fluster to enter on time, tripped over a music stand stored offstage.[37] But Tracy's approach was entirely unique: he memorized the script and auditioned without it.[38] He won the leading role, quickly discovering both his oratory skills *and* acting abilities. Tracy's first on-stage appearance came in Ripon's 1921 commencement play *The Truth*.[39] Tracy played the role of Warder. On June 23, 1921, Ripon's College Days reported:

---

[34] Davidson, *Spencer Tracy, Tragic Idol*, 23.

Larry Swindell, *Spencer Tracy* (New York: Signet/New American Library, 1971), 27.

[35] Gilpatrick, *Famous Wisconsin Film Stars*, 14.

Deschner, *The Films of Spencer Tracy*, 35.

[36] Stage acting required actors with excellent vocal quality. Louise Tracy said of her husband, "With a single line, boomed out in that strong voice of his, he could instantly command the attention of the audience" (King, *Spencer Tracy*, 12). In 1929, Warner Bros. Vitaphone Talking Pictures advertised, "At last, 'Pictures that Talk like Living People!' Vitaphone brings to you the greatest of the world's great entertainers! Screen stars! Stage stars! Opera stars! Famous Orchestras! Master musicians! You see and hear them act, talk, sing and play—like human beings in the flesh! The real, life-like talking picture" (Daniel Blum, *A New Pictorial Hisotry of the Talkies* [New York: G.P. Putnam's Sons, 1958], 9). In 1930, Tracy made two Vitaphone shorts for Warners that list his name in the credits: *Taxi Talks* and *The Hard Guy*. In *Taxi Talks*, a two-reel melodrama, he appears as a gangster who gets knifed to death by his girlfriend. The cast includes Mayo Methot (Humphrey Bogart's first wife) and Katherine Alexander. Tracy is an out-of-work married WWI vet with a hungry child in *The Hard Guy*, a one reeler also with Katharine Alexander (Kanin, *Tracy and Hepburn*, 48; Romano Tozzi, *Spencer Tracy* [New York: Pyramid, 1973], 25).

[37] Swindell, *Spencer Tracy*, 27.

[38] Davidson, *Spencer Tracy, Tragic Idol*, 23.

[39] *The Truth*, a play in four acts by Clyde Fitch, is the psychological study of a pathological liar. First performed in Cleveland, Ohio, October 1906; on Broadway, 1907; London, 1907; Broadway Revival, 1914.

The part of Warder was taken by Spencer B. Tracy of the freshman class who appeared for the first time before a Ripon audience. Mr. Tracy proved himself a consistent and unusually strong actor in this most difficult straight part. His steadiness, his reserve strength and suppressed emotion were a pleasant surprise to all.

Tracy became "enthralled with the theatre. Professor Graham provided Tracy with a list of books he should read about drama."[40] When Laurette Taylor came to Milwaukee in a touring production of her Broadway hit *Peg O' My Heart*, Tracy sat in the balcony studying her performance, impressed with her natural quality.[41]

Tracy established an alternative college drama society, Campus Players, and continued to appear in a number of Ripon plays, including *The Dregs*, as a crook. *The Dregs* was deemed unsuitable by college officials and replaced by *The Valiant*,[42] a one-act play written by Holworthy Hall and Robert Middlemass. In *The Valiant*, Tracy played the doomed convict "with surprising power and conviction."[43] Next he was cast as Philip Jordan in William Vaughn Moody's *The Great Divide*.[44] Despite

---

[40]   Davidson, *Spencer Tracy, Tragic Idol*, 24.

[41]   Andersen, *An Affair to Remember*, 98.

[42]   *The Valiant* tells the story of James Dyke, a confessed murderer who has been sentenced to die and awaits his fate on death row. The only problem is that no one knows who he really is or where he comes from, and he is determined to take his secret to the grave. The prison's warden and chaplain have nearly given up hope of discovering his true identity until the night of Dyke's execution when a strange young woman arrives requesting to see him. She may be the only key to unlocking Dyke's mysterious past. The woman leaves thinking that James is not her brother, but after she walks out, he recites lines about the Valiant. This is how we know that Dyke is her brother. He did not want to reveal his true identity so that his mother would think that her son died nobly in the war (*The Valiant*, n.d.). Also a 1929 Fox Film starring Paul Muni in his first feature-film role and Marguerite Churchill (who later appeared with Tracy in the 1931 Fox Film *Quick Millions*). Nominated for two Academy Awards.

[43]   Tozzi, *Spencer Tracy*, 15.

[44]   *The Great Divide*, a play in three acts by William Vaughn Moody, is an East-West psychological character study. *The Great Divide* originally opened on October 3, 1906, at Broadway's Princess Theatre. Henry B.

starring to more acclaim, poor grades caused him to be removed from the role.[45]

Spencer Tracy was also popular on the Ripon campus. In September 1921, he became President of West Hall/Alpha Phi Omega when the former President did not return to school. At Christmas, he appeared in the lead as the Norwegian hero Sintram[46] in *Sintram of Skagerrak*,[47] a romantic drama written by Sada Cowan and first performed on stage in 1917 at the Brooklyn Repertory Theatre, New York. He was elected to Phi Kappa Delta (Debate Honor Society), Theta Alpha Phi theatre

---

Walthall—who, like Tracy, began his career as a stage actor—appeared in a supporting role. Tracy and Walthall would later appear together in *Me and My Gal* (Fox Film Corp., 1932) and *Dante's Inferno* (Fox Film Corp., 1935). Detailed information about these Fox Films is found in *Spencer Tracy, Fox Film Actor: The Pre-Code Legacy of a Hollywood Legend* published by New England Vintage Film Society Inc., Brenda Loew, editor.

[45]   James Fisher, "A Cinemactor's Forgotten Theatrical Resume: Spencer Tracy On Stage," *New England Theatre Journal* 9 (1995): 9.

[46]   Sintram, the Norwegian hero of La Motte Fouque's romance, was the son of "Biorn of the fiery eyes" and his saintly wife, Verena. They lived in the castle of Drontheim (revised edition Cobham Brewer, n.d., 1028).

[47]   While *Sintram and His Companions* is perhaps unfamiliar to us, it was well-known and loved by the Victorians: *Little Women*'s Jo, for example, wished for the book in which it's contained *Undine and Sintram* as a Christmas present. From the first, this gothic tale is organized around a cyclical series of encounters in which the troubled Prince Sintram is harassed by two mysterious figures he eventually identifies as Death and the Devil. By the time Sintram confronts his challengers for the last time, they've already met so often they no longer hold a threat to the Prince: he has seen through all the Devil's stratagems, and the skeletal Death seems now only a not-unkind fellow traveler. Indeed, the story of Sintram is finally about how the hero manages not to defeat Death and the Devil, but how he learns to make them his "Companions" (Terri Witek, "How Robert Shaw Becomes Robert Lowell in 'For the Union Dead,'" *The Cortland Review*, Winter 2002. http://www.cortlandreview.com/features/02/12/witek.html.

fraternity, and was voted Cleverest Man and Most Talented Man on campus. He served on the 1922 All-College Prom Committee.[48]

The school's debate team traveled east (thus the name Eastern Debate Team) to debate Northwestern, Illinois Wesleyan, and Bowdoin teams. At the Bowdoin debate, Tracy was voted the Best Speaker.[49]

In the spring of 1922, after returning with the Eastern Debate Team, Tracy talked about a career as an actor. Professor Graham wrote Franklin Havers Sargent, founder of the American Academy of Dramatic Arts[50] in New York City, about a tryout. As his audition piece, Tracy rehearsed scenes from *Sintram*,[51] *The Valiant*,[52] and *The Truth*[53] as well as a personally interpreted Gettysburg Address.[54] He selected a dramatic passage from *Sintram of Skagerrak*. Sargent, who was present at the audition, immediately accepted Spencer into the Academy.[55] Tracy left Ripon.

Tracy's father paid Spencer's first semester tuition, and Tracy lived on his $30 a month pension from the government.[56] At the Academy, Tracy "studied dramatics as I'd never studied[57] anything before in my

---

[48]   Ripon College Archives, "Spencer Tracy," http://www.ripon.edu/library/ Archives/exhibits/ . . . /SpencerTracy.htm.

[49]   Ibid.

[50]   Founded in 1884, the American Academy of Dramatic Arts in New York was the first acting school in America. Students who later became successful in the motion picture industry include Cecil B. DeMille, '00; Edward G. Robinson, '13; William Powell, '13; D. W. Griffith, '15; Thelma Ritter, '22; Pat O'Brien and Spencer Tracy, '23; Agnes Moorehead and Rosalind Russell, '29; and many others.

[51]   James Fisher, *Spencer Tracy, A Bio-Bibliography* (Westport, CT: Greenwood Press, 1994), 9.

[52]   Deschner, *The Films of Spencer Tracy*, 35. Swindell, *Spencer Tracy*, 35.

[53]   Swindell, *Spencer Tracy*, 35.

[54]   Ibid.

[55]   Sargent recalled that Tracy "was manly and capable of a strong, dominating presence" (Andersen, *An Affair to Remember. The Remarkable Love Story of Katharine Hepburn and Spencer Tracy*, 100).

[56]   Deschner, *The Films of Spencer Tracy*, 35.

[57]   Charles Jehlinger was Director of Instruction for fifty years until he died in 1952. The curriculum would not have changed drastically during the 1920s (Betty Lawson, Director of External Relations, American Academy of Dramatic Art. E-mail to Brenda Loew. New York City, November 19, 2009). According to the American Academy of Dramatic

life."[58] Tracy's new friends included George Meeker, Charles Wagenheim, and Sterling Holloway. He had roles in *The Wooing of Eve*, *The Marrying of Ann Leete*, and *The Importance of Being Earnest*. Mr. and Mrs. Charles Coburn praised Tracy in a note of congratulations to

---

Arts Catalogue, 1924-1925, Academy students learned "emotion must be enough to compel the actor to give it true expression and abandon himself to its power as though he were but an instrument played upon by the spiritual forces within him; to personate a character which he cannot study at first hand the actor . . . must fall back upon imagination . . . the means of reproducing their own emotional experiences for the purpose of presenting them on stage . . . that psychological nature which exists in all of us; The Department of Life Study teaches observation and representation of people in real life . . . and teaches the students to base their art upon nature herself; the student . . . must feel these states and moods; he must surrender himself . . . until he becomes lost in his emotions and all sense of his personal limit vanishes; The criticisms of the instructor are chiefly directed against insincerity, lack of concentration and inadequacy of expression; in Vocal Expression the thought must be dominant; Characterization is the culminating study—the 'oral life study'—of motive, composition and development of human natures; the representations of the Theatre must be quite the same as the expression of life. The Truth of Life is the fundamental study of the Stage; Characterization is a search for expression of the truth of the nature represented without the interference of the personal interests and self-thought of the actor himself. The Actor's own thoughts and feelings are often quite different from those of the character to be portrayed. On the stage speech and action . . . are not essentially different from real life. The actor must have such control of his vocal and physical technique that they can always be made to serve absolutely and accurately the demands which the character exacts; the mind must be entirely freed of any prejudice, either for or against, in order that a fair understanding of what the author has endeavored to set forth can be obtained; the final result, when it reaches the audience, must be that of apparently complete spontaneity, that is, the lives of the various people in the play and their problems, conflicts, etc., must reach the audience as if they were occurring in real life then and there; The more closely we adhere to nature in our work and abstain from artifice . . . the more possible it is for us finally to reach our audience with a truthful creation. Acting is an art and no art can be obtained except by a lifetime's endeavor" (ibid., 33-41).

[58] Deschner, *The Films of Spencer Tracy*, 36.

the Academy.[59] He saw Lionel Barrymore[60] perform in *The Claw*[61] at the Broadhurst Theatre. Tracy described Barrymore's performance: "He wasn't acting at all, in the usual way. Everything he did, his little movements and gestures, was so basic and natural . . . . He was doing what Laurette Taylor did . . . just being."[62] In November 1922 Tracy made his Broadway debut at the Garrick Theatre in a bit role as a robot in Karel Capek's *R.U.R.* Fall '22 issues of Ripon's College Days reported on Tracy's success. Tracy completed his training and graduated from the Academy in March 1923.

For the next seven years, the future two-time Best Actor Oscar winner[63] performed in traveling stock companies and on Broadway as a journeyman actor. In 1930, Hollywood movie director John Ford discovered Tracy performing on Broadway in *The Last Mile* as John "Killer" Mears, Tracy's breakthrough role. Ford, who was scouting the New York stage[64] for talent, "called him 'as natural as if he didn't know a camera was there.'"[65] Ford convinced Fox Film Corporation to sign Spencer Tracy to a one-year contract for a role in Ford's picture *Up*

---

[59]   Swindell, *Spencer Tracy*, 40.

[60]   Lionel Barrymore began his stage career in the mid-1890s, appeared on Broadway in his early twenties, and also directed silent films. Barrymore returned to acting in front of the camera in 1931, winning an Academy Award for his role of an alcoholic lawyer in *A Free Soul* (1931). He appeared with Spencer Tracy in *Captains Courageous* (1937).

[61]   In November 1921 Lionel Barrymore won plaudits for his acting in a French play called *The Claw*, in which he played a politician who is ruined by a conniving woman. Critic Alexander Woollcott reported in "the Times" that the play was attended by "the most bronchial audience of the season that coughed competitively through each scene and applauded with vehemence at its conclusion" (Playbill.com).

[62]   Swindell, *Spencer Tracy*, 35.

[63]   Tracy became the first actor to win consecutive Oscars for Best Actor: in 1937 for *Captains Courageous* and in 1938 for *Boys Town*.

[64]   This was the era in which Hollywood raided Broadway in a search for new "talkie" stars. Many stage performers were signed to lucrative contracts (Tozzi, *Spencer Tracy*, 24). Those who sounded as good as they looked included Cagney, Edward G. Robinson, Claudette Colbert, Ginger Rogers, Bette Davis, Frederic March, Irene Dunne, William Powell, Paul Muni, and Barbara Stanwyck (Andersen, *An Affair to Remember, The Remarkable Love Story of Katharine Hepburn and Spencer Tracy*, 115).

[65]   King, *Spencer Tracy*, cover flap.

The River.[66] The movie was a hit, and Fox signed Tracy to a five year $350,000 contract.[67] After years of quarreling over mediocre roles, Tracy finally broke with Fox and signed with Metro Goldwyn Mayer in 1935, the studio he would remain under contract with for twenty years.

In a letter dated August 13, 1936, to Ripon College president Silas Evans, Tracy credited the theatre training he received at Ripon College for the progress of his career. He wrote, "I assure you that I am very grateful indeed for the splendid training I received at Ripon[68] and feel it is responsible for whatever progress I have made since leaving there."[69] In 1937, Tracy again credited Ripon, "Prof. Boody . . . set me on the trail which was to lead to Hollywood . . . . The idea probably never would have occurred to me . . . . I felt awkward and naturally self-conscious. But the fact that I was self-conscious made me annoyed with myself and I determined to try debating and see what it would do for me. To my surprise, I liked it. It helped me develop memory for lines that has been godsend since I started stage work, it gave me something of a stage presence and it helped me to get rid of awkwardness. Also I gradually developed the ability to speak extemporaneously, which has stood me in good stead many a time when a cue has been missed."[70]

On June 10, 1940, Dr. Silas Evans conferred upon Tracy an Honorary Doctorate in Dramatic Arts at the college's commencement exercises. In acceptance of the degree, Tracy addressed the crowd, "I owe whatever success I have had to the help and success I got at Ripon. I shall always be deeply grateful. To you of the graduating class, please bear with me.

---

[66] Tracy's salary was $1,200 a week. *Up The River* also featured Humphrey Bogart in his first movie role, the only film in which the two stars appeared together. Ford recruited Bogart away from the stage in much the same manner as he did Tracy. For a well-researched review of Tracy's performances as a Fox Film actor during the pre-Code era, read *Spencer Tracy, Fox Film Actor: The Pre-Code Legacy of a Hollywood Legend*, published by New England Vintage Film Society Inc., Brenda Loew, editor.

[67] Andersen, *An Affair to Remember, The Remarkable Love Story of Katharine Hepburn and Spencer Tracy*, 117.

[68] It is doubtful that Tracy at Ripon had real theatre courses. Most academic theatre—even as late as the 1920s—tended to be of "club" variety with little real training offered (Don Wilmeth, e-mail message to Brenda Loew, November 3, 2009).

[69] Fisher, *Spencer Tracy, A Bio-Bibliography*, 9.

[70] Spencer Tracy, "College debating team gave Spencer Tracy to the theatre; Popular movie star traces arduous climb to his first hit," D3.

When you come back, you will feel as I do. May God bless you and give you health and strength for your future work."[71] Tracy was obviously quite moved by the college's desire to honor him.[72]

In 1966, Tracy wrote a blurb for a magazine advertisement at the request of the American Academy of Dramatic Arts: "I shall always be grateful to the American Academy for what I was taught there—the value of sincerity and simplicity, unembellished and unintellectualized." That statement needs to be read and read again for its full import.[73]

Katharine Hepburn, the legendary Hollywood icon and Tracy's close friend and companion, confirmed Tracy's love for Ripon. In 1967, Ripon President Bernard Adams and Ms. Hepburn exchanged letters. In her letter dated January 8, 1968, Ms. Hepburn replied, "Your letter of November 21st touched me deeply. I have heard so much about Ripon from Spencer and I know how much his two years there meant to him and how enormously pleased he was with his doctorate."[74]

In 1977, Ripon President Bernard Adams wrote, "One of the forensic 'stars' in the early twenties was one Spencer Tracy, then a Ripon undergraduate whose photographic memory served him as well on the debate platform as it did in college dramatic productions."[75]

---

[71]   Ripon College Archives, "Spencer Tracy."

[72]   His wife, Louise, also received an honorary from Ripon in 1976 for her work in schools for the deaf.

[73]   Kanin, *Tracy and Hepburn, An Intimate Memoir*, 10.

[74]   Lee Reinsch, "Silver Screen Heart Throb Spender Tracy '24, Part of Golden Era of Movies," *Ripon Magazine*, Winter 2004, 3, Ripon College Archives.

[75]   Dr. Bernard S. Adams, "The Story of Ripon College, An Old Institution of the Highest Order," Ripon College Archives, October 24, 1977, http://www.ripon.edu/library/archives/exhibits/Adams.htm.

On March 3, 1986, close to nineteen years after his death, Tracy's friends and admirers honored him at a benefit for the American Academy of Dramatic Arts. The event marked the establishment of the Spencer Tracy Endowment Fund for Student Scholarships and featured the premiere of the documentary *The Spencer Tracy Legacy: A Tribute by Katharine Hepburn*. Hepburn, who was then seventy-six years old, "grinned mischievously" as she read Tracy's audition report from his first arrival at the Academy in 1921[76]:

> Proportions—good
> Physical Condition—very good
> Personality—sensitive but masculine
> Stage presence—good, but not technically
> Nationality—Irish Yankee
> Voice—untrained, but naturally good
> Pronunciation—fair
> Pantomime—crude but manly
> Temperament—masculine

[76] Leslie Bennetts, "Artists pay tribute to Spencer Tracy," newyorktimes.com, March 4, 1986, http://www.nytimes.com/1986/03/04/movies/artists-pay-tribute-to-spencer-tracy.html.

Act III

Spencer Tracy's Stock Company and Broadway Years

1923[77]-1930

Many call the twenties the greatest days of the American theater, and although the material Spencer Tracy worked on wasn't often memorable, he did in the space of six years work for the greatest producers—Arthur Hopkins, George M. Cohan, the Shuberts, William A. Brady, and Sam Harris, among others. Yet when he finally made his big break, it was with unknowns.

Author Larry Swindell (Swindell 1971, 65)

In those days actors playing in stock companies were doing four things simultaneously. They were *playing* a play, *forgetting* a play, *studying* a play, and *rehearsing* a play. All because each week we did a different production.

Actor Pat O'Brien[78]

Spencer Tracy: How come you'd never seen me before *The Last Mile?*

Garson Kanin: Never *seen* you? I'd never even *heard* of you.

---

[77] In 1923, in the United States, Broadway had the prestige; stock production was in its heyday . . . . Every large city had its own stock companies that traveled by bus from one town to another. The plays were mainly farces and comedies, and most were written as formula pieces geared to conventional staging and easily portable scenery . . . . Talking pictures, radio, and the Depression curtailed the life of stock theatre, yet many, including Tracy, felt that stock companies had raised the quality of American acting to levels it was never again to achieve (Swindell, *Spencer Tracy*, 45).

[78] Pat O'Brien, *The Wind at My Back: The Life and Times of Pat O'Brien* (Garden City: Doubleday & Company Inc., 1964), 61.

Spencer Tracy: You mean you didn't see me as the Ninth Robot in *R.U.R.?* Or as Holt, the Second Detective, in *A Royal Fandango?* How come you didn't come to Stamford to catch me in *The Sheepman?* And *Yellow?* I was a hit in that. Where were you? You missed *The Baby Cyclone?* And *Whispering Friends?* And those were all Broadway, buddy—big time—aside from the sensation I was in stock, in Baltimore and Trenton, and Grand Rapids and White Plains, and Providence and Cincinnati, and Lima for God's sake, Ohio. And on the road, in Chicago? And what were you doing in 1929—the year of the crash? I stayed right in style that year and did three big flops in a row: *Nigger Rich, Dread,* and *Veneer.* What do you mean, you'd never heard of me, you bastard!"[79]

On the Road

Fall 1922–Spring 1923 — Tracy is paid $10 a week for his nonspeaking part as a robot in the Theatre Guild's production of Karel Capek's science-fantasy *R.U.R., Rossum's Universal Robots.* His friend Pat O'Brien is also employed as one of the robots. During the run, Tracy gets a one-line speaking part and a $5 salary increase.[80] His salary is $42.50 a week when the show closes.[81] To pay the bills, Tracy works for months at a number of odd jobs: door-to-door salesman, piano mover, bellhop, and sparring partner at a gym.[82]

Summer 1923 — Tracy earns $20 a week in summer stock performances with the Leonard Wood Players, White Plains, New York. He has roles in *The Man Who Came Back* (two roles), *Getting Gertie's Garter* (Algy Riggs), and *Lawful Larceny.* Tracy meets another Wood Players performer Louise Treadwell. Four years older than Spencer, Louise had

---

[79] Kanin, *Tracy and Hepburn, An Intimate Memoir*, 42.

[80] Tozzi, *Spencer Tracy*, 18.
Andersen, *An Affair to Remember, The Remarkable Love Story of Katharine Hepburn and Spencer Tracy*, 102.

[81] Tracy, "College debating team gave Spencer Tracy to the theatre; Popular movie star traces arduous climb to his first hit," D3.

[82] Andersen, *An Affair to Remember, The Remarkable Love Story of Katharine Hepburn and Spencer Tracy*, 102.

already performed the lead role in a tour of *Nothing But the Truth* and as Ann Wellwyn in John Galsworthy's *The Pigeon*, a three act fantasy (Greenwich Village Theatre, February-May 1922). She played the lead in *The Man Who Came Back* and as Dotty, Seymour's wife, in the original comedy *Chains of Dew* (Provincetown Playhouse, April-May 1922). The Wood Players also travel to Fall River, Massachusetts, and Lancaster, Pennsylvania. "My pay rose to $50 a week."[83]

Fall 1923 — Tracy joins Stuart Walker's Repertory Theatre, Cincinnati, Ohio. His salary is set at $75 a week.[84] Tracy appears as Stiles in Robert Housum's *The Gypsy* [*sic*] *Trail* and as George Crooper in Booth Tarkington's *Seventeen*.[85] Spring Byington is also a member of the Company.[86] On September 12, 1923, Spencer Tracy marries Louise Treadwell between the matinee and evening performances of a play called *Buddies*.[87]

November–December 1923 — Tracy appears in small role as Holt in Broadway comedy production of Zöe Atkins original play *A Royal Fandango* starring Ethel Barrymore.[88] Tracy's salary is $75 dollars a week.[89] Edward G. Robinson also has small role. The two men become friends but never perform together again. "In 1963, Tracy suffers a heart attack, forcing him to pull out of *Cheyenne Autumn* and *The Cincinnati Kid*. Edward G. Robinson replaces him for both films."[90]

---

[83]   Tracy, "College debating team gave Spencer Tracy to the theatre; Popular movie star traces arduous climb to his first hit," D3.

[84]   Swindell, *Spencer Tracy*, 45.

[85]   *The Gipsy Trail* ran from December 1917 to March 1918 at Broadway's Plymouth Theatre. Tarkington's 1916 bestselling novel became a silent film (1916); a Broadway play starring Ruth Gordon (1918); a musical comedy (New York, 1926); a radio broadcast starring Orson Wells with the Mercury Theatre (1938); a movie with Jackie Cooper (Paramount, 1940); and a musical (New York, 1951).

[86]   Deschner, *The Films of Spencer Tracy*, 36.

[87]   Andersen, *An Affair to Remember; The Remarkable Love Story of Katharine Hepburn and Spencer Tracy*, 105.

[88]   About acting, Ms. Barrymore advised Tracy to "be yourself." She introduced Tracy to her brothers, John and Lionel, whom Tracy greatly admired (Swindell, *Spencer Tracy*, 48; Tozzi, *Spencer Tracy*, 19).

[89]   Tracy, "College debating team gave Spencer Tracy to the theatre; Popular movie star traces arduous climb to his first hit," D3.

[90]   Wikipedia Entry, "Spencer Tracy."

December 1923 — Tracy joins a stock company in Elizabeth, New Jersey. Tracy's salary increases from $20 a week to $42.50 a week.[91]

January 1924 — Tracy joins a stock company in Winnipeg, Canada. It goes out of business a short time later.

Spring 1924 — Tracy joins William. H. Wright's stock company in Pittsburgh, Pennsylvania.

Summer 1924 — W. H. Wright's stock company moves to Grand Rapids, Michigan. Tracy performs in *Page the Duke*. In June, Louise gives birth to John Ten Broeck Tracy.[92] Ten months later John is diagnosed as deaf.

Fall 1924–Winter 1925 — Under the management of W. H. Wright, Tracy joins The Montauk Players stock company at Louis F. Werba's Montauk Theatre, Brooklyn, New York. He appears in *Seven Keys to Baldpate*: "The principal role of the novelist was splendidly done by Spencer Tracy" ("7 Keys to Baldpate" Hit at Montauk, 1924); *The Bat*, a dramatic thriller; *The First Year*, an American comedy: "Spencer Tracy shone as the adoring bridegroom" (Montauk Players in "The First Year," 1924);

91 Gilpatrick, *Famous Wisconsin Film Stars*, 16.
92 Volta Voices, "IN MEMORIAM: John Ten Broeck Tracy (1924-2007),"*Alexander Graham Bell Association for the Deaf and Hard of Hearing Inc.*, 2007. http://www.highbeam.com/doc/1p3-1371792791.html.

The Breaking Point: "Spencer Tracy shines in the dual part, and skillfully handles a difficult situation which finally brings him in contact with the woman who was the cause of the shooting" (The Montauk, 1924); *A Prince There Was*, a character comedy written by George M. Cohan: "Spencer Tracy in the role of Charles Martin plays his part well" (At the Montauk, 1924); *Uncle Tom's Cabin* (Two for Uncle Tom, 1924); the leading role in David Belasco's comedy, *The Gold Diggers* by Avery Hopwood: "The Gold Diggers deals with the show girl of the present day musical comedy and gets its title from the habit of extracting money from male admirers" (In the Stocks, 1924); *Up in Mabel's Room*; *The Demi-Virgin*, a farce by Avery Hopwood: "Spencer Tracy as Wally played a principal role with more than ordinary skill" (At the Montauk, 1925); *The Cat and the Canary*; and the lead role as Lord Fancourt Babberley (Babbs) of Oxford in *Charley's Aunt*, A Farcical Comedy in Three Acts by Brandon Thomas. The Montauk Theatre Magazine Program runs an ad for coming attractions at Werba's Brooklyn—Ed Wynn in *The Grab Bag* and *Kid Boots* with Eddie Cantor.

Spring–Summer 1925 — Tracy returns to W. H. Wright's traveling stock company, The Broadway Players. Tracy plays the lead role in *Little Old New York* at The Regent Theatre, Grand Rapids, Michigan.

September–October 1925 — Tracy appears in *The Sheepman*, which closes prior to its scheduled Broadway opening.

November 1925–January 1926 — Tracy joins Frank McCoy's Trent Theatre Stock Company, Trenton, New Jersey. He appears[93] in *The Best*

---

[93]   Reviews: *Trenton Times*, Nov. 10: "Spencer Tracy assumed the title role—the same role that Mr. Cohan himself had in his original company. And Mr. Tracy was true to his part, acting with an exactness that several times brought him rounds of applause from a fair-sized, first-night audience"; *Trenton Times*, Nov. 12: "Mr. Tracy is being enthusiastically received at every performance. The part of the song and dance man is one of the most difficult to handle and required an unusually large amount of study. It is a long role and many of the speeches in it are the *longest* ever written for a part"; *Evening Times*, Dec. 8 (*The Back Slapper*): "Spencer Tracy and Ethel Remey have the leading parts, as usual, and it hurts us to see Mr. Tracy, ordinarily such a gentlemanly personage, trying to enact the part of a villain, a tyrannical husband, in the second and last acts"; Dec. 29 (*Buddies*): "Spencer Tracy, as the tongue-tied bashful 'Babe' had the audience with him from the very start, and when he finally managed to, by accident, gasp

People, George M. Cohan's *The Song and Dance Man*, *The Back Slapper*, *Shipwrecked*, *Chicken Feed*, *Buddies*, *Wedding Bells*, *Quincy Adams Sawyer*, *The Family Upstairs*.[94]

Spring–Summer 1926 — Tracy rejoins W. H. Wright Company, Grand Rapids, Michigan. Tracy is billed as "our popular leading man." He appears as Constable Michael Devlin, RNWMP, in Willard Mack's *Tiger Rose*, A Melodrama of the Great Northwest in Three Acts; as Billy Bartlett ("one of those boob parts you always roar at him in") in *Fair and Warmer*, A Farce Comedy in Three Acts by Avery Hopwood (Regent Theatre Week Commencing Monday, February 15, 1926); as Laurie in Louise May Alcott's *Little Women* (Regent Theatre Week Beginning Monday, March 7, 1926);[95] as Billy Felton, Barbara's husband in *Getting Gertie's Garter*, A Farce in Three Acts by Avery Hopwood and Wilson Collison; as Paul Brander in *The Love Child* by Henri Bataille;[96] as The Vicar in *The Servant In The House*, A Powerful Human Drama (Regent Theatre Week Commencing, Monday, March 22, 1926); as Senator Daniel Norcross in *Set Free*, A Drama in Four Acts (Regent Theatre Week Beginning Monday, August 3, 1926).

Remarking about this time in his career, Tracy is quoted as saying, "I had done more than fifty plays and a lot of guys without my talent, were making it on Broadway, while I was still stuck in the sticks."[97]

---

out a proposal to the girl he loved, they hung on his words with breathless anticipation."

[94] Deschner, *The Films of Spencer Tracy*, 36.

[95] Katharine Hepburn played Jo in the screen adaptation of *Little Women* (RKO, 1933) directed by George Cukor. The movie broke box-office records.

[96] *The Love Child*, which opened in November 1922 on Broadway at the George M. Cohan Theatre, was billed as "a story of a woman who has been tricked and cast aside by a man to whom she gave all—the man she loved . . . a frank play, without the mincing of words, a play with a daring motive, a play which ran for two years in Paris. It has a distinct sex appeal to every man and woman" (Regent Theatre Week Beginning Monday, March 7, 1926). MGM adapted the play for the silent screen and released it in September, 1928.

[97] King, *Spencer Tracy*, 14.

September 1926–January 1927 — Tracy appears on Broadway as Jimmy Wilkes, "an uncouth but genuine bank clerk, in Margaret Vernon's American melodrama in three acts, *Yellow*, a study of the perfect rotter," produced by George M. Cohan (*NY Times*, September 22, 1926). Chester Morris plays "Vall" Parker, a wastrel. Selena Royle, in the lead role, persuades Cohan to give Tracy a reading. Tracy receives eighth billing. The part is a turning point for Tracy: it introduces him to George M. Cohan, who has a great influence on his acting. Tracy later said of Cohan, "The old master taught me everything I know about underplaying[98] and timing." The admiration was mutual: Cohan remarked during a rehearsal[99] of *Yellow*, "Spencer Tracy, you're the best damned actor I ever saw."[100] "That was the day I decided to stay on the stage."[101]

---

[98]   "Underplay": to act (a role) subtly or with restraint (The Free Dictionary).

[99]   According to Damon Runyon, who was present and wrote about it. Cohan also pointed out Lynne Overman's, Grant Mitchell's, and Walter Houston's mannerisms to Tracy, "all those little touches that add up to total characterization" (Swindell, *Spencer Tracy*, 59). Years earlier, Tracy and Overman had become good friends while on the road. Tracy claimed Overman made him aware of instinct as an actor's ruling force (ibid., 50).

[100]   Davidson, *Spencer Tracy, Tragic Idol*, 40.
      King, *Spencer Tracy*, 14.
      Swindell, *Spencer Tracy*, 56.

[101]   Kanin, *Tracy and Hepburn, An Intimate Memoir*, 37.

Winter 1927 — Tracy appears in William A. Brady's Chicago production of Sidney Howard's *Ned McCobb's Daughter*. On Broadway, Edward G. Robinson and Alfred Lunt were opening night cast members (November '26-April '27). Carole Lombard was cast in the role of Jennie, a waitress and mistress, in the 1928 talkie.

April-June 1927 — Tracy rejoins the W. H. Wright stock company, Lima, Ohio. Tracy plays leading roles opposite his wife, Louise, who returns to acting. Following *Laff That Off*,[102] they appear together in *The Patsy*,[103] *The First Year*,[104] *Smilin' Through*,[105] *The Family Upstairs*,[106] *The Best People*,[107] *Chicken Feed*,[108] *The Cat and the Canary*,[109] *The Alarm Clock*,[110]

---

[102] *Laff That Off*, an original comedy play in three acts written by Don Mullally, was set in the living room of a bachelor apt occupied by three boys. It originally played at Broadway's Henry Miller Theatre: Nov. 1925-Jun. 1926.

[103] *The Patsy*, a comedy written by Barry Conners, was set in the living room of the Harrintons. Broadway opening and closing dates: Dec. 1925-Jul. 1926.

[104] *The First Year*, an original comedy in three acts by Frank Craven, was set in the Livingston Home Inn, Reading, Illinois, and Tommy's apartment. Broadway opening and closing dates: Oct. 1920-Aug. 1922.

[105] *Smilin' Through*, an original comedy fantasy by Allan Langdon Martin, was set in the Carteret Garden, Dunstable, England. Broadway opening and closing dates: Dec. 1919-May 1920.

[106] *The Family Upstairs*, a comedy in three acts written by Harry Delf, was set in the parlor of the Heller apartment. Broadway opening and closing dates: Aug. 1925-Oct. 1925. Broadway Revival 1933.

[107] *The Best People*, original comedy in three acts written by David Gray and Avery Hopwood, was set in library in home of Bronson Lenox, New York, and private dining rooms in a Broadway restaurant. Broadway opening and closing dates: Aug. 1924-Dec. 1924. Broadway Revival 1933.

[108] *Chicken Feed* or *Wages for Wives*, an original comedy in three acts by Guy Bolton, was set in Danny's living room, the Logan home, and the office of the Kester Kosy Kottage Kompany. Broadway opening and closing dates: Sept. 1923-Jan. 1924.

[109] *The Cat and the Canary*, an original melodrama in four acts by John Willard, was set in Glencliff Manor on the Hudson. Opening night cast featured Henry Hull as Paul Jones. Broadway opening and closing dates: Feb. 1922-May. 1922. Revival June 1937.

[110] *The Alarm Clock*, an original comedy in three acts by Avery Hopwood, set in a room on Bobby Brandon's house in New York City. Broadway opening and closing dates: Dec. 1923-Jan. 1924.

Applesauce,[111] and *The Whole Town's Talking.*[112] On April 12, 1927, the Lima *News* announces, "Heading the cast are Miss Louise Treadwell and Spencer Tracy, both of whom have had unlimited experience in both stock and musical comedy field."[113] Louise's return to acting proves unrewarding for both Spencer and Louise, and she retires from her acting career[114] in order to devote herself to the rearing of their son.[115]

Summer 1927 — Tracy, Pat O'Brien, Frank McHugh, and William Boyd join a Baltimore stock company[116] and open in *Tenth Avenue.*[117]

---

[111]   *Applesauce,* an original comedy in three acts by Barry Conners, was set in the Robinson home and upstairs over a drugstore. Opening night cast included Walter Connolly as Rollo Jenkins. Broadway opening and closing dates: Sept. 1925-Dec. 1925. Walter Connolly (April 8, 1887-May 28, 1940) was a successful stage actor who appeared in twenty-two Broadway productions between 1916 and 1935 and an American character actor who appeared in almost fifty films between 1914 and 1939. He had roles in two films with Tracy: *Man's Castle* (Columbia, 1933) and *Libeled Lady* (MGM, 1936) (Wikipedia, Walter Connolly).

[112]   *The Whole Town's Talking,* an original comedy by Anita Loos and John Emerson, set in the living room of the Simmons family, Toledo, Ohio. Broadway opening and closing dates: Aug. 1923-Jan. 1924. Opening night cast included Grant Mitchell who later appeared with Tracy in *20,000 Years in Sing Sing* (Warner Bros., 1932), *The Show-Off* (MGM, 1934), and *Edison, the Man* (MGM , 1940). Produced by A. H. Woods.

[113]   Deschner, *The Films of Spencer Tracy,* 39.

[114]   Deschner, *The Films of Spencer Tracy,* 39.
     King, *Spencer Tracy,* 14.
     Swindell, *Spencer Tracy,* 58.

[115]   Kanin, *Tracy and Hepburn, An Intimate Memoir,* 83.

[116]   Swindell claims *Tenth Avenue* played in Baltimore during December 1928 (Swindell, *Tracy and Hepburn, An Intimate Memoir,* 64).

[117]   O'Brien, *The Wind at My Back,* 94.
     Tozzi, *Spencer Tracy,* 21.

September 1927–Spring 1928 — Tracy appears as Gene Hurley in George M. Cohan's original Broadway farce *Baby Cyclone*,[118] at the Henry Miller Theatre. Cohan wrote the play about suburban wives battling over the same pet Pekinese dog with Tracy in mind for the lead. *Life* magazine praises Tracy's acting ease and variety and sincerity of facial expressions. The *NY Times* praises Tracy's first-rate performance. Tracy's parents see him perform three times. Tracy's father finally approves of Spencer's career.[119] The play runs for 184 days.

Spring–Fall 1928 — Tracy joins the touring company of George M. Cohan's play *Whispering Friends*, a comedy about two quarreling couples. This is Tracy's final professional association with Cohan, whose career is on the decline. Tracy's father dies of cancer during the run.

March–April 1929 — Tracy appears in the original Broadway production of *Conflict* in the role of Richard Banks, a dull clerk drafted into WWI who becomes a decorated war hero. Tracy gets the role because Clark Gable backs out. Frank McHugh, Albert Dekker, and Edward Arnold are also in the cast. Clifford Odets[120] is Tracy's understudy. *Theatre*

---

118 MGM adapted the play for the silent screen and released it in September 1928.

119 King, *Spencer Tracy*, 15.

120 Clifford Odets came to be regarded as the most gifted of the American naturalistic social-protest dramatists of the 1930s (The Free Dictionary).

magazine describes Tracy as "a standard bearer of great excellence."[121] The play runs for only thirty-seven days at the Fulton Theatre.[122]

September 1929 — Tracy appears on Broadway as Eddie Perkins in Lee Shubert's original comedy production of John McGowan's play *Nigger Rich*. The play's name means "sudden acquisition of wealth by a squanderer" but is also announced as *Parade* and *The Big Shot* before finally changed to *True Colors*. Tracy plays an ex-soldier maladjusted to civilian life and receives excellent notices. He is described as an actor "of the thermodynamic school" (*NY Times*, September 21, 1929). The play is withdrawn from production after eleven performances "due to protests from several unspecified negro societies" (*NY Times*, September 23, 1929). Tracy next appears in the Sam Harris production of *Dread*, which plays in Washington DC and Brooklyn. Tracy's character is both a war hero and a scoundrel who betrays women and eventually goes insane.[123] In the cast is Madge Evans, who, together with Grant Mitchell, later co-star with Tracy in *The Show Off* (MGM, 1934).

December 1929 — On December 3, Tracy replaces lead player Henry Hull[124] in Hugh Stanislaus Stange's Broadway production of *Veneer*, which opened 11.12.29. Tracy plays a cheap braggart who seduces then walks out on a naïve girl.[125] *Veneer* closes after thirty-one performances.[126]

Odets was later hired to write screenplays in Hollywood, where he met and married two-time Oscar-winning actress Luise Rainer. Later, Tracy (who had just won the Oscar for *Captains Courageous*) and Rainer co-starred in Director Frank Borgaze's urban melodrama *Big City* (MGM, 1937).

[121] Deschner, *The Films of Spencer Tracy*, 41.

[122] Davidson, *Spencer Tracy, Tragic Idol*, 47.

[123] Tozzi, *Spencer Tracy*, 22.
Deschner, *The Films of Spencer Tracy*, 41.

[124] Henry Hull later played Dave Morris in *Boys Town* (1938) and Bennett in *Stanley & Livingstone* (1939), two MGM films starring Spencer Tracy. Tracy won his second consecutive Academy Award Oscar for Best Actor for his *Boys Town* performance as Father Flanagan.

[125] Tozzi, *Spencer Tracy*, 22.

[126] In 1929, Tracy appeared in three flops: *Conflict*, *Nigger Rich*, and *Veneer*. The Wall Street Crash that led to the Great Depression began on Thursday, October 24, 1929.

February 13, 1930–October 1930 — Tracy appears on Broadway at the Sam H. Harris Theatre in an original tragedy *The Last Mile,*[127] as John "Killer" Mears, directed by twenty-three-year-old Chester Erskine, who later said of Tracy, "He was the best actor I'd worked with up to then—or since . . . the triumph was Tracy's."[128] Based on the true story of convict Robert Blake, who wrote down his thoughts while awaiting execution on Death Row, *The Last Mile* is far removed from the comedies and farces so popular at the start of the Great Depression. The play is an overnight success on Broadway, and Tracy, who thought this was another flop, is catapulted to stardom. The *New York Times* wrote, "Mears is a killer acted with muscular determination by Spencer Tracy and acted well."[129] The program of *The Last Mile* lists Tracy's biography on page 14:[130]

who's who in the cast

SPENCER TRACY is much better known for comedy than for the ringleader of a mutiny which he portrays in this drama. In "Yellow," "The Baby Cyclone" and "Whispering Friends" he had important roles which were all in the light vein. His two parts before that had been quite slight ones—a Robot in "R.U.R." and a reporter in "The Royal Fandango." His first heavy acting was done in "Ned McCobb's Daughter." Then, in "Conflict," he was a war hero. His top-seargeant [*sic*] in "Nigger Rich" marked a temporary return to comedy. In "Veneer," where he played the role originated by Henry Hull, Tracy offered another serious interpretation. "The Last Mile" presents him in the most intense vein he has yet attempted.

Director John Ford sees Tracy perform six times and arranges a one-picture contract for his Fox Film Corporation comedy about a prison escape, *Up the River.*[131] Tracy's salary is $1,000 a week for six

---

[127] The "last mile" is a common expression for doomed convicts on their way to the electric chair or gas chamber (Davidson, *Spencer Tracy, Tragic Idol,* 48).

[128] Kanin, *Tracy and Hepburn, An Intimate Memoir,* 43.

[129] Davidson, *Spencer Tracy, Tragic Idol,* 49.

[130] Also in the cast is Joseph Calleia as Tom D'Amoro (Cell 1). Calleia later co-starred with Spencer Tracy, Jean Harlow, and Mickey Rooney in *Riff Raff* (MGM, 1935), playing the role of a lecherous womanizer.

[131] "Panic struck Hollywood when sound was introduced. Many silent stars failed to make the transition; either they possessed too strong a foreign

weeks' work. Thomas Mitchell replaces Tracy as Mears.[132] Ford later spots Humphrey Bogart in another play and also signs him up. *Up the River* is the only film Tracy and Bogart appear together in.[133] Impressed with Tracy, Fox executives offer Tracy a multi-year contract.

November 10, 1945–January 19, 1946—Tracy returns to the Broadway stage in the leading role as Morey Vinion, a journalistic crusader and investigating GI, in Robert E. Sherwood's *The Rugged Path*—an original political drama set at the White House and in the Philippines "having to do with that esteemed liberal's first hand observation of World War II . . . an . . . always honest report on several vitally important aspects of a democracy at war." The play opens in Providence, Rhode Island, followed by Washington, Boston, and New York City. Tracy's notices are highly flattering. Business at the box office booms; however, Tracy dreads the New York critics and has mental reservations about the play. At first greatly enthusiastic, he wonders if *The Rugged Path* is the best drama for his temporary return to the legitimate theatre.[134] As it turns out, *The Rugged Path* is his final appearance on the stage.

---

accent or their voices did not record well on the primitive equipment. Melodramatic silent screen acting seemed ludicrous . . . . The Broadway stage was raided for actors who could speak lines . . . . Hollywood moguls sought to capture the entertainment dollars of the American middle class" (Ronald L. Davis, *John Ford, Hollywood's Old Master* [USA: University of Oklahoma Press, 1995], 61). When the voices of silent screen idols Vilma Banky, John Gilbert, and numerous other stars proved uncongenial to the new technology, there was a rush to sign up stage-trained actors who would be able to make a smooth adjustment to microphone technique. Often an actor with an uncertain future on Broadway and only a handful of plays under his belt found himself the object of the studios' bidding wars. Spencer Tracy, Katharine Hepburn, Humphrey Bogart, Bette Davis, Barbara Stanwyck, and Claudette Colbert were a few of the struggling stage actors who would soon find themselves pulling into Pasadena on the Super Chief . . . contemplating a brighter future (Brian Kellow, *The Bennetts: An Acting Family* [USA: The University Press of Kentucky, 2004], 115).

[132] Tozzi, *Spencer Tracy*, 26.

[133] King, *Spencer Tracy*, 17.

[134] Mantle Burns, ed., *The Best Plays of 1945-46 and the Year Book of the Drama in America* (New York: Dodd, Mead and Company, 1946), 308-309.

Curtain Call

Spencer Tracy's Legendary Naturalness: An Acting Legacy That Lives On— What They Said

Regarded for decades by his peers as the consummate film actor,[135] Tracy's natural acting style is legendary—a legacy that endures to this day. Tracy's work continues to influence actors and stir audiences . . . . His legacy to the world . . . is a legacy he would be proud to acknowledge.[136]

Spencer Tracy
In his own words

Like most of the younger stage actors I took my inspiration from the screen. To me there had always been something strained about play acting . . . . In life we are more casual, more repressed . . . . A normal conversation has few rising inflections. It is my opinion that the screen is a more natural medium of expression than the theater and that it strives harder to effect realism . . . . The screen is a more intimate art because it lets you into the confidence of players; you can almost see their minds working, hear their whispering and see their moods in their eyes—three advantages impossible to duplicate on the stage . . . . My first notices commented on the ease with which I spoke my lines. The real reason I made an impression was this: I spoke as the normal man would under similar dramatic conditions. As a result many thought I was establishing a new technique but I wasn't. I merely brought the average man to the stage; a fellow everyone understood and liked because he was real. (*Hartford Courant*, September 10, 1933)

•

I took to the stage like a duck to water.[137]

---

[135]   Leslie Bennetts, "Artists pay tribute to Spencer Tracy."

[136]   Tozzi, *Spencer Tracy*, 11.

[137]   Spencer Tracy, "College debating team gave Spencer Tracy to the theatre; Popular movie star traces arduous climb to his first hit," D3.

•

I'm Spencer Tracy with some deference to the character. When a person says he's an actor—he's a personality. The whole idea is to show your personality. There are people who are much better technically, but who cares? Nobody cares . . . . The only thing an actor has to offer a director and finally an audience is his instinct. That's all . . . . What any good actor does is crawl into the part he's playing and play it as completely as he can. He catches the character and is that character consistently.[138]

•

I've finally narrowed it down to where, when I begin a part, I say to myself, this is Spencer Tracy as a judge, or this is Spencer Tracy as a priest or as a lawyer, and let it go at that. Look, the only thing an actor has to offer a director and finally an audience is his instinct.[139]

•

When someone sees me, he knows it's Tracy. I'm not trying to become someone else. I watch David Susskind looking down his nose, talking about what acting is. I can't explain what it is. I had a wonderful teacher in George M. Cohan, and he couldn't explain it. My three years with George M., they were the most important. Cohan[140] said to me,

---

[138]   Fisher, *Spencer Tracy, A Bio-Bibliography*, 5.

[139]   Deschner, *The Films of Spencer Tracy*, 23.

[140]   Cohan, known as "the man who owned Broadway," called Tracy the finest young actor he had ever seen. John McCabe, Cohan biographer, suggested that "Tracy's acting derived essentially from Cohan." In the 1940s, Hollywood columnist Sidney Skolsky pointed to Cohan's mannerisms in Tracy's performances. Cohan had encouraged Tracy's instinctive relaxed naturalness. Tracy's natural instinct for comedy grew under Cohan's guidance (Fisher, "A Cinemactor's Forgotten Theatrical Resume: Spencer Tracy On Stage," 12). George M. Cohan considered Tracy his protégé in Tracy's early acting days. Tracy was always one of his favorite actors. Author John McCabe says, "He had even expressed his keen disappointment to Spencer Tracy over his young protégé's giving up the theatre for the artistically less rewarding world of motion pictures." Tracy had appeared in two Cohan productions appearing on Broadway—both *Yellow* with Chester Morris and *The Baby Cyclone* with Grant Mitchell (Volta Voices, "IN

"Spencer, you have to act less." (Excerpt from an interview by Jack Nugent, *Newsweek*, January 9, 1961)[141]

•

A good performance depends on the role, and what the actor brings of himself to it. And him alone. I bring Spencer Tracy to it. Nobody else can bring Spencer Tracy to it because they're not me. I'm the best Spencer Tracy in the world. If they want to give me an award for that, I've truly earned it.

•

The Last Mile was my real smash hit, and while I was in it I made tests for all the studios—Universal, MGM, Fox, Warners.[142] Nobody ever said a word—they never even called to tell me I was lousy. In those days they loaded you with makeup for a screen test. I wasn't exactly pretty, anyway, so I probably ended up looking like a gargoyle. They most likely threw the film in the ashcan, but I didn't care very much because I never thought I'd be a movie actor; I had no ambition in that direction and was perfectly happy on the stage.[143]

•

The kids keep telling me I should try this new "Method Acting" but I'm too old, I'm too tired and I'm too talented to care.[144]

MEMORIAM: John Ten Broeck Tracy [1924-2007]," *Alexander Graham Bell Association for the Deaf and Hard of Hearing Inc.*, 2007. http://www.highbeam.com/doc/1p3-1371792791.html).

[141] Deschner, *The Films of Spencer Tracy*, 31.

[142] Tracy made two shorts for Warners: as a a gangster in *Taxi Talks*, a two reel melodrama, with Mayo Methot, (Humphrey Bogart's first wife) and Katherine Alexander; and as an out of work married WWI vet with a hungry child in *The Hard Guy*, a one reeler, also with Katharine Alexander (Kanin 48)

[143] Fisher, *Spencer Tracy*, 14.

[144] The Internet Movie Database, "Biography for Spencer Tracy," http://www.imdb.com/name/nm0000075/bio.

Chester Erskine
Director
The Last Mile (1930)
Broadway play that projected Spencer Tracy to stardom

This is a true insight into his own work—Spencer did not act roles, the roles acted Spencer. His performances were part of him. They were him. "The best movie actor in the world," wrote an effusive journalist—just after Spencer Tracy had been nominated for an Academy Award for *Father of the Bride* in 1950. A lot of people, including most of his fellow actors, would agree to this. The notable exception was Spencer himself: "A good performance depends on the role, and what the actor brings of himself to it. And him alone. I bring Spencer Tracy to it. Nobody else can bring Spencer Tracy to it because they're not me. I'm the best Spencer Tracy in the world. If they want to give me an award for that, I've truly earned it." He came upon this special approach during rehearsals of *The Last Mile* in 1930, a landmark play of the time in which society's right to take the life of even a murderer was questioned. It was directed by me in a new style of realism—one that I had successfully introduced into several previous productions, a true realism born out of a world in economic depression, a world impatient with euphemism. The play is about a convicted murderer awaiting execution in the death house of an American prison, who chooses to die in violent protest rather than by passive compliance. Spencer had previously appeared in a potpourri of plays in repertory and in New York. He was a promising actor who occasionally showed flashes of true talent. I had seen a few of his performances, and was not overly impressed by him as a candidate for the lead in *The Last Mile*. I was just about to dismiss him, when something about our too brief casting interview stayed with me. Since it was getting on to dinner-time I invited him to join me at a theatrical haunt. There, in a less strained atmosphere, I was suddenly made aware as we were talking that beneath the surface, here was a man of passion, violence, sensitivity and desperation: no ordinary man, and just the man for the part.

•

On the play's opening night, I stationed myself at the back of the auditorium. I suddenly saw him, after a hesitant start, realize his power as he felt the audience drawn into the experience of the play and respond to the measure of his skill and the power of his personality. I knew that he had found himself as an actor, and I knew that he knew it. The play—and his performance—projected Tracy to permanent stardom. It was inevitable, of course, that the new realism of the theatre would pass to films, then in the transitional period from silent pictures to dialogue pictures. The film director John Ford came to New York and saw *The Last Mile*. He was fascinated by Tracy and invited him to make a picture. It turned out to be *Up the River*, a slapstick prison comedy of no quality. It was an unfortunate start for Spencer. Fox, the company to which he was under contract, typecast him in similar roles and inferior material, though his performances rose far above the banal level of the films. Eventually a respite (inspired by film critics who complained of this misuse of his talent) came in the form of several interesting pictures. In particular there was *The Power and the Glory*, a brilliant study by Preston Sturges of an industrialist's rise to power, in which Spencer came to maturity as a film actor in a role worthy of him.

John Ford
Director
Up The River (Fox Film Corporation, 1930)
The Last Hurrah (Columbia, 1958)

He directed *me* twice . . . . He was a great actor—the greatest, I guess—in my time.[145]

Humphrey Bogart
Lifelong friend
Appeared with Tracy in their feature film debuts
Up The River (Fox Film Corporation, 1930)

As far as actors go—living ones—I'd say Spence is the best by far . . . . Professionally I rate him tops . . . . Spencer *does* it, that's all. Feels it. Says it. Talks. Listens. He means what he says when he says it, and if you think that's easy, try it.[146]

---

[145] Kanin, *Tracy and Hepburn, An Intimate Memoir*, 51.
[146] Ibid.

Clark Gable
Co-starred with Tracy in
San Francisco (MGM, 1936)
Test Pilot (MGM, 1938)
Boom Town (MGM, 1940)

He mesmerizes you. Those eyes of his—and what goes on behind them.[147] The guy's good and there's nobody in this business who can touch him, so you're a fool to try.[148] Whenever I'm asked what my definition of a professional is in our business, I tell 'em to go talk to Spence.[149]

James Cagney
Member, informal group of actors
Hollywood columnist Sidney Skolsky called the Irish Mafia.
They preferred to call their group the Boy's Club.
Original Members: Spencer Tracy, Frank McHugh,
James Cagney, Pat O'Brien
Added members: Lynne Overman, Ralph Bellamy, Frank Morgan[150]

Spence? He's the most difficult son of a bitch I've ever known. And the best. Certainly the best actor.[151] He doesn't have any mannerisms of his own . . . . With him every character he plays develops his *own* mannerisms and idiosyncrasies.[152]

Joan Bennett
Co-starred with Tracy in
She Wanted a Millionaire (Fox Film Corporation, 1932)
Me and My Gal (Fox Film Corporation, 1932)
Father of the Bride (MGM, 1950)
Father's Little Dividend (MGM, 1951)

[147] Ibid.
[148] Swindell, *Spencer Tracy*, i.
[149] The Internet Movie Database.
[150] McCabe, *Cagney*, 127.
[151] Andersen, *An Affair to Remember, The Remarkable Love Story of Katharine Hepburn and Spencer Tracy*, 110.
Kanin, *Tracy and Hepburn, An Intimate Memoir*, 244.
[152] Kanin, *Tracy and Hepburn, An Intimate Memoir*, 244.

Everything he did seemed so natural and simple; he could strike the right emotional chord without straining . . . . He always came to the set with his lines letter perfect and saw no real reason to rehearse, fearing it would rob his performance of spontaneity . . . . [153] The truth of the scene occurred at the very moment he spoke.[154]

Hume Cronyn
Appeared in a supporting role with Tracy in
The Seventh Cross (MGM, 1944)

His method seemed to be as simple as it is difficult to achieve. He appeared to do nothing. He listened, he felt, he said the words without forcing anything. There were no extraneous moves. Whatever was provoked in him emotionally was seen in his eyes. He was praised for his naturalness, for being "so real" but it wasn't real. Acting never is. His was a finely honed craft.[155]

Angela Lansbury
Appeared in a supporting role with Tracy and Hepburn in
State of the Union (MGM, 1948)

His greatness as an actor had a lot to do with his own persona. He had an extraordinary understanding of the common man, which he was, and which he always played . . . . He understood the person he enacted, had a brilliant knowledge of all his reactions—and never let his own personal demons intrude on the character.[156]

Elizabeth Taylor
Co-starred with Tracy in
Father of the Bride (MGM, 1950)
Father's Little Dividend (MGM, 1951)

---

[153] Brian Kellow, *The Bennetts: An Acting Family* (USA: The University Press of Kentucky, 2004), 158, 161.

[154] Fisher, *Spencer Tracy, A Bio-Bibliography*, 16.

[155] Ibid., 40.

[156] Davidson, *Spencer Tracy, Tragic Idol*, 5.

His acting seemed almost effortless, it seemed almost as if he wasn't doing anything, and yet he was doing everything. It came so subtly out of his eyes, every muscle in his face—he was a *film* actor.[157]

Jean Simmons
Co-starred with Tracy in
The Actress (MGM, 1953)

When I was with him in *The Actress*—playing his daughter—well, I confess I'd never known anything like it . . . . All at once, he looked at me and he wasn't the star—he was my father. *My* father. And I wasn't me—I was his daughter . . . . One never quite got used to it. To him.[158]

Edward Dmytryk
Director
Broken Lance (Twentieth Century Fox, 1954)
The Mountain (Paramount, 1956)

You believe him. Audiences believe him, and *in* him. They never feel the strain of acting in him, so they can relax and enjoy it. Of course, it's all an illusion. Actually, he works as hard as anyone I know—but it's all inside. Hidden. You never see the strings.[159]

Robert Wagner
Appeared with Tracy in
The Broken Lance (Twentieth Century Fox, 1954)
The Mountain (Paramount, 1956)

He was always in character. It was always inside, this interior kind of life that he had (*The Spencer Tracy Legacy*, 1984).

---

[157]   Nick Sambides Jr., "Spencer Tracy: The Forgotten Great," *New York Times*, http://movies.nytimes.com/movie/270251.

[158]   Kanin, *Tracy and Hepburn, An Intimate Memoir*, 51.

[159]   Ibid.

Richard Widmark
Appeared in a supporting role with Tracy in
Broken Lance (Twentieth Century Fox, 1954)
Appeared in the main cast with Tracy in
Judgment at Nuremberg (MGM, 1961)

It's what every actor tries to strive for—to make it so simple, so real that anybody in the audience can say, "Oh, I could do that"—if you can ever achieve that kind of grace in acting you're on the way. And Tracy did it from the very beginning.[160]

John Sturges
Director
Bad Day at Black Rock (MGM, 1955)
The Old Man and the Sea (Warner Bros., 1958)

Tracy, very often, became the role he was playing in a film offstage as well as on not that he would be the part but the part was always within him (*The Spencer Tracy Legacy*).

Ernest Borgnine
Appeared in the main cast with Tracy in
Bad Day at Black Rock (MGM, 1955)

Like old Spencer Tracy said, "Don't forget your words and don't bump against the furniture." It's the best advice you can have.[161]

Dina Merrill
Recalled her screen debut with Tracy in
Desk Set (Twentieth Century Fox, 1957)

My very first scene was with Spence and I remember being mesmerized by his naturalness. He was the ideal screen actor—so natural that he made it seem totally spontaneous and effortless. His concentration was total—a great and meaningful lesson for a young actress.[162]

---

[160]   Nick Sambides Jr., "Spencer Tracy: The Forgotten Great," *New York Times*, http://movies.nytimes.com/movie/270251.

[161]   Simon Hayes, "Interview: Hollywood Legend Ernest Borgnine," May 7, 2009, http://www.wharf.co.uk/2009/05/interview-hollywood-legend-ern.html.

[162]   Fisher, *Spencer Tracy, A Bio-Bibliography*, 57.

Burt Reynolds
A young Burt Reynolds watched scenes being filmed
by Spencer Tracy
on the set of *Inherit the Wind* (MGM, 1961)
and later recalled Tracy's advice

"Don't let anybody catch you at it. Don't act. Just behave." He always said, "Less is more on screen. Most actors never learn how much gold is in a scene just by listening." I could never catch Tracy acting. You don't see the work. He simply is on screen (TCM).

Sir Laurence Olivier
Spencer Tracy and Laurence Olivier
share the record in the number of their nominations
for the Academy Award for Best Actor[163]

I've learned more about acting from watching Tracy than in any other way.[164] He has great truth in everything he does.[165]

Frank Sinatra
Co-starred with Tracy in
The Devil at 4 O'Clock (Columbia, 1961)
and later recalled Tracy's words of advice

Be on time, know your words and hit the chalk mark. Just react. Acting to me has always been reacting. Listen like hell all the time.[166] I don't believe people should "act." They should read lines as natural as they do in a conversation with somebody. The only thing about acting you have to know is to know your words, find your mark and be on time.[167]

[163] Wikipedia Entry, "Academy Award for Best Actor."

[164] Davidson, *Spencer Tracy, Tragic Idol*, dust jacket flap.

[165] *Celebrating Ten Years of Daily Celebrations: Spencer Tracy, Love an Idea.* http:// www.dailycelebrations.com/082200.htm.

[166] Leslie Bennetts, "Artists pay tribute to Spencer Tracy," newyorktimes. com, March 4, 1986. http://www.nytimes.com/1986/03//04/movies/artists-pay-tribute-to-spencer-tracy.html.

[167] *The Spencer Tracy Legacy: A Tribute by Katharine Hepburn*, Educational Broadcasting Corp. and Turner Entertainment Co., 1986.

Garson Kanin
In collaboration with his wife, actress Ruth Gordon, wrote the classic
Spencer Tracy/Katharine Hepburn film comedies
Adam's Rib (MGM, 1949) and *Pat and Mike* (MGM, 1952)
and the screenplay for
The Actress (MGM, 1953)
in which Tracy played Ruth Gordon's father.
Author, *Tracy and Hepburn: An Intimate Memoir* (Bantam, 1972)

Spencer was a true intellectual, but he believed that acting should be a matter of instinct rather than design. He would study his parts secretly and thoroughly and think about them, but when it came to actual performance he would let go and follow his instinct. "It's the only thing I have, really," he often said.[168] . . . It was his (George M. Cohan's) influence on Spencer's style that helped Spencer to evolve that remarkable relaxation, that seeming ease. This was, of course, an illusion. In order to achieve the effect of relaxed spontaneity, Spencer would frequently tear himself apart inside.[169]

Robert Osborne
Turner Classic Movies Prime Time Host

"The Method." Those are words which struck terror into the souls of many a Hollywood actor in the 1950s, exactly as the phrase "Talking Pictures" sobered up numerous film players in the late 1920s . . . . What was and is "the Method"? It's a process by which actors behave naturally, stripping themselves of all artifice, using their emotional memory of past experiences and feelings to create a character's motivation. (It's worth noting that the man considered one of the greatest of all screen actors, Spencer Tracy, had been giving naturalistic performances for years, using a method quite his own.)[170]

---

[168]   Kanin, *Tracy and Hepburn, An Intimate Memoir*, 10.

[169]   Ibid., 59.

[170]   Robert Osborne, "Robert Osborne on Method Acting," *Now Playing, A Viewer's Guide to Turner Classic Movies*, January 2010:3.

BIBLIOGRAPHY

Adams, Dr. Bernard S. "The Story of Ripon College, An Old Institution of the Highest Order." *Ripon College Archives*. October 24, 1977. http://www.ripon.edu/library/archives/exhibits/Adams.htm (accessed November 7, 2009).

American Academy of Dramatic Arts. *Annual Catalogue*. New York, 1924-1925.

Andersen, Christopher. *An Affair to Remember, The Remarkable Love Story of Katharine Hepburn and Spencer Tracy*. New York: Avon, 1997.

Anderson, Joan Wester. *Forever Young, The Authorized Biography of Loretta Young*. Allen, TX: Thomas More Publishing, 2000.

Arliss, George. Introduction. In *The Illusion of the First Time in Acting*, by William H. Gillette. New York: Dramatic Museum of Columbia University, 1915.

Bennetts, Leslie. "Artists pay tribute to Spencer Tracy." newyorktimes.com. March 4, 1986. http://www.nytimes.com/1986/03/04/movies/artists-pay-tribute-to-spencer-tracy.html (accessed Jan. 23, 2010).

Blum, Daniel. *A New Pictorial History of the Talkies*. New York: G. P. Putnam's Sons, 1958.

Cagney, James. *Cagney by Cagney*. New York: Doubleday & Company, 1976.

Celebrating Ten Years of Daily Celebrations: Spencer Tracy, Love an Idea. http://www.dailycelebrations.com/081100.htm (accessed November 22, 2009).

Champlin, Charles. "Hepburn & Tracy." *The Milwaukee Journal Sentinel*, July 3, 2003.

Davidson, Bill. *Spencer Tracy, Tragic Idol*. New York: E. P. Dutton, 1987.

Davis, Ronald L. *John Ford, Hollywood's Old Master*. University of Oklahoma Press, 1995.

Deschner, Donald. *The Films of Spencer Tracy*. New York: Cadillac Publishing Co. Inc., 1968.

ECONOMICexpert.com. "Topics: Naturalism [article about the theatrical movement]." www.economicexpert.com. http://www.economicexpert.com/a/Naturalism.html (accessed November 16, 2009).

Erskine, Chester. *Spencer Tracy, The Face of Integrity—Biography*. http://www.leninimports.com/spencer_tracy.html (accessed November 21, 2009).

Eyman, Scott. *The Speed of Sound: Hollywood and the Talkie Revolution, 1926-1930*. New York: Simon and Schuster, 1997.

Fisher, James. "A Cinemactor's Forgotten Theatrical Resume: Spencer Tracy On Stage." *New England Theatre Journal*, vol. 6, 1995.

_____. *Spencer Tracy, A Bio-Bibliography*. Westport, CT: Greenwood Press, 1994.

Gillette, William. *The Illusion of the First Time in Acting*. New York: Dramatic Museum of Columbia University, 1915.

Gilpatrick, Kristin. *Famous Wisconsin Film Stars*. Oregon, WI: Badger Books Inc., 2002.

Grobel, Laurence. *The Houstons*. New York: Avon Books, 1989.

Hall, Holworthy, and Robert Middlemass. "The Valiant." http://en.wikipedia.org/wiki/The_Valiant_(play)#Summary   (accessed November 9, 2009).

Hartford Courant. "Spencer Tracy says screen has helped his art—He learned 'naturalness' while on stage from studying films." Sep. 10, 1933:D3.

Hayes, Simon. "Interview: Hollywood Legend Ernest Borgnine." May 7, 2009. http://www.wharf.co.uk/2009/05/interview-hollywood-legend-ern.html (accessed November 20, 2009).

Highbeam Research. "Spencer Tracy. Archive Photos." 1996. http://www.highbeam.com (accessed November 11, 2009).

Kanin, Garson. *Tracy and Hepburn, An Intimate Memoir*. New York: Bantam Books Inc., 1972.

Kellow, Brian. *The Bennetts: An Acting Family*. The University Press of Kentucky, 2004.

King, Alison. *Spencer Tracy*. New York: Crescent Books, 1992.

Lawson, Betty, Director of External Relations, American Academy of Dramatic Art. *E-mail to Brenda Loew*. New York City, November 19, 2009.

Mantle, Burns, ed. *The Best Plays of 1945-46 and the Year Book of the Drama in America*. New York: Dodd, Mead and Company, 1946.

Matthews, Brander. Notes. *The Illusion of the First Time in Acting*, by William H. Gillette. New York: Dramatic Museum of Columbia University, 1915.

McArthur, Benjamin. *Actors and American Culture, 1880-1920*. Philadelphia: Temple University Press, 1984.

McCabe, John. *Cagney*. New York: Carroll & Graf, 1999.

Metro Goldwyn Mayer. "Frank Capra's State of the Union." *Life Magazine*, April 19, 1948:56.

New England Vintage Film Society Inc. Edited by Brenda Loew. *Spencer Tracy, Fox Film Actor: The Pre-Code Legacy of a Hollywood Legend*. Bloomington, IN: Xlibris Corporation, 2009.

Nochimson, Martha. "Chapter 5 Katharine Hepburn and Spencer Tracy." In *Screen Couple Chemistry: The Power of 2*, 184-233. Austin TX: University of Texas Press, 2002.

Nolan, Martin F. "No one has replaced Spencer Tracy as the master of believability. The actor's actor." *Boston Globe*, April 5, 2000.

O'Brien, Pat. *The Wind at My Back: The Life and Times of Pat O'Brien*. Garden City: Doubleday & Company Inc., 1964.

Osborne, Robert. "Robert Osborne on Method Acting." *Now Playing, A Viewer's Guide to Turner Classic Movies*, Jan. 2010:3.

Playbill.com. "Reference: At This Theatre Broadhurst Theatre (Broadway)." http://www.playbill.com/reference/theatre_info/2156.html (accessed November 11, 2009).

"Pre-MGM Spencer Tracy." *Films in Review*, Nov./Dec. 1995: 2-23.

Regent Theatre. *Playbill*. Week Commencing Monday, February 15, 1926.

Regent Theatre. *Playbill*. Week Beginning Monday, March 7, 1926.

_____. *Playbill*. Week Commencing Monday, March 22, 1926.

_____. *Playbill*. Week Beginning Monday, August 3, 1926.

Reinsch, Lee. "Silver Screen Heart Throb Spencer Tracy '24, Part of Golden Era of Movies." *Ripon Magazine*, Winter 2004: 1-11.

Rev. E. Cobham Brewer, LLD. *The Reader's Handbook of Famous Names in Fiction, Allusions, References, Proverbs, Plots, Stories, and Poems*. Philadelphia: J. B. Lippincott & Company.

Riis, Johannes. "Naturalist and Classical Styles in Early Sound Film Acting." *Cinema Journal 43 No. 3*, Spring 2004: 3-17.

Ripon College Archives. "Archives > Online Exhibits > Campus Life Through the Decades > 1920s > Spencer Tracy." *Spencer Tracy*. www.ripon.edu/library/Archives/exhibits/ . . . /SpencerTracy.htm (accessed December 12, 2009).

S. D., Trav. *No Applause—Just Throw Money, or, The Book That Made Vaudeville Famous*. New York: Faber and Faber Inc., 2005.

Sambides, Nick Jr. "Spencer Tracy: The Forgotten Great." *New York Times*. http://movies.nytimes.com/movie/270251/Spencer-Tracy-The-Forgotten-Great/overview (accessed November 20, 2009).

Schatz, Thomas. *Hollywood Genres: Formulas, Filmmaking, and the Studio System*. New York: McGraw-Hill, 1981.

Sherwood, Robert E. "The Rugged Path." *The Best Plays of 1945-1946*, by Burns Mantle, editor, 308-344. New York: Dodd Mead and Company, 1969.

Swindell, Larry. *Spencer Tracy*. New York: Signet/New American Library, 1971.

TCM . *Burt Reynolds on Spencer Tracy*. http://www.youtube.com/watch?v=D4FTdempF4U (accessed November 22, 2009).

The Brooklyn Daily Eagle. "'7 Keys to Baldpate" at Montauk Theatre." Nov. 2, 1924: 2E.

_____. "'7 Keys to Baldpate' Hit at Montauk." Nov. 4, 1924: 6.

_____. "'A Prince There Was' at Montauk Theater." Dec. 7, 1924: 2E.

_____. "'The Breaking Point' Offered at Montauk." Nov. 30, 1924: 2E.

_____. "'Uncle Tom's Cabin' Comes Here Again." Dec. 16, 1924: 8.

_____. "At the Montauk." Dec. 9, 1924: 11.

_____. "At the Montauk." Jan. 13, 1925: 14.

_____. "In Mabel's Room." Jan. 6, 1925: 8.

_____. "In Stock." Jan. 11, 1925: 2E.

_____. "In Stock." Jan. 18, 1925: E3.

_____. "In the Stocks." Dec. 28, 1924: 2E.

_____. "Montauk Players in 'The First Year.'" Nov. 23, 1924: 2E.

_____. "Montauk Players in 'The First Year.'" Nov. 25, 1924: 11.

_____. "Montauk Presents 'Uncle Tom's Cabin.'" Dec. 14, 1924: 2E.

_____. "The Bat Presented at the Montauk." Nov. 9, 1924: E3.

_____. "The Gold Diggers." Dec. 30, 1924: 7.

_____. "The Montauk." Dec. 2, 1924: 14.

_____. "Two for Uncle Tom." Dec. 23, 1924: 9.

The Free Dictionary. "Adventure—Definition of adventure." The Free Online Dictionary, Thesaurus and Encyclopedia. http://www.thefreedictionary.com/Adventure (accessed Jan. 23, 2010).

_____. "Odets, Clifford." The Free Online Dictionary, Thesaurus and Encyclopedia. http://encyclopedia2.thefreedictionary.com/Odets,+Clifford (accessed November 11, 2009).

_____. "underplay—Definition of underplay." The Free Online Dictionary, Thesaurus and Encyclopedia. http://www.thefreedictionary.com/underplay (accessed November 30, 2009).

The Internet Movie Database. "Biography for Spencer Tracy." http://www.imdb.com/name/nm0000075/bio (accessed Dec. 5, 2009).

The Spencer Tracy Legacy: A Tribute by Katharine Hepburn. Educational Broadcasting Corp. and Turner Entertainment Co., 1986.

Tozzi, Romano. *Spencer Tracy*. New York: Pyramid, 1973.

Tracy, Spencer. "College debating team gave Spencer Tracy to the theatre; Popular movie star traces arduous climb to his first hit." *Hartford Courant*, Feb. 21, 1937: D3.

_____. "Spencer Tracy labels his career 'Hitch Hiking to Hollywood'; Opens own story in days when he attended 15 or 18 schools." *Hartford Courant*, Feb. 14, 1937: D1.

_____. "Ups and downs of being on top of the heap in Hollywood related by Spencer Tracy in last chapter of career story." *Hartford Courant*, Feb. 28, 1937: D5.

Volta Voices. "IN MEMORIAM: John Ten Broeck Tracy (1924-2007)." *Alexander Graham Bell Association for the Deaf and Hard of Hearing Inc.* 2007. http://www.highbeam.com/doc/1P3-1371792791.html (accessed November 26, 2009).

Wayne, Jane Ellen. *The Leading Men of MGM*. New York: Carol and Graf, 2005.

Wikipedia. "Academy Award for Best Actor." http://en.wikipedia.org/wiki/Academy_Award_for_Best_Actor (accessed Jan. 23, 2010).

_____. "Spencer Tracy." http://en.wikipedia.org/wiki/Spencer_Tracy (accessed November 12, 2009).

_____. "Wall Street Crash of 1929." http://en.wikipedia.org/wiki/Wall_Street_Crash_of_1929 (accessed November 11, 2009).

_____. "Walter Connolly." http://en.wikipedia.org/wiki/Walter_Connolly (accessed November 11, 2009).

Wilmeth, Don. E-mail to author. Nov. 3, 2009.

Witek, Terri. "How Robert Shaw Becomes Robert Lowell in 'For the Union Dead.'" *The Cortland Review*. Winter 2002. http://www.cortlandreview.com/features/02/12/witek.html (accessed September 13, 2009).

The Morgan Brothers— Ralph, Frank . . . and *Carlyle*

Valerie A. Yaros

*If you have to act, you have to act and no one can stop you . . . .
Until he quits this life, the bred in the bone actor never voluntarily
quits acting. He can't.*

—Ralph Morgan, 1933[1]

On June 19, 2010, the Hollywood Division of the Screen Actors Guild honored actress Gloria Stuart for her role in the Guild's founding years, her upcoming one hundredth birthday, and her service on its board of directors in the 1930s. Actress Frances Fisher, one of her co-stars in James Cameron's 1997 blockbuster *Titanic*, presented her with a bronze comedy/tragedy statuette named for the first president of Screen Actors Guild: Ralph Morgan. Ms. Stuart was the sole person still living who served with him on the board of directors in 1930s Hollywood.

Ralph Morgan, overshadowed in motion picture history by his brother Frank's stellar career, and so often relegated to roles as the "secret murderer" in low-budget films, remains a "star" at Screen Actors Guild. The Ralph Morgan Award keeps his name alive at the union he

---

[1] Jessie Henderson, "True Actors Can't Quit Job, Says Morgan: Law Degree and Parental Opposition Failed to Halt Career," *Ogden Standard-Examiner*, January 22, 1933.

so courageously helped found in 1933. Courage and self-sacrifice were just two hallmarks of Ralph Morgan's character.

Frank Morgan, his youngest brother, earned movie immortality when MGM's *The Wizard of Oz* took on a life of its own, becoming one of Hollywood's most enduring popular films; and *Oz* dolls, figurines, calendars, and other items were produced bearing Frank's likeness. A two-time Oscar nominee, he evolved into one of Metro-Goldwyn-Mayer's most popular character actors in the 1930s and '40s, as well as a radio star. And in 1933, a year after his arrival in Hollywood, he joined brother Ralph and stars like Eddie Cantor, Robert Montgomery, Fredric March, Adolphe Menjou, Boris Karloff, Groucho Marx, Ann Harding, Chester Morris, Ralph Bellamy, and Spencer Tracy on the Screen Actors Guild's board of directors.

When Hollywood called the Morgan brothers from Broadway—Ralph in 1931 with Frank heading west the following year—they were stage veterans in their forties. Frank, who had been a minor movie star in non-Hollywood silent films in the 1910s, had assumed a *second* motion picture career in New York: *talkies* this time. Ralph, who also had several 1910s and '20s silent films to his credit, initially came to Hollywood under contract to Fox Films, and then "freelanced," with occasional returns to the local and Broadway stage over the next twenty years—he was never able to get "the theatre" out of his blood. Both on and off screen the brothers wore signet rings by Tiffany & Co., bearing their family crest, on their right pinkie fingers—Ralph's in gold and Frank's in platinum—which can be spotted in many of their films. Frank wears his as "Professor Marvel" in *The Wizard of Oz*.[2]

Hollywood fans and journalists confused their identities for years, writing of Ralph as Frank and Frank as Ralph—which baffled the brothers. Ralph explained to writer Grace Kingsley in 1934: "When we were on the stage we didn't have any trouble about our identities being confused, but the screen does something that brings out family resemblances. Our fan mail is mixed up all the time. I'm constantly getting letters telling me how good I am in Frank's pictures and doubtless he gets letters telling him how bad he is in my pictures!"[3]

But in spite of some similar facial features, they were hardly twins. Horror film star Boris Karloff, who served with them on the Screen

---

[2]   Frank Morgan's family crest ring is now with his grandson, George Morgan Jr., in Hawaii.

[3]   Grace Kingsley, "This Mistaken Identity Gag Isn't Funny to the Morgans," *Los Angeles Times*, February 2, 1934.

Actors Guild board, recalled, "What a pair those two brothers were! As unalike in appearance and temperament as any two human beings could possibly be, but united in one thing at least . . . their devotion to the cause of their fellow actors, great or small."[4]

Ralph, born in 1883, was Frank's elder by seven years, and he climbed the theatrical ladder steadily—becoming a Broadway leading man while Frank was still playing "catch up." Frank caught up to Ralph in 1924 with the Broadway hit *The Firebrand*, and the two brothers were "neck and neck" on stage until the late 1920s, when Frank pulled ahead with a string of Broadway successes. Although Ralph headed for Hollywood first, he never regained his acting status, even as a movie contract player; and Fox failed to cast him in any light comic roles, like he had enjoyed in many stage productions. One term of Ralph's original Fox contract was that, in addition to growing a fuller mustache, he would have his teeth straightened.[5] Rather than comply, he evidently handled the problem in his own way: when smiling onscreen, he never displayed his teeth. This, combined with his deep-set serious eyes, had the unfortunate effect of making him appear sinister, or a man with something to hide. Frank's teeth needed no such cosmetic enhancements, allowing him to flash his dazzling grin in film after film.

When Ralph Morgan came to Hollywood, over a dozen years had passed since actor Warner Oland gave him his first professional role, in 1908, in Henrik Ibsen's *Love's Comedy*. How appropriate that Ralph's first Hollywood film, *Charlie Chan's Chance*, should star none other than Oland himself.[6] While Ralph commenced filming *Charlie Chan's Chance*, brother Frank was still cavorting on Broadway in the long-running musical revue *The Band Wagon* with Fred Astaire and his sister, Adele Astaire. Fred would be soon headin' to Hollywood himself, where he'd find the perfect screen partner: a blonde actress-dancer that Frank had appeared with in the talkie comedy *Queen High* in 1930: Ginger Rogers.

Ralph Morgan's early Hollywood career was mixed; and the major "prestige pictures" in which he appeared in 1932, like *Rasputin and the Empress*, with John, Ethel, and Lionel Barrymore, where he played Czar

---

4   Boris Karloff, "Oaks from Acorns," *Screen Actor*, October-November, 1960, 10.

5   Ralph Morgan Fox Films contract, 20th Century Fox legal files, University of California, Los Angeles.

6   *Charlie's Chan's Chance* is believed to be a "lost" film, but a re-creation of the production, using stills and a shooting script, is available as a DVD bonus on 20th Century Fox's *Charlie Chan Collection*, volume 3 on the disc of the film *The Black Camel*.

Nicholas II, and *Strange Interlude*, reprising his stage role as "Charlie Marsden," with Norma Shearer, Clark Gable, and Alexander Kirkland, were made on loan-out to MGM. He was also cast that year as a Chinese character in MGM's *The Son-Daughter*, again with Warner Oland. The Fox publicity department made sure Ralph gave press interviews, posed for "photo ops," often with his pretty actress-daughter Claudia, and he played a mix of lead and supporting roles for his home studio in 1932 and 1933: a kindly doctor in *Humanity*, a magician in *Trick for Trick*, a wealthy despicable faithless husband in *Walls of Gold*, another Chinese character in *Shanghai Madness* with Spencer Tracy, and Tracy's friend "Henry" in *The Power and the Glory*. On loan to Warner Bros., Ralph's role in *The Kennel Murder Case* set the tone for so many future portrayals as he is revealed as the killer sought by William Powell. But a "breakthrough role" was never to be his. And his involvement as a Screen Actors Guild leader starting in 1933 was, if anything, an impediment to furthering his Hollywood success.

In January 1934, *Photoplay* writer Judith Stone noted the contrast between the brothers' careers to date, remarking that the "tables have been turned" on them: "Frank, who played small bits on the stage while his brother was matinee idol of Broadway, has been getting the fat, juicy roles onscreen. And Ralph, the stage success, has had many ineffectual and rather unimportant parts. Frank, you will remember, was handed one conspicuously plump role after another: With Lupe Velez in *The Half-Naked Truth*. With Alice Brady in *Broadway to Hollywood*. With Jean Harlow in *Bombshell*. The role of the philandering publisher, with Ann Harding and Myrna Loy in *When Ladies Meet*. On the other hand, Ralph's parts have not been strong—even when the film was important. Take, for example, the sad-faced ineffectual Czar in *Rasputin and the Empress*, and the pathetic Uncle Charlie in *Strange Interlude*. Fortunately, Ralph's Hollywood breaks are getting better—with his stronger roles in *The Power and the Glory* and *7 Lives Were Changed*."[7]

Ralph's "breaks" did little for him: Fox released *Seven Lives Were Changed* as *Orient Express*, starring Heather Angel and Norman Foster, but Ralph's role as Dr. Richard Czinner did nothing to advance him. After the early 1930s—with few exceptions like *The Magnificent Obsession*, *Anthony Adverse*, and *Mannequin*—he would be largely relegated to "B" pictures and low-budget independent productions and serials. By late 1934, no longer under contract to Fox, Ralph accepted roles from

---

[7]   Judith Stone, "A Pair of Wuppermanns," *Photoplay*, January 1934, 106.

"Poverty Row" studios Monogram, and Mascot Pictures—which Frank *never* would have or needed to do.

In the fall of 1936, not yet "typed" as a *villain*, but frustrated with his roles to date, Ralph admitted to *Movie Classic* interviewer Clark Warren (who had seen Ralph perform on the New York stage for seven years in a row) that he felt he was "futilely trying to defend myself against Hollywood casting directors who insist on 'typeing' [*sic*] me from their own ideas of what roles I should play . . . . 'Typeing' is an evil in pictures. And, it has ruined many an otherwise promising career." Mr. Warren noted, "It has been a strange quirk of fate that Frank Morgan, who gained his fame on the stage as an actor of straight dramatic parts should become one of the really few genuine comedians in pictures. And that Ralph Morgan, who was famed for his comedy ability on the stage, should be 'typed' in pictures as a straight dramatic actor. Ever since Frank Morgan burst forth before a delighted public with that marvelously droll performance of the Duke in *The Affairs of Cellini* [which would bring his first Oscar nomination] he has been called upon time and time again to play the same sort of amusing character." By the same token, ever since Ralph Morgan recreated his original stage role of 'Uncle Charley' [*sic*] in *Strange Interlude* and contributed that splendid characterization of the Czar Nicholas in *Rasputin* with the three Barrymores—John, Lionel, and Ethel—he has been doomed by the picturepickers to play sad, gentle oldsters with the same charming, wistful appeal of your favorite dear old college professor." Warren closed his article with a prediction that came half-true: "I am likewise sure that he would be a happier actor if the movie moguls would let him be a comedian or a villain, occasionally."[8]

In 1936, young actress Kay Linaker, with a handful of film credits, was cast as Ralph's wife in a small Fox picture, *Crack Up*, with Peter Lorre. Amazed that Ralph sustained a positive attitude while acting in films that most would consider a "comedown" from productions like *Rasputin and the Empress*, she asked him to explain. Ralph told the young actress that "everything that is offered to you—no matter what walk of life you're in—is a gift from the 'giver of gifts.' Now, the 'giver of gifts' is any force that you believe is the controlling force . . . . You are given a gift of every opportunity to earn a living, or further your career in any way that you want to, *whatever* you're doing. Now, don't worry about 'why' you were given this. You're given this opportunity so that either you can *learn* something, you can help someone *else* learn something, you can have a revelation of what is supposed to happen in other areas

8   Clark Warren, "The House of Morgan," *Movie Classic*, October 1936, 21-21, 58.

than in the work area. But it is a *gift*. And if you don't follow that gift, and do the very, very best that you can—not bothering to ask questions *why*—just do the very best job that you can . . . . Pretty soon the giver of gifts is going to get sick and tired of offering things, and it will *stop*."[9]

The "giver of gifts" heaped few material riches on Ralph. But it provided a reliable steady income for himself and his wife in competitive, fickle Hollywood, and that was fine with him.

In the 1930s and '40s, Hollywood richly rewarded gregarious Frank Morgan, who would shine in support of stars at Hollywood's most glamorous studio—Metro-Goldwyn-Mayer—in productions like

9   Kay Linaker (1913-2008), in telephone conversation with the author, May 13, 2001. In 1945, she married Howard Phillips and, as Kate Phillips, co-wrote the screenplay for *The Blob* (1958) starring Steve McQueen. Linaker made three films with Ralph Morgan: *Crack Up* (1936), *The Outer Gate* (1937), and *Close Call for Ellery Queen* (1942). In 1956, she attended Ralph's funeral at the "Little Church Around the Corner," in New York.

Naughty Marietta (1935) with Jeanette MacDonald and Nelson Eddy; *The Great Ziegfeld* (1936) with William Powell; *The Last of Mrs. Cheyney* (1937) with his fellow Screen Actors Guild officers Robert Montgomery, Joan Crawford, and Franchot Tone; Jean Harlow's final film *Saratoga* (1937) with Clark Gable; *Rosalie* (which Frank played on Broadway) with Nelson Eddy and Eleanor Powell (1937); *Sweethearts* (1938), another MacDonald-Eddy production; *The Wizard of Oz* (1939); *The Shop Around the Corner* (1940) with James Stewart and Margaret Sullavan; *The Broadway Melody of 1940* with Fred Astaire and Eleanor Powell; and dramas like *The Mortal Storm* (1940), again with James Stewart; *Tortilla Flat* (1940), with his pal Spencer Tracy, John Garfield, and Hedy Lamarr for which he'd receive his second Oscar nomination; *The Human Comedy* (1943) with Mickey Rooney, plus *Casanova Brown* with Gary Cooper; and *The Three Musketeers* (1948) with Lana Turner and Gene Kelly.

These two hard-working actors never "retired," but performed until illness or death ended their work. As they began their theatrical careers in the early years of the twentieth century, however, the "Morgan brothers" were on their way not as "character actors" but as stage juveniles and young leading men—slender, handsome, clean-shaven—and unbeknownst to most Hollywood fans, there had been *three* of them.

Yes—three. Fate granted Ralph and Frank Morgan long careers on stage, screen, and even radio; but Fate was not kind to the third actor-brother, of whom few ever heard—*Carlyle* Morgan—his life cut short in 1919 by a bullet through the brain in Germany in the aftermath of the Great War, a tale mysterious and dramatic enough for any motion picture.

In "real life," they were not "Morgans" at all but Wuppermanns: Raphael, Carlos, and Francis—three of eleven children of Spanish, German, and English ancestry born to George and Josephine Hancox Wuppermann into New York's upper-middle-class *white* Harlem.[10] Mr.

---

[10]   Three of the Wuppermann siblings died in early childhood: Zoyla Dolores (six months), George Diogratias (two years, four months), and George Herbert (seven days). All are buried at Green-Wood Cemetery, Brooklyn, New York. The eight who survived to adulthood were Elisa, Adolph Edward, Josephine, Marguerite, Zoyla, Ralph, Carlos, and Frank. The Wuppermanns' five-story Harlem brownstone, at 35 West 124th Street, just past the northwest corner of Mount Morris Park (also known as Marcus Garvey Park), no longer survives. Ralph, Carlos, and Frank were born here on, respectively, July 6, 1883; November 29, 1887; and June 1, 1890. The townhouse to which they moved in 1902, at 309 West 100th Street, and

and Mrs. Wuppermann were importers and distributors of Dr. Seigert's Angostura Bitters, and Mr. Wuppermann was also president of the R. D. Cortina Company language academy and book publishers. The Wuppermanns also counted a famous relation, via marriage: wealthy railroad baron E. H. Harriman (1848-1909). His eldest brother, John Neilson Harriman, married Mrs. Wuppermann's sister, Elizabeth Granger Hancox; and in 1870, the "Morgan" brothers' parents were joined in marriage by E. H. Harriman's father, the Reverend Orlando Harriman. Carlos and Frank were the youngest Wuppermann children, and the two brothers grew quite close.

Little Raphael's beautiful Spanish name embarrassed him, and by the time he was nine years old, in 1892, he insisted on using "Ralph."[11] As he later explained it to Hollywood journalist Grace Kingsley, "Can you imagine a bunch of kids playing baseball yelling 'Catch the ball, Raphael!'"[12] And if Ralph could unload his given name, little brother could soon discard Francis for "Frank"—and he did.

---

vacated in 1907, still stands. In 1900, while the Wuppermanns were still in Harlem, a much poorer young neighbor, Loretta Cooney, lived exactly one block to the north, on busy West 125th Street (the 1900 U.S. Census gives the address as 45-47 West 125th and the biography by Taylor's daughter, *Laurette: The Intimate biography of Laurette Taylor*, gives Fifty-Two West 125th Street). Loretta Cooney would become the legendary actress Laurette Taylor of *Peg O' My Heart* and *The Glass Menagerie*. Ralph would star with her in a drama, *The National Anthem*, in New York from January to April 1922. Edward Arnold (1890-1956, b. Gunther Schneider), who acted in the 1910s with both Ralph and Frank, moved to Harlem with his family about 1900 at Park Avenue and East 121st Street, near Mount Morris Park.

[11] Ralph's father, George Diogracia Wuppermann (son of Adolph Christian Wuppermann and Zoyla Gomez), was half-Spanish, born in Venezuela in 1838. He named Ralph after a merchant-friend, Raphael Kühner. The September 21, 1892, manifest for the ship *The City of Paris* on which the family returned to America after spending over a year abroad lists Raphael as "Ralph" Wuppermann, but mixes up the ages of the children, listing nine-year-old Ralph as seven, four-year-old Carlos as nine, and two-year-old toddler Francis (Frank) as six. Their forty-two-year-old mother, Josephine, is listed as age fifty-four.

[12] Grace Kingsley, "This Mistaken Identity Gag Isn't Funny to the Morgans," *Los Angeles Times*, February 2, 1934.

Without Ralph to blaze the theatrical trail in 1908, however, odds are excellent that Frank would never have followed his elder brother onto the "wicked" stage. Millions would have missed the delightful escape from daily cares in the Great Depression of the thirties, and World War II in the forties, laughing at Frank's film and radio performances, or be deeply moved by his surprisingly serious turns in *The Human Comedy*, *The Mortal Storm*, and *Tortilla Flat*. And of course his role as the Wizard and other characters in MGM's legendary *The Wizard of Oz*. And without Ralph, actor Kenneth Thomson would have had a tougher time in 1933 creating the Screen Actors Guild, of which Ralph became first president.

Frank would follow Ralph into the profession in early 1914, but he played *drama* as much as comedy,[13] and it would be ten years before he developed his distinctive comic "persona" and trademark chuckle, starting in 1924 with his shining comic turn as the Duke in Edwin Justus Mayer's Broadway hit *The Firebrand* (which Frank would film as *The Affairs of Cellini* in 1934).[14]

And without supportive brother Carlos, *Carlyle* Morgan, twenty-four-year-old Ralph might never have found the courage in 1908 to shed the profession of attorney that his parents had so expensively educated him, and chase his theatrical dream before it was too late to try.

There was no history of "actor folk" in the Wuppermann or Hancox ancestry, but for Papa Wuppermann, the culprit was clearly on *his* side of the family: German literary giant Johann Wolfgang von Goethe. Ah yes, Goethe *had* died in 1832—six years before Papa's birth—but it was surely the artistic Goethe blood in the Frankfurt branch of Papa's German family tree that had lured his sons astray. Bewildered Papa could only conclude: "It *must* be Goethe."[15]

---

[13] In addition to Frank Morgan's dozens of comic and dramatic roles in vaudeville and stock, half of the Broadway plays he appeared in before *The Firebrand* were dramas: *Mr. Wu* (1914), *The White Villa* (1921), *The Triumph of X* (1921), *The Dream Maker* (1921), and *The Lullaby* (1923).

[14] Frank Morgan's son, George (1916-2003), recalled the laugh's origins to the author: Frank was drinking at a New York speakeasy, probably with Edwin Justus Mayer, when something struck him as hilarious and produced a series of peculiar guffaws—"I can *use* that!" he marveled—and this style of laughter would serve him for twenty-five more years of stage, film, and radio comedy.

[15] George Morgan, in various conversations, 1999-2002, confirmed the "It must be Goethe" story. Genealogical history book: Macco, H. F. *Geschichte*

So how did three boys from a non-theatrical family get from Harlem to Broadway and, for two of them, to Hollywood?

The "acting bug" (or, if you will, the artistic "Goethe bug") bit fifteen-year-old Ralph Wuppermann at New York's Madison Square Theatre (not the Garden) in early 1899 at his first legitimate New York production: the comedy *Because She Loved Him So*, adapted from a French play by the stage's future Sherlock Holmes, William Gillette. Of course, to an upper-middle-class family like the Wuppermanns the theatre was only respectable to *attend*, not to enter as a profession.[16]

So Ralph contented himself, temporarily, with the substitute of so many young stage-struck folk: amateur theatre. Soon after *Because She Loved Him So*, teenage Ralph Wuppermann stepped onto a Harlem stage—in the parish house of the family's Holy Trinity Church—in a production for the church's Young Men's Club. The following year, on February 8, 1900, he again trod the parish house boards, as comic lead in *A Cure for the Fidgets*. *Harlem Life* magazine praised the boy's efforts: "The acting done by Mr. Wuppermann as Finnikin Fussleton, was but a repeat of his clever work of last year, and a reminder of his elder brother's [Edward] ambitious work a few years ago. Assisted by Miss [Alice H] Cole and Miss [Anna B] Arnold this young man made 'A Cure for the Fidgets' a very amusing farce . . . . A large and fashionable audience greeted each player with prolonged applause, and flowers were in abundance."[17]

Ralph must have been "over the moon." No doubt, most of the large Wuppermann clan were there applauding him, including twelve-year-old Carlos and nine-year-old Frank.[18] *Frank's* passion, in these years,

---

der Familie Wuppermann, 1911, also reveals the Goethe family connection.

[16] Grace Kingsley, "This Mistaken Identity Gag Isn't Funny to the Morgans," *Los Angeles Times*, February 2, 1934.

[17] Source for both of Ralph Wuppermann's stage performances: *Harlem Life*, February 1900. Holy Trinity Church is now St. Martin's Episcopal Church at 122nd Street and Lenox Avenue. The famous "Delany Sisters," Sadie and Bessie, of the best-selling 1993 book *Having Our Say: the Delany Sisters' First 100 Years*, attended it in later years. The Holy Trinity congregation moved north to the Inwood area of New York City, where the church records, including the Wuppermann boys' baptisms, now reside.

[18] Two plays were held at the Holy Trinity parish house that evening, and the first, *Ici on Parle Français*, featured another member of the Young Men's Club in the character part of "Victor Dubois," who would later join Ralph in the Phi Gamma Delta fraternity at Columbia: Gerald Stuart O'

however, was not acting but *singing*—he became a "boy soprano" at the family's next church, All Angels (to which they transferred after moving out of Harlem in early 1902), and fashionable St. Thomas Church. He also sang for vacationers in Allenhurst, New Jersey, where the family built a twelve-bedroom summer home on Elberon Avenue in 1901. Carlos, a bookish boy and violin player, with dark brown eyes like Papa, fancied *himself* a singer, musician, poet, and writer.

Ralph continued amateur theatricals in the springtime Varsity Shows of Columbia University, which he entered in the fall of 1900, where his slight build and flair for comedy brought him many roles. *Female* roles. None of which prepared him for the dapper, often villainous parts awaiting him in 1930s Hollywood. Encased in corsets, dresses, blonde wigs, long gloves, and high heels, handsome Ralph Wuppermann twirled, sang, and skipped across the stage of Varsity Show venues like the Carnegie Lyceum and New Jersey's Montclair Club.

By 1903, fifteen-year-old Carlos had followed Ralph to Columbia University and was soon initiated into the Omega Chapter of his elder brother's fraternity, Phi Gamma Delta. Ralph continued his girlish Varsity Show performances, and New York papers like the *Tribune* and the *Sun* responded with commentary that would have made him blush with embarrassment in distinguished later years. He was notable as "Genevieve de Vou, a Broadway Show Girl" in Roi Cooper Megrue's *Isle of Illusia* in March of 1904: "R.K. Wupperman [*sic*] . . . was feminine and girlish and sang a song called 'Queenie.'"[19] "His agile skittishness may have been equaled but certainly never surpassed by any Broadway show girl."[20]

After Ralph graduated Columbia in spring, 1904, he informed Papa that he'd chosen a profession: the theatre.

Ralph recalled Papa's displeasure: "The fact that an actor simply has to act is a lesson I learned when my father opposed my own ambition to go on the stage . . . . My father was an importer and both he and my mother entertained old-fashioned views regarding the stage as a profession. When I suggested that I'd like to be an actor, my father looked astounded and promptly put his foot down on the idea. He was a

---

Loughlin (source: play review in *Harlem Life*, February 1900). His namesake son, actor Gerald S. O'Loughlin, born in 1921, played Lt. Ed Ryker on the 1970s hit TV series, "The Rookies."

[19]   *New York Sun*, March 15, 1904.

[20]   *New York Sun*, 2nd edition, March 20, 1904.

swell dad, and when he suggested that law would be more dignified as a career I reluctantly took up a course in law at Columbia University."[21]

So dutiful Ralph Wuppermann returned to Columbia as a law major, while brother Carlos contributed poems, short stories, and plays to the University's literary magazine, the *Columbia Monthly*, of which he became managing editor at the beginning of 1906. By now, Frank was away from both the City and his brothers as a boarding student at the Pawling School where he became the hockey team's goalie.[22]

Law student Wuppermann garnered more Varsity Show reviews, such as for *The Khan of Kathan*: "The action is dislocated in a mythical island where no American girl has ever set foot, until the arrival of Joy, who set down a fairly heavy foot early in the first act, which foot belongs off stage to a young man named Raphael Kuhner Wuppermann. Joy had beautiful blond locks and a complexion that it is to be hoped will come off."[23] For his final Varsity Show role in 1906, *The Conspiritors*, the *New York Sun* reviewer observed, "Among the veterans in the feminine roles is R.K. Wupperman [*sic*] . . . who has donned skirts in several previous shows. Wupperman makes a young lady of the soubrette type, vivacious and talkative. He enjoys the reputation of being able to manipulate a cigarette in true womanly fashion, without danger to the frills and laces on his costume. His part is Madge Fairmont, a dashing young lady from the wilds of Texas, who has seen the wild life of the plains and has not forgotten it. Wupperman well portrays the dash and nonchalance of the Texas girl and is expected to make a big hit."[24] But Ralph's feminine footwear was not without hazards, as the *New York Sun* reviewer noted, "Raphael Kuhner Wupperman [*sic*] as Maude [*sic*] Fairmont from Texas found his unfamiliar high heels in his way when he did a sprinting act and turned his ankle, limping a bit through the first act. He sang 'The Windlass and the Bell Buoy' to the satisfaction of everybody, apparently."[25]

The Varsity Shows brought invaluable connections to Ralph, Carlos, and later Frank, through fellow Columbia students like future *Wizard of*

---

[21]   Jessie Henderson, "True Actors Can't Quit Job, Says Morgan: Law Degree and Parental Opposition Failed to Halt Career," *Ogden Standard-Examiner*, January 22, 1933.

[22]   Original photos of Frank at Pawling School, including on the hockey team, are at Screen Actors Guild.

[23]   *New York Tribune*, March 14, 1905.

[24]   *New York Sun*, March 11, 1906.

[25]   Ibid., March 13, 1906.

Oz screenplay contributor Edgar Allan Woolf;[26] playwright Roi Cooper Megrue, who would have multiple Broadway successes including Ralph's breakthrough play *Under Cover*; and future Hollywood film composer Roy Webb (six-time Oscar nominee) and his brother, writer-director Kenneth S. Webb, who would craft the comic operas that Frank would perform in his final years as an amateur actor.

After graduation, Ralph began his dreary law career, but his heart lay in the theatre. Ralph explained to a journalist in 1933: "After I secured my law degree I practiced law for nearly two years, but all the time I didn't want to be an attorney. When I first told my father that I just had to try to act, he lectured me severely. No argument I could advance convinced him—which shows I wasn't cut out for the law. Even two years later, when I had made good I was merely tolerated at home."[27]

In the summer of 1907, Frank was on break from the Pawling School; Carlos was completing a year of studies in Germany at the University of Leipzig; and vacationing attorney Ralph Wuppermann donned dresses again in one of his final amateur productions, the comedic *Jersey-land* at the Deal Casino north of Allenhurst, on the New Jersey shore. A *Pittsburgh Press* reviewer noted that "in the second part, Ralph Wupperman [*sic*] gave some clever impersonations of actresses."[28] So far, Ralph Wuppermann/Morgan's stage image had more in common with then up-and-coming female impersonator Julian Eltinge than he may have wished!

Fall of 1907 changed everything. In early September, Ralph's Ibsen-loving brother Carlos returned from a year in Germany at the

---

[26]   As well as *The Wizard of Oz* screenplay, writer Edgar Allan Woolf's association with Frank Morgan included the vaudeville sketch *The Last of the Quakers* (1914), with Frank's first profession role; co-authoring the book for the Broadway musical *Rock a Bye Baby* (1918) starring Frank and Louise Dresser; and the screenplay for the feature film *Broadway to Hollywood* (1933) with Frank and Alice Brady. On June 25, 1906, just after Ralph Morgan graduated from Columbia, architect Stanford White was murdered by Harry K. Thaw during the presentation of Woolf's playlet *Mamzelle Champagne*, on the Roof Garden of the White-designed Madison Square Garden. Thaw was the husband of White's former paramour, ex-artist's model, and showgirl Evelyn Nesbit.

[27]   Jessie Henderson, "True Actors Can't Quit Job, Says Morgan: Law Degree and Parental Opposition Failed to Halt Career," *Ogden Standard-Examiner*, January 22, 1933.

[28]   *Pittsburgh Press*, August 25, 1907.

University of Leipzig, fired up with enthusiasm for *socialism*, and ready to resume his studies at Columbia. [29]

The great Russian dramatic actress Alla Nazimova opened in New York at the Bijou Theatre in Norwegian playwright Henrik Ibsen's *The Master Builder* on September 22, 1907. Nazimova followed with Ibsen's *A Doll's House*, and Ralph attended many performances of both. It was a welcome break from the law office and quite possible that Carlos—that lover of Ibsen's works—accompanied him on these outings and may have suggested them himself. Ralph met Nazimova's co-star, Warner Oland, who would lift Ralph Wuppermann from the amateur ranks to the professional stage.[30]

In 1936, Ralph described the fateful 1907 meeting to an interviewer: "It wasn't long after I graduated that I was spending the twenty-five dollars a week I earned in a law office for theater tickets. Alla

---

[29]   Soon after his return to Columbia in the fall of 1907, Carlos Wuppermann befriended a fellow student who'd transferred from Rutgers and also fancied himself a lover of the drama, a writer of verse, and, for a while, a socialist: Alfred Joyce Kilmer, who went by "Joyce." In 1913, *Poetry* magazine published the poem that made Joyce Kilmer famous: *Trees*. According to the author's conversation with the late Carlos Wuppermann Cook (1920-2003), son of the Morgan brothers' sister, Zoyla, Carlos often had Kilmer over to the Wuppermann home for meals, and they both attended lectures by anarchist Emma Goldman. Kilmer also crafted a small piece of amusing verse about Carlos, reproduced in Kenton Kilmer's *Memories of My Father, Joyce Kilmer.*

[30]   Nazimova first performed her Ibsen dramas, *A Doll's House* and *Hedda Gabler*, in New York in November 1906 through April 1907, when Carlos Wuppermann had just left America for Germany. Ralph evidently did not attend these performances, but only Nazimova's Ibsen productions, with Warner Oland, *after* Carlos's September 1907 return to America. In 1915, the Bijou Theatre, where Ralph saw Nazimova, was demolished and replaced with an office building. Ralph Morgan would later tell interviewers that during this period he had also done amateur work with the "New York Comedy Club," but the author has discovered no organization by that exact name. New York had a professional "Comedy Club" of vaudeville performers, but Ralph was not yet a professional. Nor does his name appear in the extensive records of New York's Amateur Comedy Club. Donald Brian, who opened on Broadway in *The Merry Widow* on October 22, 1907, with whom Ralph would co-star in 1920 in the musical comedy *Buddies*, also recalled meeting Ralph at this time.

Nazimova . . . became so curious over seeing me in the front row of her Ibsen repertoire nearly every night, that she finally sent her manager to bring me backstage. I still think she originally thought I was crazy. And, I know my parents did. At any rate, Warner Oland happened to be visiting in her dressing room that night. A remark he made to me at that time helped me immeasurably to make the decision that was to change the course of my life. Kindly Warner said 'With your love of the theatre and your understanding, you belong in the profession.'"[31]

Warner Oland became Ralph Morgan's "angel"—casting him and acting alongside him in an Ibsen play: *Love's Comedy*, its first professional production in English on an American stage. On March 23, 1908, Ralph skipped the law office and made his *Love's Comedy* debut that afternoon at the Hudson Theatre—and he didn't have to don a dress to do it! But he did choose a new name for himself. "Wuppermann" was too distinctive, and he could not humiliate his disapproving parents by using it onstage. So although in later years he would tell journalists that he chose the name "Morgan" from a popular actor he admired, "A. E. Morgan," no such professional actor appears to have existed. Ralph was not above harmless fibbing and it is likelier that he actually chose the name from that of a fellow student a year his senior at the private Trinity School that he, Carlos, and Frank attended before college days: *Ralph Morgan*.[32]

In the spring and summer of 1908, Ralph joined the Giffen Players in Richmond, Virginia, learning the "ropes" as a stock company juvenile, and discovered that discipline and stamina, which he fortunately had in abundance, were as much a requirement as talent to survive as a stage actor. Frank, meanwhile, entered Cornell University as a business major that fall—far from the lights of Broadway.

A year after *Love's Comedy*, Ralph had his first legitimate Broadway opening night, on March 15, 1909, in *The Bachelor* at Maxine Elliott's Theatre. Old Columbia pal Roi Cooper Megrue sent him an encouraging note, declaring, "I earnestly hope tonight is the start of a real career. Go in and win."[33]

---

[31]   Clark Warren, "The House of Morgan," *Movie Classic*, October 1936, 58.

[32]   Trinity School yearbooks reveal the existence of this "Ralph Morgan" a year ahead of Ralph Wuppermann. The New York Public Library for the Performing Arts has a page from the *Love's Comedy* program, showing the stage name "Ralph Morgan." Call number: Programme MWEZ + NC 743, page 19.

[33]   Roi Cooper Megrue to Ralph Morgan. New York Public Library for the Performing Arts. Text of letter listed in card catalog under "Megrue."

Ralph was still the family's sole actor. For in 1909, Frank was studying business at Cornell, but not for much longer—he would soon return home to work for his father and elder brother, Edward. Carlos continued an artistic student year, contributing poems, stories, and plays to the *Columbia Monthly*, and at last deposited his first stage play for copyright with the Library of Congress: *Lassalle's Death*, on German socialist leader Ferdinand Lassalle, who died in a duel in 1864. Carlos was a liberal, not a "radical," yet attended lectures on modern drama given in New York by anarchist Emma Goldman, and was prominently involved with the Inter-Collegiate Socialist Society with fellow Columbia students like writer Randolph Bourne. Fluent in Spanish, Carlos also co-translated Jose Echegaray's Spanish-language play *Mariana* for Moods Publishing Company in 1909. Carlos realized the power of good plays to not only "entertain," but to influence and transform, as they had done for him. Foreign playwrights like Ibsen, Sudermann, and Maeterlinck particularly inspired him; and he realized the best plays had the power to bring "light" to another human soul. Playwriting, he felt, was his "calling."

By 1910, Carlos Wuppermann was convinced that to become a good playwright, he must also learn stagecraft as an *actor*. He was soon cast as handsome young teacher-poet "Herr Strubel" in the Columbia University Graduate Dramatic Association's production of Hermann Sudermann's 1907 one-act play *The Far-Away Princess*. The *Columbia Spectator* reviewer noted that he "gave an eloquent interpretation of the poet's fervor and brought out the pathetic element with great skill."[34]

As the summer of 1910 drew to a close, Ralph was in love—with an *actress*, who had been on the stage longer than he. He met this smiling blue-eyed blonde daughter of Norwegian immigrants, Miss Georgiana Louise Iverson, while with the James Neill Stock Company in St. Paul. She was known onstage as "Grace Arnold," but Ralph would soon learn to use her nickname: "Daisy."[35] Enhancing his joy, he was hired to portray a lawyer—"Raymond Floriot"—for a road company of Henry W. Savage's production of his Broadway success, *Madame X*. That August, Ralph

---

[34] "Old Grads on the Boards," *Columbia Spectator*, May 16, 1910. That same year, one of Carlos Wuppermann's poems, "Friendship," was included in a volume of poetry, *The Younger Choir*, along with poems by such Columbia University colleagues as Joyce Kilmer, George Cronyn, B. Russell Herts, and Shaemas O'Sheel.

[35] Two "Grace Arnolds" have screen credits: British actress Grace Arnold (1899-1979), with dozens of film and television roles, and Ralph's wife (1886-1948) with one: *The Penny Philanthropist* (1917).

kept his bride-to-be, who was still with the Neill Company in St. Paul, Minnesota, lovingly apprised of his thoughts, hopes, and worries. He wrote, "If anything should happen that they should need a 'Raymond' in the NY company They [*sic*] would more likely call me in than the man out west—altho' of course that is a very remote possibility."[36]

Ralph wrote "Grace" of the younger brothers she had yet to meet: "Both Frank and Carlos my two brothers are up at Lake Mohonk now evidently having the time of their lives—Carlos comes back at the end of this week, and Frank stays a week longer. By the way, Grace dear, I left that play of my brother's in your drawer; you will bring it home with you, won't you—I am not in any hurry for it now—Good bye Sweetheart for the present—may the beautiful angels watch over my darling and keep her always safe and happy—I send you all my love dear—as ever your Ralph."

But all was not smooth at *Madame X* rehearsals, as Ralph shared with his betrothed: "Yesterday's rehearsal was the most trying one we have had yet—all afternoon and evening—and a new man rehearsed us—well he was just a little bit to the bad with booze and he insisted upon stopping us on every line and giving us different intonations and business—I know the piece so well now that I knew half the things he told me were absolutely wrong—Talk about 'patsy lines,' well I couldn't say one line to please him—everyline [*sic*] I had was a patsy line—at last he got me so nervous and tired out that I became hysterical and when he would correct me I could only laugh at him like a silly idiot—I wasn't the only one who was in that condition—Mr. Bonelli, who plays my father—and three or four others of the principal characters felt just the same way . . . just at present we are all absolutely in the air and have no idea what we are really to do."

Ralph married Daisy in New York on September 15, 1910, in a small ceremony at the Church of the Transfiguration, known with great affection by actors as their "Little Church Around the Corner." Carlos was best man, and Daisy chose a fellow actress from the James Neill Stock Company to be her maid of honor: a Washington DC girl named

---

36   Ralph Morgan to "Grace Arnold," Screen Actors Guild. In a few months, Ralph would indeed replace the original "Raymond," William Elliott, in the NY company of *Madame X*. A dozen of Ralph's 1910 letters to "Grace" were donated to the Guild by Frances Tannehill Clark, an actress friend of Ralph and Daisy's daughter, Claudia Morgan. Mrs. Clark's half-sister, actress Myrtle Tannehill (1886-1977), appeared on Broadway with Frank Morgan and William Gillette in *The Dream Maker* (1921-22).

Edith Prescott Luckett. None of the four that afternoon could have foreseen that young Edith Luckett would become mother-in-law to an as yet unborn president of the United States: Ronald Reagan.[37] Ralph had little time to waste as he had to return to *Madame X* duties, and Carlos and their sister Josephine were to depart with their parents for an automobile tour. So Ralph asked Frank to inform Mama and Papa of the marriage—by telegram—and Frank complied with a simple message: "Have just married Daisy. Please wish us luck." But he neglected to identify *who* had married Daisy, and signed the telegram with his own name: *Frank*.[38]

Restless Frank, now twenty years old, had not yet "found himself." He found no satisfaction working for his father and brother Edward, or in his job selling advertising on the *Boston Traveler*, obtained through his brother-in-law, Clarence Nickerson Cook, who did the same work, or in any of his other "odd jobs." He decided to head west, finally landing as a ranch hand at the massive Placita Ranch in Las Vegas.

Carlos continued amateur acting in May 1911 as Prof. Ebenezer Goodly in the comedy *What Happened to Jones*, again with Columbia's Graduate Dramatic Association. On the eighth of May, Ralph opened at the Manhattan Opera House in *Madame X*'s New York company, as he had replaced the original "Raymond," William Elliott. Dorothy Donnelly, who originated the title role, continued as the star. A month later, on June 12, 1911, Ralph became a father for the first and only time, as Daisy gave birth—with great difficulty—to the little actress-to-be that they named Claudeigh Louise Wuppermann (Claudia Morgan).

1912 was productive for the Morgan/Wuppermann brothers. Carlos' first book of poetry, *Quiet Places*, published by his Irish-American friend, the fiery socialist-poet, Shaemas O'Sheel, appeared at the beginning of the year and garnered encouraging reviews in newspapers and magazines such as the *Cleveland Plain Dealer*, *Hartford Courant*, *American Review of Reviews*, *The Independent*, and even *The Nation*.[39] Frank was back in New

---

[37]   Record confirming marriage of Ralph and Daisy, with Carlos Wuppermann and Edith Luckett as witnesses, are in the archives of the Church of the Transfiguration, the "Little Church Around the Corner," New York, New York.

[38]   Grace Kingsley, "This Mistaken Identity Gag Isn't Funny to the Morgans," *Los Angeles Times*, February 2, 1934. When George Morgan read the story, he laughed until tears came to his eyes.

[39]   The unnamed subject of many of Carlos Wuppermann's *Quiet Places* poems was a beautiful Barnard College graduate, Jessie Isabelle Cochran,

York at last—acting and singing in Kenneth and Roy Webb's amateur comic opera *The Dancing Parson*. Carlos commenced rehearsing another Columbia University Graduate Dramatic Association production, *Her Big Assignment*; and on the evening of April 14, Ralph and Daisy opened in Chicago in a play, *The Glass House*, hours before the magnificent new *RMS Titanic* struck an iceberg in the frigid North Atlantic and sank the following morning.

The *New-York Tribune* reviewer gave Carlos accolades for *Her Big Assignment* in a May 17,1912, review, declaring that he "easily carried away the honors." Soon after, Ralph joined the Mary Servoss Players in Grand Rapids, Michigan, receiving an enthusiastic review for his role in George M. Cohan's *Forty-Five Minutes from Broadway* that sounds like a description of brother Frank in later years: "Ralph Morgan was capital as Kid Burns, dancing, singing and gagging with the ease of a regular musical show comedian." [40] By late fall of 1912, Ralph was again on Broadway, in the comedy-drama *The Master of the House*, with Mary Servoss, followed by the title role in a short-lived play, *A Rich Man's Son*; and at the close of the year, he accepted the leading part in a road company of Cohan's hit *Broadway Jones*.

1913 was Frank Wuppermann's final year as an amateur actor. On the sixth of March, while Ralph was touring the country in *Broadway Jones* with Edith Luckett, Frank and Carlos appeared in *Trelawny of the "Wells"* at the Plaza Hotel for the St. Christopher's League, with Carlos as Tom Wrench and Frank in a lesser role, unnamed by the *New York Times*. Two months later, Frank was acting and singing in yet another amateur Kenneth and Roy Webb comic opera, *The Forbidden City*, at Wallack's Theatre.[41] But May 28 brought Frank not another play but a future bride: Just three weeks after *The Forbidden City*, he met a bewitching blue-eyed blonde teenager, who resided in a New Jersey castle, and would become his wife: young suffragist and expert horsewoman Alma

---

with whom Carlos acted in the Columbia University Graduate Dramatic Association plays *The Far-Away Princess* and *What Happened to Jones*. At this time, Carlos also hand wrote a twenty-page love poem to her, entitled *Madonna*, which is now in possession of one of her granddaughters, Janice Lebel. Miss Cochran (1889-1975) bore a dramatic resemblance to British film actress Helena Bonham Carter (born 1966).

[40]   *Grand Rapids Press*, June 3, 1912.

[41]   *New York Times*, May 7, 1913. As with the Bijou, where Ralph saw Nazimova in 1907, Wallack's Theatre was also demolished in 1915 and replaced with an office building.

Rose Muller. It was just four days before Frank's twenty-third birthday. The occasion was the graduation dance for the all-girls Gardner School, attended by Rosamond Whiteside, the daughter of actor Walker Whiteside, a neighbor of the Wuppermanns' in Hastings-on-Hudson, New York.[42] If there's such a thing as "love at first sight," Frank had it and spent his summer courting Miss Muller who was staying in the City under the "supervision" of an aunt.

Ralph, an avid baseball fan, was cast in a baseball comedy, *The Girl and the Pennant*, co-written by the great New York Giants pitcher himself, thirty-three-year-old Christy Mathewson, which made its Broadway bow at the Lyric on October 23, 1913. Reviews were good, yet the play ran but a few weeks. However, in December 1913, Ralph and two of his *Girl and the Pennant* cast members, matinee idol William Courtenay and ingenue Lola Fisher, opened in Boston in what would become the first major "hit" of Ralph's career—a Roi Cooper Megrue comic melodrama starring Courtenay as Stephen Denby: *Under Cover*. Ralph played "Monty Vaughn," described by Megrue as "a good looking young man of twenty five or twenty six years with a slight mustache which he is continually fussing with. He is Denby's opposite—timid, high-strung, nervous, but basically not really a coward." Lola Fisher played Ralph's love interest, Nora Rutledge. December 19, 1913, was Frank's final turn as an amateur actor in *His Excellency, the Governor* for the St. Christopher's League at the Plaza Hotel.[43]

As 1914 began, nearly six years had elapsed since Ralph's professional debut—and now it was Frank's turn. Columbia alum Edgar Allan Woolf had a part for Frank in a vaudeville sketch he'd written starring Miss Hermine Shone: *The Last of the Quakers*.[44]

---

[42]   The Wuppermann family moved to Hasting-on-Hudson in late 1911 or early 1912. Their house, which they dubbed "Miramonte," still stands at 18 Calumet Avenue.

[43]   *New York Times*, December 20, 1913.

[44]   In 1939, twenty-five years after *The Last of the Quakers*, Edgar Allan Woolf would contribute to the screenplay of Frank's latest film, *The Wizard of Oz*. Numerous sources, including *Who's Who in the Theatre*, state that Frank graduated from the American Academy of Dramatic Arts in 1914, but this has not proved correct. No information originating from Frank or M-G-M ever mentions the AADA, and it was evidently another "Frank Morgan" who graduated in March 1914, while Frank Wuppermann was already in *The Last of the Quakers*. Actor Frank Grant Mills (1895-1973), later just "Grant Mills," used the professional name of "Frank Morgan" first, and

Whereas Ralph had changed his last name to avoid family embarrassment, Frank kept "Wuppermann"—almost. He shortened his surname by dropping the final *n*. He now experienced the theatrical rigors and hardships that Ralph had known for nearly six years, and he dashed off a short sweet telegram to his beloved Alma: "Have not time to eat or sleep but think of you always with love. Frank."[45] Pleasing Alma spurred Frank on; and even when he failed onstage, he wished her to know, admitting to his "Own Baby Sweetheart," that "I gave a terrible performance this afternoon—nobody knows what was the matter with me—but tonight I shall surprise them—for you have been thinking of me & you are going to write and oh! I am happy."[46] Three weeks later, on March 11, 1914, twenty-three-year-old Frank and eighteen-year-old Alma married at All Saints Episcopal Church in Hoboken, New Jersey. *Secretly*, as Ralph and Daisy had initially done in 1910, but this marriage, which would also last a lifetime, would remain secret more than six months.

Over the next few months of 1914, Frank toured the country in *The Last of the Quakers*, as Alma sailed to Europe to study art. Ralph remained in Boston in *Under Cover* where he became a "union man" for the first time—joining the one year-old Actors' Equity Association. That summer, Carlos and Rosamond Whiteside performed together in a play at Hastings-on-Hudson and her father, actor Walker Whiteside, gave Frank thrilling news. While on a *Last of the Quakers* hiatus, Frank visited Mr. Whiteside who told him the role of the teenage boy in his upcoming play, *Mr. Wu*, was his! If he came through rehearsals adequately.[47] Mere months after his debut as a professional, Frank was going to Broadway!

---

appeared in two of Roi Cooper Megrue's Broadway plays often incorrectly attributed to Frank Morgan/Wuppermann: *Under Fire* (1915) and *Under Sentence* (1916). Confirmation of this fact was through scrapbook clippings belonging to Grant Mills. Mills may also be the "Frank Morgan" credited in the 1914 production of *A Woman Killed with Kindness* at the Lyceum—also often misrepresented as Frank Morgan/Wuppermann's first professional stage appearance—but this has not yet been ascertained.

[45]   Wuppermann, Frank. Telegram to Alma Muller, January 22, 1914. Uncat ZA File Morgan. Yale Collection of American Literature, Beinecke Rare Book, and Manuscript Library, Yale University.

[46]   Ibid. Undated letter postmarked Feb. 22, 1914.

[47]   Ibid. May 25, 1914.

But by the end of July 1914, as Frank resumed touring with *The Last of the Quakers*, a storm cloud broke: Europe was at war. And Alma was in Germany.

Frank was in a panic for his young wife's safety as Americans began leaving Europe however they could. *Mr. Wu* was to open in October, but Frank's foremost thoughts were for Alma. Alma and her father, Rudolph Muller, were finally able to get passage to America on the SS *Red Cross* just two days before Frank's Broadway opening. On October 14, 1914, Frank made his Broadway debut in *Mr. Wu*, as Alma and her father were sailing back across the Atlantic. For the first time, Ralph and Frank were both on Broadway: Ralph in *Under Cover*, which had opened at the Cort Theatre in August, and Frank at Maxine Elliott's Theatre. To Frank's relief, the beloved bride he had not seen in over six months had arrived home safely, and sent him a telegram to meet her at the Knickerbocker Hotel. But Frank's joy was shattered: Alma insisted she no longer loved him and the secret marriage was over.

Desperate and determined, Frank placed a wedding announcement in the *New York Times* and was somehow able to draw the attention of the press, through the Wuppermanns' family connection to the Harrimans. He journeyed to her family's home, Muller Castle in Monticello, New York, with Carlos and their eldest brother, Edward, in tow, to plead with Alma to change her mind.[48] Reporters besieged Muller Castle for interviews, and newspapers across the country carried sensational headlines like "Bride Secretly Wed Longs for Freedom,"[49] "Eloper Prefers Convent to Hubby . . . Spurns Nephew of Mrs. Harriman,"[50] "Bride Spurns Harriman's Nephew."[51] And there were whisperings of a possible *rival* to Frank: a dark and handsome young six-feet-tall visitor to the Muller home named Norman Kaiser.[52]

Mr. Wu soon closed, and that December 1914 at the Cort Theatre, the now-unemployed and rejected Frank played Ralph's *father* in a one-act curtain raiser before *Under Cover* that Ralph co-wrote with another Columbia alum, George Cronyn, called *The Greaser*.

---

[48] Sadly, Muller Castle was demolished in June 2006.

[49] *New York Times*, November 1, 1914.

[50] *Middletown Times*, November 2, 1914

[51] *Fort Wayne News*, November 27, 1914.

[52] Norman Kaiser (1894-1956), a childhood school friend of Alma's, became famous on the silent screen as actor Norman Kerry—and a lifelong friend of Frank and Alma's. Kerry would be a pallbearer at Frank's 1949 funeral.

By February 1915, as Ralph left *Under Cover* to rehearse and tour a new comedy, *A Full House*, the third Wuppermann brother made his Broadway bow: Carlos, who had been acting professionally with a stock company in Yonkers, succeeded Ralph as "Monty Vaughn," bearing a new stage name he would not continue to use: "Carliss Wupperman." Lola Fisher continued as "Monty's love interest," Nora. And Carlos's involvement with the Intercollegiate Socialist Society paid off that month as well, when one of its founders Upton Sinclair, famous author of *The Jungle*, requested permission to reproduce Carlos's poem *Tonight* in his new anthology of social protest literature, *The Cry For Justice*—for which Jack London was writing the introduction.[53] At month's end, Carlos deposited another full-length play for copyright at the Library of Congress, *The Triumph of X*, which would be produced in New York only after his death.

In an eerie foreshadowing of his near future, several of Carlos's comic "*Under Cover* lines dealt with shooting. 'Monty Vaughn' declares: 'Gee, if I don't get shot, I'm the happiest man in the world,' and at another point, Lola Fisher's 'Nora' pleads with him: 'Don't get shot, Monty dear,' to which Carlos would have replied: 'Believe me, I'll try not to.'"[54]

Frank's luck turned around in 1915—he joined Lucille La Verne's stock company in Richmond, Virginia, then Savannah, Georgia—and Alma and he were reunited. The *Oakland Tribune* carried an interview with Alma, revealing a passionate Frank that would have been most alien to those who would only know the befuddled, white-haired middle-aged comic character actor of future years. Alma explained her return to Frank: "He made me love him. He is the greatest love-maker in

---

[53]   Permission form from Carlos Wuppermann to Upton Sinclair. Upton Sinclair papers, Lilly Library Manuscript Collections, Indiana University. Carlos's poem, *Tonight*, appeared in the book's "Out of the Depths" section and read: "TONIGHT the beautiful, chaste moon/From heaven's height/Scatters over the bridal earth/Blossoms of white; And spring's renewed glad charms unfold/Endless delight. Such mystic wonder the hushed world wears, Evil has fled Far, far away; in every heart God reigns instead . . . . Tonight a starving virgin sells Her soul for bread." *Tonight* was one of the works eliminated by the editors of Barricade Books's 1996 revised, "updated" paperback edition of *The Cry for Justice*, to which more recent material was added.

[54]   All dialogue from *Under Cover: A Melodrama in Four Acts*, by Roi Cooper Megrue.

the world. You've seen him make love on the stage? Well that's nothing. You should have seen him when he wooed me . . . . I married Frank Wupperman because I loved him. I knew it for weeks before I became his wife. I did not like his profession. My parents had taught me to look upon the stage as on another world. But I met Frank one glorious night and then it was different. There is not such another love-maker in the world. I loved Frank with all my heart, but because my mother objected I told her I did not. We parted again and finally he went to Richmond to fill a theatrical engagement. Then came the real test. I tried to stay with my parents but my love for Frank was too great. I came to him and nothing shall ever part us again." Her imposing mother, Mrs. Elizabeth Worth Muller—known as the leading suffragist of Sullivan County, New York—sternly added, "He drove us nearly to distraction with telegrams and telephone calls day and night. Alma was driven nearly crazy. Then we were threatened with a suit for alienating Alma's affections, and we made up our minds that she should take her place with her husband for a year. For that period she is dead to us."[55]

One of Frank's fellow LaVerne company players would make quite a screen career for himself in the future and become a Screen Actors Guild president as well: Edward Arnold. Arnold reminisced decades later about that 1915 season: "Frank Morgan was the only member of the cast who owned a Prince Albert coat and a top hat, with all the proper accessories for daytime occasions. So, much against his inclination, we induced Frank to don his elegant attire and saunter up and down the main street when the [Easter] service was over. Thus we hoped to give people the idea of the prosperity of the company in general and convey to all and sundry our individual gentility. Frank, a fine-looking chap, made the right impression on the throng with his attractive wife on his arm, and was recognized by many of the passers-by. Business, however, didn't improve."[56]

Shortly after Frank and Alma's return from the South, Papa George Wuppermann died at home in Hastings-on-Hudson on June 12, 1915—the fourth birthday of his granddaughter, Claudeigh (Ralph's daughter, Claudia Morgan). Nine months after Papa's death, Alma would give birth to a son whom she and Frank would name for him: *George.*

---

[55] *Oakland Tribune*, April 20, 1915.
[56] Arnold, Edward. *Lorenzo Goes to Hollywood*. New York: Liveright Publishing, 1940, 46.

As 1915 continued, Ralph debuted in his first "flicker": the film was either The *Master of the House*, which he had done on Broadway, or perhaps *The Man Trail* for Essanay. (*Moving Picture World* and other sources of the time do not list Ralph in the *Man Trail* credits, and his appearance has yet to be truly verified.) He also reprised his role of "Raymond Floriet" in the first motion picture of *Madame X*, starring the original "Madame X," Dorothy Donnelly, with whom he had acted in 1911. Frank and Carlos were hired together as actors for a road company of *A Full House* that Ralph had played on Broadway earlier that year, and in late 1915, Carlos joined Walker Whiteside's company in *The Typhoon*, which would take him all the way to the west coast before his return to New York in 1916. The Great War continued to devastate Europe, and in spare moments in the *Typhoon* tour, Carlos worked with a fellow cast member, young English actor Leonard Mudie, on a one-act play about a shell-shocked British soldier-hero. They would ironically title it *Laughing Harry*.

1916 marked multiple milestones in Frank's life: he became a father on March 16, and he also made his motion picture debut for Vitagraph in a production called *The Suspect*, with film star Anita Stewart. The writer/director/co-star was young S. Rankin Drew, who would direct Frank in a total of four films.[57] At year's end, after using "Francis Morgan" in three moving pictures, he at last became "Frank Morgan" onscreen for a Fox Films production with June Caprice: *A Modern Cinderella*, released at the start of 1917.

---

[57]   Frank would later tell journalists how he had gone to Vitagraph Studios in Brooklyn to see about obtaining film work and was mistaken for Miss Stewart's frequent co-star Earle Williams. But Frank never revealed why *Vitagraph* in the first place. The answer may lie in another Columbia University connection: Director William P. S. Earle (a Phi Gamma Delta fraternity brother of Ralph and Carlos) started work for Vitagraph a few months before Frank's visit to the studio, so it is possible that he may have extended the invitation.

Carlos Wuppermann, meanwhile, spent part of 1916 after *The Typhoon* touring in vaudeville with popular actress Henrietta Crosman in the comic one-act play *Cousin Eleanor*, playing a young father. Famous pugilist-turned-performer James J. Corbett was on the bill with them in Ohio, and Carlos wrote his sister Josephine about him—and an embarrassing stage mishap, as well: "James J. Corbett is on the bill with us this week and has the dressing-room next to mine. He comes in frequently to tell me his 'throubles' as an actor in English that was forcefully and wonderfully made in the greatest part of the emeral' isle. He is a thoroughly likable, good-hearted, gregarious sort of chap with a smile for everyone. He has a wonderful physique and is the youngest looking man of fifty I ever saw . . . . A funny thing happened last night in the performance. I am supposed to run wildly out of the house with the baby in my arms. Last night I did my usual stunt of tripping, and fell flat while the baby [a rag doll] landed on its head. Shrieks of laughter from the audience while Miss Crosman went into hysterics. Imagine what would have happened if it had been a real baby!"[58]

---

[58] Carlos Wuppermann to sister Josephine Wuppermann, handwritten letter September 1, 1916. Screen Actors Guild collection. Gift of Janie Johnson, Santa Ynez, California, 2008.

In 1917 America at last entered the Great War. As the year began, Carlos was acting in a comedy that would never make Broadway, *Stocks and Stockings*, bearing a new stage name: *Carlyle Morgan*. Perhaps in the increased anti-German climate, as America headed toward war after Germany resumed unrestricted submarine warfare and the infamous "Zimmermann telegram" was intercepted, it was safer for the German surname "Wuppermann" to depart.

Ralph was in Chicago in 1917 and starred in *Laughing Harry* by "Carlyle Morgan and Leonard Mudie," at the Actors' Fund Fair, March 9, with Edward Arnold in the cast as well. At the end of the month Guy Bates Post, and some of his *Masquerader* cast members, played *Laughing Harry* for the Actors' Fair in Boston, and the *Boston Globe* declared it the "most interesting of the one-act plays."[59] *Laughing Harry* played the Harlem Opera House in May, and the *New York Clipper* reviewer expressed that it was "excellently well-acted and well-written, but these advantages only serve to bring out the horrible result of war all the more realistically."[60] As Congress ratified the Selective Service Act—the draft—Carlos soon withdrew *Laughing Harry* from production as it was unwise to continue offering a play with so much as a hint of antiwar sentiment.

Frank and Carlos registered for the draft on June 5. Ralph by then was "over-age" until the following year, when the draft age was expanded. Frank was working for Goldwyn Studios on the film *Baby Mine*, and soothed his pre-draft board apprehension with liquor. Carlos, unemployed since the failure of *Stocks and Stockings*, gave his profession to the draft board as "actor." Two weeks later, Carlos enlisted. He joined the Bellevue Hospital Medical Corps and continued polishing his one-act play, *The Wife of a Genius*, while waiting for his training to begin. Frank began filming another motion picture: *Raffles, the Amateur Cracksman*, starring John Barrymore, who would remain Frank's friend for life.[61] *Light in Darkness*, with Frank and teenage Shirley Mason, was soon released as Frank's sixth film, and he had become a popular motion picture actor. That fall, Frank left New York for Massachusetts to join the Northampton Players.

---

59 *Boston Globe*, April 1, 1917.
60 *New York Clipper*, May 9, 1917,
61 *Raffles, the Amateur Cracksman* is available on DVD through Grapevine Video of Phoenix, Arizona.

On the chilly, windy morning of February 26, 1918, Carlos shipped out of New York for Europe with the Bellevue Medical Corps on one of the late *Titanic*'s sister ships, RMS *Olympic*. He would never return.

Carlos spent his first months overseas in Vichy, France, where the Bellevue Medical Corps became part of Base Hospital, No. 1. In addition to work as a French/English translator, stretcher-bearer unloading trains of wounded soldiers, and general hospital and office worker, he entertained hospitalized soldiers as a singer, with his "rich, baritone voice."[62] But he was restless and felt that, with so many sacrificing their lives in the war effort, he could be of greater service in another area. Carlos applied to enter counterintelligence work in the Corps of Intelligence Police on the advice of an officer who felt Carlos had three major qualifications for the potentially dangerous job: he was college educated, multilingual (German, French, and Spanish) and . . . *an actor.*[63]

Frank opened on Broadway for the first time since *Mr Wu* in 1914—this time as Frank *Morgan* in the musical comedy *Rock-a-Bye Baby*, on May 22, 1918. But Frank got shocking news in June: he learned that S. Rankin Drew, who had directed him in four films, and became an aviator in France's Lafayette Flying Corps, had died in aerial combat. In response, Carlos wrote to their mother: "I was sorry to read in yesterday's paper of Rankin Drew's death. It must have been quite a shock to Frank. He was certainly a highly gifted and likable fellow."[64]

At the end of summer 1918 Ralph was in his second Broadway stage hit—an even more successful comedy than *Under Cover*: *Lightnin'* starring Frank Bacon as "Lightnin' Bill Jones" with Ralph in a key role as yet another *attorney*, "John Marvin." By October, Carlos was a sergeant with the Corps of Intelligence Police in France, and Frank snagged a plum role as male lead in a road company of the Broadway

---

[62] The description of Carlos Wuppermann's singing voice comes from page 1 of the privately printed *Carlos Siegert Wuppermann: A Few of His Letters and Other Data, 1887-1919*, which states: "He also had a rich baritone voice to the cultivation of which he devoted much time and study." In several letters home to his mother, he mentioned singing at the hospital, as well as receiving voice tips there from an associate, American opera singer Raymond Loder.

[63] *Carlos Siegert Wuppermann: A Few of His Letters and Other Data, 1887-1919*, 28. Letter to mother, May 19, 1918, from Vichy, France.

[64] *Ibid.*, page 39. Carlos Wuppermann to mother, June 16, 1918 from Vichy, France.

drama *The Man Who Came Back*, in a part originated by Henry Hull. His co-star was film and stage actress Dorothy Bernard.[65] Carlos delightedly wrote their mother that *The Man Who Came Back* "should suit [Frank] to perfection and furnish him with an excellent opportunity to add to his growing reputation."[66]

War hostilities ceased as an armistice between Germany and the Allies was signed in France on November 11, 1918—more than four years of death and destruction over. As 1918 turned to 1919, Frank continued his success in *The Man Who Came Back*. Carlos was so proud of his little brother's work that he wrote Mama a prediction from his station with the U.S. Army of Occupation in Trier, Germany: "I am certainly delighted to hear of the success Frank has made in *The Man Who Came Back*. The hardest part of his career lies behind him now. Underneath his carefree, 'go as you please' artistic temperament he has tremendous will power and that, now that it seems to have been fully awakened, combined with his natural gifts should take him to the top of the ladder."[67] As Carlos completed the letter that March, he had just over a month to live.

At the end of May 1919, as Frank's *The Man Who Came Back* was making its way back east, Mama Josephine Wuppermann received a package from the postman that left her reeling. Ralph, who knew the Third Assistant Secretary of War Frederick Keppel, from his former tenure as Dean of Students at Columbia University, urgently telegraphed Keppel the next morning: "My Mother received Thursday morning a diary and small book of poems belonging to my brother Carlos Wuppermann. Package was sent by 1st Lieutenant Quinby Infantry Advance GHI [*sic*] AEF Tier [*sic*] Germany. Please investigate and let me know immediately. Mother in critical condition."[68] No communication from Carlos had been received in weeks, and days would pass before

---

65   At this time, Frank's *The Man Who Came Back* co-star, Dorothy Bernard, and her husband, actor A. H. Van Buren, had an eight-year-old daughter, "Midge." In 1933, Midge Van Buren would become the first employee of Screen Actors Guild.

66   *Carlos Siegert Wuppermann: A Few of His Letters and Other Data, 1887-1919*, 64. Letter to mother, October 30, 1919, from unnamed location in France.

67   *Carlos Siegert Wuppermann: A Few of His Letters and Other Data, 1887-1919*, 89. Letter to mother, March 2, 1919, from Treves (Trier), Germany.

68   May 23, 1919, telegram Ralph Morgan to Frederick Keppel. National Personnel Records Center, St. Louis, Carlos Wuppermann, army personnel file.

the Wuppermann family would have any answers. Frank was still far away, in Minnesota, with *The Man Who Came Back*.

Before his return to New York, Frank was interviewed by Marie Canel for the *Duluth News-Tribune*, who gushed over his "ravishing dimples" and declared, "If Frank Morgan goes back to the screen and is starred and is given a good director, within a short time he'll be one of the most popular movie heroes that we have with the possible exception of Eugene O'Brien and Wallace Reid. He combines all the attributes for film work—he photographs well, is attractive, understands screen work and has the ability to act." Frank was less enthusiastic about movies and explained his preference for the stage: "But really I like the legitimate best. It gives a person much better opportunities for real acting. The principal requisites for screen acting are merely ability to photograph well and to do what your director tells you—that's about all, and on the stage one has opportunities to more effectively put his own personality and ideas into the work . . . in motion pictures we have some wonderful directors, but for every really good one there are a hundred who aren't good." Frank reassured Miss Canel that he was considering two film offers after his imminent return to New York, and she was delighted, declaring, "And if he should go back to films, we know you're going to be so glad—he's so youthful and just the type of leading man every girl dreams about at some time or other in her young life."[69]

But a terrible surprise awaited Frank Morgan on his return to New York, unless he had received it beforehand: Carlos was confirmed dead—and had been since the fifteenth of April.[70]

Six weeks after learning of Carlos's death, Ralph opened in *The Five Million* at Broadway's Lyric Theatre. In a painful coincidence, his role was that of a man believed killed in the war who surprisingly returns very much alive. A month later, on August 7, 1919, Actors' Equity declared a strike, and Ralph and his fellow *Five Million* cast members walked off the show.[71] Both Ralph and Frank participated in the month-long strike

---

[69] *Duluth News-Tribune*, June 8, 1919.

[70] In a letter from Carlos's sister Josephine Wright Wuppermann to Carlos's friend, jailed conscientious objector Roderick Seidenberg at U.S. Disciplinary Barracks, Fort Douglas, Utah, January 20, 1920, Josephine tells him the family was "unofficially" told he was dead on May 31, 1919. Roderick Seidenberg and Mabel Dwight Collection, University of Baltimore.

[71] Two of the *Five Million* cast members were James Gleason and his wife, Lucile Webster Gleason, who would join Ralph on the first board of directors of Screen Actors Guild in 1933.

activities, and in 1920, Ralph was elected to the Council of the Actors' Equity Association—the first step on his path to creating the Screen Actors Guild.

Josephine Wuppermann, their mother, hired a private investigator to try to uncover how Carlos had really died. The Army's conclusion, ignoring any evidence to the contrary, was that he had shot himself through the left temple. A suicide. The fact that Carlos was *right*-handed and there was no trace of powder marks was set aside as irrelevant. The investigator identified a likely suspect, an Intelligence Police associate of Carlos's, and Frank was determined to draw a confession from the young man he believed to be his brother's killer. But his bold plan—to get the fellow drunk enough to "talk"—failed.[72]

In spring 1921 G. P. Putnam's Sons posthumously published a book of Carlos Wuppermann's spiritual essays, entitled *The Deeper Faith*, bringing its deceased author positive reviews. Reverend Malcolm James MacLeod, who had known Carlos and was himself an author of numerous books, wrote that "Wuppermann was a mystic and a poet and he always looks deep down into the soul of things. If he had lived he undoubtedly would have taken a high place among the constructive thinkers and makers of human thought."[73]

Determined that his brother's theatrical labors should not be forgotten, Frank convinced actress Jessie Bonstelle to produce Carlos's play, *The Triumph of X*, in Detroit with her stock company that summer. The production was followed by a Broadway bow at a small Shubert House, the Comedy Theatre, in August, with Frank in the lead male role. But *The Triumph of X* failed to "draw" and closed after a few weeks. Ralph's Broadway appearance this month also failed: *The Poppy God*, with Ralph playing a drug addict. August 1921 would be the only time all three Morgan brothers had their names on Broadway productions,

---

[72] Details on Carlos Wuppermann's death, including lack of powder marks, are in his death investigation report transcript, and the autopsy report in the National Archives, College Park, Maryland. A document in his army personnel file revealed his *right*-handedness, and the author's conversations with the late George Morgan and Carlos Wuppermann Cook produced details of the hiring of the unnamed private investigator and Frank's attempt in New York to get the "suspect" drunk to pull a confession from him. The suspect admitted nothing.

[73] Reverend MacLeod's remarks appear on the front of the *Deeper Faith* dust jacket. Carlos dedicated *The Deeper Faith* to "J.I.C."—again, the beautiful Jessie Isabelle Cochran.

and none succeeded. In November, Frank followed *The Triumph of X* with William Gillette and Myrtle Tannehill in the melodrama *The Dream Maker* with a better run: over eighty performances.

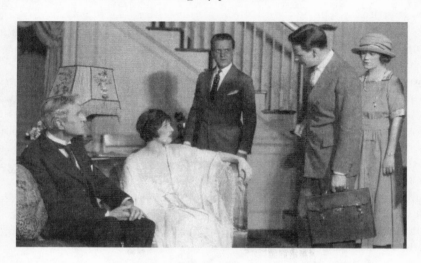

1924 was a banner Broadway year for Ralph and Frank. Ralph gave Carlos life again, in his way, through a magical performance as "Tony Dorning" in Martin Brown's drama *Cobra* with Louis Calhern as "Jack" and Judith Anderson as "Elise" (the deadly female "cobra" of the title). A theatrical paper revealed the secret in an article entitled "Ralph Morgan Plays His Brother": "Ralph Morgan, who plays with convincing tenderness the chief role in 'Cobra,' told me that he was playing his own brother. 'The finest lad that ever lived . . . . He was the pure idealist I have tried to show in "Cobra."'"[74] Ralph received the best reviews of his career. From the *New York Evening Post*, coincidentally Carlos' favorite newspaper: "Mr. Morgan . . . really behaved admirably in the part. He acted amazingly, as if he believed every word Mr. Brown made him say, and when he began softly to cry about Elise and her doings it was enough to tear your heart out. He seems honestly to forget that he's in the theatre and becomes as straightforward and likable a chap as Mr. Brown can conveniently manage." And the *New York Times* declared, "[Jack's] chum and partner is an idealist, manly at heart, but abashed before all women—a character played by Ralph Morgan with a

---

[74]   "Ralph Morgan Plays His Brother," unsourced, undated clipping in Ralph Morgan Scrapbook collection, New York Public Library for the Performing Arts.

spiritual insight and emotional intensity that are positively beautiful."
Even humorist Robert Benchley was moved to tears by Ralph's *Cobra*
performance, admitting, "When . . . Ralph Morgan brought to bear his
heart-breaking throat-work, we succumbed entirely to the spell. We
once predicted that if Mr. Morgan ever had a role again that was half-way
tragic, we should be the first man in a New York audience to sob out
loud. Well, he did, and we did."[75] Ralph's portrayal was so popular that
a local men's clothing wholesaler even named a sweater for him.[76] That
summer, Ralph even served briefly as acting president of Actors' Equity
during the absence in Europe of its president, John Emerson.

On October 15, 1924, five and a half years after Carlos Wuppermann
predicted that Frank's "will power" and "natural gifts should take him
to the top of the ladder," they did. Frank opened on Broadway in Edwin
Justus Mayer's *The Firebrand* at the Morosco. *The Firebrand* launched
thirty-four-year-old Frank as a supreme stage comic in role of Duke
Alessandro de Medici. *New York Times* critic Stark Young was initially
lukewarm, as Frank's performance in the first act was unremarkable:
"undefined and loose" he described it. Perhaps it was only "first night
jitters," but Frank pulled out all stops from the second act onward; and
critic Young was impressed, describing the Frank Morgan that future
movie and radio fans would come to love, the comic persona that would
carry him through the twenty-five remaining years of life and career.
Stark Young enthused that "Frank Morgan . . . sets out from the second
curtain on to give the audience the most likable booby of a Prince
imaginable, a noble loon, absurd, scatter-brained, afraid of his wife,
and all the while ironically inadequate to the necessities of his high
station."[77]

The Firebrand cast also brought Frank a life-long pal: future legendary
movie gangster Edward G. Robinson, who played the Duke's cousin,

---

[75]   Robert Benchley, *Life* magazine, May 8, 1924, 20.

[76]   Paramount Pictures released *Cobra* as a silent film in 1925, with an altered
plot and some changed character names: instead of Louis Calhern's "Jack
Race" character, it was Rudolph Valentino as "Count Rodrigo Torriani."
Judith Anderson's seductive "Elise" was portrayed by screen vamp
Nita Naldi. Ralph Morgan's "Tony Dorning" character received a new
name, "Jack" Dorning, and was played by twenty-four-year-old Casson
Ferguson—who portrayed Ralph's "Raymond Floriet" stage character in
the second 1920 film version of *Madame X*. In 1929, both Mr. Ferguson and
his young actress-wife died of pneumonia within two days of each other.

[77]   Stark Young, "E. J. Mayer's First Play," *New York Times*, October 16, 1924.

Ottaviano de Medici. But Eddie was saddened to observe that his new friend—letter-perfect in his lines, never missing a cue—was, in fact, an alcoholic.[78] The pressures and sorrows in these five years since Carlos's sudden death, combined with a culture of drinking—which Prohibition did nothing to curb—had caught up with Frank, and only his iron will and professionalism kept it from harming his work.

The next five years, 1925 through 1929, found Frank in a combination of stage hits and misses. In 1925, Ralph and Frank supported Thomas Meighan in the Paramount feature film *The Man Who Found Himself*, but did not play brothers. In 1926, they appeared together on Broadway (for the first time since the one-act *Under Cover* curtain raiser, *The Greaser*, in 1914), with Estelle Winwood in the comedy *A Weak Woman*, from January to March; but the play was not a "hit." Again, they did not play brothers. By September 1926, Frank hit another "jackpot" with *Gentlemen Prefer Blondes*. But Frank left the production in a few months to take a dramatic role in *Puppets of Passion*, which opened in February 1927. The drama failed after just twelve performances, while *Gentlemen Prefer Blondes* was still packing 'em in.[79]

Ralph's stage luck was no better, playing a troubled ex-baseball player in the drama *Damn the Tears* in January 1927. It closed after just eleven performances.[80]

Frank followed February's *Puppets of Passion* failure with another when his next drama, *Hearts are Trumps*, folded after twenty performances in April 1927. Frank did better in August 1927 when he and one of his *Gentlemen Prefer Blondes* co-stars, Edna Hibbard, played in the melodrama *Tenth Avenue* at the Eltinge Theatre, running over eighty performances. Next around Frank's corner was another comic Broadway smash: Florenz Ziegfeld's *Rosalie*, starring Marilyn Miller, which opened at the beautiful New Amsterdam theatre on January 10, 1928.

A month after Frank's *Rosalie* opening, Ralph appeared in the mystery *The Clutching Claw* beginning February 14, 1928. The following day, Brooks Atkinson's review appeared in the *New York Times* with a blunder—perhaps a "first"—that would become all too common in Hollywood a few years later: misidentifying Ralph as Frank. Atkinson

---

[78] Robinson, Edward G. *All My Yesterdays*. New York: Hawthorne Books, 77. Robinson recalled that, during *The Firebrand*, Frank loved his bourbon and "more than once I had to make him up and guide him onstage where he would instantly sober up and play splendidly."

[79] "The Final Figures," *New York Times*, June 5, 1927.

[80] Ibid.

wrote, "As the omniscient amateur detective, Frank Morgan becomes a little mousy as the evening advances."[81]

In 1929, Ralph took over Tom Powers's role of "Charles Marsden" in the Theatre Guild's production of Eugene O'Neill's long difficult *Strange Interlude*, and toured with the production across the country. By early spring, the company was in Los Angeles while his union, Actors' Equity, was surveying Hollywood film players in "talkies" to determine if there was sufficient support for Equity. In October 1929, the unimaginable happened: Wall Street "Laid an Egg" (as *Variety* described it) as the stock market took the most severe crash in its history. The resulting Great Depression would bring massive unemployment—including for theatre actors.

1930 brought the "talking picture" debuts of both Morgan brothers, and another successful Broadway comedy for Frank as the star of *Topaze*, which opened in February. Frank also signed to a motion picture contract with Paramount Pictures—in *New York*, not Hollywood. Frank surely got less sleep than usual in the winter, spring, and summer of 1930 as he performed in *Topaze* at night and commuted to Paramount's Astoria Studios in Long Island during the day to shoot multiple films: *Belle of the Night* (a short with "Dorothy McNulty" who would change her name to Penny Singleton and star in the *Blondie* comedies); *Dangerous Nan Megrew*, with "Boop Boop a Doop" girl Helen Kane; *Queen High* with Charlie Ruggles; *Laughter* with Nancy Carroll, and *Fast and Loose* with Carole Lombard, Miriam Hopkins, and Charles Starrett. Ralph had yet to appear in a talking feature, but he made his "talkie" debut in a "Vitaphone Varieties" short entitled *Excuse the Pardon*, portraying a man released to his wife and young son after nine years in prison.

As 1930 continued, and the economy worsened, more Broadway actors were lured to Hollywood, and one was Frank's friend Ralph Bellamy. Bellamy was noticed in a short-lived (eleven performances) Broadway comedy, *Roadside*, and offered a Hollywood contract. In October, Frank had finished his New York run of *Topaze* and was continuing the play in Chicago, where Bellamy had to change trains for the trip west. Frank met him at the train station and saw the "deserter" off with harsh words indeed, as Bellamy later recalled: "My friend Frank Morgan, who was playing in *Topaze* in Chicago, came to the Santa Fe station to see me off with the most vituperative language, including calling me a prostitute,

---

81   J. Brooks Atkinson, "The Play: Foiling the Clutching Claw," *New York Times*, February 15, 1928.

selling out for money."[82] Evidently, Frank felt "movie work" was fine in New York, but not *Hollywood*.

As 1930 drew to an end, Ralph filmed a very small role at the Astoria Studios in his first talking *feature* film: Paramount's *Honor Among Lovers*.

In July 1931, Ralph played "Tony Dorning as Carlos" one more time as he was engaged to perform in *Cobra*, at the Westchester Theatre in Mount Vernon, New York. Two days after the opening, he signed the movie contract with Fox Films and *drove* with Daisy across the country to Hollywood that fall. Frank was in no hurry to head for Hollywood, for in June he had opened in another Broadway hit: *The Band Wagon*, with Fred and Adele Astaire. And besides, hadn't he told Ralph Bellamy exactly what he thought of actors deserting the stage for Hollywood?

In the spring of 1932, Ralph Bellamy would have had a good laugh if he had read any of the multiple newspapers carrying syndicated Hollywood columnist Louella Parsons's story on Monday May 23. Miss

82   Bellamy, Ralph. *When the Smoke Hit the Fan*. Garden City, NY: Doubleday & Company, 1979, 109. Bellamy's memory failed him on one point: Frank did not come to Hollywood "six months later," but almost two years afterwards.

Parsons gave the latest scoop on his old buddy, Frank Morgan, who'd called Bellamy a "prostitute" and a "sellout" for taking that Hollywood movie contract in 1930. She announced, "One of New York's finest actors, Frank Morgan to be exact, has been signed by Irving Thalberg. Frank has been so busy on the stage with *Topaze* and *The Band Wagon* and other notable successes that he has found it difficult to leave Broadway, but his brother, Ralph, is here and a Hollywood enthusiast. So Frank has also signed a movie contract."

After *The Band Wagon*, Frank completed his final Broadway engagement, as star of the short-lived comic revue *Hey Nonny Nonny*; and in August 1932, he and Alma set off for Hollywood, leaving teenage son George behind at boarding school. Unlike Ralph, Frank would never return to Broadway.

Now *both* Morgan brothers were in Hollywood, and the identity confusion began. There was ample employment for them, but also dissatisfaction with the working conditions these two longtime members of Actors' Equity Association encountered and observed. And as the Great Depression continued, with resulting reductions in salary for many Hollywood actors and actresses, combined with long workweeks and scant time for proper sleep between calls back to the set, a "storm" brewed. One of Franklin Roosevelt's first acts as new president in 1933 was to halt the wave of bank failures by ordering all banks in the country to be closed for four days. The Hollywood studios reacted swiftly and announced plans to deal with the crisis by cutting the pay of their actors—contract, freelance, or day player—by 50 percent. It proved the "last straw," and a handful of Equity members met to discuss a solution. That solution became the Screen Actors Guild with Ralph Morgan as its first president. Cautious Frank, so often risk-averse, delayed in joining his brother as a Guild member until more famous names signed up but, once in, fought faithfully alongside Ralph for the Guild's recognition. It took nearly four years, as Ralph and Frank combined Guild work with roles in dozens of films, before the Guild achieved its first contract with the Hollywood studios.

On May 9, 1937, thousands of Screen Actors Guild members gathered at the local boxing arena—the Hollywood Legion Stadium—to hear the news from the Guild's president, movie star Robert Montgomery: after almost four years of resistance, movie executives Louis B. Mayer and Joseph Schenck had agreed to recognize the Guild and bring the other studio heads to agreement. As they say, "the crowd went wild."

Ralph Morgan, as cofounder and first Guild president, took the stadium stage and announced, "You can stop, maybe, an army of a million men, but you can't stop a right idea when its time has come. Your idea, and your ideals, have come tonight. After three [sic] long years, I am happier tonight than ever before in our struggle for independence, harmony, and peace in this branch of the profession which we all love so dearly. The fulfillment of these ideas and ideals is due, almost completely, to your loyalty and your cooperation. Through me, the Board expresses its deepest and sincerest gratitude to every one of you. Our duty after this week shall be to protect those ideals and those ideas."

Frank Morgan who, "electrified the audience" after "comparing this night to the Equity strike of 1919," delivered the evening's concluding speech with "your Board has been sitting almost constantly from the beginning of this week until now, waiting anxiously as the negotiating committee went to and from the producers, interviewing the highest officials. We have had days and hours of exalted optimism and days and hours of deep gloom. There is nothing we can lose as long as we have face-to-face across the table with producers, the fine men on our negotiating committee. I would like to have a rising vote from you for the glorious work of these men, and nobody will give a damn if you cheer."[83]

In 1938, Frank began appearing in the radio program *Good News*; and on September 22, 1938, MGM announced Frank's casting in one of their latest films: *The Wizard of Oz*. By March of 1939, principal filming was complete. *Oz* gave Frank multiple costumes and multiple roles: Professor Marvel ("I never do anything without consulting my crystal first"); an Emerald City doorman ("Who rang that bell?!"); a carriage cab driver ("He's the Horse of a Different Colour, you've heard tell about"); a place guard ("Go home! The Wizard says, 'Go away!'"); and, of course, the Great and Powerful Wizard of Oz himself ("I'm a humbug"). *The Wizard of Oz* had its Hollywood premiere at Sid Grauman's Chinese Theatre on August 15, 1939.

But just four months later, a car crash in New Mexico nearly claimed Frank's life, just before Christmas. On December 20, Frank's black chauffer, Mr. Will Martin, was at the wheel when one of the brand-new tires blew out on Highway 80, east of Deming, New Mexico. Mr. Martin lost control of the auto as it skidded into the sandy shoulder of the road and flipped over, violently hurling Alma and George out, while Frank and his driver remained inside. The steering wheel crushed Mr. Martin's chest, and this good man died at the hospital from internal

---

[83] "Guild Wins!" *Screen Guild Magazine*, May 1937, 8, 40.

injuries. Frank was shaken, Alma's leg was broken, and George received a severe concussion; but the Morgan family still had their lives.[84]

It is not known how this escape from death affected Frank personally, and he continued his work in MGM comic roles and in his *Good News/Maxwell House Coffee Time* radio programs. But in the four years following the New Mexico accident and Mr. Martin's death, he took those notably serious parts in *The Mortal Storm* (1940), *Tortilla Flat* (1942), and *The Human Comedy* (1943). On June 13, 1946, two weeks after Frank's fifty-sixth birthday, he suffered a serious personal loss as one of his dearest friends, character actor Charlie Butterworth, died in a car accident at a Sunset Boulevard intersection. Frank continued to wear his cheerful, energetic public "mask," but he had been doing fewer films and was growing weary inside. In January 1947, with just two and a half more years of life left to him, he told a reporter that when his MGM contract ran out, three years hence, he and Alma would travel the world; and when he returned, he would "act in movies when he feels like it—one or two a year."[85]

Frank's behavior became erratic in the remaining months of his life, and an alarmed Alma asked their doctor, Ralph Tandowsky, for help. But it was evidently too late: Frank did not wake up on the morning of September 18, 1949. Looking much older than his fifty-nine years, his body gave out at last. No autopsy was performed, and his cause of death was given as "cerebral thrombosis."[86]

Ralph, widowed when Daisy died in 1948, outlived his youngest brother by nearly seven years. Developing a lung ailment, he moved back to New York to be with daughter Claudia; and the day before Claudia's birthday, June 11, 1956, Ralph Morgan passed from this life. The funeral was held where he'd married Daisy in 1910, when Edith Luckett and Carlos stood by his side: the "Little Church Around the Corner." Three days later, he was interred in the family plot at Brooklyn's Green-Wood

---

84   The late George Morgan, in conversation with the author, filled in details of the 1939 car accident.

85   "Screen Morgan Not the Real Thing," *Portland* [Maine] *Sunday Telegram and Sunday Press Herald,* January 19, 1947.

86   Frank and Alma's son, the late George Morgan, described Frank's disturbing behavior to the author. Frank had threatened to leave everything, including MGM and Alma, and sail around the world on his yacht. He was obviously under great stress, in addition to depression, for which no solution was found in time.

Cemetery; and the three "Morgan" brothers—Ralph, Carlyle, and Frank—were together again at last.[87]

Three lives unselfishly lived: Ralph created an actors' union, Carlos sacrificed his life in service to his country, and Frank brought hearty laughter to millions. These three actors left this world a better place than they found it. And when an actor does an exceptional job, it warrants a standing ovation. Well done, Wuppermann boys!

Bibliography

Archival Sources

Amateur Comedy Club, New York, NY.

Church of the Transfiguration ("Little Church Around the Corner") archives, New York, NY.

Columbia University Archives, New York, NY.

Holy Trinity Church Inwood, New York, NY.

Lilly Library, Indiana University. Upton Sinclair Manuscripts.

National Archives and Records Administration, College Park, MD.

National Personnel Records Center, St. Louis, MO. Carlos Wuppermann army personnel file.

New York Public Library for the Performing Arts: Ralph Morgan scrapbooks.

Screen Actors Guild: Frank Morgan, Ralph Morgan, Carlos Wuppermann collections.

Trinity School, New York.

University of Baltimore, Lansdale Library, Roderick Seidenberg and Mabel Dwight Collection.

Yale University, Collection of American Literature, Beinecke Rare Book and Manuscript Library, Uncat ZA file Morgan.

Books

Arnold, Edward. *Lorenzo Goes to Hollywood*. New York: Liveright Publishing Corporation, 1940.

Carlos Siegert Wuppermann: A Few of His Letters and Other Data, 1887-1919. Privately printed, n.d.

---

[87] Most of the Wuppermann and Hancox family are buried in Green-Wood Cemetery, lot number 14447, section 168.

Courtney, Margaret. *Laurette: The Intimate Biography of Laurette Taylor*. New York & Toronto: Rinehart & Company, 1955.

Echegaray, Jose. *Mariana*. Translated by Federico Sarda and Carlos D. S. Wuppermann. New York: Moods Publishing Company, 1909.

Foster, Charles. *Donald Brian: The King of Broadway*. St John's, Newfoundland: Breakwater Books, 2005.

Kilmer, Kenton. *Memories of My Father, Joyce Kilmer*. Brunswick, NJ: Joyce Kilmer Centennial, 1993.

Macco, H. F. *Geschichte der familie Wuppermann*. 1911.

Robinson, Edward G. *All My Yesterdays*. New York: Hawthorne Books, 1973.

Tjomsland, Anna. *Bellevue in France*. New York: Froben Press, 1941.

Wuppermann, Carlos. *The Deeper Faith*. New York and London: G. P. Putnam's Sons, 1921

_____. *Quiet Places*. New York: Shaemas O'Sheel, 1912.

Newspapers and Periodicals

American Review of Reviews
Brooklyn Eagle
Cleveland Plain-Dealer
Columbia Monthly
Columbia Spectator
Duluth News-Tribune
Fort Wayne News
Grand Rapids Press
Harlem Life
Hartford Courant
Independent
Life (1883-1936 magazine)
Los Angeles Times
Middletown Times
Modern School
Moods
Movie Classic
Moving Picture World
Nation
New York Clipper
New York Dramatic Mirror
New York Evening Post
New York Sun

New York Times
New York Tribune
Oakland Tribune
Ogden Standard-Examiner
Phi Gamma Delta
Photoplay
Pittsburgh Press
Screen Actor
Screen Guild Magazine

Contributors

Abigail Adams lives in Woodland Park, Colorado. She enjoys hiking, drawing, nature, and writing. She is currently writing a book of short fiction stories and a children's book about rabbits.

Ben Bergin lives, writes, acts, directs, and broadcasts in New York City and has been doing so four years since he moved from Doncaster, in the north of England. He writes a weekly column on British Culture in New York for the website examiner.com; podcasts for the Cincinnati Bengals during the NFL season (bengalspodcast.com); and, alongside Liz Curtis, runs the production company Benbokis Productions as Managing Director and Artistic Director. As well as several plays and screenplays, he authored the children's narrative poem "The Turtle and the Panda," and has contributed to various magazines, such as *The Mountaineer*, which most recently published his "Journal of an Englishman Abroad."

A professional singer, actor, and dancer, as well as a published writer and playwright, **Matthew Bowerman** has appeared in commercials, films, national tour, and Off-Broadway productions. He is the recipient of a 2007 Emmy Award as Writer/Director for Best Educational Feature Short for his anti-bullying piece *BusSTOP*, as well as a 2008 CINE Golden Eagle Film Award for the same work. Currently, Matthew is writing/directing four new pieces on CyberBullying and Teacher Character Education/Role Modeling with the Educational Channel of Baltimore County Public Schools. His educational films, geared at all three levels of public education, have been used in Health curriculum, as well as at the state and national education levels. His work earned him a 2010 Gifted and Talented Educator as Leader Award in Maryland. Matthew earned his Bachelor of Science in Theatre from Towson University,

Masters in Educational Leadership/Theatre Education from College of Notre Dame, and will complete his postgraduate degree in Globalized Leadership for Changing Populations with a concentration in Performing Arts Education in 2011 from College of Notre Dame. He is married to Claire, a professional actress and model, and they have three marvelous children.

Elizabeth Engel grew up in Needham Massachusetts. She attended the University of Vermont, where she developed a passion for writing and the arts. Elizabeth Engel is a freelance writer of fiction and nonfiction and currently resides in New York City.

Helaine Feldman is a principal in the New York—based communications firm, Dick Moore and Associates, working with such clients as Actors' Equity Association and the American Federation of Television and Radio Artists, among others. She is a member of the League of Professional Theatre Women, the Drama Desk, a past Board member of the Coalition of Professional Women in the Arts & Media, and is listed in *Who's Who of American Women*.

James Fisher is Professor of Theatre and Head of the Department of Theatre at UNCG, where he received an MFA in Acting/Directing in 1976. He has authored several books, including *The Historical Dictionary of the American Theater: Contemporary*; *Understanding Tony Kushner*; *The Historical Dictionary of the American Theater: Modernism* (co-authored with Felicia Hardison Londré); bio-bibliographies of Spencer Tracy, Al Jolson, and Eddie Cantor; *The Theatre of Tony Kushner: Living Past Hope*; *The Theatre of Yesterday and Tomorrow: Commedia dell'arte on the Modern Stage*; three "In an Hour" books on Eugene O'Neill, Thornton Wilder, and Arthur Miller; and he has contributed book chapters and essays to a wide range of publications on theatre and film. Among his many directing credits are *Angels in America*, *Holiday*, *Chapter Two*, *Mere Mortals*, *1776*, *The Illusion*, *The Complete Works of William Shakespeare (Abridged)*, *Glengarry Glen Ross*, *Mister Roberts*, *The Notebook of Trigorin*, *Tartuffe*, *Accidental Death of an Anarchist*, *True West*, *Bus Stop*, *The School for Wives*, *Mrs. Warren's Profession*, and his own adaptation of Plautus's *The Braggart Soldier*. Also an actor, Fisher most recently played Sheridan Whiteside in *The Man Who Came to Dinner* and is the recipient of the 2007 Betty Jean Jones Award for Excellence in the Teaching of American Theatre from the American Theatre and Drama Society.

Maurizio Giammarco received his MA in Creative Writing and PhD in English from Temple University and has taught courses in film, drama, literature, and creative writing at the university for eighteen years. From 2005 to 2007 he taught drama, acting, rehearsal and production, and writing at Rosemont College on a full-time basis, and where he was also the theater program director. During his tenure there, he supervised the one-act play festival held every Oktoberfest and directed the school's annual spring production: in 2006 he staged *Anton in Show Business* by Jane Martin; in 2007 he staged *The Trojan Women* by Euripides. In 2007 he returned to Temple University, and in addition to teaching there as a full-time lecturer in the Intellectual Heritage Program, he was a visiting professor at Haverford College, where he taught introductory and advanced courses in fiction writing, as well as classes in screenwriting, terrorism in international film, and food and society. His articles and theater and film reviews have appeared in *The Temple News*, *Reel Visions*, *City Weekly Paper*, and *The Journal of Modern Literature*. He has written and directed short films, both fiction and documentary, which have been shown at university festivals as well as in Philadelphia, New Jersey, Italy, and Sicily.

Immediately after graduating from Pittsburgh's Point Park College (now a university) with a degree in journalism, **Zanne Hall** was one of four Americans accepted by London's Royal Academy of Dramatic Art to study theatre. After leaving London, she moved to New York City and pursued dualistic careers in writing and theatre, finally combining them as a playwright. She is a member of the Dramatists Guild and has won several playwriting awards, including a National Federation of Community Broadcasters Award for her radio drama "The Arctic Crusoe," which aired on various National Public Radio stations across the United States. She now resides in Kew Gardens, New York, with her husband who is a *New York Post* financial writer and their three cats. She looks forward to the day when they will all move to Pittsburgh, her hometown and a progressive city that has weathered many potential setbacks to be named as one of the top U.S. places to live.

Erik Hanson graduated from Sacred Heart University in with a BA in Media Studies and a Masters of Arts in Teaching (K-6). In 2002, his monologue, *Reminisce*, was published in *Horizons Literary Magazine*. In the summer of 2004, The Eclectic Company Theatre had an equity production of his play, *After School Special*, in North Hollywood. His one-act play, *Acronym*, was staged for an AIDS benefit at the Spartanburg

Little Theatre in South Carolina. The Gallery Players of Brooklyn staged his play *The Sex of Our Lives* as part of their Eighth Annual Black Box New Play Festival. In June 2005, his collection of plays, *The Gray Area*, had a four-week run at Theatre-Studio Incorporated in Manhattan. In October of 2005, his play *The Ethan Hawke Thing* was staged for the AT/ WAS Theatre Company, and The Native Aliens Theatre Group in New York City staged his play *Suburban Soldier*. In August of 2006, his play *Cabin Echoes* premiered at The Complex in West Hollywood. Madair Productions staged his play *Marital Bliss* during the Project Playwright II series in November 2006 at the Access Theatre in New York. His play *Same Only Different* was a semi-finalist for the 2007 Eugene O'Neill Conference. His play *To Darfur* was published by Smith and Kraus Publishing in *The Best Ten-Minute Plays of 2008* (three actors or more). His play *Property of Africa* was staged in May of 2008 during the Tenth Annual Boston Theater Marathon. At present, he is an adjunct professor in the English department at Sacred Heart University.

Michael D. Jackson is a theatre artist, having worked in nearly every aspect of the profession. He has written theatre criticism for *Off Off Broadway Review*, has directed numerous productions in New York and California, and is a playwright. His theatre journalism appears in *New York Stages: A Journal of New Millennium Theatre*. A collection of his plays can be found in *Making Progress*. His play *Three Women* is published in *Best Plays of the Strawberry One Act Festival, Vol. III*, and *A Taste of Heaven* received the Excellence in Playwriting honor at the New York International Fringe Theatre Festival. Michael received his MA in Theatre Arts from California State University, Sacramento. He is a licensing agent with Music Theatre International where he has also adapted musicals for the company's education programs.

Audrey Johnson has been an intern with New England Vintage Film Society Incorporated since September 2009. Audrey's primary responsibility with this publication was to assist the editor by compiling a reference list for each submitted essay. She has loved the opportunity to learn not only of the grandeur of vintage productions, but also of the impact they have had on our films and entertainment in the present day. Audrey graduated in May 2008 with a BS in Psychology from the University of Mary Washington located in Fredericksburg, Virginia. Following graduation, Audrey took a position working on the McCain-Palin presidential campaign out of national headquarters in Crystal City, Virginia. She currently works with the volunteer-based nonprofit StandUp for Kids, serving as the Director of Public Relations, in Boston, Massachusetts.

Cinzi Lavin is a musical dramatist whose production *On This River* (for which she wrote the script, score, and lyrics) won a state award for outstanding contribution to Massachusetts arts and culture. Her subsequent musical, *Toilers of the Sea: The Life of Joshua James*, a biographical drama about the most highly decorated civilian lifesaving crew commander in U.S. history, was awarded a state grant. As a humor columnist and essayist, her works have appeared in several publications including the NEVFS's *Spencer Tracy: Fox Film Actor*. Born in Manhattan and educated in Texas, her postgraduate study focused on dramatic theory and criticism. After college, she ran off and joined a comedy troupe and later worked as an actress in Dallas. An accomplished musician, she has performed at Madison Square Garden and taught at several private music schools across the United States. She lives in Hull, Massachusetts, with three spoiled houseplants who prefer to remain anonymous.

Brenda Loew founded and serves as President of New England Vintage Film Society Incorporated. Brenda lectures on classic films, organizes public library displays of classic film memorabilia, and offers classic film screening programs at adult education centers and retirement communities. Brenda is the editor of *Spencer Tracy, Fox Film Actor: The Pre-Code Legacy of a Hollywood Legend*—endorsed by Turner Classic Movies host, Robert Osborne—and *Playbills To Photoplays: Stage Performers Who Pioneered the Talkies*. Brenda's early interest in performing on stage was recognized by the Boston Children's Theatre, which, following her audition, immediately accepted her for their summer Teen Stagemobile Touring Company productions. A former tenured public school speech therapist, Brenda is an award-winning public access television producer, writer, and publisher. She has appeared as a guest on numerous television and radio shows for her political activism. An animal lover, Brenda owns five cats and is a volunteer with the Newton Massachusetts Animal Rescue Team (NMART). A graduate of Boston University, Brown University, and Northeastern University, Brenda is the great niece of the late theatre chain and entertainment mogul E. M. Loew, who once owned the largest chain of indoor and "open air" theatres east of the Mississippi, the Latin Quarter nightclubs in New York, Boston, and Palm Island (Miami) and Bay State Raceway in Foxboro, Massachusetts—currently the site of Gillette Stadium, home of the New England Patriots. Brenda's association with New England Vintage Film Society Incorporated maintains the Loew family connection to show business.

Jan Merlin and **William Russo** have collaborated on several Hollywood history books and *The Paid Companion of J. Wilkes Booth*, published as a documentary novel and forthcoming from Bluewater Productions as a graphic novel. Mr. Merlin, Emmy Award-winning writer, has acted on stage, in movies, and in several hundreds of live and filmed television appearances. He is the recipient of the 2009 Southern Motion Picture Council Halo Award. His published works include *Ainoko*, *Gunbearer (Parts 1 and 2)*, *Crackpots*, *Gypsies Don't Lie*, and *Shooting Montezuma: A Hollywood Monster Story*. Dr. Russo, a professor of literature and film studies in New England, has taught writing and published *Riding James Kirkwood's Pony*, *Booth and Oswald*, as well as *Audie Murphy, Vietnam, and the Making of The Quiet American*. Russo also contributed to the previous New England Vintage Film Society book *Spencer Tracy: Fox Film Actor*.

Lauren Milberger is an actor/writer, originally from Scotch Plains, New Jersey, and grew up with a love of comedy. As an actor, some of Lauren's roles include Joan in Elaine May's *The Way of All Fish*, Jill in *Butterflies Are Free*, and Lala in *The Last Night of Ballyhoo*. Other appearances include Caryl Churchill's *The Skriker* (Kennedy Center), *Tango 'Til They're Sore* (The Flea Theater), *Keanu Reeves Saves the Universe* (People's Improv Theatre), and *Corelone: The Shakespeare Godfather* (NY Fringe Festival). Lauren has worked with such New York City improv groups as *National Comedy Theatre* and *Manhattan Comedy Collective*. In Film and TV, Lauren has appeared in a promo for Oxygen TV and the mockumentary *The Royal We*, and she was infamously cut as Gilda Radner from the film *Chapter 27*, starring Jared Leto and Lindsay Lohan. As a writer, Lauren has written a few unproduced screenplays and unpublished essays and one produced play, *The Onion: First Date*, a two-character play in which she also appeared, mounted as part of The Southern Slam Festival at the Warehouse Theater, South Carolina. Currently, Lauren is working on a full-length play about George Burns and Gracie Allen, and recently appeared in an industry workshop reading as Gracie Allen. Lauren received her Masters from the New School, Actors Studio, and is a graduate of the Second City NY Conservatory Program. Lauren currently resides in New York City where she awaits the return of Vaudeville. Visit www.laurenmilberger.com for more info.

Howard Oboler received his BA Degree from Cornell, where he was elected to Phi Beta Kappa, and awarded a Fulbright Scholarship for study abroad. The major portion of his business career was spent at Ernst & Young where he was employed as a management consultant. After retiring, he enrolled in the graduate program in American Studies at Columbia University and received his MA Degree in1996. For the past twelve years Mr. Oboler has been teaching adult education courses at FAU, PBCC, and at other venues in South Florida. He also lectures at NYU and the 92nd Street Y in New York City.

Susanne Robertson—pianist, musicologist, writer, educator and lecturer—is a lifelong resident of Massachusetts. She is a magna cum laude graduate of UMass Lowell (BS) and Indiana University (MM in musicology) where she held a research assistantship under Dr. Hans Tischler. She is an accomplished classical pianist with extensive recital experience. Highlights of her qualifications include thirty-two (32) years' experience as a multi-level music educator (K-12) in the Billerica, Massachusetts, public schools and two (2) years' experience as a choral instructor at Emmanuel College in Boston. She is an experienced director of award-winning choral ensembles recognized by the American Choral Director's Association and the Massachusetts Instrumental and Choral Conductors Associations. She is an accomplished director of many music theater productions: *Li'l Abner*; *Guys and Dolls*; *The Pajama Game*; *Hello, Dolly!*; *Oklahoma*; *Bye, Bye Birdie*; *Carousel*; *Anything Goes*; *South Pacific*; *Fiddler on the Roof*, *The Sound of Music*; *Once Upon a Mattress*; *Annie Get Your Gun*; *How to Succeed in Business Without Really Trying*; *Brigadoon*; *State Fair*; *and Mame*. Susanne is a published author. Representative works include *Programme: Lowell Musicale—A Musical Portrait of the Spindle City*, written under the auspices of Lowell National Historical Park, U.S. Development of the Interior, and the Massachusetts Cultural Council. Her current work-in-progress is *Charms of the Muse*, a biographical survey of four (4) artistic women writers, scholars, and composers, whose work flourished in Victorian New England. She was consultant and participant in the Lowell National Historical Park documentary film *The Lowell Offering—Arts in the Merrimack Valley*. She has presented papers and/or workshops for the Tsongas Industrial History Center in Lowell; the Massachusetts Music Educators Association; Lowell National Historical Park, and the Lowell Conference on Women's History: Race, Ethnicity, Gender and Class. In addition, she is a freelance writer of poetry and short stories. She and her husband, Richard, reside in Billerica, Massachusetts. She has two daughters, Kelley and Meghan, both of whom are vitally involved with theater and the arts.

Judy Samelson has called *Playbill®* magazine home for over thirty years. She was editor of the national theatre publication from 1993 to 2009 and is currently a regular contributor to its website, Playbill.com, writing features and a column about performing arts books. Her love of classic Hollywood dates back to her early childhood when she was nurtured on a steady diet of Humphrey Bogart, Bette Davis, Spencer Tracy, Cary Grant, Barbara Stanwyck, Ingrid Bergman, Edward G., et al., via WOR-TV Channel 9's *Million Dollar Movie*, New York City's local television haven for movie lovers (nowadays she gets her 24/7 fix from cable's Turner Classic Movies). She was thirteen years old when she first encountered Katharine Hepburn in 1967. Thinking she was going to see a new Sidney Poitier movie called *Guess Who's Coming to Dinner*, Judy emerged from the darkened theatre two hours later with one burning question: *who* was that woman? From that day forward, Hepburn's life and work became a source of endless hours of discovery, enjoyment, fascination, and admiration. She was thrilled to have seen Hepburn on stage in three productions—*Coco* (1969), *A Matter of Gravity* (1976), and *The West Side Waltz* (1981)—as well as at rare public appearances such as the Film Society of Lincoln Center's tribute to her frequent director and longtime friend George Cukor (1978), the premiere of her pet film project *The Spencer Tracy Legacy* at Broadway's Majestic Theatre (1986), and *Night of 100 Stars III* at Radio City Music Hall (1990). She remembers a backstage meeting with the star after one of those performances as a high point in her life. She owns an extensive collection of material relating to Hepburn's life and career, including items from Sotheby's Katharine Hepburn Estate auction, about which she wrote for the Bryn Mawr College Bulletin. Judy is also an honorary member of the board of the Katharine Hepburn Cultural Arts Center in Old Saybrook, Connecticut, and serves on its museum committee. She has contributed articles to the theatre's Capital Campaign Brochure as well as the program for its 2009 Opening Night Gala.

Val Sherman entered the School of the Arts at Columbia University to pursue screenwriting full-time, after working in film and theatre as a writer, director, and producer for close to fifteen years. His accomplishments include Associate Producer of *Old Wicked Songs* (Pulitzer Prize finalist for Drama, 1996), *Broadway Loves Lucy* (writer, producer), and presenting the American premiere of the English play

New Boy (2002). Val is the author of several feature screenplays and teleplays and has written, directed, and produced three short films. His spec script, "30 Rock: Seeing Is Believing," was recognized as a Faculty Select, in addition to being awarded Best Teleplay, as part of the 2009 Columbia University Film Festival. Val is a graduate of the University of Pennsylvania. He currently has a screenplay in development.

Jon Steinhagen is a Resident Playwright at Chicago Dramatists, the 2009 winner of the Julie Harris Award for Playwriting, and winner of four Joseph Jefferson Awards for his work in Chicago theater as writer, actor, or musical director. His recent works include the play *The Analytical Engine* and the musical *The Teapot Scandals*. He was a recent finalist for the inaugural Noël Coward Award, is a company member of Signal Ensemble Theatre in Chicago, and a member of the Dramatists Guild. He teaches at the Theatre Building Chicago Musical Writers Workshop, and is currently working on a book that will profile pre-Code Hollywood film characters.

Performer, writer, and producer **Trav S. D.** is the author of over one hundred plays (for stage, screen, and radio), three hundred published articles, and the book *No Applause, Just Throw Money, The Book That Made Vaudeville Famous* (Faber & Faber, 2005). A frequent radio guest and public speaker, his voice has been heard on the *Leonard Lopate Show* (WNYC), *The Sound of Young America* (NPR), *The Joey Reynolds Show* (WOR), *Cat Radio Café* (WBAI), and a dozen others throughout the country. He has contributed to *American Theater*, the *Village Voice*, *Time Out New York*, the *New York Sun*, *Reason*, and many others, and currently has a monthly column that runs in the *Villager*, *Downtown Express*, and *Chelsea Now*. His plays include *Willy Nilly*, a musical about the Manson Family that was a hit of the 2009 NY International Fringe Festival, and *House of Trash*, published in *Plays and Playwrights 2001*. His works have been presented at Joe's Pub (the Public Theatre); Theater for the New City; LaMama; the Ohio Theatre (Soho Think Tank); HERE; Dixon Place; the Brick; and, regionally and internationally, in London, Portland, Minneapolis, Austin, Seattle, and Providence. He also presented hundreds of New York's top variety acts through his American Vaudeville Theatre.

Kal Wagenheim is a journalist (formerly with the *New York Times*), author and translator of eight books and ten plays and screenplays. His biography of Babe Ruth was adapted for an NBC-TV film. His plays *Bavarian Rage, Coffee With God* and *We Beat Whitey Ford* have been produced Off-Off-Broadway. His one-act play *Coffee With God* is now being filmed for broadcast on New Jersey cable TV and for submission to festivals. He has also taught creative writing at Columbia University and the State Prison in Trenton, New Jersey. Member: PEN American Center and The Dramatists Guild of America.

Don B. Wilmeth (PhD, University of Illinois, 1964) is Asa Messer Professor Emeritus and Emeritus Professor of Theatre and of English, Brown University, retiring in 2003 after thirty-six years there, sixteen as chair of the theatre department. He is the author, editor, coeditor, or series editor of over four dozen books, including the award-winning three-volume *Cambridge History of American Theatre*, which has been issued in a paperback edition, and *George Frederick Cooke: Machiavel of the Stage*. He has contributed to dozens of reference works, including over fifty essays to *World Book Encyclopedia*. For a dozen years he was series editor for Cambridge University Press's "Studies in American Theatre and Drama" and is currently editor of Palgrave Macmillan's "Studies in Theatre and Performance History." In 2007 he completed a new edition of the *Cambridge Guide to American Theatre*, a standard in the field. For a decade he was an advisor to the Shaw Festival in Ontario, Canada. In recent years, in addition to Brown, he has taught at Smith College, Tufts University, and Trinity University (Texas), and been a distinguished speaker at various universities and professional meetings, including the Universities of Indiana, Washington, Wisconsin, and venues in Japan, England, Russia, and Canada. He is considered a pioneer in the serious study of American popular entertainment (he has been an on-screen interviewee for PBS specials on Houdini and Annie Oakley) and an established authority on the history of American theatre and drama (he was recently termed the "dean of American theatre history"). A former president of the American Society for Theatre Research and dean emeritus of the College of Fellows of the American Theatre, Don recently served as vice president of the International Shaw Society and as a member of the board of the Theatre Library Association. He is the recipient of career and research recognitions from the New England Theatre Conference, the Association for Theatre in Higher Education, the Society for Theatre Research (UK), the American Society for Theatre Research, and the Theatre Library Association. ATHE also honored him for his work as an editor. He was a Guggenheim Fellow and is a member of Phi Beta Kappa. In 2008 Brown University bestowed upon him the William Williams Award, the most prestigious honor given by the Brown

University Library. It is presented on an irregular basis to individuals who have provided extraordinary support for the Brown library. Wilmeth is also an actor (recently Buffalo Bill in *Annie Get Your Gun* and Captain Hook in the musical *Peter Pan*) and director and an ardent collector of theatre and entertainment ephemera and memorabilia, as well as books on the history of the theatre (over five thousand). He has mounted recent exhibits drawn from his collection at Franklin Pierce University, the Cheshire County (NH) Historical Society, and at Brown's John Hay Library.

Valerie A. Yaros is an historical film, photo and library researcher, writer, and the historian for Screen Actors Guild, in Los Angeles. She served for four years as the Guild's representative on the Library of Congress's National Film Preservation Board, and is a board member and former Secretary of Hollywood Heritage. Among her television documentary film credits are PBS's *Making Sense of the Sixties*, Kevin Costner's *500 Nations*, and *The Projection Racket* for the BBC's *Timewatch* series. She is the "unofficial" historian for the Wuppermann/Morgan family and has spent the past decade in extensive research and travel to sources outside Los Angeles including the National Archives in Washington DC and College Park, Maryland; Library of Congress; Columbia University; The Players, Amateur Comedy Club; Museum of the City of New York; Trinity School; Hastings Historical Society (Hastings-on-Hudson); Green-Wood Cemetery; New York Public Library; and Wuppermann family members and associates in Maryland and New York.

Index

D

W

The Barrymores

1878-1959

Edwards Brothers,Inc!
Thorofare, NJ 08086
20 December, 2010
BA2010354